ACT
Quick Start
Guide

Welcome to *ACT Premier 2014!*

In this Quick Start Guide, we'll walk you through everything you'll need to know to take advantage of the book, DVD, and online resources. We'll help you prep smarter and score higher.

You've taken the first steps toward maximizing your ACT score—now what?

Kaplan's *ACT Premier* gives you everything you need for test day. Here's a handy checklist to get your studying on track:

☐ **Register your online companion** for extra practice, Live Online classroom events, chapter-specific tutorial videos, sample essays for the Writing section, and more.

☐ **Take the online diagnostic quiz** to figure out your strong and weak areas.

☐ **Build your study plan.**

☐ **Review** English, Reading, Math, and Science concepts.

☐ **Practice, practice, practice** with our full-length tests in the book and online.

☐ **Watch the DVD containing** instruction and tips from elite Kaplan teachers.

▶ YOUR *ACT PREMIER* BOOK

Kaplan's *ACT Premier* is packed with resources to help you get ready for test day.

It's got:

- A targeted review of key ACT terms and concepts

- Tips and strategies for each exam section and question type

- Lots of test practice (including four full-length exams in the book and two online)

▶ TAKE ADVANTAGE OF KAPLAN EXCLUSIVES

These powerful tools will help you score higher on test day!

ACT Expert Tutor Tips	ACT Perfect Score Tips
Inside each, you'll find proven test tips provided by Kaplan's expert ACT instructors.	Inside each of these, you'll find advice and strategies from a Kaplan student who earned a perfect score on the ACT.

▶ SMARTPOINTS™

SmartPoints rank the skills and topics that are tested most often on the ACT. They help you focus your test prep on the areas that will earn you the most points on test day.

How does it work? We ranked the most tested topics and crucial ACT skills using our exclusive SmartPoints bars system. The more SmartPoint bars an item has (from one bar to five bars), the more important it likely will be on test day.

As you go through this book, you'll see SmartPoints skills and topics discussed throughout.

Look for the SmartPoints bars as you study:

Use SmartPoints to prioritize your ACT studies:

- Customize your study plan according to your strengths and weaknesses, giving extra time to items with higher SmartPoints rankings.

- If you're short on time, focus your study on items with higher SmartPoints rankings first, and review items with lesser rankings as time allows.

Using Your ACT Online Companion

1 REGISTER YOUR ONLINE COMPANION

The online companion gives you access to even more test prep, including two full-length practice tests, Fast Fact videos, registration for a Live Online event, a diagnostic quiz, fresh new quizzes every month, and more!

Register your online companion using these simple steps:

1. Go to kaptest.com/booksonline.
2. Follow the on-screen instructions. Please have a copy of your book available.

2 TAKE THE ONLINE DIAGNOSTIC QUIZ

The diagnostic quiz will help you to do the following:

- **Identify your strengths and weaknesses.** This will help you target your practice time so you can work on the areas where you need help.

- **Develop your ACT study plan.** Once you review the results of your diagnostic quiz, you know where you went wrong. Build your study plan based on your needs and schedule.

  - Check your answers carefully, noting how many questions you got right and wrong, how long it took you to answer each question, and how often you skipped questions.

  - Look for patterns. Were you stronger in some areas than others?

- **Know what to expect on test day.** The diagnostic quiz provides you with a sample of each question type, so you'll know just what's waiting for you on test day.

- **Reinforce key concepts and sharpen your skills.**

3 GET TO KNOW THE ACT AND CREATE YOUR STUDY PLAN

Remember, your *ACT Premier* program is designed to meet your individual needs.

What does that mean?

- **You're in control.** Study how and when it works best for you.

- **You can customize your study.** We've made your ACT program interactive—you get to mix things up by jumping between the book and the online resources.

Take some time to familiarize yourself with some of the key components of your *ACT Premier* book. It's got all the tools you'll need to conquer the ACT exam on test day.

4 JOIN A LIVE ONLINE SESSION

Kaplan's ACT Live Online sessions are interactive, instructor-led ACT prep lessons that you can participate in from anywhere you can access the Internet.

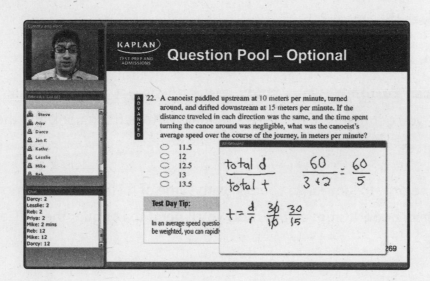

ACT Live Online sessions are held in a state-of-the-art virtual classroom—actual lessons in real time, just like a physical classroom experience. Interact with your teacher and other classmates using audio, instant chat, whiteboard, polling, and screen-sharing functionality. And just like courses at Kaplan centers, ACT Live Online sessions are led by experienced Kaplan instructors.

To register for an ACT Live Online event:

Once you've signed in to your student home page, open your Syllabus.

1. In the Syllabus window, go to the "Live Online Registration" menu option.

2. Click on the link. A separate window will appear with registration instructions.

ACT Live Online events are scheduled to take place throughout 2013. Please check your online companion for dates and times! **Please note:** Registration begins one month before the session date. Be sure to sign up early, since spaces are reserved on a first come, first serve basis.

5 WATCH THE FAST FACT VIDEOS

In Fast Fact videos, one of Kaplan's highly rated ACT tutors explains and reinforces the most important concepts from each chapter.

Fast Fact videos can only be accessed through your online companion.

Here's how:

1. Once you've signed into your student home page, open your Syllabus.

2. In the Syllabus window, go to the "Fast Fact Videos" menu option.

3. Click on the link for the video you'd like to see. A separate window will appear with your video.

GOOD LUCK!

TIPS FOR CUSTOMIZING YOUR STUDY PLAN

The most effective study plan will adapt to your individual needs. Here are some helpful tips:

- ☐ Start with a review of the content you're weakest in and include quizzes on these weaker topics to boost your skills and understanding.

- ☐ Devote time to reinforcing content strengths through lesson reviews and practice quizzes.

- ☐ Use full-length practice tests as milestones. There are six full-length Practice Tests in the program—don't plan on saving them all for the final weeks. Test yourself periodically and chart your progress.

- ☐ Think about the topics on which you need to focus. Plan to read those lessons in the book, take practice sets, and review answer explanations.

- ☐ As time permits, go back to the question types that you aced so you can keep the material sharp.

- ☐ Take time to practice your essay writing. Understanding the essay requirements and practicing your writing will help you deliver a great essay on test day.

- ☐ Reevaluate your strengths and weaknesses regularly. If they change, adjust your plan accordingly.

ACT®

PREMIER

2014 Edition

Kaplan offers resources and options to help you prepare for the PSAT, SAT, ACT, AP exams, and other high-stakes exams. Go to www.kaptest.com or scan this code below with your phone (you will need to download a QR code reader) for free events and promotions.

snap.vu/m87n

Related Titles for College-Bound Students

AP Biology

AP Calculus AB & BC

AP Chemistry

AP English Language & Composition

AP English Literature & Composition

AP Environmental Science

AP European History

AP Human Geography

AP Macroeconomics/Microeconomics

AP Physics B & C

AP Psychology

AP Statistics

AP U.S. Government & Politics

AP U.S. History

AP World History

ACT Strategies, Practice, and Review

ACT Premier

ACT English and Reading Workbook

ACT Math and Science Workbook

ACT Strategies for Super Busy Students

SAT Strategies, Practice, and Review

SAT Premier

12 Practice Tests for the SAT

SAT 2400

SAT Critical Reading Workbook

SAT Math Workbook

SAT Writing Workbook

SAT Comprehensive Vocabulary

SAT Strategies for Super Busy Students

Frankenstein: A Kaplan SAT Score-Raising Classic

The Tales of Edgar Allan Poe: A Kaplan SAT Score-Raising Classic

Dr. Jekyll and Mr. Hyde: A Kaplan SAT Score-Raising Classic

The Scarlet Letter: A Kaplan SAT Score-Raising Classic

The War of the Worlds: A Kaplan SAT Score-Raising Classic

Wuthering Heights: A Kaplan SAT Score-Raising Classic

SAT Score-Raising Dictionary

SAT Subject Test: Biology E/M

SAT Subject Test: Chemistry

SAT Subject Test: Literature

SAT Subject Test: Mathematics Level 1

SAT Subject Test: Mathematics Level 2

SAT Subject Test: Physics

SAT Subject Test: Spanish

SAT Subject Test: U.S. History

SAT Subject Test: World History

ACT®

PREMIER

2014

KAPLAN
PUBLISHING
New York

© 2013 by Kaplan, Inc.

Published by Kaplan Publishing, a division of Kaplan, Inc.
395 Hudson St., 4th Floor
New York, NY 10014

Excerpt from *History of Western Civilization: A Handbook*, Sixth Edition, copyright © 1986 by William H. McNeil. Reprinted by permission of the University of Chicago Press.

Excerpt from *Invitation to the Theatre*, copyright © 1967 by George Kernodle. Harcourt, Brace & World, Inc.

Excerpt from *Remains of the Day*, copyright © 1989 by Kazuo Ishiguro. Reprinted by permission of Alfred A. Knopf, a division of Random House, Inc.

Excerpt from *Light and Color in Nature and Art*, copyright © 1983 by Samuel J. Williamson. Reprinted by permission of John Wiley & Sons.

Excerpt from *A History of Women Artists*, copyright © 1975 by Hugo Munsterberg; Clarkson N. Potter, a division of Random House, Inc. Reprinted by permission of the author's family.

Excerpt from "The Return of the Big Cats," by Mac Margolis, *Newsweek*, December 11, 2000, copyright © 2000 by Newsweek, Inc. Reprinted by permission.

Excerpt from *Music Through the Ages*, by Marion Bauer and Ethel R. Peyser, edited by Elizabeth E. Rogers, copyright © 1932 by Marion Bauer and Ethel R. Peyser, renewed © 1960 by Ethel R. Peyser. Revised edition copyright © 1967 by Elizabeth E. Rogers and Clair Lingg. Reprinted by permission of G.P. Putnam's Sons, a division of Penguin Group (USA), Inc.

Excerpt from "The Solar Inconstant," by John Horgan, *Scientific American*, September 1988, copyright © 1988 by *Scientific American*. Reprinted by permission of *Scientific American*. All rights reserved.

Excerpt from "Architects and Power: The Natural Market for Architecture," by Robert Gutman, *Progressive Architecture*, December 1992. Reprinted by permission of Penton Media, Inc.

Printed in the United States of America

10 9 8 7 6 5 4 3

ISBN-13: 978-1-61865-059-7

Kaplan Publishing books are available at special quantity discounts to use for sales promotions, employee premiums, or educational purposes. For more information or to order books, please call the Simon & Schuster special sales department at 866-506-1949.

Contents

Welcome to
Kaplan ACT: Premier

Are you ready to conquer the ACT?

Kaplan knows the ACT exam is important to you. A great score on the ACT can help you stand out from the crowd when applying to colleges and can also help you get scholarships and financial aid to pay for it all.

Kaplan has more than 75 years of experience getting students ready for exams. We've spent decades building a powerful arsenal of test-taking tools designed with *you* in mind, and the book you now hold in your hands contains everything you need to score higher on the ACT.

The name of this book says it all: The 2014 edition of *Kaplan ACT: Premier* includes proven ACT strategies, six realistic ACT Practice Tests (four in the book and two online), a DVD of elite Kaplan teachers providing instruction and tips, and in-depth review of all tested material. Kaplan's exclusive ACT tools work. Use them to your advantage, and get ready to score higher on the ACT!

LET'S GET STARTED!

Kaplan ACT: Premier has everything you need to get ready for test day, but how you use it is *your* choice. Kaplan realizes that no one knows your test-prep needs better than you, so we've designed this book to put you in control of the variety and amount of study that best suits your needs.

This book is designed to allow you to determine the path your test prep takes. Use it front to back or jump around and focus on the test sections that you need the most help with—it's your call.

On top of all the great test prep inside the book, we've put a diagnostic test online to help you determine your test strengths and weaknesses and focus your study plan. This is a great place to get started.

TAKE THE ONLINE DIAGNOSTIC QUIZ

Taking the online diagnostic quiz is a great way to figure out where your ACT skills stand and how to structure your study time between now and test day. Take the quiz and see what test sections are your strongest and which may require the most prep.

Here's how to access your ACT diagnostic quiz online:

1. Go to kaptest.com/booksonline.
2. Follow the on-screen instructions. Please have a copy of your book available.

BUILD YOUR ACT STUDY PLAN

Okay, so you've taken the diagnostic quiz. Now what? Well, now that you have a good idea which test sections are your strongest and which need the most attention, you are ready to make the most of this book and build your study plan.

YOUR ACT STUDY PLAN—5 STEPS TO SUCCESS

1. Carefully go through the lessons in this book, paying close attention to the ones that focus on the test sections you were weakest in on your diagnostic quiz.

2. Take the end-of-chapter practice sets to see how well you're progressing. Be sure to read the answer explanations carefully—they'll help you figure out where you might have gone wrong during your problem solving.

3. Don't be afraid to review challenging lessons and concepts more than once. Isn't doing well on the ACT worth the extra study time?

4. Take time to practice your writing skills for the ACT essay. Use the strategies provided in this book to wow the essay graders on test day!

5. Once you're comfortable with the various ACT question types and test material, dive into the full-length Practice Tests at the back of the book. Test yourself under realistic test-day conditions and chart your progress. If your strengths and weaknesses change, adjust your study plan.

KAPLAN'S GOT YOU COVERED!

In addition to all the proven test-prep material in this book, based on decades of experience preparing students for the ACT, we've asked some of Kaplan's premier test experts to provide you with exclusive advice, tips, and strategies for scoring higher on the ACT.

Whenever you see these icons:

we recommend you read the quote carefully and follow the advice given as you get ready for test day.

These helpful hints come from the following sources:

Kaplan Expert Tutor Tips

One of Kaplan's expert ACT tutors provides valuable insight on how you can make the most of your ACT prep and score higher.

Kaplan Perfect Score Tips

Did you know that in any given year, less than .0001 percent of test takers get a perfect ACT score? It's a pretty rare and impressive feat and one which a Kaplan student recently achieved! Our very own perfect score whiz gives you the secret to her ACT success!

Good luck on test day!

PART ONE

ACT Basics

CHAPTER 1

Introduction to the ACT

Before you plunge into studying for the ACT, let's take a step back and look at the big picture. What's the ACT all about? How can you prepare for it? How is it scored? This chapter will answer these questions and more.

The ACT is an opportunity, not a barrier. In fact, you should be grateful that you have to take it. Really. A strong ACT score is one credential that doesn't depend on things you can't control. It doesn't depend on how good your high school is. It doesn't depend on how many academic luminaries you know, or how rich and famous your family is, or whether any of your teachers are gullible enough to swear in a letter of recommendation that you're the greatest scientific mind since Isaac Newton. No, your ACT score depends on only you.

> **EXPERT TUTOR TIP**
> If you have two weeks or fewer to prep for the ACT, don't panic. The first thing you should do is become familiar with the test. This chapter is the place to start.

Granted, the ACT is a tough exam, but you should be grateful for that, too. Really. If the ACT were easy, everyone would do well. A good score wouldn't mean much. However, because it is so challenging, the ACT can be your single best opportunity to show what you can do and prove to colleges that you are the candidate of choice—for admission, for advanced placement, for scholarships.

It's important, though, that you take the test in the right spirit. Don't be timid in the face of the ACT or let it bully you. You've got to take control of the test. Our mission in this book is to show you exactly how to do that.

It helps to think of the ACT challenge as a contest—not only between you and the test, but also between you and that other person trying to get your spot in college. The ACT, after all, is meant to provide a way for all college applicants to compete on an even playing field. How do you compete successfully in a fair academic fight?

You train—harder and smarter than the next person. First, you learn whatever knowledge and skills you need to know. Also, just as importantly, you learn how to show what you know, in ways that the test is designed to reward. You learn how to be a savvy test taker.

> ✔️ **PERFECT SCORE TIP**
> The best thing you can do for yourself is really get to know the test. The ACT is a very predictable test, and being familiar with it will help you with both time and nerves on test day.

FOUR KEYS TO ACT SUCCESS

There are four basic keys to achieving ACT success. Following any of these by itself will improve your score. Following all four together will make you nothing less than awesome.

1. Learn the Test

The ACT is very predictable. You'd think the test makers would get bored after a while, but they don't. The same kinds of questions, testing the same skills and concepts, appear every time the ACT is given.

Because the test specifications rarely change, you can learn in advance what to expect on every section. Just a little familiarity can make an enormous difference on the ACT. Here are a few ways in which learning the test will boost your score:

- **You'll learn the directions.** Why waste valuable time reading directions when you can have them down pat beforehand? You need every second during the test to answer questions and get points.

- **You'll learn the difficulty range of questions.** The typical ACT test taker only gets about half the questions right. Knowing this will stop you from panicking when you hit an impossible science passage or trigonometry question. Relax! You can skip many tough questions on the ACT and still get a great score! Also, once you know that the questions aren't arranged in order of difficulty, you'll know that just beyond that awful question will be one, two, or even three easy questions that you can get right with no sweat at all.

- **You'll learn how to get extra points by guessing.** Unlike other standardized tests, the ACT has no wrong-answer penalty. Knowing that simple fact can boost your score significantly. If you can't answer a question, guess.

- **You'll learn what makes a high-scoring essay.** If you are taking the optional Writing test, learning how it is scored will help you craft a good essay.

We'll help you get a better understanding of the ACT in the next chapter, entitled "The Subject Tests: A Preview."

> **PERFECT SCORE TIP**
> The ACT will not penalize you for a wrong answer. So answer every question, and don't lose possible points by leaving questions blank.

2. Learn the Kaplan Methods and Strategies

The ACT isn't a normal exam. Most normal exams test your memory. Instead the ACT tests problem-solving skills in a standardized-test format. Therefore, arming yourself with the Kaplan Methods and Strategies will earn you points!

Most students miss a lot of ACT questions for no good reason. They see a tough-looking question, say to themselves, "Uh-oh, I don't remember how to do that," and start to gnaw on their No. 2 pencils.

However, many ACT questions can be answered without perfect knowledge of the material being tested. Often, all you need to do to succeed on the ACT is to think strategically and creatively. We call this kind of strategic, creative frame of mind the ACT Mind-Set.

How do you put yourself into the ACT Mind-Set? You continually ask yourself questions such as: "What does this mean? How can I put this into a form I can understand and use? How can I do this faster?" Once you develop some savvy test-taking skills, you'll find yourself capable of working out problems that, at first reading, might have scared you half to death! In fact, we'll show you how you can sometimes get right answers when you don't even understand the question or the passage.

> **PERFECT SCORE TIP**
> Don't let tough questions scare you. The Kaplan Methods and Strategies will help teach you how to tackle them. And remember: You don't need to know every question to do well.

There are many, many specific strategies you can use to boost your score. For instance, here are just a few things you'll learn:

- **You'll learn the peculiarities of the ACT format.** Except for the Writing test, the ACT is a multiple-choice test. The correct answer is **always** right there in front of you. We'll show you how to develop specific tactics for each question type to maximize your chances of selecting the correct answer. The wrong answers often take predictable forms. For example, in the English section the shortest answer is the correct answer surprisingly often. Knowing statistical information like this can give you an important edge.

- **You'll learn a plan of attack for each subject test.** We'll show you some really useful ways of attacking each subject test. You'll learn how to do "question triage"—deciding which questions to do now and which to save for later. You'll learn the Kaplan Method—designed to get you points quickly and systematically—for each ACT subject test. You'll learn gridding techniques to avoid any answer sheet disasters.

- **You'll learn "unofficial" ways of getting right answers fast.** On the ACT, nobody cares how you decide which choice to select. The only thing that matters is picking the right answer. That's different from the way it works on most high school tests, where you get credit for showing that you've done the questions the "right" way (that is, the way you were taught to do them by your high school teacher). We'll show you how to find creative shortcuts to the correct answers—"unofficial" methods that will save you precious time and net you extra points.

> ☑ **PERFECT SCORE TIP**
> Test-taking tips can only take you so far if you don't know the material. Figure out which topics you need the most help on, and make sure to focus time on learning or refreshing those topics.

The basic test-smart techniques and strategies for the whole test are covered in the chapter called "Taking Control: The Top Ten Strategies." The Kaplan Methods and Strategies for each subject test, plus specific hints, techniques, and strategies for individual question types, are found in the Skill-Building Workouts. These are then summarized in the Strategic Summaries.

3. Learn the Material Tested

The ACT is designed to test skills and concepts learned in high school and needed for college. Familiarity with the test, coupled with smart test-taking strategies, will take you only so far. For your best score, you need to sharpen up the skills and content-related knowledge that the ACT tests.

The good news is that most of the content on the ACT is pretty basic. You've probably already learned most of what the ACT expects you to know, but you may need help remembering. That's partly what this book is for—to remind you of the knowledge you already have and to build and refine the specific skills you've developed in high school. Here are just a few of the things we'll remind you of:

- **You'll learn how to read graphs and tables.** Many Science questions rely on your ability to use data presented in the form of graphs and tables. (We'll teach you how to read graphs and tables in Science Workout 1.)

- **Have you met any FANBOYS lately?** Don't know? Well, this is the acronym for the conjunctions used with a comma to connect two independent clauses in a sentence. We know you want to know more about this, so here's a sneak preview: FANBOYS help you remember **F**or, **A**nd, **N**or, **B**ut, **O**r, **Y**et, **S**o. For more grammar rules, check out English Workout 3.

- **If your math "engine" is rusty when it comes to triangles, probabilities, algebraic expressions**, and more, we'll get you up and running. The three Math Workout chapters and the 100 Key Math Concepts for the ACT will have that engine purring again in no time.

- **You'll learn how to do trigonometry problems.** Do you remember exactly what a cotangent is? A cosine? We didn't think so. But there are four trig problems on every ACT. (You can learn about trigonometry problems in 100 Key Math Concepts for the ACT, items 96–100.)

- **You'll learn the difference between *lie* and *lay*.** Is it "I lay down on the couch" or "I lie down on the couch"? You may want to lie down yourself if you encounter such issues on the ACT, but don't fret. We'll remind you of the common grammar traps the test lays for you. (For a discussion of this tested issue, see Classic Grammar Rule #9 in English Workout 3.)

4. Practice, Practice, Practice

Practice creates confidence. On test day, you need to have all the Kaplan Methods and Strategies and the tested concepts in your brain and to be relaxed and ready to go. Reading and understanding the contents of this book are key, but there's one more step. For the Kaplan Methods to be most effective on test day, you need to make them part of your everyday routine. The best way to do that is to practice as much as possible.

Test day often becomes THE DAY. You're in a room full of people, all in a state of anticipation and nervousness—the anxiety is contagious! Don't let the moment take over and make you forget what you know about doing well. Your best ally is the confidence that practice gives you.

Note: If you don't have time to practice with all of the sections, you can (and should!) practice in the areas you feel weakest.

These specifics we've discussed comprise what we call the ACT knowledge base. The components of this knowledge base are reviewed along the way throughout this book. The resources in this book and online summarize this information for the two sections of the ACT that explicitly test knowledge: English and Math.

In sum, then, follow these four keys to ACT success:

1. **Learn the test.**
2. **Learn the strategies.**
3. **Learn the material tested.**
4. **Practice, practice, practice.**

If you do, you'll find yourself just where you should be: in full command of your ACT test-taking experience. Count on it.

> ✓ **PERFECT SCORE TIP**
> Don't be tricked into thinking the ACT is a test based solely on intelligence. Anyone can do well on this test if he or she really studies for it.

WHAT IS THE ACT?

As you know, the ACT is a standardized test. That means it tests predefined concepts in predictable ways. For example, the ACT English section always includes ten questions that test punctuation. The ACT Math section always includes four questions that test trigonometry. The format of the ACT is also predictable. For example, the Reading section always includes four passages, each with ten questions. The Science section always includes seven passages; one of those will always present conflicting viewpoints and will feature seven questions. You'll learn more about the tested concepts and the predictability of the ACT as you work with this book. For now, though, you should understand one thing—the more you know about how the test is written and structured, the more in control you'll feel on test day. Sure, you can work only on the Math section when the proctor announces, "You have the next 60 minutes to work on Section 2." However, you don't necessarily need to work on the questions in their exact order. In fact, you shouldn't. The methods and strategies you'll learn in this book are designed to put you in control of your test-taking experience and earn you the most points possible in each section. Your success begins with knowing exactly what to expect on the ACT.

So, before anything, take some time and get to know this test. Let's start with the basics. The ACT is a three-hour exam (three and a half hours if you take the optional Writing test) taken by high school juniors and seniors for admission to college. It is not an IQ test; it's a test of problem-solving skills—which means that you can improve your performance by preparing for it.

But let's be realistic about ACT scores. It's a neat and easy way of comparing all students numerically, no matter what their academic backgrounds and no matter how much grade inflation exists at their high schools. You know the admissions people are going to take a serious look at your test scores.

The ACT consists of four subject tests: English, Math, Reading, and Science, as well as the optional Writing test. All the subject tests are primarily designed to test skills rather than knowledge, though some knowledge is required—particularly in English, for which a familiarity with grammar and usage is important. In Math, you will need to know the basic math concepts taught in a regular high school curriculum. The Writing section tests your ability to clearly communicate your position on an issue.

▶ OVERVIEW OF THE ACT

- The ACT is about three hours long (three and a half with the Writing test).
- There will be a short break between the Math and Reading subtests.
- The ACT consists of a total of 215 scored multiple-choice questions and one optional essay.
- The exam is comprised of four subject tests and an optional Writing test:
    - English (45 minutes, 75 questions)
    - Math (60 minutes, 60 questions)
    - Reading (35 minutes, 40 questions)
    - Science (35 minutes, 40 questions)
    - Writing (30 minutes, 1 essay question)

ACT FAQS

Here are some quick answers to the questions students ask most frequently about the ACT.

How Is the ACT Scored?

The ACT is scored differently from most tests you take at school. Your ACT score on a test section is not reported as the total number of questions you answered correctly, nor does your ACT score indicate the percentage of questions you answered correctly. Instead, the test makers add up all of your correct answers in a section to get what's called your raw score for that section. They then use a conversion chart, or scale, that matches up a particular raw score with what's called a scaled score. The scaled score is the number that gets reported as your score for that ACT subtest. For each version of the ACT administered, the test maker uses a unique conversion chart that equates a particular raw score with a particular scaled score.

> **EXPERT TUTOR TIP**
> Most ACT test takers score between 17 and 23. A score below 17 will seriously limit your choice of colleges. Any score above 23 will be an asset in your quest for admission to a competitive college.

ACT scaled scores range from 1 to 36. Nearly half of all test takers score within a much narrower range: 17–23. Tests at different dates vary slightly, but the following data is based on a recent administration of the test and can be considered typical.

ACT Approximate Percentile Rank*	Scaled (or Composite) Score	Percentage of Questions Correct
99%	31	90%
90%	26	75%
76%	23	63%
54%	20	53%
28%	17	43%

*Percentage of ACT takers scoring at or below given score

Notice that to earn a score of 20 (the national average), you need to answer only about 53 percent of the questions correctly. On most tests, getting only a bit more than half the questions right would be terrible. Not so on the ACT. A score of 20 puts you in the middle range of test takers.

> **EXPERT TUTOR TIP**
> Just a few questions right or wrong on the ACT can make a big difference. Answering only five extra questions correctly on each subject test can move you from the bottom of the applicant pool into the middle or from the middle up to the top.

The score table includes two very strong scores: 26 and 31. Either score would impress almost any college admissions officer. A 26 would put you in the top 10 percent of the students who take the exam, and a 31 would put you in the top 1 percent. Even a 31 requires getting only about 90 percent of the questions right! The best student in your high school will probably get at least a dozen questions wrong. The ACT includes questions that even your smartest teachers might get wrong.

If you earn a score of 23, you'll be in about the 76th percentile. That means that 76 percent of the test takers did as well as, or worse than, you did—in other words, that only 24 percent did better than you. It means you're in the top quarter of the people who take the ACT. That's a good score, but notice that to earn this score, you need only about 63 percent of the questions correct. On most tests, a score of 63 is probably a D or an F. But on the ACT, it's about a B+.

How Many ACT Scores Will You Get?

The ACT scaled score we've talked about so far is technically called the composite score. While it's really important, you actually receive 12 different scores when you take the ACT: the composite score, 4 (or 5) subject scores, and 7 subscores. Though the subject scores can play a role in decisions at some schools, the subscores usually aren't important for most people, so feel free to ignore the following chart if you don't feel like looking at it.

Here's the full battery of ACT scores (1–36) you'll receive. Few people (except your parents, maybe) will care about anything except your composite score for college admissions, though some schools use subscores for course placement.

English Score (1–36)	Usage/Mechanics subscore (1–18); Rhetorical Skills subscore (1–18)
Math Score (1–36)	Pre-Algebra/Elementary Algebra subscore (1–18); Algebra/Coordinate Geometry subscore (1–18); Plane Geometry/Trigonometry subscore (1–18)
Reading Score (1–36)	Social Sciences/Sciences subscore (1–18); Arts/Literature subscore (1–18)
Science Score (1–36)	There are no subscores in Science.
(Optional) Writing Score (2–12)	There are no subscores in Writing.
(Optional) Combined English-Writing Score (1–36)	There are no subscores for the Combined English-Writing score. This score does not count toward your composite score, but colleges will see it.

How Do Colleges Use Your ACT Score?

The most important score is typically the composite score (which is an average of the four major subject scores). This is the score used by most colleges and universities in the admissions process. The subject scores and subscores may be used for advanced placement or occasionally for scholarships, but they are primarily used by college advisors to help students select majors and first-year courses.

Although many schools deny that they use benchmark scores as cutoffs, we're not sure we really believe them. Big Ten universities and colleges with similarly competitive admissions generally decline to accept students with composite scores below 22 or 23. For less competitive schools, the benchmark score may be lower than that; for some very selective schools, the cutoff may be higher.

To be fair, no school uses the ACT as an absolute bar to admission; for most applicants, though, a low ACT score is decisive. As a rule, only students whose backgrounds are extremely unusual or who have overcome enormous disadvantages are accepted if their ACT scores are below the benchmark.

> **✔ PERFECT SCORE TIP**
> Many people are scared of taking the Writing test because they compare it to the SAT Writing section. The two tests are very different—so be sure to read chapter 16 before making your choice.

Should You Take the Optional Writing Test?

You should decide whether to take the ACT Writing test based on the admissions policies of your target schools and on the advice of your high school guidance counselors. A list of colleges requiring the test is maintained on the ACT website, www.act.org/aap/writing. If you are unsure about what schools you will apply to, you should plan to take the Writing test. However, testing will be available later if you decide not to take the Writing test and discover later that you need it.

> **✔ PERFECT SCORE TIP**
> Many schools prefer that you take the ACT Writing test. If you don't know yet where you will be applying, consider taking this optional test to reduce the chances you will have to take the ACT again.

How Do Schools Use the Optional Writing Test?

The ACT Writing test may be used for either admissions or course placement purposes or sometimes both. Students who take the Writing test will receive an English score, a Writing subscore, and a combined English-Writing score on a 1–36 scale. (The combined English-Writing score is not averaged into the composite score.) Copies of the essay (with the graders' comments) will also be available online for downloading. Schools that do not require the Writing test will also receive the Combined English-Writing score for students who have taken the Writing test, unless the school specifically asks *not* to receive those results.

Should You Guess on the ACT?

The short answer? Yes! The long answer? Yes, of course!

As we saw, ACT scores are only based on the number of correct answers. Questions that you leave blank and questions you answer incorrectly simply don't count. Unlike some other standardized tests, the ACT has no wrong answer penalty. That's why you should **always** guess on every ACT question you can't answer, even if you don't have time to read it. Though the questions vary enormously in difficulty, harder questions are worth exactly the same as easier ones, so it pays to guess on the really hard questions and spend your time breezing through the really easy ones.

Can You Retake the Test?

You can take the ACT as many times as you like. You can then select whichever test score you prefer to be sent to colleges when you apply. However, you cannot take advantage of this option if, at the time you register for the test, you designate certain colleges to receive your scores. Thus, it is crucial that you not designate any colleges when you register for the test. You can (for a small additional fee) have ACT scores sent to colleges at any time after the scores are reported.

EXPERT TUTOR TIP
When you sign up for the ACT, you can choose colleges to receive your score. Unless time is of the essence, don't do it, even though the first four score reports are sent for free. Wait until you get your score, then send it out (for a small additional fee) if you're happy. If you hate your score, you can take the test again and send only the new, improved score.

Unless you don't have enough money for that small extra fee, or you're taking the ACT under the wire and you need your scores to reach your target schools ASAP, give yourself the freedom to retake the test. What this means, of course, is that even if you blow the ACT once, you can give yourself another chance without the schools of your choice knowing about it. The ACT is one of the few areas of your academic life in which you get a second chance.

PERFECT SCORE TIP
The ACT is offered many times per year, so think hard about which test date will give you the most time to prepare. For example, I took it in September because I knew during the school year I would not have enough time to give my studying the attention it deserved.

ACT REGISTRATION OVERVIEW

- **To get a registration packet, see your guidance counselor, or contact:**

    ACT Registration
    301 ACT Drive
    P.O. Box 414
    Iowa City, IA 52243-0414
    Phone: (319) 337-1270
    Web: www.act.org

- **You can also register online at www.actstudent.org.**

- **Students with disabilities or with other special circumstances can call (319) 337-1332.**

> **GO ONLINE**
> Visit the test maker's website at www.act.org for the latest information on test registration, fees, and content.

- **The basic fee at press time for the ACT is $35 without the Writing test and $50.50 with the Writing test in the United States.** (For students testing outside the 50 United States, the fee is $65, $80.50 for the ACT with Writing test.) Call (319) 337-1448 for more information on taking the test outside the United States.

  This price includes reports for you, your high school, and up to four college choices. There are additional fees for late registration, standby testing, changing test centers or test dates, and additional services and products.

- **In the United States, the ACT is administered in September, October, December, February, April, and June.** (The February date is not available in the state of New York.) In selected states, the ACT is also offered in late September. Register early to secure the time you want at the test center of your choice and to avoid late registration fees.

- **You may take the ACT as often as you wish.** Many students take it twice, once as a junior and again as a senior. There are no limitations on how many times you can take the ACT, but there are some restrictions on how often you can test. For example, you can test only once per national test date.

- **Be sure you take your test center admission ticket and acceptable identification with you to the test center.** Acceptable forms of identification are a photo ID or a recently published photo with your full name printed. Unacceptable forms of identification are a birth certificate, Social Security card, or any other ID without photo. You will not be admitted without acceptable identification.

- **Check with ACT, Inc., for all the latest information on the test.** Every effort is made to keep the information in this book up-to-date, but changes may occur after the book is published.

- **Go online (act.org) to make sure you know ALL the ACT regulations for test day.** For example, all electronic devices (including cell phones) must be turned off from the time you're admitted to the test until you're dismissed after testing concludes.

Note: Violations of these rules, such as an alarm going off or a phone ringing in the test room, may result in your dismissal from the room and the nonscoring of your answer sheet.

- **You might be considering whether to take the ACT, the SAT, or both.** For more information on the SAT, go to the College Board's website at www.collegeboard.com.

> ✓ **PERFECT SCORE TIP**
> The ACT and SAT are very different tests. Many people have an affinity for one over the other. Try some sample questions from each, and decide which one works best for you.

TAKING THE PLAN EXAM

Students should also be aware of the PLAN® exam, which offers a preview of the format and content of the material found on the ACT. A student's success on this exam is often an accurate predictor of success on the ACT. The PLAN exam helps students decide which courses to take in their junior and senior years of high school; it also helps them consider certain career paths prior to college, based on their strengths or weaknesses as indicated by their scores. The PLAN is generally offered to students in the fall of their sophomore year. To learn more, visit PLAN's website for student information at www.actstudent.org/plan.

▶ IF YOU LEARNED ONLY FIVE THINGS IN THIS CHAPTER...

1. The ACT consists of four required subject tests (English, Math, Reading, and Science), plus an optional Writing test.

2. Total testing time is about three hours, plus half an hour for Writing.

3. All questions are multiple-choice except on the Writing test (one essay question).

4. There is no penalty for a wrong answer, so you should guess.

5. ACT composite scores range from 1–36.

CHAPTER 2

The Subject Tests: A Preview

Okay, you've seen how the ACT is set up. But to really do well, you've got to know something about the ACT subject tests.

As we'll see, the questions in every subject test vary widely in difficulty. Some are so easy that most elementary school students could answer them. Others would give even Einstein a little trouble. Recall: **The questions are not arranged in order of difficulty.** That's different from some other tests, in which easier questions come first. Skipping past hard questions is very important, since otherwise you may **never** reach easy ones toward the end of the exam.

Here's a preview of the types of questions you'll see on the subject tests. We'll keep them toward the easy end of the difficulty scale here, but later, in the Skill-Building Workouts, we'll challenge you with tougher questions.

After we look at the four required subject tests, we'll give you a preview of the optional Writing test.

 **PERFECT SCORE TIP**
The structure of the ACT is very predictable. Know the order, number of questions, and time for each section cold by the time you get to test day.

ENGLISH

The English test lasts 45 minutes and includes 75 questions. That works out to about 30 seconds per question. When it comes down to it, though, you should spend less time on easier questions and more on harder questions. The test is divided into five passages, each with about 15 questions.

Note: You're not tested on spelling or vocabulary here. Rather, the ACT is designed to test your understanding of the conventions of English—punctuation, grammar, sentence structure—and of rhetorical skills. Rhetorical skills are more strategic things like organizing the text and making sure it's consistently styled and concise.

Students nearly **always** get more questions correct in English than in any other section. That tends to make them think that English is a lot easier than the rest of the ACT. Alas, it's not that simple. Because most students do well, the test makers have much higher expectations for English than for other parts of the test. They know that it's generally easier to get English questions right than, say, Science questions. That's why, to earn an average English subscore (a 20, say), you have to get almost two-thirds of the questions right, while on the rest of the test you need to get only about half of them right.

The Format

More than half of the English questions follow a standard format. A word, phrase, or sentence in a passage is underlined. You're given four options: to leave the underlined portion alone (NO CHANGE, which is **always** the first choice) or to replace it with one of three alternatives.

Example

...Pike's Peak in Southwest Colorado

is named before Zebulon Pike, an
    37
early explorer. He traveled through
    37
the area, exploring...

37. A. NO CHANGE
    B. before Zebulon Pike became
        an explorer, and he
    C. after Zebulon Pike, when he
    D. after Zebulon Pike. He

The right answer for number 37 is choice D. The other choices all have various problems: grammatical, stylistic, logical. Only choice D makes the sentence sensible and correct.

Notice that a single question can test several kinds of writing errors. We find that about a third of the English questions test your ability to write concisely (we call them Economy questions), about another third test for logic and sense (Sense questions), and only the remaining third test hard-and-fast rules of grammar (Technicality questions). There's a lot of overlap between these question types, so don't worry too much about categories. We provide them simply to give you an idea of the kinds of errors you'll be expected to correct.

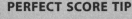
PERFECT SCORE TIP
In English passages, always read the options in context, pretending you are saying them out loud. Often, the mistake will become clear to you when you say it to yourself.

TO OMIT OR NOT TO OMIT

Some English questions offer, as one of the alternatives, the chance to completely omit the underlined portion, usually as the last of the four choices.

Example

Later, Pike fell while valiantly defending America in the War of 1812. <u>It goes</u> 40 <u>without saying that this took place after</u> 40 <u>he discovered Pike's Peak.</u> He actually 40 died near York (now called Toronto)…

40. F. NO CHANGE
    G. Clearly, this must have occurred subsequent to his discovering Pike's Peak.
    H. This was after he found Pike's Peak.
    J. OMIT the underlined portion

In this case, choice J is correct. The idea really does "go without saying." For that reason, it shouldn't be stated. On recent ACTs, when OMIT has appeared as an answer choice, it's been correct more than half of the time. Before choosing OMIT, however, read the passage text *without* the underlined portion to ensure the passage is clear and correct when it is left out. When offered as a choice, OMIT is often correct, but not always.

> ✔ **PERFECT SCORE TIP**
> Answer A or F in many English questions is NO CHANGE. Remember that this is sometimes the answer. If you are sure the sentence is completely correct, select this answer instead of making up nonexistent grammar problems.

The Directions

The directions on the English test illustrate why there's an advantage to knowing them beforehand. The directions are long and complicated. Here's what they'll look like, but take our advice—don't bother reading them. We'll show you what you'll need to do. Then, while everyone else is reading the directions on test day, you'll be racking up points.

> ✔ **PERFECT SCORE TIP**
> OMIT is often the correct answer, so don't be scared to think of part of the passage as unnecessary. There will be more tips about this in the first English Workout.

Directions: In the five passages that follow, certain words and phrases are underlined and numbered. In the right-hand column, you will find alternatives for the underlined parts. In most cases, you are to choose the one that best expresses the idea, makes the statement appropriate for standard written English, or is worded most consistently with the style and tone of the passage as a whole. If you think the original version is best, choose NO CHANGE. In some cases, you will find in the right-hand column a question about the underlined part. You are to choose the best answer to the question.

You will also find questions about a section of the passage or about the passage as a whole. These questions do not refer to an underlined portion of the passage, but rather are identified by a number or numbers in a box.

> ✓ **PERFECT SCORE TIP**
> Don't waste valuable time reading the directions on test day, or miss valuable points by not following them. Most directions are not that complicated—so make sure you know them cold before test day.

For each question, choose the alternative you consider best and fill in the corresponding oval on your answer grid. Read each passage through once before you answer the questions that accompany it. For many questions, you must read several sentences beyond the underlined portion to determine the answer. Be sure that you have read enough ahead each time you answer a question.

Nonstandard-Format Questions

Some ACT English questions—about 20 per test—don't follow the more typical format of presenting you with an underlined portion and three possible revisions. A Nonstandard-Format question might appear with an underlined part of the passage and ask you to determine which choice is the LEAST acceptable alternative to the underlined part. Another nonstandard-format question might ask you which of the offered choices best accomplishes a specific goal. You might also be asked whether you should add or delete material, and then choose the appropriate reason for adding or deleting it. For questions like these, it's important to read very carefully! Here's an example of how question 40, which you saw earlier, could be presented as a Nonstandard-Format question.

Example

...Later, Pike fell while valiantly defending America in the War of 1812. [40] He actually died near York (now called Toronto)...

40. Suppose the author considered adding the following sentence at this point: "It goes without saying that this occurred after he discovered Pike's Peak." Given the overall purpose of the passage, would this sentence be appropriate?

F. No, because the sentence adds nothing to the meaning of the passage.

G. No, because the passage is not concerned with Pike's achievements.

H. Yes, because otherwise the sequence of events would be unclear.

J. Yes. Though the sentence is not needed, the author recognizes this fact by using the phrase "it goes without saying."

The correct answer for this question is choice F. Though choice G correctly states that the sentence doesn't belong in the passage, it offers a pretty inappropriate reason. The passage *is* concerned with Pike's achievements. Choices H and J are wrong because they recommend including a sentence that is clearly redundant.

Many of the nonstandard questions occur at the end of a passage. Some ask about the meaning, purpose, or tone of individual paragraphs or of the passage as a whole. Others ask you to evaluate the passage. And still others ask you to determine the proper order of words, sentences, or paragraphs that have been scrambled in the passage.

We think you'll like the English subject test. It can actually be fun. We'll cover strategies for the English question types in the English Workouts.

MATH

The Math test is 60 minutes long and includes 60 questions. That works out to one minute per question, but you'll want to spend less time on easy questions and more on the tough ones.

The Format

All of the Math questions have the same basic multiple-choice format. They ask a question and offer five possible choices (unlike questions on the other subject tests, which have only four choices each).

> ✔ **PERFECT SCORE TIP**
> While studying, if you come across any questions for which you do not know or remember the material, review it! Especially in math, tricks can only get you so far if you don't remember the math behind them.

The questions cover a full range of math topics, from pre-algebra and elementary algebra to plane geometry and even a little bit of trigonometry. If you have specific weaknesses in any of these areas, the 100 Key Math Concepts for the ACT section at the end of this book will help.

Although the Math questions aren't ordered in terms of difficulty, questions drawn from elementary school or junior high tend to come earlier in the section, while those from high school math curricula tend to come later. But this doesn't mean that the easy questions come first and the hardest ones come later. We've found that high school subjects tend to be fresher in most students' minds than things they were taught years ago, so you may actually find the later questions easier. (Do *you* remember the math you learned in seventh grade?)

The Directions

Here's what the Math directions will look like:

> **Directions:** Solve each problem, choose the correct answer, and then fill in the corresponding oval on your answer document.
>
> Do not linger over problems that take too much time. Solve as many as you can, then return to the others in the time you have left for this test.
>
> You are permitted to use a calculator on this test. You may use your calculator for any problems you choose, but some of the problems may best be done without using a calculator.

Note: Unless otherwise noted, all of the following should be assumed:

1. Illustrative figures are NOT necessarily drawn to scale.

2. Geometric figures lie in a plane.

3. The word *line* indicates a straight line.

4. The word *average* indicates arithmetic mean.

Again, when it comes to directions on the ACT, the golden rule is: ***Don't read them on test day!*** You'll already know what they say by the time you take the test.

The Math directions don't really tell you much anyway. Of the four special notes at the end of the Math directions, #2, #3, and #4 almost go without saying. Note #1—that figures are *not* necessarily drawn to scale—seems pretty scary, but in fact, the vast majority of ACT figures *are* drawn to scale. As we'll see, this has significant implications for how to guess on geometry questions.

> ✓ **PERFECT SCORE TIP**
> The use of a calculator is discussed later. You should be familiar with your calculator, and learn when using it is really necessary for you.

READING AND DRAWING DIAGRAMS

We find that about a third of the Math questions either give you a diagram or describe a situation that should be diagrammed. For these questions, the diagrams are crucial.

Example

1. The figure below contains five congruent triangles. The longest side of each triangle is 4 meters long. What is the area of the whole figure?

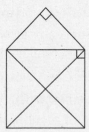

   A. 12.5 square meters

   B. 15 square meters

   C. 20 square meters

   D. 30 square meters

   E. Cannot be determined from the given information.

> **EXPERT TUTOR TIP**
> In ACT Math questions, the answer choice "cannot be determined" is rare. When it does appear, it's usually wrong. "Cannot be determined" is **almost always** wrong in a question that comes with a diagram or for which you can draw one.

The key to this question is to let the diagram tell you what you need to know: Each triangle represents one-quarter of the area of the square and the sides of the *square* are 4 meters (you can figure this out because the top side of the square is the hypotenuse—or longest side—of the triangle that makes the "roof"). Since the area of a square can be found by squaring its side, the area of the square is 16 square meters. Thus, each triangle has an area one-fourth as much—4 square meters. Since the whole figure consists of *five* triangles, each with area 4, the total area is 5 × 4 = 20. The answer is C.

HOW TO APPROACH A STORY PROBLEM

We find that about another third of the Math questions are story problems like the following:

Example

2. Evan drove halfway home at 20 miles per hour, then sped up and drove the rest of the way at 30 miles per hour. What was his average speed for the entire trip?

   F.   20 miles per hour

   G.   22 miles per hour

   H.   24 miles per hour

   J.   25 miles per hour

   K.   28 miles per hour

A good way to comprehend—and resolve—a story problem like this is to think of a real situation just like the one in the story. For example, what if Evan had 120 miles to drive? (You should pick a distance that's easily divisible by both rates.) He would go 60 miles at 30 mph, then 60 miles at 20 mph. How long would it take? Well, 60 miles at 30 mph is two hours; 60 miles at 20 mph is three hours. That's a total of 120 miles in five hours; 120 divided by 5 gives an average speed of 24 mph. The correct answer is thus choice H. (Note: We'll show you alternative ways to answer questions like this later on.)

> ✔ **PERFECT SCORE TIP**
> Don't let variables or abstract stories confuse you. When you see them, calm down and make them simpler by putting real numbers in for the variables. You'll learn more about this Picking Numbers Strategy in Math Workout 1.

GETTING THE CONCEPT

Finally, we find that about a third of the questions directly ask you to demonstrate your knowledge of specific math concepts.

Example

3. If angles A and B are supplementary, and the measure of angle A is 57°, what is the measure, in degrees, of angle B?

    A. 33
    B. 43
    C. 47
    D. 123
    E. 147

This question simply requires that you know the concept of supplementary angles. Two angles are *supplementary* when they form a straight line—in other words, when they add up to 180°. Thus, question 3 boils down to this: What number, added to 57, makes 180? The answer is choice D, 123.

These three types of Math questions, of course, will be discussed more fully in the Math Workouts.

READING

The Reading test is 35 minutes long and includes 40 questions. It contains four passages, each followed by ten questions. You should allow three minutes (or less) to read and mark up the passage. You will then have about 30 seconds per question.

The Format

There are four categories of reading passages: Prose Fiction, Social Science, Humanities, and Natural Science. You'll get one passage in each category. The passages are about 1,000 words long and are written at about the same difficulty level as college textbooks and readings. After each passage, you'll find ten questions.

The Social Science, Humanities, and Natural Science passages are usually well-organized essays. Each has a very specific purpose. Questions expect you to recognize this purpose, to comprehend specific facts contained in the passage, and to understand the structure of the essay. Prose Fiction passages require you to understand the thoughts, feelings, and motivations of fictional characters, even when these are not explicitly stated in the passage (we'll have a special section on Prose Fiction passages in Reading Workout 3).

There are really only three different categories of Reading questions:

1. Specific Detail questions (What does the author say?)
2. Inference questions (Why is this included? What conclusions can you make?)
3. Big Picture questions (What's the overall topic?)

> ✓ **PERFECT SCORE TIP**
> Unlike reading on the SAT, ACT Reading will always have the same format. You will always have four passages, and they will always appear in this order: Prose, Social Science, History, Natural Science.

The Directions

The Reading directions are general:

> **Directions:** There are four passages in this test. Each passage is followed by several questions. After reading a passage, choose the best answer to each question and fill in the corresponding oval on your answer document. You may refer to the passages as often as necessary.

There's nothing stupefying here, but nothing very substantive either. We'll be a little more specific and strategic than the test makers when we suggest a plan of attack in the three Reading Workouts.

> ✓ **PERFECT SCORE TIP**
> You do not have to do the readings in order. For example, if you always have trouble with Prose but are very good at Natural Science, do Natural Science first to make sure you don't run out of time to get those easy points. Develop a personal order that works for you, especially if you have trouble with time.

NAILING DOWN THE DETAILS

Specific Detail questions ask about things stated explicitly in the passage. Your challenge is the following:

- Find the exact place in the passage where the answer can be found. If the question doesn't give line references to help, you will be glad you marked up the passage.
- Remember the ABCs: **A**bbreviate margin notes, **B**racket key sentences, and **C**ircle key words and phrases.
- Match the detail from the text in the passage with the correct answer (by locating either similar words or paraphrasings).

Note: Many wrong choices will be designed to trip you up by including details from other parts of the passage or by using the same wording as the passage while distorting the meaning. Questions in the ACT Reading section are written to have three wrong answers and *only* one right answer. Some answer choices may appear to be half-right, half-wrong; remember, if an answer choice has *anything* wrong with it, then it cannot be the correct answer! Look for the one choice that is flawless.

Two important points to keep in mind:

1. There is one right answer, but there will be other tempting answers.
2. "Refer to the passage" in the Reading directions means that it's a good idea to look at the text before you try to answer the question. Predict before you peek! That is, predict in your own words, or by pointing to a specific phrase in the passage, what you think the answer will be before you look at the choices provided.

Example

When we say "Bach," we almost always refer to Johann Sebastian Bach (1685–1750), but in fact the name "Bach" belongs to a whole family of Baroque German musicians...

(*7 paragraphs and 950 words omitted*)

The works of Johann Christian Bach, J. S. Bach's son, clearly prefigure the rich musical developments that followed the Baroque period. Thus, it is both surprising and unfortunate that the rest of J. S. Bach's family isn't more well known.

6. According to the author, J. S. Bach is the best-known:
   F. German Baroque musician.
   G. member of a musical family.
   H. organist in German history.
   J. composer of Lutheran hymns.

7. Johann Christian Bach was:
   A. born earlier than Johann Sebastian Bach.
   B. a composer of the "Romantic" school of music.
   C. a composer whose works are transitional in style.
   D. well known during his own lifetime.

✔ **PERFECT SCORE TIP**
Always make sure you read the entire question and answer. The incorrect answers are made to look tempting on purpose, so avoid picking them based on key words.

The answer for question 6 is G. Both the first and last sentences in the passage refer to J. S. Bach as the most famous member of a whole family of musicians. You might think J. S. Bach is the best-known German Baroque musician (choice F), but that's not what the passage says, so it's wrong.

The answer for question 7 is choice C. At the end of the passage, the author says that Johann Christian's work "prefigure[d]" the music that followed the Baroque. Thus, it must have had some Baroque characteristics and some new aspects. In other words, it was transitional.

✓ **PERFECT SCORE TIP**
Remember, the scorers do not care about your opinions or ideas about the passage. Base all your answer choices on what is explicitly written in the passage—not your own knowledge of the material.

MAKING AN INFERENCE

Most Reading passages also include a large number of Inference questions, which require you to make an inference from the passage (to "read between the lines"). They differ somewhat from Specific Detail questions. For one thing, students usually consider them harder. An example of each follows.

Example

...though schizophrenia and multiple personality disorder (MPD) may be related, and are often confused by laymen, the two terms have radically different meanings...

32. Which of the following best expresses the relationship between schizophrenia and multiple personality disorder?

F. They are two terms that describe essentially the same phenomenon.

G. The two disorders have nothing in common.

H. Though the two have some similarities, they are fundamentally different.

J. The two are not exactly alike, but are very close.

33. Suppose that a patient has been diagnosed with schizophrenia. Based on the passage, which of the following is LEAST likely?

   A. The patient's doctors immediately assume that the patient also suffers from MPD.

   B. The patient is a layman.

   C. The patient denies that he has MPD.

   D. The patient is related to someone with MPD.

> ✓ **PERFECT SCORE TIP**
> Note trick words such as *except* or *least likely.* Circle them when you read them in questions so you don't mistakenly answer the opposite question.

Note the differences between Specific Detail and Inference questions: 32, a Specific Detail question, requires that you understand the explicitly stated idea that schizophrenia and MPD have some connection but are not the same. That's what choice H says. Question 33, on the other hand, requires you to apply the idea that the two disorders are different. If they are, it's highly unlikely that doctors would simply assume that a patient suffering from one disorder must suffer from the other. Therefore, choice A is least likely—and therefore correct. The other choices may or may not be true, and nothing in the passage leads us to think one way or the other about them. Question 33 is what we'd call a garden-variety Inference question.

> ✓ **PERFECT SCORE TIP**
> Even when the test asks you to infer an answer, the answer will be based on the passage and what the author says. Do not make unsubstantiated judgments on the reading.

GETTING THE BIG PICTURE

Although the majority of Reading questions are Specific Detail and Inference questions, the Reading subtest also includes another type of question that we call Big Picture questions. Some Big Picture questions ask about the passage as a whole, requiring you to find the purpose, tone, or structure of the passage. Others ask you to evaluate the writing. Here's a typical Big Picture question that might have appeared with the Bach family passage we talked about earlier.

Example

9. The author's main point in the passage is to:

    A. show that many of the lesser-known members of the Bach family also influenced music history.

    B. argue that J. C. Bach was actually a greater composer than his father, J. S. Bach.

    C. demonstrate that musical talent **always** runs in families.

    D. dispute the claim that the Bach family was the best-known family of German Baroque musicians.

In order to answer this kind of question, you've got to have a good sense of the Big Picture—the shape and flow of the whole passage. Of course, we printed only a few selected lines from the passage, but that should have been enough to lead you to choice A as the answer. The first line definitely indicates that the subject of the passage is going to be the entire Bach family, with a focus on the ones who aren't as well known as the famous J. S. Bach.

SCIENCE

The Science test is 35 minutes long and includes 40 questions. It has seven passages, each with five to seven questions. This breaks down to approximately five minutes per passage.

No, you don't have to be a scientist to succeed on the ACT Science test. You don't have to know the atomic number of cadmium or the preferred mating habits of the monarch butterfly. All that's required is common sense (though a knowledge of standard scientific processes and procedures sure does help). You'll be given passages containing various kinds of scientific information—drawn from the fields of biology, chemistry, physics, geology, astronomy, and meteorology—which you'll have to understand and use as a basis for inferences.

The Format

On the Science section of the test, the seven passages are broken down as follows:

- Three passages (each with five questions) about tables and graphs
- Three passages (each with six questions) about experiments
- One passage (with seven questions) that presents opposing viewpoints on the same issue

The Directions

Here's what the Science directions will look like:

Directions: There are seven passages in this test. Each passage is followed by several questions. After reading a passage, choose the best answer to each question and fill in the corresponding oval on your answer document. You may refer to the passages as often as necessary. You are NOT permitted to use a calculator on this test.

> ✔ **PERFECT SCORE TIP**
> The biggest ACT myth is about the Science section: this section is NOT based on scientific knowledge, but scientific skills like analyzing experiments and graphs. You do not need to memorize the periodic table to do very well.

Notice the similarity between these directions for Science and those for Reading. The ACT Science and Reading subtests actually test similar skills and require a similar approach—first read the passage quickly to get the big picture, then refer back to the passage to research the relevant information as you answer each question.

ANALYZING DATA

About two-thirds of the questions on the Science subtest require you to read data from graphs or tables. In easier questions, you need only report the information. In harder questions, you may need to draw inferences or note patterns in the data.

> **EXPERT TUTOR TIP**
> We'll show you the best strategic way to attack this subject test in the three Science Workouts.

Example

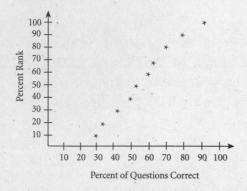

1. A test taker who scores in approximately the 40th percentile has correctly answered about what fraction of the questions?

   A. $\dfrac{9}{10}$

   B. $\dfrac{2}{3}$

   C. $\dfrac{1}{2}$

   D. $\dfrac{1}{5}$

2. Which of the following best describes the relationship between percentile rank and percent of questions correct?

   F. As percentile rank increases, percent of correct questions also increases.

   G. Percentile rank is inversely proportional to the percent of correct questions.

   H. As percentile rank increases, the percent of correct questions decreases.

   J. As percentile rank decreases, percent of correct questions usually, but not always, also decreases.

The correct answer to question 1 is choice C. The point for the 40th percentile is slightly above the 50 percent point on the horizontal axis (percent or questions correct). Fifty percent is the same as $\dfrac{1}{2}$. Note that this question involves a little simple arithmetic (translating a percent into a fraction)—not uncommon for Science questions.

In question 2, the correct answer is choice F. The points that are higher on the graph (higher percentile) are always farther to the right (higher percentage of correct questions). Note that choices G and H say essentially the same thing (we'll discuss direct and inverse proportionality in Science Workout 1), and thus are wrong for the same reason: they get the relationship backwards. Choice J is wrong because it says that the percent of correct questions does not **always** decrease as percentile rank decreases.

> ✔️ **PERFECT SCORE TIP**
> Don't panic if you read the names of chemicals you don't recognize. This section is based on reading comprehension, and you don't need to know all of the chemistry, biology, and physics.

CONDUCTING EXPERIMENTS

Other Science questions require that you understand the way experiments are designed and what they prove. For example, part of a passage might describe an experiment as follows:

Example

EXPERIMENT 1

A scientist adds one drop of nitric acid to Beakers A, B, and C. Each beaker contains water from a different stream. The water in Beaker A came from Stream A, that in Beaker B came from Stream B, and that in Beaker C came from Stream C. Precipitates form in Beakers B and C, but not in Beaker A.

12. Which of the following could properly be inferred on the basis of Experiment 1?

F. Stream A is more polluted than Streams B and C.

G. Streams B and C are more polluted than A.

H. Stream A contains material that neutralizes nitric acid.

J. Streams B and C contain some substance that reacts in the presence of nitric acid.

The correct answer is choice J. Since a precipitate forms when nitric acid is added to Beakers B and C, which contain water from Streams B and C, something in these streams must be involved. However, we don't know that it is pollution, so choice F and G are unwarranted. We don't know exactly *why* no precipitate formed in Beaker A, so choice H is also an unwarranted conclusion. Scientists *hate* unwarranted conclusions.

> ✔️ **PERFECT SCORE TIP**
> Remember that like Reading, Science questions will never ask you to make inferences too far beyond what is given. Analyze the data, but DO NOT make unjustified conclusions.

THE PRINCIPLE OF THE THING

The remaining Science questions require you either to logically apply a principle or to identify ways of defending or attacking a principle. Often, the question will involve two scientists stating opposing views on the same subject, but this is not **always** the case. A passage might describe a theory that most V-shaped valleys are typically formed by water erosion through soft rock and ask these two Principle questions:

Example

16. Which of the following is most likely to be a V-shaped valley?

    F. A valley formed by glaciers

    G. A river valley which is cut into very hard basalt

    H. A valley formed by wind erosion

    J. A river valley in a region of soft shale rocks

17. Which of the following discoveries would most weaken the theory of V-shaped valley formation given in the passage?

    A. Certain parts of many valleys formed by water that are U-shaped

    B. A group of V-shaped valleys almost certainly formed by wind erosion

    C. A group of U-shaped valleys formed by water erosion in hard rock

    D. A group of valleys on Mars that appear to be V-shaped but that are not near any running water

In question 16, the correct answer is choice J, since this is consistent with the passage as described. The correct answer in question 17 is choice B. Finding V-shaped valleys not formed by water erosion would tend to weaken the theory that they are formed this way. The other answers do not offer evidence about V-shaped valleys on Earth, and thus are irrelevant to a theory about them.

We'll be showing you strategies for each kind of Science question in the three Science Workouts.

WRITING

The Writing test is 30 minutes long and includes one essay. You'll be given a topic or issue on which you must take a position, supporting your point of view with examples and evidence.

You don't have to be a great creative writer to succeed on the ACT Writing test. Instead, you have to show that you can focus on an issue and argue your point of view in a coherent, direct way with concrete examples. Furthermore, the essay graders are not primarily concerned with your grammar and punctuation skills. In terms of writing, clarity is what they are looking for. You are being tested on your ability to communicate in writing.

> ✔ **PERFECT SCORE TIP**
> Organization is the key to success on the Writing section. Get used to reading a question and immediately developing three body paragraphs and a thesis. This will not only make for a better essay, but will also let you finish it in the allowed time.

One of the biggest challenges of the Writing test is the time frame. With only 30 minutes to read about the issue, plan your response, draft the essay, and proofread it, you have to work quickly and efficiently. Coming up with a plan and sticking to it are key to succeeding on the Writing test.

The Format

The Writing test consists of one prompt that lays out the issue and gives directions for your response. There are no choices of topic; you have to respond to the topic that's there. Don't worry too much about not knowing anything about the issue you have to write about. Test makers try to craft topics that will be relevant to high school students and about which they can be expected to have a point of view.

> ✔ **PERFECT SCORE TIP**
> ACT essay topics always deal with "high school situations," so don't worry about not understanding the topics. Read the entire prompt and feel free to use the background info it gives you.

The Directions

Here's what the Writing test directions will look like:

This is a test of your writing skills. You will have thirty (30) minutes to write an essay in English. Before you begin planning and writing your essay, read the writing prompt carefully to understand exactly what you are being asked to do. Your essay will be evaluated on the evidence it provides of your ability to express judgments by taking a position on the issue in the writing prompt; to maintain a focus on the topic throughout the essay; to develop a position by using logical reasoning and by supporting your ideas; to organize ideas in a logical way; and to use language clearly and effectively according to the conventions of standard written English.

You may use the unlined pages in this test booklet to plan your essay. These pages will not be scored. *You must write your essay in pencil on the lined pages in the answer folder.* Your writing on those lined pages will be scored. You may not need all the lined pages, but to ensure you have enough room to finish, do NOT skip lines. You may write corrections or additions neatly between the lines of your essay, but do NOT write in the margins of the lined pages. *Illegible essays cannot be scored, so you must write (or print) clearly.*

If you finish before time is called, you may review your work. Lay your pencil down immediately when time called.

DO NOT OPEN THIS BOOKLET UNTIL TOLD TO DO SO.

> ✔ **PERFECT SCORE TIP**
> The questions will always ask you to take a position. Don't try to argue both opinions or feel tied to the one you agree with. For example, in my essay, I argued a stance I do not agree with personally, but I found it an easier topic for an organized and complete essay.

Writing Test Skills

The graders realize you're writing under time pressure, and they expect you to make some mistakes. **The content of your essay is not relevant; readers are not checking your facts, nor will they judge you on your opinions. They only want to see how well you can communicate a relevant, coherent point of view.**

The test makers identify the following as the skills tested on the Writing test:

- **Stating a clear perspective on an issue.** This means answering the question in the prompt.
- **Providing supporting evidence and logical reasoning.** This means offering relevant support for your opinion and building an argument based on concrete details and examples.
- **Maintaining focus and organizing ideas logically.** You've got to be organized, avoid digressions, and tie all your ideas together in a sensible way.
- **Writing clearly.** This is the only skill addressing your ability to write directly, and it's limited to clarity.

> 📶 **GO ONLINE**
> Try writing an ACT-style essay using one of the sample prompts and model essays in the online companion.

The Writing test is not principally a test of your grammar and punctuation (which are tested in the English section)—colleges want to see your reasoning and communication skills. To learn more about how to plan and draft a high-scoring essay, review the Writing Workout.

▶ IF YOU LEARNED ONLY FIVE THINGS IN THIS CHAPTER...

1. The ACT English test includes 75 questions to be answered in 45 minutes. It tests your knowledge of grammar and usage. You'll be asked to fix errors in passages and sometimes to comment on the passage as a whole.

2. The ACT Math test consists of 60 questions to be answered in 60 minutes. Topics include pre-algebra, elementary and intermediate algebra, coordinate and plane geometry, and trigonometry. Questions are not given in order of difficulty.

3. The ACT Reading test includes 40 questions to be answered in 35 minutes. The questions refer to four passages: Prose Fiction, Social Sciences, Humanities, and Natural Sciences.

4. The ACT Science test is comprised of 40 questions to be answered in 35 minutes. There are seven passages with related questions that ask you to analyze and interpret experiments, figures, and scientists' viewpoints. There will be only one to three questions that call on you to use your existing science knowledge.

5. The ACT Writing test consists of one essay prompt that asks you to take a stand on an issue. You have 30 minutes to write a clear and persuasive essay, supported with evidence from your experience, reading, current events, or other sources.

CHAPTER 3

Taking Control:
The Top Ten Strategies

Now that you've got some idea of the kind of challenges you face on the ACT, it's time to start developing strategies for managing them. In other words, you've got to start developing your ACT Mind-Set.

> **EXPERT TUTOR TIP**
> This chapter will help you to take control of the ACT. You should read this chapter even if you have less than two weeks to prep.

The ACT, as we've just seen, isn't a normal test, which requires you to rely almost exclusively on your memory. On a normal test, you'd see questions like this:

> The "golden spike," which joined the Union Pacific and Central Pacific Railroads, was driven in Ogden, Utah, in May 1869. Who was president of the United States at the time?

To answer this question, you have to resort to memory dredging. Either you know the answer is Ulysses S. Grant or else you don't. No matter how hard you think, you'll **never** be able to answer this question if you can't remember your history.

But the ACT doesn't test your long-term memory. The answer to every ACT question can be found on the test. Theoretically, if you read carefully and understand the words and concepts the test uses, you can get almost any ACT question right.

> **PERFECT SCORE TIP**
> Never let hard questions scare you. You can control your own test taking experience, and this next chapter will show you how to manage these hard questions.

Notice the difference between the regular-test question on the previous page and the ACT-type question below:

Example

1. What is the product of n and m^2, where n is an odd number and m is an even number?

    A. An odd number

    B. A multiple of 4

    C. A noninteger

    D. An irrational number

    E. The square of an integer

Aside from the obvious distinction (this question has answer choices, while the other one does not), there's another difference: the ACT question mostly tests your ability to understand a situation rather than your ability to passively remember a fact. Nobody expects you to know off the top of your head what the product of an odd number and the square of an even number is. But the ACT test makers do expect you to be able to roll up your sleeves and figure it out (as we'll do below).

THE ACT MIND-SET

Most students take the ACT with the same mind-set that they use for normal tests. With their brains on "memory mode," students often panic and give up because they can't seem to remember enough. **But you don't need to remember a ton of picky little rules for the ACT. Don't give up on an ACT question just because your memory fails.**

> **EXPERT TUTOR TIP**
> The mind-set for the ACT is creative problem-solving mode. Don't rely too heavily on your memory. Instead, use your brain's creative thinking cells. The ACT Mind-Set isn't too different from the one you'd use to play chess, work a crossword, or do a sudoku puzzle.

On the ACT, if you understand what a question is really asking, you can almost always answer it. For instance, take the previous math problem. You might have been thrown by the way it was phrased. "How can I solve this problem?" you may have asked yourself. "It doesn't even have numbers in it!"

The key here, as in all ACT questions, is taking control. Take the question and wrestle it into a form you can understand. Ask yourself: What's really being asked here? What does it mean when they say something like "the product of n and m^2"?

Well, you might start by putting it into words. You might say something like this: "I've got to take one number times another. One of the numbers is odd, and the other is an even number squared. Then I've got to see what kind of number I get as an answer." Once you put the question in your own terms like this, it becomes much less intimidating—and much easier to get right. You'll realize that you don't have to do complex algebraic computations with variables. All you have to do is substitute numbers.

So do it! Try picking some easy-to-use numbers. Say that n is 3 (an odd number) and m is 2 (an even number). Then m^2 would be 4, because 2^2 is 4. And $n \times m$ would be 3×4, which is 12—a multiple of 4, but not odd, not a noninteger, not an irrational number, and not a perfect square. The only answer that can be right, then, is B.

See what we mean about figuring out the answer creatively rather than passively remembering it? True, there are some things you had to remember here—what even and odd numbers are, how variables and exponents work, and maybe what integers and irrational numbers are. But these are very basic concepts. Most of what you're expected to know on the ACT is like that: basic.

> **EXPERT TUTOR TIP**
> ACT questions are puzzles to solve. Don't think: "Can I remember?" Think: "Let me figure this thing out!"

Of course, basic doesn't always mean easy. Many ACT questions are built on basic concepts but are tough nonetheless. The previous problem, for instance, is difficult because it requires some thought to figure out what's being asked. This isn't only true in Math—it's the same for every part of the ACT.

The creative, take-control kind of thinking we call the ACT Mind-Set is something you want to bring to virtually every ACT question you encounter. As we'll see, being in the ACT Mind-Set means reshaping the test-taking experience so that you are in the driver's seat.

It means:

- Answering questions **if** you want to (by guessing on the impossible questions rather than wasting time on them).

- Answering questions **when** you want to (by skipping tough but doable questions and coming back to them after you've gotten all of the easy questions done).

- Answering questions **how** you want to (by using "unofficial" ways of getting correct answers fast).

That's really what the ACT Mind-Set boils down to: taking control, being creative, and solving specific problems to get points as quickly and easily as you can.

What follows are the top ten strategies you need to do just that.

> **GO ONLINE**
> With two full-length Practice Tests and eight section-length Practice Tests online, you'll get plenty of opportunities to practice the strategies in this chapter.

TEN STRATEGIES FOR MASTERING THE ACT

1. Do Question Triage

In a hospital emergency room, the triage nurse is the person who evaluates each patient and decides which ones get attention first and which ones should be treated later. You should do the same thing on the ACT.

Practicing triage is one of the most important ways of controlling your test-taking experience. There are some questions on the ACT that most students could **never** answer correctly, no matter how much time or effort they spent on them.

Example

57. If $\sec^2 x = 4$, which of the following could be $\sin x$?

    A. 1.73205

    B. 3.14159

    C. $\sqrt{3}$

    D. $\dfrac{\sqrt{3}}{2}$

    E. Cannot be determined from the given information.

Clearly, even if you could manage to come up with an answer to this question, it would take some time (if you insist on doing so, refer to the following explanation). But would it be worth the time? We think not.

This question clearly illustrates our point: do question triage on the ACT. The first time you look at a question, make a quick decision about how hard and time-consuming it looks. Then decide whether to answer it now or skip it and do it later.

• If the question looks comprehensible and reasonably doable, do it right away.

- If the question looks tough and time-consuming, but ultimately doable, skip it, circle the question number in your test booklet, and come back to it later.
- If the question looks impossible, forget about it. Guess and move on, **never** to return.

This triage method will ensure you spend the time needed to do all the easy questions before getting bogged down with a tough problem. Remember, every question on a subject test is worth the same number of points. It's pointless to spend three minutes struggling on a hard question that you might not even get right when you could move on to two or more easier questions that you could answer correctly instead!

> **EXPERT TUTOR TIP**
> The key to question triage is to evaluate questions quickly. If you linger over these decisions, you will lose valuable time on test day.

Answering easier questions first has another benefit: it gives you confidence to answer harder ones later. Doing problems in the order you choose rather than in the order imposed by the test makers gives you control over the test. Most students don't have time to do all of the problems, so you've got to make sure you do all of the ones you can easily score on!

DO YOU KNOW YOUR TRIG?

Okay, since you're reading this, it's obvious that you want to know the answer to the trig question we just looked at. The answer is choice D. Here's how we got it:

$\sec^2 x = 4$	given
$\sec x = 2$ or -2	square root both sides
$\cos x = \dfrac{1}{2}$ or $-\dfrac{1}{2}$	$\cos x = \dfrac{1}{\sec x}$
$\cos^2 x = \dfrac{1}{4}$	square both sides
$\sin^2 x = 1 - \dfrac{1}{4}$	$\sin^2 x + \cos^2 x = 1$
$\sin^2 x = \dfrac{3}{4}$	$\sin^2 x = 1 - \cos^2 x$
$\sin x = \sqrt{\dfrac{3}{4}}$ or $-\sqrt{\dfrac{3}{4}}$	square root both sides
$\sin x = \dfrac{\sqrt{3}}{2}$ or $-\dfrac{\sqrt{3}}{2}$	$\sqrt{4} = 2$

So answer choice D is correct. But if you got it right, don't congratulate yourself quite yet. How long did it take you to get it right? So long that you could have gotten the answers to two easy questions in the same amount of time?

> **EXPERT TUTOR TIP**
> Let's say you took three minutes to get a tough question right. That might feel good, but you would actually be better off if you had skipped the tough question and, in the same amount of time, answered two or three easier questions correctly.

DEVELOP A PLAN OF ATTACK

For the English, Reading, and Science sections, the best plan of attack is to do each passage as a block. Make a longish first pass through the questions (call it the "triage pass"), doing the easy ones, guessing on the impossible ones, and skipping any that look like they might cause trouble. Then make a second pass (call it the "cleanup pass"), and do those questions you think you can solve with some elbow grease.

> **PERFECT SCORE TIP**
> In Reading and Science, try to finish each passage before moving on, as you will waste time rereading the passage if you skip between readings.

For Math, you use the same two-pass strategy, except that you move through the whole subject test twice. Work through the doable questions first. Most, but not all, of these will probably be toward the beginning. Then come back and attack the questions that look possible but tough or time-consuming.

No matter what subject test you're working on, **you should take pains to grid your answers in the right place.** It's easy to misgrid when you're skipping around, so be careful. And of course: *Make sure you have an answer gridded for every question by the time the subject test is over!*

2. Put the Material into a Form You Can Understand and Use

ACT questions are rarely presented in the simplest, most helpful way. In fact, your main job for many questions is to figure out what the question means so you can solve it.

Since the material is presented in such an intimidating way, one of your best strategies for taking control is to recast (reword) the material into a form you can handle better. This is what we did in the math problem about "the product of n and m^2." We took the question and reworded it in a way we could understand.

MARK UP YOUR TEST BOOKLET

This strategy should be employed on all four subject tests. For example, in Reading, many students find the passages overwhelming: 85 to 90 lines of dense verbiage for each one! The secret is to put the passages into a form you can understand and use. Circle or underline the main idea, for one thing. Make yourself a road map of the passage, labeling each paragraph so you understand how the ideas all fit together. That way, you'll also know—later, when you're doing the questions—where in the passage to find certain types of information you need.

> **EXPERT TUTOR TIP**
> Write all over your test booklet. Crossing out wrong answers eliminates confusion and helps you to see clearly which answer is correct. Underlining key points when reading passages helps you to determine the main Idea.

REWORD THE QUESTIONS

You'll find that you also need to do some recasting of the *questions*. For instance, take this question from a Science passage:

Example

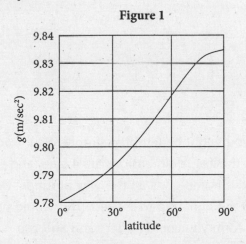

Figure 1

15. According to Figure 1, at approximately what latitude would calculations using an estimated value at sea level of $g = 9.80$ m/sec² produce the least error?

    A.   0°

    B. 20°

    C. 40°

    D. 80°

At what latitude would the calculations using a value of $g = 9.80$ m/sec² produce the least error? Yikes! What does that mean?

Take a deep breath. Ask yourself: where would an estimate for g of 9.80 m/sec² produce the least error? In a latitude where 9.80 m/sec² is the real value of g. If you find that latitude, then using 9.80 m/sec² as an estimate there would produce no error at all!

So, in other words, what this question is asking is: at what latitude does $g = 9.80$ m/sec²? Now that's a form of the question you can understand. In that form, you can answer it easily: choice C, which you can get just by reading the chart.

DRAW DIAGRAMS

Sometimes putting the material into usable form involves drawing with your pencil. For instance, take a look at the following math problem.

Example

2. Jason bought a painting with a frame 1 inch wide. If the dimensions of the outside of the frame are 5 inches by 7 inches, which of the following could be the length of one of the sides of the painting inside the frame?

    F. 3 inches

    G. 4 inches

    H. $5\frac{1}{2}$ inches

    J. $6\frac{1}{2}$ inches

    K. 7 inches

Just looking at the question the first time, you might be tempted simply to subtract 1 from the outside dimensions and think that the inside dimensions are 4 by 6 (and pick choice G). Why isn't this correct? Because the frame goes all the way around—both above and below the painting, and both to the right and to the left. This would have been clear if you had put the problem in a form you could understand and use.

For instance, you might have visualized the situation by actually sketching out the painting frame:

When you draw the picture frame like this, you realize that if the outside dimensions are 5 by 7, the inside dimensions must be 3 by 5. Thus, the correct answer is choice F.

So remember: on the ACT, you've got to put everything into a form that you can understand and use.

3. Ignore Irrelevant Issues

It's easy to waste time on ACT questions by considering irrelevant issues. Just because an issue looks interesting, or you're worried about something, doesn't make it important.

Example

...China was certainly one of the cradles of civilization. It's obvious that, China has a long history. As is the case with other ancient cultures, the early history of China is lost in mythology...

14. F. NO CHANGE
    G. It's obvious that China has a long history.
    H. Obviously; China has a long history.
    J. OMIT the underlined portion.

In this question, the test makers are counting on you to waste time worrying about punctuation. Does that comma belong? Can you use a semicolon here? These issues might be worrisome, but there's a bigger issue here—namely, does the sentence belong in the passage at all? No, it doesn't. If China has an ancient culture and was a cradle of civilization, it must have a long history, so the sentence really is obvious. Redundancy is the relevant issue here, not punctuation. Choice J is correct.

Remember, you've got limited time, so don't get caught up in issues that won't get you a point.

 PERFECT SCORE TIP
In English, identify the tested issue. Don't get distracted by other mistakes.

4. Check Back

Remember, the ACT is not a test of your memory, so don't make it one. All of the information you need is in the test itself. Don't be afraid to refer to it. Much of the information is too complex to accurately remember anyway.

In Reading and Science, always refer to the place in the passage where the answer to a question can be found. The question stem will often contain a line reference or a reference to a specific table, graph, or experiment to help you out. Your chosen answer should match the passage—not in exact vocabulary or units of measurement, perhaps, but in meaning.

> **EXPERT TUTOR TIP**
> If there's no line reference in a Reading question, you'll need to use your notes to help you know where to look for help with the answer.

Example

Isaac Newton was born in 1642 in the hamlet of Woolsthorpe in Lincolnshire, England. But he is more famous as a man of Cambridge, where he studied and taught…

7. Which of the following does the author imply is a fact about Newton's birth?

    A. It occurred in Lincoln, a small hamlet in England.
    B. It took place in a part of England known for raising sheep.
    C. It did not occur in a large metropolitan setting.
    D. It caused Newton to seek his education at Cambridge.

You might expect the right answer to be that Newton was born in a hamlet, or in Woolsthorpe, or in Lincolnshire. But none of those are offered as choices. Choice A is tempting but wrong. Newton was born in Lincolnshire, *not* Lincoln. Choice B is actually true, but it's wrong here. As its name suggests, Woolsthorpe was once known for its wool—which comes from sheep, but the question asks for something implied in the passage.

The correct answer here is choice C because a hamlet is a small village. That's not a large metropolitan setting.

> **PERFECT SCORE TIP**
> Even if you have the best memory in the world, don't waste points by trusting your memory of the passage. Always refer to where each answer is found in the passage.

Checking back is especially important in Reading and Science because the passages leave many people feeling adrift in a sea of details. Often, the wrong answers will be misplaced details taken from different parts of the passage. They are things that don't answer the question properly but that might sound good to you if you aren't careful. By checking back in the passage, you can avoid choosing such tempting wrong choices.

There's another important lesson here: **don't pick a choice just because it contains key words you remember from the passage.** Many wrong choices, like D in the previous question, are distortions—they use the right words but say the wrong things. Look for answer choices that contain the same ideas you find in the passage.

> **EXPERT TUTOR TIP**
> Researching Reading questions is important because the correct answer directly relates to the passage. Incorrect answers, **even if true**, don't relate well to either the passage OR the question.

One of the best ways to avoid choosing misplaced details and distortions is to refer to the passage.

5. Answer the Right Question

This strategy is a natural extension of the last. As we said, **the ACT test makers often include among the wrong choices for a question the correct answer to a different question.** Under time pressure, it's easy to fall for one of these red herrings, thinking that you know what's being asked for when really you don't.

> **PERFECT SCORE TIP**
> If you do not understand a question, take time and read it again. The extra five seconds is better than trying to answer a question that was not asked and getting an incorrect answer.

Example

7. What is the value of $3x$ if $9x = 5y + 2$ and $y + 4 = 2y - 10$?

   A. 5
   B. 8
   C. 14
   D. 24
   E. 72

To solve this problem, we need to find y first, even though the question asks about x (because x here is given only in terms of y). You could solve the second equation like this:

$y + 4 = 2y - 10$ given
$\quad 4 = y - 10$ by subtracting y from both sides
$\quad 14 = y$ by adding 10 to both sides

But choice C, 14, isn't the right answer here because the question doesn't ask for the value of y—it asks about x. We can use the value of y to find x, however, by plugging the calculated value of y into the first equation:

$9x = 5y + 2$ given
$9x = 5(14) + 2$ because $y = 14$
$9x = 70 + 2$
$9x = 72$

But E, 72, isn't the answer either because the question doesn't ask for $9x$. It doesn't ask for x either, so if you picked B, 8, you'd be wrong as well. Remember to refer to the question! The question asks for $3x$. So we need to divide $9x$ by 3:

$9x = 72$ from above
$3x = 24$ dividing by 3

Thus, the answer is D.

Always check the question again before choosing your answer. Doing all the right work but then getting the wrong answer can be seriously depressing. So make sure you're answering the right question.

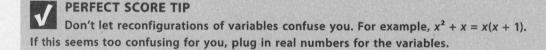

✓ PERFECT SCORE TIP
Don't let reconfigurations of variables confuse you. For example, $x^2 + x = x(x + 1)$. If this seems too confusing for you, plug in real numbers for the variables.

6. Look for the Hidden Answer

On many ACT questions, the right answer is hidden in one way or another. An answer can be hidden by being written in an unexpected way. For example, you might work out a problem and get .5 as your answer, but then find that .5 isn't among the answer choices. Then you notice that one choice reads $\frac{1}{2}$. You've found the hidden answer! It pays to think flexibly about numbers.

There's another way the ACT can hide answers. **Many ACT questions have more than one possible right solution, though only one correct answer choice is given. The ACT will hide that answer by offering one of the less obvious possible answers to a question.**

Example

2. If $3x^2 + 5 = 17$, which of the following could be the value of x?

   A. −3
   B. −2
   C. 0
   D. 1
   E. 4

You quickly solve this very straightforward problem like so:

$3x^2 + 5 = 17$ given
$3x^2 = 12$ by subtracting 5
$x^2 = 4$ dividing by 3
$x = 2$ taking square root of both sides

Having gotten an answer, you confidently look for it among the choices. But 2 isn't a choice. The explanation? This question has two possible solutions, not just one. The square root of 4 can be either 2 or −2. Thus, B is the answer.

Keep in mind that though there's only one right answer choice for each question, that right answer may not be the one that occurs to you first. A common mistake is to pick an answer that seems sort of like the answer you're looking for, even when you know it's wrong. Don't settle for second best. If you don't find your answer, don't assume that you're wrong. Try to think of another right way to answer the question.

7. Guess Intelligently

An unanswered question is always wrong, but even a wild guess may be right. On the ACT, a guess can't hurt you, but it can help. In fact, smart guessing can make a big difference in your score. **Always** guess on every ACT question you can't answer. Never leave a question blank.

You'll be doing two different kinds of guessing during your two sweeps through any subject test:

1. Blind guessing (which you do mostly on questions you deem too hard or time-consuming even to try).

2. Strategic guessing (which you do mostly on questions that you do some work on but can't make headway with).

When you guess blindly, you just choose any letter you feel like choosing (many students like to choose B for Bart; few choose H for Homer). When you guess in a strategic way, on the other hand, you've usually done enough work on a question to eliminate at least one or two choices. If you can eliminate any choices, you'll up the odds of guessing correctly.

> **EXPERT TUTOR TIP**
> If you guess blindly, you have one chance in four (or one in five on the Math) of getting the question right. If you can eliminate one or two choices as definitely wrong, you can improve those odds.

Here are some fun facts about guessing: If you were to work on only half of the questions on the ACT but get them all right, then guess blindly on the other half of the questions, you would probably earn a composite ACT score of around 23 (assuming you had a statistically reasonable success rate on your guesses). A 23 would put you in roughly the top quarter of all those who take the ACT. It's a good score. And all you had to do was answer half the questions correctly.

On the other hand, if you were to hurry and finish all the questions but get only half of them right, you'd probably earn only a 19, which is below average.

How? Why are you better off answering half and getting them all right instead of answering all and getting only half right?

Here's the trick. The student who answers half the questions right and skips the others can still take guesses on the unanswered questions—and odds are this student will have enough correct guesses to move up four points, from a 19 to a 23. But the student who answers all the questions and gets half wrong doesn't have the luxury of taking guesses.

In short: **guess if you can't figure out an answer for any question!**

> **EXPERT TUTOR TIP**
> Get the points you deserve on the questions you can answer. But don't worry about the ones you have to guess on. Odds are good that you'll guess some correctly. And those correct guesses will increase your score just as much as if you'd figured out the answers.

8. Be Careful with the Answer Grid

Your ACT score is based on the answers you select on your answer grid. Even if you work out every question correctly, you'll get a low score if you misgrid your answers. So be careful! Don't disdain the process of filling in those little "bubbles" on the grid. Sure, it's mindless, but under time pressure, it's easy to lose control and make mistakes.

It's important to **develop a disciplined strategy for filling in the answer grid.** We find that it's smart to grid the answers in groups rather than one question at a time. What you should do is this: as you figure out each question in the test booklet, circle the answer choice you come up with. Then, transfer those answers to the answer grid in groups of five or more (until you get close to the end of the section, when you should start gridding answers one by one).

> **PERFECT SCORE TIP**
> I found it helpful to grid after each Reading passage and after every two pages of Math. Gridding too often can be distracting to your concentration, but there is nothing worse than running out of time to grid your answers.

Gridding in groups like this cuts down on errors because you can focus on this one task and do it right. It also saves time you'd otherwise spend moving papers around, finding your place, and redirecting your mind. Answering ACT questions takes deep, hard thinking. Filling out answer grids is easy, but you have to be careful, especially if you do a lot of skipping around. Shifting between hard thinking and careful book-keeping takes time and effort.

In English, Reading, and Science, the test is divided naturally into groups of questions— the passages. It makes the most sense to circle your answers in your test booklet as you work them out. Then, when you're finished with each passage and its questions, grid the answers as a group.

In Math, the strategy has to be different because the Math test isn't broken up into natural groups. Mark your answers in the test booklet, and then grid them when you reach the end of each page or two. Since there are usually about five math questions per page, you'll probably be gridding five or ten math answers at a time.

No matter what subject test you're working on, though, if you're near the end of a subject test, start gridding your answers one at a time. You don't want to be caught with ungridded answers when time is called.

During the test, the proctor should warn you when you have about five minutes left on each subject test. But don't depend on proctors! **Rely on your own watch.** When there are five minutes left on a subject test, start gridding your answers one by one. With a minute or two left, start filling in everything you've left blank. Remember: even one question left blank could cut your score.

> ✔ **PERFECT SCORE TIP**
> When gridding, don't be a hero and try to remember eight answers in your head and transfer them to your grid. Work deliberately, but one place you cannot afford to lose points is in gridding your answers.

9. Use the Letters of the Choices to Stay on Track

One oddity about the ACT is that even-numbered questions have F, G, H, J (and, in Math, K) as answer choices, rather than A, B, C, D (and, again, E in Math). This might be confusing at first, but you can make it work for you. **A common mistake with the answer grid is to accidentally enter an answer one row up or down. On the ACT, that won't happen if you pay attention to the letter in the answer.** If you're looking for an A and you see only F, G, H, J, and K, you'll know you're in the wrong row on the answer grid.

Another advantage of having answers F through K for even-numbered questions is that it makes you less nervous about patterns in the answers. It's common to start worrying if you've picked the same letter twice or three times in a row. Since the questions have different letters, this can't happen on the ACT. Of course, you could pick the first choice (A or F) for several questions in a row. This shouldn't worry you. It's common for the answers in the same position to be correct three times in a row, and even four times in a row isn't unheard of.

> ✔ **PERFECT SCORE TIP**
> Especially if you have time problems, realize that gridding does take time. Use an actual answer grid when you take a practice test to get a feel for whether you will have trouble finishing the actual test.

10. Keep Track of Time

During each subject test, you really have to pace yourself. On average, English, Reading, and Science questions should take about 30 seconds each. Math questions should average less than one minute each. Remember to take into account the fact that you'll probably be taking two passes through the questions.

> **EXPERT TUTOR TIP**
> Spend your test time wisely! English, Reading passages: about nine minutes each (including questions); Science passages: about five minutes each (including questions); Math questions: about 30–60 seconds each, depending on the difficulty.

Set your watch to 12:00 at the beginning of each subject test so it will be easy to check your time. Again, don't rely on proctors, even if they promise that they will dutifully call out the time every 15 minutes. Proctors get distracted once in a while.

More basic questions should take less time, and harder ones will probably take more. In Math, for instance, you need to go much faster than one per minute during your first sweep. But at the end, you may spend two or three minutes on each of the harder problems you work out.

TAKE CONTROL

You are the master of the test-taking experience. A common thread in all ten strategies is: take control. That's Kaplan's ACT Mind-Set. Do the questions in the order you want and in the way you want. Don't get bogged down or agonize. Remember, you don't earn points for suffering, but you do earn points for moving on to the next question and getting it right.

The ACT Is NOT School

You have spent at least 11 years in school at this point. There, you learned some techniques that won't help you on the ACT. (Want two good examples? "Don't guess on a test" and "If you show your work on math problems, you'll get partial credit.") Many of these school-driven methods don't work well on the ACT. In fact, they work *against* you.

On ACT test day, don't fall into the trap of familiar school habits. Test day is an exciting and stressful event. We strongly suggest that you practice using the ten strategies in this chapter so that you're rehearsed and confident for test day.

Just reading and understanding these strategies before the test doesn't mean you'll remember to do them effectively on test day. The ACT Mind-Set will work only if you use it, so practice!

As you practice, time yourself. Buy or borrow a digital watch, and get used to working with it so it doesn't beep at the wrong moment. Your cell phone will be turned off during the test, so you won't be able to use that as a timekeeper.

Practicing the various sections of the test at home and taking at least one entire Practice Test in one sitting are the best ways to make sure you're comfortable with the test and ready to get your highest scores on test day.

> **GO ONLINE**
> Before going on to the subject-specific workouts, take the online diagnostic quiz if you haven't already. You'll learn where to focus your study time.

BASIC STRATEGY REFERENCE SHEET

The Four Keys to ACT Success

1. LEARN THE TEST

- Learn the directions before test day.
- Become familiar with all the subject tests.
- Get a sense of the range of difficulty of the questions.

2. LEARN THE KAPLAN METHODS AND STRATEGIES

- Develop a plan of attack for each subject test.
- Develop a guessing strategy that works for you.
- Find "unofficial" ways of finding answers fast.

3. LEARN THE MATERIAL TESTED

- Bone up on weak areas.
- Find out what is and isn't part of the ACT knowledge base.
- Use the ACT Resources section to review important Math and English concepts.

4. PRACTICE, PRACTICE, PRACTICE

The Top Ten Strategies

1. Do question triage.
2. Put the material into a form you can understand and use.
3. Ignore irrelevant issues.
4. Check back.
5. Answer the right question.
6. Look for the hidden answer.
7. Guess intelligently.
8. Be careful with the answer grid.
9. Use the letters of the choices to stay on track.
10. Keep track of time.

▶ IF YOU LEARNED ONLY TWO THINGS IN THIS CHAPTER...

1. Remember the ACT Mind-Set: Take control of your test experience.
2. Know the four keys to ACT success and the top ten strategies.

PART TWO

Skill-Building Workouts

CHAPTER 4

English Workout 1: When in Doubt, Take It Out

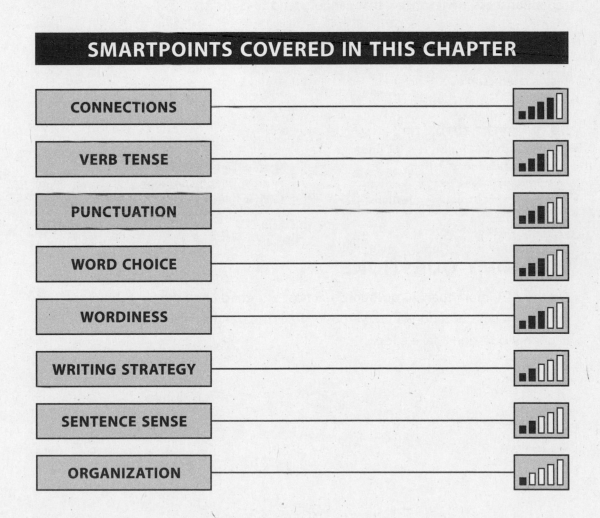

SMARTPOINTS COVERED IN THIS CHAPTER

CONNECTIONS

VERB TENSE

PUNCTUATION

WORD CHOICE

WORDINESS

WRITING STRATEGY

SENTENCE SENSE

ORGANIZATION

Think back to the last paper you had to write. Maybe your teacher assigned something like ten pages. You wrote and you wrote and ended up with six pages. It was the night before the paper had to be turned in; you were out of research and ideas. You knew what to do: pad it.

You're not alone. Almost all of us have padded papers at one time or another. The recipe for padding, in fact, is practically universal: You repeat yourself a few times. You trade short phrases for long-winded verbiage. You add a few offbeat ideas that don't really belong. Presto! Your six-page paper is transformed into a ten-page paper.

The ACT test makers know that most students pad. In fact, many of the English questions on the ACT are testing for the very same bad writing habits—long-windedness, repetitiousness, irrelevance—that padders tend to cultivate.

Once you know what ACT English is testing, you can easily avoid making these common English mistakes. More than any other part of the exam, the ACT English subject test is predictable.

 EXPERT TUTOR TIP

The ACT English test includes:

- 10 punctuation questions
- 12 grammar and usage questions
- 18 sentence structure questions
- 12 strategy questions
- 11 organization questions
- 12 style questions

ECONOMY QUESTIONS

On the ACT, more than 20 questions—almost one-third of all the English items—test your awareness of redundancy, verbosity, relevance, and similar issues. We call these Economy questions. Take a look.

Example

ACT ENGLISH: SHORTER IS OFTEN BETTER!

On recent ACTs, the shortest answer has been <u>correct,</u>
<u>and absolutely right,</u> for about half of all English

questions. Because this is <u>true,</u> a student who knows no

English at all could earn <u>—and justly so—</u>an English
subject score of about 15. Such a student could

compare the choices carefully and choose the <u>single</u>
<u>shortest one</u> every time. Where the answers are the
same length, the student could pick at random. On
recently published ACTs, guessing in this way would have
yielded between 35 and 38 correct answers out of 75
questions. Of course, you're going to <u>be doing</u> much

better than that. You actually <u>are capable of speaking</u>
<u>the English language.</u> You may not know every little
rule of English usage, but you certainly know something. Obviously, getting the question right because

1. A. NO CHANGE
    B. correct
    C. right, that is, correct,
    D. correct, absolutely, and right,

2. F. NO CHANGE
    G. truthfully factual
    H. factually correct
    J. factual—and true too—

3. A. NO CHANGE
    B. —quite justly, in fact—
    C. and justify
    D. OMIT the underlined portion.

4. F. NO CHANGE
    G. singularly shortest one
    H. uniquely short item
    J. shortest one

5. A. NO CHANGE
    B. do
    C. achieve
    D. be achieving

6. F. NO CHANGE
    G. possess the capability of speaking English.
    H. possess the capability of speaking in the land called England.
    J. speak English.

you know the <u>right answer</u> is better than getting it
7

right because you guessed well.

    Still, you should always remember that the

ACT test makers <u>like</u> the shortest answers. Why?
8

Why should the ACT make life so easy for you?

<u>Why can't history or science classes in high school</u>
9

<u>be so easy?</u> Usually, the best way to write something
9

really is the shortest way to write it. The ACT can't

help that, <u>any more than you can help the fact that</u>
10

<u>you must take the ACT to get into college.</u> Good
10

7. A. NO CHANGE
  B. best choice to select
  C. most correct answer of the choices given
  D. answer considered as correct

8. F. NO CHANGE
  G. have a habit of liking
  H. habitually tend to like
  J. are in the habit of liking

9. A. NO CHANGE
  B. Why isn't history or science?
  C. History and science aren't so easy, either!
  D. OMIT the underlined portion.

10. F. NO CHANGE
  G. just as you are helpless to avoid the requirement of taking the ACT
  H. whether or not they'd want to
  J. OMIT the underlined portion and end the sentence with a period after *that*.

writing is concise and <u>clear</u>. There are many rules of
11
English, but many of them grow from one dominant

principle: use only the words you need to say what

you mean. 12

11. A. NO CHANGE
    B. clearly better
    C. translucent, like clear water
    D. clear. Thus it is short and to the
        point.

12. Suppose the author considers adding
    this final sentence: "Thus, if you
    can't say something nice, don't say
    anything at all." Would this be an
    effective conclusion for the paragraph?

    F. Yes, because this concept is
        needed to explain the meaning of
        the previous sentence.

    G. Yes, because it adds an uplifting
        moral tone to an otherwise
        depressing, amoral text.

    H. Yes, because this thought is
        relevant to the next paragraph.

    J. No, because the paragraph is not
        concerned with being nice.

Answers

1.	B	7.	A
2.	F	8.	F
3.	D	9.	D
4.	J	10.	J
5.	B	11.	A
6.	J	12.	J

The shortest answer happens to be correct in all 12 of the questions above. Note that OMIT, where it is an option, is the shortest answer since taking the material out leaves a shorter text than leaving anything in. In question 12, choice J is the shortest answer since it leaves the proposed final sentence off entirely.

Redundancy

In questions 1–4, the wrong (long) answers are redundant—they make the passage say the same thing twice. **The ACT is very strict about redundancy: Never let the text in a sentence repeat itself.**

Verbosity

In questions 5–8, the wrong (long) answers are verbose, which means overly wordy. They may have more words, but they are no clearer than the short answers and don't add meaning. **This is another rule the ACT is very strict about: the best way to write something is the shortest way, as long as it doesn't violate any rules of writing mechanics (like grammar or punctuation) or contain language that's either too formal or informal to match the style of the passage.**

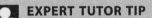 **EXPERT TUTOR TIP**
On recent ACTs, the shortest answer has been correct on about one-half of all English questions.

Irrelevance

Questions 9–12 test relevance. The wrong (long) answers introduce irrelevant concepts. The paragraph is about ACT English questions and how to answer them—it's not about history or science classes, the necessity of taking the ACT, or that lovely translucence of clear water. **Omit the ideas that are not directly and logically tied in with the purpose of the paragraph or passage.**

With Economy questions, the shortest answer is correct with great frequency. If you suspect Economy is the tested issue, consider these questions:

- Is the underlined part redundant? Check the nonunderlined part of the passage to see if it contains words that repeat the meaning of the underlined part.
- Is the underlined part verbose? See if there is an answer choice that is shorter and still expresses the same meaning.
- Is the underlined part relevant? Ask yourself if it fits with the topic of the paragraph and the purpose of the passage as a whole.

Because the ACT values conciseness, remember: **when in doubt, take it out.**

> ✓ **PERFECT SCORE TIP**
> In English, every single word and sentence should have a unique purpose. If the underlined portion is not absolutely necessary, it is probably redundant or irrelevant.

Keep It Short—on All English Questions

Questions on which the lengths of the answers vary greatly and questions that contain the answer choice OMIT are usually Economy questions. For these questions, you should be especially inclined to choose the shortest choice. For the other questions, the shortest answer is not nearly as often correct.

As we'll see in later workouts, the other English questions mostly test your ability to spot nonsense, bad grammar, and bad punctuation. Even in these cases, the rule "when in doubt, take it out" still holds. Even for questions testing issues other than writing economy, some answer choices are wrong simply because they're too long.

Because the issue of writing economy is so important to English questions of all kinds, we've made it the linchpin for our recommended approach to the English subject test. **When approaching English questions, the very first question you should ask yourself is: "Does this stuff belong here? Can the passage or sentence work without it?"**

> **AVAILABLE ONLINE**
> The online companion includes two section-length ACT English Practice Tests. Hone your skills with these before tackling a full-length Practice Test.

Reading the Passage as You Go

Read the passage as far as you find necessary to answer each question, and then answer each one in turn. *Don't skip over sentences without questions in them*—you'll need to understand the whole passage when you answer the questions at the end.

> ✓ **PERFECT SCORE TIP**
> Get into a "grammar mind-set." For the weeks before I took the ACT, I got used to notic-ing all the grammar mistakes in my life. While sometimes annoying to my family, immediately noticing agreement and other mistakes really helped me notice these mistakes on test day.

THE KAPLAN METHOD FOR ACT ENGLISH

Here's the Kaplan Method for ACT English questions.

STEP 1: Read until you have enough information to identify the issue.

Although the instructions on the ACT will tell you to read the whole passage and then answer the questions about it, our advice is to answer each question as soon as you've read far enough in the passage to do so. For some questions, you'll only need to read a sentence to find the issue. What's an "issue," you ask? Think of the issue as the reason the test makers included the question—what are you being tested on? Issues are not necessarily errors, because some sentences have no errors, and some English questions test your understanding of the passage as a whole.

STEP 2: Eliminate answer choices that do not address the issue.

Now that you've identified the issue that the question is testing, read through the answers to see which ones do not address the issue. Once these are eliminated, you may have one or two options left. Then move on to Step 3.

STEP 3: Plug in the remaining answer choices to select the most correct, concise, and relevant choice.

Finally, try out the remaining answer choices by "plugging" them into the sentence or paragraph and seeing how they work. This may mean reading the questions without the underlined phrase to see if OMIT is the best choice. The best choice will be grammatically correct, concise, and will make sense with the rest of the passage. This applies to any Big Picture questions, too.

Read the passage as far as you find necessary to answer each question, and then answer each one in turn. *Don't skip over sentences without questions in them—you'll need to understand the whole passage when you answer the questions at the end.*

Practice Being Economical

Now try the next practice passage, keeping in mind the approach you just learned.

THE OLDEST NFL TEAM

The Phoenix Cardinals are the <u>oldest, most long-</u>

<u>established, longest-playing</u> football club in the

National Football League (NFL). They began as

the Racine Avenue Cardinals on Chicago's South

Side sometime in the 1870s or <u>1880s, during the</u>

<u>nineteenth century.</u>

    At that time, the Cardinals were an amateur

team <u>that did not play for money.</u> There was

nothing in the world which so much as resembled

pro football in those days. The Racine Avenue

Cardinals played amateur ball all through the late

1800s <u>and the game they played was football,</u>

<u>no doubt about it.</u>

1. A. NO CHANGE
   B. oldest
   C. most long-established
   D. longest-playing

2. F. NO CHANGE
   G. 1880s
   H. the nineteenth century
   J. during the 1880s

3. A. NO CHANGE
   B. that played for the pure joy of the sport.
   C. that played on a nonprofessional level.
   D. OMIT the underlined portion and end the sentence with a period.

4. F. NO CHANGE
   G. nothing anything like
   H. no such thing as
   J. not even a dream of

5. A. NO CHANGE
   B. no doubt about it.
   C. to be assured it was football.
   D. OMIT the underlined portion and end the sentence with a period.

None of the other clubs in the NFL was formed before the league itself was established in 1919. When the NFL was first established, the Cardinals remained aloof and thumbed their noses at it.
<u>aloof and thumbed their noses at it.</u>
6
Professional football had a bad reputation, and

the Cardinals were <u>greatly prideful</u> of their
7
record as amateurs. However, in 1921, the Cardinals decided to join the NFL. They were required to play a "game to the death" with the Chicago Tigers <u>(the Detroit Tigers are a baseball</u>
8
<u>team).</u> Whichever team won would be allowed
8

to stay in Chicago; the other team would <u>have</u>
9
<u>to move.</u> The Cardinals won. The Tigers moved
9
away and soon went bankrupt. The Cardinals are thus the only NFL team that won their franchise on the football field.

Ironically, the team that fought to stay in Chicago eventually moved away. The Cardinals were rarely as <u>successfully able to win games</u>
10
<u>or make money</u> as the Chicago Bears, their
10

6. F. NO CHANGE
   G. aloof.
   H. aloof and tried to ignore it.
   J. off in their own corner.

7. A. NO CHANGE
   B. full of great pride
   C. proud
   D. gratefully proud

8. F. NO CHANGE
   G. (not to be confused with the Detroit Tigers, a baseball team).
   H. (not the more famous modern-day Detroit Tigers baseball team).
   J. OMIT the underlined portion and end the sentence with a period.

9. A. NO CHANGE
   B. be forced to move along
   C. be legally obliged, by injunction, to relocate their franchise
   D. be obligated to be moving out

10. F. NO CHANGE
    G. successful at winning
    H. winning or profitable, a team,
    J. successful

crosstown rivals. Fans gradually deserted the

Cardinals, so the team moved—to St. Louis in

1958 and to Phoenix in 1986, seeking a more

profitable market. Maybe Phoenix <u>is the place</u>
                                      11
<u>in which</u> the Cardinals are destined to stay.
  11
Some people say that the name "Cardinal" was

a nineteenth-century name for a mythical bird

that arose from its own ashes <u>in the fireplace,</u>
                                    12
and that the Cardinals date back to have begun

on Racine Avenue <u>(or maybe not).</u> Chicago was
                       13
proud to rise from its ashes like the mythical

Cardinal. The <u>name that is more common</u> for
                        14

11. A. NO CHANGE
    B. is the place at which
    C. is where
    D. OMIT the underlined portion.

12. F. NO CHANGE
    G. that had consumed it
    H. created by the fire that had consumed it
    J. OMIT the underlined portion.

13. A. NO CHANGE
    B. according to ironic legend.
    C. resulting from violations of the fire code and a cow in a barn.
    D. OMIT the underlined portion and end the sentence with a period.

14. F. NO CHANGE
    G. common name
    H. name that is famous
    J. common way of speaking

that mythical firebird is the Phoenix. [15]

15. Suppose the author wishes to add a new paragraph at the end of the existing passage quickly summarizing the history of Canadian football. Would this be appropriate, in light of the content and style of the rest of the passage?

A. Yes, because it is only fair to mention Canadian football at least once in the passage.

B. Yes, because the Phoenix Cardinals now play Canadian football.

C. No, because the passage does not focus on sports history.

D. No, because the passage has nothing to do with Canadian football.

Answers

1.	B	9.	A
2.	G	10.	J
3.	D	11.	C
4.	H	12.	J
5.	D	13.	D
6.	G	14.	G
7.	C	15.	D
8.	J		

Did you notice anything about all of these questions? For the first 14, you only needed to read one sentence to answer each question. Imagine how long it would have taken to read the whole passage once and then go back and analyze each sentence. By using Step 1 of the Kaplan Method, you could take it one sentence at a time. Did you notice anything else? The correct answer usually made the sentence shorter and more concise. OMIT always makes the answer shorter but isn't always correct. In 11, if you omit the phrase "is the place in which," the sentence doesn't make any sense, meaning that you'd correct it in Step 3 of the three-step approach. (Note: This passage is not typical—most ACT passages don't consist exclusively of Economy questions—but we used this passage to drive home the point about choosing concise answers on the English subject test.)

EXPERT TUTOR TIP
Remember that OMIT is **always the shortest answer.**

Many students might object to answer J in question 10, because the word *successful* alone does not indicate the kind of success meant. Use common sense. Winning and making money would definitely make a professional football team successful. Thus, the concepts of winning and profitability are implicit in the notion that the Cardinals are (now) a successful team. **The ACT expects you to cut anything that isn't absolutely needed.**

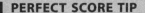
PERFECT SCORE TIP
Do not defend something if the passage could make sense without it. The ACT will never ask you to add any unnecessary details or description.

> ## IF YOU LEARNED ONLY THREE THINGS IN THIS CHAPTER...
>
> 1. Read until you have enough information to identify the issue, eliminate choices that do NOT address the issue, and test each remaining choice to find the correct answer.
>
> 2. When approaching questions, ask yourself: Why did the test makers include this question? What issue is this question testing?
>
> 3. Many English questions test redundancy, verbosity, and irrelevance. Start with the shortest answer.

CHAPTER 5

English Workout 2: Make It Make Sense

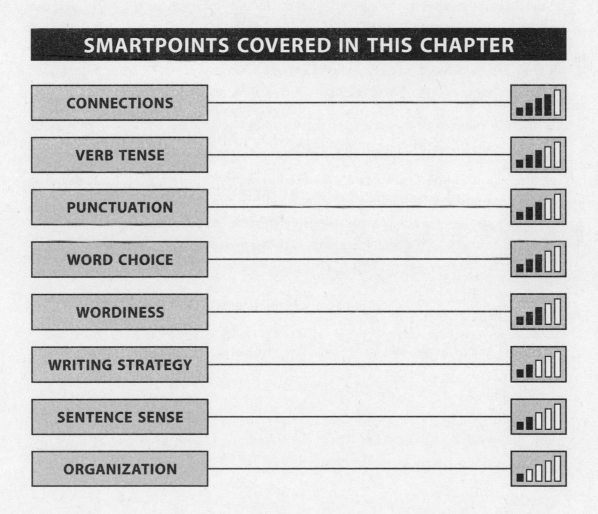

SMARTPOINTS COVERED IN THIS CHAPTER

CONNECTIONS

VERB TENSE

PUNCTUATION

WORD CHOICE

WORDINESS

WRITING STRATEGY

SENTENCE SENSE

ORGANIZATION

In English Workout 1, we saw that the ACT expects you to use your words efficiently and that, in fact, the shortest answer is correct remarkably often. Obviously, however, the shortest answer is sometimes wrong. What could make it wrong? It may not mean what it says.

Take this example: "Abraham Lincoln's father was a model of hardworking self-sufficiency. He was born in a log cabin he built with his own hands." Well, that's a cute trick, being born in a cabin you built yourself. Presumably, the writer means that Abe was born in a cabin that his father built. But the literal meaning of the example is that the father somehow managed to be born in a cabin that he himself had built.

It's possible, of course, to analyze this example in terms of the rules of apostrophe use and pronoun reference. But that's not practical for the ACT, even for a student who has good grammar skills. There isn't time to carefully analyze every question, consider all the rules involved, and decide on an answer. You have to do 75 English questions in only 45 minutes—that's almost 2 questions per minute.

But there *is* plenty of time to approach examples like this one in a more pragmatic way. Ask yourself, *Do these words make sense?*

For the ACT, it's important to care. You need to adjust your mind-set. After deciding whether or not the selection in a question is concise and relevant (Step 1 in the three-step method), the next step is to make sure that the sentence *says* exactly what it's supposed to *mean*. If it doesn't, your job is to make it do so. In other words, make it make sense.

> ✔ **PERFECT SCORE TIP**
> If you can't find a mistake in an underlined sentence, consider logic. A sentence may sound like English but actually have a logical inconsistency, which makes it not make sense.

We at Kaplan have a name for questions that test errors of meaning—**Sense questions.** Once you get the hang of them, these questions can actually be fun. They're often funny once you see them. The following passage gives examples of the most common kinds of Sense questions you'll find on the ACT.

> ✔ **PERFECT SCORE TIP**
> In the Reading section, skimming and not noting small problems is a good thing. In English, you must pay close attention to all words near the underlined part.

Passage I

ROBINSON CRUSOE: FICTION AND FACT

Most people—even those who've never read
Daniel Defoe's *Robinson Crusoe*—are familiar
with the strange story of the sailor shipwrecked
on a far-flung Pacific island. Relatively few of
them, however, know that Crusoe's <u>story. It was</u>
₁
actually based on the real-life adventures of a
Scottish seaman, Alexander Selkirk. Selkirk
came to the Pacific as a member of a 1703
privateering expedition led by a captain named
William Dampier. During the voyage, Selkirk
became dissatisfied with conditions aboard ship.
<u>After a bitter quarrel with his captain, he put</u>
₂
<u>Selkirk ashore</u> on tiny Mas a Tierra, one of the
₂
islands of Juan Fernandez, off the coast of Chile.
Stranded, Selkirk lived there alone—in much

the <u>same manner as</u> Defoe's Crusoe—until 1709,
₃
when he was finally rescued by another English
privateer. Upon his return to England, Selkirk

found himself a <u>celebrity, his</u> strange tale had
₄

1. A. NO CHANGE
    B. story: was
    C. story, was
    D. story was

2. F. NO CHANGE
    G. Quarreling with his captain, the
       boat was put ashore
    H. Having quarreled with his captain,
       Selkirk was put ashore
    J. Having quarreled with his captain,
       they put Selkirk ashore

3. A. NO CHANGE
    B. same manner that
    C. identical manner that
    D. identical way as

4. F. NO CHANGE
    G. celebrity, but his
    H. celebrity. His
    J. celebrity his

already become the talk of pubs and coffeehouses throughout the British Isles. The story even reached the ears of Richard Steele, who featured it in his periodical, *The Tatler*. Eventually, <u>he became</u> the subject of a best-selling book,
5
A Cruizing Voyage Round the World, by Woodes

Rogers. <u>While</u> there is some evidence that Defoe,
6
a journalist, may actually have interviewed Selkirk personally, most literary historians believe that it was the reprinting of the Rogers book in 1718 that served as the real stimulus for Defoe's novel.

In *Crusoe*, which <u>has been published</u> in
7
1719, Defoe took substantial liberties with the Selkirk story. For example, while Selkirk's

presence on the island was of course <u>known for</u>
8
<u>many people</u> (certainly everyone in the crew
8
that stranded him there), no one in the novel is aware of Crusoe's survival of the wreck and presence on the island. Moreover, while Selkirk's exile lasted just six years, Crusoe's goes on for a much more dramatic, though less credible, twenty-eight <u>(over four times as long)</u>. However,
9
Defoe's most blatant embellishment of the tale is the invention of the character of Friday, for whom there was no counterpart whatsoever in the real-life story.

5. A. NO CHANGE
   B. Selkirk became
   C. his became
   D. he becomes

6. F. NO CHANGE
   G. But since
   H. And therefore
   J. OMIT the underlined portion and start the sentence with *There*.

7. A. NO CHANGE
   B. was published
   C. had been published
   D. will have been published

8. F. NO CHANGE
   G. widely known among people
   H. known about many people
   J. known to many people

9. A. NO CHANGE
   B. (much longer)
   C. (a much longer time, of course)
   D. OMIT the underlined portion.

Because of its basis in fact, *Robinson*
10

Crusoe is often regarded as the first major novel

in English literature. Still popular today, contem-
11

porary audiences enjoyed the book as well.
11

In fact, two sequels, in which Crusoe returns

to the island after his rescue, were eventually

published. Though to little acclaim. Meanwhile,
12

Selkirk himself never gave a hoot about returning
13

to the island that had made him famous.

Legend has it that he never gave up his eccentric

living habits, spending his last years in a cave

teaching alley cats to dance in his spare time.

One wonders if even Defoe himself could have

invented a more fitting end to the bizarre story

of his shipwrecked sailor.

10. F. NO CHANGE
    G. Despite
    H. Resulting from
    J. As a consequence of

11. A. NO CHANGE
    B. Still read today, Defoe's contem-
       poraries also enjoyed it.
    C. Viewed by many even then as a
       classic, the book is still popular
       to this day.
    D. Much read in its day, modern
       audiences still find the book
       compelling.

12. F. NO CHANGE
    G. published, though
    H. published although
    J. published; although

13. A. NO CHANGE
    B. evinced himself as desirous of
       returning
    C. could whip up a head of steam
       to return
    D. expressed any desire to return

Questions 14–15 ask about the preceding passage as a whole.

14. Considering the tone and subject matter of the preceding paragraphs, is the last sentence an appropriate way to end the essay?

    F. Yes, because it is necessary to shed some doubt on Defoe's creativity.

    G. Yes, because the essay is about the relationship between the real Selkirk and Defoe's fictionalized version of him.

    H. No, because there is nothing "bizarre" about Selkirk's story as it is related in the essay.

    J. No, because the focus of the essay is more on Selkirk himself than on Defoe's fictionalized version of him.

15. This essay would be most appropriate as part of a:

    A. scholarly study of 18th-century maritime history.

    B. study of the geography of the islands off of Chile.

    C. history of privateering in the Pacific.

    D. popular history of English literature.

Answers

1.	D	9.	D
2.	H	10.	G
3.	A	11.	C
4.	H	12.	G
5.	B	13.	D
6.	F	14.	G
7.	B	15.	D
8.	J		

Please note that in the explanations that follow, we treat the questions not in numerical order but rather in groups according to the tested issue. We do this to help you better understand the concepts behind the questions. The more easily you can spot the tested issue—the concept the ACT requires you to understand to answer the question correctly—the more confident you'll feel on test day.

Sense Questions vs. Economy Questions

Most of the time, we don't usually care much if an author isn't clear. We have learned to interpret what the writer meant to say and move on. On the ACT, test takers *must* care and make sure that what is written is the same as what the author meant. Sense questions may seem harder than the Economy questions—the shortest answers aren't necessarily right.

Step 1 is all you needed in question numbers 1, 3, 7, 9, 10, and 13. "When in doubt, take it out" worked for these. As we saw in English Workout 1, questions that include an OMIT option, and those in which some of the answers are much longer than others, are usually testing writing economy.

In the rest of the questions in this passage, the answers differ in other ways. They may join or fragment sentences, rearrange things, or add words that affect the meaning of the sentences. When the answers are all about the same length, as in most of the questions here, the question is more likely to test sense. Consider the shortest answer first, but don't be as quick to select it and move on. Think about the effect each choice has on the *meaning* of the sentence, and pick longer answers if the shortest one doesn't make sense.

GRAMMAR RULES AND SENSE QUESTIONS

▪▫▫▫ **SENTENCE SENSE**

▪▪▫▫ **CONNECTIONS**

The ACT test makers include questions like those in Passage I to test many different rules of writing mechanics. Though it's *not necessary* to think about rules to answer the questions, being familiar with them will help. **The more ways to think about a question you have, the more likely you are to find the right answer.**

> **EXPERT TUTOR TIP**
> Students tend to reject informal writing as incorrect, but ACT passages are written at various levels of formality. Some are as stiff as textbooks. Others are as casual as a talk with friends. Pay attention to the tone of the words. Are they serious? Are they laid-back? Stay with the author's tone. Don't **always** stay formal.

We'll discuss some of these examples in groups based on what they're designed to test. That way we can briefly discuss the rules and also show you how the basic strategic approach of "make it make sense" can get you the answers without a lot of technical analysis. Let's start with **question 1.**

Completeness

▪▪▪▫ **CONNECTIONS**

▪▫▫▫ **SENTENCE SENSE**

▪▪▫▫ **PUNCTUATION**

Question 1 tests sentence sense.

Rule at work: Every sentence must contain a subject and a predicate verb and express a complete thought.

...Relatively few of them, however, know that Crusoe's <u>story. It was</u> actually based
                                    1
on the real-life adventures of a Scottish
Scottish seaman, Alexander Selkirk.

1. A. NO CHANGE
   B. story: was
   C. story, was
   D. story was

If the underlined section for question 1 were left as it is, the second sentence of the passage would be incomplete. It wouldn't make sense. "Relatively few people know that Crusoe's story" what? To make it make sense, you've got to continue the sentence so it can tell us what few people know about Crusoe's story. The three alternatives all do that, but choice B introduces a nonsensical colon, while choice C adds a comma when there's no pause in the sentence. Choice D, however, continues the sentence—adding nothing unnecessary but making it complete.

When you are testing a sentence for completeness, don't just look to see if it has a subject and verb.

Question 12 tests the same concept:

…In fact, two sequels, in which Crusoe returns to the island after his rescue, were eventually published. Though to 12 little acclaim.	12. F. NO CHANGE G. published, though H. published although J. published; although

Here, the fragment should be more obvious, since the clause that's trying to pass itself off as a sentence—"Though to little acclaim"—contains neither a subject nor a verb. That's the technical reason it's wrong, and if you recognized this, great. On a more intuitive level, it just doesn't make sense to say, as a complete thought: "Though to little acclaim."

Clearly, that fragment has to be connected to the sentence before it, so choices F and J are wrong, since both would leave the fragment isolated. Choice H goes too far in the other direction, omitting any punctuation at all between the fragment and the main body of the sentence, and that's no good. The correct choice, G, does just what we need it to do: it connects the fragment logically to the main sentence, but it provides a comma to represent the pause between the two.

Sentence Structure

Rule at work: A sentence can have two thoughts, but they must be combined correctly (see below). If none of the answer choices does this, select the choice that creates two separate sentences.

…Upon his return to England, Selkirk found himself a celebrity, his strange 4 tale had already become the talk of pubs and coffeehouses throughout the British Isles.	4. F. NO CHANGE G. celebrity, but his H. celebrity. His J. celebrity his

Here we have two complete thoughts: (1) Selkirk found himself a celebrity upon his return, and (2) his tale was bandied about the pubs and coffeehouses. You can't just run these two complete thoughts together with a comma, as the underlined portion does. And you certainly can't just run them together *without* a comma or anything else, as choice J does. You can relate the two thoughts with a comma and a linking word (*and*, for instance), but choice G's inclusion of the word *but* makes no sense. It implies a contrast, while the two complete thoughts are actually very similar. Thus, you should create two sentences, one for each thought. That's what correct choice H does.

Rule at work: There are three ways to connect complete thoughts.

1. Use a semicolon.
2. Use a comma with a FANBOYS (For, And, Nor, But, Or, Yet, So) conjunction.
3. Make one of the two thoughts *in*complete (or dependent).

Working with these three possibilities for question 4, you might have seen any of these correct answer choices:

1. Selkirk found himself a celebrity*;* his strange tale had already…
2. Selkirk found himself a celebrity, *for* his strange tale had already…
3. Selkirk found himself a celebrity *because* his strange tale had already…

> ✔ **PERFECT SCORE TIP**
> If considering independent versus dependent clauses seems too confusing for you, just think, "If I put a period in the middle of this sentence and did not change any words, would the two new sentences make sense?" If the answer is yes, the sentence is a run-on.

Modifiers

SENTENCE SENSE

Question 2 tests modifier problems:

…After a bitter quarrel with his captain,
₂

he put Selkirk ashore on tiny Mas a Tierra,
₂

one of the islands of Juan Fernandez…

2. F. NO CHANGE
   G. Quarreling with his captain, the boat was put ashore
   H. Having quarreled with his captain, Selkirk was put ashore
   J. Having quarreled with his captain, they put Selkirk ashore

Rule at work: A modifier, or describer, is any word or group of words that describes another. Any and all describers must clearly relate to (be close to) whatever they are referring to.

> ✓ **PERFECT SCORE TIP**
> Misplaced modifiers are a common ACT trick. If multiple answers sound right to you, consider, "Is every modifying phrase placed near the word it logically modifies?"

Sentences become confused if a descriptive word, phrase, or clause is separated from the verb, noun, pronoun, etc. that it should be connected to. In the underlined portion of question 2, the phrase "after a bitter quarrel with his captain" should describe the person (or pronoun) that follows next. It doesn't.

The *he* who put Selkirk ashore must be the captain, but it can't be the captain who had "a bitter quarrel with his captain." That doesn't make sense (unless the captain quarrels with himself). Put the thing modified next to the thing modifying it. The person who quarreled with his captain was Selkirk—not the boat and not *they*, whoever *they* are—so choice H is correct.

If you recognized the problem with question 2 as a misplaced modifier, that's great. Fantastic, even. However, you didn't have to know the technicalities to get the right answer here. You just had to make the sentence make sense.

Question 11 tests a similar problem:

...Still popular today, contemporary
audiences enjoyed the book as well.

11. A. NO CHANGE
    B. Still read today, Defoe's contemporaries also enjoyed it.
    C. Viewed by many even then as a classic, the book is still popular to this day.
    D. Much read in its day, modern audiences still find the book compelling.

The way the sentence is written, it basically means that contemporary audiences are "still popular today." That doesn't make sense. The *intended* meaning is that the *book* is still popular today, as it was then. Choice C fixes the sense problem by putting its modifier—"viewed by many even then as a classic"—next to the thing it modifies—"the book." Notice that the other choices all misplace their modifiers in the same way, making them modify "Defoe's contemporaries" (in B) and "modern audiences" (in choice D).

> **EXPERT TUTOR TIP**
> Sentences should make sense. You'll be richly rewarded on test day if you learn to recognize misplaced modifiers, ambiguous pronouns, and correct sentence structure.

As a rule of thumb, you should **always** make sure that modifiers are as close as possible to the things they describe.

Idiom (Accepted Word Form and Choice)

WORD CHOICE

Rule at work: The correct preposition can vary depending on the sense of the sentence. Many phrases in English are correct because people have agreed to use them in a certain way. No overall rules apply. To master these, listen to what sounds right, or if English is not your native language, remember them one by one.

Question 3 tests idiom, or accepted uses of English words. Many words have special rules.

…Stranded, Selkirk lived there alone—in much the <u>same manner as</u> Defoe's
₃
Crusoe—until 1709, when he was finally rescued by another…

3. A. NO CHANGE
   B. same manner that
   C. identical manner that
   D. identical way as

The sentence as written actually makes sense. Selkirk lived in "much the same manner as" Defoe's Crusoe. The idiom "much the same" calls for *as* to complete the comparison between Selkirk's and Crusoe's ways of life. Note how choices B and C would create completeness problems—in much the same (or identical) manner that Defoe's Crusoe what? Choice D, meanwhile, sounds strange. In English, we just don't say "in much the identical way as" because the word *identical* is an absolute. You can't be more or partially identical; you either are or aren't identical to something else. Even if you didn't analyze choice D this carefully, it should have just sounded wrong to your ear. (In English Workout 3, we'll show you how "trusting your ear" can be a great way to get correct answers on the English subject test.)

Question 8 tests another idiom problem:

…For example, while Selkirk's presence on the island was of course <u>known for many people</u> (certainly everyone in the crew that stranded him there), no one in the novel is aware of Crusoe's survival of the wreck and presence on the island.

₈

8. F. NO CHANGE
    G. widely known among people
    H. known about many people
    J. known to many people

The underlined portion as written is unidiomatic. Selkirk's presence wasn't known *for* many people—it was known *by,* or known *to,* many people. When you're known *for* something, that means you have a reputation for doing such and such. That makes no sense in this context. Choice J *does* make sense, since it points out that Selkirk's presence on the island was known *to* many people—that is, it was something that many people knew about. Choice G is unidiomatic; we just wouldn't say "among people" here, since it's not specific enough. That sounds as if we're talking about people as a species. Choice H would have been acceptable if it had read "known about *by* many people," but without the *by,* the correction just wouldn't make sense.

> ✓ **PERFECT SCORE TIP**
> If you are a native English speaker, the key to idioms is really trusting your ear. Chances are, incorrect idioms will jump out at you if you trust what you hear.

Idiom is a tough topic if you're not a native speaker. You have to think very carefully about the meaning of every word. But if you *are* a native speaker, **use your many years of hearing English as a guide.** Choose the correction that makes sense and doesn't sound weird.

Pronouns

▃▃▁▁▁ **WORD CHOICE**

▃▁▁▁▁ **SENTENCE SENSE**

▁▁▁▁▁ **ORGANIZATION**

Rule at work: A pronoun must agree with the person or thing it is referring to, in person, gender, and number (singular or plural). The reference must be clear; if there is *any* confusion, the sentence must be fixed.

Sometimes, the test will throw you a sentence in which the meaning of a pronoun is unclear. You won't be sure to whom or what the pronoun is referring. That's the kind of problem you were given in **question 5:**

…The story even reached the ears of Richard Steele, who featured it in his periodical, *The Tatler*. Eventually, he became the subject of a best-selling book…

5. A. NO CHANGE
   B. Selkirk became
   C. his became
   D. he becomes

The *intended* meaning of the pronoun *he* here is Selkirk. But what's the closest male name to the pronoun? Richard Steele, the publisher of *The Tatler*. Your job is to make it clear whom the pronoun is referring to. Choice B takes care of the problem by naming Selkirk explicitly. Choice C would create a sense problem—his *what* became the subject of a book? Meanwhile, D shifts the verb tense into the present, which makes no sense since this book was written over 250 years ago!

 PERFECT SCORE TIP
Ambiguous pronouns are never right. If *he* or *they* are used, make sure it is obvious whom these pronouns are describing.

Mistakes of sense often involve pronouns. Make a habit of checking every underlined pronoun as you go along. What does the pronoun stand for? Can you tell? If not, there's an error. Does it make sense? If not, there's an error. Make sure it's perfectly clear to what or to whom all pronouns refer.

Logic

 WORD CHOICE

 SENTENCE SENSE

 ORGANIZATION

Think about words like *therefore, despite, however,* and *because.* Such words are structural clues. They serve as signposts in the passage to let you know where the author is going and how all of the pieces logically fit together. If the author uses the structural clue *on the other hand,* that means a contrast is coming up; if he or she uses the clue *moreover,* that means that a continuation is coming up—an addition that is more or less in the same vein as what came before.

Many ACT English questions mix up the logic of a piece of writing by giving you the wrong structural clue or another logic word. That's what's tested in **question 10:**

...<u>Because of</u> its basis in fact,
     10
Robinson Crusoe is often regarded as

the first major novel in English literature.

10. F. NO CHANGE
    G. Despite
    H. Resulting from
    J. As a consequence of

As written, this sentence means that *Crusoe* was regarded as the first major novel because it was based on fact. But that makes no sense. If it was based on fact, that would work against its being regarded as a novel. There's a contrast between "basis in fact" (which implies nonfiction) and "first major novel" (which implies fiction). To show that contrast logically, you need a contrast word like *despite*. That's why choice G is correct here.

> **EXPERT TUTOR TIP**
> The ACT test makers love to include questions about transitions between clauses, sentences, and paragraphs. Learn to recognize the logic and direction of a piece of writing—this will help you on the English and Reading tests.

Question 6 also tests logic:

...the subject of a best-selling book,

A Cruizing Voyage Round the World,

by Woodes Rogers. <u>While</u> there is
                        6
some evidence that Defoe, a journalist,

may actually have interviewed Selkirk

personally, most literary historians

believe that it was the reprinting of the

Rogers book in 1718 that served as the

real stimulus for Defoe's novel.

6. F. NO CHANGE
   G. But since
   H. And therefore
   J. OMIT the underlined portion and start the sentence with *There*.

The structural clue should convey a sense of contrast with the previous sentence. Even though Defoe may have interviewed Selkirk, many believe Defoe's main source was the book by Rogers. *While* provides the needed contrast, making NO CHANGE the correct answer.

Choices G and H have *since* and *therefore* which are cause-and-effect words, which make no sense in context. Choice J omits a key word and creates a run-on sentence—two independent clauses that are combined improperly. Remember, don't pick OMIT simply because it's there!

Verb Usage

.ıı00 VERB TENSE

.ıı00 WORD CHOICE

.ıı00 SENTENCE SENSE

Rules at work:

1. Use the simplest tense possible. In most cases, the present, past, and future tenses are all you need.
2. Change tenses only if the sentence doesn't make sense as written.
3. Make sure the verb is singular if it has a singular subject and plural if the subject is plural.

Verbs have an annoying habit of changing form depending on who's doing the action and when that person is doing it. Example: "I *hate* verbs; he *hates* verbs; and we both *have hated* verbs ever since we were kids." **You have to be very careful to make sure verbs match their subject and the tense of the surrounding context.**

…In *Crusoe*, which <u>has been published</u>
7
in 1719, Defoe took substantial liberties with the Selkirk story.

7. A. NO CHANGE
   B. was published
   C. had been published
   D. will have been published

The publication of *Robinson Crusoe* is something that took place in 1719—the past, in other words. So the underlined portion, which puts the verb in the present perfect tense, is flawed. Choices C and D, meanwhile, would put the verb into tenses normally used to convey a complex time relationship. Choice C makes it seem as if publication of the book happened before Defoe took his liberties with the story, but that's nonsensical. The liberties were taken in the writing of the book. Choice D, meanwhile, does strange things with the time sequence. The book was published in the past; Defoe also took his substantial liberties in the same past. So just use the simple past tense, choice B.

Tone

 **WORD CHOICE**

WRITING STRATEGY

Rule at work: Every writer of an ACT English passage has a voice, or tone. This voice is usually either casual (conversational) or factual (informational). Be sure to make choices that fit the author's voice.

As we said earlier, the passages in the English subject test vary in tone. Some are formal, others are informal. Usually, you'll know which is which without having to think about it. If a passage contains slang, a few exclamation points, and a joke or two, the tone is informal; if it sounds like something from a textbook, the tone is probably formal.

Good style requires that the tone of a piece of writing be at the same level throughout. Sometimes the underlined portion might not fit the tone of the rest of the passage. If so, it's up to you to correct it. Look at **question 13**:

…Meanwhile, Selkirk himself never <u>gave</u> <u>a hoot about returning</u> to the island that
13
had made him famous.

13. A. NO CHANGE
    B. evinced himself as desirous of returning
    C. could whip up a head of steam to return
    D. expressed any desire to return

Selkirk "never gave a hoot" about going back? No way! Slang doesn't belong in this passage. Choose D because it uses a straightforward, factual tone that fits the passage. The NO CHANGE choice is silly. Choice B is too wordy and formal. Choice C is also slang.

> **EXPERT TUTOR TIP**
> Don't pick an answer just because it sounds "fancy." Pick commonsense, everyday words that express the meaning the author intends. Don't worry if it sounds plain.

NONSTANDARD-FORMAT QUESTIONS

WRITING STRATEGY

ORGANIZATION

The Nonstandard-Format questions ask about the passage as a whole. Keep in mind the main point of the passage—the gist—as well as the overall tone and style. For an entire passage to make sense, it has to be consistent throughout, both in content and in tone and style.

Judging the Passage

Question 14 asks you to judge the passage. Was the last sentence an appropriate ending or not?

14. Considering the tone and subject matter of the preceding paragraphs, is the last sentence an appropriate way to end the essay?

    F. Yes, because it is necessary to shed some doubt on Defoe's creativity.

    G. Yes, because the essay is about the relationship between the real Selkirk and Defoe's fictionalized version of him.

    H. No, because there is nothing bizarre about Selkirk's story as it is related in the essay.

    J. No, because the focus of the essay is more on Selkirk himself than on Defoe's fictionalized version of him.

Think of the passage as a whole. It has been comparing Selkirk's real life with the one that Defoe made up for the character of Robinson Crusoe. Therefore, ending in this way, with an ironic reference wondering whether Defoe could have written a more fitting end to Selkirk's life, is perfectly appropriate. The answer to the question is yes (eliminating choices H and J). Choice G restates the point of the passage and is the best answer.

Reading Comprehension Questions

If you thought **question 15** looked like a Reading question hiding in the English part of the exam, you were right. As mentioned in ACT Basics, one reason that you should keep thinking about what the passage means—rather than focusing on picky rules of grammar or punctuation—is that **the English section includes some questions that test your reading comprehension skills.**

15. This essay would be most appropriate as part of a:

    A. scholarly study of 18th-century maritime history.

    B. study of the geography of the islands off of Chile.

    C. history of privateering in the Pacific.

    D. popular history of English literature.

What was this passage principally about? How Defoe's *Robinson Crusoe* was loosely based on the life of a real shipwrecked sailor, Alexander Selkirk. Would that kind of thing belong in a study of geography (choice B)? No. The focus is on the fictionalization of a historical life, not on the physical features of the islands off Chile. The passage isn't principally about privateering or maritime history either, so choices C and A are wrong as well. This passage is about the relationship between a true story and a famous fictionalized story. Its tone isn't overly scholarly, so it probably belongs in a popular history of English literature (choice D).

Structure and Purpose

The English section will also have questions that test your grasp of overall structure and purpose in a piece of prose. The test makers scramble the order of the sentences in a paragraph (or of the paragraphs in a passage). The question then asks you to decide on the best order for the scrambled parts. Take a look at this new question:

[1] Only recently has new evidence led many scientists to question the accepted division between birds and dinosaurs. [2] Traditionally, they have been placed in entirely separate classes within the subphylum *Vertebrata*. [3] Birds and dinosaurs don't have many obvious similarities. [4] Birds formed the class *Aves*, while dinosaurs constituted two orders, *Saurischia* and *Ornithischia*, within the class *Reptilia*.

16. To best fulfill the author's purpose, the order of the sentences in the paragraph should be:

    F. 1, 2, 3, 4.

    G. 2, 3, 4, 1.

    H. 3, 2, 4, 1.

    J. 3, 2, 1, 4.

Here again, the goal is to make it make sense. All of the sentences in this paragraph relate to the differences between birds and dinosaurs. Sentence 3 best introduces this idea. Notice that two of the answer choices begin with sentence 3—H and J. The other two can be eliminated.

Look again at the logic of the sentences. Because sentence 4 elaborates on the distinction introduced in sentence 2, sentence 4 should immediately follow sentence 2. Only choice H has them in that order, so H looks like the answer.

Just to check, you'll want to read the entire paragraph in the order suggested by choice H. And if you do, you'll notice that the paragraph makes perfect sense, with sentence 3 introducing the topic, sentences 2 and 4 showing how that topic has been traditionally viewed, and sentence 1 coming in naturally to show how that traditional view is no longer valid.

For questions like this, it's usually a good idea to start by trying to figure out the first (and sometimes the last) sentence because first and last sentences usually have the most obvious functions in an ACT-style paragraph.

EXPERT TUTOR TIP

If you don't know where to start on an organization question, look at the answers that begin with the same number (H and J), compare the two, and eliminate one or both answers.

▶ IF YOU LEARNED ONLY TWO THINGS IN THIS CHAPTER...

1. Consider the meaning of a sentence. If it doesn't make sense, there's probably a grammatical mistake. The correct answer will make sense.

2. Nonstandard-Format questions ask you to judge the passage and consider it as a whole. You may be asked about paragraph structure and function.

CHAPTER 6

English Workout 3: Look and Listen

In the first two English Workouts, we discussed English questions that hinged on economy and sense. There are some English questions—we call them Technicality questions—that may seem harder because they test for the technical rules of grammar, requiring you to correct errors that don't necessarily harm the economy or sense of the sentence. Don't worry. You don't have to be a grammar whiz to get these questions right. Luckily, you can often detect these errors because they "sound funny." **Most of the time on the ACT, it's safe to trust your ear.**

LISTEN TO THE CHOICES

Which of the following "sounds right" and which "sounds funny"?

- Bob doesn't know the value of the house he lives in.
- Bob don't know the value of the house he lives in.

The first sounds a lot better, right? For many of these questions, all you need to do is "listen" carefully in this way.

> **EXPERT TUTOR TIP**
> You can spot questions that test grammar rules because the answers are roughly the same length. Read the sentences carefully, looking and listening for clues to the error.

Your ear can help you determine the tone of a passage. For example, if the passage starts off "You'll just love Bermuda—great beaches, good living…" it won't end like this: "and an infinitely fascinating array of flora and fauna which may conceivably exceed, in range and scope, that of any alternative…" It's too formal. Pick something like this: "You'll just love Bermuda—great beaches, good living, and lots of awesome plants and animals."

> ✓ **PERFECT SCORE TIP**
> The best preparation for the English sections is really to enter a grammar "hyper mode" where you recognize grammar mistakes around you. If you are used to doing this in everyday life, common verb or agreement errors will pop out to you on the test.

Although ACT passages differ in level of formality, they all are designed to test standard English—the kind used by people in most of America. Test takers who speak regional or ethnic dialects may therefore find it more difficult to follow their ears on some ACT questions. In much of the South, for instance, it's common to use the word *in* with the word *rate,* like this: "Mortality declined *in* a rate of almost 2 percent per year." Most speakers of English, however, use the word *at* with *rate,* like this: "Mortality declined *at* a rate of…" Fortunately, ACT questions testing issues like this are rare. Even if you do speak a nonstandard dialect, you probably know what standard English sounds like. The dialect used on most television and radio programs would be considered standard.

In the following short passage, use your eyes and ears.

Passage II

THE HISTORY OF HALLOWEEN

Halloween was first celebrated among various Celtic
                                    1
tribes in Ireland in the fifth century B.C. It traditionally took place on the official last day of summer—October

31, and was named "All-Hallows' Eve." It was believed
2
that all persons who had died during the previous year returned on this day to select persons or animals to inhabit for the next twelve months, until they could

pass peaceful into the afterlife.
3

On All-Hallows' Eve, the Celts were dressing up as
                                      4
demons and monsters to frighten the spirits and tried

1. A. NO CHANGE
   B. among varied
   C. between the various
   D. between various

2. F. NO CHANGE
   G. 31—and
   H. 31. And
   J. 31; and

3. A. NO CHANGE
   B. pass peacefully
   C. passed peacefully
   D. be passing peaceful

4. F. NO CHANGE
   G. were dressed
   H. dressed
   J. are dressed

to make their homes <u>as coldest</u> as possible to prevent any
5
stray ghosts from crossing their thresholds. Late at night,

the townspeople typically gathered outside the village,

where a druidic priest would light a huge bonfire to

frighten away ghosts and to honor the sun god for the

past summer's harvest. Any villager <u>whom was</u> suspected
6

of being possessed would be captured, after which <u>they</u>
7
might be sacrificed in the bonfire as a warning to other

spirits seeking to possess the living. When the Romans

invaded the British Isles, they adopted Celtic—not

Saxon—Halloween rituals, but they outlawed human

sacrifice in A.D. 61. Instead, they used effigies for their

sacrifices. In time, as <u>belief in</u> spirit possession waned,
8

Halloween rituals lost their serious aspect and <u>had been</u>
9
instead performed for amusement.

Irish immigrants, fleeing from the potato famine

in the 1840s, <u>brought there</u> Halloween customs to the
10
United States. In New England, Halloween became a

night of costumes and practical jokes. Some favorite

5. A. NO CHANGE
   B. colder
   C. coldest
   D. as cold

6. F. NO CHANGE
   G. whom were
   H. who was
   J. who were

7. A. NO CHANGE
   B. it
   C. he or she
   D. those

8. F. NO CHANGE
   G. belief for
   H. believing about
   J. belief of

9. A. NO CHANGE
   B. having been
   C. have been
   D. were

10. F. NO CHANGE
    G. brought they're
    H. brought their
    J. their brought-in

pranks <u>included unhinging</u> front gates and overturning
                11
outhouses. The Irish also introduced the custom of

carving jack-o'-lanterns. The ancient Celts probably

began the tradition by hollowing out a large turnip,

carving it with a demon's face, and lighting it from

inside with a candle. Since there were <u>far less</u> turnips in
                                            12
New England than in Ireland, the Irish immigrants were

forced to settle for pumpkins.

Gradually, Halloween celebrations spread to other

regions of the United States. Halloween has been a

popular holiday ever since, <u>although these days it's</u>
                                        13

principal celebrants are children <u>rather than</u> adults.
                                        14

11. A. NO CHANGE
     B. include unhinging
     C. had included unhinged
     D. includes unhinged

12. F. NO CHANGE
     G. lots less
     H. not as much
     J. far fewer

13. A. NO CHANGE
     B. although these days its
     C. while now it's
     D. while not it is

14. F. NO CHANGE
     G. rather then
     H. rather
     J. else then

Key to Passage II

	Answer	Issue
1.	A	*among/between* distinction
2.	G	commas and dashes mixed
3.	B	use of adjectives and adverbs
4.	H	wrong verb tense
5.	D	comparative/superlative
6.	H	*who/whom* confusion
7.	C	pronoun usage error
8.	F	preposition usage
9.	D	tense problem with *to be*
10.	H	*they're/there/their* mix-up
11.	A	wrong verb tense
12.	J	*less/fewer* confusion
13.	B	*it's/its* confusion
14.	F	*then/than* confusion

GRAMMAR RULES TO KNOW

The rest of this workout is designed to help you build your own "flag list" of common errors on the ACT that your ear might not catch. Consider each classic error. If it seems like common sense to you (or, better, If the error just sounds like bad English to you, while the correction sounds like good English), you probably don't have to add it to your flag list. On the other hand, if it doesn't seem obvious, add it to your list.

As we'll see, making things match works in two ways. Some rules force you to match one part of the sentence with another part. Other rules force you to match the right word or word form with the intended meaning.

> ✔ **PERFECT SCORE TIP**
> Depending on if the people around you use correct grammar, your ear may or may not give you correct answers. Even if you generally have correct grammar, knowing the rules will help make you more confident in yourself. So be sure to review the grammar rules in this section.

RULE 1: Number Agreement

The most tested agreement rule on the ACT is this: Singular nouns must match with singular verbs and pronouns, and plural nouns must match with plural verbs and pronouns. A common error in this area involves the use of the word *they*. It's plural, but in everyday speech, we often use it as a singular.

> **WRONG:** "If a student won't study, they won't do well."
>
> **PROBLEM:** A *student* (singular) and *they* (plural) don't agree.
>
> **CORRECTION:** "If students won't study, they won't do well," or "If a student won't study, he or she won't do well."

> ✔ **PERFECT SCORE TIP**
> Take out surrounding words and just say the subject and the verb. Other words can hide verb mistakes, but a verb that doesn't match its subject will become clearer if you just say it after its subject.

RULE 2: Pronouns in Compounds

Another common agreement or matching error concerns compounds, which are phrases that join two words with *and* or *or*.

> **WRONG:** "The fool gave the wrong tickets to Bob and I."
>
> **PROBLEM:** *I* is a subject; it can't be the object of the preposition *to*.
>
> **CORRECTION:** "The fool gave the wrong tickets to Bob and me."

Hint: Try dropping the rest of the compound (Bob and). "The fool gave the wrong tickets to I" should sound funny to you.

RULE 3: Commas or Dashes (Parenthetical Phrases)

Parenthetical phrases must begin and end with the same punctuation mark. Such phrases can be recognized because without them the sentence would still be complete. For instance: "Bob, on his way to the store, saw a large lizard in the street." If you dropped the phrase "on his way to the store," the sentence would still be complete. Thus, this phrase is parenthetical. It could be marked off with commas, parentheses, or dashes. But the same mark is needed at both ends of the phrase.

> **WRONG:** "Bob—on his way to the store, saw a lizard."
>
> **PROBLEM:** The parenthetical phrase starts with a dash but finishes with a comma.
>
> **CORRECTION:** "Bob, on his way to the store, saw a lizard."

RULE 4: Commas (Run-Ons and Comma Splices)

You can't combine two sentences into one with a comma (though you can with a semicolon or conjunction).

WRONG: "Ed's a slacker, Sara isn't."

PROBLEM: Two sentences are spliced together with a comma.

CORRECTION: "Ed's a slacker, but Sara isn't." Or "Ed's a slacker; Sara isn't." Or "Ed, unlike Sara, is a slacker."

RULE 5: Fragments

This rule goes hand in hand with the previous one. **A sentence must have at least one "major event."** A fragment is writing that could be a subordinate part of a sentence but not a whole sentence itself.

WRONG: "Emily listened to music. While she studied."

PROBLEM: "She studied" would be a sentence, but *while* makes this a fragment.

CORRECTION: "Emily listened to music while she studied."

RULE 6: Punctuation

The ACT doesn't test tricky rules of punctuation. However, it does expect you to know what the punctuation marks mean and to match their use to their meanings. Here are some common punctuation marks and their meanings:

Use a **comma** (,) or **commas** to do the following:

- Set off items in a list of three or more items
- Combine two independent clauses with a FANBOYS conjunction (For, And, Nor, But, Or, Yet, So)
- Set off an introductory phrase from the rest of the sentence
- Separate nonessential information (something that could be considered a parenthetical phrase) from the rest of the sentence

Use a **semicolon** (;) to do the following:

- Combine two independent clauses when a FANBOYS word is not present
- Separate items in a series or list if those items already include commas

Use a **colon** (:) to introduce or emphasize a short phrase, quotation, example, explanation, or list.

Use a **dash** (—) or **dashes** to set off an explanatory or parenthetical phrase in a sentence.

Use an **apostrophe** (') to do the following:

- Indicate the possessive form of a noun
- Stand in for a missing letter or letters in a contraction

> **EXPERT TUTOR TIP**
> Most test takers need some review of punctuation. Brush up on your skills with English Review for the ACT on your online syllabus.

RULE 7: *-ly* Endings (Adverbs and Adjectives)

The ACT expects you to understand the difference between adverbs (which often end in -*ly*) and adjectives. The two are similar because they're both modifiers. They modify, refer to, or describe another word or phrase in the sentence. Nouns and pronouns must be modified by adjectives, while other words, especially verbs and adjectives themselves, must be modified by adverbs.

WRONG: "Anna is an extreme gifted child, and she speaks beautiful too."

PROBLEM: *Extreme* and *beautiful* are adjectives, but they're supposed to modify an adjective (*gifted*) and a verb (*speaks*) here, so they should be adverbs.

CORRECTION: "Anna is an extremely gifted child, and she speaks beautifully too."

RULE 8: *Good* or *Well*

In everyday speech, we often confuse the words *good* and *well*. But *good* is an adjective (it modifies a noun or pronoun); *well* is an adverb (it can modify verbs and adjectives).

WRONG: "Joe did good on the ACT."

PROBLEM: *Good* is an adjective, but here it's modifying a verb (*did*), so use an adverb.

CORRECTION: "Joe did well on the ACT."

One exception: *well* can also be used as an adjective when it means "healthy." So: "Joe was well again by the morning of the ACT" is correct, even though *well* is modifying the noun *Joe*.

> ☑ **PERFECT SCORE TIP**
> Perhaps the most ingrained grammar mistake is the answer of "Good" to the question, "How are you doing?" Especially when it comes to *good* vs. *well*, do not trust your ear, as it is often wrong. Just remember *good* is an adjective and will modify a noun while *well* modifies a verb.

RULE 9: *Lie, Lay, Laid, Lain*

The words *lay* and *lie* are easy to confuse because they look alike and have similar meanings. The key difference in meaning is point of view. If the speaker is doing something without a direct object, he is *lying*. If the speaker is doing it to something else, he is *laying*. For example, "I will go lie down" (not *lay* down), but "I will lay this pencil on the desk" (not *lie* it).

It gets worse. The past tense of *lay* is *laid*. That's not too hard. The confusing word is *lie*. The past tense of *lie* is *lay*; when used for special tenses (with the words *had, have,* or *been,* for example), the form is *lain*. Thus, you'd say, "I lay down" (meaning you, yourself, took a rest at some time in the past) or "I have lain down for a nap every afternoon for years now." You'd say, "I laid that pencil on the desk yesterday, just as I have laid it on the desk every day for years now."

Don't confuse *lie* with the word *lie* that relates to dishonesty. The past tense of *lie* (meaning to tell an untruth) is *lied*. The following example uses all the various forms correctly:

> "I lied. I said that I had lain down, but I hadn't. In fact, I had just laid the pencil down. After I lied, though, I lay down to repent for having lied."

Try not to get bogged down with *lie* and *lay*. If you don't get it, don't sweat it. It will account for one question if it appears at all.

RULE 10: *In, Of, To, For* (Idiomatic Preposition Use)

Whenever you see a preposition, double-check to make sure it makes sense and that it matches with the other words. Many words require particular prepositions.

WRONG:	"She tried to instill on me a respect to the law." "I want to protect you in all dangers."
PROBLEM:	The prepositions don't match the verbs.
CORRECTION:	"She tried to instill in me a respect for the law." "I want to protect you from all dangers."

RULE 11: *Who* or *Whom*

Many students fear the words *who* and *whom* more than any other grammatical conundrum. Fear no more. There's an easy way to remember when to use them: they work the same way *he* and *him* work. Turn the sentence into a question as we've done in the example below. If the answer to the question is *he,* the form should be *who.* If the answer is *him,* the form should be *whom.* Notice that the *m*s go together.

WRONG: "Always remember who you're speaking to."

PROBLEM: *Who* is wrong. Ask: Speaking to who? Speaking to him, not to he. So it should be *whom.*

CORRECTION: "Always remember whom you're speaking to."

Some students try to avoid the who/whom problem by using the word *which* instead. Don't. It's not nice to call people "whiches." **Never** use the word *which* for a person.

> ✓ **PERFECT SCORE TIP**
> The Kaplan strategy for distinguishing between *who* and *whom* was very helpful for me. I substituted *he* and *him,* and a difficult grammar concept became manageable.

RULE 12: *Its* or *It's* (Apostrophe Use)

Apostrophes are used primarily for two purposes: possessives and contractions. When you make a *noun* (not a pronoun) possessive by adding an *s,* you use an apostrophe. Examples: *Bob's, the water's, a noodle's.* You **NEVER** use an apostrophe to make a pronoun possessive—pronouns have special possessive forms. You'd never write *her's.* When you run two words together to form a single word, you use an apostrophe to join them. For example: *you'd, he's, they're.*

Apostrophes also have a few unusual uses, but luckily they're almost **never** tested on the ACT. So master the basics and you're in good shape. The most common apostrophe issue on the ACT is usage of the words *its* and *it's.* A good way to remember which is which is that *its* and *it's* follow the same rule as do *his* and *he's.* Both *its* and *his* are possessive pronouns—so they have *no* apostrophes. Both *it's* and *he's* are contractions—so they *do* have apostrophes.

WRONG: "The company claims its illegal to use it's name that way."

PROBLEM: *It's* is a contraction of *it is*; *its* is the possessive form of *it.*

CORRECTION: "The company claims it's illegal to use its name that way."

> ✓ **PERFECT SCORE TIP**
> Distinguishing *its* from *it's* was very important on my test. It is not a difficult concept, but it may help you get several questions correct on the ACT.

RULE 13: *There, Their,* or *They're* and *Are* or *Our* (Proper Word Usage)

Some students confuse the words *there, their,* and *they're.* **Remember that contractions use apostrophes—so *they're* is the contraction for *they are.*** You can tell which is *there* because it's spelled like *here,* and the words *here* and *there* match. (*Their* means "of or belonging to them"; you'll just have to remember that one the old-fashioned way.)

Students also frequently confuse the words *are* (a verb) and *our* (a possessive). You can remember that *our* is spelled like *your,* which is also possessive.

RULE 14: *Sang, Sung, Brang, Brung,* etc. (Verb Forms)

When the answers differ because of different forms of the same or similar verbs (for example, *live, lives, lived*), ask yourself *who* did it and *when* did they do it? We would say "I now live" but "he now lives." In these sentences, the *who* is different—and so the verb changes. Similarly, we would say "I now live" but "I lived in the past." In these sentences, the *when* is different—so the verb changes.

Most verbs are regular in this way, with only the endings *s* and *d* to worry about. You use the *s* when the subject is *he, she,* or *it* and the time is now (present tense). You use the *d* for times in the past. For times in the future, or several steps backward in time, there are no special endings. You use the words *will, will have, have,* and *had* for these time sequences. "I *will* live. I *will have* lived for 25 years by the time the next century begins. I *had* lived in Nebraska, but we moved. I *have* lived in Indiana since then."

However, a few verbs are irregular. They have special forms. For example, we say *sang* rather than *singed* and *have sung* rather than *have singed* or *have sang.* Each of these verbs must be learned separately.

One irregular verb commonly tested on the ACT is *bring.*

WRONG:	"I've brung my umbrella to work."
PROBLEM:	*Brang* and *brung* aren't used in standard English.
CORRECTION:	"I've brought my umbrella to work."

RULE 15: *Be* and *Was* (Forms of the Verb *To Be*)

The ACT tests the use of proper verb forms, especially of the verb *to be*. You must use the following forms. Memorize them if you have to:

Present Tense:	I *am*, we *are*, you *are*, they *are*, he/she/it *is*
Past Tense:	I *was*, we *were*, you *were*, they *were*, he/she/it *was*
Future Tense:	I/we/you/they/he/she/it *will be*
Perfect Tense:	I/we/you *have been*, he/she/it *has been*
Past Perfect:	I/we/you/he/she/it *had been*
Future Perfect:	I/we/you/he/she/it *will have been*

You decide which form (*am, are, is, were, was, will be, have been, had been, will have been*) is correct by determining what the subject is and what the tense is. (*Tense* refers to time: present, past, or future.) In many dialects, the words *be* and *was* are used instead of the special forms given. For example, many speakers might say, "They *be* going home" or "They *was* going home." On the ACT, the correct form is "They *are* (or *were*) going home."

> ✓ **PERFECT SCORE TIP**
> The verb *to be* is commonly conjugated incorrectly in everyday life. Review the rules and make a concerted effort to use them correctly when speaking—it will pay off on test day.

RULE 16: *-ing* Endings (Unidiomatic Verb Use)

Don't use *-ing* endings where they aren't needed. They are used to indicate repeated or continuous action and shouldn't be used for a single action that occurs once.

WRONG:	"When I left for the store, I was forgetting my list."
PROBLEM:	The *-ing* ending isn't necessary.
CORRECTION:	"When I left for the store, I forgot my list."

RULE 17: -er and -est, More, and Most (Comparatives and Superlatives)

Whenever you see the endings -er or -est, or the words more or most, double-check to make sure they're used correctly. Words with -er or with more should be used to compare only two things. If there are more than two things involved, use -est or most.

WRONG:	"Bob is the fastest of the two runners."
PROBLEM:	The comparison is between just two things, so -est is inappropriate.
CORRECTION:	"Bob is the faster of the two runners."

Don't use the words more or most if you can use the endings instead. Say "I think vanilla is tastier than chocolate," not "I think vanilla is more tasty than chocolate." Never use both more or most **and** an ending. Don't say "Of the five flavors of frozen yogurt I've eaten, strawberry delight is the most tastiest." Just say it's "the tastiest."

A note on than and then: Than is used in comparisons such as "Bob is faster than Jim." Then refers to time, as in "Bob ran and then stopped."

RULE 18: Between or Among

Make sure that you use the word between only when there are two things involved. When there are more than two things, or an unknown number of things, use among.

WRONG:	"I will walk among the two halves of the class." "I will walk between the many students in class."
PROBLEM:	Use between for two things and among for more than two.
CORRECTION:	"I will walk between the two halves of the class." "I will walk among the many students in class."

RULE 19: Less or Fewer

Make sure that you use the word less only for uncountable things. When things can be counted, they are fewer.

WRONG:	"I have fewer water than I thought, so I can fill less buckets."
PROBLEM:	You can count buckets; you can't count water.
CORRECTION:	"I have less water than I thought, so I can fill fewer buckets."

HINT: People are **always** countable, so use fewer when writing about them.

> **GO ONLINE**
> For a more thorough account of the grammar points you should know for the ACT, refer to the English Review for the ACT section of your online syllabus.

IF YOU LEARNED ONLY THREE THINGS IN THIS CHAPTER...

1. You can recognize some grammar mistakes because they sound strange. Listening is a great tool in the English section.

2. Other grammar mistakes break rules in context. To find these, you must read the sentence carefully to determine the correct punctuation, word, phrase, or clause.

3. Grammar rules tested by the ACT are relatively few. Refer to the quick outline provided in this chapter to learn them.

CHAPTER 7

Math Workout 1:
The End Justifies the Means

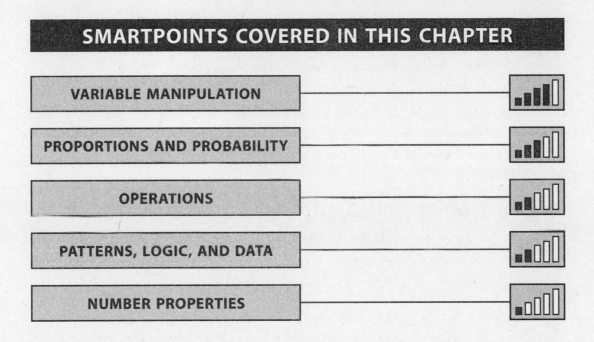

SMARTPOINTS COVERED IN THIS CHAPTER

VARIABLE MANIPULATION

PROPORTIONS AND PROBABILITY

OPERATIONS

PATTERNS, LOGIC, AND DATA

NUMBER PROPERTIES

Your goal on the Math subject test is to get as many correct answers as you can in 60 minutes. It doesn't matter what you do (short of cheating, naturally) to get those correct answers.

You don't have to do every problem the way your math teacher would. **Be open to clever and original solution methods.** All that matters is that your methods be quick and that they get you a solid number of correct answers. How many correct answers you need depends on what kind of score you're aiming for, but chances are you don't have to get so many right as you might think to get a good score. Yes, it's a tough test, but it's graded on a curve.

> **EXPERT TUTOR TIP**
> Here's how to use this chapter if you don't have much time. Learn the Kaplan Method for ACT Math, trying the sample questions that follow. Read the sidebars throughout the whole chapter for quick ACT Math strategy tips.

As we've pointed out, the ACT is different from the typical high school test. On a typical high school math test, you get a series of problems just like the ones you've been doing in class. Because you're being tested on a relatively narrow scope of topics, you're expected to get almost every question right.

ACT Math is different. The scope of what's tested is deliberately wide so that every student will get an opportunity to demonstrate his or her strengths, wherever they may lie.

> **PERFECT SCORE TIP**
> Remember that no one will be checking your method of doing problems. Don't feel compelled to do unnecessary algebra when you know a simpler way to solve the problem.

The average ACT student gets fewer than half of the Math questions right. **You need only about 40 correct answers to get your Math score over 25—just 2 right out of every 3 questions gets you a great score!**

THE ACT MATH MIND-SET

According to an old legend at MIT, a physics professor once asked the following question on a final exam: *How could a barometer be used to determine the height of a tower?*

To answer the question, most students worked out complex equations based on the fact that air pressure (which is what a barometer measures) decreases at higher altitudes. But one student made three suggestions instead:

1. Measure the length of the barometer, then use the barometer as a ruler and measure the tower.

2. Drop the barometer and time its fall, keeping in mind that the acceleration of falling objects is about 32 ft/sec².

3. Find the person who built the tower and say, "I'll give you a nice barometer if you tell me how tall your tower is."

Guess which student got an A…

On the ACT, as in college and beyond, you'll sometimes be called upon to do more than merely regurgitate memorized facts and unquestioningly follow prepackaged procedures. True, some ACT Math questions are straightforward: as soon as you understand what the question's asking, you know what to do. But more challenging—and more fun (really)—are the ACT Math questions that aren't what they seem at first glance. These are the questions that call for creative solutions.

 EXPERT TUTOR TIP
The ACT Math test includes:
- 24 pre-algebra and elementary algebra questions (corresponding roughly to the 100 Key Math Concepts for the ACT, #1–65)
- 10 intermediate algebra questions (100 Key Math Concepts for the ACT, #66–70)
- 8 coordinate geometry questions (100 Key Math Concepts for the ACT, #71–77)
- 14 plane geometry questions (100 Key Math Concepts for the ACT, #78–95)
- 4 trigonometry questions (100 Key Math Concepts for the ACT, #96–100)

Don't Be Obedient

On the ACT, there's no partial credit. All that matters is the right answer. It makes no difference how you find it. In fact, as we'll see, it's sometimes safer and faster if you don't do ACT problems the "right" way—the way you've been taught in school. For a lot of ACT Math problems, there's more than one way to find the answer. And many of these other ways are faster than the so-called right way.

If you do every problem the way your algebra teacher would want you to, you may earn his or her undying gratitude, but you won't achieve your goal of getting as many correct answers as possible. **You don't have time to use the textbook approach on every question.** You don't have time to write out every step.

✓ **PERFECT SCORE TIP**
Learn the correct amount of work to write down on math problems. Writing down some steps will help lessen your confusion, but writing too much will make it harder for you to find the right answer.

Pick Numbers

Sometimes you can get stuck on an algebra problem because it's too general or abstract. A good way to get a handle on such a problem is to make it more explicit by temporarily substituting numbers for the variables.

Example

1. If a is an odd integer and b is an even integer, which of the following must be odd?

    A. $2a + b$
    B. $a + 2b$
    C. ab
    D. a^2b
    E. ab^2

Rather than try to think this one through abstractly, it's easier to pick numbers for a and b. There are rules that predict the evenness or oddness of sums, differences, and products, but there's no need to memorize those rules. When it comes to adding, subtracting, and multiplying evens and odds, what happens with one pair of numbers generally happens with all similar pairs.

Just say, for the time being, that $a = 1$ and $b = 2$. Plug those values into the answer choices, and there's a good chance only one choice will be odd:

    A. $2a + b = 2(1) + 2 = 4$
    B. $a + 2b = 1 + 2(2) = 5$
    C. $ab = (1)(2) = 2$
    D. $a^2b = (1)^2(2) = 2$
    E. $ab^2 = (1)(2)^2 = 4$

Choice B was the only odd one for $a = 1$ and $b = 2$, so it *must* be the one that's odd no matter *what* odd number a and even number b actually stand for.

Backsolve

With some ACT Math problems, it may actually be easier to try out each answer choice until you find the one that works, rather than attempt to solve the problem and then look among the choices for the answer. Because this approach involves working backward from the answer choices to the question stem, it's called backsolving.

Example

2. All 200 tickets were sold for a particular concert. Some tickets cost $10 apiece, and the others cost $5 apiece. If total ticket sales were $1,750, how many of the more expensive tickets were sold?

   F. 20
   G. 75
   H. 100
   J. 150
   K. 175

There are ways to solve this problem by setting up an equation or two, but if you're not comfortable with the algebraic approach to this one, why not just try out each answer choice?

Start with choice H. If 100 tickets went for $10, then the other 100 went for $5. 100 at $10 is $1,000, and 100 tickets at $5 is $500, for a total of $1,500—too small. There must have been more than 100 $10 tickets.

Which answer do we try next? Because F and G are even smaller than H, try choice J next. If 150 tickets went for $10, then the other 50 went for $5. So 150 tickets at $10 is $1,500, and 50 tickets at $5 is $250, for a total of $1,750—that's it! The answer is J. On test day, the answers will also go in order from smallest to largest (or largest to smallest) allowing you to eliminate wrong answers without trying them out.

Backsolving your way to the answer may not be a method you'd show your algebra teacher with pride—but your algebra teacher won't be watching on test day. Remember, all that matters is right answers—it doesn't matter how you get them.

> **EXPERT TUTOR TIP**
> You will not get credit for anything you write under "DO YOUR FIGURING HERE." You get credit only for answers correctly gridded into the bubbles on your answer sheet.

Be a Thinker—Not a Number Cruncher

One reason you're given limited time for the Math subject test is that the ACT is testing your ability to think, not your willingness to do a lot of mindless calculations. So one of your guiding principles for ACT Math should be: **work less, but think harder.**

If you want to get the best score you can, be on the lookout for quicker ways to solve problems. Here's an example that could take a lot more time than it needs to:

Example

3. When $\frac{4}{11}$ is converted to a decimal, the 50th digit after the decimal point is:

   A. 2

   B. 3

   C. 4

   D. 5

   E. 6

It seems that when you convert $\frac{4}{11}$ to a decimal, there are at least 50 digits after the decimal point. The question asks for the 50th. One way to answer this question would be to divide 11 into 4, carrying the division out to 50 decimal places. That method would work, but it would take forever. It's not worth spending that much time on one question.

No ACT Math question should take more than a minute to solve. There has to be a faster way to solve this problem. There must be some kind of pattern you can take advantage of, some kind of pattern with a decimal. How about a *repeating* decimal?!

In fact, that's exactly what you have here. The decimal equivalent of $\frac{4}{11}$ is 0.3636363636…

The 1st, 3rd, 5th, 7th, and 9th digits are each 3. The 2nd, 4th, 6th, 8th, and 10th digits are each 6. Put simply, odd-numbered digits are 3s and even-numbered digits are 6s. The 50th digit is an even-numbered digit, so it's a 6 and the answer is E.

What looked at first glance like a fractions and decimals problem turned out to be something of an odds and evens problem. If you don't use creative shortcuts on problems like this one, you'll get bogged down, you'll run out of time, and you won't get a lot of correct answers.

> **EXPERT TUTOR TIP**
> Underlining what the question is asking will help you to make sure you choose the correct answer.

Question 3 demonstrates how the ACT designs problems to reward clever thinking and to punish students who blindly "go through the motions." But how do you get yourself into a creative mind-set on the Math test? For one thing, you have to take the time to understand thoroughly each problem you decide to work on. Most students are so nervous about time that they skim each math problem and almost immediately start computing with their pencils. But that's the wrong way of thinking. **Sometimes you have to *take* time to *save* time.** A few extra moments spent understanding a math problem can save many extra moments of computation or other drudgery.

✔ **PERFECT SCORE TIP**
As will be discussed later, a calculator can be your biggest aid or your greatest weakness. Use it to eliminate timely and costly calculation mistakes but not as a substitute for thinking about a problem.

THE KAPLAN METHOD FOR ACT MATH

At Kaplan, we've developed this take-time-to-save-time philosophy into a method for ACT Math problems. The approach is designed to help you find the fast, inventive solutions that the ACT rewards. The steps are:

STEP 1: What Is the Question?

Focus first on the question stem (the part before the answer choices), and make sure you understand the problem. Sometimes you'll want to read the stem twice or rephrase it in a way you can better understand. Think to yourself: "What kind of problem is this? What am I looking for?"

To understand an ACT Math problem, you first have to understand the language. Mathematicians are generally very precise in their use of language. They choose their words carefully and mean exactly what they say. You don't need to memorize definitions (you'll **never** have to recite one on the ACT), but you do need to understand what the question writer means.

✔ **PERFECT SCORE TIP**
Understanding the question is key. I know how tempting it is to start looking at answer choices before you really know what the question is looking for, but I promise this will not help you.

STEP 2: What Information Am I Given?

Now that you know what the question is asking, you need to figure out how to get from the problem to the answer. The best way to approach problems on the ACT is to ask yourself two things:

1. What information is provided in the question stem? Look at what information you're given along with what the question is asking. Do you have all of the information you need to answer the question like you would in a straightforward arithmetic or algebra problem? Are there additional computations you need to make in order to get to the answer? Note to yourself what information you have and what you may still need.

2. In what format do the answers appear? Take a quick look at the answers—not to choose an answer yet, just to check out the format of your options. This will help you organize your thinking. For example, you may think that you need to solve for x in an equation, but then you see that all of the answers are given in terms of x, so you don't actually need to find x, just come up with a formula. Additionally, if you are given information in fractions and see answers in decimals, you'll know that you need to convert from one to the other at some point.

For some questions, it will be clear to you what information you have and what you may need to do to find the answer. For others, you may not have all of the information you need and will need to do some computations before you can answer the question. That brings us to Step 3.

STEP 3: What Can I Do with the Information?

Think for a moment and decide on a plan of attack. Don't start crunching numbers until you've given the problem a little thought. There are three ways to solve the problem:

1. Use your math skills. If you know what to do, go for it!

2. Picking numbers. Are there variables in the answer choices that you can pick numbers for?

3. Backsolving. Are there numbers in the answer choices that you can use to figure out which one has to be the correct answer?

 EXPERT TUTOR TIP
Examine the diagram if you are given one, or make your own.

STEP 4: Am I Finished?

Once you get an answer, check the question again. Have you fully answered the question? Some questions may require several steps, and you may miss the last step if you don't check before you select. The test makers know to offer tempting answer choices for students who don't recheck the question. For example, you may need to find the area of a circle and you've only determined the radius—and the radius might be an answer choice! Since you will have identified the question in Step 1, double-checking that you're finished should take only a few seconds, and it can make a real difference on test day. Once you're sure, circle the answer in your test book and fill in the answer grid.

If you are stuck, skip the problem on the first pass through the test. Get all your easy points first! When you come back, if you still don't know how to approach the problem, try guessing strategically. In other words, are there any answer choices that you know couldn't possibly be the answer? Eliminate as many as you can before you choose an answer. Each answer choice you eliminate gets you one step closer to the correct answer!

Each of these steps can happen in a matter of seconds; it may not always be clear when you've finished with one step and moved on to the next. Sometimes you'll know how to attack a problem the instant you read and understand it.

> 🛜 **GO ONLINE**
> You can find the Kaplan Method for ACT Math on your downloadable study sheet, for review on the go.

Using the Kaplan Method

Here's how the Kaplan Method could be applied to question 3.

STEP 1: What Is the Question?

First, we made sure we understood what the problem was asking for: the 50th digit after the decimal point in the decimal equivalent of a certain fraction. Because we knew what *digit* and *decimal equivalent* meant, it took only a second to understand what the problem was asking.

STEP 2: What Information Am I Given?

In this case, you were given a fraction and were asked to convert it into a decimal and find the 50th digit after the decimal point. The answers were all single digits from 2 to 6.

STEP 3: What Can I Do with the Information?

Most crucially, we analyzed the situation and thought about a plan of attack before we tried to solve the problem. We realized that the obvious method would take too long, so we figured out a creative approach that got us an answer of 6 in just a few seconds.

STEP 4: Am I Finished?

Before choosing an answer, we reread the question to be sure that we had answered it fully. In this case, the question was pretty straightforward, but others may not be.

Finally, we looked at the answer choices, found 6, and selected choice E.

The Kaplan Method isn't a rigid procedure; it's a set of guidelines that will keep you on track, moving quickly, and evading pitfalls.

Example

4. If the sum of five consecutive even integers is equal to their product, what is the greatest of the five integers?

   F.   4
   G. 10
   H. 14
   J.   16
   K. 20

STEP 1: What Is the Question?

Before you can begin to solve this problem, you have to figure out what it's asking. You'll need to know the meanings of *sum, product, consecutive, even,* and *integer.* Put the question stem into words you can understand. What the question stem is really saying here is that when you add up these five consecutive even integers, you get the same thing as when you multiply them.

STEP 2: What Information Am I Given?

We are not given any numbers in the problem, but we *are* told that we'll be working with consecutive even integers. The difference between each integer in this series will be 2. A quick glance at the answer choices and we see that they are all positive. Good to know.

STEP 3: What Can I Do with the Information?

How are we going to figure out what these five numbers are? We could set up an equation:

$$x + (x - 2) + (x - 4) + (x - 6) + (x - 8) = x(x - 2)(x - 4)(x - 6)(x - 8)$$

But there's no way you'll have time to solve an equation like this! So don't even try. Come up with a better way.

Let's stop and think logically about this one for a moment. When we think about sums and products, it's natural to think mostly of positive integers. With positive integers, we would generally expect the product to be *greater* than the sum.

But what about negative integers? Hmm. Well, the sum of five negatives is negative, and the product of five negatives is also negative. Generally the product will be "more negative" than the sum, so with negative integers, the product will be less than the sum.

So when will the product and sum be the same? How about right at the boundary of positive and negative—that is, around 0? The five consecutive even integers with equal product and sum are: –4, –2, 0, 2, and 4.

$$(-4) \times (-2) \times 0 \times 2 \times 4 = (-4) + (-2) + 0 + 2 + 4$$

The product and sum are both 0. Ha! We've done it!

How to backsolve: The question asks which is the greatest of the integers, so you start with the greatest answer choice: K. If the largest number is 20, then the other numbers must be 18, 16, 14, 12. Their sum is $20 + 18 + 16 + 14 + 12 = 80$. 20 times 18 is already 360, so we know that choice K is not correct and that it is WAY too big! Let's try the next smallest choice, H (14). We want to add: $14 + 12 + 10 + 8 + 6 = 50$. Still too big, because 10 times 6 is already 60. So let's try 4, choice F. $4 + 2 + 0 + (-2) + (-4) = 4 \times 2 \times 0 \times (-2) \times (-4) = 0$. It works!

> **EXPERT TUTOR TIP**
> If you don't have any idea how to solve this problem, ask yourself, "Can I pick numbers? Can I backsolve?" There are numbers in the answer choices, so you should backsolve.

STEP 4: Am I Finished?

We found the answer by thinking logically about the question and confirmed our answer by backsolving. The question asks for the greatest of five integers, which is 4, choice F. If you didn't read the question carefully, you might be tempted to look for the sum and product of the five integers—fortunately, that's not an option, but for other questions, a tempting answer may be a choice.

You've probably encountered every math term that appears on the ACT sometime in your high school math career, but you may not remember exactly what every one of them means. The Math Glossary in the ACT Resources section of your online syllabus is a complete but compact list of the terminology you need for ACT Math problems. Look it over. Jot down the terms you're not sure of for future reference. And be sure to use the online glossary to look up any unfamiliar term you encounter while practicing with ACT Math questions.

> ☑ **PERFECT SCORE TIP**
> Math is one section where actual knowledge of material is necessary. If any terms you read here are unfamiliar to you, learn them! Don't waste precious easy points because you don't know the definition of basic terms.

Definition Alert

As you refresh your memory of key terminology, watch out for technicalities. Here are a few examples of such technicalities (by the way, these are great for stumping your know-it-all friends):

- *Integers* **include 0 and negative whole numbers.** If a question says "*x* and *y* are integers," it's not ruling out numbers like 0 and –1.

- *Evens and odds* **include 0 and negative whole numbers.** Zero and –2 are even numbers; –1 is an odd number.

- *Prime numbers* **do not include 1.** The technical definition of a prime number is a positive integer with exactly two distinct positive integer factors. Two is prime because it has exactly two positive factors: 1 and 2. It's also the smallest, and the only even, prime number. Four is not prime because it has three positive factors (1, 2, and 4)—too many! And 1 is not prime because it has only one positive factor (1)—too few!

- *Remainders* **are integers.** If a question asks for the remainder when 15 is divided by 2, don't say "15 divided by 2 is 7.5, so the remainder is .5." What you should say is: "15 divided by 2 is 7 with a remainder of 1."

- *The $\sqrt{}$ symbol represents the positive square root only.* The equation $x^2 = 9$ has two solutions: 3 and –3. But when you see $\sqrt{9}$, it means positive 3 only.

- *Rectangles* **include squares.** The definition of a rectangle is a four-sided figure with four right angles. It doesn't matter if the length and width are the same or not—if it has four right angles, it's a rectangle. When a question refers to "rectangle ABCD," it's not ruling out a square.

Example

5. What is the value of $x^2 + 3x - 9$ when $x = -3$?

   A. -27
   B. -9
   C. -6
   D. 0
   E. 9

STEP 1: What Is the Question?

You've probably seen dozens of problems just like this. If so, then you realize right away that what it's asking is, "What do you get when you plug $x = -3$ into $x^2 + 3x - 9$?"

STEP 2: What Information Am I Given?

In this question, we're given an algebra problem and a value for x. We're given three negative integers for answer choices, along with 0 and 3.

STEP 3: What Can I Do with the Information?

Because we have a value for x, we can just plug it into the algebra problem and solve:

$$x^2 + 3x - 9 = (-3)^2 + 3(-3) - 9$$
$$= 9 + (-9) - 9$$
$$= -9$$

STEP 4: Am I Finished?

Rereading the problem tells us we've done exactly what it asked; our answer, -9, is choice B.

So this is a case where you knew exactly what to do as soon as you understood what the question was asking. Sometimes you're not so lucky. Let's look at a case where the method of solution is not so obvious, even after you understand the stem:

NUMBER PROPERTIES

Example

6. Which is the greatest of the numbers 1^{50}, 50^1, 2^{25}, 25^2, 4^{10}?

    F. 1^{50}

    G. 50^1

    H. 2^{25}

    J. 25^2

    K. 4^{10}

STEP 1: What Is the Question?

It's not hard to figure out what the question is asking: which of five numbers is the greatest? But the five numbers are all written as powers, some of which we don't have time to calculate. Yikes! How are we going to compare them?

STEP 2: What Information Am I Given?

Here you're given five integers of different values with exponents of different values. Since you're asked to find the greatest of the numbers, you can't rely on the answers to be in ascending value as they usually are for ACT questions—that would be too easy.

STEP 3: What Can I Do with the Information?

If all the powers had the same base or the same exponent, or if they could all be rewritten with a common base or exponent, we could compare all five at once. As it is, though, we should take two at a time.

> ◎ **KAPLAN'S TARGET STRATEGY**
> Step 3 is where you'll be doing most of your serious thinking. The other two Math Workouts will address this step in greater detail.

Compare 1^{50} and 50^1 to start: $1^{50} = 1$, while $50^1 = 50$, so there's no way choice F could be the biggest.

Next, compare 50^1 and 2^{25}. We don't have time to calculate 2^{25}, but we can see that it doesn't take anywhere near 25 factors of 2 to get over 50. In fact, 2^6 is 64, already more than 50, so 2^{25} is much more than 50. That eliminates G.

Choice J, 25^2, doesn't take too long to calculate: $25 \times 25 = 625$. How does that compare to 2^{25}? Once again, with a little thought, we realize that it doesn't take 25 factors of 2 to get over 625. That eliminates J.

The last comparison is easy because choice K, 4^{10}, can be rewritten as $(2^2)^{10} = 2^{20}$, which is clearly less than 2^{25}. That eliminates choice K.

> **EXPERT TUTOR TIP**
> Whenever plugging negative numbers into your calculator, always make sure to put them in parentheses. Not using them will lead to a wrong answer!

STEP 4: Am I Finished?

Check the question—we were asked for the greatest of the numbers. The answer is H and we are finished.

> **EXPERT TUTOR TIP**
> Use your calculator to fly right through Example 6. If you don't use a calculator all the time in school, start practicing so you are familiar with it by test day.

Know When to Skip

At any time during the four-step process, you could choose to cut bait and skip the question. **Almost everyone should skip at least some questions the first time through.**

> **EXPERT TUTOR TIP**
> The fastest way to a higher score on the ACT is to get all your easy points first—skip those hard problems, and go back to them later if you have time.

If you know your own strengths and weaknesses, you can sometimes choose to skip a question while still in Step 1: Understand. For example, suppose you **never** studied trigonometry. Maybe you think that a secant is something that sailors sing while climbing up the yardarms. Well, the ACT includes exactly four trigonometry questions, and it's not hard to spot them. Why waste a second on such questions? Skip them! You don't need those four measly questions to get a great score. And since you know a second visit later won't help any, you might as well go ahead and make some random guesses.

> ## KAPLAN'S TWO-PASS PLAN FOR ACT MATH
>
> We recommend that you plan two passes through the Math test.
>
> - **First pass:** Examine each problem in order. Do every problem you understand. Don't skip too hastily—sometimes it takes a few seconds of thought to see how to do something—but don't get bogged down. Never spend more than a minute on any question in the first pass. This first pass should take about 45 minutes.
>
> - **Second pass:** Use the last 15 minutes to go back to the questions that stumped you the first time. Sometimes a fresh look is all you need—after going away and then coming back, you'll sometimes suddenly see what to do. In most cases, though, you'll still be stumped by the question stem, so it's time to give the answer choices a try. Work by process of elimination, and guess. Be sure to select an answer for every question, even if it's just a blind guess.

It can be harder to decide when to skip a question if you understand it, but then get stuck in Step 2: Analyze. Suppose you just don't see how to solve it. Don't give up too quickly. Sometimes it takes 30 seconds or so before you see the light. But don't get bogged down either. Never spend more than a minute on a question the first time through the section. No single question is worth it. Be prepared to leave a question and come back to it later. Often, on the second try, you'll see something you didn't see before. That old lightbulb will light up over your head and you'll be on your way.

Of course, eventually, you're going to grid in an answer choice for every question, even the ones you don't understand. **The first time through the section, you should concentrate on the questions you understand.**

> **EXPERT TUTOR TIP**
> Making two passes through the Math test means you'll never run out of time before seeing every question.

Don't plan on visiting a question a third time; it's inefficient to go back and forth that much. Every time you leave a question and come back to it, you have to take at least a few seconds to refamiliarize yourself with the problem. **Always** grid in an answer choice on the second pass—even if it's just a wild guess. At the end of the second pass, every question should be answered.

Don't worry if you don't work on every question in the section. The average ACT test taker gets fewer than half of the problems right. You can score in the top quarter of all ACT test takers if you can do just half of the problems on the test, get every single one of them right, and guess blindly on the other half. If you did just one-third of the problems and got every one right, then guessed blindly on the other 40 problems, you would still earn an average score.

> **✓ PERFECT SCORE TIP**
> I skipped multiple questions on my first time through. When I returned to them the second time, I found that they often became clearer to me. It is possible to get a very good score even if the solution to every problem does not pop out at you.

Don't Make Careless Mistakes

Most students don't worry much about careless errors. Because in school (where you show your work) you can earn partial credit, many students think that careless errors somehow "don't count." Not so on the ACT. There are only so many problems you'll know how to do. Some of the problems will be impossible for you, so you'll make or break your score on the problems you can do. You can't afford to miss one easy problem!

Unless math is a very strong area for you, the best way to maximize your score is to work on the questions you deserve to get correct. Don't worry about getting to every problem (though, of course, you should mark an answer for every problem on your answer grid, even if it's a blind guess).

Even if math is a strong area for you, don't get complacent on easy problems—that causes careless errors. For strong students, the easy problems may be the most challenging. You have to find a way to answer them quickly and accurately in order to have time for the tougher ones. You won't have time for the hard problems unless you save some time on the easy ones.

Here's a question that's not hard to understand but is hard to solve if you don't remember the rules for simplifying and adding radicals:

⦿ NUMBER PROPERTIES

Example

7. $\dfrac{\sqrt{32} + \sqrt{24}}{\sqrt{8}} = ?$

    A. $\sqrt{7}$

    B. $\sqrt{2} + \sqrt{3}$

    C. $2 + \sqrt{3}$

    D. $\sqrt{2} + 3$

    E. 7

STEP 1: What Is the Question?

The question wants you to simplify the given expression, which includes three radicals. In other words, turn the radicals into numbers you can use, then work out the fraction.

> **✓ PERFECT SCORE TIP**
> Sometimes radicals can be intimidating. Remember that even if you forget the rules, there are simpler ways to deal with them, such as using known radicals to estimate, or if worse comes to worst, using your calculator to get estimates.

STEP 2: What Information Am I Given?

You're given a fraction with numbers under a radical in the numerator and denominator. If you looked at the problem and had no idea what to do, a glance at the answers would help. The answers are not given in fractional terms so you know you can simplify the fraction to eliminate the denominator. Additionally, the choices include the numbers 7, 2, and 3, either alone or under radicals. Think about how the numbers under the radicals can be factored into those numbers as you approach Step 3.

STEP 3: What Can I Do with the Information?

The best way to solve this problem would be to apply the rules of radicals—but what if you don't remember them? Don't give up; you can still guesstimate. In the question stem, the numbers under the radicals are not too far away from perfect squares. You could round $\sqrt{32}$ off to $\sqrt{36}$, which is 6. You could round $\sqrt{24}$ to $\sqrt{25}$, which is 5. And you could round $\sqrt{8}$ off to $\sqrt{9}$, which is 3. So the expression is now

$\frac{6+5}{3}$, which is $3\frac{2}{3}$. That's just a guesstimate, of course—the actual value might be something a bit less or a bit more than that.

> **EXPERT TUTOR TIP**
> This problem can also be solved using a calculator. If you plug this into your calculator, you get 3.73. Then put each of the answer choices into your calculator to see which one matches.

STEP 4: Am I Finished?

Reread the question, then look at the answer choices. Choice A ($\sqrt{7}$) is less than 3, so it's too small. Choice B ($\sqrt{2} + \sqrt{3}$) is about 1.4 + 1.7, or just barely more than 3, so it seems a little small, too. Choice C ($2 + \sqrt{3}$) is about 2 + 1.7, or about 3.7—that's very close to our guesstimate! We still have to check the other choices. Choice D ($\sqrt{2} + 3$) is about 1.4 + 3, or 4.4—too big. And choice E, 7, is obviously way too big. Looks like our best bet is choice C—and C in fact is the correct answer.

> **PERFECT SCORE TIP**
> My biggest problem on the Math section was trying to go too fast. In practice, I would often get questions wrong simply because I went too fast and missed an important word in the question or made an arithmetic mistake. These mistakes are not worth it—trust me.

TO CALCULATE OR NOT TO CALCULATE

You are permitted to use a calculator on the Math section. The good news is that you never *absolutely need* to use a calculator on the ACT. No Math question requires messy or tedious calculations. But while the calculator can't answer questions for you, it can keep you from making computational errors on questions you know how to solve. The bad news, however, is that a calculator can actually cost you time if you overuse it. Take a look at this example:

Example

8. The sum of all the integers from 1 to 44, inclusive, is subtracted from the sum of all the integers from 7 to 50, inclusive. What is the result?

   F.   6
   G.   44
   H.   50
   J.   264
   K.   300

You could add all the integers from 1 through 44, and then all the integers from 7 through 50, and then subtract the first sum from the second. And then punch in all the numbers into the calculator. And then hope you didn't hit any wrong buttons.

But that's the long way...and the *wrong* way. That way involves hitting over 250 keys on your calculator. It'll take too long, and you're too likely to make a mistake. The amount of computation involved in solving this problem tells you that there must be an easier way. Remember, no ACT problem absolutely requires the use of a calculator.

Look at the problem again: a calculator *can* help you on this question, but you have to think first. Both sums contain the same number of consecutive integers, and each integer in the first sum has a corresponding integer 6 greater than it in the second sum. Here's the scratchwork:

$$
\begin{array}{cc}
1 & 7 \\
+2 & +8 \\
+3 & +9 \\
\cdot & \cdot \\
\cdot & \cdot \\
\cdot & \cdot \\
+42 & +48 \\
+43 & +49 \\
+44 & +50 \\
\end{array}
$$

This means there are 44 pairs of integers which are each 6 apart. So the total difference between the two sums will be the difference between each pair of integers times the number of pairs. Now you can pull out your calculator, punch in "6 × 44 =," and get the correct answer of 264 with little or no time wasted. Mark J in your test booklet and move on.

> **EXPERT TUTOR TIP**
> If a problem seems to involve a lot of calculation, look for a quicker way. Try to spot a pattern that will help you save some time.

Of course, there will be many situations on the ACT in which using a calculator can save you time. Here's a trig question that's much easier with a calculator:

Example

9. sin 495° =

    A. $-\dfrac{\sqrt{2}}{2}$

    B. $-\dfrac{1}{2}$

    C. $\dfrac{1}{2}$

    D. $\dfrac{\sqrt{2}}{2}$

    E. $\dfrac{3\sqrt{2}}{2}$

Without a calculator, this is a very difficult problem. To find a trigonometric function of an angle greater than or equal to 90°, sketch a circle of radius 1 which is centered at the origin of the coordinate grid. Start from the point (1, 0) and rotate the appropriate number of degrees counterclockwise. When you rotate counterclockwise 495°, you rotate 360° (which brings you back to where you started), and then an additional 135°. That puts you midway into the second quadrant. Now you need to know whether sine is positive or negative in the second quadrant. Pretty scary, huh?

> ✓ **PERFECT SCORE TIP**
> One of my biggest weaknesses is simple arithmetic, so my calculator was very helpful in eliminating these mistakes. Still, I had to be sure that I had a plan for how to do most problems without a calculator, and then use it just to check my math.

With a calculator, this problem becomes simple. Just punch in "sin 495°" and you get 0.7071067811865. Choices A and B are negative, so they're out, and 0.7071067811865 is clearly not equal to $\dfrac{1}{2}$, so choice C is also wrong. That leaves only choices D or E. Now, with respect to choice E: $\sqrt{2}$ is greater than 1, so if you multiply it by another number greater than 1 (namely $\dfrac{3}{2}$), the result is obviously greater than 1. So you can eliminate choice E, leaving D as the correct answer. With a calculator, you can get this question right without really understanding it.

> **EXPERT TUTOR TIP**
> When doing trig functions, make sure that your calculator is in degree mode—unless the answers contain π, in which case you have to use radians.

The key to effective calculator use is practice, so don't run out the night before the test to buy a fancy new calculator. If you don't already have a calculator (and intend to use one on the test), buy one now. Unless you're studying math or science in college, you won't need anything more complex than trig functions. You're better off bringing a straightforward model you're familiar with than an esoteric model you don't know how to use.

Practicing with your calculator is the best way to get a sense of where it can help and save time. Here's a brief guide to spotting those calculator-friendly Math questions.

Example

10. $(7.3 + 0.8) - 3(1.98 + 0.69) =$

   F.   −0.99
   G.   −0.09
   H.   0
   J.   0.09
   K.   0.99

This problem basically involves straightforward computation, so you'd be right if you reached for your calculator. However, if you just start punching the numbers in as they appear in the question, you will come up with the wrong answer. When you're performing a string of computations, you know that you need to follow the right order of operations. The problem is, your calculator might not know this. Some calculators have parentheses keys and do follow the order of operations, so it's important to know your calculator and what its capabilities are. See 100 Key Math Concepts for the ACT, #7 for further explanation of PEMDAS.

> **EXPERT TUTOR TIP**
> Some calculators automatically follow the proper order of operations, but others don't. Know before test day what your calculator can and cannot do.

If your calculator doesn't follow the order of operations, you'd need to perform the operations within parentheses separately and proceed carefully from there. You'd get 8.1 − 3(2.67). Multiplication comes before subtraction, so you'd get 8.1 − 8.01, and then finally 0.09, choice J.

Example

11. A certain bank issues three-letter identification codes to its customers. If each letter can be used only once per code, how many different codes are possible?

    A.   26

    B.   78

    C.   326

    D. 15,600

    E. 17,576

Just manipulating the numbers in this problem will get you nowhere, but once you arrive at the setup, a calculator is very useful.

For the first letter in the code, you can choose any of the 26 letters in the alphabet. For the second letter, you can choose from all the letters in the alphabet except the one you used in the first spot, so there are $26 - 1 = 25$ possibilities. For the third, there are $26 - 2 = 24$ possibilities. So the total number of different codes possible is equal to $26 \times 25 \times 24$. Using your calculator, you find that there are 15,600 codes—choice D.

Example

12. Which of the following fractions is greater than 0.68 and less than 0.72?

    F. $\dfrac{5}{9}$

    G. $\dfrac{7}{11}$

    H. $\dfrac{2}{3}$

    J. $\dfrac{5}{7}$

    K. $\dfrac{3}{4}$

Here, you have to convert the fractions to decimals and see which one falls in the range of values given in the question. If you're familiar with common decimal/fraction conversions, you might know that choice K, $\frac{3}{4}$, is equal to 0.75 (too large) and choice H, $\frac{2}{3}$, is approximately 0.67 (too small). But you'd still have to check out the other three choices. Your calculator can make short work of this, showing you that choice F, $\frac{5}{9}$, equals $0.\overline{55}$; choice G, $\frac{7}{11}$, equals $.\overline{63}$; and choice J, $\frac{5}{7}$, is approximately 0.71. Only 0.71 falls between 0.68 and 0.72, so choice J is correct.

GO ONLINE
Your downloadable study sheet contains key math formulas and concepts.

▶▶ IF YOU LEARNED ONLY FOUR THINGS IN THIS CHAPTER...

1. Look for the quickest ways to solve problems. Sometimes this requires creative thinking.

2. Use the answer choices to help you. If you are stuck, can you plug numbers in for the variables or use the numbers in the answer choices to get to the correct answer?

3. Follow Kaplan's Two-Pass Plan: Skip problems that are more difficult, and come back to them after you've finished the easy ones.

4. Practice with your calculator so you are comfortable using it—and understand when it is faster not to use it.

CHAPTER 8

Math Workout 2: Shake It Up!

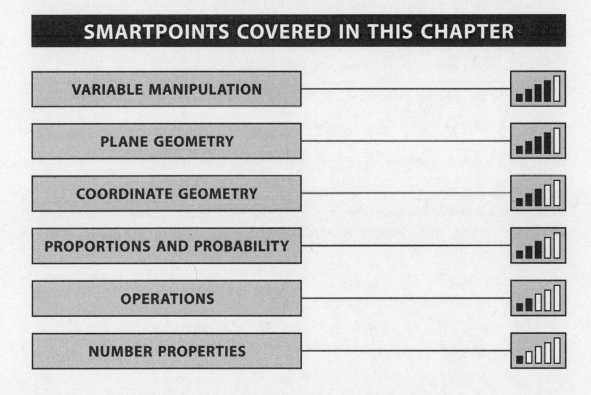

SMARTPOINTS COVERED IN THIS CHAPTER

- VARIABLE MANIPULATION
- PLANE GEOMETRY
- COORDINATE GEOMETRY
- PROPORTIONS AND PROBABILITY
- OPERATIONS
- NUMBER PROPERTIES

The main idea of Math Workout 1 was: Don't jump in headfirst and start crunching numbers until you've given a problem some thought. Make sure you know what you're doing—*and* that what you're doing won't take too long.

As we saw in Math Workout 1, sometimes you'll know how to proceed as soon as you understand the question. A good number of ACT algebra and coordinate geometry questions are straightforward textbook questions you may already be prepared for.

TEN TEXTBOOK ALGEBRA AND COORDINATE GEOMETRY QUESTIONS

📶 **VARIABLE MANIPULATION**

📶 **COORDINATE GEOMETRY**

When you take the ACT, you can be sure you'll see some of the following questions with only slight variations. You'll find answers and explanations for these questions in the 100 Key Math Concepts for the ACT section.

1. **Evaluate an algebraic expression.** *(See 100 Key Math Concepts for the ACT, #52)*
   Example: If $x = -2$, then $x^2 + 5x - 6 = ?$

2. **Multiply binomials.** *(See 100 Key Math Concepts for the ACT, #56)*
   Example: $(x + 3)(x + 4) = ?$

3. **Factor a polynomial.** *(See 100 Key Math Concepts for the ACT, #61)*
   Example: What is the complete factorization of $x^2 - 5x + 6$?

4. **Simplify an algebraic fraction.** *(See 100 Key Math Concepts for the ACT, #62)*
   Example: For all $x \neq \pm 63$, $\dfrac{x^2 - x - 12}{x^2 - 9} = ?$

5. **Solve a linear equation.** *(See 100 Key Math Concepts for the ACT, #63)*
   Example: If $5x - 12 = -2x + 9$, then $x = ?$

6. **Solve a quadratic equation.**
   (See 100 Key Math Concepts for the ACT, #66)
   Example: If $x^2 + 12 = 7x$, what are the two possible values of x?

7. **Solve a system of equations.**
   (See 100 Key Math Concepts for the ACT, #67)
   Example: If $4x + 3y = 8$ and $x + y = 3$, what is the value of x?

8. **Solve an inequality.**
   (See 100 Key Math Concepts for the ACT, #69)
   Example: What are all the values of x for which $-5x + 7 < -3$?

9. **Find the distance between two points in the (x, y) coordinate plane.**
   (See 100 Key Math Concepts for the ACT, #71)
   Example: What is the distance between the points with (x, y) coordinates $(-2, 2)$ and $(1, -2)$?

10. **Find the slope of a line from its equation.**
    (See 100 Key Math Concepts for the ACT, #73)
    Example: What is the slope of the line with the equation $2x + 3y = 4$?

These questions are all straightforward and traditional. They could have come out of a high school algebra textbook, so do these questions the way you were taught. In case you'd like to review them, you'll find all the standard approaches succinctly summarized in 100 Key Math Concepts for the ACT. We're not so concerned in these workouts with problems you may already know how to solve. Here, we're going to focus on several situations where the quick and reliable solution method is not so obvious.

> **GO ONLINE**
> Get more coordinate geometry practice with the online workshop and quiz available through your online syllabus.

> ✔ **PERFECT SCORE TIP**
> Basic algebra is a must-know for ACT Math. If any of these concepts seem unfamiliar to you, be sure to read about them in the 100 Key Math Concepts.

THREE WAYS TO SHAKE IT UP

It's bound to happen at some point on test day. You look at a math problem and you don't see what to do. Don't freak out. Think about the problem for a few seconds before you give up. **When you don't see the quick and reliable approach right away, shake the problem up a little.** Try one of these "shake-it-up" techniques:

1. **Restate.**
2. **Remove the disguise.**
3. **Try eyeballing.**

1. Restate the Problem

Often, the way to get over that stymied feeling is to change your perspective. Have you ever watched people playing Scrabble®? In their search to form high-scoring words with the letters on their seven tiles, they continually move the tiles around in their racks. Sometimes a good word becomes apparent only after rearranging the tiles. One might not see the seven-letter word in this arrangement:

> R E B A G L A

But reverse the tiles and a word almost reveals itself:

> A L G A B E R

The tiles can spell ALGEBRA.

The same gimmick works on the ACT, too. **When you get stuck, try looking at the problem from a different angle.** Try rearranging the numbers, changing fractions to decimals, factoring, multiplying out, or redrawing the diagram—anything that might give you the fresh perspective you need to uncover a good solution method.

Here's a question you might not know what to do with at first glance:

 OPERATIONS

Example

1. Which of the following is equivalent to $7^{77} - 7^{76}$?

    A. 7

    B. 7^{77-76}

    C. $7^{77 \div 76}$

    D. $7(77 - 76)$

    E. $7^{76}(6)$

Here's a hint: *Think of an easier problem testing the same principles.* The important thing to look for is the basic relationships involved—here, we have exponents and subtraction. That subtraction sign causes trouble, because none of the ordinary rules of exponents (see 100 Key Math Concepts for the ACT, #47–48) seem to apply when there is subtraction of unlike terms.

Another hint: How would you work with $x^2 - x$? Most test takers could come up with another expression for $x^2 - x$: they'd factor to $x(x - 1)$. Or if the problem asked for $x^{77} - x^{76}$, they'd factor to $x^{76}(x - 1)$. The rule is no different for 7 than for x. Factoring out the 7^{76} gives you: $7^{76}(7 - 1)$, which is $7^{76}(6)$, or choice E.

> **EXPERT TUTOR TIP**
> If you are using a graphing calculator, you can use your calculator to solve Example 1.

Sometimes an ACT algebra question will include an expression that isn't of much use in its given form. The breakthrough in such a case may be to restate the expression by either simplifying it or factoring it.

> **✔ PERFECT SCORE TIP**
> If the first way you think of to solve a problem is not working, don't be afraid to try a different one. Often, rephrasing a problem you are stuck on will make it become clearer.

Part Two: Skill-Building Workouts
Math Workout 2: Shake It Up!

137

NUMBER PROPERTIES

Example

2. If $\frac{x}{2} - \frac{x}{6}$ is an integer, which of the following statements must be true?

   F. x is positive.

   G. x is odd.

   H. x is even.

   J. x is a multiple of 3.

   K. x is a multiple of 6.

Re-express: $\frac{x}{2} - \frac{x}{6} = \frac{3x}{6} - \frac{x}{6} = \frac{2x}{6} = \frac{x}{3}$

This form of the expression tells us a lot more. If $\frac{x}{3}$ is an integer, then x is equal to three times an integer:

$\frac{x}{3} =$ an integer

$x = 3 \times$ an integer

In other words, x is a multiple of 3, choice J.

2. Remove the Disguise

Sometimes it's hard to see the quick and reliable method immediately because the true nature of the problem is hidden behind a disguise. Look at this example:

VARIABLE MANIPULATION

Example

3. What are the (x, y) coordinates of the point of intersection of the line representing the equation $5x + 2y = 4$ and the line representing the equation $x - 2y = 8$?

   A. $(2, 3)$

   B. $(-2, 3)$

   C. $(2, -3)$

   D. $(-3, 2)$

   E. $(3, -2)$

This may look like a coordinate geometry question, but do you really have to graph the lines to find the point of intersection? Remember, the ACT is looking for creative thinkers, not mindless calculators! Think about it for a moment—what's the special significance of the point of intersection, the one point that the two lines have in common? That's the one point whose coordinates will satisfy *both* equations.

EXPERT TUTOR TIP

Although this question turned out not to be a real coordinate geometry problem, the test makers do have a soft spot in their hearts for coordinate geometry. Typically 8 or more of the 60 Math questions involve coordinate geometry. It's hard to get a top score without getting at least some of these questions right. Use 100 Key Math Concepts for the ACT #71–77 to review the relevant rules and formulas.

So what we realize now is that this is not a coordinate geometry question at all, but a system-of-equations question. All it's really asking you to do is solve the pair of equations for *x* and *y*. The question has nothing to do with slopes, intercepts, axes, or quadrants. It's a pure algebra question in disguise.

Now that we know we're looking at a system of equations, the method of solution presents itself more clearly. The first equation has $a + 2y$, and the second equation has $a - 2y$. If we just add the equations, the *y* terms cancel:

$$\begin{array}{r} 5x + 2y = 4 \\ x - 2y = 8 \\ \hline 6x = 12 \end{array}$$

If $6x = 12$, then $x = 2$. Plug that back into either of the original equations, and you'll find that $y = -3$. The point of intersection is $(2, -3)$, and the answer is C.

EXPERT TUTOR TIP

When you have a system of equations, you can solve it by:

• Combination
• Substitution
• Graphing

The previous example demonstrates combination.

▁▂▃▄ VARIABLE MANIPULATION

Example

4. A geometer uses the following formula to estimate the area A of the shaded portion of a circle, as shown in the figure below, when only the height h and the length of the chord c are known:

$$A = \frac{2ch}{3} + \frac{h^3}{2c}$$

What is the geometer's estimate of the area, in square inches, of the shaded region if the height is 2 inches and the length of the chord is 6 inches?

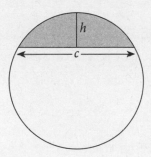

   F. 6

   G. $6\frac{2}{3}$

   H. $7\frac{1}{2}$

   J. $8\frac{2}{3}$

   K. 12

At first glance, this looks like a horrendously esoteric geometry question. Who ever heard of such a formula? But when you think about the question a bit, you realize that you don't really have to understand the formula. You certainly don't have to remember it—it's right there in the question.

> **🧑 EXPERT TUTOR TIP**
> If you look at this problem and you freak out the first time through the test, skip it. Hopefully you'll realize how easy it is on your second pass. Don't waste valuable time freaking out about one problem.

In fact, this is not really a geometry question at all. It's just an "evaluate the algebraic expression" question in disguise. All you have to do is plug the given values $h = 2$ and $c = 6$ into the formula:

$$A = \frac{2ch}{3} + \frac{h^3}{2c}$$

$$= \frac{2(6)(2)}{3} + \frac{(2)^3}{2(6)}$$

$$= 8 + \frac{2}{3} = 8\frac{2}{3}$$

Choice J is correct.

The people who wrote this question wanted you to freak out at first sight and give up. Don't give up on a question too quickly just because it looks like it's testing something you never saw before. In many such cases, it's really a familiar problem in disguise.

3. Stuck? Try Eyeballing

There is another simple but powerful strategy that should give you at least a 50-50 chance on almost any diagram question: **When in doubt, use your eyes. Trust common sense and careful thinking; don't worry if you've forgotten most of the geometry you ever knew.** For almost half of all diagram questions, you can get a reasonable answer without solving anything: just eyeball it.

The Math directions say, "Illustrative figures are NOT necessarily drawn to scale," but in fact they almost **always** are. You're never really *supposed* to just eyeball the figure, but it makes a lot more sense than random guessing. Occasionally, eyeballing can help you narrow down the choices.

EXPERT TUTOR TIP
It pays to learn the approximate value of these three irrational numbers:
$\sqrt{2} \approx 1.4$
$\sqrt{3} \approx 1.7$
$\pi = 3.14$

Here's a difficult geometry question that you might just decide to eyeball:

▂▃▅▇ PLANE GEOMETRY

Example

5. In the figure below, points A, B, and C lie on a circle centered at O. Triangle AOC is equilateral, and the length of OC is 3 inches. What is the length, in inches, of arc ABC ?

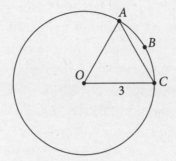

   A. 3

   B. π

   C. 2π

   D. 3π

   E. 6π

STEP 1: What Is the Question?

There's an equilateral triangle that connects the center and two points on the circumference of a circle. You're looking for the length of the arc that goes from A to C.

STEP 2: What Information Am I Given?

You know the length of OC is 3 inches and that AOC is an *equilateral* triangle, that is, a triangle where all sides are equal lengths and all interior angles are 60 degrees. All but one of the answer choices are given in terms of π, so it's likely that a calculation with π would help you find the answer if you were to do a calculation using a formula. But read on, in Step 3 we'll show you that you don't actually need to use a formula to figure this one out!

STEP 3: What Can I Do with the Information?

What you're "supposed" to do to answer this question is recall and apply the formula for the length of an arc. But suppose you don't remember that formula (most people don't). Should you give up and take a wild guess?

No. You can eyeball it. Since you understand that *equilateral* means all sides are equal, you know that side $\overline{AC}$ is 3 inches long. Now look at arc *ABC* compared to side $\overline{AC}$. Suppose you were an ant, and you had to walk from *A* to *C*. If you walked along line segment $\overline{AC}$, it would be a 3-inch trip. About how long a walk would it be along arc *ABC*? Clearly more, but not much more, than 3 inches.

STEP 4: Am I Finished?

Now look at the answer choices. Choice A is no good—you know the arc is more than 3 inches. All the other choices are in terms of π. Just think of π as "a bit more than 3," and you will quickly see that only one answer choice is in the right ballpark. Choice B—π—would be a bit more than 3, which sounds pretty good. Choice C—2π—would be something more than 6. Already that's way too big. Choices D and E are even bigger. It sure looks like the answer has to be B—and it is.

> **GO ONLINE**
> If you have forgotten any of the geometry terms discussed in this workout, look them up in the Math Glossary of your online syllabus.

Not many ACT students would be able to solve question 5 the textbook way. If you could, great! Solving the problem is **always** more reliable than eyeballing. But when you *don't* know how to solve a diagram problem, or if you think it would take forever to get an answer, eyeballing and eliminating answer choices sure beat wild guessing. Sometimes, as with question 5, you might even be able to narrow the choices down to the one that's probably correct.

> **EXPERT TUTOR TIP**
> Answer choices are in order. If the first number you try doesn't work, the process of plugging in that first number might tell you whether you'll need a smaller or a larger number. So when backsolving, start with the middle choice (C or H) to be safe.

TYPICAL STORY PROBLEMS

We find that about one-third of the questions on the Math test are Story Problems. Though some Story Problems present unique situations that must be analyzed on the spot, others are just variations on familiar themes.

Percent Problems

In Percent Problems, you're usually given two numbers and asked to find a third. The key is to identify what you have and what you're looking for. In other words, identify the part, the percent, and the whole.

> **EXPERT TUTOR TIP**
> Be prepared: Problems involving percentages, averages, ratios, and probability appear frequently on the ACT Math test.

Put the numbers and the unknown into the general form:

Part = Percent × Whole

Usually the part is associated with the word *is,* and the whole is associated with the word *of.*

📊 PROPORTIONS AND PROBABILITY

Example

6. In a group of 250 students, 40 are seniors. What percentage of the group are seniors?

    F. 1.6%

    G. 6.25%

    H. 10%

    J. 16%

    K. 40%

The percent is what we're looking for ("What percentage…"); the whole is 250 ("…of the group…"); and the part is 40 ("…are seniors"). Plug these into the general formula:

Part = Percent × Whole

$$40 = 250x$$

$$x = \frac{40}{250} = .16 = 16\%$$

The answer is J.

Many ACT Percent Problems concern percent change. To increase a number by a certain percent, calculate that percent of the original number and add it on. To decrease a number by a certain percent, calculate that percent of the original number and then subtract. For example, to answer the question, "What number is 30 percent greater than 80?" first find 30 percent of 80—that's 24—and add that on to 80: 80 + 24 = 104.

> **EXPERT TUTOR TIP**
>
> When a quantity is increased or decreased by a percent *more than once*, you cannot simply add and subtract the percents to get the answer. In this kind of percent problem:
>
> • The first percent change is a percent of the starting amount.
> • The second percent change is a percent of the new amount.

The ACT has ways of complicating percent change problems. Especially tricky are problems with multiple changes, such as a percent increase followed by another percent increase or a percent increase followed by a percent decrease.

PROPORTIONS AND PROBABILITY

Example

7. If a positive number is increased by 70 percent, and then the result is decreased by 50 percent, which of the following accurately describes the net change?

   A. A 20 percent decrease

   B. A 15 percent decrease

   C. A 12 percent increase

   D. A 20 percent increase

   E. A 120 percent increase

To get a handle on this one, pick a number. Suppose the original number is 100. After a 70 percent increase, it rises to 170. That number, 170, is decreased by 50 percent, which means it's reduced by half to 85. The net change from 100 to 85 is a 15 percent decrease—choice B.

> **PERFECT SCORE TIP**
>
> One of the most common mistakes on percentages is thinking that taking 25 percent off twice is the same as taking 50 percent off—it is not. To avoid this, try pretending you began with 100 dollars and then doing the percentage manipulations in the question.

Average Problems

Instead of giving you a list of values to plug into the average formula, ACT Average Problems often put a slight spin on the question. They tell you the average of a group of terms and ask you to find the value of the missing term. Here's a classic example:

PROPORTIONS AND PROBABILITY

Example

8. To earn a B for the semester, Linda needs an average of at least 80 on the five tests. Her average for the first four test scores is 79. What is the minimum score she must get on the fifth test to earn a B for the semester?

   F. 80
   G. 81
   H. 82
   J. 83
   K. 84

The key to almost every Average Problem is to use the sum. Sums can be combined much more readily than averages. An average of 80 on five tests is more usefully thought of as a combined score of 400. To get a B for the semester, Linda's five test scores have to add up to 400 or more. The first four scores add up to $4 \times 79 = 316$. She needs another 84 to get that 316 up to 400. The answer is K.

> **EXPERT TUTOR TIP**
> Backsolving is a fast way to work through average problems. Question 8 asks for the minimum score, so start with 80. Try plugging that in for the fifth test score.

Weighted Average Problems

Another spin ACT test makers put on Average Problems is to give you an average for part of a group and an average for the rest of the group, and then ask for the combined average.

PROPORTIONS AND PROBABILITY

Example

9. In a class of 10 boys and 15 girls, the boys' average score on the final exam was 80 and the girls' average score was 90. What was the average score for the whole class?

   A. 83
   B. 84
   C. 85
   D. 86
   E. 87

Don't just average 80 and 90 to get 85. That would work only if the class had exactly the same number of girls as boys. In this case, there are more girls, so they carry more weight in the overall class average. In other words, the class average should be somewhat closer to 90 (the girls' average) than to 80 (the boys' average).

As usual with averages, the key is to use the sum. The average score for the whole class is the total of the 25 individual scores divided by 25. We don't have 25 scores to add up, but we can use the boys' average and the girls' average to get two subtotals.

If 10 boys average 80, then their 10 scores add up to 10×80, or 800. If 15 girls average 90, then their 15 scores add up to 15×90, or 1,350. Add the boys' total to the girls' total: $800 + 1,350 = 2,150$. That's the class total, which can be divided by 25 to get the class average: $\frac{2,150}{25} = 86$. The answer is D.

Probability Problems

Probabilities are part-to-whole ratios. The whole is the total number of possible outcomes. The part is the number of favorable outcomes. For example, if a drawer contains two black ties and five other ties and you want a black tie, the total number of possible outcomes is 7 (the total number of ties), and the number of favorable outcomes is 2 (the number of black ties). The probability of choosing a black tie at random is $\frac{2}{7}$.

> **EXPERT TUTOR TIP**
> The probability of what *will* happen is not affected by what already *has* happened. Whenever you flip a coin, the probability is $\frac{1}{2}$ that it will be heads. Even if you flip the coin and get heads 10 times in a row, the probability is still $\frac{1}{2}$ on the 11th flip. Of course, the odds against 11 heads in a row are huge, but once the first 10 flips are history they're no longer relevant.

WHAT TO DO NEXT

Because more than half the Math questions on the ACT involve algebra, it's a good idea to solidify your understanding of the basics before test day. Focus on #52–70 in 100 Key Math Concepts for the ACT. Keep things in perspective. **Geometry questions are important, too, but algebra questions are more important.**

▶ IF YOU LEARNED ONLY THREE THINGS IN THIS CHAPTER...

1. You should be familiar with the ten textbook algebra and coordinate geometry problems.

2. Some ACT Math problems will be disguised so that their method of solution isn't obvious.

3. Be familiar with the formulas for calculating percentages and averages.

CHAPTER 9

Math Workout 3: Figuring It Out

SMARTPOINTS COVERED IN THIS CHAPTER

| PLANE GEOMETRY |
| COORDINATE GEOMETRY |

Every ACT Math subject test has about 14 geometry questions and exactly four trigonometry questions. Depending on what kind of score you're aiming for, you don't need to spend too much time working on trigonometry problems, but you definitely want to spend some time brushing up on your geometry skills.

Fortunately, a good number of the geometry questions are straightforward. Nothing is distorted or disguised. With these questions, you know what to do—if you know your geometry—the instant you understand them.

TEN TEXTBOOK GEOMETRY QUESTIONS

PLANE GEOMETRY

COORDINATE GEOMETRY

Here's a set of ten such questions. When you take the ACT, you will see quite a few questions just like these—possibly reworded and certainly with different numbers and figures. Use these questions to find out how well you remember your geometry.

✓ **PERFECT SCORE TIP**
If you are aiming for a top Math score, you will need the trig questions. Luckily, normally three of the four can be answered simply by knowing SOHCAHTOA (sin = opposite/hypotenuse, cos = adjacent/hypotenuse, tan = opposite/adjacent). I took the ACT before taking trigonometry and did not think the trig questions were much to worry about. Still, if the trig sections look hard to you—review them. That one question can be really important if you are looking for a very high score.

Example

1. In the figure below, line t crosses parallel lines m and n. What is the degree measure of $\angle x$?

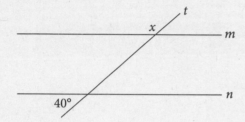

A. 40
B. 50
C. 60
D. 130
E. 140

2. What is the slope of the line perpendicular to the equation $4x + 3y = 9$?

F. $-\dfrac{4}{3}$

G. $-\dfrac{3}{4}$

H. $\dfrac{4}{3}$

J. $\dfrac{3}{4}$

K. 3

3. In the figure below, $\angle B$ is a right angle and the lengths of AB, BC, and CD are given in units. What is the area of $\triangle ACD$, in square units?

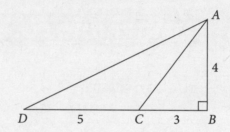

A. 10
B. 12
C. 16
D. 20
E. 32

4. In the figure below, $\triangle ABC$ is similar to $\triangle DEF$. $\angle A$ corresponds to $\angle D$, $\angle B$ corresponds to $\angle E$, and $\angle C$ corresponds to $\angle F$. If the given lengths are of the same unit of measure, what is the value of x?

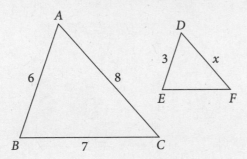

F. 3
G. 3.5
H. 4
J. 5
K. 6

5. In $\triangle ABC$ below, $\angle B$ is a right angle. If $\overline{AB}$ is 1 unit long and $\overline{BC}$ is 2 units long, how many units long is $\overline{AC}$?

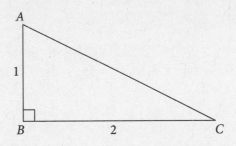

A. $\sqrt{3}$
B. $\sqrt{3}$
C. 2
D. $\sqrt{5}$
E. 3

6. Point P (–3, 5) and point Q (0, 1) are points on the x-y coordinate plane. What is the distance between points P and Q?

F. 4
G. 5
H. 6
J. 7
K. 8

7. In the figure below, $\overline{BE}$ is perpendicular to $\overline{AD}$, and the lengths of $\overline{AB}$, $\overline{BC}$, $\overline{CD}$, and $\overline{BE}$ are given in inches. What is the area, in square inches, of trapezoid ABCD ?

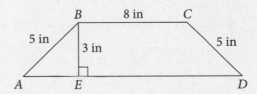

A. 24
B. 30
C. 32
D. 34
E. 36

8. What is the area, in square inches, of a circle with a diameter of 8 inches?

F. 4π
G. 8π
H. 16π
J. 32π
K. 64π

9. In the circle centered at O in the figure below, the measure of $\angle AOB$ is 40°. If $\overline{OA}$ is 9 units long, how many units long is minor arc AB?

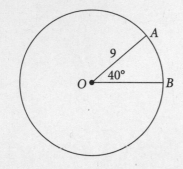

A. π

B. 2π

C. 9

D. 9π

E. 40

10. In the figure below, $ABCD$ is a square and $\overline{AB}$ is a diameter of the circle centered at O. If $\overline{AD}$ is 10 units long, what is the area, in square units, of the shaded region?

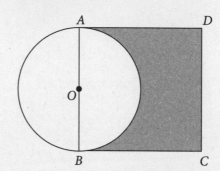

F. $100 - 50\pi$

G. $100 - 25\pi$

H. $100 - \dfrac{25\pi}{2}$

J. $100 - 10\pi$

K. $100 - 5\pi$

Scoring

10 correct: You have a solid grounding in geometry. Straightforward textbook geometry questions are no problem for you. Skip ahead to the section called Tackling More Complex Geometry questions.

8–9 correct: You have a pretty good grasp of the geometry you need to know for the ACT. Before moving on to the discussion of more complex geometry, read the explanations that follow for the questions you got wrong, and study the appropriate pages of the 100 Key Math Concepts for the ACT section at the back of this book.

0–7 correct: You have gaps in your knowledge of geometry. Before you can hope to get much out of our discussion of more complex geometry, you had better solidify your geometry foundations. Look at the explanations that follow, and study the corresponding pages of the 100 Key Math Concepts for the ACT section at the back of this book.

Answers

1.	E	6.	G
2.	J	7.	E
3.	A	8.	H
4.	H	9.	B
5.	D	10.	H

Answers and Explanations

1. When a transversal crosses parallel lines, the four acute angles formed are all equal, the four obtuse angles formed are all equal, and any angles that are not equal are supplementary. The angle marked x is obtuse, so it's supplementary to the given 40° angle. $180 - 40 = 140$. The answer is E. (*100 Key Math Concepts for the ACT, #79*)

2. First, you need to put the equation you are given into $y = mx + b$ form. When you do this, you can see that the slope of this line is $-\frac{4}{3}$. We are looking for the slope of the line perpendicular to this line. That means that we need the opposite reciprocal slope, which is $\frac{3}{4}$, choice J.

3. The formula for the area of a triangle is $A = \frac{1}{2}bh$. To apply this formula, you need the base and the height. Here, you can use CD for the base and AB for the height. So: Area $= \frac{1}{2}(CD)(AB) = \frac{1}{2}(5)(4) = 10$. The answer is A. (*100 Key Math Concepts for the ACT, #83*)

4. In similar triangles, corresponding sides are proportional. DE corresponds to AB, and DF corresponds to AC, so we can set up this proportion:

$$\frac{AB}{DE} = \frac{AC}{DF}$$

$$\frac{6}{3} = \frac{8}{x}$$

$$6x = 3 \times 8$$

$$6x = 24$$

$$x = 4$$

The answer is H. (*100 Key Math Concepts for the ACT, #82*)

5. The Pythagorean theorem says: $(leg_1)^2 + (leg_2)^2 = (hypotenuse)^2$. Here, the legs have lengths of 1 and 2, so plug them into the formula:

$$(1)^2 + (2)^2 = (hypotenuse)^2$$
$$1 + 4 = x^2$$
$$x^2 = 5$$
$$x = \sqrt{5}$$

The answer is D. (*100 Key Math Concepts for the ACT, #84*)

6. There are a couple of ways to solve a distance problem. If you can remember the formula, great! Plug the coordinates into the distance formula:

$$\sqrt{(x_1 - x_2)^2 + (y_2 - y_1)^2}$$

to get

$$\sqrt{(0 - (-3))^2 + (1 - 5)^2} = \sqrt{(-3)^2 + (4)^2} = \sqrt{9 + 16} = \sqrt{25} = 5$$

If you can't, you can still get this problem correct. Draw a quick graph and plot the two points that you are given. See if you can make a triangle once you draw the points, and then determine the lengths of the two legs. You will need to solve for the hypotenuse, but you know how to do this—the Pythagorean theorem! You might also recognize the Pythagorean triplet (3-4-5). Any way you solve it, you will get 5, choice G.

7. The formula for the area of a trapezoid is $A = \left(\dfrac{b_1 + b_2}{2}\right)h$, where b_1 and b_2 are the lengths of the parallel sides. You could think of it as the height times the average of the bases. You're given the height (3 inches), one base (8 inches), and enough information to figure out the other base. Notice that $\triangle ABE$ is a 3-4-5 triangle, so $AE = 4$ inches. And if you were to drop an altitude down from point C, you'd get another 3-4-5 triangle on the right:

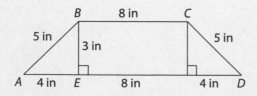

EXPERT TUTOR TIP

If you don't remember the formula for the area of a trapezoid, break it into shapes that you do know the area formulas for—triangles and a rectangle.

Now you can see that the bottom base is 16 inches. Plug these numbers into the formula:

$$A = \left(\frac{b_1 + b_2}{2}\right)h$$
$$= \left(\frac{8 + 16}{2}\right) \times 3$$
$$= 12 \times 3 = 36$$

The answer is E. (*100 Key Math Concepts for the ACT, #87*)

8. The formula for the area of a circle is $A = \pi r^2$, where r is the radius. If the diameter is 8 inches, then the radius is 4 inches, which we plug into the formula:

$$A = \pi r^2$$
$$= \pi(4)^2$$
$$= 16\pi$$

The answer is H. (*100 Key Math Concepts for the ACT, #91*)

9. The central angle of minor arc *AB* is 40°, which is $\frac{1}{9}$ of the whole circle's 360°. The length of minor arc *AB*, therefore, is $\frac{1}{9}$ of the whole circle's circumference.

$$C = 2\pi r = 2\pi(9) = 18\pi$$
$$\frac{1}{9}C = \frac{1}{9}(18\pi) = 2\pi$$

The answer is B. (*100 Key Math Concepts for the ACT, #90*)

> **EXPERT TUTOR TIP**
> The length of an arc is only a fraction of the length around the circle (the circumference). The fraction is the angle divided by 360.

10. The shaded region is equal to the area of the square minus the area of the semicircle. The area of the square is $10 \times 10 = 100$. The radius of the circle is half of 10, or 5, so the area of the whole circle is $\pi(5)^2 = 25\pi$, and the area of the semicircle is $\frac{25\pi}{2}$. The square minus the semicircle, then, is: $100 - \frac{25\pi}{2}$. The answer is H. (*100 Key Math Concepts for the ACT, #87, #91*)

TACKLING MORE COMPLEX GEOMETRY QUESTIONS

Not all ACT geometry questions are straightforward. The test writers have ways of further complicating them. It's not **always** obvious at first what the question is getting at. Sometimes you really have to think about the figure and the given information before that lightbulb goes on in your head. Often, the inspiration that brings illumination is finding the hidden information.

 PLANE GEOMETRY

Example

1. In the figure below, $\triangle ABC$ is a right triangle and $\overline{AC}$ is perpendicular to $\overline{BD}$. If $\overline{AB}$ is 6 units long, and $\overline{AC}$ is 10 units long, how many units long is $\overline{AD}$?

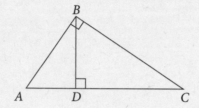

   A. 3
   B. $2\sqrt{3}$
   C. 3.6
   D. 4
   E. $3\sqrt{2}$

> ✔ **PERFECT SCORE TIP**
> If the question gives you lengths of sides, write them on the diagram. I found this often made solutions or other hints more obvious to me.

At first, this looks like a Pythagorean theorem question. In fact, the two given sides of $\triangle ABC$ identify it as the 6-8-10 version of the 3-4-5 special right triangle. (*100 Key Math Concepts for the ACT, #85*) So we know that $\overline{BC} = 8$. So what? How's that going to help us find $\overline{AD}$?

> ✔ **PERFECT SCORE TIP**
> If you are stuck on a triangle problem, the two most common solutions involve either the Pythagorean theorem or similar triangles, so be sure to look for ways to use either of those.

The inspiration here is to realize that this is a "similar triangles" problem. We don't see the word *similar* anywhere in the question stem, but the stem and the figure combined actually tell us that all three triangles in the figure—$\triangle ABC$, $\triangle ADB$, and $\triangle BDC$—are similar. We know the triangles are similar because they all have the same three angles. Here are the three triangles separated and oriented to show the correspondences:

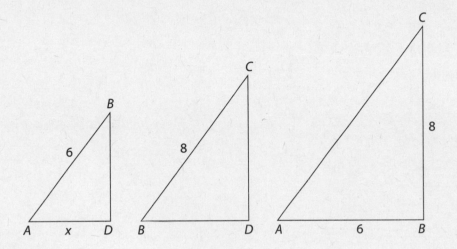

In this orientation, it's easy to set up the proportion that will solve the problem:

$$\frac{10}{6} = \frac{6}{x}$$

$$10x = 36$$

$$x = 3.6$$

The answer is C.

.ıll◧ PLANE GEOMETRY

Example

2. In the figure below, the area of the circle centered at O is 25π, and $\overline{AC}$ is perpendicular to $\overline{OB}$. If $\overline{AC}$ is 8 units long, how many units long is $\overline{BD}$?

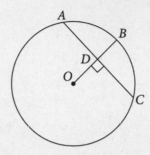

F. 2

G. 2.5

H. 3

J. 3.125

K. 4

This is a tough one. It's not easy to see how to get BD from the given information. You can use the area—25π—to figure out the radius, and then you'd know the length of OB:

$$Area = \pi r^2$$
$$25\pi = \pi r^2$$
$$25 = r^2$$
$$r = 5$$

So you know $\overline{OB} = 5$, but what about $\overline{BD}$? If you knew $\overline{OD}$, you could subtract that from $\overline{OB}$ to get what you want. But do you know $\overline{OD}$? This is the place where most people get stuck.

The inspiration that will lead to a solution is that you can take advantage of the right angle at *D*. Look what happens when you take a pencil and physically add $\overline{OA}$ and $\overline{OC}$ to the figure:

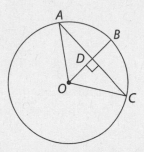

EXPERT TUTOR TIP
The radius will be the key to solving almost any ACT problem involving circles. If you get stuck, try drawing a radius to see if that helps you.

$\triangle OAD$ and $\triangle OCD$ are right triangles. And when we write in the lengths, we discover some special right triangles:

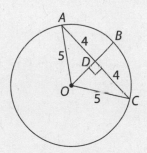

Now it's apparent that $\overline{OD} = 3$. Since $\overline{OB} = 5$, $\overline{BD}$ is $5 - 3 = 2$. The answer is F.

Figureless Problems

Some ACT geometry problems present an extra challenge because they don't provide a figure. You have to figure it out for yourself. Try this one:

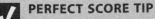 **PLANE GEOMETRY**

Example

3. If one side of a right triangle is 3 units long, and a second side is 4 units long, which of the following could be the length, in units, of the third side?

   A. 1
   B. 2
   C. $\sqrt{7}$
   D. $3\sqrt{2}$
   E. $3\sqrt{3}$

The key to solving most figureless problems is to sketch a diagram, but sometimes the test makers deliberately give you less information than you might like. Question 3 is the perfect example—it gives you two sides of a right triangle and asks for the third. Sounds familiar. And the two sides it gives you—3 and 4—*really* sound familiar. It's a 3-4-5, right?

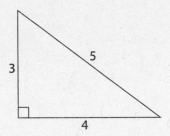

So the answer's 5…

Whoops! There's no 5 among the answer choices! What's going on?!

Better check back. Notice that the question asks, "Which of the following *could* be the length…" That *could* is crucial. It suggests that there's more than one possibility. Our answer of 5 was too obvious. There's another one somewhere.

> ✓ **PERFECT SCORE TIP**
> Remember that there are multiple ways to draw diagrams. If the one you picked isn't working, try another instead of trying to do weird manipulations to an incorrect picture.

Can you think of another way of sketching the figure with the same given information? Who says that the 3 and 4 have to be the two legs? Look at what happens when you make one of them—the larger one, of course—the *hypotenuse*:

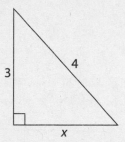

This is not a 3-4-5 triangle, because in a 3-4-5, the 3 and the 4 are the legs. This is no special right triangle; to figure out the length of the third side, resort to the Pythagorean theorem:

$$(leg_1)^2 + (leg_2)^2 = (hypotenuse)^2$$
$$3^2 + x^2 = 4^2$$
$$9 + x^2 = 16$$
$$x^2 = 7$$
$$x = \sqrt{7}$$

The answer is C.

Many Steps and Many Concepts

Some of the toughest ACT geometry questions are ones that take many steps to solve and combine many different geometry concepts. The following is an example:

📶 **PLANE GEOMETRY**

Example

4. In the figure below, $\overline{AB}$ is tangent to the circle at A. If the circumference of the circle is 12π units and $\overline{OB}$ is 12 units long, what is the area, in square units, of the shaded region?

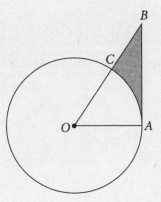

F. $18\sqrt{3} - 6\pi$

G. $24\sqrt{3} - 6\pi$

H. $18\sqrt{3} - 2\pi$

J. $12\pi - 12$

K. $243 - 2\pi$

This is about as hard as they come on the ACT. It is by no means clear how the given information—the circumference of the circle and the length of $\overline{OB}$ —will lead you to the area of the shaded region.

So what do you do? Give up? No. *Don't* give up immediately unless you're really short on time or you know for sure you can't do the problem.

So then should you just plow ahead blindly and figure out every length, angle, and area you can and see where that leads you? *Well, not exactly.* It would be better to be more systematic.

The key to success with a circuitous problem like this is to focus on your destination—what you're looking for—and think about what you need to get there. Then go back to the given information and see what you can do to get you going in the right direction. Think about where you're headed before you take even one step; otherwise, you may just have to backtrack.

Your goal in question 4 is to find the area of the shaded region. That region is a shape that has no name, let alone an area formula. Like most shaded regions, this one is in fact the difference between two familiar shapes with names and area formulas. Think of the shaded region in question 4 as:

(the area of $\triangle AOB$) − (the area of sector AOC)

So now you know you need to figure out the area of the triangle and the area of the sector.

First, the triangle. You are explicitly given $\overline{OB}$ = 12. You are also given that $\overline{AB}$ is tangent to the circle at A, which tells you that $\overline{OA}$ is a radius and that $\angle OAB$ is a right angle. So if you can figure out the radius of the circle, you'll have two sides of a right triangle, which will enable you to figure out the third side, and then figure out the area.

You can get the radius from the given circumference. Plug what you know into the formula and solve for r:

$$\text{Circumference} = 2\pi r$$
$$12\pi = 2\pi r$$
$$r = \frac{12\pi}{2\pi} = 6$$
$$\overline{OA} = 6$$

Aha! So it turns out that $\triangle AOB$ is no ordinary right triangle. Since one leg—6—is exactly half the hypotenuse—12—you're looking at a 30°-60°-90° triangle. By applying the well-known side ratios (1:$\sqrt{3}$:2) for a 30°-60°-90° triangle (*100 Key Math Concepts for the ACT, #85*), you determine that $\overline{AB} = 6\sqrt{3}$. Now plug the lengths of the legs in for the base and altitude in the formula for the area of a triangle, and you'll get:

$$\text{Area} = \frac{1}{2}bh$$
$$= \frac{1}{2}(6\sqrt{3})(6)$$
$$= 18\sqrt{3}$$

Already it looks like the answer is going to be F or H—they're the choices that begin with $18\sqrt{3}$. You could just guess choice F or H and move on, but if you've come this far, you might as well go all the way.

Next, you need to determine the area of the sector. Fortunately, while working on the triangle, you figured out the two things you need to get the area of the sector: the radius of the circle (6) and the measure of the central angle (60°). The radius tells you that the area of the whole circle (πr^2) is 36π. And the central angle tells you that the sector is $\frac{60}{360}$, or $\frac{1}{6}$ of the circle. One-sixth of 36π is 6π. So the area of the shaded region is $18\sqrt{3} - 6\pi$, choice F.

> **GO ONLINE**
> Brush up on your trig. Try the online trigonometry workshop and test yourself with the online quiz.

▶ IF YOU LEARNED ONLY THREE THINGS IN THIS CHAPTER...

1. You should be familiar with the ten textbook geometry questions.

2. When dealing with "disguised" geometry questions, use the figure and the question stem to find the information you need. It may not be stated directly.

3. If a geometry question doesn't have a figure, it usually helps to draw one.

CHAPTER 10

Reading Workout 1: Know Where You're Going

Reading skills are crucial on every part of the ACT, not just on the Reading test. Savvy ACT-style reading Is certainly useful for the English and Science tests. Even your work on many of the Math problems will benefit from the skills discussed as follows, so don't ignore the Reading Workouts, even if you think you're an ace reader.

The kind of reading rewarded by the ACT is special. You probably know how to do it already, but you may be reluctant to do it on a standardized test. You may think that success on a test like this requires that you read very slowly and deliberately, making sure you remember everything. Well, we at Kaplan have found that this kind of reading won't work on the ACT. In fact, It is a sure way to run out of time halfway through the Reading test.

 EXPERT TUTOR TIP
The ACT Reading test includes:

- One Prose Fiction passage with ten questions
- One Social Sciences passage with ten questions
- One Humanities passage with ten questions
- One Natural Sciences passage with ten questions

THE KEY TO ACTIVE ACT READING

The real key to ACT Reading is to read quickly but actively, getting a sense of the gist or main idea of the passage and seeing how everything fits together to support that main idea. You should constantly try to think ahead. Look for the general outline of the passage—determine how it's structured. Don't worry about the details. You'll come back for those later.

> ✅ **PERFECT SCORE TIP**
> Remember that on the ACT, the goal of reading is very different than it is in English class. No one is looking for original ideas or deep reading—just for you to get the main ideas.

Fast, active reading, of course, requires a little more mental energy than slow, passive reading, but it pays off. Those who dwell on details—who passively let the passage reveal itself at its own pace—are sure to run out of time. Don't be that kind of reader! Make the passage reveal itself to you on your schedule, by skimming the passage with an eye to structure rather than detail. Look for key words that tell you what the author is doing so that you can save yourself time. For instance, read examples very quickly, just glancing over the words. When an author says "for example," you know that what follows is an example of a general point. Do you need to understand that specific example? Maybe, maybe not. If you do, you can come back and read the verbiage when you're attacking the questions. You'll know exactly where the author gave an example of general point *x* (or whatever). If you *don't* need to know the example for any of the questions, great! You haven't wasted much time on something that won't get you a point.

> 👤 **EXPERT TUTOR TIP**
> Here's how to use this chapter if you don't have much time. Learn the Kaplan Method for ACT Reading. Try the sample passage that follows. Check your answers. If you need more help, go back and read the whole chapter.

You actually do this kind of "reading" all the time, and not just when you're reading a book or newspaper. When you watch TV or see a movie, for instance, you can often figure out much of what's going to happen in advance. You see the bad guys run out of a bank with bags of money in their hands, and you can guess that the next thing they'll do is get into a car and drive away in excess of the speed limit. You see a character in an old sitcom bragging to his friends about how great a driver he is, and you know that he's bound to get into a fender bender before the next commercial. **This ability to know where something is going is very valuable. Use it on the ACT.**

To help you know where an author is going, pay careful attention to structural clues. Words like *but, nevertheless,* and *moreover* help you get a sense of where a piece of writing is going. Look for signal phrases (like *clearly, as a result,* or *no one can deny that*) to determine the logic of the passage. The details, remember, you can come back for later, when you're doing the questions. **What's important in reading the passage is getting a sense of how those details fit together to express the point or points of the passage.**

✓ **PERFECT SCORE TIP**
The key to ACT Reading is main ideas. At the end of every paragraph and passage, you should be able to give a very brief summary of what it was about. This will really help with the questions.

EXPERT TUTOR TIP
Read actively, with an eye toward where the author is going. Don't worry about remembering the details. You can (and should) always refer to them later.

Practice Knowing Where You're Going

In the following exercise, try to fill in the word or phrase that should come next. For most, there are many possible answers, so don't worry about getting the "right" answer.

1. You'd think that the recipe for a strawberry soufflé would be complicated, but my friend's version was _____.

2. I can't believe my good luck! The one time in my life I buy a lottery ticket, I _____.

3. A parked car burns no fuel and causes no pollution. Once the ignition is turned on, however, _____.

4. As their habitat is destroyed, wild animals _____.

5. The new word-processing program was far easier to use than the old one. Moreover, the accompanying instruction booklet explained the commands in a _____ way.

6. The new word-processing program was far easier to use than the old one. On the other hand, the accompanying instruction booklet explained the commands in a _____ way.

Answers

- In Sentence 1, the active reader would probably complete the sentence by saying that the friend's version was "actually quite simple" or something similar. How do you know what's coming next here? The structural clue *but* tips you off. *But* tells you that a contrast is coming up. You'd think the recipe would be complicated, *but* it's "actually quite simple."

- In Sentence 2, on the other hand, there's no real structural clue to help you out. However, the *meaning* of the sentence should make clear what's coming up. Because the speaker is marveling at his good luck, he must have won some money. A likely completion would be something like: The one time in my life I buy a lottery ticket, I "win the jackpot."

- In sentence 3, we have another contrast, signaled by the clue *however*. A parked car doesn't burn fuel or pollute, so the answer has to be something like "the car starts burning gas and polluting."

- Sentence 4 demonstrates again that you don't need explicit structural clues to stay ahead. Sometimes all you need is common sense. What do you think would happen to animals whose habitat had been destroyed? Would they thrive? Celebrate? Buy a condo in Florida? No, they'd probably "start dying out." They might even "become extinct."

- Sentences 5 and 6 show clearly how you can use an author's language to anticipate what point he or she is going to make next. Here, we have identical sentences, except for one small (but very important) difference. One of the sentences in question 5 includes the word *moreover*, indicating continuation or the addition of similar information. The blank should be something close to "in a clear and easy-to-understand" way. It makes sense that "The program was easy to use; moreover, the instructions were easy to understand." The connection in question 6, "on the other hand," indicates contrast. The sentences make sense only if you fill in the blank with "a confusing and unclear" way.

Create a Passage Map

The best way to read actively is to take quick notes, marking up the passage as you go. You don't have time to write extensively in the margin, nor do you want to underline too many sentences. After all, *if you underline everything, nothing stands out on the page.* Your goal is to create flags that wave at you when you are looking for the answers to the questions in the passage.

The fastest way to create your passage map is to follow the ABCs of Active Reading:

> **A**bbreviate margin notes.
> **B**racket key sentences.
> **C**ircle key words and phrases.

Abbreviate margin notes. Develop your own shorthand notes, such as *opin* (opinion), *contr* (contrast or comparison), *hist* (history), *bio* (early years). You must be able to understand what you've written. Otherwise, the notes won't be helpful.

Bracket key sentences. These may (or may not) be the first and last sentences of a paragraph. You are looking for any sentences that express key themes, conclusions, or opinions (of either the author or of the characters in the passage). If you string these bracketed sentences together, you will have highlighted the author's train of thought.

Circle key words and phrases. These are the structural clues or flags (*however, therefore, on one hand…on the other hand*), as well as proper names, dates, key actions, etc.—the signposts of each paragraph. For example, if a passage were about child development, you'd want to circle the key ages discussed in each paragraph. Thus, circling *six months, one year, age two through five* would help you know where to look for the answers to questions about those ages.

> ✓ **PERFECT SCORE TIP**
> I found labeling each paragraph with its main topic helped me quickly know where to look when answering questions.

THE KAPLAN METHOD FOR ACT READING

These steps are tried-and-true. If you learn and practice them, you'll be able to read all four passages successfully and have time to answer all the questions. When test day rolls around, you'll be glad you've got these steps to follow.

The key to this section is being in control of timing—how much time you spend reading the passage (about three minutes) and answering the questions (an average of 30 seconds per question).

If you divide 40 questions into 35 minutes, you'll see that you have $8\frac{3}{4}$ minutes per passage. As you practice, it will be clear that one or two passages take more (or less) time than the others. So your goal is an average of just under 9 minutes per passage. How do you learn to do this? Practice. Practice. Practice.

For the ACT, however, you have a special purpose: to answer specific multiple-choice questions. And we've found that the best way to do that is to read each passage quickly and actively for general understanding, then refer to the passage to answer individual questions. Every ACT test taker can succeed by following the Kaplan Method:

STEP 1: Actively read the passage, taking notes as you go.

STEP 2: Examine the question stem, looking for clues.

STEP 3: Predict the answer and select the choice that best matches your prediction.

For most students, these three steps should together take up about nine minutes per passage. Spend three of those nine minutes on prereading. Spend the remaining time considering the questions and referring to the passage to check your answers. As we mentioned in the ACT Basics section, you'll probably want to take two sweeps through the questions for each passage, getting the doable ones the first time around, coming back for the harder ones.

STEP 1: Actively Read the Passage, Taking Notes as You Go

Read the whole passage before trying to answer the questions. Remember to "know where you're going," anticipating how the parts of the passage fit together. In this preread, the main goals are to:

- Understand the gist of the passage (the main idea)
- Take notes and create a road map of the passage

You may want to underline key points, jot down notes, circle structural clues— whatever it takes to accomplish the two goals above. It's a good idea to label each paragraph to fix in your mind how the paragraphs relate to one another and what aspect of the main idea is discussed in each. That could be your road map.

Two important reminders: The road map will be your guide to finding answers in the passage once you approach the questions. Do what works for you and don't get bogged down in the details. Most of the details in the passage aren't required for answering the questions, but you will want to keep straight who said what and why.

Most of the details in the passage aren't required for answering the questions, so why waste time worrying about them?

> **EXPERT TUTOR TIP**
> Mark up the passages! Have a system worked out in which you use different symbols to mean different things. For example, circle names, box numbers and dates, underline key sentences, and draw arrows to lists of details. Once you know your system, you can find the facts you are looking for faster.

STEP 2: Examine the Question Stem, Looking for Clues

Approaching the Reading questions requires self-discipline. Most test takers have an almost irresistible urge to immediately jump to the answer choices to see what "looks okay." That's not a good idea. Don't peek at the answer choices.

Read the question stem to identify what the test maker is asking. Which of the following is it about?

- A detail (what happened)
- The passage as a whole (the Big Idea)
- A conclusion (reading between the lines)
- A specific word or phrase used in the passage

Analyzing what the question stem is asking is very important because the test makers will offer you choices that don't answer the question at hand. It is easy to get the right answer—if you know what you are looking for.

How do you know what you're looking for? There will be clues in the question stem. These clues could be as straightforward as a line reference or as vague as the phrase "as stated in the passage." In both cases, though, you know that you'll be able to find the answer in the passage. That's where your notes come in handy.

In Reading, think about the question stem without looking at the choices. In most questions, you won't be able to remember exactly what the passage said about the matter in question. That's okay. In fact, even if you do think you remember, don't trust your memory. Instead refer to the passage.

Now's the time when your passage map comes to your aid. Your notes are all waiting to help you find the answers to the ten questions. Once you've found the right spot in the passage...

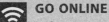 **GO ONLINE**
Refer to your downloadable study sheet to review the Kaplan Three-Step Method for ACT Reading—anywhere, anytime.

STEP 3: Predict the Answer and Select the Choice That Best Matches Your Prediction

It's extremely important in Reading to **make a habit of answering the question in your own words** (based on your checking of the passage) *before* looking at the answer choices. Predict before you pick. Most students waste enormous amounts of time thinking about answer choices in Reading. If you do that, you'll **never** finish, and you'll get so confused you'll probably get many questions wrong.

Once you have an answer in your head based on what you've read and rechecked in the passage, match it to one of the answer choices. Avoid trying to see if they "look right."

You don't want to think very hard about each choice if you can help it. They're intended to confuse you, after all, so don't think about them any more than you absolutely have to.

Now practice the Kaplan Method on the full-length ACT passage that follows. We're going to give you added incentive to use it by first showing you the questions *without* answer choices. That way you can practice the Kaplan Method for ACT Reading and won't be tempted to read the answers before answering the question in your own words. The same questions in ACT style, *with* answer choices, will follow the passage. But try to answer them in fill-in-the-blank format first.

Passage I

SOCIAL SCIENCE

This passage is taken from the book *History of Western Civilization, A Handbook,* ©1986 by William H. McNeill. Reprinted by permission of the University of Chicago Press.

By the tenth century most of northern Europe was divided into farming units known as manors…

Line
(5) Almost always a manor comprised four parts: arable, meadow, waste, and the village area itself. The arable was of course the land which grew the crops on which the inhabitants of the manor subsisted. To maintain fertility and keep down weeds it
(10) was necessary to fallow a part of the cultivated land each year. It was, therefore, usual (though not universal) to divide the arable into three fields. One such field was planted with winter grain, a second with spring
(15) grain, and the third left fallow; the following year, the fallow field would be planted with winter grain, the field in which winter grain had been raised was planted with spring grain, and the third field left fallow.
(20) By following such a rotation, the cycle was completed every three years. Since the fallow field had to be plowed twice in the year in order to keep down the weeds, and the others had to be plowed once, work for the
(25) plow teams extended almost throughout the year. Plowing stopped only at times when all hands were needed to bring in

the harvest, or when the soil was too wet to be plowed, or was frozen. The amount
(30) of land that could be tilled was fixed fairly definitely by the number of plows and plow teams which the manor could muster; and official documents sometimes estimated the wealth and value of a manor in terms of the
(35) number of plows it possessed.

The three great fields lay open, without fences, but were subdivided into numerous small strips (often one acre in size, i.e., the amount of one day's plowing) which
(40) individual peasants "owned." The strips belonging to any one individual were scattered through the three fields in different parts, perhaps in order to assure that each peasant would have strips plowed
(45) early and late, in fertile and infertile parts of the arable land.

Custom severely restricted the individual's rights over his land. The time for plowing and planting was fixed by custom
(50) and each peasant had to conform, since he needed his neighbor's help to plow his strips and they needed his. Uniform cropping was imperative, since on a given day the village animals were turned into the fields to graze

(55) after the harvest had been gathered, and if some individual planted a crop which did not ripen as early as that of his neighbors, he had no means of defending his field from the hungry animals. If his crop ripened
(60) sooner, on the other hand, it could not be garnered without trampling neighboring fields. Moreover, the very idea of innovation was lacking: men did what custom prescribed, cooperated in the plowing and
(65) to some extent in the harvesting, and for many generations did not dream of trying to change.

The meadow was almost as important as the arable for the economy of the village.
(70) Hay from the meadow supported the indispensable draught animals through the winter. The idea that hay might be sown did not occur to men in medieval times; consequently they were compelled to rely on
(75) natural meadows alone. One result was that in many manors shortage of winter fodder for the plow teams was a constant danger. It was common practice to feed oxen on leaves picked from trees, and on straw from the
(80) grain harvest; but despite such supplements the draught animals often nearly starved in winter. In some cases oxen actually had to be carried out from their winter stalls to spring pastures until some of their strength
(85) was recovered and plowing could begin. Thus on many manors meadow land was even more valuable than the arable and was divided into much smaller strips (often the width of a scythe stroke).
(90) The waste provided summer pasture for various animals of the manor: pigs, geese, cattle, and sheep. The animals of the whole manor normally grazed together under the watchful eyes of some young children or
(95) other attendants who could keep them from wandering too far afield, and bring them back to the village at night. The waste also was the source of wood for fuel and for building purposes, and helped to supplement

(100) the food supply with such things as nuts, berries, honey, and rabbits...

The fourth segment of the manor was the village itself, usually located in the center of the arable near a source of
(105) drinking water, and perhaps along a road or path or footpath leading to the outside world. The cottages of medieval peasants were extremely humble, usually consisting of a single room, with earthen floor
(110) and thatched roof. Around each cottage normally lay a small garden in which various vegetables and sometimes fruit trees were planted. In the village streets chickens, ducks, and dogs picked up a precarious
(115) living.

QUESTIONS

1. The description of the near starvation of the oxen (lines 82–85) serves to:

2. According to the passage, the fact that the peasants' individual strips of land were unfenced subdivisions of larger fields required each peasant to:

3. According to the second paragraph (lines 4–35), the fallow part of the arable had to be plowed a total of how many times in any given calendar year?

4. The passage suggests that the practice of peasants owning strips "scattered through the three fields in different parts" (lines 42–43) was instituted in order to:

5. On the basis of the information in the passage, it may be inferred that people in medieval times did not think of sowing hay because:

6. As it is used in line 61, the word *garnered* means:

7. According to the passage, if one of the arable's three great fields were left fallow one year, it would be:

8. Which of the following conclusions is suggested by the fourth paragraph (lines 47–67)?

9. According to the passage, a manor's value might be judged according to the number of its plows because:

10. According to the passage, summer pasture for a manor's geese would be provided:

YOUR ANSWERS

1. The description of the near starvation of the oxen (lines 82–85) serves to:

   A. demonstrate how difficult life on the manor was in tenth century northern Europe.

   B. showcase how important work animals were to medieval manors.

   C. emphasize how important natural meadows were to feeding the work animals.

   D. explain why uniform cropping was a critical practice that ensured survival on the medieval manor.

2. According to the passage, the fact that the peasants' individual strips of land were unfenced subdivisions of larger fields required each peasant to:

   F. follow a fixed planting schedule so as to be able to harvest crops at the same time as the other peasants.

   G. harvest crops independently of his neighbors.

   H. limit the size of strips to what could be plowed in a single day.

   J. maintain small garden plots in order to provide his family with enough food.

3. According to the second paragraph (lines 4–35), the fallow part of the arable had to be plowed a total of how many times in any given calendar year?

   A. One

   B. Two

   C. Four

   D. Six

4. The passage suggests that the practice of peasants owning strips "scattered through the three fields in different parts" (lines 42–43) was instituted in order to:

   F. divide resources fairly evenly.

   G. preserve the wealth of elite land-owners.

   H. protect the three fields from overuse.

   J. force neighbors to work only their own lands.

5. On the basis of the information in the passage, it may be inferred that people in medieval times did not think of sowing hay because:

   A. hay sowing had not been done in the past.

   B. the need for more hay was not great enough to warrant the extra work.

   C. northern Europeans did not yet have the necessary farming techniques for successful hay cultivation.

   D. the tight schedule of cultivating the arable meant that the peasants had no time to cultivate extra crops.

6. As it is used in line 61, the word *garnered* means:

   F. planted.

   G. watered.

   H. gathered.

   J. plowed.

7. According to the passage, if one of the arable's three great fields were left fallow one year, it would be:

   A. left fallow for two more years in succession.

   B. planted the next year with winter grain only.

   C. planted the next year with spring grain only.

   D. planted with either winter or spring grain the next year.

8. Which of the following conclusions is suggested by the fourth paragraph (lines 47–67)?

   I. An individual was free to cultivate his own land in any way he wished.

   II. The manor was run according to tradition.

   III. Successful farming required cooperative methods.

   F. I and II only

   G. I and III only

   H. II and III only

   J. I, II, and III

9. According to the passage, a manor's value might be judged according to the number of its plows because:

   A. the more plows a manor had, the less land had to be left fallow.

   B. plows, while not in themselves valuable, symbolized great wealth.

   C. manors with sufficient plows could continue plowing throughout the year.

   D. the number of plows a manor owned determined how much land could be cultivated.

10. According to the passage, summer pasture for a manor's geese would be provided:

   F. next to cottages, within the village.

   G. on the fallow field of the arable.

   H. on the communal ground of the waste.

   J. on the whole of the meadow.

The Lay of the Land

Well, how'd you do? Did you remember to refer to the passage? You probably found that you had to do a more thorough check for some questions than for others.

This passage, like most nonfiction passages on the ACT, is organized in a fairly logical way around the main idea, which you might have expressed as "the structure and common practices of the medieval manor." Here's one possible road map you might have come up with:

- Paragraph 1 (just a single sentence, really): Intro to the topic of medieval manors (divided, as cited in the first sentence of next paragraph, into arable, meadow, waste, and village)

- Paragraphs 2, 3, and 4: Discussion of the arable and the practices associated with it

- Paragraph 5: Discussion of the meadow

- Paragraph 6: Discussion of the waste

- Paragraph 7: Discussion of the village

It should be obvious why, in your prereading step, you really need to get some sense of the layout of the passage like this. **Many questions don't contain specific line references to help you locate information, and if you don't have a road map of the passage in your head or on paper, you might get lost.**

Following is a key to the ten questions attached to this passage.

Key to Passage I

(NONFICTION—SOCIAL STUDIES)

	Answer	Refer to	Type	Comments
1.	C	Lines 68–89	Function	The entire paragraph supports this claim.
2.	F	Lines 52–59	Detail	"Uniform cropping was imperative…"
3.	B	Lines 21–23	Detail	Don't confuse fallow with planted fields.
4.	F	Lines 43–46	Inference	Every peasant got some fertile and some infertile land—inferably, to be fair to each.
5.	A	Lines 62–67, 72–75	Inference	No line reference, so you had to have a sense of the structure to find this.
6.	H	Lines 59–62	Vocab-in-Context	Use context. The crop is ripe, so it must be ready to be gathered.
7.	B	Lines 13–19	Detail	No line reference; otherwise, no problem.

8.	H	Lines 47–67	Inference	I: lines 47–52 say the opposite II: lines 48–52 III: lines 52–62 Statement I is false, so that means F, G, and J are wrong. That means H must be the answer.
9.	D	Lines 33–35	Detail	No line reference; number of plows = amount of land.
10.	H	Lines 90–92	Detail	Whole paragraph devoted to describing waste.

EXPERT TUTOR TIP

A few ACT questions—like question 8 in this passage—are Roman numeral questions. You're given three or four statements, each labeled with a Roman numeral. The idea is to treat each one as a true/false statement. Decide which statements are true, and then select the choice that includes only those statements. Often, you can save yourself some time on these questions. For instance, in question 8: Once you decide that Statement I is false, you can eliminate choices F, G, and J, all of which include Statement I. Thus, you can get your answer, choice H, without even looking at Statements II and III.

▶ IF YOU LEARNED ONLY THREE THINGS IN THIS CHAPTER...

1. Read the passage actively and take notes to create a passage map. Note the purpose of each paragraph and the passage overall.

2. Carefully read the question stems (*only*) to determine the type of question being asked.

3. Look for the correct answer in the passage—don't try to answer from memory. Predict an answer first, then look for the answer that best matches your prediction.

CHAPTER 11

Reading Workout 2: Look It Up!

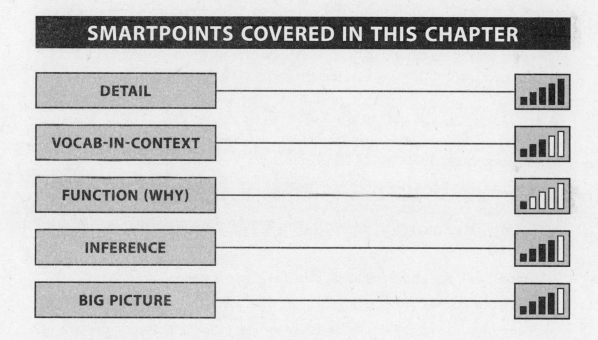

SMARTPOINTS COVERED IN THIS CHAPTER

DETAIL

VOCAB-IN-CONTEXT

FUNCTION (WHY)

INFERENCE

BIG PICTURE

In Reading Workout 1, we discussed general strategies for approaching ACT Reading. Now let's look more closely at the types of questions you'll encounter.

The three main types of Reading questions are:

SPECIFIC QUESTIONS

DETAIL

VOCAB-IN-CONTEXT

FUNCTION (WHY)

INFERENCE QUESTIONS

   [..ılıll] INFERENCE

BIG PICTURE QUESTIONS

   [..ılıll] BIG PICTURE

THE KAPLAN METHOD (AGAIN)

Don't forget to use the Kaplan Method for ACT Reading that we discussed in Reading Workout 1. Here's a reminder of how it works:

STEP 1: Actively Read the Passage, Taking Notes as You Go

In other words, quickly work through the passage (*before* trying to answer the questions) in less than three minutes. Read actively, and assemble a passage map or overall idea of how the passage is organized. Use your pencil to mark the passage and take notes.

> ☑ **PERFECT SCORE TIP**
> Prereading is much easier if you have an idea what the passage is about. Make sure to always read the brief intro provided at the beginning of each passage.

STEP 2: Examine the Question Stem, Looking for Clues

Before plunging into the answer choices, take a moment to understand what kind of question it is. They are:

- **Detail:** Asks about the "what" as stated in the passage
- **Vocab-in-Context:** Asks about the meaning of a word or words as used in context
- **Function:** Asks about why a word, sentence, or example is used in the passage
- **Inference:** Asks you to read between the lines to draw a conclusion that is not explicitly stated
- **Big Picture:** Asks about the overall point of the whole passage or of one paragraph

Refer to the passage to find the answer. You don't need to refer to the whole passage—just where the answer to a question can be found. Sometimes a line reference will be included in the question; otherwise, rely on your road map of the passage.

STEP 3: Predict the Answer and Select the Choice That Best Matches Your Prediction

Do this *before* looking at the answer choices. Then, with an answer in mind, it'll be easier to spot the correct choice.

IMPORTANT QUESTION TYPES

Try the following typical ACT nonfiction passage, this one from the Humanities. Afterward, we'll discuss selected questions from this set as examples of Specific Detail, Inference, and Big Picture questions.

Passage II

HUMANITIES

This passage is taken from the book *Invitation to the Theatre,* Third Edition, © 1985 by George Kernodle. Reprinted by permission of Wadsworth, a division of Thomson Learning.

Tragedy was the invention of the Greeks. In their Golden Age, the fifth century before Christ, they produced the world's greatest
Line dramatists, new forms of tragedy and
(5) comedy that have been models ever since, and a theatre that every age goes back to for rediscovery of some basic principles...

Since it derived from primitive religious rites, with masks and ceremonial costumes,
(10) and made use of music, dance, and poetry, the Greek drama was at the opposite pole from the modern realistic stage. In fact, probably no other theatre in history has made fuller use of the intensities of art. The
(15) masks, made of painted linen, wood, and plaster, brought down from primitive days the atmosphere of gods, heroes, and demons. Our nineteenth- and twentieth-century grandfathers thought masks must have been
(20) very artificial. Today, however, we appreciate their exciting intensity and can see that in a large theatre they were indispensable. If they allowed no fleeting change of expression during a single episode, they could give for
(25) each episode in turn more intense expression than any human face could. When

Oedipus comes back with bleeding eyes, the new mask could be more terrible than any facial makeup the audience could endure,
(30) yet in its sculpted intensity more beautiful than a real face.

Most essential of all intensities, and hardest for us to understand, was the chorus. Yet many playwrights today are
(35) trying to find some equivalent to do for a modern play what the chorus did for the Greeks. During the episodes played by the actors, the chorus would only provide a background of group response, enlarging
(40) and reverberating the emotions of the actors, sometimes protesting and opposing but in general serving as ideal spectators to stir and lead the reactions of the audience. But between episodes, with the actors out
(45) of the way, the chorus took over. We have only the words, not the music or dance, and some translations of the odes are in such formal, old-fashioned language that it is hard to guess that they were accom-
(50) panied by vigorous, sometimes even wild dances and symbolic actions that filled an orchestra which in some cities was sixty

to ninety feet in diameter. Sometimes the chorus expressed simple horror or lament.
(55) Sometimes it chanted and acted out, in unison and in precise formations of rows and lines, the acts of violence the characters were enacting offstage. When Phaedra rushes offstage in *Hippolytus* to hang herself
(60) from the rafters, the members of the chorus, all fifteen of them, perform in mime and chant the act of tying the rope and swinging from the rafters. Sometimes the chorus tells or reenacts an incident of history or legend
(65) that throws light on the situation in the play.

Sometimes the chorus puts into specific action what is a general intention in the mind of the main character. When Oedipus resolves to hunt out the guilty person and
(70) cleanse the city, he is speaking metaphorically, but the chorus invokes the gods of vengeance and dances a wild pursuit.

On the printed page, the choral odes seem static and formal, lyric and philosoph-
(75) ical, emotional letdowns that punctuate the series of episodes, like intermissions between two acts of a play. The reader who skips the odes can get the main points of the play. A few are worth reading as independent
(80) poems, notably the famous one in *Antigone* beginning, "Many are the wonders of the world, but none is more wonderful than man." Some modern acting versions omit the chorus or reduce it to a few background
(85) figures. Yet to the Greeks the odes were certainly more than mere poetic interludes: the wild Dionysian words and movements evoked primitive levels of the subconscious and at the same time served to transform
(90) primitive violence into charm and beauty and to add philosophical reflections on the meaning of human destiny.

For production today, we can only improvise some partial equivalent. In Athens
(95) the entire population was familiar with choral performances. Every year each of the tribes entered a dithyramb in a contest, rehearsing five hundred men and boys for weeks. Some modern composers have
(100) tried to write dramatic music for choruses: the most notable examples are the French composer Darius Milhaud, in the primitive rhythms, shouts, and chants of his operatic version of the *Oresteia*; George Gershwin, in
(105) the Negro funeral scenes of *Porgy and Bess*; and Kurt Weill, in the African choruses for *Lost in the Stars*, the musical dramatization of Alan Paton's novel, *Cry, the Beloved Country*. For revivals of Greek tragedies we
(110) have not dared use much music beyond a few phrases half shouted, half sung, and drumbeats and suggestive melodies in the background.

A quick preread of the passage should have given you a sense of its general organization:

- *First paragraph:* introduces the topic of Greek tragedy.
- *Second paragraph:* discusses use of masks (artificial but intense).
- *Third and fourth paragraphs:* discuss use of chorus (also artificial but intense).
- *Fifth paragraph:* expands discussion to choral odes.
- *Sixth paragraph:* concludes with discussion of how Greek tragedy is performed today and how it has influenced some modern art.

That's really all the road map you need going into the questions. Aside from that, you should take away the author's main point: Greek tragedy included many artificial devices, but these devices allowed it to rise to a high level of intensity.

1. Combined with the passage's additional information, the fact that some Greek orchestras were 60 to 90 feet across suggests that:

   A. few spectators were able to see the stage.
   B. no one performer could dominate a performance.
   C. choruses and masks helped overcome the distance between actors and audience.
   D. Greek tragedies lacked the emotional force of modern theatrical productions.

2. The phrase "fuller use of the intensities of art" (line 14) most nearly means:

   F. employment of brightly illuminated effects.
   G. good use of powerful, dramatic effects of music, dance, and poetry.
   H. the enjoyment of strong elements of effects on stage.
   J. the utilization of dramatic interactions.

3. The description of the chorus's enactment of Phaedra's offstage suicide (lines 58–63) shows that, in contrast to modern theater, ancient Greek theater was:

   A. more violent.
   B. more concerned with satisfying an audience.
   C. more apt to be historically accurate.
   D. less concerned with a realistic portrayal of events.

4. It can be inferred that one consequence of the Greeks' use of masks was that:

   F. the actors often had to change masks between episodes.
   G. the characters in the play could not convey emotion.
   H. the actors wearing masks played nonspeaking roles.
   J. good acting ability was not important to the Greeks.

5. Which of the following is supported by the information in the second paragraph (lines 8–31)?

   A. Masks in Greek drama combined artistic beauty with emotional intensity.

   B. The use of masks in Greek drama was better appreciated in the 19th century than it is now.

   C. Masks in Greek drama were used to portray gods but never human beings.

   D. Contemporary scholars seriously doubt the importance of masks to Greek theater.

6. The author indicates in lines 69–70 that Oedipus's resolution "to hunt out the guilty person and cleanse the city" was:

   F. at odds with what he actually does later in the performance.

   G. misinterpreted by the chorus.

   H. dramatized by the actions of the chorus.

   J. angrily condemned by the chorus.

7. According to the passage, when actors were present on stage, the chorus would:

   A. look on silently as spectators.

   B. inevitably agree with the actors' actions.

   C. communicate to the audience solely through mime.

   D. react to the performance as an audience might.

8. The main point of the fifth paragraph (lines 73–92) is that choral odes:

   F. should not be performed by modern choruses.

   G. have a meaning and beauty that are lost in modern adaptations.

   H. can be safely ignored by a modern-day reader.

   J. are only worthwhile in *Antigone*.

9. The passage suggests that modern revivals of Greek tragedies "have not dared use much music" (line 110) because:

   A. modern instruments would appear out of place.

   B. to do so would require a greater understanding of how choral odes were performed.

   C. music would distract the audience from listening to the words of choral odes.

   D. such music is considered far too primitive for modern audiences.

10. The author discusses *Porgy and Bess* and *Lost in the Stars* in order to:

   F. show how two modern plays reenact ancient Greek tragedies.

   G. demonstrate the use of music in modern plays.

   H. give examples of two modern-day playwrights who used musical choruses in their dramas.

   J. illustrate how music evokes subconscious emotions in modern-day plays.

Now let's take a look at selected questions, which fall into three categories.

Specific Questions

⬛ **DETAIL**

⬛ **VOCAB-IN-CONTEXT**

⬛ **FUNCTION**

Questions 2, 6, 7, and 10 are typical Specific questions. Some Specific questions give you a line reference to help you out; others don't, forcing you either to start tearing your hair out (if you're an unprepared test taker) or else to seek out the answer based on your sense of how the passage is laid out (one of the two key reasons to preread the passage).

> **EXPERT TUTOR TIP**
> The answers are in the passage. Focus your attention on locating them. Your mind-set should be: "Find the answer," not "Remember the answer." Locate them using your trusty road map.

Question 2 is a Vocab-in-Context question. This stem refers to a word or phrase in the passage and asks you to select the answer that is closest to the meaning in *context*.

Read a little before line 12. Greek drama "made use of music, dance, and poetry" (line 10). This reference matches choice G, which is the correct answer.

Note: The best answer is not a direct definition of the words. Look instead for the answer that would make the most sense. To check your answer, plug it into the sentence.

Question 6 provides a line reference (lines 69–70), but to answer the question confidently, you should have also read a few lines *before* and a few lines *after* the cited lines. There, you would have read: "Sometimes the chorus puts into action what is a general intention in the mind of the main character. When Oedipus resolves…" Clearly, the Oedipus example is meant to illustrate the point about the chorus acting out a character's intentions. So choice H is correct—they are dramatizing (or acting out) Oedipus's resolution. (By the way, choice G might have been tempting, but there's no evidence that the chorus is misinterpreting, just that they're "putting a general intention into specific action.")

Question 7 is a Specific question *without* a line reference. Such questions are common on the ACT, and they require that you have a good sense of the structure of the passage as a whole so that you can locate the place where the question is answered. The mention of the chorus in the question should send you to paragraph 3. If you marked this paragraph with the ABC method we've discussed, a quick glance over should lead you to the sentence that begins on line 37, where the author claims that the chorus serves to "lead the reactions of the audience"—captured by choice D.

Question 10 is another type of Specific question: Function. These questions ask why an author uses a word, phrase, or detail in the passage. You can spot these questions because you'll see phrases like, "is used to," "is meant to," and "in order to" in the question stem.

Question 10 asks why the author mentions the modern plays *Porgy and Bess* and *Lost in the Stars* in the passage. It is important to remember that WHY something is discussed is different from WHAT is discussed. The road map after the passage and the topic sentences in lines 93–109 in the passage indicate the main idea for the final paragraph is the modern use of the chorus. Choice H is the right answer.

Note: While choices G and J may be true, they are not the reason why the author mentions these plays. Choice F is false—they are not reenactments of Greek tragedies.

Inference Questions

.ıll❲ INFERENCE

With Inference questions, your job is to combine ideas logically to make an inference—something that's not stated explicitly in the passage but that is definitely said implicitly. Often, you'll see a word like *suggest, infer, inference,* or *imply* in the question stem to tip you off.

To succeed on Inference questions, you have to read between the lines. Common sense is your best tool here. You use various bits of information in the passage as evidence for your own logical conclusion.

> ✔ **PERFECT SCORE TIP**
> While Inference questions will ask you to read between the lines, remember that they will never ask you to make conclusions outside the scope of the passage, so be sure all your answers have a basis in the reading.

Questions 1, 3, and **5** require that you combine information from more than one place in the passage. **Question 1** has no line references to help; a quick survey of the passage tells you that C is the only compatible answer. **Question 3** research might lead to a prediction of "the chorus emphasizes what's happening on stage," pointing you to answer D. **Question 5** research leads you to the key word *intensity*, which you examined previously for question 2, and which appears in only one answer choice.

Note: The relationship between questions 2 and 5 is a good example of how answering one question can help you with the answer to another. Thus, you may find that if you skip a question the first time, you can answer it during a second pass.

Question 4 provides no line reference, but the mention of masks should have sent you to the second paragraph of the passage. Lines 23–24 explain that masks "allowed no fleeting change of expression during a single episode." Treat that as your first piece of evidence. Your second comes in lines 24–26: "they [the masks] could give for each episode in turn more intense expression than any human face could." Put those two pieces of evidence together—masks can't change expression *during* a single episode, but they can give expression for each episode *in turn*.

> **EXPERT TUTOR TIP**
> Making inferences often requires that you combine bits of information from different parts of the passage. Common sense will then lead you to an appropriate inference—one that's not too extreme.

Clearly, the actors must have changed masks between episodes so that they could express the different emotions that different episodes required. Choice F is correct.

One warning: Keep your inferences as close to the passage as possible. Don't make wild inferential leaps. An inference should follow naturally and inevitably from the evidence provided in the passage.

Big Picture Questions

BIG PICTURE

About one-third of the ACT Reading questions are Detail questions and most of the rest are Inference questions. But there are also a few questions that test your understanding of the theme, purpose, and organization of the passage as a whole. Big Picture questions tend to look for:

- **Main point or purpose of a passage or part of a passage**
- **Author's attitude or tone**
- **Logic underlying the author's argument**
- **Relationship between different parts of the passage**
- **Difference between fact and opinion**

One way to see the Big Picture is to read actively. As you read, ask yourself, "What's this all about? What's the point of this? Why is the author saying this?"

> **EXPERT TUTOR TIP**
> If you're still stumped on a Big Picture question after reading the passage, try doing the Detail and Inference questions first. They can help you fill in the Big Picture.

Question 8 asks for the main idea of a particular paragraph—namely, the fifth—which our general outline indicates is the paragraph about choral odes. Skimming that paragraph, you find reference to how the odes seem to us modern people—"static and formal" (line 74), "like intermissions between two acts of a play" (lines 76–77). Later, the author states, by way of contrast (note the use of the clue word *yet*): "Yet to the Greeks the odes were certainly more than mere poetic interludes." Clearly, the author wants to contrast our modern static view of the odes with the Greeks' view of them as something more. That idea is best captured by choice G.

FIND AND PARAPHRASE...AND OTHER TIPS

The previous examples show that your real task in Reading is not what you might expect. **Your main job is to find the answers.** Perhaps a better name for the Reading subtest would be "find and paraphrase." But students tend to think that their task in Reading is to "comprehend and remember." That's the wrong mind-set.

Don't Be Afraid to Skip

Now that you've done a couple full-length passages and questions, you've probably encountered at least a few questions that you found unanswerable. **What do you do if you can't find the answer in the passage, or if you can find it but don't understand, or if you do understand but can't see an answer choice that makes sense? Skip the question.** Skipping is probably more important in Reading than in any other ACT subject test. Many students find it useful to skip as many as half of the questions on the first pass through a set of Reading questions. That's fine.

> **PERFECT SCORE TIP**
> I found skipping questions during the first pass the most useful in Reading. Don't spend too much time on one question the first time through.

When you come back to a Reading question the second time, it usually makes sense to use the process of elimination. The first time around, you tried to find the *right* answer but you couldn't. So now try to identify the three *wrong* answers. Eliminating three choices is slower than finding one right choice, so don't make it your main strategy for Reading. However, it is a good way to try a second attack on a question.

Another thing to consider when attacking a question for a second time is that the right answer may have been hidden. Maybe it's written in an unexpected way, with different vocabulary, or maybe there is another good way that you haven't thought of to answer the question. Remember that it's still important to avoid getting bogged down when you come back to a question. **Be willing to admit that there are some problems you just can't answer. Guess if you have to.**

Here's a key to the Greek tragedy passage so that you can check the answers to the questions not discussed previously.

Key to Passage II
(NONFICTION—HUMANITIES)

	Answer	Refer to	Type	Comments
1.	C	Lines 20–22, 34–53	Inference	Q-stem emphasizes distance between audience and stage; masks and choruses help to enlarge the action so that it can be understood from a distance.
2.	G	Lines 8–26	Vocab-in-Context	Must make sense in context.
3.	D	Lines 58–62	Inference	Combine info from lines 8–12, 58–63, 85–92.
4.	F	Lines 23–26	Inference	Discussed above.
5.	A	Lines 8–31	Inference	Combine info from lines 12–14, 27–31.
6.	H	Lines 69–70	Detail	Don't overthink the answer.
7.	D	Lines 37–44	Detail	No line reference. Be careful.
8.	G	Lines 73–92	Big Picture	Which answer echoes the passage?
9.	B	Lines 107–111	Inference	Be sure to consult all your notes for the last paragraph.
10.	H	Lines 99–109	Function	"Some modern composers have tried to write dramatic music for choruses."

IF YOU LEARNED ONLY THREE THINGS IN THIS CHAPTER...

1. Preread the passage and make a road map: know what each paragraph is saying.

2. Refer to your road map when you attack the questions, and **always** refer back to the passage to find the answer.

3. Reading questions can ask about specific details of a passage, what a passage implies, and its overall structure and argument.

CHAPTER 12

Reading Workout 3: Subject Matters

Now that you've learned the general approach to ACT Reading and the approach for each of the specific question types, let's look more closely at the two passage types that give students the most trouble—the Prose Fiction passage and the Natural Sciences passage.

The passage breakdown for the ACT Reading test is as follows:

- Prose Fiction—one passage per test
- Nonfiction—three passages per test, one each in:
  - **Social Sciences**
  - **Humanities**
  - **Natural Sciences**

Your approach will be essentially the same for all three nonfiction passages, since they're all well-organized essays. Your approach to the Prose Fiction passage, however, will be somewhat different.

What follows are two full ACT Reading passages—one Prose Fiction passage and one Natural Sciences passage (which, for convenience, we'll call just Science)—complete with questions. We'll talk about specific strategies for each, but just as importantly, we'll talk about how you can bring together everything you've learned so far and combine this knowledge into a plan of attack for *all* Reading passages. At the end of the workout, we'll also show you how to salvage a few extra points if you find yourself near the end of the test with not enough time to read the final passage.

> ☑ **PERFECT SCORE TIP**
> You do not have to read the four Reading passages in order! Figure out your best and start there. If prose is hard for you and takes a while, do it last even though it is first in the test book.

THE PROSE FICTION PASSAGE

The Prose Fiction passage differs from the three nonfiction passages in that it is not a well-structured essay designed to communicate ideas in a logical, orderly way. It is, usually, a story in which characters fully equipped with their own motivations and emotions interact with each other in revealing ways. For that reason, the Prose Fiction passage won't break down into an orderly outline or road map, so don't even try to characterize the function of each paragraph. Pay attention instead to the *story*.

In the Prose Fiction passage, almost all of the questions relate to the characters. Your job is to find the answers to the following questions:

- **Who are these people?** What are they like? How are they related to each other?
- **What is their state of mind?** Are they angry? Sad? Reflective? Excited?
- **What's going on?** What's happening on the surface? What's happening beneath the surface?
- **What's the author's attitude toward the characters?**

Most of the passages focus on one person or are written from the point of view of one of the characters. Figure out who this main character is and pay special attention to what he or she is like. **Read between the lines to determine unspoken emotions and attitudes. Little hints—a momentary frown, a pointed or sarcastic comment—are sometimes all you have to go on, so *pay attention*.** In fact, you'll probably want to spend more time prereading the Prose Fiction passage than you do any of the other three passages. It's important to get a good feel for the tone and style of the passage as a whole before going to the questions.

> 👤 **EXPERT TUTOR TIP**
> Fiction passages focus on the characters. Who are they? What are they like? What do they think about each other? Watch what they say and do in the passages.

Fortunately, the questions that accompany these passages tend to go more quickly than those for the other passages, so you'll be able to make up some of that time you lose reading the passage.

Make It a Movie in Your Head

Try to make the passage into a movie! Imagine the scenes, the characters, the events. In the Prose Fiction passage, it should be easy to imagine the story unfolding like a movie. Pay careful attention not only to what the characters say but also how they say it.

> ✓ **PERFECT SCORE TIP**
> I found imagining the prose passage as a movie very helpful. It helped keep me awake and engaged while reading it so I was more prepared for the questions.

And don't forget to read actively, as always. Don't just read and then react. Once you have an idea of the personality of the characters, you should be able to respond to the questions. What should you do if you are struggling to understand what's going on? Go to the questions and let the line and paragraph references guide you to important words, phrases, and sentences. One or two questions should help you discover the meaning of the passage. Don't forget to guess on a question you're not sure of.

The Real Thing: Practice Passage

What follows is a typical ACT Prose Fiction passage, complete with questions. Before trying it, you might want to glance back at the techniques discussed in our first Reading Workout. Review the Kaplan Reading Method. **Spend about three minutes prereading (a little more, actually, since this is the Prose Fiction passage). Then do whichever questions you can figure out quickly. Skip any hard or time-consuming problems and come back to them later.**

When you work on the questions, constantly refer to the passage. Plan to spend much more time with your eyeballs pointed at the passage than at the questions. And don't forget to answer the questions in your own words (based on what you've preread and reread in the passage) *before* you look at the answers.

Passage III

PROSE FICTION

I recall a mist starting in as I crossed the lawn that afternoon. I was making my way up to the summer house for the purpose of
Line clearing away the remains of his lordship's
(5) taking tea there with some guest a little while earlier. I can recall spotting from some distance... Miss Kenton's figure moving about inside the summerhouse. When I entered she had seated herself on one of the
(10) wicker chairs scattered around its interior, evidently engaged in some needlework. On closer inspection, I saw she was performing repairs to a cushion. I went about gathering up the various items of crockery from
(15) amidst the plants and the cane furniture, and as I did so, I believe we exchanged a few pleasantries, perhaps discussed one or two professional matters. For the truth was, it was extremely refreshing to be out in the
(20) summerhouse after many continuous days in the main building and neither of us was inclined to hurry with our tasks... In fact, I was looking out over the lawn to where the mist was thickening down around the poplar
(25) trees planted along the cart-track, when I finally introduced the topic of the previous year's dismissals. Perhaps a little predictably, I did so by saying:

"I was just thinking earlier, Miss Kenton.
(30) It's rather funny to remember now, but you know, only this time a year ago, you were still insisting you were going to resign. It rather amused me to think of it." When I finally turned to look at her, she was gazing
(35) through the glass at the great expanse of fog outside.

"You probably have no idea, Mr. Stevens," she said eventually, "how seriously I really thought of leaving this house. I felt so
(40) strongly about what happened. Had I been anyone worthy of any respect at all, I dare say I would have left Darlington Hall long ago." She paused for a while, and I turned my gaze back out to the poplar trees down
(45) in the distance. Then she continued in a tired voice: "It was cowardice, Mr. Stevens. Simple cowardice. Where could I have gone? I have no family. Only my aunt. I love her dearly, but I can't live with her for a day
(50) without feeling my whole life is wasting away. I did tell myself, of course, I would soon find some situation.

"But I was so frightened, Mr. Stevens. Whenever I thought of leaving, I just saw
(55) myself going out there and finding nobody who knew or cared about me. There, that's all my high principles amount to. I feel so ashamed of myself. But I just couldn't leave, Mr. Stevens. I just couldn't bring myself to
(60) leave."

Miss Kenton paused again and seemed to be deep in thought. I thus thought it opportune to relate at this point, as precisely as possible, what had taken place earlier
(65) between myself and Lord Darlington. I proceeded to do so and concluded by saying:

"What's done can hardly be undone. But it is at least a great comfort to hear his lordship declare so unequivocally that it
(70) was all a terrible misunderstanding. I just thought you'd like to know, Miss Kenton,

since I recall you were as distressed by the episode as I was."

"I'm sorry, Mr. Stevens," Miss Kenton
(75) said behind me in an entirely new voice, as though she had just been jolted from a dream, "I don't understand you." Then as I turned to her, she went on: "As I recall, you thought it was only right
(80) and proper that Ruth and Sarah be sent packing. You were positively cheerful about it."

"Now really, Miss Kenton, that is quite incorrect and unfair. The whole matter
(85) caused me great concern, great concern indeed. It is hardly the sort of thing I like to see happen in this house."

"Then why, Mr. Stevens, did you not tell me so at the time?"
(90)   I gave a laugh, but for a moment was rather at a loss for an answer. Before I could formulate one, Miss Kenton put down her sewing and said:

"Do you realize, Mr. Stevens, how
(95) much it would have meant to me if you had thought to share your feelings last year? You knew how upset I was when my girls were dismissed. Do you realize how much it would have helped me? Why, Mr.
(100) Stevens, why, why, why do you always have to pretend?"

I gave another laugh at the ridiculous turn the conversation had suddenly taken. "Really, Miss Kenton," I said, "I'm not sure
(105) I know what you mean. Pretend? Why, really...."

"I suffered so much over Ruth and Sarah leaving us. And I suffered all the more because I believed I suffered alone."

1. According to the passage, the author thinks Mr. Stevens is:

   A. worthy of respect.

   B. not considerate of Miss Kenton's feelings.

   C. too formal in his demeanor.

   D. disloyal to his friends.

2. The statement "Had I been anyone worthy of any respect at all, I dare say I would have left Darlington Hall long ago" (lines 40–44) can be interpreted to mean:

   F. no one at Darlington Hall truly respects Miss Kenton.

   G. Miss Kenton has little respect for Mr. Stevens.

   H. Miss Kenton feels she betrayed her principles by staying.

   J. Miss Kenton senses that Mr. Stevens feels superior to her.

3. According to the passage, the intent of Mr. Stevens's recollection of Miss Kenton's desire to resign (lines 29–33) is most likely to:

   A. open up a discussion of an event that had upset Miss Kenton.

   B. turn the conversation to the professional topic of furniture repair.

   C. indulge in nostalgic reminiscences of happier days.

   D. irritate Miss Kenton by mocking the seriousness of that desire.

4. Mr. Stevens gives "a laugh" (line 90) because he is suddenly:

   F. amused.

   G. insecure.

   H. suspicious.

   J. sarcastic.

5. The main point of Miss Kenton's references to her own family (lines 48–52) is that:

   A. she would have nowhere to turn if she left her job.

   B. children often reject those they should love.

   C. she was afraid of discovering that she did not love her aunt.

   D. life becomes very tedious when one visits relatives.

6. What is it that Mr. Stevens describes as "done" (line 66)?

   F. Lord Darlington's earlier conversation with him

   G. Miss Kenton's talk of leaving Darlington Hall

   H. Ruth and Sarah's dismissal

   J. Any talk of Miss Kenton's dismissal

7. As he is revealed in the passage, Mr. Stevens is:

   A. bored with their conversation in the summer house.

   B. increasingly hostile to Miss Kenton's depiction of his actions.

   C. uncomfortable with expressing his deep affection for Miss Kenton.

   D. unaware of how his past behavior had affected Miss Kenton.

8. Which of the following would be out of character for the narrator?

   I. Pointing out to Miss Kenton why she was unfairly characterizing his actions

   II. Spending time thinking about Miss Kenton's accusations

   III. Ridiculing Miss Kenton for poorly repairing the cushion

   F. I only

   G. II only

   H. I and II only

   J. III only

9. Miss Kenton interacts with Mr. Stevens in a way that can best be described as:

   A. sincere but formal.

   B. indifferent but polite.

   C. timid but angry.

   D. patronizing but kindly.

10. At the end of the passage, Miss Kenton asks, "Why, Mr. Stevens, why, why, why do you always have to pretend?" (lines 98–100) What specific action of Mr. Stevens does she have in mind?

    F. His apparent cheerfulness at Ruth and Sarah's dismissal

    G. His simulation of great affection for her

    H. His phony concern for her own future employment

    J. His empty expressions of sympathy for her own suffering

Answers and Explanations

Paragraphs in the Prose Fiction passage move the story forward. Your prereading road map should center on answers to four main questions about character, actions, and attitudes. They are:

1. **Who are these people?** The first paragraphs are peppered with hints about who these people are. Lines 3–6 discuss Mr. Stevens "clearing away the remains of his lordship's taking tea." Lines 12–13 describe Miss Kenton "performing repairs to a cushion." Lines 29–32 discuss her previous plans for resigning. Clearly, Mr. Stevens and Miss Kenton are servants (we later learn—in lines 64–65—that their employer is Lord Darlington).

2. **What is their state of mind?** We read of "the previous year's dismissals" (lines 26–27) and Miss Kenton's intentions to leave the house (lines 37–39) as a result of them. She "felt so strongly about what happened" (lines 39–40), but she was afraid to take the step of actually leaving in protest ("It was cowardice," she admits in line 46). It sounds like some other servants were dismissed unfairly last year and that this upset Miss Kenton. Apparently, Mr. Stevens also found the incident distressing (lines 71–72), but Miss Kenton hadn't realized this at the time.

3. **What's going on?** These are obviously very formal people, but there are strong emotions rumbling beneath the surface. It's clear that Miss Kenton is very upset because she didn't realize that Mr. Stevens disapproved of the dismissals, too ("Do you realize, Mr. Stevens, how much it would have meant to me if you had thought to share your feelings last year?"—lines 93–96. And later: "Why, Mr. Stevens, why, why, why do you always have to pretend?"—lines 98–100). We get the impression that Mr. Stevens is not a man who very readily shows his feelings and emotions—as Miss Kenton puts it, he always *pretends*.

4. **What is the author's attitude toward the characters?** Often, there will be a question asking about the author's point of view. Be careful here—don't confuse what the characters think about each other with what the author thinks. The two may not be the same.

Note: The first question here is about Writer's View. Your best bet is to skip the question and leave it for last.

Notice how many inference-type questions there are. This is typical of the Prose Fiction passage, where so much information is conveyed implicitly—between the lines. In most cases, you have to read around the specific line references in order to find your answer. If you've done your preread properly, however, you should be able to knock off most of the questions quickly.

Key to Passage III

(PROSE FICTION)

▮▮▮▯ INFERENCE

▮▮▯▯ BIG PICTURE

▮▮▮▮ DETAIL

▮▮▮▮ WRITER'S VIEW

	Answer	Refer to	Type	Comments
1.	B	First two paragraphs	Writer's View	Stevens says he was "amused" and thought it "funny" that she wanted to resign her position. Miss Kenton replies very seriously to his words, saying she doesn't understand him and how could he be so cheerful if he disapproved of the two firings. Miss Kenton has plainly suffered, and Mr. Stevens has not reacted kindly to her pain. The author's sympathy is with Miss Kenton, not Mr. Stevens.
2.	H	Lines 40–44, 55–56	Inference	"There, that's all my high principles amount to," she says.
3.	A	Lines 29–33, 60–65	Inference	Lines 60–65 show that Mr. Stevens has just been discussing this subject with Lord Darlington and now wants to discuss it with Miss Kenton.
4.	G	Lines 89–90	Inference	He is "at a loss for an answer" and clearly not laughing out of amusement.
5.	A	Lines 47–48	Detail	"Where could I have gone? I have no family."
6.	H	Lines 66–72	Detail	Refers to "the previous year's dismissals," first mentioned in lines 25–27.
7.	D	Throughout	Big Picture	Mr. Stevens's nervous laughs hint that he had no idea how deeply Miss Kenton was affected.
8.	J	Throughout	Inference	I: He does this in lines 82–86. II: He wishes to respond to the accusations in lines 78–81. III: This kind of blatant harshness would be uncharacteristic of so discreet and proper a man.
9.	A	Throughout	Big Picture	Miss Kenton freely expresses her feelings to him throughout, so she is sincere. But she **never** loses her formal language and demeanor.
10.	F	Lines 98–100, 73–81	Inference	She wishes that he "had thought to share [his] feelings"; she was under the impression that he was "positively cheerful about [the dismissals]."

THE NATURAL SCIENCES PASSAGE

The Science passage in the Reading subject test emphasizes reading. Here, it is more important understanding ideas than analyzing experiments and data.

Approaching the Science passage is really not any different from approaching the other nonfiction passages, since all are well-organized essays that lay out ideas in a straight-forward, logical way. However, you may be more likely to find unfamiliar vocabulary in Science passages. ***Don't panic*. Any unfamiliar terms will usually be defined in the passage or else will have definitions inferable from context.**

> ✓ **PERFECT SCORE TIP**
> Often, the Natural Science passage will be difficult and have a lot of unfamiliar scientific knowledge in it. Just remind yourself that you don't have to understand all the science behind it. The answer to almost every question is found in the passage and is within your grasp.

Don't Get Lost!

In the Science passage, it's easy to lose yourself in complex details. Don't do it. **It's *especially* important not to get bogged down in the Science passage!** Many students try to understand and remember everything as they read, but that's not the right ACT mind-set. In your preread of the passage, just get the gist and the outline; don't sweat the details. As always, use line references in the questions when possible. They will lead you back to the details that are important. You'd be surprised how many questions you can answer on a passage you don't really understand.

The Real Thing: Practice Passage

The next passage is a typical ACT-style Science passage with questions. Attack it with the same Kaplan Method you use for other passages. Don't worry if you don't understand everything. Your only goal is to get a sense of the passage and its outline.

Passage IV

NATURAL SCIENCE

This passage is excerpted from *Light and Color in Nature and Art*, © 1983 by Samuel J. Williamson. Reprinted by permission of John Wiley & Sons, Inc.

Atoms can be excited in many ways other than by absorbing a photon. The element phosphorous spontaneously combines with oxygen when exposed to air. There is
(5) a transfer of energy to the phosphorous electrons during this chemical reaction, which excites them to sufficiently high energy states that they can subsequently emit light when dropping into a lower
(10) state. This is an example of what is termed chemiluminescence, the emission of light as a result of chemical reaction.

A related effect is bioluminescence, when light is produced by chemical reactions
(15) associated with biological activity. Biolumi- nescence occurs in a variety of life forms and is more common in marine organisms than in terrestrial or freshwater life. Examples include certain bacteria, jellyfish,
(20) clams, fungi, worms, ants, and fireflies. There is considerable diversity in how light is produced. Most processes involve the reaction of a protein with oxygen, catalyzed by an enzyme. The protein varies
(25) from one organism to another, but all are grouped under the generic name luciferin. The enzymes are known as luciferase. Both words stem from the Latin lucifer meaning light-bearing. The various chemical steps
(30) leading to bioluminescence are yet to be explained in detail, but in some higher organisms the process is known to be activated by the nervous system.

The firefly is best understood. Its light organ is located near the end of
(35) the abdomen. Within it luciferin is combined with other atomic groups in a series of processes in which oxygen is converted into carbon dioxide. The sequence

culminates when the luciferin is split off
(40) from the rest, leaving it in an excited state. The excess energy is released as a photon. The peak in the emission spectrum lies between 550 and 600 nm depending on the type of luciferase. This flash produced
(45) by the simultaneous emission of many photons serves to attract mates, and females also use it to attract males of other species, which they devour.

Certain bacteria also produce light
(50) when stimulated by motion. This is why the breaking sea or a passing boat generate the greenish light seen in some bodies of water such as Phosphorescent Bay in Puerto Rico. Some fish have a symbiotic relationship
(55) with bacteria. The "flashlight fish" takes advantage of the light created by bacteria lodged beneath each eye. Certain other fish produce their own bioluminescence, which serves as identification. However, the
(60) biological advantage, if any, of biolumines- cence in some other organisms such as fungi remains a mystery.

Triboluminescence is the emission of light when one hard object is sharply struck
(65) against another. This contact, when atom scrapes against atom, excites electrons and disrupts electrical bonds. Light is then created when the electrons find their way to lower states. Triboluminescence is not to be
(70) confused with the glow of small particles that may be broken off by the impact. Such "sparks" are seen as a result of their high temperature. Light given off by hot objects is known as thermoluminescence, or incandes-
(75) cence.

Another form of thermoluminescence is the basis for dating ancient ceramic objects.

Quartz and other constituents of clay are continually irradiated by naturally occurring (80) radioactive elements (e.g., uranium and thorium) and by cosmic rays. This produces defects in the material where electrons may be trapped. Heating pottery to 500°C releases the trapped electrons, which can (85) then migrate back to their original atoms, where on returning to an atomic orbit they then emit a photon. The intensity of thermoluminescence is therefore a measure of the duration of irradiation since the time when (90) the pottery had been previously fired.

Excitation is also possible by other means. The passage of an electrical current (electroluminescence) is one. The impact of high energy particles is another. The (95) *aurora borealis* and its southern counterpart the *aurora australis* arise when a stream of high energy particles from the sun enters the Earth's upper atmosphere and literally shatters some of the molecules of (100) the air. This leaves their atoms in excited states, and the light subsequently given off is characteristic of the atoms. Although the oxygen molecule, a major constituent of our atmosphere, has no emission in the visible, (105) the oxygen atom can emit photons in either the red or green portions of the spectrum. Other atoms contribute to light at other wavelengths.

11. According to the information in the sixth paragraph (lines 76–90), the brighter the thermoluminescence of a heated piece of ancient pottery:

  A. the younger the piece is.

  B. the older the piece is.

  C. the less irradiation has occurred within the piece's clay.

  D. the fewer electrons have become trapped within the clay.

12. If an ancient ceramic bowl is heated to 500°C, light is emitted when certain electrons:

  F. release radioactive elements found in the clay.

  G. scrape against other electrons.

  H. become superheated.

  J. return to their former atoms.

13. Compared to bioluminescence, chemiluminescence is NOT produced by:

  A. organic proteins that have been catalyzed.

  B. a chemical reaction.

  C. any reaction involving oxygen.

  D. a change in energy states.

14. It can be inferred from the passage that the description of the firefly's production of light is a good example of the degree to which researchers understand:

  F. why light attracts fireflies.

  G. how a chemical process can trigger bioluminescence.

  H. how female fireflies attack male fireflies.

  J. how to measure the intensity of a firefly's bioluminescence.

15. In both chemiluminescence and bioluminescence, photons are emitted:

  A. as excess energy.

  B. only by certain marine organisms.

  C. only when luciferase is present.

  D. only when phosphorous is present.

16. Based on details in the passage, the word *excited* as used in line 1 means:

    F. split off from a molecule.

    G. agitated until glowing.

    H. raised to a higher energy level.

    J. heated to the point of disintegra-
        tion.

17. In discussing the creation of the two kinds of aurora, the passage asserts that the oxygen molecule "has no emission in the visible [spectrum]" (line 104) but also states that "the oxygen atom can emit photons in either the red or the green portions of the spectrum" (lines 105–106). Is the passage logically consistent?

    A. Yes, because visible light is emitted after the oxygen molecules have been broken apart into oxygen atoms.

    B. Yes, because the passage presents factual information and therefore cannot be illogical.

    C. No, because the oxygen molecule forms the largest part of the atmo-sphere and scientific theories must account for its invisible emissions.

    D. No, because the writer has failed to adequately differentiate between the oxygen molecule's behavior and that of the oxygen atom.

18. Assume that two meteors have collided and shattered. Astronomers see both a burst of light and then a subsequent glow. Such a visual phenomenon could best be explained as the result of:

    > I. chemiluminescence.
    >
    > II. triboluminescence.
    >
    > III. thermoluminescence.

    F. II only

    G. II and III only

    H. I and III only

    J. I, II, and III

19. Based on information presented in the passage, which of the following is a hypothesis, rather than a fact?

    A. Fireflies use bioluminescence to attract mates.

    B. Thermoluminescence and tribo-luminescence are two distinctly different kinds of light emission.

    C. A firefly's type of luciferase determines the peak of its light emission's intensity.

    D. All organisms that produce biolumi-nescence do so for some biological advantage.

20. According to the last paragraph (lines 91–108), both the *aurora borealis* and the *aurora australis*:

    F. arise from the effect of high energy particles on atoms.

    G. occur without the presence of oxygen.

    H. emit light due to the presence of electrical currents.

    J. are visible from the surface of the Earth.

Answers and Explanations

Feeling a little numb? Unless you're a real science buff, you probably found this passage a lot less exciting than the atoms did. And you may have found yourself adrift in a sea of bewildering terms—*chemiluminescence, luciferin, aurora australis.*

We hope, though, that you didn't panic. You could still get points—and lots of them—from this passage even if all that you took away from your preread was a sense that the passage was mainly about things in nature glowing when their atoms are excited. That, and a sense of a road map, was really all you needed. Most of the questions were answerable by referring to the appropriate lines in the passage and paraphrasing what you read there.

Here's a possible road map for the passage:

- **First paragraph:** Introduction of idea of excited atoms releasing photons (i.e., luminescence). Discusses *chemiluminescence* (resulting from a chemical reaction).
- **Second paragraph:** Discusses *bioluminescence* (associated with biological activity—that is, with things that are alive).
- **Third paragraph:** Example of *bioluminescence*—fireflies.
- **Fourth paragraph:** More examples of *bioluminescence*—sea life.
- **Fifth paragraph:** Discusses *triboluminescence* (things hitting each other) and *thermoluminescence* (hot objects).
- **Sixth paragraph:** Example of *thermoluminescence*—refired ceramic objects.
- **Seventh paragraph:** Concludes with discussion of *electroluminescence* (associated with electrical currents).

Basically, the author is giving us a rundown on the various kinds of luminescence in nature. When the questions ask about one kind or another, you simply refer to the appropriate paragraph and lines.

Following is a key to the answers for this passage. Notice how you could have gotten an answer to number 12, for instance, *even if you were totally confused*. If you found 500° in the passage (line 83), the sentence more or less spelled out the answer for you, requiring a minimum of paraphrasing.

Key to Passage IV

(NONFICTION—NATURAL SCIENCES)

📶 INFERENCE

📶 DETAIL

📶 BIG PICTURE

	Answer	Refer to	Type	Comments
11.	B	Lines 76–90	Inference	More time since last firing to trap more electrons, creating brighter glow
12.	J	Lines 76–87	Detail	"migrate back to their original atoms"
13.	A	Paragraph 2	Detail	Be careful with the reversal word NOT in the question. Organic means "having to do with life."
14.	G	Lines 22–33, 33–48	Inference	Remember, passage is about luminescence, not fireflies.
15.	A	Lines 4–12, 44–47	Inference	B and C aren't chemi-; D isn't bio-. Only A is both.
16.	H	Lines 2–12, 65–77	Detail	Lines 4–10 say it all.
17.	A	Lines 91–108	Detail	Note difference between oxygen molecule and oxygen atom.
18.	G	Lines 63–75	Inference	I: No, since no chemical reaction II: Yes, since impact reaction III: Yes, since "subsequent glow" (probably a heat reaction)
19.	D	Throughout	Big Picture	Any statement about "all organisms" is probably a hypothesis, since no one can verify what's true of every organism in existence.
20.	F	Lines 65–77	Detail	"a stream of high energy particles from the sun"

EMERGENCY STRATEGY FOR TEST DAY

If you have less than four minutes left and you've still got an entire passage untouched, you need to shift to last-minute strategies. Don't try to preread the passage; you'll just run out of time before you answer any questions. Instead, scan the questions without reading the passage and look first for the ones that mention line numbers or specific paragraphs. You can often get quick points on these questions by referring back to the passage as the question stem directs, reading a few lines around the reference, and taking your best shot.

Of course, the most important thing is to make sure you have gridded in at least a random guess on every question. If some of your blind guesses are right (as some of them statistically *should* be), they'll boost your score just as much as well-reasoned, thought-out answers would!

> ✓ **PERFECT SCORE TIP**
> Remember that the most important thing to do on the ACT is to answer every question. Even if you have time trouble and don't finish a section—guess!

▶ IF YOU LEARNED ONLY TWO THINGS IN THIS CHAPTER...

1. In the Prose Fiction passage, concentrate on who the characters are and what they are doing. What are the characters' attitudes toward each other? What is the author's attitude toward the characters?

2. For Natural Science passages, ask yourself, "What's new?" in each paragraph. Don't get bogged down in details or terminology. All you need is the general idea of how the paragraphs fit together.

CHAPTER 13

Science Workout 1: Look for Patterns

SMARTPOINTS COVERED IN THIS CHAPTER

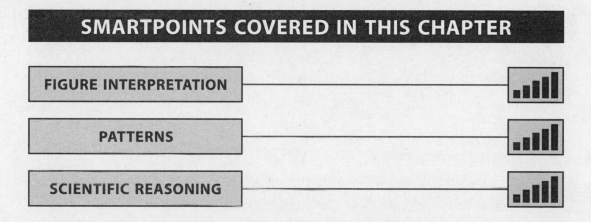

FIGURE INTERPRETATION

PATTERNS

SCIENTIFIC REASONING

The Science subject test causes a lot of unnecessary anxiety among ACT takers. Many people get so overwhelmed by the terminology and technicality of the passages that they just give up. What they fail to realize is that Science is a little like the reverse of Math. In Math, you'll remember, we said that many of the questions are difficult problems based on elementary principles. In Science, on the other hand, many of the questions are elementary problems based on difficult material. So it's important not to panic if you don't understand the passage in Science. You can often get many of the questions right on a passage, even if you find it virtually incomprehensible!

> **EXPERT TUTOR TIP**
> The ACT Science test covers biology, chemistry, Earth/space sciences, and physics. It includes:
> • Three Data Representation passages with five questions each
> • Three Experiment passages with six questions each
> • One Conflicting Viewpoints passage with seven questions

Many ACT takers also tend to rely too heavily on what they've learned in school when approaching the Science subject test. But as we've said, remembering facts is not the mind-set the ACT will reward. You couldn't possibly know the answers to ACT Science questions in advance: You have to pull them out of the passages. **All the information you need to answer the questions is right on the page.**

Worrying about science knowledge can be a problem no matter how good or bad your science background is. Students who have done poorly in science tend to panic because they think they don't know enough. Students who have done well in science might know **too** much. Some questions include wrong choices that are scientifically correct but don't relate to the passages. Choosing such answers will not earn you points on the ACT. Try not to rely primarily on your knowledge of science. Instead, use your ability to pull information from the passages.

> **EXPERT TUTOR TIP**
> Here's how to use this chapter if you don't have much time. Learn the Kaplan Method for ACT Science. Try the sample passage later in this chapter, then read the section called Reading Tables and Graphs.

ACT Science requires many of the same skills that ACT Reading does. The strategies discussed in Reading Workout I will therefore also work well for many Science passages. The most important difference between Reading and Science is that the details you have to find in the Science passages almost all relate to numbers or scientific processes, and they are often contained in graphs and tables rather than in paragraph form.

- **Reading graphs, tables, and research summaries.** Many questions involve accurately retrieving data from only one graph or table. Others involve combining knowledge from two different graphs or tables. Still others involve understanding experimental methods well enough to evaluate information contained in summaries of experiments.

- **Looking for patterns in the numbers that appear.** Do these numbers get bigger or smaller? Where are the highest numbers? The lowest? At what point do the numbers change? A little calculation is sometimes required, but not much. In Science, you won't be computing with numbers so much as thinking about what they mean.

In Science, as in Reading, it's crucial to consider the questions and at least try to answer them before looking at the answer choices. Refer to the passage to find the answer, and try to match it with one of the choices. **Use the process of elimination** as a fallback strategy for hard questions—but don't make it your main approach.

> ✔ **PERFECT SCORE TIP**
> A common myth is that the ACT Science section is based on science knowledge. It is really another reading comprehension section, not a test of your scientific knowledge.

THE KAPLAN METHOD FOR ACT SCIENCE

STEP 1: Map the passage, identifying and marking the purpose, method, and results of the experiment.

STEP 2: Scan the figures, identifying variables and patterns.

STEP 3: Find support for the answer in the passage.

In Science, you have seven shorter passages to do instead of the four longer ones in Reading. Each passage should take you an average of five minutes to complete. We recommend using just about one minute or so to preread the passage, and then a total of about four minutes to consider the questions and refer to the passage (that's about 40 seconds per question). Notice that you spend less time prereading than in Reading.

STEP 1: Map the Passage, Identifying and Marking the Purpose, Method, and Results of the Experiment

As with the Reading test, you'll want to read and map the passage so you can easily find information once you attack the questions. Some of the material covered is extremely technical, and you'll just get frustrated trying to understand it completely. So it's crucial that you skim to get a general idea of what's going on and—just as importantly—to get a sense of where certain types of data can be found.

> ✔ **PERFECT SCORE TIP**
> I often find the intro is the most useful part of the whole reading. Don't try to understand everything in them, but definitely make sure to read all the intros as they will give you background for the rest of the passages.

Almost all Science passages have the same general structure. They begin with an introduction—**always** read it first to orient yourself. Some passages relate to material you may have already studied in high school. If you're familiar with the concepts, you may not need to do more than skim the introduction. If not, you'll want to read it more carefully. But remember, don't focus on details. In the introduction, mark the *purpose* of the experiment. Whether you bracket it, circle it, or put a "P" next to it doesn't really matter. The only important thing is that somehow you note its location in case a question refers to it. The purpose will answer the question "Why was this experiment performed?"

After reviewing the introduction, quickly scan the rest of the passage. Take note of the *method* of the experiment(s). The method will answer the question "How was the experiment set up?" How is the information presented? Graphs? Diagrams? Are there experiments? What seems to be important? Size? Shape? Temperature? Speed? Chemical composition? Don't worry about details and don't try to remember it all. Plan to refer to the passage just as you would in Reading.

Example

> Scientists researching the relationship between birds and dinosaurs have chosen to carefully examine three fossils dating from the Jurassic period: an *archaeopteryx* (the oldest known bird) at the British Museum in London, a *compsognathus* (a dinosaur) at the Field Museum in Chicago, and a *teleosaurus* (a crocodile) at the National Museum in Beijing. All three creatures were about the same size as a turkey.

Remember to read actively. Ask yourself: Why would the scientists choose these three creatures? Since the scientists are studying birds and dinosaurs, the first two choices seem natural. But why should they include a crocodile? Maybe the National Museum in Beijing had a special deal on crocodile bones? More likely it's because crocodiles are somewhat like dinosaurs, but not extinct.

Finally, note the *results* of the experiment with an "R" next to the section—whether that's a paragraph, figure, or both. You don't need to fully comprehend the results just yet; you only need to indicate where they can be found so you can easily answer questions about them later.

STEP 2: Scan the Figures, Identifying Variables and Patterns

As you preread the passage, make sure you know what any tables and graphs in the passage are meant to represent. You only need to scan them to get a sense of what kind of data is contained in each graph and table, but don't read the data carefully yet. You may want to take note of general trends in the data, but don't waste time taking in information that may not be relevant to the questions. **Remember, your goal is to answer questions, not to learn and remember everything that goes on in the passage.**

> **EXPERT TUTOR TIP**
>
> If you need to know the meaning of a special scientific term, the test will usually define it. If the test doesn't tell you what a word means, you can usually figure it out from the context (or else you won't need to know it).

STEP 3: Find Support for the Answer in the Passage

Most of your time in Science will be spent considering questions and referring to the passage to find the answers. Here's where you should do most of your really careful reading. **It's essential that you understand exactly what the question is asking.** Then go back to the passage and get a sense of what the answer should be before looking at the choices.

There are three basic kinds of Science questions:

1. **Figure Interpretation questions.** For these questions, you'll almost certainly be going back to the graphs. They are usually among the easiest on the Science test. Knowing the headings of each figure will help make these questions that much easier.

2. **Patterns questions.** These are usually medium difficulty. You have to look beyond just the data that is presented in the figures to see what the patterns are in the data.

3. **Scientific Interpretation questions.** These questions are usually among the hardest on the test because they are based on what is in the text versus what is in the figures. Here, you must apply a scientific principle or identify ways of defending or attacking a principle. This includes making predictions based on a given theory or showing how a hypothesis might be strengthened or weakened by particular findings. (These questions will be especially important for the Conflicting Viewpoints passage, discussed in Science Workout 3.)

As we mentioned, one possible pitfall in answering the questions is relying too heavily on your own knowledge of science. In answering questions, use your knowledge of scientific *methods* and *procedures*. But don't rely heavily on any knowledge of specific facts. For example, the following question might have appeared with the previous passage excerpt:

▮▮▮▮ SCIENTIFIC REASONING

Example

1. The dinosaur studied by the scientists, *compsognathus*, was:

   A. definitely a reptile.

   B. definitely a bird.

   C. about the size of a turkey.

   D. larger than *archaeopteryx* or *teleosaurus*.

If you know that dinosaurs are usually classified as reptiles, choice A would be very tempting. But it's wrong—the passage doesn't say that. In fact, if we had seen the rest of this passage, we would have learned that the researchers were questioning whether dinosaurs should be classified as reptiles or birds. What the passage *does* say is that all three of the creatures tested are turkey sized, making the correct choice C.

As in Reading, you have to be diligent about referring to the passage. Your prereading of the passage should have given you an idea of where particular kinds of data can be found. Sometimes the questions themselves will direct you to the right place.

Be careful not to mix up units when taking information from graphs, tables, and summaries. Don't confuse *decreases* and *increases*: Many questions will hinge on whether you can correctly identify the factors that decrease and the ones that increase. Incorrect answers will often put a *decrease* where an *increase* should be and vice versa. **Read the questions carefully!**

> **▮ EXPERT TUTOR TIP**
> Reading the question carefully is the most important step. If you miss a little word such as *not*, you will get the question wrong.

The answers to the Science questions are there in the passage. As mentioned in Step 2, don't rely too much on your own knowledge of science. Instead, think of paraphrasing the information in the passage.

> **✔ PERFECT SCORE TIP**
> The words *not* and *except* will show up in question stems, and missing them is an easy way to get a question wrong. Pay attention to these words and circle them when you see them.

Once you've paraphrased the information and matched it to an answer choice, double-check the question to make sure that you've actually answered the question asked.

Many of the questions in Science are reversal questions. Always look for words such as *not* and *except* in the questions.

READING TABLES AND GRAPHS

Most of the information in ACT Science passages is presented in tables or graphs, usually accompanied by explanatory material. Knowing how to read data from tables and graphs is critical to success on the Science subject test! In order to read most graphs and tables, ask yourself:

- What does the figure show?
- What are the units of measurement?
- What is the pattern in the data?

Let's say you saw the following graph in a Science passage:

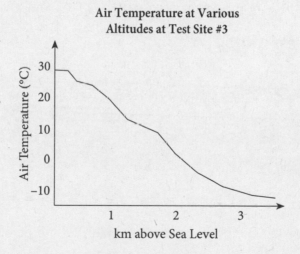

- **What does the figure show?** Most graphs and tables have titles that tell you what they represent. For some, though, you may have to get that information from the introduction. Here, the graph is representing how cold or hot the air is at various altitudes above a certain Test Site #3.

- **What are the units of measurement?** Note that distance here is measured in *kilometers*, not miles or feet. Temperature is measured in degrees *Celsius*, not Fahrenheit.

- **What is the pattern in the data?** The pattern of the data in this graph is pretty clear. As you rise in altitude, the temperature drops—the higher the altitude, the lower the temperature. (As we'll see later, this kind of trend is called an *inverse variation*.)

The sloping line on the graph represents the various temperatures measured at the various altitudes. To find what the measured temperature was at, say, 2 km above sea level, find the 2 km point on the x-axis and trace your finger directly up from it until it hits the line. It does so at about the level of 3°C. In other words, at an altitude of 2 km above sea level at Test Site #3, the air temperature was about 3°C.

> **EXPERT TUTOR TIP**
> Get plenty of practice reading and interpreting data presented in graphs and tables. This is one of the most frequently tested topics in ACT Science.

Be careful with units of measurement. Most passages use the metric system, but a few may use traditional or British units of measure. You won't be expected to remember oddball unit conversions such as 8 furlongs = 1 mile or 2.54 cm = 1 in, and passages that use special units of measure, such as microns or parsecs, will define these units if necessary. But don't assume that all the units in the graphs match the units in the questions. For instance, try the following question:

FIGURE INTERPRETATION

Example

2. At what altitude did the meteorologists measure an air temperature of 10°C?

   F. 1.4 m

   G. 140 m

   H. 1,400 m

   J. 14 km

Many test takers solving the problem above would find the point on the line at the level of 10°C on the y-axis, trace their fingers down to the x-axis, see that the altitude would be about halfway between 1 and 2 (a little closer to 1, maybe), and then quickly choose F. This is incorrect; F gives you 1.4 *meters*, while the graph figures are given in *kilometers*. Remember to translate the data! A kilometer is 1,000 meters, so 1.4 kilometers would be 1.4 times 1,000 meters = 1,400 meters. That's choice H.

You should follow a similar procedure with tables of information. For instance, in the introduction to the passage in which the following table might have appeared, you would have learned that scientists were trying to determine the effects of two pollutants (Pb and Hg, lead and mercury) on the trout population of a particular river.

Table 1

Location	Water Temperature (°C)	Presence of Pb (parts per million)	Presence of Hg (parts per million)	Population Density of Speckled Trout (# per 100 m³)
1	15.4	0	3	7.9
2	16.1	0	1	3.5
3	16.3	1	67	0
4	15.8	54	3	5.7
5	16.0	2	4	9.5

- **What does the figure show?** Here, each row represents the data from a different numbered location on the river. Each column represents different data: water temperature, presence of the first pollutant, presence of the second pollutant, population of one kind of trout.

- **What are the units of measurement?** Temperature is measured in degrees Celsius. The two pollutants are measured in parts per million (or ppm). The trout populations are measured in average number per 100 cubic meters of river.

- **What is the pattern in the data?** Glancing at the table, it looks like locations where the Hg concentration is high (as in Location 3), the trout population is virtually nonexistent. This would seem to indicate that trout find a high Hg concentration incompatible. But notice the location where the other pollutant is abundant—in Location 4. Here, the trout population seems to be more in line with other locations. That would seem to indicate that this other pollutant—Pb—is NOT quite so detrimental to trout populations (though we'd have to do more studies if it turned out that all of the trout in that location had three eyes).

How Tables and Graphs Relate

To really understand tables and graphs, it helps to see how the same information can be represented in both. For instance, look at the next table and graph:

CONCENTRATION OF *E. COLI* IN COOKING POOL B	
Distance from Effluent Pipe 3	**1,000s of *E. coli* per Centiliter**
0 m	0.4
5 m	5.6
10 m	27.6
15 m	14.0
20 m	7.5

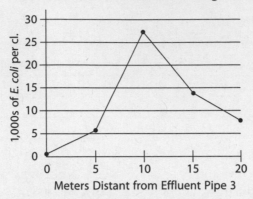

Concentration of *E. coli* in Cooling Pool B

The previous table and graph represent the exact same data. And here's yet another way of depicting the same data, in a bar chart:

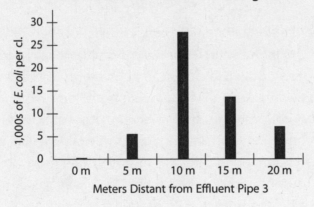

Concentration of *E. coli* in Cooling Pool B

Remember that data can be represented in many different ways. But however it appears in the passage, whether it be in tables, graphs, or charts, you'll have to read and translate it to answer the questions.

EXPERT TUTOR TIP
No matter what the figure looks like, you still ask yourself the same questions:
1. What does the figure show?
2. What are the units of measurement?
3. What is the pattern in the data?

PERFECT SCORE TIP
If you do not have much experience reading graphs—practice! Being able to read graphs is one of the most necessary skills on this section.

Look for Patterns and Trends

When you first examine a graph or table, don't focus on exact numbers. **Look for *patterns* in the numbers. But don't assume that there is *always* a pattern or trend:** Finding that there isn't a pattern is just as important as finding that there is one. When looking for patterns and trends, you should keep three things in mind:

1. EXTREMES

Extremes—or maximums and minimums—are merely the highest and lowest points that things reach. In tables, the minimums and maximums will be represented by relatively high and low numbers. In graphs, they will be represented by highs and lows on the *x*- and *y*-axes. In bar charts, they will be represented by the tallest and shortest bars.

Look back at Table 1. What location on the river has the maximum concentration of Hg? Of Pb? A glance at the numbers tells you that Location 3—with 67 ppm—represents the maximum for Hg, while Location 4—with 54 ppm—represents the maximum for Pb.

How can taking note of maximums and minimums help you spot patterns in the data? Look again at Table 1. Notice that the maximum concentration of Hg, 67 ppm, just happens to coincide with the *minimum* for trout population—0 per 100 m³. That's a good indication that there's some cause and effect going on here. Somehow, a maximum of Hg concentration correlates with a minimum of trout population. The obvious (though not airtight) conclusion is that a high concentration of Hg is detrimental to trout populations. And this kind of finding is much more evident when you look at maximums and minimums.

2. CRITICAL POINTS

To find out how critical points can help you evaluate data, take another look at the graph representing the concentration of *E. coli* (a common type of bacterium) in Cooling Pool B.

Concentration of *E. coli* in Cooling Pool B

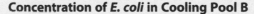
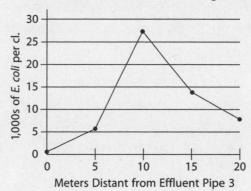

Notice how the concentration is low very near Effluent Pipe 3. From there, it rises until about 10 meters away from the pipe, then it falls again, tapering off as you get farther from the pipe. There's a critical point, then, right around 10 meters from Effluent Pipe 3. Somehow, that vicinity is most conducive to the growth of *E. coli*. As you move closer to or farther away from that point, the concentration falls off. So, in looking to explain the data, you'd want to focus on that location—10 meters from the pipe. What is it about that location that's so special? What makes it the hot new place for *E. coli* to see and be seen?

3. RELATIONSHIPS

Being able to recognize relationships within a figure will lead directly to earning more points on test day. Look at the figure below.

Hours of Sunlight	Air Temperature (Fahrenheit)		
	Chamber 1	**Chamber 2**	**Chamber 3**
2	73.23	75.67	78.87
4	71.23	75.79	79.78
6	69.23	74.76	81.34
8	67.23	79.87	82.12
10	65.23	80.65	83.06

> **EXPERT TUTOR TIP**
> Learn to recognize patterns in data, and you'll be able to answer most ACT Science questions on test day. Look for extremes, critical points, and variation.

What happens in Chamber 1? What do you think the temperature is going to be after 12 hours of sunlight? Do you notice the pattern? The temperature goes down by 2 degrees for every 2 hours of sunlight. The temperature is going to be 63.23 degrees.

As the number of hours of sunlight increases, what happens to the temperature in Chamber 2? When you look at the data, there doesn't appear to be a relationship. This is a valid answer.

Based on the data, what do you think the temperature will be after one hour of sunlight in Chamber 3? Well, as the number of hours of sunlight increase, the temperature in the chamber increases. So if you had to predict what would happen after only one hour of sunlight, then according to the table, it is going to be less than 78.87 degrees.

Before you tackle a real Science passage, let's review the Kaplan Method for the Science section. Note how similar it is to the steps for the Reading section. However, here you spend only one minute prereading (actively reading) the passage.

THE REAL THING: PRACTICE PASSAGE

Let's take a look at a full-fledged Science passage that requires these skills. Give yourself about seven minutes to do the passage and the questions (on the actual test, you'll want to move a bit faster).

Passage I

Although the effective acceleration due to gravity at the Earth's surface is often treated as a constant ($g = 9.80$ m/sec²), its actual value varies from place to place because of several factors.

First, a body on the surface of any rotating spheroid experiences an effective force perpendicular to the rotational axis and proportional to the speed of rotation. This centrifugal force, which counteracts gravity, varies with latitude, increasing from zero at the poles to a maximum at the equator. In addition, because the Earth "bulges" at the equator, a body at equatorial sea level is farther from the center of the Earth than is a body at polar sea level. Figure 1 shows the variation of mean values of g at sea level resulting from both effects; the contribution from "bulging" is about half that from rotation.

Figure 1

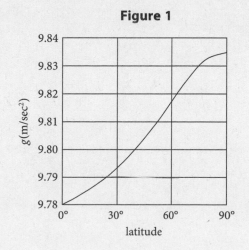

Measurements of *g* also vary depending on local rock density and altitude. Table 1 shows the effect of altitude on *g* at various points above sea level.

Table 1

Altitude above Sea Level (km)	g (m/sec²)
1	−0.0031
5	−0.0154
10	−0.0309
25	−0.0772
30	−0.1543

 EXPERT TUTOR TIP
Don't forget to ask yourself:
1. What does the figure show?
2. What are the units of measurement?
3. What is the pattern in the data?

 FIGURE INTERPRETATION

Examples

3. If the Earth's density were uniform, at approximately what latitude would calculations using an estimated value at sea level of $g = 9.80$ m/sec² produce the least error?

   A. 0°

   B. 20°

   C. 40°

   D. 80°

4. According to Table 1, what would the change in gravity (in m/sec²) be at 2 km above sea level?

   F. −0.0001

   G. −0.0030

   H. −0.0081

   J. −0.0165

📶 PATTERNS

5. Given the information in the passage, which of the following figures most closely approximates the value of g at a point 10 km high along the equator?

   A. 9.75 m/sec²

   B. 9.80 m/sec²

   C. 9.81 m/sec²

   D. 9.87 m/sec²

6. Suppose that the Earth stopped rotating but still "bulged." Based on information from the passage, the value of g at sea level at the equator would be:

   F. exactly 9.80 m/sec².

   G. greater than 9.78 m/sec².

   H. exactly 9.78 m/sec².

   J. less than 9.78 m/sec².

7. According to the information in Figure 1, the value of g:

   A. changes by a greater average amount per degree latitude between 30° and 60° than it does near the equator or poles.

   B. changes by a greater average amount per degree latitude near the equator or poles than it does between 30° and 60°.

   C. increases by an average of 5.8 m/sec² per degree latitude from the equator to the poles.

   D. decreases by an average of 3.1×10^{-3} m/sec² per degree latitude from the equator to the poles.

Answers

1. A
2. H
3. C
4. H
5. A
6. G
7. A

Answers and Explanations

This was actually a relatively simple, straightforward Science passage, but the terminology may have been intimidating nonetheless. The introduction tells you that the issue here is gravity and how its pull (in other words, the acceleration due to gravity) changes because of several factors. Those factors—and the changes they cause—are represented in Figure 1 (which deals with the factor of latitude) and Table 1 (which deals with the factor of altitude).

Analyzing Figure 1, you should have seen that the graph is supposed to show how g (the acceleration due to gravity) is affected by latitude (i.e., north-south location on the globe). The higher the latitude (the greater the distance from the equator), the greater the value of g. As the curves at the beginning and ending of the line in Figure 1 tell you, the increase in g is slower near the equator and near the poles.

Notice how you could have answered **question 3** just by understanding Figure 1. Question 3 asks, assuming the Earth's density were uniform, "at what latitude would calculations using an estimated value at sea level of $g = 9.80$ m/sec^2 produce the least error?" First, figure out what that question is asking. You remember this question; we mentioned it in ACT Basics. It's simply asking you: Where would you get an actual value of g closest to 9.80 m/sec^2? Find 9.80 on the y-axis of the graph, follow across until you intersect with the curved line, and see where you are on the x-axis. That turns out to be about a third of the way from 30° to 60° latitude. In other words, choice C, 40°, is the answer.

> **EXPERT TUTOR TIP**
> Remember, you score points by answering the questions correctly, not by understanding the passages completely. You can get points on a Science passage, even if you don't understand it!

Question 4 is simply asking you to figure out the pattern in Table 1. To find out what the change in g at 2 km is, you would need to look at the table between 1 km and 5 km. There is only one answer choice that falls between the values of −0.0031 and −0.0154, and that is choice H, −0.0081.

We'll get to **question 5** soon.

Question 6 requires more applications of principles and is yet another question that can be answered by simply reading Figure 1. It asks you to suppose that rotation effects (one of the two factors affected by latitude) ceased, but that the Earth still bulged at the equator. What would be the value of g? Well, again, rotation tends to "counteract" gravity, so it would have a depressing effect on g. Without rotation, then, g would be less depressed—it would go up, in other words. That means (reading from Figure 1 again) that g at 0° latitude (the equator) would, in the absence of rotation, go up from its current value of 9.78. That's why choice G is correct.

Question 7 (not to get monotonous) can also be answered just by reading Figure 1. It asks you to describe what the graph tells you about the value of g. As we saw, the value rises slowly as you head away from 0° latitude (the equator), rises more rapidly in the middle latitudes, and slows down again near 90° latitude (the poles). That's best described by choice A. (Choice B gets it backwards—remember to read the choices carefully!) Choices C and D would involve you in some extensive calculations, at the end of which you'd realize that they were not true. But there's no reason to get that far. If you find yourself doing extensive calculation, you should know that you're on the wrong track. ACT Science will involve simple calculation only.

Notice how you could have answered four of the five questions with just a rudimentary grasp of the introduction and an understanding of how to read Figure 1 and Table 1.

The other question, **question 5**, requires that you read both Figure 1 and Table 1 properly. It asks for the value of g at the equator (that information comes from Figure 1), but at an altitude of 10 km above sea level (that information comes from Table 1). Figure 1 tells you that the value of g at the equator at sea level would be 9.78 m/sec². But at 10 km above sea level, according to Table 1, g would be slightly lower—0.0309 m/sec² lower to be precise. So 9.78 minus 0.0309 would be about 9.75 m/sec². That's choice A.

Look for Patterns

The previous passage and questions should convince you of one thing: to do well on Science, you have to be able to read graphs and tables, paying special attention to trends and patterns in the data. Sometimes that's all you need to do to get most of the points on a passage.

▶ IF YOU LEARNED ONLY THREE THINGS IN THIS CHAPTER...

1. The information you need is given in the passages—don't rely on your outside knowledge of science.

2. Approach Science passages like Reading passages: read and map the passage, focus on the question stem, and find the answer in the data or scenario given.

3. When reading graphs and tables, determine what's being represented, the units of measurement, and any patterns or trends.

CHAPTER 14

Science Workout 2: Think Like a Scientist

SMARTPOINTS COVERED IN THIS CHAPTER

FIGURE INTERPRETATION	
SCIENTIFIC REASONING	

In Science Workout 1, you learned that to succeed on the ACT Science subtest, you've got to be able to spot trends and patterns in the data of graphs and tables. But that's not all you need to do well. You've also got to learn how to think like a scientist. You don't have to know very much science (though it certainly helps), but you should at least be familiar with how scientists go about getting and testing knowledge.

HOW SCIENTISTS THINK

Scientists use two very different kinds of logic, which (to keep things nontechnical) we'll call:

1. **General-to-Specific Thinking**
2. **Specific-to-General Thinking**

General-to-Specific

In some cases, scientists have already discovered a law of nature and wish to apply their knowledge to a specific case. For example, a scientist may wish to know how fast a pebble (call it Pebble A) will be falling when it hits the ground three seconds after being dropped. There is a law of physics from which it can be determined that on Earth, falling objects accelerate at a rate of about 9.8 m/sec². The scientist could use this known general principle to calculate the specific information she needs: after three seconds, the object would be falling at a rate of about 3 sec × 9.8 m/sec², or roughly 30 m/sec. You could think of this kind of logic as *general-to-specific*. The scientist uses a *general* principle (the acceleration of any object falling on Earth) to find a *specific* fact (the speed of Pebble A).

 PERFECT SCORE TIP
Most Science questions will give you data and ask you for conclusions, so focus on these skills.

Specific-to-General

But scientists use a different kind of thinking in order to discover a new law of nature. In this case, they examine many specific facts and then draw a general conclusion about what they've seen. For example, a scientist might watch hundreds of different kinds of frogs live and die and might notice that all of them developed from tadpoles. She might then announce a conclusion: all frogs develop from tadpoles. You could think of this kind of logic as *specific-to-general*. The scientist looks at many *specific* frogs to find a *general* rule about all frogs.

This conclusion is called a hypothesis, not a fact or a truth, because the scientist has not checked every single frog in the universe. She knows that there theoretically *could* be a frog somewhere that grows from pond scum or from a Dalmatian puppy. But until she finds such a frog, it is reasonable to think that her hypothesis is correct. Many hypotheses, in fact, are so well documented that they become the equivalent of laws of nature.

In your science classes in school, you mostly learn about general-to-specific thinking. Your teachers explain general rules of science to you and then expect you to apply these rules to answer questions and solve problems. Some ACT Science questions are like that as well. But a majority are not. **Most ACT Science questions test specific-to-general thinking.** The questions test your ability to see the kinds of patterns in specific data that, as a scientist, you would use to formulate your own general hypotheses. We did something like this in Science Workout 1, when we theorized—based on the trends we found in a table of data—that the pollutant Hg was in some way detrimental to trout populations.

> **EXPERT TUTOR TIP**
> Only one to three questions on the entire test will be based on your science knowledge. Everything else is based on what's in the passage.

HOW EXPERIMENTS WORK

Many ACT passages describe experiments and expect you to understand how they're designed. Experiments help scientists do specific-to-general thinking in a reliable and efficient way. Consider the tadpole researcher. In a real-world situation, what would probably happen is that she would notice some of the frogs develop from tadpoles and wonder if maybe they all did. Then she'd know what to look for and could check all the frogs systematically. This process contains the two basic steps of any experiment:

1. **Forming a hypothesis** (guessing that all frogs come from tadpoles)
2. **Testing a hypothesis** (checking the frogs to see if this guess was right)

Scientists are often interested in cause-and-effect relationships. Having formed her hypothesis about tadpoles, a scientist might wonder what *causes* a tadpole to become a frog. To test causal relationships, a special kind of experiment is needed. She must test one possible cause at a time in order to isolate which one actually produces the effect in question. For example, the scientist might inject tadpoles with several different kinds of hormones. Some of these tadpoles might die. Others might turn into frogs normally. But a few—those injected with Hormone X, say—might remain tadpoles for an indefinite time. One reasonable explanation is that Hormone X in some way inhibited whatever causes normal frog development. In other words, the scientist would hypothesize a causal relationship between Hormone X and frog development.

> **EXPERT TUTOR TIP**
> Many ACT Science questions ask you to determine the purpose of an experiment or to design one yourself. To figure out the purpose of an experiment, look to see what factor was allowed to change: That's what's being tested. To design an experiment yourself, keep everything constant except the factor you must investigate.

Method

The relationship between Hormone X and frog development, however, would not be demonstrated very well if the scientist also fed different diets to different tadpoles, kept some in warmer water, or allowed some to have more room to swim than others—or if she didn't also watch tadpoles who were injected with no hormones at all but who otherwise were kept under the same conditions as the treated tadpoles. Why? Because if the "eternal tadpoles" had diets that differed from that of the others, the scientist wouldn't know whether it was Hormone X or the special diet that kept the eternal tadpoles from becoming frogs. Moreover, if their water was warmer than that of the others, maybe it was the warmth that somehow kept the tadpoles from developing. And if she didn't watch untreated tadpoles (a control group), she couldn't be sure whether under the same conditions a normal, untreated tadpole would also remain undeveloped.

Thus, a scientist creating a well-designed experiment will:

- Ensure that there's a single variable (like Hormone X) that varies from test to test or group to group.
- Ensure that all other factors (diet, temperature, space, etc.) remain the same.
- Ensure that there is a control group (tadpoles who don't get any Hormone X at all) for comparison purposes.

Results

One of the advantages to knowing how experiments work is that you can tell what a researcher is trying to find out about by seeing what she allows to vary. That's what is being researched—in this case, Hormone X. Data about things other than hormones and tadpole-to-frog development would be outside the design of the experiment. Information about other factors might be interesting but could not be part of a scientific proof.

For example, if some of the injected tadpoles that did grow into frogs later actually turned into princes, the data from experiments about the hormone they were given would not prove what causes frogs to become princes. But this data *could* be used to design another experiment intended to explore what could make a frog become a prince.

Therefore, whenever you see an experiment in Science, you should ask yourself:

1. **What's the factor that's being varied?** That is what is being tested.
2. **What's the control group?** It's the group that has nothing special done to it.
3. **What do the results show?** What differences exist between the results for the control group and those for the other group(s)? Or between the results for one treated group and those for another differently treated group?

> ☑ **PERFECT SCORE TIP**
> I found the Kaplan Method for experiment questions very useful. It helped me focus on what components of the design were important and deserved my attention.

HANDLING EXPERIMENT QUESTIONS

Following is a full-fledged Science passage organized around two experiments. Use the Kaplan Method, but this time, ask yourself the previous three questions. Take about five or six minutes to do the passage and its questions.

Passage II

A *mutualistic* relationship between two species increases the chances of growth or survival for both of them. Several species of fungi called *mycorrhizae* form mutualistic relationships with the roots of plants. The benefits to each species are shown in the figure below.

Figure 1

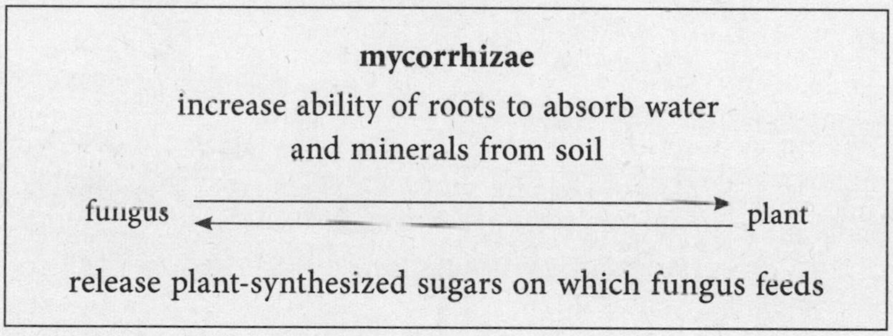

mycorrhizae

increase ability of roots to absorb water
and minerals from soil

fungus ⟵————————————⟶ plant

release plant-synthesized sugars on which fungus feeds

Some of the plant species that require or benefit from the presence of mycorrhizal fungi are noted below.

Cannot survive without mycorrhizae	Grow better with mycorrhizae
All conifers	Citrus trees
Some deciduous trees (e.g., birch, beech)	Ericaceae (heath, rhododendrons, azaleas), grapes
Orchids	Soybeans

Agronomists investigated the effects of mycorrhizae on plant growth and survival in the following studies.

STUDY 1

Three four-acre plots were prepared with soil from a pine forest. The soil for Plot A was mixed with substantial quantities of cultured mycorrhizal fungi. The soil for Plot B contained only naturally occurring mycorrhizal fungi. The soil for Plot C was sterilized in order to kill any mycorrhizal fungi. Additionally, Plot C was lined with concrete. After planting, Plot C was covered with a fabric that filtered out microorganisms while permitting air and light to penetrate. 250 pine seedlings were planted in each of the three plots. All plots received the same amount of water. The six-month survival rates were recorded in the following table.

Table 1

	Number of seedlings alive after 6 months	Utilization of available K (average)	Utilization of available P (average)
Plot A	107	18%	62%
Plot B	34	10%	13%
Plot C	0	N/A	N/A

N/A = not applicable

STUDY 2

The roots of surviving seedlings from Plots A and B were analyzed to determine how efficiently they absorbed potassium (K) and phosphorus (P) from the soil. The results were added to Table 1.

1. The most likely purpose of the concrete liner was:

   A. to block the seedlings from sending out taproots to water below the plot.

   B. to prevent mycorrhizal fungi in the surrounding soil from colonizing the plot.

   C. to absorb potassium and phosphorus from the soil for later analysis.

   D. to provide a firm foundation for mycorrhizal fungi in the plot.

2. Mycorrhizae are highly susceptible to acid rain. Given the information from the passage, acid rain is probably most harmful to:

   F. wheat fields.

   G. birch forests.

   H. orange groves.

   J. grape vines.

3. In a third study, pine seedlings were planted in soil from a different location. The soil was prepared as in Study 1. This time, the survival rates for seedlings planted in Plot A and Plot B were almost identical to each other. Which of the following theories would NOT help to explain these results?

    A. Sterilization killed all the naturally occurring mycorrhizal fungi in the new soil.

    B. The new soil was so mineral-deficient that it could not sustain life.

    C. The new soil was naturally more fertile for pine seedlings than that used in Study 1.

    D. Large quantities of mycorrhizal fungi occurred naturally in the new soil.

4. According to the passage, in which of the following ways do plants benefit from mycorrhizal associations?

    I. More efficient sugar production
    II. Enhanced ability to survive drought
    III. Increased mineral absorption

    F. I only

    G. III only

    H. II and III only

    J. I, II, and III

5. Which of the following generalizations is supported by the results of Study 2?

    A. Mycorrhizal fungi are essential for the survival of pine seedlings.

    B. Growth rates for pine seedlings may be improved by adding mycorrhizal fungi to the soil.

    C. Mycorrhizal fungi contain minerals that are not normally found in pine forest soil.

    D. Pine seedlings cannot absorb all the potassium that is present in the soil.

Answers

1. B
2. G
3. A
4. H
5. D

Answers and Explanations

Notice how many diagrams and tables were used here. That's common in experiment passages, where information is given to you in a wide variety of forms. Typically, though, the experiments themselves are clearly labeled, as Study 1 and Study 2 were here.

A quick preread of the introduction would have revealed the topic of the experiments here—the "mutualistic relationship" between some fungi and some plant roots. The fungi are called mycorrhizae ("myco" for short). The first diagram just shows you who gets what out of this relationship. The benefit accruing to the plant (the arrow pointing to the word *plant*) is an increased ability to absorb water and minerals. The benefit accruing to the *fungus* (the other arrow) is the plant-synthesized sugars on which the fungus feeds. That's the mutual benefit that the myco association creates.

Notice, by the way, that reading this first diagram alone is enough to answer **question 4**. The question is asking: what do the plants get out of the association? And we just answered that—increased ability to absorb water and minerals. Statement III is obviously correct, but so is Statement II, because increased water absorption would indeed enhance the plant's ability to survive drought (a drought is a shortage of water, after all). Statement I, though, is a distortion. We know that the fungi benefit from sugars produced by the plants, but we don't have any evidence that the association actually causes plants to produce sugar more efficiently. So I is out; II and III are in, making choice H the answer.

CAN'T LIVE WITHOUT THOSE FUNGI

Let's get back to the passage. We've just learned who gets what out of the myco association. Now we get a table that shows what *kinds* of plants enter into such associations. Some (those in the first column) are so dependent on myco associations that they can't live without them. Others (those in the second column) merely grow better with them; presumably, they could live without them.

Here again is a question we can answer based solely on information in this one table. **Question 2** tells us that mycos are highly susceptible to acid rain, and then asks what kind of plant communities would be most harmed by acid rain. Well, if acid rain hurts mycos, then the plants that are most dependent on myco fungi (that is, the ones listed in the first column) would be the most harmed by acid rain. Of the four choices, only birch forests—choice G—correspond to something in column 1 of the table. Birch trees can't even *survive* without myco fungi, so anything that hurts myco fungi would inferably hurt birch forests. (Grapevines and orange groves would also be hurt by acid rain, but not as much, since they *can* survive without myco fungi; meanwhile, we're told nothing about wheat in the passage.)

STUDY 1

Now look at the first experiment. Three plots, each with differently treated soil, are planted with pine seedlings. Plot A gets soil with cultivated myco fungi, Plot B gets untreated soil with only naturally occurring myco fungi, and Plot C gets no myco fungi at all since the soil has been sterilized and isolated (via the concrete lining and the fabric covering). Now ask yourself the three important Experiment questions:

1. **Find the factor being varied.** The factor being varied is the amount of myco fungi in the soil. Plot A gets lots; Plot B gets just the normal amount; Plot C gets none at all. It's clear, then, that the scientists are testing the effects of myco fungi on the growth of pine seedlings.

2. **Identify the control group.** The plants in Plot B, since they get untreated soil. To learn the effects of the fungi, the scientists will then compare the results from fungi-rich Plot A with the control and the results from fungi-poor Plot C with the same control.

3. **Analyze the results.** The results are listed in the first column of the table. And they are decisive: no seedlings at all survived in Plot C, 34 did in Plot B, and 107 did in Plot A. The minimums and maximums coincide. Minimum fungi = minimum number of surviving seedlings; maximum fungi = maximum number of surviving seedlings. Clearly, there's a cause-and-effect relationship here. Myco fungi probably help pine seedlings survive.

Questions 1 and 3 can be answered solely on the basis of Study 1. **Question 1** is merely a procedural question: why the concrete liner in Plot C? Well, in the analysis of the experiment above, we saw that the factor being varied was the amount of myco fungi. Plot C was designed to have none at all. Thus, one can safely assume that the concrete liner was probably there to prevent any stray myco fungi from entering the sterilized soil—choice B.

Question 3 actually sets up an extra experiment based on Study 1. The soils were prepared in the exact same way, except that the soil came from a different location.

The results? The number of surviving seedlings from Plots A and B were almost identical. What can that mean? Well, Plot A was supposed to be the fungi-rich plot, whereas Plot B (the control) was supposed to be the fungi-normal plot. But here they have the same results. However, notice that we're *not* told what those results are; it could be that no seedlings survived in any plots this time around.

The question—a reversal question—is phrased so that the three wrong choices are things that *could* explain the results; the correct choice will be the one that *can't*. Choices B, C, and D all *can* explain the results, since they all show how similar results could have been obtained from Plots A and B. If the new soil just couldn't support life—fungi or no fungi—well, Plots A and B would have gotten similar results; namely, no seedlings survive. On the other end of the spectrum, choices C and D show how the two plots might have gotten similarly *high* survival rates. If there were lots of myco fungi naturally in this soil (that's choice D), then there wouldn't be all that much difference between the soils in Plots A and B. If the soil were naturally extremely fertile for the pine seedlings (that's choice C), there must have been lots of fungi naturally present in the soil because pine trees (conifers) don't grow without fungi. So all three of these answers would help to explain similar results in Plots A and B.

Choice A, however, wouldn't help, because it talks about the sterilized soil that's in Plot C. The soil in Plot C won't affect the results in Plots A and B, so choice A is the answer here—the factor that *doesn't* help to explain the results.

STUDY 2

This study takes the surviving seedlings from Plots A and B in Study 1 and just tests how much potassium (K) and phosphorus (P) the roots have used. The results are listed in the second and third columns of the table. (Notice the N/A—not applicable—for Plot C in these columns, since there were no surviving seedlings to test in Plot C!) The data shows much better utilization of both substances in the Plot A seedlings, the seedlings that grew in a fungi-rich soil. This data would tend to support a theory that the myco fungi aid in the utilization of K and P and that this in turn aids survival in pine seedlings.

The only question that hinges on Study 2 is **question 5**. It asks what generalization would be supported by the specific results of Study 2. Notice that Study 2 involved only measuring K and P. It did not involve survival rates (that was Study 1), so choice A can't be right. And *neither* study measured growth rates, so B is out. The minerals K and P were in the control group's soil, which was natural, untreated pine forest soil, so choice C is clearly unsupported.

But the *data* did show that not all of the potassium (K) could be absorbed by pine seedlings. Only 18 percent was absorbed in Plot A, while only 10 percent was absorbed in Plot B. That's a long way from 100 percent, so choice D is a safe generalization to make.

> **EXPERT TUTOR TIP**
> Many questions on experiment passages will be answerable based solely on the data contained in a single graph or table. You can get these points with relative ease, even if you don't have time for, or don't fully understand, the experiments.

THE REAL THING: PRACTICE PASSAGE

Now that we've taken you step-by-step through a Science passage based on an experiment, it's time to try one on your own. Give yourself about six minutes for the next passage and questions. This time the explanations at the end will be very short:

Passage III

The following flowchart shows the steps used by a chemist in testing sample solutions for positive ions of silver (Ag), lead (Pb), and mercury (Hg).

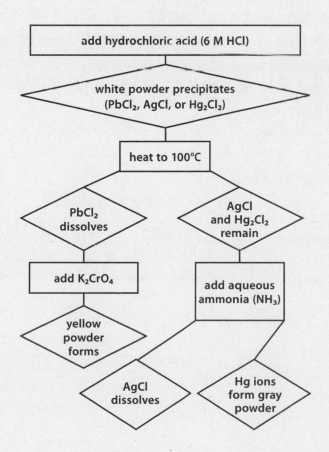

The following experiments were performed by the chemist:

EXPERIMENT 1

Hydrochloric acid (6 M HCl) was added to samples of four unknown solutions labeled 1, 2, 3, and 4. A white powder precipitated out of solutions 1, 2, and 3; no precipitate formed in solution 4.

EXPERIMENT 2

Each of the sample solutions from Experiment 1 was placed in a 100°C water bath for 15 minutes. The precipitate in solution 1 redissolved completely; solutions 2 and 3 still contained a white powder; solution 4 was unchanged. Solutions 2 and 3 were centrifuged to remove the precipitates, which were retained for further testing. Potassium chromate (K_2CrO_4) was then added to each sample. A bright yellow precipitate formed in solutions 1 and 2; none formed in solutions 3 or 4.

EXPERIMENT 3

The white powder centrifuged from solutions 2 and 3 in Experiment 2 was treated with aqueous ammonia (NH_3). The precipitate from solution 2 returned into solution, while that from solution 3 produced a gray powder.

⊙ SCIENTIFIC REASONING

6. Which conclusion is best supported by the results of Experiment 1 alone?

   F. Silver ions are present only in solution 3.

   G. No ions are present in solution 4.

   H. Lead ions are present in solutions 1, 2, and 3.

   J. No positive ions of silver, mercury, or lead are present in solution 4.

⊙ SCIENTIFIC REASONING

7. Based on the experimental results, which ions did solution 2 contain?

   A. Lead ions only

   B. Lead and silver ions only

   C. Silver and mercury ions only

   D. Silver ions only

⊙ SCIENTIFIC REASONING

8. The yellow precipitate that formed in Experiment 2 was most likely:

   F. AgCl.

   G. Hg_2Cl_2.

   H. $PbCrO_4$.

   J. Ag_2CrO_4.

⊙ FIGURE INTERPRETATION

9. The experimental results suggest that if lead chloride ($PbCl_2$) were treated with aqueous ammonia (NH_3), the results would be:

   A. a bright yellow precipitate.

   B. a light gray precipitate.

   C. a powdery white precipitate.

   D. impossible to determine from the information given.

.ıⅡⅼ FIGURE INTERPRETATION

10. A student proposed that the analysis could be carried out more efficiently by heating the samples to 100°C before adding the 6 M HCl. This suggestion is:

    F. a bad idea; since $PbCl_2$ will not precipitate out of solution at this temperature, lead ions would be undetectable.

    G. a bad idea; the hot solutions could not be safely centrifuged.

    H. a good idea; the number of steps would be reduced from 3 to 2, saving much time and effort.

    J. a good idea; the chloride-forming reaction would proceed faster, eliminating the necessity for a 15-minute water bath.

Answers

6. J
7. B
8. H
9. D
10. F

Answers and Explanations

This experiment passage was somewhat different from the preceding one. In the mycor-rhiza experiment, the scientists were thinking in specific-to-general terms (observing the growth of specific pine seedlings to come to a conclusion about the general effect of myco fungi on pine seedlings). In this series of experiments, the general principle is known—silver, lead, and mercury will precipitate or dissolve when certain things are done to them—and the scientists are using this principle to test certain substances in order to identify them. In fact, this is more like a procedure than an experiment, since there's no control group. But the same kind of experimental thinking—using the results of varying procedures to make reasonable inferences about what's happening—will get you your answers.

This passage also introduces the idea of a flowchart. Basically, the flowchart indicates an order of procedures. You follow the flowchart from top to bottom. The things in squares indicate what's done to a specimen; the things in diamonds indicate possible results.

Let's say you have an unknown substance. Following the flowchart, the first thing you do is add hydrochloric acid. If a white powder precipitates, that means there are positive ions of silver, lead, and/or mercury. (If nothing precipitates, the experiment is over; the substance is not of interest here.)

But, assuming you do get a white powder, how do you identify exactly which kind of white powder you have? You do the next procedure—heat it to 100°C. When you do this, any lead ions will dissolve, but any silver or mercury ions will remain as a powder. So the flowchart has to divide here.

If part of your specimen dissolved when heated, that doesn't necessarily mean you have lead ions. To test for that, you add K_2CrO_4. If a yellow powder forms, then you know you've got lead; if not, you've got something else.

But what about the other branch? That tells you what has to be done if you *do* have some powder remaining after heating. And what you do is add NH_3. If the powder dissolves, you've got silver ions. If it forms a gray powder, on the other hand, what you've got are mercury (Hg) ions.

The three experiments here are actually three parts of a single experiment or procedure, each one using the results of the former in the way outlined in the flowchart. The questions ask for results at various points in the procedure, so let's look at them briefly now.

Key to Passage III

	Answer	Refer to	Comments
6.	J	Experiment 1 only	If any Ag, Pb, or Hg ions were present, they would have precipitated out as powder. Note that G is too extreme (could be ions of a fourth type not within scope of the experiment). Not enough testing in Exp. 1 to determine F or H.
7.	B	All three experiments	Heating created leftover powder, so substance 2 has to have Ag or Hg or both—cut A. Addition of K_2CrO_4 left yellow precipitate, so it must contain Pb (cut C and D).
8.	H	Experiment 2	Must be lead-based, because Ag and Hg precipitates were already removed (cut F, G, and J).
9.	D	Flowchart	No evidence for what would happen—two different branches of the flowchart.
10.	F	Flowchart	If the solutions were heated first, and then the HCl was added, the $PbCl_2$ would never form; the chemist would not know whether lead ions were present.

As you've seen, not all experiments on the ACT Science subject test are specific-to-general experiments; some are general-to-specific procedures. But the same kind of strict thinking—manipulating factors to narrow down possibilities—can get you points, no matter what direction you're thinking in.

GO ONLINE
Review Science strategies on your downloadable study sheet.

EXPERT TUTOR TIP
If you get stuck on a problem, see what answer choices you can eliminate. The more you eliminate, the closer you are to the correct answer.

▶ IF YOU LEARNED ONLY THREE THINGS IN THIS CHAPTER...

1. When you encounter experiment questions, identify the factor being varied, the control group (if any), and how results vary between groups.

2. Look for Figure Interpretation questions first—they'll get you the quickest points.

3. Some scenarios ask you to make inferences about data (specific-to-general); others ask you to use general ideas to determine what will happen in a particular case (general-to-specific).

CHAPTER 15

Science Workout 3: Keep Your Viewpoints Straight

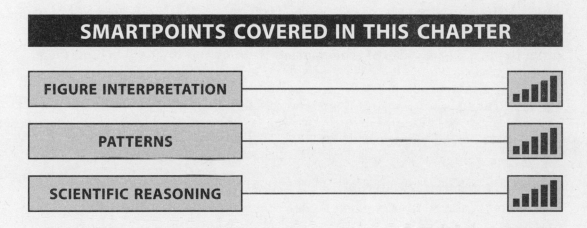

On the Science test, you'll find one Conflicting Viewpoints passage, in which two scientists propose different theories about a particular scientific phenomenon. Often, the two theories are just differing interpretations of the same data; other times, each scientist offers his own data to support his own opinion. In either case, it's essential that you know more or less what theory each scientist is proposing and that you pay careful attention to how and where their theories differ.

In Science Workout 2, we talked about how scientists think, and you should bring all of that information to bear on the Conflicting Viewpoints passage. Because the scientists are disagreeing on interpretation, it's usually the case that they're engaging in specific-to-general thinking. They're each using specific data, sometimes the *same* specific data, but they're coming to very different general conclusions.

> ✔️ **PERFECT SCORE TIP**
> On the Conflicting Viewpoints passages, I found it helpful to briefly summarize each one—just like a Reading passage. This helped keep me focused and engaged in the passage.

Your job is *not* to figure out which scientist is right and which is wrong. Instead, you'll be tested on whether you *understand* each scientist's position and the thinking behind it.

PREREADING THE CONFLICTING VIEWPOINTS PASSAGE

When tackling the Conflicting Viewpoints passage, you'll probably want to spend a little more time than usual on the prereading step of the Kaplan Reading Method. As we saw on other Science passages, your goal in prereading is to get a general idea of what's going on so that you can focus when you do the questions. But we find that **it pays to spend a little extra time with the Conflicting Viewpoints passage in order to get a clearer idea of the opposing theories and the data behind them.**

> 👤 **EXPERT TUTOR TIP**
> This passage is usually the hardest passage for students. Don't worry! There is only one passage like this, and you can save it for last if it is easier for you.

The passage will usually consist of a short introduction laying out the scientific issue in question, followed by the different viewpoints. Sometimes these viewpoints are presented under the headings Scientist 1 and Scientist 2, or Theory 1 and Theory 2, or Hypothesis 1 and Hypothesis 2.

A scientific viewpoint on the ACT will typically consist of two parts:

1. **A statement of the general theory**
2. **A summary of the data behind the theory**

Usually, the first line of each viewpoint expresses the general theory. Scientist 1's first sentence might be something like: *The universe will continue to expand indefinitely.* This is Scientist 1's viewpoint boiled down to a single statement. Scientist 2's first sentence might be: *The force of gravity will eventually force the universe to stop expanding and to begin contracting.* This is Scientist 2's viewpoint, and it clearly contradicts Scientist 1's opinion.

While it's important that you understand these basic statements of theory, it is just as important that you see how they oppose each other. In fact, you might want to circle the theory statement for each viewpoint, right there in the test booklet, to fix the two positions in your mind.

> ☑ **PERFECT SCORE TIP**
> I found it helpful to write down the opinions of each author (pro or con) so I didn't confuse them. If you confuse the two authors' opinions, you will lose valuable points, as most of the questions are based around you not mixing up their viewpoints.

After each statement of theory will come the data that's behind it. As we said, sometimes the scientists are just drawing different interpretations from the same data. But usually, each will have different supporting data. There are two different kinds of data:

1. **Data that supports the scientist's own theory**
2. **Data that weakens the opposing scientist's theory**

It's normally a good idea to identify the major points of data for each theory. You might underline a phrase or sentence that crystallizes each, or even take note of whether it primarily supports the scientist's own theory or shoots holes in the opposing theory.

Once you understand each scientist's theory and the data behind it, you'll be ready to move on to the questions. Remember that some of the questions will refer to only one of the viewpoints. **Whatever you do, *don't mix up the two viewpoints!*** A question asking about the data supporting Theory 2 may have wrong answers that perfectly describe the data for Theory 1. If you're careless, you can easily fall for one of these wrong answers.

THE REAL THING: PRACTICE PASSAGE

What follows is a full-fledged, ACT-style Conflicting Viewpoints passage. Give yourself six minutes or so to read the passage and do all seven questions.

Passage IV

Tektites are natural, glassy objects that range in size from the diameter of a grain of sand to that of a human fist. They are found in only a few well-defined areas, called strewn fields. Two theories about the origin of tektites are presented here.

SCIENTIST 1

Tektites almost certainly are extraterrestrial, probably lunar, in origin. Their forms show the characteristics of air-friction melting. In one study, flanged "flying saucer" shapes similar to those of australites (a common tektite form) were produced by ablating lenses of tektite glass in a heated airstream that simulated atmospheric entry.

Atmospheric forces also make terrestrial origin extremely improbable. Aerodynamic studies have shown that because of atmospheric density, tektite-like material ejected from the Earth's surface would never attain a velocity much higher than that of the surrounding air, and therefore would not be shaped by atmospheric friction. Most likely, tektites were formed either from meteorites or from lunar material ejected in volcanic eruptions.

Analysis of specimen #14425 from the *Apollo 12* lunar mission shows that the sample strongly resembles some of the tektites from the Australasian strewn field. Also, tektites contain only a small fraction of the water that is locked into the structure of terrestrial volcanic glass. And tektites never contain unmelted crystalline material; the otherwise similar terrestrial glass produced by some meteorite impacts **always** does.

SCIENTIST 2

Nonlocal origin is extremely unlikely, given the narrow distribution of tektite strewn fields. Even if a tightly focused jet of lunar matter were to strike the Earth, whatever was deflected by the atmosphere would remain in a solar orbit. The next time its orbit coincided with that of the Earth, some of the matter would be captured by Earth's gravity and fall over a wide area.

There are striking similarities not only between the composition of the Earth's crust and that of most tektites but also between the proportions of various gases found in the Earth's atmosphere and also the vesicles of certain tektites.

Tektites were probably formed by meteorite impacts. The shock wave produced by a major collision could temporarily displace the atmosphere above. Terrestrial material might then splatter to suborbital heights and undergo air-friction melting upon reentry. And tektite fields in the Ivory Coast and Ghana can be correlated with known impact craters.

.ııl SCIENTIFIC REASONING

1. The discovery that many tektites contain unmelted, crystalline material would:

   A. tend to weaken Scientist 1's argument.

   B. tend to weaken Scientist 2's argument.

   C. be incompatible with both scientists' views.

   D. be irrelevant to the controversy.

2. Which of the following is a reason given by Scientist 2 for believing that tektites originate on the Earth?

   F. The density of the Earth's atmosphere would prevent any similar lunar or extraterrestrial material from reaching the Earth's surface.

   G. Tektites have a composition totally unlike that of any material ever brought back from the moon.

   H. Extraterrestrial material could not have been as widely dispersed as tektites are.

   J. Material ejected from the moon or beyond would eventually have been much more widely distributed on Earth.

3. Scientist 1 could best answer the point that some tektites have vesicles filled with gases in the same proportion as the Earth's atmosphere by:

   A. countering that not all tektites have such gas-filled vesicles.

   B. demonstrating that molten material would be likely to trap some gases while falling through the terrestrial atmosphere.

   C. suggesting that those gases might occur in the same proportions in the moon's atmosphere.

   D. showing that similar vesicles, filled with these gases in the same proportions, are also found in some terrestrial volcanic glass.

4. How did Scientist 2 answer the argument that tektite-like material ejected from the Earth could not reach a high enough velocity relative to the atmosphere to undergo air friction melting?

   F. By asserting that a shock wave might cause a momentary change in atmosphere density, permitting subsequent aerodynamic heating

   G. By pointing out that periodic meteorite impacts have caused gradual changes in atmospheric density over the eons

   H. By attacking the validity of the aerodynamic studies cited by Scientist 1

   J. By referring to the correlation between tektite fields and known impact craters in the Ivory Coast and Ghana

5. The point of subjecting lenses of tektite glass to a heated airstream was to:

   A. determine their water content.

   B. see if gases became trapped in their vesicles.

   C. reproduce the effects of atmospheric entry.

   D. simulate the mechanism of meteorite formation.

6. Researchers could best counter the objections of Scientist 2 to Scientist 1's argument by:

   F. discovering some phenomenon that would quickly remove tektite-sized objects from orbit.

   G. proving that most common tektite shapes can be produced by aerodynamic heating.

   H. confirming that active volcanoes once existed on the moon.

   J. mapping the locations of all known tektite fields and impact craters.

7. Which of the following characteristics of tektites is LEAST consistent with the theory that tektites are of extraterrestrial origin?

   A. Low water content

   B. "Flying saucer" shapes

   C. Narrow distribution

   D. Absence of unmelted material

Answers

1. A
2. J
3. B
4. F
5. C
6. F
7. C

Answers and Explanations

Your preread of the introduction should have revealed the issue at hand—namely, tektites, which are small glassy objects found in certain areas known as strewn fields. The conflict is about the *origin* of these objects: In other words, where did they come from?

 EXPERT TUTOR TIP
Keep viewpoints straight:

1. Read the intro and Scientist 1 passage.
2. Answer questions that say Scientist 1.
3. Read Scientist 2 paragraph.
4. Answer Scientist 2 questions.
5. Answer any other questions.

Scientist 1's theory is expressed in his first sentence: "Tektites almost certainly are extraterrestrial, probably lunar, in origin." Put that into a form you can understand: Scientist 1 believes that tektites come from space, probably the moon. On the other hand, Scientist 2 has an opposing theory, also expressed in her first sentence: "Nonlocal origin is extremely unlikely." In other words, it's unlikely that tektites came from a nonlocal source; they probably came from a *local* source, i.e., right here on Earth. The conflict is clear. One says that tektites come from space; the other says they come from Earth. You might have even labeled the two positions "space origin" and "Earth origin."

Scientist 1 presents three points of data:

1. Tektite shapes show characteristics of "air-friction melting" (supporting the theory of space origin).

2. "Atmospheric forces" wouldn't be great enough to shape tektite-like material ejected from Earth's surface (weakening the theory of Earth origin).

3. Tektites resemble moon rocks gathered by *Apollo 12* but not Earth rocks (strengthening the theory of space origin).

Scientist 2 also presents three points of data:

1. Any matter coming from space would "fall over a wide area" instead of being concentrated in strewn fields (weakening the theory of space origin).

2. There are "striking similarities" between tektites and the composition of the Earth's crust (strengthening the theory of Earth origin).

3. "Meteorite impacts" could create shock waves, explaining how terrestrial material could undergo air-friction melting (strengthening the theory of Earth origin by counteracting Scientist 1's first point).

Obviously, you won't have time to write out the supporting data for each theory the way we've done above. But it is important to circle or bracket the key phrases in the data descriptions ("air-friction melting," *"Apollo 12,"* etc.) and number them. **What's important is that you have an idea of what data supports which theory.** The questions, once you get to them, will then force you to focus.

> **EXPERT TUTOR TIP**
> Active Reading in the Conflicting Viewpoints passage will make it easier to find the information you need to answer questions correctly.

Question 1 asks how it would affect the scientists' arguments if it were discovered that many tektites contain unmelted crystalline material. Well, Scientist 1 says that tektites never contain unmelted crystalline material and that the terrestrial glass produced by some meteorite impacts *always* does. Therefore, by showing a resemblance between tektites and Earth materials, this discovery would weaken Scientist 1's argument for extraterrestrial origin. **Choice A is correct.**

For **question 2**, you had to identify which answer choice was used by Scientist 2 to support the argument that tektites are terrestrial in origin. You should have been immediately drawn to choice J, which expresses what we've identified above as Scientist 2's first data point. Notice how choice F is a piece of evidence that Scientist 1 cites. (Remember not to confuse the viewpoints!) As for choice G, Scientist 2 says that tektites *do* resemble Earth materials, but never says that they *don't* resemble lunar materials. And choice H gets it backwards; Scientist 2 says that extraterrestrial material *would* be widely dispersed and that the tektites are *not* widely dispersed, rather than vice versa.

> **EXPERT TUTOR TIP**
> Many Conflicting Viewpoints questions relate to *evidence* (or *data*). You may be asked: What was presented? Why? Would it help or hurt a scientist's claim?

For **question 3**, you need to find the best way for Scientist 1 to counter the point that some tektites have vesicles filled with gases in the same proportion as the Earth's atmosphere. First, make sure you understand the meaning of that point. The idea that these gases must have been trapped in the vesicles (little holes) while the rock was actually being formed is being used by Scientist 2 to suggest that tektites are of terrestrial origin. Scientist 1 *could* say that not all tektites have such gas-filled vesicles—choice A—but that's not a great argument. If any reasonable number of them *do*, Scientist 1 would have to come up with an alternative explanation (Scientist 2 **never** claimed that *all* tektites contained these vesicles). But if, as choice B suggests, Scientist 1 could demonstrate that molten material would be likely to trap some terrestrial gases while falling through Earth's atmosphere, this would explain how tektites might have come from beyond Earth and still contain vesicles filled with Earth-like gases. Choice C is easy to eliminate if you know that the moon's atmosphere is extremely thin and totally different in composition from Earth's atmosphere. Unlike correct choice B, it doesn't explain how the trapped gas made it to Earth. Finally, since it's Scientist 2 who claims that tektites are terrestrial in origin, choice D, showing that similar gas-filled vesicles occur in some terrestrial volcanic glass, this wouldn't help Scientist 1 at all.

In **question 4**, you're asked how Scientist 2 answered the argument that tektite-like material ejected from the Earth could not reach a high enough velocity to undergo air-friction melting. Well, that was Scientist 2's third data point. The shock wave produced by a major meteorite collision could momentarily displace the atmosphere right above the impact site (meaning the air moved out of the way for a brief time). So when the splattered material reentered the atmosphere, it would undergo air-friction melting. That's basically what choice F says, making it the correct answer.

In **question 5**, the concept of subjecting lenses of tektite glass to a heated airstream was mentioned toward the beginning of Scientist 1's argument. The point was to simulate the entry of extraterrestrial tektite material through Earth's atmosphere, which is closest to choice C.

Question 6 shows again why it pays to keep each scientist's viewpoint straight. You can't counter the objections of Scientist 2 to Scientist 1's argument unless you know what Scientist 2 was objecting to. Scientist 2's first data point is the only one designed to shoot holes in the opposing viewpoint. There, Scientist 2 takes issue with the idea that lunar material could strike the Earth without being dispersed over a far wider area than the known strewn fields. But, as correct choice F says, if researchers found some force capable of removing tektite-sized objects from orbit *quickly*, it would demolish the objection that Scientist 2 raises in her first paragraph. The tektite material would strike the Earth or be pulled away quickly, instead of remaining in a solar orbit long enough to be captured by the Earth's gravity and subsequently be distributed over a wide area of the Earth.

Question 7 wasn't too tough if you read the question stem carefully. You want to find the tektite characteristic that is LEAST consistent with the theory that tektites came from the moon or beyond. This is Scientist 1's theory, so you want to pick the answer choice that doesn't go with his argument. Scientist 1's evidence *does* include tektites' low water content, "flying saucer" shapes, and absence of unmelted material. The only answer choice that he didn't mention was the narrow distribution of the strewn fields. And with good reason. That's part of Scientist 2's argument *against* an extraterrestrial origin. So the correct answer is choice C.

> **EXPERT TUTOR TIP**
> If a passage looks very difficult for you, skip it. Do the easy passages first, then come back to the passages that look like they are harder.

THE DEEP END: FACING TOUGH SCIENCE PASSAGES

Now we're going to do something very cruel. We're going to throw you a Science passage of such technical difficulty that you will want to go screaming for the exit before you finish reading it.

> **PERFECT SCORE TIP**
> I know how stressful the Science section can get. It is the fourth section, and you are given passages about things you could never hope to understand. Take a deep breath when you get to difficult Science questions, and remember that you have strategies to tackle them.

We're doing this for a reason. Sometimes on the ACT Science test, you'll find yourself encountering a bear of a passage—one that seems entirely incomprehensible. **The secret to success with these passages is:** *don't panic.* As we'll show you, you can get points on even the most difficult Science passage in the entire history of the ACT—as long as you keep your cool and approach it in a savvy, practical way. Here's the passage:

Passage V

Neutrinos (n) are subatomic particles that travel at approximately the speed of light. They can penetrate most matter, because they are electrically neutral and effectively massless.

Generally accepted theory holds that the nuclear reactions that power the sun create vast quantities of neutrinos as byproducts. Three proposed stages

(PPI, PPII, and PPIII) of the most important solar reaction are shown in Figure 1, along with their neutrino-producing subpaths. Equations for the subpaths are shown in Table 1, as are the predicted neutrino energies and fluxes.

Figure 1

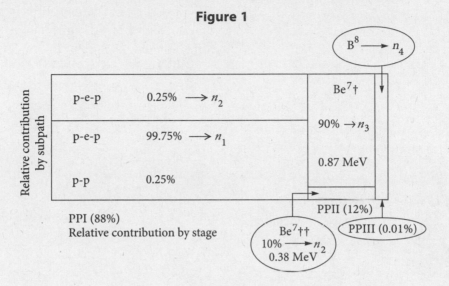

Table 1

Subpath name	Subpath equation	Neutrino energy (MeV)	Expected flux on Earth (10^{10} cm^{-2} sec^{-1})
p-p	$_1H^1 + {_1}H^1 \longrightarrow {_1}H^2 + \beta^+ + n$	0.42	6.06781
p-e-p	$_1H^1 + \beta^- + {_1}H^1 \longrightarrow {_1}H^2 + n$	1.44	0.01524
Be^7†	$_4Be^7 + \beta^- \longrightarrow {_3}Li^7 + n$	0.87	0.43924
Be^7††	$_4Be^7 + \beta^- \longrightarrow {_3}Li^7 + n$	0.38	0.04880
B^8	$_5B^8 \longrightarrow {_4}Be^8 + \beta^+ + n$	14.05*	0.00054

†Be^7 subpath 1
††Be^7 subpath 2

*Maximum

.ıll FIGURE INTERPRETATION

8. According to the information presented in the passage, which of the following stages or subpaths should contribute the smallest portion of the total solar neutrino flux on Earth?

F. p-p

G. PPI

H. PPII

J. PPIII

｜ FIGURE INTERPRETATION

9. Of the neutrinos that are produced in the subpaths described in the passage, which type can have the greatest energy?

   A. n_1

   B. n_2

   C. n_3

   D. n_4

｜ PATTERNS

10. Based on the information presented in the passage, the percentage of solar neutrinos produced by Be^7 subpath 2 is approximately:

    F. 1.2%.

    G. 10%.

    H. 12%.

    J. 90%.

｜ FIGURE INTERPRETATION

11. Solar neutrinos are detected through a reaction with $_{37}Cl$ for which the minimum neutrino energy is approximately 0.8 MeV. Of the neutrinos discussed in the passage, this method would detect:

    A. all of the neutrinos produced in PPI and PPII.

    B. some of the neutrinos produced in PPI, PPII, and PPIII.

    C. only neutrinos produced in Be^7 subpath 1 of PPII.

    D. only neutrinos produced in PPIII.

｜ SCIENTIFIC REASONING

12. The symbol β represents a beta particle, a particle emitted during nuclear decay. Beta particles may be positively or negatively charged. During which of the following subpaths are beta particles emitted?

    I. p-p

    II. p-e-p

    III. B^8

    F. II only

    G. I and III only

    H. II and III only

    J. I, II, and III

Answers

8. J
9. D
10. F
11. B
12. G

Answers and Explanations

Confused? If you aren't, you should stick close to your phone, because the Nobel Prize committee will probably be calling sometime soon! On the other hand, if you *are* confused, don't sweat it. **As we said in ACT Basics, some ACT questions are so hard that even your *teachers* would have a hard time getting them correct.**

> ☑ **PERFECT SCORE TIP**
> The most important thing to remember for Science is that you do not have to understand everything that is said. For example, you do not have to have any idea whatsoever what PPIII is to answer question 8. In fact, they don't expect you to.

The good news is that you don't have to understand a passage to get a few questions right. Here's how you might have approached the previous passage:

GETTING POINTS EVEN IF YOU DON'T GET THE POINT

Your preread of the introduction should have told you that the passage is about neutrinos coming from the sun. But that may be all you were able to get from this gibberish. You may have been in a total fog looking at Figure 1 and Table 1. But if you didn't panic, you might have noticed a few things: First, that whatever Figure 1 illustrates, there are some really big parts and some really small parts. If you look at the *x*-axis of the chart, you'll see that, whatever PPI, PPII, and PPIII are, the first is 88 percent, the second only 12 percent, and the third only 0.01 percent.

Is that tiny, vague insight enough to get a point? Yes! Look at **question 8**. It asks which stage or subpath contributes the *smallest* portion of flux. Well, look for a small portion. PPIII's figure of 0.01 percent is a very small number, whatever it's supposed to be referring to, so PPIII would be a good guess here. And indeed, choice J is correct for question 8.

What about Table 1? This is a little easier to understand, especially if you ignore the column about subpath equations. But "neutrino energy" sounds like something we can comprehend. Apparently, each subpath produces a different level of neutrino energy. Some have high energy (like B^8, with 14.06), and some have low energy (like Be^7††, with only 0.38). Energy is mentioned in **question 9**. Which type of neutrinos can have the greatest energy? Well, if B^8 were a choice, we'd pick that. But the choices are *n*s, not Bs. Well, try to find B^8 somewhere in the other chart—Figure 1. There, we find it somehow associated with n_4 neutrinos. So take a gamble; choose n_4—which is choice D—for this question. If you did that, you'd still have gotten another point, still without really understanding much more than before.

You're hot; keep it going. **Question 10** refers to Be^7 subpath 2. You may have noticed in the note under Table 1 that the Be^7 with two little dagger marks signifies subpath 2. So far, so good. Notice that the choices are all percentages. Where are percentages mentioned? In Figure 1. So find Be^7 with two dagger marks in Figure 1. You find it in the area of PPII, which is 12 percent of the *x*-axis in that chart. But notice that Be^7 with two dagger marks represents only *part* of that part of the figure— 10 percent, to be exact. So 10 percent of 12 percent would be 1.2 percent. That's choice F. It's also the correct answer.

Things get a little harder with **question 11**, but you still might have gotten the answer if you used common sense. Here we get some mumbo jumbo about $_{37}Cl$, but the part of the question that should have caught your eye was the bit about a minimum neutrino energy of 0.8 MeV. Neutrino energy was represented in the third column of Table 1. According to that table, only three subpaths have an energy greater than 0.8—p-e-p (with 1.44), Be^7 with one dagger mark (with 0.87), and B^8 (the champion, with 14.06). Unfortunately, the answer choices aren't expressed in those terms; they're expressed in terms of PPI, II, and III, so we're going to have to translate from table to figure again, just as we did with **question 9**.

Take p-e-p first. That's part (but not all) of the PPI portion of Figure 1. Be^7 with one dagger mark, similarly, is part (but not all) of the PPII portion. And B^8 is all of the PPIII portion. So there are at least parts of PPI, PPII, and PPIII implicated here. That should have led you to choice B, which would have gotten you yet another point. Notice that choice A is inaccurate because it talks about *all* of something in PPI and PPII and doesn't mention PPIII at all. Choices C and D, meanwhile, seem too limited, since they only mention one of the PP areas (whatever they are). So B is definitely the right answer choice.

Finally, **question 12** talks about beta particles. Well, that little beta symbol appears only in the subpath equation column of Table 1. There, we find beta symbols in the equations for *all* of the subpaths in the table. That may have led you to believe that all three Roman numerals should be included, and no one would have blamed you for choosing choice J (I, II, and III). You would have been wrong, but you can't win them all when you're winging questions you don't really understand.

Of course, if you noticed that the question was asking for beta particles *emitted,* and if you knew that in the subpath equations everything *before* the arrow is what you start with while everything *after* the arrow is what you finish with, you might have been able to make a better guess. You would have realized that those equations with a beta symbol *before* the arrow were ones in which a beta particle was *absorbed,* while those with a beta symbol *after* the arrow were ones in which a beta particle was *emitted*. In that case, then, you would have seen that the equations for p-p and B^8 do have beta particles emitted, while the equation for p-e-p does not. That might have led you to choice G—I and III only—which is the correct answer.

Six questions, six points—and all without understanding the passage in any deep or thorough way. Of course, if you understand the mysteries of neutrino flux and p-e-p subpaths, congratulations. You're probably enough of a science whiz to ace the subject test anyway. But if you're like most ACT test takers, you won't understand everything the passages talk about. Sometimes you'll even find yourself totally lost.

The moral of the story, of course, is **don't give up on a passage just because you don't understand it.** You may not be able to get *every* point associated with the passage, but you may be able to get at least one or two (or three or four). Remember: The test is designed in such a way that you can *figure out* many of the questions, even if you don't know the subject area.

Let's conclude now with another quick point about getting quick points. If you're nearly out of time and you've still got a whole Science passage left, you need to shift to last-minute strategies. As in Reading, don't try to preread the passage, or you'll just run out of time before you answer any questions. Instead, scan the questions without reading the passage and look first for the ones that require only reading data off of a graph or table. You can often get a couple of quick points just by knowing how to find data quickly.

Again, the most important thing is to make sure you have gridded in at least a random guess on every question.

> ✔ **PERFECT SCORE TIP**
> The advice that cannot be repeated enough times is to answer every question. If you are running out of time, be sure to guess on every answer. Even one lucky guess could boost your score.

> ## IF YOU LEARNED ONLY THREE THINGS IN THIS CHAPTER...
>
> 1. Each ACT Science test has one Conflicting Viewpoints passage in which two scientists debate an issue.
>
> 2. Spend more time prereading Conflicting Viewpoints passages. Determine each scientist's view and identify the supporting and undermining evidence.
>
> 3. You can get many Science questions right even when you don't understand the entire passage. Don't panic when faced with a tough passage.

CHAPTER 16

Writing Workout: Write What Counts

A growing number of colleges want an assessment of your written communication skills. If you consider yourself a good writer and are accustomed to scoring well on essays, there may be a temptation to skip this chapter. Don't—top scores are not given out easily, and writing a scored first draft in under a half hour is unlike most of your past writing experiences.

In addition, the ACT essay is not a typical essay that you are used to writing in school. For example: you are allowed (even encouraged) to use the first person *I* and *we* in your argument. Personal experiences are excellent ways to back up your position. If you need to embroider the facts a little to make your point, no one is going to fact-check your essay.

> **GO ONLINE**
> Your online companion contains two practice essay prompts (in addition to the one in this chapter). After you test yourself, evaluate your essays by comparing them to the model essays provided.

Let's start with the basics.

JUST THE FACTS

Writing has **always** been an essential skill for college success. The ACT includes an optional Writing test. Some colleges require it; others do not. **Before registering for the ACT, find out if the schools to which you're applying want applicants to take the Writing test.**

The ACT English test measures knowledge of effective writing skills, including grammar, punctuation, organization, and style. The Writing test complements that evaluation of technical skill with an example of your simple, direct writing.

How the ACT Essay Is Scored

Your essay will be graded on a holistic scale of 1–6 (6 being the best). Graders will be looking for an overall sense of your essay, not assigning separate scores for specific elements like grammar or organization. Two readers read and score each essay; then those scores are added together to arrive at your Writing subscore (from 2–12). If there's a difference of more than a point between the two readers' scores, your essay will be read by a third reader.

Statistically speaking, there will be few essays that score 6. If each grader gives your essay a 4 or 5, that will place you at the upper range of those taking the exam.

> ✔ **PERFECT SCORE TIP**
> I suggest taking the Writing section if you think there is any chance a college you want to go to might want it. Being forced to retake such a long test sounds more painful than just preparing for Writing in the first place.

What Should I Do?

The readers realize you're writing under time pressure and so expect you to make some mistakes. **The facts in your essay are not important; readers are not checking your facts. Nor will they judge you on your opinions. They want to see how well you can communicate a relevant, coherent point of view.**

The test makers identify the following as the skills tested in the Writing test:

- **Answer the question in the prompt.** State a clear perspective on an issue.

- **Build an argument.** Assemble supporting evidence logically with relevant, specific points.

- **Maintain focus and organize your specific points logically.** Avoid digressions and be sure to draw everything together in a concluding paragraph.

- **Address the complexity of the issue.** Discuss BOTH sides of the argument. Don't ignore the opposite side.

- **Write clearly.** Make sure your argument is easy to follow. Grammar rules are not the point of the essay; however, errors that interfere with the essay's argument will hurt your score.

Can I Prepare for the Essay?

The underlying skill in the Writing test is speed. On the ACT, you have only 30 minutes, and you must accomplish a lot in that time. It takes practice to read the prompt, organize your position with relevant ideas and facts, write a concluding paragraph—and proofread!

> ☑ **PERFECT SCORE TIP**
> The key to the ACT essay really is clarity. The graders want to see if you can logically put together an argument, and they don't want to waste their time trying to decode cryptic language, so make your points clear and obvious.

Do You Need to Prepare for the Essay?

The ACT essay is not like other writing experiences. It's a first draft that will be graded. Not only must it be complete and well organized, but it must also be easy for a grader to see that it is complete and well organized (and the grader may spend as little as a minute reading your essay). That's a lot to do in 30 minutes, so preparation and practice are essential.

> 👤 **EXPERT TUTOR TIP**
> By the way, practicing the ACT essay also reinforces what you've learned for the English test and strengthens your Reading test skills: in Reading, you take an argument apart; in Writing, you put together an argument.

THE KAPLAN METHOD FOR THE ACT ESSAY

STEP 1: Prompt
STEP 2: Plan
STEP 3: Produce
STEP 4: Proofread

If you plan your essay and adhere to your plan when you write, the result will be solidly organized. Between now and test day, you can't drastically change your overall writing skills—and you probably don't need to. **If your plan is good, all you need to do in the writing and proofreading steps is draw on your strengths and avoid your weaknesses.** Get to know what those are as you practice.

Write what counts: To maximize your score, use the Kaplan Method to help you focus on writing what the scorers will look for—*and nothing else.*

Step	A High-Scoring Essay	A Low-Scoring Essay
Prompt	clearly develops a position on the prompt	does not clearly state a position
Plan	supports with concrete, relevant examples	is general, repetitious, or overly simplistic
Produce	maintains clear focus and organization	digresses or has weak organization
Proofread	shows competent use of language	contains errors that reduce clarity

Kaplan has found this approach useful in our many years of experience with hundreds of sample essay statements on a wide range of tests. Let's look at what the test makers tell you about how the essays are scored.

To score Level 4, you must:

- Answer the question
- Support ideas with examples
- Show logical thought and organization
- Avoid major or frequent errors that make your writing unclear

Organization and clarity are key to an above-average essay. If the reader can't follow your train of thought—if ideas aren't clearly organized or if grammatical errors, misspellings, and incorrect word choices make your writing unclear—you can't do well.

To score Level 5, all you have to add to a 4 is:

- Address the topic in depth

In other words, offer more examples and details. The test graders love specific examples, and the more concrete your examples are, the more they clarify your thinking and keep you focused.

To score Level 6, all you have to add to a 5 is:

- Make transitions smoother and show variety in syntax and vocabulary

Use words from the prompt to tie paragraphs together, rather than relying exclusively on connectors like *however* and *therefore*. Vary your sentence structure, sometimes using simple sentences and other times using compound and complex ones. Adding a few college-level vocabulary words will also boost your score.

Now let's apply the Kaplan Method to a practice prompt:

> **EXPERT TUTOR TIP**
> Note that you can't earn a 5 or 6 (10 or 12) if you haven't met the basic requirements for a 4 (8). Think of the requirements as building blocks to higher scores.

STEP 1: Prompt

The ACT Writing prompt usually relates to a topic that is familiar to high school students. It will outline an issue that teenagers are likely to have an opinion on.

> **PERFECT SCORE TIP**
> You must take a position on the Writing section. Graders like to see decisiveness no matter what the opinion may be. In other words, don't try to toe the line and support both pro and con—pick one.

If, by chance, the prompt describes a situation you feel strongly about, be sure to present your argument in a careful, thoughtful manner. Do NOT write an overly emotional response.

> **EXPERT TUTOR TIP**
> The assignment is not to write something vaguely inspired by the information given—that's where many good, creative writers go wrong.

Spend less than a minute reading the prompt on test day.

Here's an example of a typical ACT Writing prompt:

> In many high schools, the administration provides guidelines for the publication of student newspapers. These guidelines often determine which topics can and cannot be discussed in the newspaper and prohibit use of language that the administration deems inappropriate. Many administrators and teachers feel that these restrictions enable them to provide a safe learning environment for students. Others feel that any restriction on the student newspaper is a violation of freedom of speech. In your opinion, should high schools place restrictions on student newspapers?
>
> In your essay, take a position on this question. You may write about either one of the two points of view given, or you many present a different point of view on this question. Use specific reasons and examples to support your position.

STEP 2: Plan

Take five or six minutes to build a plan before you write. This step is critical—a successful plan leads directly to a high-scoring essay. Focus on what kinds of reasoning and examples you can use to support your position.

> ✓ **PERFECT SCORE TIP**
> Organization is the biggest gift you can give yourself on the essay. "Clever ideas" are nowhere near as important as having a solid road map that is obvious to the readers. To avoid wasting time, make sure you do not start writing without knowing your three points and how you will support them.

Note: If you find you have more examples for a position different from the one you thought you would take originally, *change your position*.

There is no one way to plan an essay. One method is to draw a large "T" on the page and align examples and ideas on either side of the line. So you might have the following notes on the prompt we started with in Step 1:

NEWSPAPERS IN SCHOOL

Safe learning environment (more control)	Freedom of speech (less control)
can have faculty advisor monitor coverage to make sure issues are clearly, fairly, and *tastefully* presented	add coverage of state, local elections, & discussion of school issues imp't to students
Administration can get its side heard, too.	help prepare students to be adults who know how to think and to vote
promotes safe discussion, improves student morale, and avoids protests	air debates about student rights ex. dress code ex. off-campus lunch privileges
	Students have rights and should be acknowledged.

Conclusion: Everyone benefits from freedom of speech in a school newspaper.

Information banks: Don't wait until test day to think of examples you can use to support your ideas. Regardless of what question is raised in the prompt, you will draw your support from the things you know best and are most comfortable writing about—things that you know a fair amount of concrete detail about.

Refresh your memory about your favorite or most memorable books, school subjects, historical events, personal experiences, activities—anything. By doing so, you strengthen mental connections to those ideas and details—that will make it easier to connect to the right examples on test day.

Structure your essay: Plan a clear introduction, a distinct middle section, and a strong conclusion. **Choose your best examples, decide in what order you'll handle them, and plan your paragraphs.**

With that in mind, we suggest:

- Use an effective *hook* to bring the reader in.
- Use regular *transitions* to provide the glue that holds your ideas together.
- End with a *bang* to make your essay memorable.

Using a "hook" means avoiding an essay that opens (as thousands of other essays will): "In my opinion, … because …" Try a more general statement that introduces one or more of the key words you will use from the prompt.

Using the "T" model presented earlier, you might use the following sentence:

A student newspaper should help students learn to think and express themselves.

A "bang" means a closing that ties the three example paragraphs together. A good choice can be a clear, succinct statement of your thesis in the essay or a vivid example that's right on point.

To conclude the planned "T" essay, you might finish with:

Both students and the administration would benefit from a school newspaper that covers a broad array of topics.

 PERFECT SCORE TIP
Every reader is going to read thousands of essays, so make yours memorable. A good hook and interesting writing will help wake up your reader and boost your score.

Let's plan for our prompt using a paragraph-by-paragraph method. The answer we've chosen is this:

I agree that restrictions on student newspapers violate freedom of speech, and I also believe restrictions impede student learning.

This position clearly responds to the assignment, and adding some reasoning not taken directly from the prompt immediately tells the reader "I have ideas of my own."

Next, working with our proposed response, comb your memory or your imagination for supporting reasons and examples to use. We'll use:

Point: Student newspapers should mimic real life newspapers.

Point: Not being in the school paper doesn't mean it's not discussed.

Point: Students can avoid "harming" others as well as adults.

Point: Censorship is anti-democratic.

Fill in the details. Jot down any notes you need to ensure that you use the details you've developed, but don't take the time to write full sentences. When you have enough ideas for a few supporting paragraphs, decide what your introduction and conclusion will be and the order in which you'll discuss each supporting idea.

Here's our sample plan:

Para 1: I agree with "free speech." Student newspapers should prepare for real life.

Para 2: Press is treated specially in real life.

Para 3: Potential harm not a good argument.

Para 4: Censorship vs. democracy

Para 5: Better to have discussion out in the open.

Para 6: Restate thesis.

If you take our advice and use examples that are very familiar to you, you won't have to write much in your plan in order to remember the point being made. **Learn how brief you can make your notes and still not lose sight of what you mean to say.**

 EXPERT TUTOR TIP
Save your best example for last and stress its relative importance.

A good plan:

- Responds to the prompt
- Has an introduction
- Has strong examples, usually one per paragraph
- Has a strong conclusion

In addition to writing practice essays, practice just making plans on your own whenever you have a few spare minutes, using ideas for changes in high school curriculum, events, lifestyle, and activities, such as: longer vs. shorter class sessions; students should/ should not be allowed off campus during the school day; study halls should/should not be eliminated; vocational options vs. all college prep. The more you think in advance about how you might discuss a variety of potential issues, the easier it will be to write your ACT essay on test day.

STEP 3: Produce

Appearances count. In purely physical terms, your essay will make a better impression if you fill a significant portion of the space provided and if it is clearly divided into three to five reasonably equal paragraphs (except that the final paragraph can be short). **Use one paragraph for your introduction, one for each example or line of reasoning, and one for your conclusion so your essay will be easy for readers to follow.**

Write neatly. Graders will give you a zero if your essay is hard to read—and negative feelings affect holistic scoring. If your handwriting is a problem, print.

Stick with the plan. Resist any urge to introduce new ideas—no matter how good you think they are—or to digress from the central focus or organization of each paragraph.

> **EXPERT TUTOR TIP**
> The ACT essay isn't the place for creative writing. Make your writing direct, persuasive, and error-free. Give the graders what they are looking for.

Think twice, write once. Write mentally before you write on paper. If your essays are littered with misspellings and grammatical mistakes, you may get a low score simply because the reader cannot follow what you are trying to say.

Use topic sentences. Each paragraph should be organized around a topic sentence that you should finish in your mind before you start to write. These may begin:

- *I believe…*
- *One example…*
- *Another example…*
- *Another example…*
- *Therefore, we can conclude…*

You don't have to write it this way in the essay, but completing these sentences in your mind ensures that you focus on what idea organizes each paragraph.

> **PERFECT SCORE TIP**
> Topic sentences are very important in ACT essays. The reader should be able to read just the topic sentences of each paragraph and get your major arguments, so make sure these sentences are clear.

Choose words carefully. Use vocabulary that you know well. Inserting new or fancy words that you have learned recently often sticks out. The result of unfamiliar words in an essay is the opposite of what you want: awkward, confusing thoughts. Instead of impressing the graders, you have made a mess. Two more points here:

1. Avoid using *I* excessively.
2. Avoid slang.

Use transitions. Think about the relationship between ideas as you write, and spell them out clearly. This makes it easy for the readers to follow your reasoning, and they'll appreciate it. **Use key words from the prompt as well as the kinds of words you've learned about in Reading that indicate contrast, opinion, relative importance, and support.**

Essay length. While many poor essays can be quite long, there will be few 6 essays under about 300 words, so take this into consideration as you practice. The length of an essay is no measure of its quality. However, it's hard to develop an argument in depth—something the graders look for—in one or two short paragraphs. **Don't ramble, digress, or write off topic just to make your essay longer.** Practice writing organized essays with developed examples, and you'll find yourself writing more naturally.

Don't sweat the small stuff. Do not obsess over every little thing. If you cannot remember how to spell a word, do your best and just **keep going**. Even the top scoring essays can have minor errors. The essay readers understand that you are writing first drafts and have no time for research or revision.

STEP 4: Proofread

Always leave yourself two or three minutes to review your work—the time spent will definitely pay off. Very few of us can avoid the occasional confused sentence or omitted word when we write under pressure. Quickly review your essay to be sure your ideas are clearly stated.

Don't hesitate to make corrections on your essay—these are timed first drafts, not term papers. But keep it clear: use a single line through deletions and an asterisk to mark where text should be inserted.

> ☑ **PERFECT SCORE TIP**
> Do you notice that most of your sentences tend to be relatively simple and begin with a subject followed by a passive verb? This is a problem. Varying sentence structure and writing in active voice will not only make your essay more enjoyable, but can be the difference between a 5 and a 6.

You don't have time to look for every minor error or to revise substantially. Learn the types of mistakes you tend to make and look for them. Some of the most common mistakes in students' essays are those found in the English test questions.

COMMON ERRORS

- Omitted words
- Sentence fragments
- Subject-verb agreement or verb tense errors
- Misplaced modifiers
- Pronoun agreement errors
- Misused words—especially homonyms like *their* for *there* or *they're*
- Spelling errors

> **EXPERT TUTOR TIP**
> Use a caret ∧ or an asterisk * to insert a word or words. Write a backward P or ¶ to create a new paragraph, and cross words out with one line. Don't make a mess!

COMMON STYLE PROBLEMS

- Choppy sentences (combine some)
- Too many long, complex sentences (break some up)
- Too many stuffy-sounding words (replace some with simple words)
- Too many simple words (add a few college-level words)

> **EXPERT TUTOR TIP**
> On test day, use 6–7 minutes for planning and 23–24 minutes for writing and proof-reading. Try writing practice essays in 20 minutes to make the real essay seem easier.

KNOW THE SCORE: SAMPLE ESSAYS

The best way to be sure you've learned what the readers will look for is to try scoring some essays yourself.

> **EXPERT TUTOR TIP**
> Don't cheat yourself by reading our explanation without first deciding what holistic grade you would give the sample essay.

The graders will be scoring holistically, not checking off "points"—but to learn what makes a good essay, it may help to consider these questions, based on the test makers' scoring criteria:

- Does the author answer the question?
- Is the author's position clearly stated?
- Does the body of the essay support and develop the position taken?
- Are there at least three supporting paragraphs?
- Is the relevance of each supporting paragraph clear?
- Does the writer address the other side of the argument?
- Is the essay organized, with a clear introduction, middle, and end?
- Does the author start a new paragraph for each new idea?
- Is each sentence in a paragraph relevant to the point made in that paragraph?
- Are transitions clear?
- Is the essay easy to read? Is it engaging?
- Are sentences varied?
- Is vocabulary used effectively? Is college-level vocabulary used?

> ✔ **PERFECT SCORE TIP**
> I know it is tempting to copy the prompt in your essay. The readers will notice and you will be penalized! There is nothing worse than copying the prompt in your essay, as it is not only painfully obvious that you don't have your own ideas, but it wastes time and space, and readers will simply disregard it. Do not copy the prompt!

Let's look at a sample essay based on the prompt and plan we've been looking at.

Sample Essay 1

In many high schools, the administration has provided guidelines for the publication of student newspapers. These guidelines often determine which topics can and cannot be discussed in the newspaper, and prohibit what the administration deems inappropriate language. Many administrators and teachers feel that these restrictions enable them to provide a safe, appropriate learning environment for students. Others feel that any restriction on the student newspaper is a violation of freedom of speech. In my opinion, students should be free to write on any topic.

Firstly, restrictions will not stop certain topics being talked about. Students will always discuss topics that they are interested in. Second, students are more aware of what is or is not appropriate than the administration might think. A newspaper is there to tell news and students will therefore write about the news.

Finally and most importantly, a right such as freedom of speech should not be checked at the school door. Students not being able to cognizant and value rights such as these if they are not taught their importance in school. So high schools should not place restrictions on student newspapers.

Score: _____ /6

It should have been fairly easy to see that this isn't a strong essay. We'd give it a score of 2 out of 6. The author does state a clear opinion, but half of the essay is a direct copy of the prompt—the graders will notice this and won't be impressed by it. The time and space spent just quoting the prompt was completely wasted—it earned the writer zero points.

The rest of the essay is organized and uses transition words (*firstly* and *finally*). The author states her thesis, follows with three supporting reasons, and then a conclusion. However, none of this is discussed fully enough—no concrete details or examples are given. In the second paragraph, for instance, the author should have added an example demonstrating that students are aware of what is appropriate or an example of topics that students will discuss in the paper.

The language is understandable, but there are significant errors affecting clarity. For instance, the second sentence of paragraph 3 is a fragment—there is no verb. Some vocabulary words are used without a clear understanding of their meaning: In paragraph 3, "not being able to cognizant" is incorrect; perhaps the student meant "not being able to understand."

This essay looks like the writer couldn't think of good ideas, waited too long to start writing, and had to write in a hurry.

Let's try another better essay. Read quickly and select a score before reading our evaluation.

Sample Essay 2

Many high schools place restrictions on appropriate topics and language for student newspapers. Many people disagree with these restrictions. While arguments can be made for either side, I believe that newspapers, as part of the school, should be placed under guidelines of the school.

First, a high school necessarily has stricter rules than normal society. These rules are not in place to punish students. They protect them and providing a suitable learning environment. In this way, when students leave high school they will have grown from children to adults, ready to succeed in the larger world. For example, the strict time schedule, with exactly three or four minutes given between classes, prepares students for strict schedules in the broader world.

Second, students interested in journalism should have instruction in how to write and publish newspaper articles. A student newspaper, which for obvious reasons has limited scope, is a perfect laboratory for students to experiment with journalistic writing. The administration and faculty dedicated to the newspaper can guide students in choosing appropriate topics, such as student elections. Then they can write articles on politics in the future. Imagine a student whose high school teacher taught the proper techniques for reporting on the race for student council president, joining a major news organization and reporting on the United States Presidential election.

Lastly, students may not realize the harm which their writing may cause. In my school, a student discovered a teacher's affair and "reported" on it in a story on the student's TV network, before the school could interfere. The teacher's career was destroyed and his marriage fell apart. Perhaps he deserved it, but student television should not have been the vehicle that ruined his life. The student reporter felt terribly in the end, as she had not thought through the consequences of her story. The same consequences could occur in a student newspaper that was restricted by no guidelines from the school.

Therefore, while many people argue that freedom of speech is a right too precious to give up, it is more important to provide guidelines for young people.

Score: _____ /6

Okay, now how do you want to score this essay?

This sample exceeds the basic requirements for a 4; it's a 5.

This essay addresses the assignment. The writer's position is clear, and the personal example in the fourth paragraph provides good support. The organization is good, and the author uses transition words. Each paragraph discusses a different aspect of the writer's argument. Let's look at why it doesn't rate a 6.

Some of the support isn't explained enough. The second paragraph, for example, doesn't show the connection between strict schedules and restrictions on newspaper reporting—the subject of the essay. The idea, in paragraph 3, of a student growing up to be a presidential reporter is interesting, but it doesn't particularly address the idea of restrictions. The final paragraph doesn't tie back to the main argument about newspapers; it only generally mentions "guidelines for young people."

The author's writing is good, but unexceptional. There are a few examples of complex sentences. For example, in paragraph 3: "A student newspaper, which for obvious reasons has limited scope, is a perfect laboratory for students to experiment with journalistic writing." The essay includes grammar mistakes, however, such as in paragraph 2: "They protect them and providing a suitable learning environment." In paragraph 3, the sentence "Then they can write articles on politics in the future" includes the ambiguous *they*, which could refer to the administration and teachers or the students.

> **EXPERT TUTOR TIP**
> To get from a 4 to a 5, you need fully developed examples and logic. To get to a 6, you also need lively, mostly error-free writing.

Let's look at another essay. Read it quickly and decide how you would score it.

Sample Essay 3

School administrations and teachers who support restrictions believe that these restrictions are needed to form an appropriate learning environment. But I agree with those who oppose such restrictions because they violate freedom of speech and these limits impede student progress and success after high school.

Despite the true need for rules in high schools, newspapers should be exempt. Students need discipline in the form of detention for misbehavior or demerits for poor study, but the student newspaper should not be a part of that system. Rather, it should mimic "real world" journalism.

Student editors, usually seniors aged seventeen or eighteen, are well aware of the overall environment in which they publish, and understand what is or is not appropriate. High school should give students practice at being cognizant of the larger arena in which they act. The few negative incidents that free press will admittedly cause will teach students that in life, one must take responsibility for one's actions.

Therefore, the argument for freedom of speech in student newspapers advances substantial educational goals for students, as well as our unalienable right of freedom of speech. This right, however, is paramount. The American public school is an extension of the American government and community, and censorship is inconsistent with American democracy. Again, students need to be prepared for the world they will live in; depriving them of rights that are promoted in the greater community prepares students poorly for life after high school.

Finally, censoring information in the student newspaper will not remove the subject from student discussion. Rather, it will remove a balanced, informative viewpoint, and often make the "inappropriate" action more desirable and "cool." Placing restrictions on student newspapers would be a serious mistake that would hinder students from learning what it is to participate in a free society.

Score: _____ /6

Did you recognize this as an essay similar to the plan we did earlier?

Para 1: I agree with "free speech." Student newspapers should prepare for real life.

Para 2: Press is treated specially in real life.

Para 3: Potential harm not a good argument.

Para 4: Censorship vs. democracy

Para 5: Not discussing in press doesn't mean not discussing in school.

This essay is pretty good—it would earn a 4. The position is clearly stated, and some supporting reasoning is given.

However, the reasoning is too general and the writing is too ordinary to earn the top score. Let's see how it could be improved.

TURNING A 4 INTO A 6

The essay plunges right into the two points of view offered in the prompt. It could be improved by introducing the issue with a general statement, like:

Many students, parents, and school administrators are debating the proper role of student newspapers. Should their language and content be restricted?

In the last sentence of the first paragraph, the writer introduces some additional reasoning *not* included in the prompt. That's excellent, but it would be better to make it clear where the position from the prompt ends and the author's position begins, perhaps like this:

> But I agree with those who oppose such restrictions because they violate freedom of speech. I would further argue that these limits impede student progress and success after high school.

The second paragraph is relevant and organized—it covers one of the two positions offered in the prompt. But it would be better if the writer tied this argument more clearly to something specific in the prompt, perhaps with an opening sentence using language from the prompt, like:

> Some people claim that high school students need strict guidelines in order to prepare for life after school.

Moreover, at the end of the paragraph, the reference to mimicking "real world" journalism would be improved by telling the reader what "real world" journalism is:

> Rather, it should mimic "real world" journalism, which strives to provide valid, balanced reporting on events important to the public, or in this case the student body.

The third paragraph addresses the view in the prompt that students can cause harm by printing inappropriate articles. Again, it should be made clearer what part of the prompt this paragraph is responding to, with a first sentence like:

> Others believe that students may cause unintended harm with newspaper articles written on controversial subjects. I think that is laughable.

Paragraph four is pretty good, as is. It states clearly what the author considers the most important argument. The fifth paragraph raises good arguments, but leaves them undeveloped. It would be best to provide an example of what type of story would help promote "balanced, informative" discussion to counteract "inappropriate…cool" actions, like:

> For instance, a reporter for my high school paper researched and wrote an in-depth story on the increasing drug problem among students. The administration quickly intervened and stopped the story, declaring that drugs were an inappropriate topic for student discussion. This story, however, would have focused discussion on a crucial issue for students, so that they can make the right choice when offered drugs or when they see friends using drugs. Unfortunately, this is a situation most students will face, and they need to be prepared. Suppressing the story made drugs seem even more rebellious and mysterious and most importantly did not give students facts with which they could prepare.

This makes it clear why the writer saved this argument for the last—an important, detailed example.

Finally, since this writer offers a fair number of supporting ideas, it would also be a good idea to add some transitions that establish the relative importance of those ideas. For example, in the third paragraph:

> First of all, student editors, usually seniors aged seventeen or eighteen, are well aware of the overall environment in which they publish, and understand what is or is not appropriate. But even more importantly, high school should give students practice at being cognizant of the larger arena in which they act.

> ✓ **PERFECT SCORE TIP**
> Remember that your personal opinion really is irrelevant. Write your essay on the topic you can support the best, as they will grade how you write not what you think.

Here's how this essay would look with the improvements we've suggested.

> Many students, parents, and school administrators are debating the proper role of student newspapers. Should their language and content be restricted? School administrations and teachers who support restrictions believe that these restrictions are needed to form an appropriate learning environment. But I agree with those who oppose such restrictions because they violate freedom of speech. I would further argue that these limits impede student progress and success after high school.
>
> Some people claim that high school students need strict guidelines in order to prepare for life after school. Despite the true need for rules in high schools, newspapers should be exempt. Students need discipline in the form of detention for misbehavior or demerits for poor study, but the student newspaper should not be a part of that system. Rather, it should mimic "real world" journalism, which strives to provide valid, balanced reporting on events important to the public, or in this case the student body.
>
> Others believe that students may cause unintended harm with newspaper articles written on controversial subjects. I think that is laughable. First of all, student editors, usually seniors aged seventeen or eighteen, are well aware of the overall environment in which they publish, and understand what is or is not appropriate. But even more importantly, high school should give students practice at being cognizant of the larger arena in which they act. The few negative incidents that free press will admittedly cause will teach students that in life, one must take responsibility for one's actions.

Therefore, the argument for freedom of speech in student newspapers advances substantial educational goals for students, as well as our unalienable right of freedom of speech. This right, however, is paramount. The American public school is an extension of the American government and community, and censorship is inconsistent with American democracy. Again, students need to be prepared for the world they will live in; depriving them of rights that are promoted in the greater community prepares students poorly for life after high school.

Finally, censoring information in the student newspaper will not remove the subject from student discussion. Rather, it will remove a balanced, informative viewpoint, and often make the "inappropriate" action more desirable and "cool." For instance, a reporter for my high school paper researched and wrote an in-depth story on the increasing drug problem among students. The administration quickly intervened and stopped the story, declaring that drugs were an inappropriate topic for student discussion. This story, however, would have focused discussion on a crucial issue for students so that they can make the right choice when offered drugs or when they see friends using drugs. Unfortunately, this is a situation most students will face, and they need to be prepared. Suppressing the story made drugs seem even more rebellious and mysterious and most importantly did not give students facts with which they could prepare.

Placing restrictions on student newspapers would be a serious mistake that would hinder students from learning what it is to participate in a free society.

This is now a 6 essay. It addresses the task both fully and concretely. It addresses both sides of the argument, refutes two opposing arguments, and then moves to the bulk of the author's own reasoning. The first paragraph introduces all the lines of reasoning that will be used, demonstrating to the reader that the writer knew right from the start where this essay was headed. The development of ideas is clear and logical and the paragraphs reflect this organization.

> **EXPERT TUTOR TIP**
> There are no right or wrong opinions. You can earn a 6 with an essay for or against the issue raised in the prompt.

The author shows a high level of skill with language. The transitions between paragraphs are clear and guide the reader through the reasoning. The sentence structure varies throughout the passage and is at times complex.

So what did we do to our 4 to make it a 6?

- We added examples and detail.

- We varied sentence structure and added stronger vocabulary (*strives*, *laughable*, *intervened*, and *suppressing*).

- While length alone doesn't make a 6, we've added detail to our original essay.

- The conclusion, rather than being lost in the fifth paragraph, is now a strong, independent statement that concisely sums up the writer's point of view.

Remember that your graders will be reading *holistically*. They will not be grading you by assigning points to particular aspects of your writing. However, as you practice essay writing, you can build an otherwise humdrum essay into a 6 by working on specific elements, with the net effect of giving your essay that 6 glow.

PREPARING FOR THE ESSAY

Information Banks

Don't wait until test day to think about what subjects you can draw on for your examples to create animated and engaging essays. Examples can be drawn from anywhere: your life experience, a story you saw on the news, etc. So prepare yourself by refreshing your memory about your favorite subjects—collect examples that can be used for a variety of topics.

Don't hesitate to use your examples broadly. If the topic is about school, that doesn't mean you have to use school-based examples. It's better to write about things that you are comfortable with and know a lot about—but be sure to make it clear how they are relevant to the topic.

Read Op-Ed Essays

Newspapers and blogs have op-ed (opinion-editorial) articles. These present arguments and opinions on a wide range of topics. Some will present their arguments well, others will not. Make a point of reading and evaluating them. Ask yourself:

- What is the author's point?

- How is it supported?

- Is the argument convincing? If not, why?

Follow a Practice Regimen

Don't try to cut corners. Learn the Kaplan Method and practice writing at least one essay a week; last minute cramming will not be effective. If you intend to maximize your score, you must establish and adhere to a practice schedule. Practice at the same time of day that you will be writing on test day.

Be hard on yourself. **Always** time yourself to internalize the necessary pacing. Don't allow yourself any extra minutes to complete an essay.

Never start to write until you have a complete plan, and then adhere to your plan.

Always reserve two minutes to look over the essay and make needed additions or corrections.

> ✔ **PERFECT SCORE TIP**
> Writing an essay fast can be very challenging if you are not used to it. If this scares you, practice! Go to a quiet place and give yourself 25 minutes to write a sample essay. Make sure you handwrite it, as you will have to on the test.

Self-Evaluation

After each practice essay, score yourself based on the guidelines provided. As part of your self-evaluation, determine which types of examples are most useful to you and what types of errors you make most often. Then analyze how well you followed the Kaplan Method in constructing your essays and what you might focus on to improve. Do you have a tendency to rush your plan, or do you find that you haven't left two minutes to proofread at the end? **Practice to make your pacing reliable.**

Get a Second Opinion

Ask someone else to read and critique your practice essays. If you know someone else who's taking the ACT, you might agree to assist each other in this way. Knowing whether another person can follow your reasoning is the single most important learning aid you can have for the essay.

> ✔ **PERFECT SCORE TIP**
> I really recommend getting a second opinion on practice essays. I know I write many things that I believe are clear but that others cannot understand. If you are not good at judging your own clarity and logic, have someone else help you.

If You're Not a "Writer"

While the essay is optional, many colleges require the ACT essay. Remember that the essay is set up so that *everyone* can do well on it. You don't have to be an expert writer to formulate a good argument and support it well. Plain, clear language will go a long way toward getting a good score.

> **EXPERT TUTOR TIP**
> If you're down to the wire, allow yourself a few minutes to plan and then write, based on that plan, no matter how much you wish you could think of other ideas. Remember that the essay tests your ability to convey those ideas—not the ideas themselves.

If English Is Your Second Language

The ACT essay can be a special challenge for the international student or ESL student here in the United States. On the ACT, you will be taking a position on the prompt, something that sometimes, but not **always**, happens on the TOEFL® (Test of English as a Foreign Language). However, plan your essay using all the tools in this chapter and write according to your plan. Make a special point of spending time proofreading your practice essays when you finish them, and edit anything that makes your writing unclear. There's a strong connection between your English reading skills and your writing skills, so keep reading as well (and don't forget to look for material for your information banks while you read).

PRACTICE ESSAY

Try out the Kaplan Method on the following essay prompt. After you're finished, read your essay, and if possible, have someone else read it as well. You can compare it to the model essay that follows the lined pages. Good luck!

Many city councils have introduced proposals that would give them the power to ban certain books from the children's and young adult sections of local public libraries. Some citizens support such proposals because they hope to limit young people's exposure to inappropriate materials. However, other people believe that these measures are equivalent to censorship. In your opinion, should the government have the right to restrict the materials available to young people in libraries?

In your essay, take a position on this question. You may write about either one of the two points of view given, or you may present a different point of view on this question. Use specific reasons and examples to support your position.

_____

_____

_____

_____

_____

_____

_____

_____

_____

_____

_____

_____

Model Essay

Here's one possible way to approach this essay prompt. Remember that the opinion you express is less important than the way you present it. Notice how this response includes a logically arranged argument with specific examples.

In some districts, city councils and other governing bodies have suggested that they be given the power to ban certain teen and children's books from public libraries. While some citizens believe that it would be beneficial for an outside party to screen the books that are available to young people, others are upset at what they see as censorship of the library's offerings.

Leaving the question of censorship aside, I believe that decisions about which books are appropriate for young people should be left to the young people themselves and their parents, not to city councils or librarians. Young people's reading levels and maturity levels can vary dramatically even within the same age group, and parents are the best judges of what kinds of books are suitable for their children. The proposal to have the city council make these decisions also fails to take into account the huge variations in parents' own preferences for their children; the idea of inappropriateness is a very subjective one. While some parents may agree with the city council's decisions, others may feel that the city council bans too many books, or even too few. In the end, parents must be responsible for knowing what books their children are reading and making their own decisions about those books' appropriateness within the context of their own values.

Additionally, whether certain books are appropriate or not, it's unrealistic to think that removing "objectionable" material from public libraries will keep young people from ever encountering that kind of material. Between television, the Internet, and interactions with friends and classmates, young people encounter all sorts of situations that may not necessarily be age appropriate. It's understandable that adults are concerned, but trying to keep potentially objectionable books away from young readers doesn't ensure that they won't encounter the language or situations used in those books elsewhere. To my mind, the best solution is for adults to encourage young people to analyze these situations thoughtfully, ask questions, and form their own opinions, rather than trying to shield them from the realities of the world.

Finally, although certain books contain elements that some people may find offensive or upsetting, those elements don't necessarily outweigh the literary merits of the books in question. One example of this is *Huckleberry Finn*, which all of the students at my school read as a requirement in English classes. It is widely recognized as a classic of American literature, even though it also includes portrayals of African-American characters that many people find offensive. The historical context that is necessary to understand *The Diary of Anne Frank* may be upsetting to younger readers, but the diary is still a significant historical document. Many books with controversial content are still worth reading, and a policy that screens out books based on their potential to offend may exclude important works of literature from libraries.

In conclusion, I believe that the power to make determinations about a book's appropriateness should lie not with a city council or a librarian, but with young readers and their parents. The role of a library is to make information available, not to make or enforce judgments about what its patrons should or should not be reading.

▶ IF YOU LEARNED ONLY FOUR THINGS IN THIS CHAPTER...

1. You should be familiar with the Kaplan Method for the ACT Essay: pause to know the prompt, plan, produce, and proofread.

2. The Writing test asks you to take a position on the issue in the prompt. The best essays knock down the opposing arguments and positively support the side you take.

3. Support your view with relevant and clearly organized evidence. Examples will come from your own experiences.

4. Pacing is crucial to getting all your ideas on paper. Be sure to leave yourself two or three minutes to proofread.

PART THREE

Ready, Set, Go

CHAPTER 17

Strategic Summaries

ENGLISH TEST

The English subject test:

- Is 45 minutes long

- Includes five passages, representing a range of writing styles and levels of formality

- Consists of 75 questions, divided among the five passages, which test many points of grammar, punctuation, writing mechanics, usage, and rhetorical skills by proposing ways of expressing information underlined at various points in the passages; we divide the questions strategically into three groups:

    1. **Economy questions**
    2. **Sense questions**
    3. **Technicality questions**

There are also some Nonstandard-Format questions that require different strategies, as outlined in Special Strategies below.

The questions **do *not* get harder** as you proceed through the section.

> ✔ **PERFECT SCORE TIP**
> If you haven't read the rest of this book, remember two important things about the ACT—there is no guessing penalty, and the questions do not get harder as you go in the section.

Mind-Set

- **When in doubt, take it out.** Make sure that everything is written as concisely as possible. If you think something doesn't belong in a sentence, it probably doesn't, so choose an answer that leaves it out.

- **Make it make sense.** Make sure that each answer you choose creates a sentence or paragraph that is logical. Consider sentence formation, making sure that you use complete sentences and not fragments. When connection words are tested, think about how ideas relate logically. For an answer choice to be right in ACT English, it must create a sentence that is logically *and* grammatically correct.

- **Trust your eyes and ear.** Mistakes in grammar often sound or look bad to your ear. Trust that instinct. Don't choose the answer that "sounds fancy," choose the one that "sounds right." Review the Grammar Rules to Know in English Workout 3.

The Kaplan Method

For each question, ask yourself three things. Note that you may actually have your answer before getting to all three questions:

STEP 1: Read until you have enough information to identify the issue. Don't read the whole passage before attacking the questions; instead, take the English test one sentence or issue at a time. As you approach each question, ask yourself, "What issue is this question testing?"

STEP 2: Eliminate choices that do NOT address the issue. Read through each answer to see if it addresses the issue you identified in Step 1. If not, cross it out and move on. Try to eliminate as many answer choices as possible. For those you don't eliminate…

STEP 3: Plug in the remaining choices, and choose the one that is most correct, concise, and relevant. The ACT test makers want short, simple, easy-to-understand prose. Make sure the answer you choose sounds right.

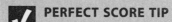

PERFECT SCORE TIP
On the English section, remember to get used to recognizing common errors and trusting your ear.

Special Strategies

A few questions will require you to rearrange the words in a sentence, the sentences in a paragraph, or even the paragraphs in a passage. Others may ask questions about the meaning of all or part of the passage, or about its structure. Your approach to these Nonstandard-Format questions should be:

1. **Determine your task.** What are you being asked to do?
2. **Consider the passage as a whole.** Read the sentences around the numbered question. You need to know the various points made there. Most passages will have a well-defined theme, laid out in a logical way. Choose the answer that

expresses this theme or the arrangement of elements that best continues the logical "flow" of the passage.

3. **Predict your answer.** As in Reading, you should have an idea of what the answer is before looking at the choices.

Timing

We recommend that you *not* skip around in the English subject test. Although you can certainly use the usual Two-Pass Approach, you might prefer to go straight from beginning to end, answering all of the questions as you go. Unlike in other sections, in English you'll usually have at least a sense of what the right answer should be rather quickly. Remember, even the correct answer will start to sound wrong if you think about it too much!

Set your watch to 12:00 at the beginning of the subject test. Although you should go faster if you can, here's roughly where you should be at the following checkpoints.

12:09 . . . . . One passage finished and answers gridded in

12:18 . . . . . Two passages finished and answers gridded in

12:27 . . . . . Three passages finished and answers gridded in

12:36 . . . . . Four passages finished and answers gridded in

12:45 . . . . . Five passages finished and answers for the entire section gridded in

Note that you should do at least some work on all 75 English questions, and make sure you have at least a guess gridded in for every question when time is called.

When You're Running Out of Time

If you have no time left even to read the last few questions, choose the shortest answer for each one. Remember that OMIT, when it appears, counts as the shortest answer.

Scoring

Your performance on the English subject test will be averaged into your ACT Composite Score, weighted equally with your scores on the other three major subject tests. You will also receive:

- English subject score—from 1 to 36—for the entire English subject test
- Usage/Mechanics subscore—from 1 to 18—based on your performance on the questions testing grammar, usage, punctuation, and sentence structure

- Rhetorical Skills subscore—from 1 to 18—based on your performance on the questions testing strategy, organization, and style

- Writing subscore—from 2 to 12—based on the optional Writing test

- Combined English-Writing score—from 1 to 36—if you take the optional Writing test

MATH TEST

The Math subject test:

- Is 60 minutes long

- Consists of 60 questions, which test your grasp of pre-algebra, algebra, coordinate geometry, plane geometry, and trigonometry; we break down the questions into the following three strategic categories:

   1. **Diagram questions**
   2. **Story questions**
   3. **Concept questions**

The math concepts **do get more advanced** as you proceed through the section.

Mind-Set

- **The end justifies the means.** That means getting as many correct answers as quickly as possible. If that means doing straightforward questions in a straight-forward way, that's fine. But many questions can be solved faster by using Kaplan Methods, such as backsolving and picking numbers.

- **Take time to save time.** It sounds paradoxical, but to go your fastest on the Math test, you've got to slow down. Never dive in headlong, wildly crunching numbers or manipulating equations without first giving the problem some thought.

- **When in doubt, shake it up.** ACT Math questions are not always what they seem at first glance. Sometimes all you need is a new perspective to break through the disguise.

GO ONLINE
Find the Kaplan Method for approaching each section of the ACT on your download-able study sheet.

The Kaplan Method

STEP 1: What is the question? First, focus on the question stem and make sure you understand the problem. Underlining what the question is asking might help you. If it is a word problem and you are completely lost, try taking notes. You will pull out the information that is necessary to solve the problem. Think to yourself: "What kind of problem is this? What am I looking for? What am I given?"

STEP 2: What information am I given? You're given information in the question stem and in the answer choices. Pay attention to the format of these to figure out the best approach to the question.

STEP 3: What can I do with the information?

- Think for a moment and decide on a plan of attack.

- **Straightforward math.** Do you know how to solve the problem using your math knowledge? Go for it!

- **Picking numbers.** Are there variables in the answer choices? If so, is there a way to pick numbers for the variable to help you get to the right answer?

- **Backsolving.** Are there numbers in the answer choices? What is the question asking for? (That is what the numbers in the answer choices represent.) Is there a way to use the answer choices to get to the right answer?

- **Guess strategically.** If you're really not sure, you can guess—you don't lose points for incorrect answers on the ACT. Try to eliminate as many incorrect choices as you can before guessing, and mark the question in your booklet so you can return to it at the end of the Math test and try again.

STEP 4: Am I finished? Before you select an answer, reread the question. Are you answering the right question? Did you miss any steps? Most importantly, does it match one of the answer choices? If so, circle the answer in your test book and fill in the appropriate bubble on your answer grid. If you are stuck, circle the problem in your test book and move on to get all your "easy" points first! Come back to this problem after you have gone through the entire test.

Special Strategies

We offer several recommendations for what to do when you get stuck. If after a few moments of thought you find you still can't come up with a reasonable way of doing the problem, try one of these techniques:

- **Restate.** When you get stuck, try looking at the problem from a different angle. Try rearranging the numbers, changing decimals to fractions, fractions to decimals, multiplying out numbers, factoring problems, redrawing a diagram, or anything that might help you to look at the problem a bit differently.

- **Remove the disguise.** Find out what the question is really asking—it might not be what the problem appears to ask at first. See Math Workout 2 for some examples!

- **Try eyeballing.** Even though the directions warn you that diagrams are "not necessarily" drawn to scale, eyeballing is a surprisingly effective guessing strategy. Unless a problem says "Note: Not drawn to scale," you can assume that it is drawn to scale! Use that to help you eliminate answer choices that you know are wrong!

> ✔️ **PERFECT SCORE TIP**
> Remember that the textbook way to solve a problem is not always the best in Math. Try to simplify problems by plugging in numbers for variables and restating difficult problems.

Timing

Remember the Two-Pass Approach. **Spend about 45 minutes on your first pass through the Math subject test: Do the easier questions, guess on the questions you know you'll never get, and mark the tough ones that you'll want to come back to.** Spend the last 15 minutes picking up those questions that you skipped on the first pass.

We recommend that you grid your answers at the end of every page or two. In the last five minutes or so, start gridding your answers one by one. And make sure that you have an answer (even if it's a blind guess) gridded for every question by the time the test is over.

Don't worry if you have to guess on a lot of the Math questions. You can miss a lot of questions on the subject test and still get a great score. **Remember that the average ACT test taker gets fewer than half the Math questions right!**

When You're Running Out of Time

If at some point you realize you have more questions left than you have time for, be willing to skip around, looking for questions you understand right away. Pick your spots. Concentrate on the questions you have the best chance of correctly answering. Just be sure to grid an answer—even if it's just a wild guess—for every question.

Scoring

Your performance on the Math subject test will be averaged into your ACT Composite Score, equally weighted with your scores on the other three major subject tests. You will also receive:

- Math subject score—from 1 to 36—for the entire Math subject test
- Pre-Algebra/Elementary Algebra subscore—from 1 to 18
- Intermediate Algebra/Coordinate Geometry subscore—from 1 to 18
- Plane Geometry/Trigonometry subscore—from 1 to 18

READING TEST

The Reading subject test:

- Is 35 minutes long
- Includes four passages:
  - Three Nonfiction passages (one each in Social Science, Humanities, and Natural Science, though there is no significant difference among them except subject matter)
  - One Prose Fiction passage (an excerpt from a short story or novel)
- Consists of 40 questions, 10 on each passage, which include:
  - Detail questions
    - Specific Information
    - Vocab-in-Context
    - Function (Why)
  - Inference questions
  - Big Picture questions

The questions do *not* get harder as you go through the section.

> ☑ **PERFECT SCORE TIP**
> On the Reading section, remember to be able to summarize each paragraph and passage after prereading so you have a road map to help you with answering questions.

Mind-Set

- **Know where the passage is going.** Read the passages actively, and pay attention to structural clues and key words and sentences. The easiest way to do this is to create a road map.

- **Conquer the questions.** Look up the answers; don't be tempted by the choices.

The Kaplan Method

STEP 1: Actively read the passage, taking notes as you go. Try to understand the gist of the passage. Get a sense of the overall structure of the passage. Create a road map to make referring back easier.

STEP 2: Examine the question stem, looking for clues. Understand the question first, without looking at the answer choices that are offered. Remember that many wrong choices are designed to mislead test takers who just jump past the question stem and start comparing choices to each other.

STEP 3: Predict the answer and select the choice that best matches your prediction. Always refer to the passage before answering the question. If the question includes line references, read around them. Only then look at the choices. Make sure your answer matches the passage in meaning.

Answer the question in your own words before looking at the choices and match your answer with one of the choices. Having an answer in mind will keep you from falling for tempting but wrong answers—predict before you peek!

> **EXPERT TUTOR TIP**
> Once you've finished reading a passage and its questions, put it out of your mind. There's no connection at all between passages, so don't carry your stress or doubt to the next one. Approach each passage as if it were the only one. Stay active and confident—you're doing great!

Special Strategies

THE PROSE FICTION PASSAGE

When you preread the passage, pay attention to the characters, especially the main character. Read between the lines to determine unspoken emotions and attitudes. Ask yourself:

- **Who are these people?** What are they like? How do the characters relate to each other?

- **What is their state of mind?** Are they angry, sad, reflective, excited?

- **What's going on?** What's happening on the surface? What's happening beneath the surface?

- **What is the author's attitude toward the characters?** What words indicate a particular tone? Do any phrases suggest the author is either approving of or critical of one of the characters?

NONFICTION PASSAGES

Don't be thrown by unfamiliar vocabulary or topics. The Natural Science passage may take you into strange territory. Everything you need to know will be covered in the passage. If you find a difficult term, odds are the definition will be given to you in context (or else it simply might not matter what the word means). You can still get lots of questions right, even if you don't fully understand the passage. Remember, you can find all the answers in the passage.

Timing

You might want to take a few seconds at the beginning of the subject test to page through the passages, gauging the difficulty of each one. At first glance, you may wish to skip an entire passage if it seems very difficult.

We recommend that you treat each passage and its questions as a block. Take two passes through each block before moving on to the next. (Skip around if you like, but watch your answer grid if you do!) Get the easy questions on the first pass through and save the tougher ones for the second pass. Just make sure to keep track of time.

Set your watch to 12:00 at the beginning of the subject test. Although you should go faster if you can, here's roughly where you should be at the following checkpoints:

12:09 . . . . . One passage finished and answers gridded in

12:18 . . . . . Two passages finished and answers gridded in

12:27 . . . . . Three passages finished and answers gridded in

12:35 . . . . . Four passages finished and answers for entire section gridded in

Take about 30 seconds (average) per question. Some questions take more time than others (ones with Roman numerals in them and ones that have EXCEPT are examples). If you feel the need to spend a lot of time to get the right answer, don't. Either guess, or skip and come back. (Don't forget to do so.)

Do the best you can to finish all four passages, but don't panic if you don't. Develop a fallback position to use, if you fall short (see the tips that follow). If, during practice, you often don't get to *many* of the questions, approach all the passages this way:

1. **Learn to spot the easier questions and answer these quickly.**
2. **Address the ones you might be able to get with more research.**
3. **Guess randomly on the ones you would need lots of time for.**

Note: If you are a slow reader and have trouble with the ABCs of Active Reading, this method may help.

Don't panic if you can't finish all four passages. Make sure you do a good job on at least three passages—and remember to grid answers (even if they're blind guesses) for all questions by the end. Even if you try all four passages, you probably won't really work on all 40 questions. For many questions, you'll just have to guess. Just make sure you guess on the tough ones and actually work on the easy ones!

When You're Running Out of Time

If you have less than five minutes left for the last passage, do the following:

1. **Look for questions with specific line references and do them.**
2. **Refer to the cited location in the passage and answer the question as best you can, based on what you see there.**
3. **Make sure you have gridded in an answer for every question before time is called.**

Scoring

Your performance on the Reading subject test will be averaged into your ACT Composite Score, weighted equally with your scores on the other three major subject tests. You will also receive:

- Reading subject score—from 1 to 36—for the entire Reading subject test
- Social Science/Sciences subscore—from 1 to 18—based on your performance on the nonfiction passages drawn from Social Studies and Natural Sciences
- Arts/Literature subscore—from 1 to 18—based on your performance on the Nonfiction passage (drawn from the Humanities) and on the Prose Fiction passage

SCIENCE TEST

The Science subject test:

- Is 35 minutes long
- Includes seven passages or sets of scientific information, involving graphs, tables, and research summaries, and typically, one of the passages involves two conflicting viewpoints on a single scientific issue
- Consists of 40 questions, divided among the seven passages. We divide the questions strategically into three categories:

    1. **Figure Interpretation questions**
    2. **Patterns questions**
    3. **Scientific Reasoning questions**

The questions **do *not* get harder** as you proceed through the section.

Mind-Set

- **Look for patterns.** Usually, the exact data contained in Science passages is not as important as are changes in the data. Look for extremes (maximums and minimums), critical points (points of change), and variation (direct and inverse).
- **Know your direction.** There are two kinds of scientific reasoning—general-to-specific and specific-to-general. **Always** be aware of when scientists are inferring a specific case from a general rule and when they are using specific data to form a (general) hypothesis.
- **Refer, don't remember.** Don't even think of trying to remember data. It's **always** there, right on the page, for you to refer to when needed.

The Kaplan Method

STEP 1: Map the passage, identifying and marking the purpose, method, and results of the experiment. What is being researched? What are the scientists varying? What are the scientists keeping constant? Don't get bogged down in the details, and don't worry about understanding everything.

STEP 2: Scan figures, identifying variables and patterns. You don't need to study these closely, just note what each figure is telling you about the purpose, methods, or results of the experiment. That way you'll know where to look when answering the questions.

Consider the question stem. Make sure you understand exactly what the question is asking. Get a sense of what the answer should be without looking at the choices, many of which are designed to mislead you if you're indecisive.

STEP 3: Find support for the answer in the passage. Always refer back to the passage before looking at the choices and selecting one. Make sure you read charts and graphs accurately and that you do not confuse different kinds of units. It helps to answer the question in your own words. Don't rely too much on your knowledge of science. Match your answer with one of the choices.

> ✓ **PERFECT SCORE TIP**
> Remember that you do not have to understand all the science in the Science section to do well, so don't let difficult concepts throw you.

Special Strategies

READING TABLES AND GRAPHS

When reading tables and graphs, you should ask yourself:

- What does the figure show?
- What are the units of measurement?
- What is the pattern in the data?

EXPERIMENTS

Remember how experiments work. There is typically (though not always) a control group plus an experimental group or groups. In a well-designed experiment, the only difference between the groups will be a variation in the factor that's being tested. Ask yourself:

- What's the factor that's being varied?
- What's the control group, if any?
- What do the results show? What differences exist between the results for one group and those for another?

CONFLICTING VIEWPOINTS PASSAGE

Spend a little more time than usual on the prereading step of this passage. Focus on the two points of view. What are the scientists arguing about? What do they agree on, if anything? What do they differ on? Identify the following for each scientist:

- **Basic theory statement** (usually the first sentence of each scientist's presentation)
- **Major pieces of data behind the theory** (keeping in mind whether each supports the scientist's own theory or weakens the opposing scientist's theory)

Timing

Some Science passages are a lot harder than others, and they're not arranged in order of difficulty, so you might want to **take a few seconds at the beginning of the subject test to page through the passages, gauging the difficulty of each one.** You may wish to skip an entire passage if it seems very difficult (but remember that a very difficult passage may have very easy questions).

As in Reading, treat each passage and its questions as a block, taking two passes through each block before moving on to the next. Get the easy questions on the first pass through and save the tougher ones for the second pass. Some questions will probably be impossible for you to answer; take an educated guess on these.

Set your watch to 12:00 at the beginning of the subject test. Although you should go faster if you can, here's where you should be at the following checkpoints:

12:05	One passage finished and answers gridded in
12:10	Two passages finished and answers gridded in
12:15	Three passages finished and answers gridded in
12:20	Four passages finished and answers gridded in
12:25	Five passages finished and answers gridded in
12:30	Six passages finished and answers gridded in
12:35	Seven passages finished and answers for the entire section gridded in

Don't spend time agonizing over specific questions. Avoid thinking long and hard about the answer choices. If you've spent a minute or so on a question and don't seem to be making any headway, make your best guess and move on.

Don't panic if you can't finish all seven passages, but try to do a good job on at least five of them. Make sure you remember to grid answers (even if they're blind guesses) for all questions by the end.

When You're Running Out of Time

If you have fewer than three minutes left for the last passage, do the following:

1. **Look for questions that refer to specific experiments or to specific graphs or tables.**

2. **Refer to the cited location in the passage and answer the question as best you can, based on what you see there.**

3. **Make sure you have gridded in an answer for every question before time is called.**

Scoring

Your performance on the Science subject test will be averaged into your ACT Composite Score, weighted equally with your scores on the other three major subject tests. You will also receive:

- A Science subject score—from 1 to 36—for the entire Science subject test

Unlike the other three subject scores, the Science score is not divided into subscores.

WRITING TEST

The Writing test:

- Is optional (check with the schools to which you are applying and with your guidance counselor about whether you should take the test)

- Is 30 minutes long

- Includes just one prompt about which you must write an essay that must:
  - State a point of view on the issue
  - Support the point of view with concrete, relevant examples
  - Provide a clear and coherent argument, which includes a discussion of the opposite point of view

Mind-Set

Don't wait until test day to think of examples you can use to support your ideas. Regardless of what question is raised in the prompt, you will draw your support from the things you know best and are most comfortable writing about—things that you can describe in concrete detail.

Refresh your memory about school subjects, current events, personal experiences, and activities—anything. By doing so, you strengthen mental connections to those ideas and details—that will make it easier to connect to the right examples on test day.

The Kaplan Method

1. **Prompt.** Read about the issue and take a position on it. There is no right or wrong answer, but make sure you address the issue. In other words, answer the question.

2. **Plan.** Take up to six or seven minutes to plan the essay before you write. Focus on what kinds of reasoning and examples you can use to support your position. If you find you have more examples for a position different from the one you thought you would take, *change your position*.

3. **Produce.** Write your draft, sticking closely to your plan. The essay should have three to five well-developed paragraphs with topic sentences and supporting details. Include an introductory paragraph stating your position and a concluding paragraph. Write neatly.

4. **Proofread.** Always leave yourself two minutes to review your work—the time spent will definitely pay off. Very few of us can avoid the occasional confused sentence or omitted word when we write under pressure. Quickly review your essay to be sure your ideas are clearly stated.

 **PERFECT SCORE TIP**
Remember to write a "textbook essay" with a clear structure, topic sentences, well-developed examples, and sentence variation.

Helpful Strategies

You must be very focused in order to write a complete, coherent essay in 30 minutes. During the planning stage, use one of the two following strategies:

1. **Draw a "T" and list your argument on either side of it** (your stance on one side and your arguments addressing the other side on the other). See page 262. This method will help you decide if you have enough to back up your stance. You may find you need to take the opposite point of view!

   OR

2. **List the topic of each paragraph** you plan to write, noting the segments of the argument that you want to make.

Stick to the plan as you write the essay. Don't change the plan in midstream if another idea suddenly comes to you; it might derail the essay. Keep your focus on the issue and don't digress.

Make the structure of your essay very easy for the reader to see. Have an introductory paragraph, two or three middle paragraphs, each focused on one example or bit of evidence, and a concluding paragraph.

Write neatly. Graders will give you a poor grade if it's hard to decipher. If your handwriting is a problem, print.

Timing

With only 30 minutes, efficient use of time is critical. Divide your time as follows:

6–7 minutes—Read the prompt and plan the essay.

20–21 minutes—Draft the essay, sticking to the plan.

3 minutes—Proofread and correct any errors.

When You're Running Out of Time

Running out of time doesn't mean only that you'll have to guess on the last few questions as it does on the other tests; it means your essay won't be as complete and coherent as it should be. If you do start running out of time, leave out one of your example paragraphs and go on to the concluding paragraph. Even when you're rushed, try to allow one to two minutes to proofread for errors that affect clarity.

Scoring

Two trained readers read and score each of your essays on a scale of 1–6; then those scores are added together to arrive at your Writing subscore (from 2–12). If there's a difference of more than a point between the two readers' scores, your essay will be read by a third reader. Readers evaluate the essays holistically, judging the overall quality of each, not assigning separate scores for specific elements like grammar or organization.

A combined English-Writing score will also be recorded. Two-thirds of this score is based on your English score and one-third is based on your Writing subscore. The combined English-Writing score does not count toward your composite score.

Statistically speaking, there will be few essays that score 12 out of 12. If each grader gives your essay a 4 or 5 (making your subscore 8 or 10), that will place you at the upper range of those taking the exam.

CHAPTER 18

Last-Minute Tips

Is it starting to feel like your whole life is a buildup to the ACT? You've known about it for years, you've worried about it for months, and now you've spent at least a few hours in solid preparation for it. As the test gets closer, you may find your anxiety is on the rise. Don't worry. After the preparation you've received from this book, you're in good shape for test day.

> ✔ **PERFECT SCORE TIP**
> If it is close to the test and you know there is one specific section you are not prepared for, do as many practice problems from that section as possible. Practice really does bring you closer to perfection.

To calm any pretest jitters you may have (and assuming you've left yourself at least some breathing time before your ACT), let's go over a few last-minute strategies for the few days before and after the test.

> **EXPERT TUTOR TIP**
> If you have less than two weeks to prep for the ACT, read this chapter. It tells you how to use your time wisely before, during, and after the test.

THREE DAYS BEFORE THE TEST

- If you haven't already done so, take one of the full-length Practice Tests in this book under timed conditions. If you have already worked through all the tests in the book, try an actual published ACT (your guidance counselor might have one). You can also find practice questions on the official ACT website at www. actstudent.org.

- Try to use all of the techniques and tips you've learned in this book. Take control. Approach the test strategically and confidently.

WARNING: Don't take a full practice ACT unless you have at least 48 hours left before the test! Doing so will probably exhaust you, hurting your scoring potential on the actual test! You wouldn't run a marathon the day before the real thing, would you?

TWO DAYS BEFORE THE TEST

- **Go over the results of your Practice Test.** Don't worry too much about your score or whether you got a specific question right or wrong. Remember—the Practice Test doesn't count. But do examine your performance on specific questions with an eye to how you might get through each one faster and with greater accuracy on the actual test to come.

- **After reviewing your test, look over the Strategic Summaries.** If you feel a little shaky about any of the areas mentioned, quickly read the relevant workouts.

- **This is the last study day—review a couple of the more difficult principles we've covered, do a few more practice problems, and call it quits.** It doesn't pay to make yourself crazy right before the test. Besides, you've prepared. You'll do well.

> **EXPERT TUTOR TIP**
> Guard against being easily distracted during the test—by traffic outside or a sniffling neighbor. Try practicing in a coffee shop or with the door to your room open.

THE DAY BEFORE THE TEST

- **Don't study.**
- **Get together an "ACT survival kit" containing the following items:**
  - Watch (preferably digital)
  - At least three sharpened No. 2 pencils
  - Pencil sharpener
  - Two erasers
  - Photo ID card (if you're not taking the test at your high school, make sure your ID is official)
  - An approved calculator
  - Your admission ticket
  - Snack and a bottle of water—there's a break, and you'll probably get hungry
  - Confidence!

- **Know exactly where you're going and how you're getting there.** It's a good idea to visit your test center sometime before test day so that you know what to expect on the big day.

> ☑ **PERFECT SCORE TIP**
> Make sure you prepare the things you will need the day before. It is not worth getting stressed the morning of because you cannot find your calculator or pencils.

- **Relax!** Read a good book, take a bubble bath, watch TV. Exercise can be a good idea early in the afternoon. Working out makes it easier to sleep when you're nervous, and it also makes many people feel better. Of course, don't work so hard that you can't get up the next day!

> ☑ **PERFECT SCORE TIP**
> You have worked too hard for this test to give it all up by going out the night before. Relax the night before and get a good night's sleep so you are ready for the next morning.

- **Get a good night's sleep.** Go to bed early and allow for some extra time to get ready in the morning.

THE MORNING OF THE TEST

- **Eat breakfast.** Protein is brain food, but don't eat anything too heavy or greasy. Don't drink a lot of coffee if you're not used to it; bathroom breaks cut into your time, and too much caffeine—or any other kind of drug—is a bad idea.

> ☑ **PERFECT SCORE TIP**
> Be sure to bring food for breaks, and eat a sufficient breakfast. I find foods such as peanut butter and raisins give me the lasting energy needed for such a grueling test. Be careful of eating sugar, as it only gives short-term energy.

- **Dress in layers** so that you can adjust to the temperature of the test room.
- **Read something.** Warm up your brain with a newspaper or a magazine. Don't let the ACT be the first thing you read that day.
- **Be sure to get there early.** Allow yourself extra time for traffic, mass-transit delays, and any other possible problems.
- **If you can, go to the test with a friend** (even if he or she isn't taking the test). It's nice to have somebody supporting you right up to the last minute.

DURING THE TEST

- **Don't get rattled.** If you find your confidence slipping, remind yourself how well you've prepared. You've followed the keys to ACT success, and you have practiced. You know the test; you know the strategies; you know the material tested. You're in great shape, as long as you relax!

- **Even if something goes really wrong, don't panic.** If the test booklet is defective—two pages are stuck together or the ink has run—try to stay calm. Raise your hand, and tell the proctor you need a new book. If you accidentally misgrid your answer page or put the answers in the wrong section, again, don't panic. Raise your hand, and tell the proctor. He or she might be able to arrange for you to regrid your test after it's over, when it won't cost you any time.

> ☑ **PERFECT SCORE TIP**
> Calm down during the test. Take a deep breath if you are getting stressed, and remember that you are prepared and have an arsenal of tools to help increase your chances of answering even the toughest problems.

Good luck! With all of your practice and Kaplan's strategies under your belt, we know you'll do great on the ACT.

AFTER THE TEST

Once the test is over, put it out of your mind. If you don't plan to take the ACT again, shelve this book and start thinking about more interesting things.

You might walk out of the ACT thinking that you blew it. This is a normal reaction. Lots of people—even the highest scorers—feel that way. You tend to remember the questions that stumped you, not the many that you knew. If you're really concerned, call us for advice. Also call us if you had any problems with your test experience—a proctor who called time early, a testing room whose temperature hovered just below freezing. We'll do everything we can to make sure that your rights as a test taker are preserved!

However, we're positive that you performed well and scored your best on the exam because you followed our ACT Premier Program. Be confident that you were prepared, and celebrate in the fact that the ACT is a distant memory.

If you want more help or just want to know more about the ACT, college admissions, or Kaplan prep courses for the ACT, give us a call at 800-KAP-TEST or visit us at www. kaptest.com. We're here to answer your questions and to help you in any way we can. Also, be sure to return one last time to your online syllabus and complete our survey. We're only as good as our successful students!

> ✓ **PERFECT SCORE TIP**
> Congratulations! You're done! Schedule something fun to do after the test as a reward for your hard work—and don't fret about score reports. Don't beat yourself up if you don't think you did your best.

PART FOUR

Practice Tests and Explanations

ENGLISH TEST

45 Minutes—75 Questions

Directions: In the following five passages, certain words and phrases are underlined and numbered. In the right-hand column are alternatives for each underlined portion. Select the one that best conveys the idea, creates the most grammatically correct sentence, or is the most consistent with the style and tone of the passage. If you decide that the original version is best, select NO CHANGE. You may also find questions that ask about the entire passage or a section of the passage. These questions will correspond to small numbered boxes in the text. For these questions, decide which choice best accomplishes the purpose set out in the question stem. After you've selected the best choice, fill in the corresponding oval in your Answer Grid. For some questions, you'll need to read the context in order to answer correctly. Be sure to read until you have enough information to determine the correct answer choice.

You will also find questions about a section of the passage or about the passage as a whole. These questions do not refer to an underlined portion of the passage, but rather are identified by a number or numbers in a box.

For each question, choose the alternative you consider best and fill in the corresponding oval on your answer document. Read each passage through once before you begin to answer the questions that accompany it. For many of the questions, you must read several sentences beyond the question to determine the answer. Be sure that you have read enough ahead each time you choose an alternative.

Passage I

ORIGINS OF URBAN LEGENDS

[1]

Since primitive times, societies have created,
1

and told legends. Even before the development
1

of written language, cultures would orally pass

down these popular stories.

1. A. NO CHANGE
   B. created then subsequently told
   C. created and told
   D. created, and told original

[2]

2̲ These stories served the dual purpose of

entertaining audiences and of transmitting values

and beliefs from generation to generation. Indeed
                                           ‾‾‾‾‾‾
                                              3
today we have many more permanent ways of

handing down our beliefs to future generations,

we continue to create and tell legends. In our

technological society, a new form of folktale has

emerged: the urban legend.
        ‾‾‾
         4

[3]

Urban legends are stories we all have heard;

they are supposed to have really happened,

but are never verifiable however. It seems that
              ‾‾‾‾‾‾‾‾‾‾‾‾‾‾‾‾‾
                      5
the people involved can never be found.

Researchers of the urban legend call the elusive

participant in such supposed "real-life" events a

FOAF—a Friend of a Friend.

[4]

Urban legends have some characteristic

features. They are often humorous in nature

2. Suppose that the author wants to insert a sentence here to describe the different kinds of oral stories told by these societies. Which of the following sentences would best serve that purpose?

   F. These myths and tales varied in substance, from the humorous to the heroic.

   G. These myths and tales were often recited by paid storytellers.

   H. Unfortunately, no recording of the original myths and tales exists.

   J. Sometimes it took several evenings for the full story to be recited.

3. A. NO CHANGE

   B. However,

   C. Indeed,

   D. Although

4. F. NO CHANGE

   G. it is called the

   H. it being the

   J. known as the

5. A. NO CHANGE

   B. verifiable, however.

   C. verifiable, furthermore.

   D. verifiable.

GO ON TO THE NEXT PAGE ⟹

with a surprise ending and a conclusion. One
<u>_____</u>
                            6
such legend is the tale of the hunter who was

returning home from an unsuccessful hunting

trip. On his way home, he accidentally hit and

killed a deer on a deserted highway. Even though

he knew it was illegal, he decided to keep the

deer, and he loads it in the back of his station
         <u>_____</u>
                7
wagon. As the hunter continued driving, the deer,

he was only temporarily knocked unconscious by
<u>_____</u>
   8
the car, woke up and began thrashing around. The

hunter panicked, stopped the car, ran to the ditch,

and watched the enraged deer destroy his car.

[5]

One legend involves alligators in the sewer

systems of major metropolitan areas. According

to the story, before alligators were a protected

species, people vacationing in Florida purchased
<u>_____</u>
      9
baby alligators to take home as souvenirs.

Between 1930 and 1940, nearly a million alligators
<u>_____</u>
                          10
in Florida were killed for the value of their skin,
<u>_____</u>
                          10
used to make expensive leather products such as
<u>_____</u>
                          10
boots and wallets. After the novelty of having a
<u>_____</u>
         10
pet alligator wore off, many people flushed their

baby souvenirs down toilets. Legend has it that

the baby alligators found a perfect growing and

6. F. NO CHANGE
   G. ending.
   H. ending, which is a conclusion.
   J. ending or conclusion.

7. A. NO CHANGE
   B. loaded it in
   C. is loading it in
   D. had loaded it in

8. F. NO CHANGE
   G. which being
   H. that is
   J. which was

9. A. NO CHANGE
   B. species; people
   C. species. People
   D. species people

10. F. NO CHANGE
    G. Because their skin is used to make
       expensive leather products such as
       boots and wallets, nearly a million
       alligators in Florida were killed
       between 1930 and 1940.
    H. Killed between 1930 and 1940, the
       skin of nearly a million alligators
       from Florida was used to make
       expensive leather products such as
       boots and wallets.
    J. OMIT the underlined portion.

GO ON TO THE NEXT PAGE ⟹

breeding environment in city sewer systems, where they thrive to this day on the ample supply of rats.

[6]

In addition to urban legends that are told from friend to friend, a growing number of urban legends are passed along through the Internet and email. One of the more popular stories

are about a woman who was unwittingly charged
___11___
$100 for a cookie recipe she requested at an upscale restaurant. To get her money's worth,

11. A. NO CHANGE
    B. would be about
    C. is about
    D. is dealing with

this woman supposed copied the recipe for the
    ___12___
delicious cookies and forwarded it via email to everyone she knew.

12. F. NO CHANGE
    G. woman supposedly
    H. women supposedly
    J. women supposed to

[7]

Although today's technology enhances our ability to tell and retell urban legends, the Internet can also serve as a monitor of urban legends. Dedicated to commonly told urban
    ___13___
legends, research is done by many websites.
    ___13___
According to those websites, most legends, including the ones told here, have no basis in reality.

13. A. NO CHANGE
    B. Many websites are dedicated to researching the validity of commonly told urban legends.
    C. Researching the validity of commonly told urban legends, many websites are dedicated.
    D. OMIT the underlined portion.

GO ON TO THE NEXT PAGE ⇨

Questions 14–15 ask about the preceding passage as a whole.

14. The author wants to insert the following sentence:

    Other urban legends seem to be designed to instill fear.

    What would be the most logical placement for this sentence?

    F. After the last sentence of paragraph 3

    G. After the second sentence of paragraph 4

    H. Before the first sentence of paragraph 5

    J. After the last sentence of paragraph 6

15. Suppose that the author had been assigned to write an essay comparing the purposes and topics of myths and legends in primitive societies and in our modern society. Would this essay fulfill that assignment?

    A. Yes, because the essay describes myths and legends from primitive societies and modern society.

    B. Yes, because the essay provides explanations of possible purposes and topics for myths and legends from primitive societies and modern society.

    C. No, because the essay does not provide enough information about the topics of the myths and legends in primitive societies to make a valid comparison.

    D. No, because the essay doesn't provide any information on the myths and legends of primitive societies.

GO ON TO THE NEXT PAGE

Passage II

HENRY DAVID THOREAU: A SUCCESSFUL LIFE

What does it mean to be successful? <u>Do one</u>
                                        16
measure success by money? If I told you about

a <u>man: working</u> as a teacher, a land surveyor,
    17
and a factory worker (never holding any of these

jobs for more than a few years), would that man

sound like a success to you? If I told you that he

spent <u>two solitary years living alone</u> in a small
          18
cabin that he built for himself and that he spent

those years looking at plants and writing in a

diary—would you think of him as a celebrity

or an important figure? What if I told you that

<u>he rarely ventured</u> far from the town where he
      19
was born, that he was thrown in jail for refusing

to pay his taxes, and that he died at the age of

forty-five? Do any of these facts seem to point

to a man whose life should be studied and

emulated?

   You may already know about this man.

You may even have read some of his writings.

His name <u>was: Henry David Thoreau, and he</u>
                                        20
was, in addition to the jobs listed above,

a poet, an essayist, a naturalist, and a social

critic. Although the facts listed about him may

16. F. NO CHANGE
    G. Does we
    H. Does one
    J. Did you

17. A. NO CHANGE
    B. man who worked
    C. man and worked
    D. man, which working

18. F. NO CHANGE
    G. two years living alone
    H. two solitary years all by himself
    J. a couple of lonely years living in
       solitude

19. A. NO CHANGE
    B. he is rarely venturing
    C. he has rare ventures
    D. this person was to venture rarely

20. F. NO CHANGE
    G. was Henry David Thoreau and he
    H. was: Henry David Thoreau; and he
    J. was Henry David Thoreau, and he

GO ON TO THE NEXT PAGE ⟶

not seem to add up to much, he was, in fact a
<u>   21   </u>
tremendously influential person. Along with

writers such as Ralph Waldo Emerson, Mark

Twain, and Walt Whitman, Thoreau helped to

create the first literature and philosophy that

most people identify as <u>unique</u> American.
                        22

In 1845, Thoreau built a <u>cabin. Near</u> Walden
                          23
Pond and remained there for more than two

years, living alone, fending for himself, and

observing the nature around him. He kept

scrupulous notes in his diary, notes that he

later distilled into his most famous work titled

Walden. <u>*Walden* is read by many literature</u>
                        24

<u>students today.</u>
      24

[1] To protest slavery, Thoreau refused to pay

his taxes in 1846. [2] Thoreau was a firm believer

in the abolition of slavery, and he objected to the

practice's extension into the new territories of the

West. [3] For this act of rebellion, he was thrown

in the Concord jail. [25]

21. A. NO CHANGE
    B. was, in fact, a
    C. was in fact a
    D. was in fact, a

22. F. NO CHANGE
    G. uniquely
    H. uniqueness
    J. the most unique

23. A. NO CHANGE
    B. cabin. On
    C. cabin, by
    D. cabin near

24. F. NO CHANGE
    G. This book is read by many literature
       students today.
    H. Today, many literature students read
       Walden.
    J. OMIT the underlined portion.

25. What is the most logical order of
    sentences in this paragraph?
    A. NO CHANGE
    B. 3, 2, 1
    C. 2, 1, 3
    D. 3, 1, 2

GO ON TO THE NEXT PAGE

Thoreau used his writing to spread his message of resistance and activism; he published 26 an essay entitled *Civil Disobedience* (also known as *Resistance to Civil Government*). In it, Thoreau laid out his argument for refusing to obey unjust laws.

Although Thoreau's life was very brief, his works and his ideas continue to touch and 27 influence people. Students all over the country— all over the world—continue to read his essays and hear his unique voice, urging them to lead lives of principle, individuality, and freedom. [28] To be able to live out the ideas that burn in

the heart of a person—surely that is the meaning 29 of success.

26. F. NO CHANGE
    G. activism, he published:
    H. activism, he published
    J. activism, he published,

27. A. NO CHANGE
    B. he's
    C. their
    D. those

28. The purpose of this paragraph is to:
    F. explain why Thoreau was put in jail.
    G. prove a point about people's conception of success.
    H. suggest that Thoreau may be misunderstood.
    J. discuss Thoreau's importance in today's world.

29. A. NO CHANGE
    B. one's heart
    C. the heart and soul of a person
    D. through the heart of a person

Question 30 asks about
the preceding passage as a whole.

---

30. By including questions throughout the entire first paragraph, the author allows the reader to:
    F. answer each question as the passage proceeds.
    G. think about the meaning of success.
    H. assess the quality of Thoreau's work.
    J. form an opinion about greed in modern society.

GO ON TO THE NEXT PAGE

Passage III

THE SLOTH: SLOW BUT NOT SLOTHFUL

[1]

More than half of the world's <u>currently living</u>
<u>plant</u> and animal species live in tropical rain
forests. Four square miles of a Central American
rain forest can be home to up to 1,500 different
species of flowering plants, 700 species of
trees, 400 species of birds, and 125 species of
mammals. Of these mammals, the sloth is one
of the most unusual.

[2]

Unlike most mammals, the sloth is usually
upside down. A sloth does just about everything
upside down, including sleeping, eating, mating,
and giving birth. <u>Its' unique</u> anatomy allows the
sloth to spend most of the time hanging from
one tree branch or another, high in the canopy
of a rain forest tree. About the size of a large
domestic <u>cat, the</u> sloth hangs from its unusually

long limbs and long hooklike claws. <u>Specially</u>
<u>designed for limbs, the sloth's muscles seem to</u>
<u>cling to things.</u>

31. A. NO CHANGE
    B. currently existing plant
    C. living plant
    D. plant

32. F. NO CHANGE
    G. It's unique
    H. Its unique
    J. Its uniquely

33. A. NO CHANGE
    B. cat; the
    C. cat. The
    D. cat, but the

34. F. NO CHANGE
    G. The sloth's muscles seem to cling to things for specially designed limbs.
    H. The muscles in a sloth's limbs seem to be specially designed for clinging to things.
    J. OMIT the underlined portion.

GO ON TO THE NEXT PAGE

[3]

In fact, a sloth's limbs are <u>so specific</u> adapted

35

to upside-down life that a sloth is essentially

incapable of walking on the ground. <u>Instead,</u>

36

<u>they</u> must crawl or drag itself with its massive

36

claws. This makes it easy to see why the sloth

rarely leaves its home in the trees. <u>Because</u> it can

37

not move swiftly on the ground, the sloth is an

excellent swimmer.

[4]

38 A sloth can hang upside down and,

without moving the rest of its <u>body turn</u> its face

39

35. A. NO CHANGE
B. so specific and
C. so specified
D. so specifically

36. F. NO CHANGE
G. Instead, it
H. However, they
J. In addition, it

37. A. NO CHANGE
B. Despite
C. Similarly,
D. Though

38. The author wants to insert a sentence here to help connect paragraph 3 and paragraph 4. Which of the following sentences would best serve that purpose?

F. Of course, many other animals are also excellent swimmers.

G. Another unique characteristic of the sloth is its flexibility.

H. In addition to swimming, the sloth is an incredible climber.

J. Flexibility is a trait that helps the sloth survive.

39. A. NO CHANGE
B. body turns
C. body, it has the capability of turning
D. body, turn

GO ON TO THE NEXT PAGE ⟩

180 degrees so that it <u>was looking</u> at the ground.
₄₀
A sloth can rotate its forelimbs in all directions,

so it can easily reach the leaves that make up

its diet. The sloth can also roll itself up into a

ball in order to <u>protect and defend itself from</u>
₄₁

predators. <u>The howler monkey, another inhabitant</u>
₄₂
<u>of the rain forest, is not as flexible as the sloth.</u>
₄₂

[5]

The best defense a sloth has from predators

such as jaguars and large snakes, though, is its

camouflage. During the rainy season, a sloth's

thick brown or gray fur is usually covered with

a coat of blue-green <u>algae. Which</u> helps it blend
₄₃
in with its forest surroundings. Another type

of camouflage is the sloth's incredibly slow

movement: it often moves less than 100 feet

during a 24-hour period.

[6]

It is this slow movement that earned the

sloth its name. *Sloth* is also a word for laziness

or an aversion to work. But even though it

sleeps an average of 15 hours a day, the sloth

40. F. NO CHANGE
G. had been looking
H. will have the ability to be looking
J. can look

41. A. NO CHANGE
B. protect itself and defend itself from
C. protect itself so it won't be harmed by
D. protect itself from

42. F. NO CHANGE
G. Another inhabitant of the rain forest, the howler monkey, is not as flexible as the sloth.
H. Not as flexible as the sloth is the howler monkey, another inhabitant of the rain forest.
J. OMIT the underlined portion.

43. A. NO CHANGE
B. algae, which
C. algae, being that it
D. algae

isn't necessarily lazy. It just moves, upside down,

at its own slow pace through its world of rain

forest trees. [44]

44. The author is considering deleting the last sentence of paragraph 6. This change would:

    F. diminish the amount of information provided about the habits of the sloth.

    G. make the ending of the passage more abrupt.

    H. emphasize the slothful nature of the sloth.

    J. make the tone of the essay more consistent.

Question 45 asks about
the preceding passage as a whole.

---

45. The author wants to insert the following description:

> An observer could easily be tricked into thinking that a sloth was just a pile of decaying leaves.

What would be the most appropriate placement for this sentence?

    A. After the last sentence of paragraph 1

    B. After the third sentence of paragraph 2

    C. Before the last sentence of paragraph 5

    D. Before the first sentence of paragraph 6

GO ON TO THE NEXT PAGE ▷

Passage IV

FIRES IN YELLOWSTONE

During the summer of 1988, I watched Yellowstone National Park go up in flames. In June, <u>fires ignited by lightning</u> had been allowed
46
to burn unsuppressed because park officials expected that the usual summer rains would douse the flames. However, the rains never

<u>will have come</u>. A plentiful fuel supply of fallen
47
logs and pine needles was available, and winds of up to 100 mph whipped the spreading fires along and carried red-hot embers to other areas, creating new fires. By the time park officials succumbed to the pressure of public opinion and <u>decide</u> to try to extinguish the <u>flames. It's</u> too
48   49
late. The situation remained out of control in spite of the efforts of 9,000 firefighters who were using state-of-the-art equipment. By September, more than 720,000 acres of Yellowstone had been

affected by fire. <u>Nature was only able to curb</u>
50
<u>the destruction</u>; the smoke did not begin to clear
50
until the first snow arrived on September 11.

46. F. NO CHANGE
    G. fires having been ignited by lightning
    H. fires, the kind ignited by lightning,
    J. fires ignited and started by lightning

47. A. NO CHANGE
    B. came
    C. were coming
    D. have come

48. F. NO CHANGE
    G. are deciding
    H. decided
    J. OMIT the underlined portion.

49. A. NO CHANGE
    B. flames, it's
    C. flames, it was
    D. flames; it was

50. F. NO CHANGE
    G. Only curbing the destruction by able nature
    H. Only nature was able to curb the destruction
    J. Nature was able to curb only the destruction

GO ON TO THE NEXT PAGE ▷

Being that I was an ecologist who has
                      51
studied forests for 20 years, I knew that this was

not nearly the tragedy it seemed to be. Large

fires are, after all, necessary in order that the
                                  52
continued health in the forest ecosystem be
                52
maintained. Fires thin out overcrowded areas
        52
and allow the sun to reach species of plants

stunted by shade. Ash fertilizes the soil, and

fire smoke kills forest bacteria. In the case of

the lodgepole pine, fire is essential to reprodu-

tion: the pines' cone open only when exposed to
              53
temperatures greater than 112 degrees.

    The fires in Yellowstone did result in some

loss of wildlife, but overall, the region's animals

proved to be fire-tolerant and fire-adaptive.

However, large animals such as bison were often
54

seen grazing, and bedding down in meadows
        55
near burning forests. Also, the fire posed little

threat to the members of any endangered animal

species in the park.

    My confidence in the natural resilience of

the forest has been borne out in the years since

51. A. NO CHANGE
    B. Being that I am
    C. I'm
    D. As

52. F. NO CHANGE
    G. for the continued health of the
        forest ecosystem to be maintained.
    H. in order to continue the mainte-
        nance of the health of the forest
        ecosystem.
    J. for the continued health of the
        forest ecosystem.

53. A. NO CHANGE
    B. pines cones'
    C. pine's cones
    D. pine's cone

54. F. NO CHANGE
    G. Clearly,
    H. In fact,
    J. Instead,

55. A. NO CHANGE
    B. grazing; and bedding
    C. grazing: and bedding
    D. grazing and bedding

GO ON TO THE NEXT PAGE ⟶

the fires ravaged Yellowstone. <u>Judged from recent</u>
56

<u>pictures of the park</u> the forest was not destroyed;
56

<u>it</u> was rejuvenated.
57

56. F. NO CHANGE

   G. Recent pictures of the park show that

   H. Judging by the recent pictures of the park,

   J. As judged according to pictures taken of the park recently,

57. A. NO CHANGE

   B. they

   C. the fires

   D. I

Questions 58–59 ask about the preceding passage as a whole.

---

58. The writer is considering inserting the following true statement after the first sentence of the second paragraph:

> Many more acres of forest burned in Alaska in 1988 than in Yellowstone Park.

Would this addition be appropriate for the essay?

   F. Yes, the statement would add important information about the effects of large-scale forest fires.

   G. Yes, the statement would provide an informative contrast to the Yellowstone fire.

   H. No, the statement would not provide any additional information about the effect of the 1988 fire in Yellowstone.

   J. No, the statement would undermine the author's position as an authority on the subject of forest fires.

59. Suppose that the writer wishes to provide additional support for the claim that the fire posed little threat to the members of any endangered animal species in the park. Which of the following additions would be most effective?

   A. A list of the endangered animals known to inhabit the park

   B. A discussion of the particular vulnerability of endangered species of birds to forest fires

   C. An explanation of the relative infrequency of such an extensive series of forest fires

   D. A summary of reports of biologists who monitored the activity of endangered species in the park during the fire

GO ON TO THE NEXT PAGE ⇒

Passage V

MY FIRST WHITE-WATER RAFTING TRIP

[1]

White-water rafting being a favorite pastime of
                              60
mine for several years. I have drifted down many

challenging North American rivers, including

the Snake, the Green, and the Salmon, and there
                                            61
are many other rivers in America as well. I have
        61
spent some of my best moments in dangerous

rapids, yet nothing has matched the thrill I expe-

rienced facing my first rapids, on the Deschutes
                              62
River.
  62

[2]

My father and I spent the morning floating

down a calm and peaceful stretch of the Deschutes

in his wooden MacKenzie river boat. This trip

it being the wooden boat's first time down rapids,
  63

as well as mine. Rapids are rated according to a
                             64
uniform scale of relative difficulty.
              64

60. F. NO CHANGE
    G. have been
    H. has been
    J. was

61. A. NO CHANGE
    B. Salmon, just three of many rivers
       existing in North America.
    C. Salmon; many other rivers exist in
       North America.
    D. Salmon.

62. F. NO CHANGE
    G. first: rapids on the Deschutes River.
    H. first rapids; on the Deschutes River.
    J. first rapids on the Deschutes River.

63. A. NO CHANGE
    B. it happened that it was
    C. was
    D. being

64. F. NO CHANGE
    G. Rated according to a uniform scale,
       rapids are relatively difficult.
    H. (Rapids are rated according to a
       uniform scale of relative difficulty.)
    J. OMIT the underlined portion.

GO ON TO THE NEXT PAGE

[3]

Roaring, I was in the boat approaching
                        65
Whitehorse Rapids. I felt much like a novice skier
        65

peering down her first steep slope: I was scared,

but even more excited. The water churned and
                                        66
covering me with a refreshing spray. My father,
        66
towards the stern, controlled the oars. The

carefree expression he usually wore on the river

had been replaced and instead he adopted a
                    67
look of intense concentration as he maneuvered

around boulders dotting our path. To release

tension, we began to holler like kids on a roller

coaster, our voices echoing across the water as
                                68
we lurched violently about.

[4]

Suddenly we came to a jarring halt and we
                                        69
stopped; the left side of the bow was wedged
    69
on a large rock. A whirlpool whirled around

us; if we capsized, we would be sucked into the

undertow. Instinctively, I threw all of my weight

towards the right side of the tilting boat. Luckily,

65. A. NO CHANGE
    B. It roared, and the boat and I approached Whitehorse Rapids.
    C. While the roaring boat was approaching Whitehorse Rapids, I could hear the water.
    D. I could hear the water roar as we approached Whitehorse Rapids.

66. F. NO CHANGE
    G. churned, and covering me
    H. churning and covering me
    J. churned, covering me

67. A. NO CHANGE
    B. with
    C. by another countenance altogether:
    D. instead with another expression;

68. F. NO CHANGE
    G. throughout
    H. around
    J. from

69. A. NO CHANGE
    B. which stopped us
    C. and stopped
    D. OMIT the underlined portion.

it was just enough force to dislodge us, and we
―――
70

continued on down for about ten more minutes

of spectacular rapids.

[5]

Later that day, we went through Buckskin

Mary Rapids and Boxcar Rapids. When we

pulled up on the bank that evening, we saw that

the boat had received its first scar: that scar was a
―――――――――
71

small hole on the upper bow from the boulder

we had wrestled with. In the years to come,

we went down many rapids and the boat

receiving many bruises, but Whitehorse is the
―――――――
72

most memorable rapids of all. [73]

70. F. NO CHANGE
    G. it's
    H. it is
    J. its

71. A. NO CHANGE
    B. that was a
    C. which was a
    D. a

72. F. NO CHANGE
    G. received many
    H. received much
    J. receives many

73. Which of the following concluding
    sentences would most effectively
    emphasize the final point made in this
    paragraph while retaining the style and
    tone of the narrative as a whole?

    A. The brutal calamities that it
       presented the unwary rafter were
       more than offset by its beguiling
       excitement.

    B. Perhaps it is true that your first
       close encounter with white water is
       your most intense.

    C. Or, if not the most memorable, then
       at least a very memorable one!

    D. Call me crazy or weird if you want,
       but white-water rafting is the sport
       for me.

Questions 74–75 ask about the preceding passage as a whole.

74. The writer has been assigned to write an essay that focuses on the techniques of white-water rafting. Would this essay meet the requirements of that assignment?

F. No, because the essay's main focus is on a particular experience, not on techniques.

G. No, because the essay mostly deals with the relationship between father and daughter.

H. Yes, because specific rafting techniques are the essay's main focus.

J. Yes, because it presents a dramatic story of a day of white-water rafting.

75. Suppose that the writer wants to add the following sentence to the essay:

It was such a peaceful summer day that it was hard to believe dangerous rapids awaited us downstream.

What would be the most logical placement of this sentence?

A. After the last sentence of paragraph 1

B. After the last sentence of paragraph 2

C. Before the first sentence of paragraph 4

D. After the last sentence of paragraph 4

MATH TEST

60 Minutes—60 Questions

Directions: Solve each of the following problems, select the correct answer, and then fill in the corresponding oval on your Answer Grid.

Don't linger over problems that are too time-consuming. Do as many as you can, then come back to the others in the time permitted.

You may use a calculator on this test. Some questions, however, may be easier to answer without the use of a calculator.

Note: Unless the question says otherwise, assume all of the following:

1. Illustrative figures are *not* necessarily drawn to scale.
2. All geometric figures lie in a plane.
3. The term *line* indicates a straight line.
4. The term *average* indicates arithmetic mean.

---

1. In a recent survey, 14 people found their mayor to be "very competent." This number is exactly 20% of the people surveyed. How many people were surveyed?

   A. 28
   B. 35
   C. 56
   D. 70
   E. 84

DO YOUR FIGURING HERE.

GO ON TO THE NEXT PAGE

2. A train traveled at a rate of 90 miles per hour for x hours, and then at a rate of 60 miles per hour for y hours. Which expression represents the train's average rate in miles per hour for the entire distance traveled?

DO YOUR FIGURING HERE.

F. $\dfrac{540}{xy}$

G. $\dfrac{90}{x} \times \dfrac{60}{y}$

H. $\dfrac{90}{x} + \dfrac{60}{y}$

J. $\dfrac{90x + 60y}{x + y}$

K. $\dfrac{150}{x + y}$

3. In a certain string ensemble, the ratio of men to women is 5:3. If there are a total of 24 people in the ensemble, how many women are there?

A. 8
B. 9
C. 10
D. 11
E. 12

4. If $x \neq 0$, and $x^2 - 3x = 6x$, then $x = ?$

F. −9
G. −3
H. $\sqrt{3}$
J. 3
K. 9

5. The two overlapping circles below form three regions, as shown:

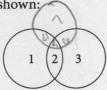

   What is the maximum number of regions that can be formed by three overlapping circles?

   A. 5

   B. 6

   C. 7

   D. 8

   E. 9

6. If $x^2 + 6x + 8 = 4 + 10x$, then x equals which of the following?

   F. −2

   G. −1

   H. 0

   J. 1

   K. 2

7. Nine less than the number c is the same as the number d, and d less than twice c is 20. Which two equations could be used to determine the value of c and d?

   A. $d - 9 = c$
      $d - 2c = 20$

   B. $c - 9 = d$
      $2c - d = 20$

   C. $c - 9 = d$
      $d - 2c = 20$

   D. $9 - c = d$
      $2c - d = 20$

   E. $9 - c = d$
      $2cd = 20$

DO YOUR FIGURING HERE.

$$x^2 - 4x + 4$$
$$(x - 2)(x - 2)$$

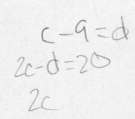

$$c - 9 = d$$
$$2c - d = 20$$
$$2c$$

GO ON TO THE NEXT PAGE

8. An ice cream parlor offers five flavors of ice cream and four different toppings (sprinkles, hot fudge, whipped cream, and butterscotch). There is a special offer that includes one flavor of ice cream and one topping, served in a cup, sugar cone, or waffle cone. How many ways are there to order ice cream with the special offer?

   F. 4
   G. 5
   H. 12
   J. 23
   K. 60

DO YOUR FIGURING HERE.

$5 \cdot 4 \cdot 3$

9. At a recent audition for a school play, 1 out of 3 students who auditioned were asked to come to a second audition. After the second audition, 75% of those asked to the second audition were offered parts. If 18 students were offered parts, how many students went to the first audition?

   A. 18
   B. 24
   C. 48
   D. 56
   E. 72

$\dfrac{1}{3}$

10. One number is 5 times another number, and their sum is −60. What is the lesser of the two numbers?

    F. −5
    G. −10
    H. −12
    J. −48
    K. −50

$x = 5y$

$x + y = 60$

$5y + y = 60$

$y = 10$

11. In the figure below, which is composed of equilateral triangles, what is the greatest number of parallelograms that can be found?

DO YOUR FIGURING HERE.

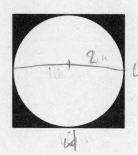

A. 6
B. 9
C. 12
D. 15
E. 18

12. The circle in the figure below is inscribed in a square with a perimeter of 16 inches. What is the area of the shaded region?

F. 4π
G. $16 - 2\pi$
H. $16 - 4\pi$
J. $8 - 2\pi$
K. $8 - 4\pi$

13. How many positive integers less than 50 are multiples of 4 but *not* multiples of 6?

A. 4
B. 6
C. 8
D. 10
E. 12

GO ON TO THE NEXT PAGE

14. What is the value of $f(3)$ where $f(x) = (8 - 3x)$ $(x^2 - 2x - 15)$?

    F.   −30
    G.   −18
    H.   12
    J.   24
    K.   30

    DO YOUR FIGURING HERE.

    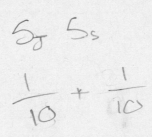

15. A class contains five juniors and five seniors. If one member of the class is assigned at random to present a paper on a certain subject, and another member of the class is randomly assigned to assist him, what is the probability that both will be juniors?

    A. $\frac{1}{10}$
    B. $\frac{1}{5}$
    C. $\frac{2}{9}$
    D. $\frac{2}{5}$
    E. $\frac{1}{2}$

16. In triangle XYZ below, $\overline{XS}$ and $\overline{SZ}$ are 3 and 12 units, respectively. If the area of triangle XYZ is 45 square units, how many units long is altitude $\overline{YS}$?

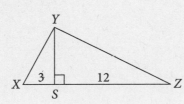

    F.   3
    G.   6
    H.   9
    J.   12
    K.   15

GO ON TO THE NEXT PAGE

17. At which *y*-coordinate does the line described by the equation $6y - 3x = 18$ intersect the *y*-axis?

    A. 2
    B. 3
    C. 6
    D. 9
    E. 18

DO YOUR FIGURING HERE.

$$y = \frac{18 + 3x}{6}$$

$$\frac{1}{2}x + 3$$

18. If $x^2 - y^2 = 12$ and $x - y = 4$, what is the value of $x^2 + 2xy + y^2$?

    F. 3
    G. 8
    H. 9
    J. 12
    K. 16

$$x = 4 + y$$

$$(4+y)^2 - y^2 = 12$$

19. What is the area in square units of the figure below?

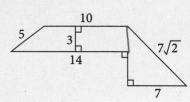

$$A = \frac{1}{2}(3)(14 + 10)$$

$$A = 36$$

$$A = \frac{1}{2}(7)(7)$$

    A. 147
    B. 108.5
    C. 91
    D. 60.5
    E. $39 + 7\sqrt{2}$

GO ON TO THE NEXT PAGE

20. A carpenter is cutting wood to make a new bookcase with a board that is 12 feet long. If the carpenter cuts off three pieces, each of which is 17 inches long, how many inches long is the remaining fourth and final board? (A foot contains 12 inches.)

    F.   36

    G.   51

    H.   93

    J.   108

    K.   144

DO YOUR FIGURING HERE.

$$\frac{17 + 17 + 17}{12}$$

21. If $x^2 - 4x - 6 = 6$, what are the possible values for x?

    A.   4, 12

    B.   −6, 2

    C.   −6, −2

    D.   6, 2

    E.   6, −2

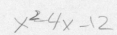

$$x^2 - 4x - 12$$

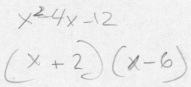

$$(x + 2)(x - 6)$$

22. If −3 is a solution for the equation $x^2 + kx - 15 = 0$, what is the value of k?

    F.   5

    G.   2

    H.   −2

    J.   −5

    K.   Cannot be determined from the information given.

$$x^2 + kx - 15 =$$

$$(x + 3)(x - 5)$$

23. If the lengths of all three sides of a triangle are integers, and one side is 7 inches long, what is the smallest possible perimeter of the triangle, in inches?

    A.   9

    B.   10

    C.   12

    D.   15

    E.   18

7 in

GO ON TO THE NEXT PAGE

24. If $0° < \theta < 90°$ and $\sin \theta = \dfrac{\sqrt{11}}{2\sqrt{3}}$, then $\cos \theta = ?$

    F. $\dfrac{1}{2\sqrt{3}}$

    G. $\dfrac{1}{\sqrt{11}}$

    H. $\dfrac{2}{\sqrt{3}}$

    J. $\dfrac{2\sqrt{3}}{\sqrt{11}}$

    K. $\dfrac{11}{2\sqrt{3}}$

25. Which of the following expressions is equivalent to $\dfrac{\sqrt{3+x}}{\sqrt{3-x}}$ for all x such that $-3 < x < 3$?

    A. $\dfrac{3-x}{3+x}$

    B. $\dfrac{3+x}{3-x}$

    C. $\dfrac{-3\sqrt{3+x}}{3-x}$

    D. $\dfrac{\sqrt{9-x^2}}{3-x}$

    E. $\dfrac{x^2-9}{3+x}$

26. In a certain cookie jar containing only macaroons and gingersnaps, the ratio of macaroons to gingersnaps is 2 to 5. Which of the following could be the total number of cookies in the cookie jar?

    F. 24
    G. 35
    H. 39
    J. 48
    K. 52

DO YOUR FIGURING HERE.

2:5

4:10

6:15

8:20

10:25

12:30

27. What is the sum of $\frac{3}{16}$ and .175?

    A. .3165
    B. .3500
    C. .3625
    D. .3750
    E. .3875

28. What is the maximum possible area, in square inches, of a rectangle with a perimeter of 20 inches?

    F. 15
    G. 20
    H. 25
    J. 30
    K. 40

5·4 20

5

29. $\dfrac{\dfrac{3}{2} + \dfrac{7}{4}}{\left(\dfrac{15}{8} - \dfrac{3}{4}\right) - \left(\dfrac{4+3}{-4+3}\right)} = ?$

DO YOUR FIGURING HERE.

A. $\dfrac{3}{8}$

B. $\dfrac{2}{5}$

C. $\dfrac{9}{13}$

D. $\dfrac{5}{2}$

E. $\dfrac{8}{3}$

30. If $x - 15 = 7 - 5(x - 4)$, then $x = ?$

F. 0
G. 2
H. 4
J. 5
K. 7

31. The sketch below shows the dimensions of a flower garden. What is the area of this garden in square meters?

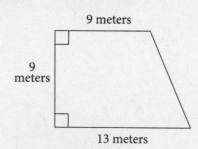

9 meters

9 meters

13 meters

A. 31
B. 85
C. 99
D. 101
E. 117

GO ON TO THE NEXT PAGE

32. What is the slope of the line described by the equation $6y - 3x = 18$?

    F. -2

    G. $-\dfrac{1}{2}$

    H. $\dfrac{1}{2}$

    J. 2

    K. 3

DO YOUR FIGURING HERE.

$y = \dfrac{18-3x}{6}$

$y = 3 - \dfrac{1}{2}x$

33. Line m passes through the point $(4, 3)$ in the standard (x, y) coordinate plane and is perpendicular to the line described by the equation $y = -\dfrac{4}{5}x + 6$. Which of the following equations describes line m?

    A. $y = \dfrac{5}{4}x - 2$

    B. $y = -\dfrac{5}{4}x + 6$

    C. $y = -\dfrac{4}{5}x - 2$

    D. $y = -\dfrac{4}{5}x + 2$

    E. $y = -\dfrac{5}{4}x - 2$

34. Line t in the standard (x, y) coordinate plane has a y-intercept of -3 and is parallel to the line having the equation $3x - 5y = 4$. Which of the following is an equation for line t?

    F. $y = -\dfrac{3}{5}x + 3$

    G. $y = -\dfrac{5}{3}x - 3$

    H. $y = \dfrac{3}{5}x + 3$

    J. $y = \dfrac{5}{3}x + 3$

    K. $y = \dfrac{3}{5}x - 3$

$5y = 3x - 4$

$y = \dfrac{3}{5}x - \dfrac{4}{5}$

GO ON TO THE NEXT PAGE

35. If $y = mx + b$, which of the following equations expresses x in terms of y, m, and b?

A. $x = \dfrac{y - b}{m}$

B. $x = \dfrac{b - y}{m}$

C. $x = \dfrac{y + b}{m}$

D. $x = \dfrac{y}{m} - bx$

E. $x = \dfrac{y}{m} + b$

DO YOUR FIGURING HERE.

$\dfrac{y-b}{xm} = x$

36. In the figure below, $\overline{AB} = 20$, $\overline{BC} = 15$, and $\angle ADB$ and $\angle ABC$ are right angles. What is the length of $\overline{AD}$?

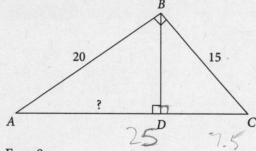

F.   9

G. 12

H. 15

J.   16

K. 25

37. In the standard (x, y) coordinate plane shown in the figure below, points A and B lie on line m, and point C lies below it. The coordinates of points A, B, and C are $(0, 5)$, $(5, 5)$, and $(3, 3)$, respectively. What is the shortest possible distance from point C to a point on line m?

DO YOUR FIGURING HERE.

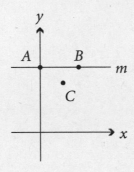

A. 2

B. $2\sqrt{2}$

C. 3

D. $\sqrt{13}$

E. 5

38. For all $x \neq 8$, $\dfrac{x^2 - 11x + 24}{8 - x} = $?

F. $8 - x$

G. $3 - x$

H. $x - 3$

J. $x - 8$

K. $x - 11$

$-1(x - 3)(x - 8)$

$-1(3 - x)(8 - x)$

39. Points A and B lie in the standard (x, y) coordinate plane. The (x, y) coordinates of A are $(2, 1)$ and the (x, y) coordinates of B are $(-2, -2)$. What is the distance from A to B?

A. $3\sqrt{2}$

B. $3\sqrt{3}$

C. 5

D. 6

E. 7

GO ON TO THE NEXT PAGE

40. In the figure below, $\overline{AB}$ and $\overline{CD}$ are both tangent to the circle as shown, and $ABCD$ is a rectangle with side lengths $2x$ and $5x$ as shown. What is the area of the shaded region?

$5x$

A ⏜ B

$2x$ $2x$

D C

F. $10\pi x^2$

G. $10x^2 - \pi x^2$

H. $10x^2 - 2\pi x$

J. $9\pi x^2$

K. $6\pi x^2$

41. If $0° < \theta < 90°$ and $\cos \theta = \dfrac{5\sqrt{2}}{8}$, then $\tan \theta = ?$

A. $\dfrac{5}{\sqrt{7}}$

B. $\dfrac{\sqrt{7}}{5}$

C. $\dfrac{\sqrt{14}}{8}$

D. $\dfrac{8}{\sqrt{14}}$

E. $\dfrac{8}{5\sqrt{2}}$

DO YOUR FIGURING HERE.

$10x^2 - x\pi$

8 x

$5\sqrt{2}$

$64 = (5(\sqrt{2}))^2 + x^2$

$25 \cdot 2$

50

$\dfrac{\sqrt{14}}{5\sqrt{2}}$

GO ON TO THE NEXT PAGE

42. Consider fractions of the form $\frac{7}{n}$, where n is an integer. How many integer values of n make this fraction greater than .5 and less than .8?

   F. 3
   G. 4
   H. 5
   J. 6
   K. 7

DO YOUR FIGURING HERE.

43. The circumference of circle X is 12π and the circumference of circle Y is 8π. What is the greatest possible distance between two points, one of which lies on the circumference of circle X and one of which lies on the circumference of circle Y?

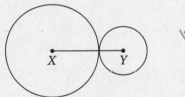

$12\pi = 2\pi r$

$6 = r$

$4 = r$

   A. 6
   B. 10
   C. 20
   D. 10π
   E. 20π

44. $\sqrt{(x^2 + 4)^2} - (x + 2)(x - 2) = ?$

   F. $2x^2$
   G. $x^2 - 8$
   H. $2(x - 2)$
   J. 0
   K. 8

$\sqrt{(x^2+4)^2} \; x^2 - 4 =$

$x^2 + 4 - (x^2 - 4)$

GO ON TO THE NEXT PAGE

45. If $s = -3$, then $s^3 + 2s^2 + 2s = ?$

    A. -15
    B. -10
    C. -5
    D. 5
    E. 33

DO YOUR FIGURING HERE.

46. How many different numbers are solutions
    for the equation $2x + 6 = (x + 5)(x + 3)$?

    F. 0
    G. 1
    H. 2
    J. 3
    K. Infinitely many

    $x^2 + 8x + 15$
    $x^2 + 6x + 9$
    $(x + 3)(x + 3)$

47. In square $ABCD$ below, $\overline{AC} = 8$. What is the
    perimeter of $ABCD$?

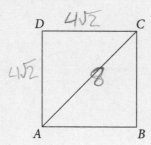

$\dfrac{8}{\sqrt{2}} \quad 4\sqrt{2}$

    A. $4\sqrt{2}$
    B. 8
    C. $8\sqrt{2}$
    D. 16
    E. $16\sqrt{2}$

GO ON TO THE NEXT PAGE

48. The front surface of a fence panel is shown below with the lengths labeled representing inches. The panel is symmetrical along its center vertical axis. What is the surface area of the front surface of the panel in square inches?

DO YOUR FIGURING HERE.

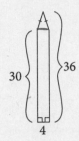

   F.   144

   G. 132

   H. 120

   J.   80

   K. $64 + 6\sqrt{5}$

49. In the figure below, O is the center of the circle, and C, D, and E are points on the circumference of the circle. If $\angle OCD$ measures 70° and $\angle OED$ measures 45°, what is the measure of $\angle CDE$?

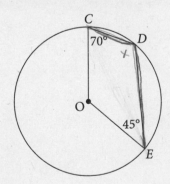

   A.   25°

   B.   45°

   C.   70°

   D.   90°

   E. 115°

GO ON TO THE NEXT PAGE

50. Which of the following systems of equations does NOT have a solution?

DO YOUR FIGURING HERE.

    F. $x + 3y = 19$
        $3x + y = 6$

    G. $x + 3y = 19$
        $x - 3y = 13$

    H. $x - 3y = 19$
        $3x - y = 7$

    J. $x - 3y = 19$
        $3x + y = 6$

    K. $x + 3y = 6$
        $3x + 9y = 7$

51. What is the 46th digit to the right of the decimal point in the decimal equivalent of $\frac{1}{7}$?

    A. 1
    B. 2
    C. 4
    D. 7
    E. 8

52. Which of the following inequalities is equivalent to $-2 - 4x \le -6x$?

    F. $x \ge -2$
    G. $x \ge 1$
    H. $x \ge 2$
    J. $x \le -1$
    K. $x \le 1$

DO YOUR FIGURING HERE.

53. If $x > 0$ and $y > 0$, $\dfrac{\sqrt{x}}{x} + \dfrac{\sqrt{y}}{y}$ is equivalent to which of the following?

   A. $\dfrac{2}{xy}$

   B. $\dfrac{\sqrt{x} + \sqrt{y}}{\sqrt{xy}}$

   C. $\dfrac{x + y}{xy}$

   D. $\dfrac{\sqrt{x} + \sqrt{y}}{\sqrt{x + y}}$

   E. $\dfrac{x + y}{\sqrt{xy}}$

54. In the diagram below, $\overline{CD}$, $\overline{BE}$, and $\overline{AF}$ are all parallel and are intersected by two transversals as shown. What is the length of $\overline{EF}$?

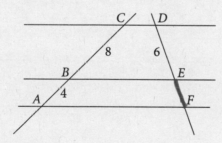

   F. 2
   G. 3
   H. 4
   J. 6
   K. 9

GO ON TO THE NEXT PAGE ⟩

55. What is the area, in square units, of the square whose vertices are located at the (x, y) coordinate points indicated in the figure below?

DO YOUR FIGURING HERE.

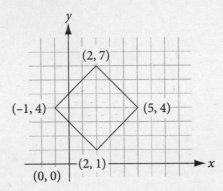

A. 9

B. 12

C. 16

D. 18

E. 24

56. Compared to the graph of $y = \cos \theta$, the graph of $y = 2 \cos \theta$ has:

F. twice the period and the same amplitude.

G. half the period and the same amplitude.

H. twice the period and half the amplitude.

J. half the amplitude and the same period.

K. twice the amplitude and the same period.

57. Brandy has a collection of comic books. If she adds 15 to the number of comic books in her collection and multiplies the sum by 3, the result will be 65 less than 4 times the number of comic books in her collection. How many comic books are in her collection?

A. 50

B. 85

C. 110

D. 145

E. 175

GO ON TO THE NEXT PAGE

58. One empty cylinder has three times the height and twice the diameter of another empty cylinder. How many fillings of the smaller cylinder would be equivalent to one filling of the larger cylinder?

(Note: The volume of a cylinder of radius r and height h is $\pi r^2 h$.)

F. 6

G. $6\sqrt{2}$

H. 12

J. 18

K. 24

59. What is the perimeter of a 30°-60°-90° triangle with a long leg of 12 inches?

A. $5\sqrt{3} + 12$

B. $4\sqrt{3} + 18$

C. $8\sqrt{3} + 18$

D. $12\sqrt{3} + 12$

E. $12\sqrt{3} + 18$

60. A baseball team scores an average of x points in its first n games and then scores y points in its next and final game of the season. Which of the following represents the team's average score for the entire season?

F. $x + \dfrac{y}{n}$

G. $x + \dfrac{y}{n+1}$

H. $\dfrac{x + ny}{n+1}$

J. $\dfrac{nx + y}{n+1}$

K. $\dfrac{n(x+y)}{n+1}$

DO YOUR FIGURING HERE.

IF YOU FINISH BEFORE TIME IS CALLED, YOU MAY CHECK YOUR WORK ON THIS SECTION ONLY. DO NOT TURN TO ANY OTHER SECTION IN THE TEST. STOP

READING TEST

35 Minutes—40 Questions

Directions: This test contains four passages, each followed by several questions. After reading each passage, select the best answer to each question and fill in the corresponding oval on your Answer Grid. You may refer to the passages while answering the questions.

Passage I

PROSE FICTION

This passage is adapted from the novel *Emma* by Jane Austen. It was originally published in 1815.

Emma Woodhouse, handsome, clever, and rich, with a comfortable home and happy disposition, seemed to unite some of the
Line best blessings of existence. She had lived
(5) nearly twenty-one years in the world with very little to distress or vex her. She was the youngest of the two daughters of a most affectionate, indulgent father, and had, in consequence of her sister's marriage, been
(10) mistress of his house from a very early period. Her mother had died too long ago for her to have more than an indistinct remembrance of her caresses, and her place had been taken by an excellent governess
(15) who had fallen little short of a mother in affection.

Sixteen years had Miss Taylor been in Mr. Woodhouse's family, less as a governess than a friend, very fond of both daughters,
(20) but particularly of Emma. Between them it was more the intimacy of sisters. Even before Miss Taylor had ceased to hold the nominal office of governess, the mildness of her temper had hardly allowed her
(25) to impose any restraint. The shadow of authority being now long passed away, they had been living together as friend and friend very mutually attached, and Emma doing just what she liked, highly esteeming Miss
(30) Taylor's judgment, but directed chiefly by

her own. The real evils, indeed, of Emma's situation were the power of having rather too much her own way, and a disposition to think a little too well of herself; these were
(35) the disadvantages which threatened alloy to her many enjoyments. The danger, however, was at present so unperceived, that they did not by any means rank as misfortunes with her.

(40)   Sorrow came—a gentle sorrow—but not at all in the shape of any disagreeable consciousness. Miss Taylor married. It was Miss Taylor's loss which first brought grief. It was on the wedding-day of this beloved
(45) friend that Emma first sat in mournful thought of any continuance. The wedding over, and the bride-people gone, she and her father were left to dine together, with no prospect of a third to cheer a long evening.
(50) Her father composed himself to sleep after dinner, as usual, and she had then only to sit and think of what she had lost.

The marriage had every promise of happiness for her friend. Mr. Weston was
(55) a man of unexceptionable character, easy fortune, suitable age, and pleasant manners. There was some satisfaction in considering with what self-denying, generous friendship she had always wished and promoted the
(60) match, but it was a black morning's work for her. The want of Miss Taylor would be felt every hour of every day. She recalled her past kindness—the kindness, the affection of sixteen years—how she had taught her

GO ON TO THE NEXT PAGE

(65) and how she had played with her from five years old—how she had devoted all her powers to attach and amuse her in health— and how she had nursed her through the various illnesses of childhood. A large

(70) debt of gratitude was owing here, but the intercourse of he last seven years, the equal footing and perfect unreserve which had soon followed Isabella's marriage, on their being left to each other, was yet a dearer,

(75) tenderer recollection. She had been a friend and companion such as few possessed: intelligent, well-informed, useful, gentle, knowing all the ways of the family, interested in all its concerns, and peculiarly

(80) interested in her, in every pleasure, every scheme of hers—one to whom she could speak every thought as it arose, and who had such an affection for her as could never find fault.

(85) How was she to bear the change? It was true that her friend was going only half a mile from them, but Emma was aware that great must be the difference between a Mrs. Weston, only half a mile from them, and

(90) a Miss Taylor in the house. With all her advantages, natural and domestic, she was now in great danger of suffering from intellectual solitude.

1. According to the passage, what are the greatest disadvantages facing Emma?

   A. Her father is not a stimulating conversationalist, and she is bored.

   B. She is lonely and afraid that Mrs. Weston will not have a happy marriage.

   C. She is used to having her way too much, and she thinks too highly of herself.

   D. She misses the companionship of her mother, her sister, and Miss Taylor.

2. The name of Emma's sister is:

   F. Mrs. Weston.

   G. Isabella.

   H. Miss Taylor.

   J. Mrs. Woodhouse.

3. As described in the passage, Emma's relationship with Miss Taylor can be characterized as:

   A. similar to a mother-daughter relationship.

   B. similar to the relationship of sisters or best friends.

   C. weaker than Emma's relationship with her sister.

   D. stronger than Miss Taylor's relationship with her new husband.

4. As used in line 33, *disposition* can most closely be defined as:

   F. a tendency.

   G. control.

   H. placement.

   J. transfer.

GO ON TO THE NEXT PAGE

5. Which of the following are included in Emma's memories of her relationship with Miss Taylor?

   I. Miss Taylor taking care of Emma during childhood illnesses

   II. Miss Taylor entertaining Emma

   III. Miss Taylor teaching her mathematics

   IV. Miss Taylor scolding her for being selfish

   A. I, III, and IV only

   B. I and III only

   C. II, III, and IV only

   D. I and II only

6. It is most reasonable to infer from Emma's realization that "great must be the difference between a Mrs. Weston, only half a mile from them, and a Miss Taylor in the house" (lines 88–90) that:

   F. Miss Taylor will no longer be a part of Emma's life.

   G. Emma is happy about the marriage because now she will have more freedom.

   H. Emma regrets that her relationship with Miss Taylor will change.

   J. Emma believes that her relationship with Miss Taylor will become stronger.

7. Based on the passage, Emma could best be described as:

   A. sweet and naïve.

   B. self-centered and naïve.

   C. self-centered and headstrong.

   D. unappreciative and bitter.

8. The passage suggests that the quality Emma values most in a friend is:

   F. charisma.

   G. devotion.

   H. honesty.

   J. intelligence.

9. How does Emma view Mr. Weston?

   A. She thinks that he is an excellent match, and it required considerable self-sacrifice not to pursue him herself.

   B. She considers him to be a respectable if somewhat average match for her friend.

   C. She sees him as an intruder who has carried away her best friend in "a black morning's work" (line 60).

   D. She believes he is an indulgent, easily swayed man, reminiscent of her father.

10. From the passage, it can be inferred that Emma is accustomed to:

   F. behaving according to the wishes of her affectionate father.

   G. taking the advice of Miss Taylor when faced with deciding upon a course of action.

   H. doing as she pleases without permission from her father or governess.

   J. abiding by strict rules governing her behavior.

GO ON TO THE NEXT PAGE ⇨

Passage II

SOCIAL SCIENCE

This passage discusses different aspects of memory from a psychological perspective.

Learning and its result, memory, are processes by which we retain acquired information, emotions, and impressions
Line that can influence our behavior. At the
(5) psychological level, memory is not a single process. Sensory memory, the first of three main systems of memory, describes the momentary lingering of perceptual information as it is initially sensed and briefly
(10) recorded. When an image strikes the eyes, it lingers in the visual system for an instant while the image is interpreted, and is quickly overwritten by new information. In the visual system this is called *iconic memory*, in
(15) the auditory system it is *echoic memory*, and in reference to touch it is *haptic memory*.

If sensory information is processed, it can move into the second main system of memory, working memory. This was once
(20) known as short-term memory (and that term is still popularly used). But working memory is viewed as a more accurate term, since this system not only stores information for short periods of time, but also enables the use
(25) and manipulation of information processed there. However, only a limited number of items can be held in working memory (the average for most people is seven), and decay of the memory occurs rapidly, although
(30) it can be held longer if the information is mentally or vocally repeated. Unless we make a conscious effort to retain it, a working memory may disappear forever.

Long-term memory is the most compre-
(35) hensive of the three, with apparently infinite capacity. Memories recorded in long-term memory are never lost, although at times there may be difficulty accessing them. There are three independent catego-
(40) ries of long-term memory which interact

extensively: *episodic* involves personal memories and details of daily life, and is closely identified with its time and place; *semantic* contains facts and general
(45) knowledge that are not tied to when or how they were learned; and *procedural* retains skills used to perform certain activities that eventually may not require conscious effort.

Although the main systems of memory
(50) are widely accepted, controversy continues about memory formation and retrieval. It was once believed that for a memory to enter long-term memory it must first be held in working memory. However, this idea
(55) has been challenged by an alternate theory suggesting that sensory memories can be directly entered into long-term memory through a pathway that runs parallel to, rather than in series with, working memory.
(60) Memories therefore can register simultaneously in both systems.

Likewise, all agree that the retrieval of long-term memories is facilitated by repetition, but there is no agreement about the
(65) accuracy of these memories. For many years, the scientific community viewed human memory as similar to computer memory, with the mind recording each detail just as it was presented. However,
(70) there is a growing consensus that our memory is sometimes flawed. An inference or assumption made by an individual when a memory is created may later be recalled as fact, or the mind may fill in details that
(75) were originally missing. Moreover, when we try to recall a particular memory, an unrelated memory may alter it through a process called interference. There is even evidence that an entirely false memory can
(80) be incorporated as a memory indistinguishable from true memories. Although for most purposes these discrepancies are harmless, concerns regarding the accuracy of human memory challenge the reliability of eyewit-
(85) ness testimony.

GO ON TO THE NEXT PAGE ⟶

11. The main purpose of the passage is to:

    A. describe the main memory systems and why they are increasingly controversial.

    B. describe the main memory systems and some views of memory formation and retrieval.

    C. demonstrate that early ideas about memory formation and retrieval were incorrect.

    D. demonstrate that theories about the main memory systems are incorrect.

12. Based on information in the passage, which of the following would be recalled from semantic long-term memory?

    F. Ballet steps

    G. A childhood birthday

    H. Multiplication tables

    J. Riding a bicycle

13. It can be reasonably inferred from the passage that, if a man in a car accident is unable to remember details of his life and family, but does remember how to perform his job, his:

    A. episodic memories have been lost.

    B. episodic memories have become inaccessible.

    C. procedural memories have been lost.

    D. procedural memories have become inaccessible.

14. The fact that the scientific community once viewed human memory as similar to computer memory is mentioned in the last paragraph in order to:

    F. illustrate that memory is now viewed as complex rather than mechanical.

    G. explain that memory is now viewed as an exact record of events.

    H. illustrate that memory is always inaccurate.

    J. explain that memories are formed the same way computers encode data.

15. A person reads, "The baseball hit the window," and when asked to recall the sentence, remembers, "The baseball broke the window." According to the passage, this is probably an example of:

    A. interference altering a memory.

    B. a memory that became inaccessible.

    C. a reader's assumption altering a memory.

    D. a completely false memory being created.

16. According to the passage, all the following are examples of episodic memory EXCEPT:

    F. the meal you ate last night.

    G. the name of an old classmate.

    H. the year your class won a trophy.

    J. the face of a stranger passed on the street.

GO ON TO THE NEXT PAGE

17. Based on information in the passage, the term *short-term memory* was most likely replaced with *working memory* in order to:

    A. refute the idea that memories in this category degrade quickly.

    B. emphasize that memories in this category can be manipulated.

    C. show that memories in this category become long-term memories.

    D. demonstrate that echoic memories are held in the visual system.

18. As it is used in the passage, the word *iconic* (line 14) most nearly means relating to:

    F. something sacred.

    G. a symbolic representation.

    H. visual sensory memory.

    J. a picture that represents a computer command.

19. According to the passage, most of the scientific community now agrees that:

    A. there are really four main categories of memory, not three.

    B. memories held in long-term memory remain forever.

    C. memories must be held in working memory before long-term memory.

    D. repetition does not affect the duration of memory.

20. According to the passage, which of the following is a characteristic of working memory?

    F. A slight echo in the ear

    G. Quick replacement by new sensory information

    H. Rapid forgetting

    J. Infinite capacity

GO ON TO THE NEXT PAGE ▷

Passage III
HUMANITIES

This passage is excerpted from *A History of Women Artists*, © 1975 by Hugo Munsterberg; Clarkson N. Potter (a division of Random House, Inc.), publisher. Reprinted by permission of the author's family.

There can be little doubt that women artists have been most prominent in photography and that they have made their greatest

Line contribution in this field. One reason for
(5) this is not difficult to ascertain. As several historians of photography have pointed out, photography, being a new medium outside the traditional academic framework, was wide open to women and offered them
(10) opportunities that the older fields did not....

All these observations apply to the first woman to have achieved eminence in photography, and that is Julia Margaret Cameron... Born in 1815 in Calcutta into an
(15) upper-middle-class family and married to Charles Hay Cameron, a distinguished jurist and member of the Supreme Court of India, Julia Cameron was well-known as a brilliant conversationalist and a woman of person-
(20) ality and intellect who was unconventional to the point of eccentricity. Although the mother of six children, she adopted several more and still found time to be active in social causes and literary activities. After
(25) the Camerons settled in England in 1848 at Freshwater Bay on the Isle of Wight, she became the center of an artistic and literary circle that included such notable figures as the poet Alfred Lord Tennyson and the
(30) painter George Frederick Watts. Pursuing numerous activities and taking care of her large family, Mrs. Cameron might have been remembered as still another rather remarkable and colorful Victorian lady had it not
(35) been for the fact that, in 1863, her daughter presented her with photographic equipment, thinking her mother might enjoy taking

pictures of her family and friends. Although forty-eight years old, Mrs. Cameron took
(40) up this new hobby with enormous enthusiasm and dedication. She was a complete beginner, but within a very few years she developed into one of the greatest photographers of her period and a giant in the
(45) history of photography. She worked ceaselessly as long as daylight lasted and mastered the technical processes of photography, at that time far more cumbersome than today, turning her coal house into a darkroom
(50) and her chicken house into a studio. To her, photography was a "divine art," and in it she found her vocation. In 1864, she wrote triumphantly under one of her photographs, "My First Success," and from then until her
(55) death in Ceylon in 1874, she devoted herself wholly to this art.

Working in a large format (her portrait studies are usually about 11 inches by 14 inches) and requiring a long exposure
(60) (on the average five minutes), she produced a large body of work that stands up as one of the notable artistic achievements of the Victorian period. The English art critic Roger Fry believed that her portraits were
(65) likely to outlive the works of artists who were her contemporaries. Her friend Watts, then a very celebrated portrait painter, inscribed on one of her photographs, "I wish I could paint such a picture as this." ...Her
(70) work was widely exhibited, and she received gold, silver, and bronze medals in England, America, Germany, and Austria. No other female artist of the nineteenth century achieved such acclaim, and no other woman
(75) photographer has ever enjoyed such success.

Her work falls into two main categories on which her contemporaries and people today differ sharply. Victorian critics were particularly impressed by her allegorical
(80) pictures, many of them based on the poems of her friend and neighbor Tennyson...

GO ON TO THE NEXT PAGE →

Contemporary taste much prefers her portraits and finds her narrative scenes sentimental and sometimes in bad taste. Yet,
(85) not only Julia Cameron, but also the painters of that time loved to depict subjects such as *The Five Foolish Virgins* or *Pray God, Bring Father Safely Home*. Still, today her fame rests upon her portraits for, as she herself
(90) said, she was intent upon representing not only the outer likeness but also the inner greatness of the people she portrayed. Working with the utmost dedication, she produced photographs of such eminent
(95) Victorians as Tennyson, Browning, Carlyle, Trollope, Longfellow, Watts, Darwin, Ellen Terry, Sir John Herschel, who was a close friend of hers, and Mrs. Duckworth, the mother of Virginia Woolf.

21. Which of the following conclusions can be reasonably drawn from the passage's discussion of Julia Margaret Cameron?

   A. She was a traditional homemaker until she discovered photography.

   B. Her work holds a significant place in the history of photography.

   C. She was unable to achieve in her lifetime the artistic recognition she deserved.

   D. Her eccentricity has kept her from being taken seriously by modern critics of photography.

22. According to the passage, Cameron is most respected by modern critics for her:

   F. portraits.

   G. allegorical pictures.

   H. use of a large format.

   J. service in recording the faces of so many twentieth century figures.

23. The author uses which of the following methods to develop the second paragraph (lines 11–56)?

   A. A series of anecdotes depicting Cameron's energy and unconventionality

   B. A presentation of factual data demonstrating Cameron's importance in the history of photography

   C. A description of the author's personal acquaintance with Cameron

   D. A chronological account of Cameron's background and artistic growth

24. As it is used in the passage, *cumbersome* (line 48) most closely means:

   F. difficult to manage.

   G. expensive.

   H. intense.

   J. enjoyable.

25. When the author says that Cameron had found "her vocation" (line 52), his main point is that photography:

   A. offered Cameron an escape from the confines of conventional social life.

   B. became the main interest of her life.

   C. became her primary source of income.

   D. provided her with a way to express her religious beliefs.

GO ON TO THE NEXT PAGE

26. The main point of the third paragraph is that Cameron:

    F. achieved great artistic success during her lifetime.

    G. is the greatest photographer who ever lived.

    H. was considered a more important artist during her lifetime than she is now.

    J. revolutionized photographic methods in the Victorian era.

27. According to the passage, the art of photography offered women artists more opportunities than did other art forms because it:

    A. did not require expensive materials.

    B. allowed the artist to use family and friends for subject matter.

    C. was nontraditional.

    D. required little artistic skill.

28. *The Five Foolish Virgins* and *Pray God, Bring Father Safely Home* are examples of:

    F. portraits of celebrated Victorians.

    G. allegorical subjects of the sort that were popular during the Victorian era.

    H. photographs in which Cameron sought to show a subject's outer likeness and inner greatness.

    J. photographs by Cameron that were scoffed at by her contemporaries.

29. According to the passage, which of the following opinions of Cameron's work was held by Victorian critics but is NOT held by modern critics?

    A. Photographs should be based on poems.

    B. Her portraits are too sentimental.

    C. Narrative scenes are often in bad taste.

    D. Her allegorical pictures are her best work.

30. The author's treatment of Cameron's development as a photographer can best be described as:

    F. admiring.

    G. condescending.

    H. neutral.

    J. defensive.

GO ON TO THE NEXT PAGE

Passage IV

NATURAL SCIENCE

This passage discusses aspects of the harbor seal's sensory systems.

The harbor seal, *Phoca vitulina*, lives amphibiously along the northern Atlantic and Pacific coasts. This extraordinary
Line mammal, which does most of its fishing at
(5) night when visibility is low and in places where noise levels are high, has developed several unique adaptations that have sharpened its acoustic and visual acuity. The need for such adaptations has been
(10) compounded by the varying behavior of sound and light in each of the two habitats of the harbor seal—land and water.

While the seal is on land, its ear operates much like the human ear, with sound waves
(15) traveling through air and entering the inner ear through the auditory canal. The directions from which sounds originate are distinguishable because the sound waves arrive at each inner ear at different times.
(20) In water, however, where sound waves travel faster than they do in air, the ability of the brain to differentiate arrival times between each ear is severely reduced. Yet it is crucial for the seal to be able to pinpoint the exact
(25) origins of sound in order to locate both its offspring and its prey. Therefore, the seal has developed an extremely sensitive quadraphonic hearing system, composed of a specialized band of tissue that extends
(30) down from the ear to the inner ear. In water, sound is conducted to the seal's inner ear by this special band of tissue, making it possible for the seal to identify the exact origins of sounds.

(35) The eye of the seal is also uniquely adapted to operate in both air and water. The human eye, adapted to function primarily in air, is equipped with a cornea, which aids in the refraction and focusing

(40) of light onto the retina. As a result, when a human eye is submerged in water, light rays are further refracted and the image is blurry. The seal's cornea, however, refracts light as water does. Therefore, in water, light
(45) rays are transmitted by the cornea without distortion, and are clearly focused on the retina. In air, however, the cornea is astigmatic, resulting in a distortion of incoming light rays. The seal compensates for this by
(50) having a stenopaic pupil, which constricts into a vertical slit. Since the astigmatism is most pronounced in the horizontal plane of the eye, the vertical pupil serves to minimize its effect on the seal's vision.

(55) Since the harbor seal hunts for food under conditions of low visibility, some scientists believe it has echolocation systems akin to those of bats, porpoises, and dolphins. This kind of natural radar involves
(60) the emission of high frequency sound pulses that reflect off obstacles such as predators, prey, or natural barriers. The reflections are received as sensory signals by the brain, which processes them into an image. The
(65) animal, blinded by unfavorable lighting conditions, is thus able to perceive its surroundings. Such echolocation by harbor seals is suggested by the fact that they emit "clicks," high frequency sounds produced in
(70) short, fast bursts that occur mostly at night, when visibility is low.

Finally, there is speculation that the seal's whiskers, or vibrissae, which are unusually well developed and highly
(75) sensitive to vibrations, act as additional sensory receptors. Scientists speculate that the vibrissae may sense wave disturbances produced by nearby moving fish, allowing the seal to home in on and capture prey.

GO ON TO THE NEXT PAGE ▷

31. The harbor seal's eye compensates for the distortion of light rays on land by means of its:

    A. vibrissae.

    B. cornea.

    C. stenopaic pupil.

    D. echolocation.

32. The passage implies that a harbor seal's vision is:

    F. inferior to a human's vision in the water, but superior to it on land.

    G. superior to a human's vision in the water, but inferior to it on land.

    H. inferior to a human's vision both in the water and on land.

    J. equivalent to a human's vision both in the water and on land.

33. According to the passage, scientists think vibrissae help harbor seals to catch prey by:

    A. improving underwater vision.

    B. sensing vibrations in the air.

    C. camouflaging predator seals.

    D. detecting underwater movement.

34. According to the passage, the speed of sound in water is:

    F. faster than the speed of sound in air.

    G. slower than the speed of sound in air.

    H. the same as the speed of sound in air.

    J. unable to be determined exactly.

35. According to the passage, which of the following have contributed to the harbor seal's need to adapt its visual and acoustic senses?

    I. Night hunting
    II. The need to operate in two habitats
    III. A noisy environment

    A. I and II only

    B. II and III only

    C. I and III only

    D. I, II, and III

36. Which of the following claims expresses the writer's opinion and not a fact?

    F. The human eye is adapted to function primarily in air.

    G. When the seal is on land, its ear operates like a human ear.

    H. The "clicks" emitted by the harbor seal mean it uses echolocation.

    J. The need for adaptation is increased if an animal lives in two habitats.

37. The passage suggests that the harbor seal lives in:

    A. cold ocean waters with accessible coasts.

    B. all areas with abundant fish populations.

    C. most island and coastal regions.

    D. warm coastlines with exceptionally clear waters.

GO ON TO THE NEXT PAGE

38. According to the passage, a special band of tissue extending from the ear to the inner ear enables the harbor seal to:

    F. make its distinctive "clicking" sounds.

    G. find prey by echolocation.

    H. breathe underwater.

    J. determine where a sound originated.

39. The author compares harbor seal sensory organs to human sensory organs primarily in order to:

    A. point out similarities among mammals.

    B. explain how the seal's sensory organs function.

    C. prove that seals are more adaptively successful than humans.

    D. prove that humans are better adapted to their environment than seals.

40. According to the passage, one way in which seals differ from humans is:

    F. that sound waves enter the inner ear through the auditory canal.

    G. the degree of refraction of light by their corneas.

    H. they focus light rays on the retina.

    J. they have adapted to live in a certain environment.

IF YOU FINISH BEFORE TIME IS CALLED, YOU MAY CHECK YOUR WORK ON THIS SECTION ONLY. DO NOT TURN TO ANY OTHER SECTION IN THE TEST. STOP

SCIENCE TEST

35 Minutes—40 Questions

Directions: This test contains seven passages, each followed by several questions. After reading each passage, select the best answer to each question and fill in the corresponding oval on your Answer Grid. You may refer to the passages while answering the questions. You may NOT use a calculator on this test.

Passage I

The table below contains some physical properties of common optical materials. The refractive index of a material is a measure of the amount by which light is bent upon entering the material. The transmittance range is the range of wavelengths over which the material is transparent.

Table 1

Physical Properties of Optical Materials				
Material	Refractive index for light of 0.589 μm	Transmittance range (μm)	Useful range for prisms (μm)	Chemical resistance
Lithium fluoride	1.39	0.12–6	2.7–5.5	Poor
Calcium fluoride	1.43	0.12–12	5–9.4	Good
Sodium chloride	1.54	0.3–17	8–16	Poor
Quartz	1.54	0.20–3.3	0.20–2.7	Excellent
Potassium bromide	1.56	0.3–29	15–28	Poor
Flint glass*	1.66	0.35–2.2	0.35–2	Excellent
Cesium iodide	1.79	0.3–70	15–55	Poor

*Flint glass is lead oxide doped quartz.

1. According to the table, which material(s) will transmit light at 25 μm?

   A. Potassium bromide only
   B. Potassium bromide and cesium iodide
   C. Lithium fluoride and cesium iodide
   D. Lithium fluoride and flint glass

2. A scientist hypothesizes that any material with poor chemical resistance would have a transmittance range wider than 10 μm. The properties of which of the following materials contradicts this hypothesis?

   F. Lithium fluoride
   G. Flint glass
   H. Cesium iodide
   J. Quartz

GO ON TO THE NEXT PAGE

3. When light travels from one medium to another, total internal reflection can occur if the first medium has a higher refractive index than the second. Total internal reflection could occur if light were traveling from:

   A. lithium fluoride to flint glass.
   B. potassium bromide to cesium iodide.
   C. quartz to potassium bromide.
   D. flint glass to calcium fluoride.

4. Based on the information in the table, how is the transmittance range related to the useful prism range?

   F. The transmittance range is always narrower than the useful prism range.
   G. The transmittance range is narrower than or equal to the useful prism range.
   H. The transmittance range increases as the useful prism range decreases.
   J. The transmittance range is wider than and includes within it the useful prism range.

5. The addition of lead oxide to pure quartz has the effect of:

   A. decreasing the transmittance range and the refractive index.
   B. decreasing the transmittance range and increasing the refractive index.
   C. increasing the transmittance range and the useful prism range.
   D. increasing the transmittance range and decreasing the useful prism range.

GO ON TO THE NEXT PAGE >

Passage II

Osmosis is the diffusion of a solvent (often water) across a semipermeable membrane from the side of the membrane with a lower concentration of dissolved material to the side with a higher concentration of dissolved material. The result of osmosis is an equilibrium—an even distribution—on both sides of the membrane. In order to prevent osmosis, external pressure must be applied to the side with the higher concentration of dissolved material. *Osmotic pressure* is the external pressure required to prevent osmosis. The apparatus shown below was used to measure osmotic pressure in the following experiments.

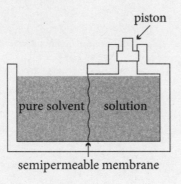

EXPERIMENT 1

Aqueous (water-based) solutions containing different concentrations of sucrose were placed in the closed side of the apparatus. The open side was filled with water. The sucrose solutions also contained a blue dye that binds to the sucrose. The osmotic pressure created by the piston was measured for each solution at various temperatures. The results are given in Table 1.

Table 1

Concentration of sucrose solution (mol/L)	Temperature K	Osmotic pressure (atm)
1.00	298.0	24.47
0.50	298.0	12.23
0.10	298.0	2.45
0.05	298.0	1.22
1.00	348.0	28.57
0.50	348.0	14.29
0.10	348.0	2.86
0.05	348.0	1.43

EXPERIMENT 2

Sucrose solutions of four different organic solvents were investigated in the same manner as in Experiment 1 with all trials at 298 K. The results are shown in Table 2.

Table 2

Solvent	Concentration of sucrose solution (mol/L)	Osmotic pressure (atm)
Ethanol	0.50	12.23
Ethanol	0.10	2.45
Acetone	0.50	12.23
Acetone	0.10	2.45
Diethyl ether	0.50	12.23
Diethyl ether	0.10	2.45
Methanol	0.50	12.23
Methanol	0.10	2.45

GO ON TO THE NEXT PAGE ⟩

6. According to the experimental results, osmotic pressure is dependent upon the:

   F. solvent and temperature only.

   G. solvent and concentration only.

   H. temperature and concentration only.

   J. solvent, temperature, and concentration.

7. According to Experiment 2, if methanol was used as a solvent, what pressure must be applied to a 0.5 mol/L solution of sucrose at 298 K to prevent osmosis?

   A. 1.23 atm

   B. 2.45 atm

   C. 12.23 atm

   D. 24.46 atm

8. A 0.10 mol/L aqueous sucrose solution is separated from an equal volume of pure water by a semipermeable membrane. If the solution is at a pressure of 1 atm and a temperature of 298 K:

   F. water will diffuse across the semipermeable membrane from the sucrose solution side to the pure water side.

   G. water will diffuse across the semipermeable membrane from the pure water side to the sucrose solution side.

   H. water will not diffuse across the semipermeable membrane.

   J. water will diffuse across the semipermeable membrane, but the direction of diffusion cannot be determined.

9. In Experiment 1, the scientists investigated the effect of:

   A. solvent and concentration on osmotic pressure.

   B. volume and temperature on osmotic pressure.

   C. concentration and temperature on osmotic pressure.

   D. temperature on atmospheric pressure.

10. Which of the following conclusions can be drawn from the experimental results?

    I. Osmotic pressure is independent of the solvent used.

    II. Osmotic pressure is only dependent upon the temperature of the system.

    III. Osmosis occurs only when the osmotic pressure is exceeded.

    F. I only

    G. III only

    H. I and II only

    J. I and III only

11. What was the most likely purpose of the dye placed in the sucrose solutions in Experiments 1 and 2?

    A. The dye showed when osmosis was completed.

    B. The dye showed the presence of ions in the solutions.

    C. The dye was used to make the experiment more colorful.

    D. The dye was used to make the onset of osmosis visible.

GO ON TO THE NEXT PAGE ⟹

Passage III

A chemist investigating the influence of molecular weight and structure on the boiling point (transition from liquid to gaseous state) of different compounds recorded the data in the tables below. Two types of compounds were investigated: organic carbon compounds (shown in Table 1) and inorganic compounds (shown in Table 2).

Table 1

Straight-Chain Hydrocarbons		
Molecular formula	Molar weight* (g/mol)	Boiling point (°C)
CH_4	16	−162
C_2H_6	30	−88
C_3H_8	44	−42
C_4H_{10}	58	0
C_5H_{12}	72	36
C_8H_{18}	114	126
$C_{20}H_{42}$	282	345

*Molar weight is the weight of one mole, or an *Avogadro's Number* of molecules ($\approx 6 \times 10^{23}$), in grams.

Table 2

Other Substances (Polar and Non-Polar)		
Molecular formula	Molar weight (g/mol)	Boiling point (°C)
N_2*	28	−196
SiH_4*	32	−112
GeH_4*	77	−90
Br_2*	160	59
CO**	28	−192
PH_3**	34	−85
AsH_3**	78	−55
ICl**	162	97

*Non-Polar: molecule's charge is evenly distributed.

**Polar: molecule's negative and positive charges are partially separated.

12. Which of the following straight-chain hydrocarbons would NOT be a gas at room temperature?

   F. C_2H_6

   G. C_3H_8

   H. C_4H_{10}

   J. C_5H_{12}

13. Which of the following conclusions is supported by the observed results?

   I. Boiling point varies directly with molecular weight.

   II. Boiling point varies inversely with molecular weight.

   III. Boiling point is affected by molecular structure.

   A. I only

   B. II only

   C. I and III only

   D. II and III only

14. Based on the data in Table 1, the boiling point of the straight-chain hydrocarbon C_6H_{14} (molecular weight 86 g/mol) is most likely:

   F. 30°C.

   G. 70°C.

   H. 130°C.

   J. impossible to predict.

GO ON TO THE NEXT PAGE

15. Based on the data in Table 2, as molecular weight increases, the difference between the boiling points of polar and non-polar substances of similar molecular weight:

    A. increases.
    B. decreases.
    C. remains constant.
    D. varies randomly.

16. A polar substance with a boiling point of 0°C is likely to have a molar weight closest to which of the following:

    F. 58
    G. 80
    H. 108
    J. 132

Passage IV

A series of experiments was performed to study the environmental factors affecting the size and number of leaves on the *Cycas* plant.

EXPERIMENT 1

Five groups of 25 *Cycas* seedlings, all from 2–3 cm tall, were allowed to grow for 3 months, each group at a different humidity level. All of the groups were kept at 75°F and received 9 hours of sunlight a day. The average leaf lengths, widths, and densities are given in Table 1.

Table 1

% Humidity	Average length (cm)	Average width (cm)	Average density* (leaves/cm)
15	5.6	1.6	0.13
35	7.1	1.8	0.25
55	9.8	2.0	0.56
75	14.6	2.6	0.61
95	7.5	1.7	0.52

*Number of leaves per 1 cm of plant stalk

EXPERIMENT 2

Five new groups of 25 seedlings, all from 2–3 cm tall, were allowed to grow for 3 months, each group receiving different amounts of sunlight at a constant humidity of 55%. All other conditions were the same as in Experiment 1. The results are listed in Table 2.

Table 2

Sunlight (hrs/day)	Average length (cm)	Average width (cm)	Average density* (leaves/cm)
0	5.3	1.5	0.32
3	12.4	2.4	0.59
6	11.2	2.0	0.56
9	8.4	1.8	0.26
12	7.7	1.7	0.19

*Number of leaves per 1 cm of plant stalk

GO ON TO THE NEXT PAGE

EXPERIMENT 3

Five new groups of 25 seedlings, all from 2–3 cm tall, were allowed to grow at a constant humidity of 55% for 3 months at different daytime and nighttime temperatures. All other conditions were the same as in Experiment 1. The results are shown in Table 3.

Table 3

Day/night temperature (°F)	Average length (cm)	Average width (cm)	Average density* (leaves/cm)
85/85	6.8	1.5	0.28
85/65	12.3	2.1	0.53
65/85	8.1	1.7	0.33
75/75	7.1	1.9	0.45
65/65	8.3	1.7	0.39

*Number of leaves per 1 cm of plant stalk

17. Which of the following conclusions can be made based on the results of Experiment 2 alone?

    A. The seedlings do not require long daily periods of sunlight to grow.

    B. The average leaf density is independent of the humidity the seedlings receive.

    C. The seedlings need more water at night than during the day.

    D. The average length of the leaves increases as the amount of sunlight increases.

18. Seedlings grown at a 40% humidity level under the same conditions as in Experiment 1 would have average leaf widths closest to:

    F. 1.6 cm.

    G. 1.9 cm.

    H. 2.2 cm.

    J. 2.5 cm.

19. According to the experimental results, under which set of conditions would a *Cycas* seedling be most likely to produce the largest leaves?

    A. 95% humidity and 3 hours of sunlight

    B. 75% humidity and 3 hours of sunlight

    C. 95% humidity and 6 hours of sunlight

    D. 75% humidity and 6 hours of sunlight

20. Which variable remained constant throughout all of the experiments?

    F. The number of seedling groups

    G. The percent of humidity

    H. The daytime temperature

    J. The nighttime temperature

21. It was assumed in the design of the three experiments that all of the *Cycas* seedlings were:

    A. more than 5 cm tall.

    B. equally capable of germinating.

    C. equally capable of producing flowers.

    D. equally capable of further growth.

22. As a continuation of the three experiments listed, it would be most appropriate to next investigate:

    F. how many leaves over 6.0 cm long there are on each plant.

    G. which animals consume *Cycas* seedlings.

    H. how the mineral content of the soil affects the leaf size and density.

    J. what time of year the seedlings have the darkest coloring.

GO ON TO THE NEXT PAGE

Passage V

The resistance (R) of a conductor is the extent to which it opposes the flow of electricity. Resistance depends not only on the conductor's resistivity (ρ), but also on the conductor's length (L) and cross-sectional area (A). The resistivity of a conductor is a physical property of the material that varies with temperature.

A research team designing a new appliance was researching the best type of wire to use in a particular circuit. The most important consideration was the wire's resistance. The team studied the resistance of wires made from four metals—gold (Au), aluminum (Al), tungsten (W), and iron (Fe). Two lengths and two gauges (diameters) of each type of wire were tested at 20°C. The results are recorded in the following table.

Table 1

Material	Resistivity (mV–cm)	Length (cm)	Cross-sectional area (mm²)	Resistance (mV)
Au	2.44	1.0	5.26	46.4
Au	2.44	1.0	1.31	186.0
Au	2.44	2.0	5.26	92.8
Au	2.44	2.0	1.31	372.0
Al	2.83	1.0	5.26	53.8
Al	2.83	1.0	1.31	216.0
Al	2.83	2.0	5.26	107.6
Al	2.83	2.0	1.31	432.0
W	5.51	1.0	5.26	105.0
W	5.51	1.0	1.31	421.0
W	5.51	2.0	5.26	210.0
W	5.51	2.0	1.31	842.0
Fe	10.00	1.0	5.26	190.0
Fe	10.00	1.0	1.31	764.0
Fe	10.00	2.0	5.26	380.0
Fe	10.00	2.0	1.31	1,528.0

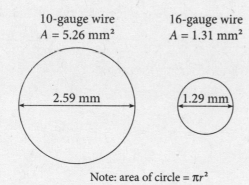

10-gauge wire
A = 5.26 mm²

16-gauge wire
A = 1.31 mm²

2.59 mm

1.29 mm

Note: area of circle = πr^2

23. Of the wires tested, resistance increases for any given material as which parameter is decreased?

A. Length

B. Cross-sectional area

C. Resistivity

D. Gauge

24. Given the data in the table, which of the following best expresses resistance in terms of resistivity (ρ), cross-sectional area (A), and length (L)?

F. $\dfrac{\rho A}{L}$

G. $\dfrac{\rho L}{A}$

H. ρAL

J. $\dfrac{AL}{\rho}$

GO ON TO THE NEXT PAGE

25. Which of the following wires would have the highest resistance?

   A. A 1-cm aluminum wire with a cross-sectional area of 0.33 mm²

   B. A 2-cm aluminum wire with a cross-sectional area of 0.33 mm²

   C. A 1-cm tungsten wire with a cross-sectional area of 0.33 mm²

   D. A 2-cm tungsten wire with a cross-sectional area of 0.33 mm²

26. According to the information given, which of the following statements is (are) correct?

   I. 10-gauge wire has a larger diameter than 16-gauge wire.

   II. Gold has a higher resistivity than tungsten.

   III. Aluminum conducts electricity better than iron.

   F. I only

   G. II only

   H. III only

   J. I and III only

27. Which of the following graphs best represents the relationship between the resistivity of a tungsten wire and its length?

A.

B.

C.

D.

Passage VI

How does evolution occur? Two views are presented below.

SCIENTIST 1

Evolution occurs by natural selection. Random mutations are continually occurring in a species as it propagates. A number of these mutations result in traits that help the species adapt to environmental changes. Because these mutant traits are advantageous, the members of the species who possess them tend to survive and pass on their genes more often than those who do not have these traits. Therefore, the percentage of the population with an advantageous trait increases over time. Long necks evolved in giraffes by natural selection. The ancestors of giraffes had necks of various sizes; however, their average neck length was much shorter than the average neck length of modern-day giraffes. Since the food supply was limited, the individuals with necks on the long range of the spectrum had access to more food (the leaves of trees) and therefore were more likely to survive and pass on their traits than individuals with shorter necks. Therefore, the proportion of the individuals with long necks is slightly greater in each subsequent generation.

SCIENTIST 2

Evolution occurs by the inheritance of acquired characteristics. Characteristics that are acquired by an individual member of a species during its lifetime are passed on to its offspring. Therefore, each generation's traits are partially accounted for by all the changes that occurred in the individuals of the previous generation. This includes changes that occurred as a result of accidents, changes in the environment, overuse of muscles, etc. The evolution of long necks of giraffes is an example. Ancestors of giraffes had short necks and consequently had to stretch their necks to reach the leaves of trees that were their main source of food. This repeated stretching of their necks caused them to elongate slightly. This trait was passed on, so that the individuals of the next generation had slightly longer necks. Each subsequent generation also stretched their necks to feed; therefore, each generation had slightly longer necks than the previous generation.

GO ON TO THE NEXT PAGE ⟩

28. Both scientists agree that:

    F. the environment affects evolution.

    G. the individuals of a generation have identical traits.

    H. acquired characteristics are inherited.

    J. random mutations occur.

29. How would the two hypotheses be affected if it were found that all of the offspring of an individual with a missing leg due to an accident were born with a missing leg?

    A. It would support Scientist 1's hypothesis, because it is an example of random mutations occurring within a species.

    B. It would refute Scientist 1's hypothesis, because it is an example of random mutations occurring within a species.

    C. It would support Scientist 2's hypothesis, because it is an example of an acquired characteristic being passed on to the next generation.

    D. It would support Scientist 2's hypothesis, because it is an example of random mutations occurring within a species.

30. Which of the following characteristics can be inherited according to Scientist 2?

    I. Fur color

    II. Bodily scars resulting from a fight with another animal

    III. Poor vision

    F. I only

    G. II only

    H. I and III only

    J. I, II, and III

31. Scientist 1 believes that the evolution of the long neck of the giraffe:

    A. is an advantageous trait that resulted from overuse of neck muscles over many generations.

    B. is an advantageous trait that resulted from a random mutation.

    C. is an advantageous trait that resulted from a mutation that occurred in response to a change in the environment.

    D. is a disadvantageous trait that resulted from a random mutation.

32. The fundamental point of disagreement between the two scientists is whether:

    F. giraffes' ancestors had short necks.

    G. evolved traits come from random mutations or from the previous generation.

    H. the environment affects the evolution of a species.

    J. the extinction of a species could be the result of random mutations.

GO ON TO THE NEXT PAGE ⟶

33. Suppose evidence was found that suggested that before the discovery of fire, human skin lacked the nerve endings necessary to detect extreme heat. Which of the following pieces of information, if true, would most seriously weaken the hypothesis of Scientist 2?

   A. Human skin is capable of generating nerve endings with new functions during life.

   B. The total number of nerve endings in the skin of a human is determined at birth and remains constant until death.

   C. An excess of nerve endings that are sensitive to extreme heat is a relatively common human mutation.

   D. No evidence exists to suggest that an excess of nerve endings that are sensitive to heat could be acquired through mutation.

34. The average height of a full-grown person today is significantly greater than was the average height of a full-grown person 1,000 years ago. If it was proven that the increase in average height was due only to evolutionary changes, how would Scientist 1 most likely explain this increase?

   F. People genetically prone to growing taller have been more likely to produce offspring over the last 1,000 years.

   G. Over the last 1,000 years, improvements in nutrition and medicine have led to greater average growth over a person's lifetime, and this growth has been passed from one generation to the next.

   H. Increased height is not a trait that can be acquired through mutation.

   J. Measurements of average height were less accurate 1,000 years ago than they are today.

GO ON TO THE NEXT PAGE

Passage VII

Bovine spongiform encephalopathy (BSE) is caused by the spread of a misfolded protein that eventually kills infected cattle. BSE is diagnosed postmortem from the diseased cavities that appear in brain tissue and is associated with the use in cattle feed of ground-up meat from scrapie-infected sheep. A series of experiments was performed to determine the mode of transmission of BSE. The results are given in the table below.

EXPERIMENT 1

Sixty healthy cows were divided into two equal groups. Group A's feed included meat from scrapie-free sheep; and Group B's feed included meat from scrapie-infected sheep. Eighteen months later, the two groups were slaughtered and their brains examined for BSE cavities.

EXPERIMENT 2

Researchers injected ground-up sheep brains directly into the brains of two groups of 30 healthy cows. The cows in Group C received brains from scrapie-free sheep. The cows in Group D received brains from scrapie-infected sheep. Eighteen months later, both groups were slaughtered and their brains examined for diseased cavities.

Table 1

Group	Mode of transmission	Scrapie present	Number of cows infected with BSE*
A	feed	no	1
B	feed	yes	12
C	injection	no	0
D	injection	yes	3

*As determined visually by presence/absence of spongiform encephalopathy

35. Which of the following hypotheses was investigated in Experiment 1?

   A. The injection of scrapie-infected sheep brains into cows' brains causes BSE.

   B. The ingestion of wild grasses causes BSE.

   C. The ingestion of scrapie-infected sheep meat causes scrapie.

   D. The ingestion of scrapie-infected sheep meat causes BSE.

36. What is the purpose of Experiment 2?

   F. To determine whether BSE can be transmitted by injection

   G. To determine whether BSE can be transmitted by ingestion

   H. To determine whether ingestion or injection is the primary mode of BSE transmission

   J. To determine the healthiest diet for cows

37. Which of the following assumptions is made by the researchers in Experiments 1 and 2?

   A. Cows do not suffer from scrapie.

   B. A year and a half is a sufficient amount of time for BSE to develop in a cow.

   C. Cows and sheep suffer from the same diseases.

   D. Cows that eat scrapie-free sheep meat will not develop BSE.

GO ON TO THE NEXT PAGE ⟶

38. A researcher wishes to determine whether BSE can be transmitted through scrapie-infected goats. Which of the following experiments would best test this?

    F. Repeating Experiment 1, using a mixture of sheep and goat meat in Group C's feed

    G. Repeating Experiments 1 and 2, replacing sheep with healthy goats

    H. Repeating Experiments 1 and 2, replacing healthy sheep with healthy goats and scrapie-infected sheep with scrapie-infected goats

    J. Repeating Experiment 2, replacing healthy cows with healthy goats

39. What is the control group in Experiment 1?

    A. Group A
    B. Group B
    C. Group C
    D. Group D

40. Which of the following conclusions is (are) supported by the experiments?

    I. Cows that are exposed to scrapie-infected sheep are more likely to develop BSE than cows that are not.

    II. BSE is only transmitted by eating scrapie-infected sheep meat.

    III. A cow that eats scrapie-infected sheep meat is more likely to develop BSE than a cow that is injected with scrapie-infected sheep brains.

    F. II only
    G. III only
    H. I and III only
    J. II and III only

WRITING TEST

30 Minutes—1 Question

Directions: This is a test of your writing skills. You will have thirty (30) minutes to write an essay in English. Before you begin planning and writing your essay, read the writing prompt carefully to understand exactly what you are being asked to do. Your essay will be evaluated on the evidence it provides of your ability to express judgments by taking a position on the issue in the writing prompt; to maintain a focus on the topic throughout the essay; to develop a position by using logical reasoning and by supporting your ideas; to organize ideas in a logical way; and to use language clearly and effectively according to the conventions of standard written English. You may use the unlined pages in this test booklet to plan your essay. These pages will not be scored. *You must write your essay in pencil on the lined pages in the answer folder.* Your writing on those lined pages will be scored. You may not need all the lined pages, but to ensure you have enough room to finish, do NOT skip lines. You may write corrections or additions neatly between the lines of your essay, but do NOT write in the margins of the lined pages. *Illegible essays cannot be scored, so you must write (or print) clearly.*

If you finish before time is called, you may review your work. Lay your pencil down immediately when time called.

DO NOT OPEN THIS BOOKLET UNTIL TOLD TO DO SO.

GO ON TO THE NEXT PAGE

ACT Writing Test Prompt

While some high schools offer art and music courses to their students, these courses are not always mandatory. Some teachers, students, and parents think that schools should emphasize traditional academic subjects like math and science, as those skills will help the students more in the future when they join the workforce. Others feel that requiring all high school students to take classes in music or the visual arts would teach equally valuable skills that the students may not learn otherwise and would also help them do better in traditional academic subject areas. In your opinion, should art or music classes be mandatory for all high school students?

In your essay, take a position on this question. You may write about either one of the two points of view given, or you may present a different point of view on this question. Use specific reasons and examples to support your position.

Use this space to *plan* your essay. Your work here will not be graded. Write your essay on the lined pages that follow.

GO ON TO THE NEXT PAGE

GO ON TO THE NEXT PAGE ⟩

_____

_____

_____

_____

_____

_____

_____

_____

_____

_____

_____

_____

_____

_____

_____

_____

_____

_____

_____

_____

_____

_____

_____

Practice Test One
ANSWER KEY

ENGLISH TEST

1. C	11. C	21. B	31. D	41. D	51. D	61. D	71. D
2. F	12. G	22. G	32. H	42. J	52. J	62. J	72. G
3. D	13. B	23. D	33. A	43. B	53. C	63. C	73. B
4. F	14. H	24. J	34. H	44. G	54. H	64. J	74. F
5. D	15. C	25. C	35. D	45. C	55. D	65. D	75. B
6. G	16. H	26. F	36. G	46. F	56. G	66. J	
7. B	17. B	27. A	37. D	47. B	57. A	67. B	
8. J	18. G	28. J	38. G	48. H	58. H	68. F	
9. A	19. A	29. B	39. D	49. C	59. D	69. D	
10. J	20. J	30. G	40. J	50. H	60. H	70. F	

MATH TEST

1. D	9. E	17. B	25. D	33. A	41. B	49. E	57. C
2. J	10. K	18. H	26. G	34. K	42. H	50. K	58. H
3. D	11. D	19. D	27. C	35. A	43. C	51. E	59. D
4. K	12. H	20. H	28. H	36. J	44. K	52. K	60. J
5. C	13. C	21. E	29. B	37. A	45. A	53. B	
6. K	14. H	22. H	30. K	38. G	46. G	54. G	
7. B	15. C	23. D	31. C	39. C	47. E	55. D	
8. K	16. G	24. F	32. H	40. G	48. G	56. K	

READING TEST

1. C	6. H	11. B	16. J	21. B	26. F	31. C	36. H
2. G	7. C	12. H	17. B	22. F	27. C	32. G	37. A
3. B	8. G	13. B	18. H	23. D	28. G	33. D	38. J
4. F	9. B	14. F	19. B	24. F	29. D	34. F	39. B
5. D	10. H	15. C	20. H	25. B	30. F	35. D	40. G

SCIENCE TEST

1. B	6. H	11. D	16. H	21. D	26. J	31. B	36. F
2. F	7. C	12. J	17. A	22. H	27. D	32. G	37. B
3. D	8. G	13. C	18. G	23. B	28. F	33. B	38. H
4. J	9. C	14. G	19. B	24. G	29. C	34. F	39. A
5. B	10. F	15. A	20. F	25. D	30. J	35. D	40. G

ANSWERS AND EXPLANATIONS

English Test

The questions fall into the following categories, according to the skills they test. If you notice that you're having trouble with particular categories, review the following:

1. REDUNDANCY: English Workout 1

2. RELEVANCE: English Workout 1

3. VERBOSITY: English Workout 1

4. JUDGING THE PASSAGE: English Workout 2

5. LOGIC: English Workout 2

6. MODIFIERS: English Workout 2

7. READING-TYPE QUESTIONS: English Workout 2

8. STRUCTURE AND PURPOSE: English Workout 2

9. TONE: English Workout 2

10. VERB USAGE: English Workout 2

11. COMPLETENESS: English Workouts 2 and 3

12. IDIOM: English Workouts 2 and 3

13. PRONOUNS: English Workouts 2 and 3

14. SENTENCE STRUCTURE: English Workouts 2 and 3

15. PUNCTUATION: English Workout 3

PASSAGE I

1. C
Punctuation

C is the most correct and concise answer choice. Choice A uses an unnecessary comma. Choice B is unnecessarily wordy. Choice D is redundant— if the societies created the legends, there is no need to describe the legends as original.

2. F
Structure and Purpose

The question stem gives an important clue to the best answer: the purpose of the inserted sentence is "to describe the different kinds" of stories. Choice F is the only choice that does this. Choice G explains how the stories were told. H explains why more is not known about the stories. Choice J describes the length of some stories.

3. D
Structure and Purpose

Answer choices A, B, and C create run-on sentences. Choice D describes a relationship that makes sense between our "many more permanent ways of handing down our beliefs" and the fact that "we continue to create and tell legends." It also creates a complete sentence.

4. F
Verbosity

Choices H and J are ungrammatical after a colon. Choices G, H, and J are unnecessarily wordy.

5. D
Redundancy

Choices A, B, and C are redundant or unnecessarily wordy. Because the contrasting word *but* is already used, *however* is repetitive and should be eliminated.

6. G

Redundancy

Choices F, H, and J are all redundant. The word *conclusion* is unnecessary because the word *ending* has already been used.

7. B

Verb Usage

Choice B is the only choice that stays consistent with the verb tense established by *knew* and *decided*.

8. J

Verb Usage

Choice F creates a run-on sentence and also makes it seem that the hunter, not the deer, "was only temporarily knocked unconscious by the car." Choices G and H use incorrect verb tenses.

9. A

Punctuation

Choice B is incorrect because the words preceding the semicolon could not be a complete sentence on their own. Choice C would create a sentence fragment. Choice D would create a run-on sentence.

10. J

Relevance

Regardless of the sequence of the words, the information provided in choices F, G, and H is irrelevant to the passage's topic of urban legends.

11. C

Verb Usage

The subject of the sentence is *One*, so the verb must be singular. Choices B and D use incorrect verb tenses.

12. G

Modifiers

Choice F creates a sentence that does not make sense. Choices H and J use the plural *women* instead of the singular *woman*.

13. B

Sentence Structure

Choice B most clearly expresses the idea that several websites research "the validity of commonly told urban legends." Because this information is relevant to the topic of urban legends, "OMIT the underlined portion" is not the best answer.

14. H

Structure and Purpose

Paragraph 4 describes an urban legend that is "humorous in nature." Paragraph 5 describes a rather frightening legend: alligators living underneath the city in the sewer system. The sentence "Other urban legends seem to be designed to instill fear" is an appropriate topic sentence for paragraph 5, and it also serves as a needed transition between paragraph 4 and paragraph 5.

15. C

Judging the Passage

Although the third and fourth sentences of paragraph 1 provide *some* general information about the purpose and topics of the myths and legends of primitive societies, no specifics are given. This makes choice C the best answer.

PASSAGE II

16. H

Verb Usage

Correct choices here could be *do you* or *does one*. The latter appears as an answer choice.

17. B
Punctuation
Choice A incorrectly uses a colon. Choices C and D are grammatically incorrect.

18. G
Redundancy
Solitary and *alone* are redundant in the same sentence. Choices H and J also have redundancy.

19. A
Modifiers
The underlined portion is clearest the way it is written.

20. J
Punctuation
The colon is incorrect, so eliminate choices F and H. Because it is a compound sentence, a comma is needed before *and*.

21. B
Sentence Structure
In fact is nonessential—it should be set off by commas.

22. G
Modifiers
American (an adjective) is the word being modified. Therefore, the adverb form of *unique* is needed.

23. D
Completeness
"Near Walden Pond..." is a long sentence fragment. The best way to fix the error is to simply combine the sentences by eliminating the period.

24. J
Logic
This paragraph and the ones that immediately follow outline Thoreau's life. His influence on the people of today is not discussed until the end of the essay. Therefore, the underlined sentence does not belong.

25. C
Logic
Sentence 3 logically follows sentence 1. Choice C is the only choice that lists this correct order.

26. F
Punctuation
There is one independent clause on each side of the semicolon, so the sentence is punctuated correctly. Choice G needs *and* after the comma to be correct. Choices H and J create run-on sentences.

27. A
Pronouns
A possessive pronoun is needed because the works belong to Thoreau. Eliminate choices B and D. Choice C relates to more than one person, so it is incorrect as well.

28. J
Judging the Passage
This paragraph discusses Thoreau's impact on modern society; only choice J expresses the correct topic.

29. B
Redundancy
Choices A, C, and D are excessively wordy.

30. G
Judging the Passage
The use of questions forces the reader to think about the answers. Choice F is too literal, and choice J is too broad for the topic of the essay. Choice H is incorrect because the author establishes the quality of Thoreau's work.

PASSAGE III

31. D
Redundancy

Because the word *live* is used later in the sentence, choices A, B, and C contain redundant information.

32. H
Pronouns

In this sentence, the *its* must be possessive because the *unique anatomy* belongs to the sloth. The word describing *anatomy* must be an adjective, not an adverb.

33. A
Punctuation

The comma is correctly used in choice A to separate the nonessential descriptive phrase "about the size of a large domestic cat" from the rest of the sentence.

34. H
Relevance

The information about the sloth's limbs is relevant to the topic, so it should not be omitted. Choice H clearly and directly expresses how the sloth's muscles are designed for clinging to things.

35. D
Modifiers

Adapted needs to be modified by an adverb, so D is the best choice.

36. G
Pronouns

Instead describes the right relationship between the two sentences. The pronouns must be consistent, and since *its* is already used in the sentence, G is the best choice.

37. D
Modifiers

D is the only choice that correctly describes the relationship between the sloth's inability to "move swiftly on the ground" and its ability to swim.

38. G
Judging the Passage

Choice G connects the sloth's unique characteristics discussed in paragraph 3 with the description of its flexibility in paragraph 4.

39. D
Punctuation

Choice D correctly uses the second comma necessary to separate the phrase "without moving the rest of its body" from the rest of the sentence. Choice C can be eliminated because it is unnecessarily wordy.

40. J
Verb Usage

J is the only choice that contains a verb tense consistent with the sentence.

41. D
Redundancy

Choices A, B, and C contain redundant information.

42. J
Relevance

This information about the howler monkey is irrelevant to the topic of the passage.

43. B
Sentence Structure

Choice A creates a sentence fragment. Choice C is unnecessarily wordy and awkward. Choice D creates a run-on sentence.

44. G
Judging the Passage
The last sentence aptly concludes the entire passage, and removing it would make the ending more abrupt.

45. C
Logic
The description of the sloth's *camouflage* is in paragraph 5.

PASSAGE IV

46. F
Verbosity
The underlined portion is best left as is. The other answer choices make the sentence unnecessarily wordy.

47. B
Verb Usage
The verb tense must agree with the tense that has been established up to this point. The passage is in the past tense, so choice B is correct.

48. H
Verb Usage
Like the answer to the previous question, the simple past tense is correct.

49. C
Verb Usage
Choice A creates a sentence fragment and uses an incorrect verb tense. Choice B also uses the wrong verb tense. Choice D incorrectly uses a semicolon, as the words preceding the semicolon do not constitute an independent clause.

50. H
Logic
In the context of the rest of the passage, only choice H makes sense. The firefighters' attempts to extinguish the flames failed; *only* nature could stop the fire with the first snowfall.

51. D
Verbosity
Choices A and B are unnecessarily wordy and awkward. Choice C creates a run-on sentence.

52. J
Verbosity
All of the other answer choices are unnecessarily wordy and/or repetitive.

53. C
Verb Usage
From the plural verb *open*, you can determine that the best answer will contain *cones*. This makes choice C the only possible answer, as the apostrophe is incorrectly used in choice B.

54. H
Logic
This is the only choice that makes sense in the context of the passage. The sighting of the large animals near burning forests is used as evidence that the animals of the region were "fire-tolerant and fire-adaptive."

55. D
Punctuation
The comma in choice A is unnecessary because the sentence has a list of only two examples, not three. The semicolon in choice B is incorrectly used because "and bedding down" does not begin an independent clause. The colon in choice C is incorrectly used because it is not being used to introduce or emphasize information.

56. G
Modifiers
The problem with "judging from recent pictures of the park" is that the phrase is modifying *forest*, and a forest obviously can't judge anything. The phrase would have been correct if the sentence read "judging from the recent

pictures of the park, I think that the forest was not destroyed." In this case, the phrase modifies *I*, the author, who is capable of judging. Choice G takes care of the problem by rewriting the sentence so that the modifying phrase is gone.

57. A
Pronouns

The pronoun refers to *forest*.

58. H
Judging the Passage

The introduction of information about fires in Alaska is unwarranted, so choices F and G can be eliminated. J is incorrect because the additional information would actually uphold the author's position as an authority.

59. D
Logic

The reports mentioned in choice D directly substantiate the author's claims much more than any of the other answer choices.

PASSAGE V

60. H
Verb Usage

Choice F creates a sentence fragment, and choice G incorrectly uses a plural verb with a singular subject. The verb tense of the paragraph makes H a better choice than J.

61. D
Relevance

The final part of the sentence, "…and there are many other rivers in America as well," is completely irrelevant to the rest of the sentence and the paragraph, in which the author discusses white-water rafting and the rivers she's rafted.

62. J
Punctuation

Choice F is wrong because *rapids* is essential information and should not be set off by commas. Choice G is wrong because what follows the colon is not an explanation. Choice H is incorrect because what follows the semicolon cannot stand alone as a sentence.

63. C
Completeness

Choices A and D create sentence fragments, and choice B is extremely awkward.

64. J
Relevance

This sentence is irrelevant to the topic of the passage.

65. D
Modifiers

This sentence makes it sound as though the author were roaring, not the rapids; *roaring* is a misplaced modifier. Choice B doesn't fix the problem because the reader has no idea what *it* refers to. Choice C has *the boat* roaring. D is the clearest choice.

66. J
Sentence Structure

The word *cover* must either be in past tense, or the structure of the sentence must change. Choice J does the latter.

67. B
Verbosity

Choice B is the simplest, most concise way of expressing the idea. Replacing "and instead he adopted" with "with" makes the sentence much less awkward.

68. F
Idioms

Choices G and J make it sound as though the author were in the water. Choice F expresses the idea more accurately than choice H does.

69. D
Redundancy

The phrase "and we stopped" is redundant because "we came to a jarring halt" says the same thing much more expressively. Omit the underlined portion.

70. F
Verb Usage

It was is fine here because the author is telling her story in the past tense. Choices G and H are the present tense, and J incorrectly introduces the possessive form.

71. D
Redundancy

The other answer choices are unnecessarily wordy; the simplest choice, D, is the best.

72. G
Verb Usage

The participle *receiving* has to be changed into a verb in the past tense, *received*, in order to be consistent with *went*. Choice G is correct as opposed to choice H because the number of bruises something has can be counted, which necessitates *many bruises*, not *much bruises*.

73. B
Logic

Choice A wouldn't work as a concluding sentence because its style and tone are off; nowhere in the passage does the writer use language such as "brutal calamities" and "beguiling excitement." Also, the writer and her father were not "unwary rafters." C contradicts the writer's main theme that nothing was as memorable as her first ride through the rapids. The tone in D, "call me crazy or weird…," is much different from the writer's. Choice B is the choice that closely matches the author's style and tone while restating the main theme of the passage.

74. F
Structure and Purpose

This essay relates a personal experience of the writer: her first time rafting down the rapids. There is very little mention of the techniques of white-water rafting, so the essay would not meet the requirements of the assignment. Choice G is wrong because the essay does not focus on the relationship between father and daughter, but on their first rafting experience together.

75. B
Judging the Passage

The sentence foreshadows things to come, so it must appear toward the beginning of the essay. That eliminates choices C and D. The second paragraph is about the peaceful setting, so choice B is the most sensible answer.

Math Test

Answer explanations for the Math test refer to 100 Key Math Concepts for the ACT, found at the end of this book.

1. D
Percentages

Key Math Concepts for the ACT, #32. You know that 14 people are 20% of the total, and you need to find 100% of the total. You could set up an equation, or you could multiply 14 by 5, since 100% is 5 times as much as 20%. The number of people surveyed is 14×5, or 70.

2. J
Average Formula

Key Math Concepts for the ACT, #41. One safe way to answer this question is by picking numbers. For instance, if you let $x = 2$ and $y = 3$, the train would have traveled $90 \times 2 + 60 \times 3 = 360$ miles in 5 hours, or $\frac{360}{5} = 72$ miles per hour. If you then plug $x = 2$ and $y = 3$ into the answer choices, it's clear that the correct answer is J. No other answer choice equals 72 when $x = 2$ and $y = 3$.

3. D
Solving a Proportion

Key Math Concepts for the ACT, #38. If the ratio of men to women is 5:3, then the ratio of women to the total is 3:3 + 5 = 3:8. Since you know the total number of string players is 24, you can set up the equation $\frac{3}{8} = \frac{x}{24}$ to find that $x = 9$. Also, without setting up the proportion, you could note that the total number of players is 3 times the ratio total, so the number of women will be 3 times the part of the ratio that represents women.

4. K
Evaluating an Expression

Key Math Concepts for the ACT, #52. In a pinch you could backsolve on this question, but this one is fairly easy to solve algebraically, like so:

$$x^2 - 3x = 6x$$
$$x^2 = 9x$$

Now you can divide both sides by x because $x \neq 0$:

$$\frac{x^2}{x} = \frac{9x}{x}$$
$$x = 9$$

5. C

With visual perception problems such as this one, the key is to play around with possibilities as you try to draw a solution. Eventually, you should be able to come up with a picture like this:

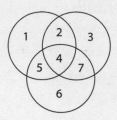

6. K
Evaluating an Expression

Key Math Concepts for the ACT, #52. This problem could be solved algebraically, but look at the answer choices. They are all simple numbers, making this a great opportunity for backsolving. Begin with choice H.

Plugging in 0, you get:

$$(0)^2 + 6(0) + 8 = 4 + 10(0)$$
$$8 = 4$$

Since 8 does not equal 4, you know this isn't the correct answer. But it is difficult to know which answer to try next. Should you aim higher or lower? If you're unsure of which direction to go, just try whatever looks easiest. Choice J, 1, looks like a good candidate:

$$(1)^2 + 6(1) + 8 = 4 + 10(1)$$
$$1 + 6 + 8 = 4 + 10$$
$$15 = 14$$

So choice J doesn't work either, but it looks like the numbers are getting closer, so you're going in the right direction. Try choice K just to be sure.

$$(2)^2 + 6(2) + 8 = 4 + 10(2)$$
$$4 + 12 + 8 = 4 + 20$$
$$24 = 24$$

Choice K is the correct answer.

7. B
Translating from English into Algebra

Key Math Concepts for the ACT, #65. Translate piece by piece:

"Nine less than c" indicates subtraction: $c - 9$.

"Nine less than c is the same as the number d": $c - 9 = d$. There's one equation.

"d less than" also indicates subtraction: $- d$.

"d less than twice c is 20": $2c - d = 20$. There's the second equation.

Choice B matches what we found.

8. K
Counting the Possibilities

Key Math Concepts for the ACT, #45. To determine the total number of possible arrangements on a question like this one, simply determine the number of possibilities for each component, and then multiply them together. There are three ways of serving the ice cream, five flavors, and four toppings. Therefore, there are $3 \times 5 \times 4 = 60$ ways to order ice cream, and choice K is correct.

9. E
Part-to-Part and Part-to-Whole Ratios

Key Math Concepts for the ACT, #37. Backsolving is a great technique to use for this problem. Start with C. The director asked 1 out of 3 students to come to the second audition and $\frac{1}{3}$ of 48 is 16, so 16 students were invited to a second audition. Then 75% of 16, which is $\frac{3}{4}(16)$ = 12 students were offered parts. The question states that 18 students were offered parts, so you already know that choice C is too small. (You can also, thus, eliminate choices A and B.) Since the director invited $\frac{1}{3}$ of the students to a second audition, the number of students at the first audition must be divisible by 3. (You can't have a fraction of a student.) That eliminates choice D, which leaves only choice E.

10. K
Multiplying/Dividing Signed Numbers

Key Math Concepts for the ACT, #6. Begin by translating the English into math: $x + 5x = -60$, $6x = -60$, so $x = -10$, and the two numbers are -10 and -50. Thus, the lesser number is -50.

By the way, this is where most people mess up. They forget that the lesser of two negative numbers is the negative number with the larger absolute value (since *less* means *to the left of* on the number line):

11. D
Special Quadrilaterals

Key Math Concepts for the ACT, #86. You're looking for the total number of parallelograms that can be found among the triangles, and parallelograms could be formed two ways from these triangles, either from two adjacent triangles or from four adjacent triangles, like so:

Begin by looking for the smaller parallelograms. If you look for parallelograms leaning in the same direction as the one we drew, you'll find three. But there are two other possible orientations for the smaller parallelogram; it could be flipped horizontally, or it could be rotated 90 degrees so that one triangle sits atop the other in the form of a diamond; both of these orientations also have three parallelograms, for a total of nine smaller parallelograms.

Now look for larger parallelograms. Perhaps the easiest way to count these is to look along the sides of the larger composite triangle. You should be able to spot two of the larger parallelograms along each side, one originating at each vertex, for a total of six larger parallelograms.

Thus, there are a total of $9 + 6 = 15$ parallelograms in all.

12. H
Areas of Special Quadrilaterals/ Area of a Circle

Key Math Concepts for the ACT, #87, #91. The square has a perimeter of 16 inches, so each side of the square is 4 inches; the area of the square is, therefore, 16 square inches. If the side of the square is 4 inches, then the diameter of the circle is also 4 inches. The radius of the circle is then 2 inches. The area of the circle is 4π square inches. The area of the shaded region is then $16 - 4\pi$ square inches.

13. C
Factor/Multiple

Key Math Concepts for the ACT, #10. The safest strategy is simply to list out the possibilities. It's also helpful to realize that multiples of both 4 and 6 are multiples of 12 (the least common multiple between the two), so skip over all multiples of 12:

4, 8, ~~12~~, 16, 20, ~~24~~, 28, 32, ~~36~~, 40, 44, ~~48~~

So there are 8 in all.

14. H
Evaluating an Expression

Key Math Concepts for the ACT, #52. Don't be intimidated by the expression $f(x)$. In this case, you should just plug in the number that appears in the parentheses for the x in the expression they have given you.

So, if $f(x) = (8 - 3x)(x^2 - 2x - 15)$, $f(3) = [8 - 3(3)]$ $[(3)^2 - 2(3) - 15]$.

Once you get to this point, just remember PEMDAS.

$[8 - 3(3)][(3)^2 - 2(3) - 15] = (8 - 9)(9 - 6 - 15) = (-1)(-12) = 12$, choice H.

15. C
Probability

Key Math Concepts for the ACT, #46. A class contains five juniors and five seniors. If one member of the class is assigned at random to present a paper on a certain subject, and another member of the class is randomly assigned to assist him, then:

The probability that the first student picked will be a junior $= \dfrac{\text{\# of Juniors}}{\text{Total \# of students}} = \dfrac{5}{10} = \dfrac{1}{2}$.

The probability that the second student picked will be a junior, given that the first student picked was a junior $= \dfrac{\text{\# of Juniors remaining}}{\text{Total \# of students remaining}}$.

So the probability that both students will be juniors $= \dfrac{1}{2} \times \dfrac{4}{9} = \dfrac{2}{9}$.

16. G
Area of a Triangle

Key Math Concepts for the ACT, #83. Since the formula to find the area of a triangle is $\dfrac{1}{2}$(base) (height), you can plug in the base and area to find the height. You know that the area of this triangle is 45 units and that the base is $3 + 12 = 15$. Let x be the length of altitude $\overline{YS}$. Plug these into the area formula to get $45 = \dfrac{15x}{2}$. Solve for x to get $x = 6$.

17. B
Using an Equation to Find an Intercept

Key Math Concepts for the ACT, #74. The y-coordinate is the point on which the x value is zero, so plug $x = 0$ into the equation:

$$6y - 3(0) = 18$$
$$6y = 18$$
$$y = 3$$

18. H
Solving a System of Equations

Key Math Concepts for the ACT, #67. This question involves common quadratics, so the key is to write these quadratic expressions in their other forms. For instance, $x^2 - y^2 = 12$, so $(x + y)$ $(x - y) = 12$. Since $x - y = 4$, $(x + y)(4) = 12$, so $x + y = 3$. Finally, $x^2 + 2xy + y^2 = (x + y)^2 = (3)^2 = 9$.

19. D
Areas of Special Quadrilaterals/ Area of a Triangle

Key Math Concepts for the ACT, #87, #83. This shape must be divided into three simple shapes. By drawing downward two perpendicular line segments from the endpoints of the side which is 10 units long, you are left with a 3 × 10 rectangle, a triangle with a base of 4 and a height of 3, and a triangle with a base of 7 and a hypotenuse of $7\sqrt{2}$. The rectangle has an area of $3 \times 10 = 30$ square units. The smaller triangle has an area of $\frac{4 \times 3}{2} = 6$ square units. The larger triangle is a 45°-45°-90° triangle, so the height must be 7. Therefore, it has an area of $\frac{7 \times 7}{2} = 24.5$ square units. The entire shape has an area of $6 + 30 + 24.5 = 60.5$ square units.

20. H
Translating from English into Algebra

Key Math Concepts for the ACT, #65. Although backsolving is certainly possible with this problem, it's probably quicker to solve with arithmetic. The board is 12 feet long, which means it is $12 \times 12 = 144$ inches. The carpenter cuts off 3 × 17 = 51 inches. That leaves $144 - 51 = 93$ inches.

21. E
Solving a Quadratic Equation

Key Math Concepts for the ACT, #66. To answer this question, begin by setting the right side of the equation equal to zero:

$$x^2 - 4x - 6 = 6$$
$$x^2 - 4x - 12 = 0$$

Now use reverse-FOIL to factor the left side of the equation:

$$(x - 6)(x + 2) = 0$$

Thus, either $x - 6 = 0$ or $x + 2 = 0$, so $x = 6$ or -2.

22. H
Solving a Quadratic Equation

Key Math Concepts for the ACT, #66. Here's another question that tests your understanding of FOIL, but you have to be careful. The question states that −3 is a possible solution for the equation $x^2 + kx - 15 = 0$, so in its factored form, one set of parentheses with a factor inside must be $(x + 3)$. Since the last term in the equation in its expanded form is −15, that means that the entire factored equation must read $(x + 3)(x - 5) = 0$, which in its expanded form is $x^2 - 2x - 15 = 0$. Thus, $k = -2$.

23. D

To solve this problem, you need to understand the triangle inequality theorem, which states: the sum of the lengths of any two sides of a triangle is always greater than the length of the third side. Therefore, the other sides of this triangle must add up to more than 7. You know from the problem that every side must be an integer. That means that the sides must add up to at least 8 inches (4 inches and 4 inches, or 7 inches and 1 inch, for example). The smallest possible perimeter is $7 + 8 = 15$.

24. F
Sine, Cosine, and Tangent of Acute Angles

Key Math Concepts for the ACT, #96. It's time to use SOHCAHTOA, and drawing a triangle might help as well. If the sine of θ (opposite side over hypotenuse) is $\frac{\sqrt{11}}{2\sqrt{3}}$, then one of the legs of the right triangle is $\sqrt{11}$, and the hypotenuse is $2\sqrt{3}$. Now apply the Pythagorean theorem to come up with the other (adjacent) leg: $(\sqrt{11})^2 + (n)^2 = (2\sqrt{3})^2$, so $11 + n^2 = 12$, which means that $n^2 = 1$, and $n = 1$. Thus, cosine (adjacent side over hypotenuse) θ is $\frac{1}{2\sqrt{3}}$.

25. D
Simplifying Square Roots

Key Math Concepts for the ACT, #49. Take a quick look at the answer choices before simplifying an expression like this one. Notice that none of these choices contain a radical sign in their denominators. So when you simplify the expression, try to eliminate that radical sign. Your calculations should look something like this:

$$\frac{\sqrt{3+x}}{\sqrt{3-x}} \times \frac{\sqrt{3-x}}{\sqrt{3-x}} = \frac{\sqrt{(3+x)(3-x)}}{\sqrt{(3-x)^2}} =$$

$$\frac{\sqrt{9-3x+3x-x^2}}{3-x} = \frac{\sqrt{9-x^2}}{3-x}$$

So choice D is correct.

26. G
Part-to-Part and Part-to-Whole Ratios

Key Math Concepts for the ACT, #37. If the ratio of the parts is 2:5, then the ratio total is $2 + 5 = 7$. Thus, the actual total number of cookies must be a multiple of 7. The only choice that's a multiple of 7 is G, 35.

27. C
Converting Fractions to Decimals

Key Math Concepts for the ACT, #29. This question is a great opportunity to use your calculator. Notice that all your choices are decimals. In order to solve, convert $\frac{3}{16}$ into a decimal and add that to .175. $\frac{3}{16} = .1875$, so the sum equals .1875 + .175 = .3625. So choice C is correct.

28. H
Areas of Special Quadrilaterals

Key Math Concepts for the ACT, #87. Remember that if you are given a perimeter for a rectangle, the rectangle with the greatest area for that perimeter will be a square. So we are looking for the area of a square with a perimeter of 20. The perimeter of a square equals $4s$, where s is the length of one side of the square. If $4s = 20$,

then $s = 5$. The area of the square equals $s^2 = 5^2 = 25$, choice H.

29. B
Adding/Subtracting, Multiplying/Dividing Fractions

Key Math Concepts for the ACT, #22, #23, #24. Be careful on this one. You can't start plugging numbers into your calculator without paying attention to the order of operations. This one is best solved on your own.

$$\frac{\frac{3}{2} + \frac{7}{4}}{\left(\frac{15}{8} - \frac{3}{4}\right) - \left(\frac{4+3}{-4+3}\right)} =$$

$$\frac{\frac{3}{2} + \frac{7}{4}}{\left(\frac{9}{8}\right) - \left(\frac{7}{-1}\right)} = \frac{\frac{13}{4}}{\frac{65}{8}} = \frac{13}{4} \times \frac{8}{65} = \frac{2}{5}$$

30. K
Solving a Linear Equation

Key Math Concepts for the ACT, #63. You could solve this algebraically for x as follows:

$$x - 15 = 7 - 5(x - 4)$$
$$x - 15 = 7 - 5x + 20$$
$$x - 15 = -5x + 27$$
$$6x = 42$$
$$x = 7$$

Remember also that if you are ever stuck, you can try to backsolve with the answer choices. Here, if you try them all out, only 7 works:

$$7 - 15 = 7 - 5(7 - 4)$$
$$-8 = 7 - 5(3)$$
$$-8 = 7 - 15$$
$$-8 = -8$$

31. C
Areas of Special Quadrilaterals, Area of a Triangle

Key Math Concepts for the ACT, #87, #83. Break strange figures like this one up into shapes that are more familiar and easier to handle. In this case, the quadrilateral can be split into a square and a right triangle. The square is 9×9, so the area of that part of the figure is 81 square meters. The right triangle has a height of 9 and a base of 4, so the area of the triangle would be $\frac{1}{2}bh = \frac{1}{2}(4 \times 9) = \frac{1}{2}(36) = 18$ square meters. So the total area of the figure is (81 + 18) square meters = 99 square meters, choice C.

32. H
Using an Equation to Find the Slope

Key Math Concepts for the ACT, #73. The easiest way to solve this question is to put it in the form $y = mx + b$, in which case m equals the slope. In other words, you want to isolate y:

$$6y - 3x = 18$$
$$6y = 3x + 18$$
$$y = \frac{3x + 18}{6}$$
$$y = \frac{1}{2}x + 3$$

So the slope equals $\frac{1}{2}$.

33. A

To answer this question, you have to know that perpendicular lines on the standard (x, y) coordinate plane have slopes that are negative reciprocals of each other. In other words, the line described by the equation $y = -\frac{4}{5}x + 6$ has a slope of $-\frac{4}{5}$, so a line perpendicular to it has a slope of $\frac{5}{4}$. This eliminates all choices but A. However, if you want to double-check, you can plug the coordinates you're given (4, 3) into the equation found in choice A.

$$3 = \frac{5}{4}(4) - 2$$
$$3 = 5 - 2$$
$$3 = 3$$

34. K
Using an Equation to Find the Slope

Key Math Concepts for the ACT, #73. Since the problem gives you the y-intercept, it is easy to look at the answer choices and rule out choices F, H, and J. Put the equation from the question in slope-intercept form to find its slope:

$$3x - 5y = 4$$
$$-5y = -3x + 4$$
$$y = \frac{-3x + 4}{-5}$$
$$y = \frac{3}{5}x - \frac{4}{5}$$

Since line t is parallel, it has the same slope. This matches choice K.

35. A
Solving a Linear Equation

Key Math Concepts for the ACT, #63. To solve for x in the equation $y = mx + b$, isolate x on one side of the equation. Begin by subtracting b from both sides. You will be left with $y - b = mx$. Then divide both sides by m, and you will be left with $x = \frac{y - b}{m}$, choice A.

36. J
Special Right Triangles

Key Math Concepts for the ACT, #85. In this figure, there are many right triangles and many similar triangles. If you know to be on the lookout for 3-4-5 triangles, it should be easy to spot that triangle ABC has sides of 15-20-25, so $\overline{AC}$ is 25. Now turn your attention to triangle ABD. Since it's a right triangle that shares $\angle BAC$ with triangle ABC, it too must be a 3-4-5 triangle. So if the hypotenuse is 20, the shorter leg ($\overline{BD}$) must have a length of 12, and the longer leg ($\overline{AD}$) must have a length of 16.

37. A

The shortest distance to line m will be a line perpendicular to m. So the distance will be the difference between the y-coordinates of point C and the nearest point on line m. Since every point on m has a y-coordinate of 5, and point C has a y-coordinate of 3, the difference is 2.

38. G

While you could try factoring the numerator, you'll find that you can't easily cancel out the denominator by doing so. Perhaps the easiest approach here is to pick numbers. Pick a simple number such as $x = 2$. Thus,

$$\frac{x^2 - 11x + 24}{8 - x} = \frac{(2)^2 - 11(2) + 24}{6} =$$

$$\frac{4 - 22 + 24}{6} = \frac{6}{6} = 1.$$

So 1 is your target number. When you plug $x = 2$ into the choices, the only choice that gives you 1 is G.

39. C

Finding the Distance between Two Points
Key Math Concepts for the ACT, #71.

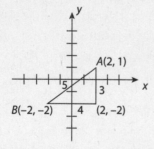

The textbook method for this problem would be to use the distance formula but that's time-consuming. Instead, it may help you to draw a picture. Draw a right triangle into the coordinate plane as we've done above. Note that the distance between the two points represents the hypotenuse of the triangle. The legs of the triangle have lengths of 3 and 4, so the distance between the two points must be 5, choice C.

40. G

Areas of Special Quadrilaterals, Area of a Circle
Key Math Concepts for the ACT, #87, #91. To find the area of the shaded region, you must subtract the area of the circle from the area of the rectangle. Since the sides of the rectangle are $2x$ and $5x$, it has an area of $2x \times 5x = 10x^2$. By examining the diagram, you can see that the circle has a diameter of $2x$, so it has a radius of x. Its area is, therefore, πx^2. The shaded region, therefore, has an area of $10x^2 - \pi x^2$.

41. B

Sine, Cosine, and Tangent of Acute Angles
Key Math Concepts for the ACT, #96. Since you are not given a diagram for this problem, it's best to draw a quick sketch of a right triangle to help keep the sides separate in your mind. Mark one of the acute angles θ. Since $\cos \theta = \frac{5\sqrt{2}}{8}$, mark the adjacent side $5\sqrt{2}$ and the hypotenuse as 8. (Remember SOHCAHTOA.) Use the Pythagorean theorem to find that the side opposite θ is $\sqrt{14}$. The problem asks you to find $\tan \theta$. Tangent $= \frac{\text{opposite}}{\text{adjacent}}$, so $\tan \theta = \frac{\sqrt{14}}{5\sqrt{2}}$, which can be simplified to $\frac{\sqrt{7}}{5}$.

42. H

This question is one where your calculator can come in handy. Divide 7 by integer values for n, and look for values between .5 and .8. Begin by looking for the integer values of n where $\frac{7}{n}$ is greater than .5. If $n = 14$, then $\frac{7}{n} = .5$, so n must be less than 14. Work through values of n until you get to the point where $\frac{7}{n} \geq .8$. When $n = 9$, $\frac{7}{n} = .778$, but when $n = 8$, $\frac{7}{n} = .875$. So the integer values that work in this case are $n = 9, 10, 11, 12,$ and 13. Five integer values work, so choice H is correct.

43. C

The points are as far apart as possible when separated by a diameter of X and a diameter of Y.

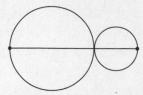

The circumference of a circle is $\pi \times$ (diameter), so the diameter of circle X is 12, and the diameter of circle Y is 8. The greatest possible distance between points then is $12 + 8 = 20$.

44. K

Adding and Subtracting Polynomials

Key Math Concepts for the ACT, #54. Begin by getting rid of the square root sign. If $y \geq 0$, then $\sqrt{y^2} = y$, so $\sqrt{(x^2 + 4)^2} = x^2 + 4$. $(x + 2)(x - 2) = x^2 - 4$, so you now have $(x^2 + 4) - (x^2 - 4) = ?$ Get rid of the parentheses, and you have $x^2 + 4 - x^2 + 4 = x^2 - x^2 + 4 + 4 = 8$.

45. A

Evaluating an Expression

Key Math Concepts for the ACT, #52. Here, you need to substitute -3 for s and solve. That gives you the expression $(-3)^3 + 2(-3)^2 + 2(-3)$, which equals $-27 + 18 - 6$, or -15. If you missed this problem, you probably made a mistake with the signs of the numbers.

46. G

Multiplying Binomials—FOIL

Key Math Concepts for the ACT, #56. Be careful on this one. Begin by simplifying the equation by FOILing one side:

$$2x + 6 = (x + 5)(x + 3)$$
$$2x + 6 = x^2 + 8x + 15$$

Then get the right side of the equation to equal zero: $x^2 + 6x + 9 = 0$.

The left side of this equation is the perfect square $(x + 3)^2$, so $(x + 3)^2 = 0$, which has only one solution, $x = -3$. Choice G is correct.

47. E

Pythagorean Theorem

Key Math Concepts for the ACT, #84. The textbook method for this would be to use the Pythagorean theorem to find the length of a side and then multiply that by 4, but there's an easier way: eyeball it! The perimeter is greater than $\overline{AC}$, so you can get rid of choices A and B. It appears to be quite a bit greater than $\overline{AC}$, more than twice as great, so choices C and D are out as well. That only leaves choice E.

If you wanted to solve this the conventional way, since the perimeter is the sum of the lengths of all the sides of the square, you need to find the length of the square's sides. Let the length of each of the square's sides be x. $\overline{AC}$ divides the square into two right triangles, so we can apply the Pythagorean theorem: $\overline{AB}^2 + \overline{BC}^2 = \overline{AC}^2$. Since $\overline{AB}$ and $\overline{BC}$ are sides of the square, they have the same length. We can write that as $x^2 + x^2 = \overline{AC}^2$. $\overline{AC} = 8$, so $2x^2 = 8^2$, $2x^2 = 64$, $x^2 = 32$, $x = \sqrt{32} = \sqrt{16 \times 2} = 4\sqrt{2}$. So each side of the square is $4\sqrt{2}$, and the perimeter of the square is $4 \times 4\sqrt{2} = 16\sqrt{2}$.

48. G

Areas of Special Quadrilaterals, Area of a Triangle

Key Math Concepts for the ACT, #87, #83. To find the area of this complex shape, you could divide it into two simple shapes by drawing a line 30 inches up, parallel to the horizontal base. This leaves you with a 4×30 rectangle and a triangle with height of 6 and a base of 4. The rectangle has an area of $4 \times 30 = 120$ square inches, and the triangle has an area of $\frac{4 \times 6}{2} = 12$ square inches. That makes a total of $120 + 12 = 132$ square inches.

49. E
Interior Angles of a Triangle

Key Math Concepts for the ACT, #80. Triangles are the secret to solving this one. Drawing $\overline{OD}$ divides quadrilateral $OCDE$ into two triangles, OCD and ODE. Both triangles are isosceles because $\overline{OC}$, $\overline{OD}$, and $\overline{OE}$ are all radii of circle O. Angles ODC and OCD have equal measures, since they're opposite equal sides, so $\angle ODC$ measures 70°. Similarly, $\angle ODE$ measures 45°. Together, angles ODC and ODE make up $\angle CDE$, so its measure is 70° + 45° = 115°.

50. K
Solving a System of Equations

Key Math Concepts for the ACT, #67. Remember that lines intersect at the point that is a solution to both equations. So equations with no common solution don't intersect—they have the same slope and are parallel. To solve this problem, search through the answer choices to find the pair of equations representing lines with the same slope. If you write the equations in K in slope-intercept form, you'll get $y = -\frac{1}{3}x + 2$, $y = -\frac{1}{3}x + \frac{7}{9}$, so the slope is clearly the same for both equations.

51. E
Repeating Decimal

Key Math Concepts for the ACT, #30. To solve a repeating decimal question, begin by determining the pattern of the decimal on your calculator. $\frac{1}{7} = 0.142857142857...$, so you know that this fraction repeats every 6 decimal places. Since we are looking for the 46th decimal place, we need to determine where in the 6-term pattern we would be at the 46th place. Divide 46 by 6, and look for the remainder. The remainder in this case is 4, so we are looking for the 4th term in the sequence, which is 8, choice E.

52. K
Solving an Inequality

Key Math Concepts for the ACT, #69. Remember that you treat an inequality exactly like an equality, except that you need to flip the sign when you multiply or divide by a negative number. In this problem, you start with the inequality $-2 - 4x \le -6x$. Add $4x$ to both sides to get $-2 \le -2x$. Divide by -2 and flip the sign to get $1 \ge x$, which matches choice K.

53. B
Adding/Subtracting Fractions

Key Math Concepts for the ACT, #22. For this problem, it would probably be easiest to pick numbers. Since you will be taking the square root of the numbers, it's easiest to pick perfect squares, like 4 and 9:

$$\frac{\sqrt{4}}{4} + \frac{\sqrt{9}}{9} = \frac{2}{4} + \frac{3}{9} = \frac{1}{2} + \frac{1}{3} = \frac{5}{6}$$

When you plug 4 and 9 into the answer choices, only B gives you $\frac{5}{6}$.

54. G
Parallel Lines and Transversals

Key Math Concepts for the ACT, #79. When transversals intersect parallel lines, corresponding line segments on the transversals are proportional. In other words, $\frac{\overline{DE}}{\overline{CB}} = \frac{\overline{EF}}{\overline{BA}}$. Thus, $\frac{6}{8} = \frac{\overline{EF}}{4}$, so $EF = 3$.

55. D
Area of a Triangle

Key Math Concepts for the ACT, #83. Divide the square into two right triangles by drawing the diagonal from (2, 7) to (2, 1). Remember that the area of each triangle is half its base times its height. Treat the diagonal as the base of a triangle. Its length is the distance from (2, 7) to (2, 1). Since the x-coordinates are the same, that distance is simply the difference between the y-coordinates, 7 − 1, or 6. The diagonal bisects the square, so the height of the triangle is half the distance from (–1, 4) to (5, 4). We already know that a diagonal of this square is 6, so half the distance is 3. Therefore, the base and height of either triangle are 6 and 3, so the area of each triangle is $\frac{6 \times 3}{2}$, or 9 square units. The square is made up of two such triangles and so has twice the area, or 18 square units.

Alternatively, you could use the Distance Formula to find the length of one side and square that side to find the area.

56. K
Graphing Trigonometric Functions

Key Math Concepts for the ACT, #100. Compared to the graph of $y = \cos \theta$, the graph of $y = 2 \cos \theta$ would have twice the amplitude and the same period, choice K. Here you are doubling y, which represents the vertical coordinates, but the θ coordinates stay the same. The amplitude of a trigonometric equation refers to how high or low the curve moves from the horizontal axis. The period refers to the distance required to complete a single wave along the horizontal axis.

57. C
Translating from English into Algebra

Key Math Concepts for the ACT, #65. To solve this problem with algebra, you need to translate each phrase into mathematics. Translated, the problem is $3(x + 15) = 4x - 65$. Solve for x to get 110. Alternatively, you could backsolve starting with the middle value:

$$3(110 + 15) = 4(110) - 65$$
$$3(125) = 440 - 65$$
$$75 = 75$$

Since the two sides are equal, choice C is correct.

58. H
Setting Up a Ratio

Key Math Concepts for the ACT, #36. You're given the formula for the volume of a cylinder in the equation so you can find the volume of both cylinders described. That turns this into a ratio problem where you're comparing the volumes of both cylinders. Pick numbers to make this question more concrete and plug them into this volume formula. Let's say the smaller cylinder has a height of 1 and a radius of 1 (diameter of 2), for a volume of $\pi(1)^2 \times 1 = \pi$. The larger cylinder would then have a height of 3 and a radius of 2 (diameter of 4), for a volume of $\pi(2)^2 \times 3 = 12\pi$. Thus, it would take 12 fillings of the smaller cylinder to fill the larger cylinder.

59. D
Special Right Triangles

Key Math Concepts for the ACT, #85. Draw a picture of the triangle, and carefully apply your knowledge of the ratio of the lengths of the sides of a 30°-60°-90° triangle ($x : x\sqrt{3} : 2x$). So if the longer leg has a length of 12, the shorter leg has a length of $\frac{12}{\sqrt{3}} = \frac{12\sqrt{3}}{\sqrt{3} \times \sqrt{3}} = \frac{12\sqrt{3}}{3} = 4\sqrt{3}$. Thus, the hypotenuse is twice this, or $8\sqrt{3}$. So the perimeter is the sum of the three sides, or $4\sqrt{3} + 12 + 8\sqrt{3} = 12\sqrt{3} + 12$.

60. J
Average Formula

Key Math Concepts for the ACT, # 41. Remember the average formula on this one. The average formula states, Average $= \frac{\text{Sum of the terms}}{\text{Number of the terms}}$. So to find the total average, find the total sum and divide it by the total number of terms. If a team averages x points in n games, then it scored nx points in n games. In the final game of the season, it scored y points. So the total sum of points for the season is $nx + y$, and the total number of games is $n + 1$. So the team's average score for the entire season is $\frac{nx + y}{n + 1}$, choice J.

Reading Test

Reading questions can be divided into four basic types: Detail questions, Inference questions, Big Picture questions, and Vocabulary-in-Context questions. As you review the answers and explanations, note which types you tend to answer correctly or incorrectly, and tailor your studying to focus on areas where you need improvement.

PASSAGE I

1. C
Detail

The answer can be found in lines 31–36: "The real evils, indeed, of Emma's situation were the power of having rather too much her own way, and a disposition to think a little too well of herself; these were the disadvantages which threatened alloy to her many enjoyments."

2. G
Detail

Isabella's name is given in line 73.

3. B
Detail

The answer can be found in lines 20–21: "Between them it was more the intimacy of sisters."

4. F
Vocabulary-in-Context

As it is used in the sentence, *disposition* means "tendency" or "inclination." It would not make sense for Emma to have choice G, control; choice H, placement; or J, transfer "to think a little too well of herself" (lines 33–34).

5. D
Detail

The answer can be found in lines 62–69: "She recalled her past kindness—the kindness, the affection of sixteen years—how she had taught her and…how she had devoted all her powers to attach and amuse her in health—and how she had nursed her through the various illnesses of childhood."

6. H
Inference

Miss Taylor will continue to be a part of Emma's life, but they will not be as close because Miss Taylor no longer lives with Emma and because Miss Taylor will be primarily concerned with her husband's, not Emma's, well-being.

7. C
Inference

Emma is self-centered, as evidenced by her description of her relationship with Miss Taylor. Among Miss Taylor's admirable qualities, Emma includes the fact that Miss Taylor was "interested in her, in every pleasure, every scheme of hers—one to whom she could speak every thought as it arose, and who had such an affection for her as could never find fault" (lines 78–84). Emma is also clearly headstrong. She is described as "having rather too much her own way" (lines 32–33).

8. G
Big Picture

Emma's description of her friendship with Miss Taylor suggests that Emma most highly values devotion in her friends.

9. B
Detail

The description of Mr. Weston is in lines 53–56: "The marriage had every promise of happiness for her friend. Mr. Weston was a man of unexceptionable character, easy fortune, suitable age, and pleasant manners." None of the other choices match this description.

10. H
Inference

The answer to the question is in lines 28–31: "Emma doing just what she liked, highly esteeming Miss Taylor's judgment, but directed chiefly by her own."

PASSAGE II

11. B
Detail

The passage presents the three main systems of memory and states that these systems are widely accepted—so eliminate choice A—but gives alternate theories about the way long-term memories are formed and possible flaws in the process. Although the passage mentions two early ideas about memory that were too simplistic, choices C and D, this is not the main focus of the passage.

12. H
Inference

Described in paragraph 3, semantic memory holds facts and general knowledge, like the multiplication tables, choice H. Ballet steps, choice F, and riding a bicycle, choice J, would be in procedural memory; a childhood memory, choice G, would be in episodic.

13. B
Inference

All the information you need is in paragraph 3. Memories of one's personal life would be held in episodic memory; therefore, the man's episodic memory was affected. Eliminate choices C and D. Long-term memories are "never lost," but they may become inaccessible; therefore, the author

would most likely agree that the man's episodic memories had become inaccessible to him.

14. F
Big Picture

While memory was once viewed as relatively simple and automatic with memories being held exactly as they were originally received, it is now believed that many factors alter the way memories are formed and retrieved (lines 69–79). Choices G and J contradict this. Choice H is too extreme.

15. C
Inference

In the last paragraph, the author states that assumptions and inferences can affect memory. A person might assume that if the ball hits a window, the window will break. Interference, choice A, is when one unrelated memory alters another. The memory described in the question is not inaccessible, choice B, but wrong. And most of the memory was still correct, not false, choice D.

16. J
Detail

This Detail question requires very careful reading. Refresh your memory by looking at *episodic* in paragraph 3. It's in long-term memory and involves personal events closely identified with a time and place. Choices F, G, and H fit that idea closely. If you're unsure, look at the description of working (short-term) memory in paragraph 2. You'll see that it includes those things briefly remembered and then lost forever—like the face of a stranger passed on the street.

17. B
Inference

Paragraph 2 describes this change in terminology. The term *short-term memory* did not accurately describe all the functions of this category of memory. *Working memory* is more accurate since, although these memories degrade quickly—eliminating choice A—these memories can also be used and manipulated as described in the second paragraph. Choice C and D confuse information in other paragraphs.

18. H
Vocabulary-in-Context

Don't panic. All you have to do is look at the line where this term is defined for you. The term doesn't relate to any of the usual meanings of the word *icon*.

19. B
Big Picture

The second sentence in paragraph 3 states, "Memories recorded in long-term memory are never lost…" Although absolute statements are often too extreme to be correct in Reading, when the passage explicitly supports an absolute statement don't be afraid to choose it. You might choose A if you mistook *short-term* and *working* memory for two separate categories. Choice C is contradicted in paragraph 4, and choice D is contradicted at the end of paragraph 2 and again at the start of paragraph 5.

20. H
Detail

Paragraph 2 states that working memories decay rapidly, which means that they are quickly forgotten. Choices F and G relate to sensory memory. Choice J is characteristic of long-term memory.

PASSAGE III

21. B
Inference

In lines 11–13, Julia Margaret Cameron is described as "the first woman to have achieved eminence in photography." The other answer choices contradict information supplied in the passage.

22. F
Detail

The answer to this question can be found in lines 82–83: "Contemporary taste much prefers her portraits…" and in lines 88–89: "today her fame rests upon her portraits…"

23. D
Detail

The dates used in the passage tell you that this is a chronological account; the author begins with Cameron's birth in 1815, tells of her marriage and then her move to England in 1848, points out that she received her first photographic equipment in 1863, describes one of her photographs from 1864, and then concludes the paragraph with her death in 1874.

24. F
Vocabulary-in-Context

The dictionary definition of *cumbersome* is "difficult to handle because of weight or bulk." Choice F most closely fits this definition, and it is the only answer choice that makes sense within the context of the sentence.

25. B
Inference

Lines 55–56 describe how Cameron "devoted herself wholly to this art," which matches choice B. Choice A contradicts information from the passage, which suggests that Cameron led anything but a conventional life. Neither the money that Cameron earned as a photographer nor her religious beliefs are discussed in the passage, making choices C and D incorrect.

26. F
Big Picture

Lines 60–63 say, "she produced a large body of work that stands up as one of the notable artistic achievements of the Victorian period." To say that she is "the greatest photographer who ever lived" goes beyond anything stated or implied in the passage. The third paragraph does not compare her importance as an artist during her lifetime to her importance today. The passage also does not state that she "revolutionized" any photographic methods.

27. C
Detail

The answer to this question can be found in lines 7–10: "photography, being a new medium outside the traditional academic framework, was wide open to women and offered them opportunities that the older fields did not…"

28. G
Detail

These titles refer to allegorical pictures, as described in lines 78–81: "Victorian critics were particularly impressed by her allegorical pictures, many of them based on the poems of her friend and neighbor Tennyson…"

29. D
Detail

The answer to this question can be found in lines 82–84: "Contemporary taste much prefers her portraits and finds her narrative scenes sentimental and sometimes in bad taste."

30. F
Big Picture

The author says that Cameron "achieved eminence" (line 12) in her field, that she "devoted herself wholly to this art" (lines 55–56), and that "no other woman photographer has ever enjoyed such success" (lines 74–75). Only choice F fits these descriptions.

PASSAGE IV

31. C
Detail

For details about the eye, look at paragraph 3. Only the cornea and stenopaic pupil are relevant, eliminating choices A and D. But the cornea, choice B, is helpful underwater, not on land.

32. G
Inference

The eye is covered in paragraph 3. The seal's cornea improves vision in the water (note the comparison to human underwater vision), but distorts light moving through the air. Another adaptation was then needed to *minimize* (line 53) distortion, but that doesn't mean distortion is completely eliminated, so the seal's vision in the air is distorted, choice G.

33. D
Detail

The vibrissae are discussed only in the last paragraph. They sense wave disturbances made by nearby moving fish, so choice D is correct. Choice B, by using the phrase "in the air," distorts information in the passage.

34. F
Detail

This is stated in the second paragraph, where the seal's hearing is discussed.

35. D
Detail

This appears in the first paragraph, which introduces the influences on the seal's adaptations. They include that the seal "does most of its fishing at night," that "noise levels are high," and that these factors are compounded by the seal's "two habitats."

36. H

Detail

Locating each of these claims in the passage, we find that choice H is *suggested* (line 68) and the subject of speculation, rather than stated as fact. All of the others are given in support of claims.

37. A

Inference

We find in the first paragraph that they live along the northern Atlantic and Pacific coasts. Since they live in both the land and water, the coastlines must be accessible. We can infer that the waters are cold rather than warm, eliminating choice D. Choices B and C are too broad.

38. J

Detail

This feature is mentioned at the end of paragraph 2. It shouldn't be confused with echolocation, which is discussed in paragraph 4, but not connected with any particular sensory organ.

39. B

Big Picture

The entire passage is about how the seal's sensory organs have adapted to life on land and in the water, making B the best choice. Generally, we are told about differences, not similarities, between the sensory organs of humans and harbor seals, eliminating choice A. The relative success of human and seal adaptation to their environments isn't discussed, thus eliminating choices C and D.

40. G

Detail

In paragraph 3, we see that human corneas refract light badly in water, and the seal's corneas perform well.

Science Test

Science questions can be divided into three basic types: Figure questions, Patterns questions, and Scientific Reasoning questions. You may also see Basic Theory questions when you review the Conflicting Viewpoints passage. As you review the answers and explanations, note which types you tend to answer correctly or incorrectly and tailor your studying to focus on areas where you need improvement.

PASSAGE I

1. B

Figure

To answer this question, you have to examine the third column of the table, transmittance range. For a material to transmit light at a wavelength of 25 μm, its transmittance range—the range of wavelengths over which the material is transparent—must include 25 μm. Only potassium bromide (0.3–29 μm) and cesium iodide (0.3–70 μm) have transmittance ranges that include 25 μm, so choice B is correct.

2. F

Figure

The material that contradicts this hypothesis is going to have poor chemical resistance but a transmittance range less than 10 μm. Lithium fluoride, choice F, fits the bill: its chemical resistance is poor, and its transmittance range is less than 6 μm wide. Choices G and J are wrong because both flint glass and quartz have excellent chemical resistance. Choice H is out because cesium iodide has a transmittance range nearly 70 μm wide.

3. D

Scientific Reasoning

The correct answer is a pair of materials in which the refractive index of the first material is greater than that of the second. In choices A, B, and C, the refractive index of the first material is less than that of the second. In choice D, however, flint glass has a refractive index of 1.66 while calcium fluoride's refractive index is only 1.43. That makes choice D the correct answer.

4. J
Scientific Reasoning

The easiest way to answer this question is to use the first couple of materials and test each hypothesis on them. Choices F and G are incorrect because the transmittance range of lithium fluoride is wider than its useful prism range. Comparing the data on lithium fluoride and calcium fluoride rules out choice H because transmittance range does NOT increase as useful prism range decreases. In fact, looking down the rest of the table, you see that transmittance range seems to decrease as useful prism range decreases. Choice J is the only one left, and the data on lithium fluoride and calcium fluoride as well as all the other materials confirms that the transmittance range is always wider than, and includes within it, the useful prism range.

5. B
Figure

According to the footnote to the table, quartz infused with lead oxide is flint glass. Comparison of the properties of pure quartz and flint glass shows that the transmittance range of flint glass is narrower than that of quartz but that its refractive index is greater. This supports choice B.

PASSAGE II

6. H
Scientific Reasoning

Use the results of both experiments to answer this question. The answer choices all involve temperature, concentration, and solvent in different combinations. To determine whether osmotic pressure is dependent upon a variable, look for a pair of trials in which all conditions except for that variable are identical. In doing so, you see that temperature and concentration affect osmotic pressure, but solvent does not.

7. C
Figure

Find methanol at 0.5 mol/L, which is in Table 2. The text above the table states that all the trials were conducted under the same temperature (298 K). Therefore, simply look across the row that you identified. The osmotic pressure is 12.23, C.

8. G
Scientific Reasoning

To figure out whether or not the sucrose solution will diffuse across the membrane under the conditions described in the question, go back to the definition of osmotic pressure given in the introduction. Once the external pressure reaches the osmotic pressure, osmosis will not occur. In order for osmosis to occur, the external pressure must be less than the osmotic pressure of the solution. The solution in this question is a 0.1 mol/L aqueous sucrose solution at 298 K; those conditions correspond to an osmotic pressure of 2.45 atm. Since the external pressure is 1 atm, which is less than the osmotic pressure, osmosis will occur. From the definition of osmosis in the passage, it is clear that the solution will diffuse from the side of the membrane with a lower concentration of dissolved material, in this case pure water, to the side with a higher concentration, in this case sucrose solution. Choice G is correct.

9. C
Figure

To determine what the scientists investigated in Experiment 1, look at what they varied and what they measured. In Experiment 1, the scientists varied the concentration and the temperature of sucrose solutions, and they measured the osmotic pressure. Therefore, they were investigating the effect of concentration and temperature on osmotic pressure, choice C. Watch out for choice A: it states what was investigated in Experiment 2, not Experiment 1.

10. F
Patterns

The results in Table 2 indicate that osmotic pressure doesn't depend on the solvent, as discussed in the explanation to question 6. So Statement I is a valid conclusion, and choice G can be eliminated. Statement II is false. The results in Table 1 indicate that osmotic pressure is dependent on concentration as well as temperature. So choice H can be ruled out. Now consider Statement III. It is not a valid conclusion because osmotic pressure is the pressure required to prevent osmosis, so osmosis occurs only if the external pressure is less than the osmotic pressure.

11. D
Figure

To answer questions that ask about the design of an experiment, look at what the scientists are trying to measure. You're told that osmotic pressure is the pressure required to prevent osmosis. In order to measure the osmotic pressure of a solution, scientists need to be able to tell when osmosis begins. If you have two clear solutions with sucrose dissolved in one of them, how can you tell when there's any movement of solvent between the two of them? If the sucrose is dyed, the blue solution will become paler when osmosis starts, i.e., when solvent moves across the membrane to create an equilibrium. Therefore, choice D is correct.

PASSAGE III

12. J
Scientific Reasoning

Even if you do not know how many °C are equivalent to room temperature, you can eliminate all of the incorrect answer choices. Choices F, G, and H all reach a boiling point at low temperatures and, therefore, would all be gases at room temperature. Choice J, at 36°C, is the only logical choice.

13. C
Patterns

To answer this question, you have to look for trends in each table and draw conclusions. This can be done by looking at the values in each category and seeing how they vary with respect to each other. If you look at Tables 1 and 2, you can see that there is a direct variation between boiling point and molecular weight: as one increases, the other increases. Therefore, Statement I is correct, Statement II is false, and you can eliminate choices B and D. Now consider Statement III. To investigate the relationship between molecular structure and boiling point, you have to keep the third variable—molecular weight—constant. Look at the data for two compounds with different molecular structures but the same molecular weight: N_2 and CO match that description and their boiling points differ. Therefore, Statement III is correct, and choice C is the correct response.

14. G
Figure

In order to answer this question, you need to establish where C_6H_{14} would fit in Table 1. It is clear from Table 1 that the boiling point increases as the molecular weight increases, so the boiling point of C_6H_{14} will be between the boiling points of molecules with greater and lesser molecular weights. The molecular weight of C_6H_{14} is 86 g/mol, so it will lie between those hydrocarbons with molecular weights of 72 g/mol and 114 g/mol. Therefore, its boiling point will be between 36°C and 126°C. G, with a value of 70°C, is the only choice that lies between these two boiling points.

15. A
Figure

N_2, a non-polar molecule, and CO, a polar molecule, have identical molecular weights and their boiling points differ by only 4°C. SiH_4 (non-polar) and PH_3 (polar) have nearly identical molecular weights as well, but the difference between their boiling points is 27°C—much greater than the difference between the boiling points of N_2 and CO, which have lower molecular weights than SiH_4 and PH_3. The difference between the boiling points of polar and non-polar substances of similar molecular weight increases as molecular weight increases, so choice A is correct.

16. H
Figure

If you refer to Table 2, you'll see that for polar substances, as the molar weight goes from 78 to 162, the boiling point goes from −55°C to 97°C. You know the molar weight has to be somewhere between 78 and 162, so F is clearly out, and G, 80, is too close to 78 to be the answer. You would expect the molar weight to be closer to 78 than 162, since 0 is closer to −55 than 97. Therefore, J, 132, is out, and choice H is the answer.

PASSAGE IV

17. A
Scientific Reasoning

The question refers to Experiment 2 only, so the correct answer will involve sunlight. Table 2 shows that the average length of the leaves

increased from 5.3 cm to 12.4 cm as the amount of sunlight increased from 0 to 3 hours per day. But as the amount of sunlight increased further, leaf size decreased. Therefore, choice D is incorrect. Neither humidity, choice B, nor water, choice C, is relevant to Experiment 2.

18. G
Figure

Table 1 gives leaf widths at 35% and 55% humidity at 1.8 cm and 2.0 cm, respectively. The leaf width at 40% humidity would most likely be between those two figures. Choice G is the only choice within that range.

19. B
Scientific Reasoning

All the answer choices involve humidity and sunlight, which were investigated in Experiments 1 and 2, respectively. In Table 1, leaf length and width were greatest at 75% humidity. In Table 2, they were greatest at three hours per day of sunlight. Combining those two conditions, as in choice B, would probably produce the largest leaves.

20. F
Scientific Reasoning

This question relates to the method of the study. Each experiment begins with a statement that five groups of seedlings were used. Therefore, choice F is correct. The other choices list variables that were manipulated.

21. D
Scientific Reasoning

Choice D is an assumption that underlies the design of all three experiments. If the seedlings were not equally capable of further growth, then changes in leaf size and density could not be reliably attributed to researcher-controlled changes in humidity, sunlight, and temperature. Choice A is wrong because all the seedlings were 2–3 cm tall. The seedlings' abilities to germinate, choice B, or to produce flowers, choice C, were not mentioned in the passage.

22. H
Scientific Reasoning

Each of the three experiments investigated a different factor related to leaf growth. To produce the most useful new data, researchers would probably vary a fourth condition. Soil mineral content would be an appropriate factor to examine. None of the other choices relate directly to the purpose of the experiments as expressed in paragraph 1 of the passage.

PASSAGE V

23. B
Figure

According to the table, decreasing the cross-sectional area of a given wire always increases resistance, so choice B is correct. Choice C is wrong because resistivity, displayed in the second column, is constant for each material and thus cannot be responsible for variations in resistance for any given material. Gauge varies inversely with cross-sectional area, so choice D is incorrect.

24. G
Patterns

Because resistance varies inversely with cross-sectional area A, as discussed in the previous explanation, the correct answer to this question must place A in the denominator. The only choice that does so is choice G.

25. D
Patterns

Compare the choices two at a time. The wires in A and B are made of the same material and have the same cross-sectional area; only their length is different. Doubling the length doubles

the resistance, so choice B would have a higher resistance than choice A. By similar reasoning, choice D would have a higher resistance than choice C. The only difference between choices B and D is the material. Even though the research team didn't test wire with a 0.33 mm² cross-sectional area, Table 1 shows that tungsten wire has higher levels of resistance than aluminum wire across all factors.

26. J
Scientific Reasoning

The larger circle represents 10-gauge wire; its diameter is 2.59 mm. The smaller circle has a diameter of only 1.29 mm, but it represents 16-gauge wire, so Statement I is true, and you can eliminate choices G and H without even checking Statements II or III. To check Statement III, the table shows that the resistance of an iron (Fe) wire is much higher than that of an aluminum (Al) wire with the same length and cross-sectional area. The first sentence of paragraph 1 defined the resistance of a conductor as "the extent to which it opposes the flow of electricity." Since iron has a higher resistance than aluminum, iron must not conduct electricity as well. Therefore, Statement III is true, and choice J is correct.

27. D
Patterns

The data indicates that the resistivity of a material doesn't change when wire length changes. Therefore, the graph of resistivity versus length for tungsten (or any other) wire is a horizontal line.

PASSAGE VI

28. F
Basic Theory

To answer this question, you have to refer to the examples presented by the scientists to find a point of agreement. Both use the example of giraffes to show how scarcity of food and the need to reach higher and higher branches led to the evolution of long necks; thus, they both agree that environment affects evolution.

29. C
Scientific Reasoning

This Principle question requires that you figure out how new evidence affects the two hypotheses. To answer it, all you have to consider are the hypotheses of the two scientists. Scientist 2 believes that characteristics acquired by an individual over a lifetime are passed on to its offspring, a theory that would be supported by this finding.

30. J
Scientific Reasoning

This question requires some reasoning. Scientist 2 states that all of the changes that occur in an individual's life can be passed on to offspring. Since he believes that any characteristic can undergo change, he must also believe that any characteristic can be inherited.

31. B
Basic Theory

You don't need any information other than the hypothesis of Scientist 1 to answer this question. He believes that random mutations continually occur within a species as it propagates and that advantageous mutations, such as long necks on giraffes, help the species adapt to environmental changes, and thus become more prevalent within the species, which is what choice B states.

32. G
Basic Theory

Here, you don't need any information other than the hypotheses of the two scientists. The crux of their disagreement is over how evolution occurs—whether through random mutations or through the inheritance of acquired characteristics.

33. B
Scientific Reasoning

Recall that Scientist 2 states that evolution occurs through the inheritance of acquired characteristics. In order to account for humans possessing nerve endings now that were not present before the discovery of fire, Scientist 2 would have to believe that new nerve endings could be acquired during a single lifetime. Choice B directly contradicts this idea and would therefore refute the hypothesis.

34. F
Scientific Reasoning

Recall that Scientist 1 explains that evolution occurs as a result of random mutation, while Scientist 2 credits the inheritance of acquired characteristics. Choice G can then be eliminated, since it is related to the explanation of the wrong scientist. Choice H would actually refute Scientist 1's hypothesis, and choice J is irrelevant. Only choice F provides a valid explanation for the increase in average height based on the random mutations described by Scientist 1.

PASSAGE VII

35. D
Figure

In Experiment 1, the researchers vary what is fed to the cows by giving them meat from scrapie-free sheep and from scrapie-infected sheep. The cows are later examined for signs of BSE. One common type of wrong answer choice for Experiment questions are choices, such as choice B for this question, that include factors that are outside the parameters of the experiment.

36. F
Figure

In Experiment 2, the researchers vary what is injected into cows' brains. Any answer choice that discusses ingestion as a focus of this experiment is wrong. This eliminates choices G, H, and J. Often, wrong answer choices for Experiment questions, such as choice G for this question, will include the appropriate information from the wrong experiment.

37. B
Scientific Reasoning

By examining the method used in a given experiment, one can determine the assumptions the researchers made in carrying out the experiment and the sources of error. Often, an error enters the experiment because of the assumptions researchers make. In Experiments 1 and 2, the researchers examined the brains of cows a year and a half after the cows were fed scrapie-infected sheep meat or were injected with scrapie-infected sheep brains. If a year and a half is not a sufficient amount of time for BSE to develop, some of the cows that were counted as not infected might have developed BSE if they had been given more time.

38. H
Scientific Reasoning

To answer this question, you need to determine how to test whether BSE can be transmitted via scrapie-infected goats. To test this, one would compare the effects of feeding cows scrapie-free goat meat with the effects of feeding cows scrapie-infected goat meat and compare the effects of injecting cows with scrapie-free goat brains with the effects of injecting them with scrapie-infected goat brains.

39. A
Scientific Reasoning

Remember that control groups are used as standards of comparison. The control group used in Experiment 1 is the group that is fed scrapie-free sheep meat. If the same proportion of Group A developed BSE as that of Group B, then the researchers would not have any evidence to support the hypothesis that the ingestion of scrapie-infected sheep meat causes BSE.

40. G
Scientific Reasoning

Since the proportion of the group of cows that ate scrapie-infected sheep meat and developed BSE was greater than the proportion of the group that were injected with scrapie-infected sheep brains and developed BSE, one can conclude that a cow that eats scrapie-infected sheep meat is more likely to develop BSE than a cow that is injected with scrapie-infected sheep brains. Mere exposure to scrapie-infected sheep, as opposed to ingestion of it, is never studied in either experiment, so conclusion I can be eliminated.

Writing Test

MODEL ESSAY

Below is an example of what a high-scoring essay might look like. Notice the author states her position clearly in the introductory paragraph and supports that position with evidence in the following paragraphs. This essay also uses transitions, some advanced vocabulary, and an effective "hook" to draw in the reader.

When people think about what students should learn in high school, they often focus on "the three Rs": reading, writing, and arithmetic. It's true that in an increasingly competitive global economy, those skills are more important than ever. However, in our society's rush to make sure students are keeping up through required standardized testing and increased computer education, are we forgetting another important aspect of education? Are we forgetting to teach our students how to think creatively and express themselves artistically? I think that requiring all high school students to take music or visual arts classes would benefit our country's students in several ways.

Learning about art and music actually helps students do better in other subjects. People often forget that studying art or music isn't just about putting paint to canvas or lips to trumpet. There is a lot of background information that students learn as well. When students study music they also have to learn a lot of history: who was the composer, where was he or she from, what was happening politically and socially during the time the music was composed, and how does the work compare historically to music by other composers. The same holds true for the visual arts; students can learn a lot from art history, not just about the artist but also about different cultures and time periods. Studies have shown that students who take music classes do better at math, maybe because these classes emphasize dividing up measures of music and counting out times.

With so much focus on standardized test scores and grade point averages, schools today emphasize individual academic performance and overlook the teaching of teamwork skills. Through playing in my high school's band, I have learned that even though it is important for me to practice so that I can play my best (and maybe move up a chair), what really matters is how we sound as a group. My bandmates and I push each other to succeed, and we get together outside of school to practice for big games and competitions. Band is also where I have made most of my friends. Participation in the arts is a great way for students to build social skills and create school spirit. It teaches students to help one another so that going to school isn't just about getting good grades for one's own benefit.

Learning about art or music is also helpful to students because it teaches them how to think creatively. When you take a photograph or paint a portrait you have to look at things in a new way, and you must try to synthesize your perception into a medium that other people can relate to. Between all the pressure to do well academically and all the social pressure teenagers face to fit in, being a teenager can be really stressful. Art and music can allow students to express their feelings in a positive, constructive way. Such classes can give students who aren't good at traditional academic subjects like math or science a chance to shine.

In conclusion, I think requiring all high school students to take music or visual arts classes would help students not only academically but socially and emotionally as well. Studying the arts actually helps students succeed in traditional subject areas, builds their confidence and social skills, and gives them the opportunity to learn to think creatively, all skills that will help them once they reach the workforce.

You can evaluate your essay and the model essay based on the following criteria, covered in chapter 16:

- Does the author answer the question?
- Is the author's position clearly stated?
- Does the body of the essay support and develop the position taken?
- Are there at least three supporting paragraphs?
- Is the relevance of each supporting paragraph clear?
- Does the writer address the other side of the argument?
- Is the essay organized, with a clear introduction, middle, and end?
- Does the author start a new paragraph for each new idea?
- Is each sentence in a paragraph relevant to the point made in that paragraph?
- Are transitions clear?
- Is the essay easy to read? Is it engaging?
- Are sentences varied?
- Is vocabulary used effectively? Is college-level vocabulary used?

Practice Test Two

ACT Practice Test Two
ANSWER SHEET

ENGLISH TEST

1. (A)(B)(C)(D) 11. (A)(B)(C)(D) 21. (A)(B)(C)(D) 31. (A)(B)(C)(D) 41. (A)(B)(C)(D) 51. (A)(B)(C)(D) 61. (A)(B)(C)(D) 71. (A)(B)(C)(D)
2. (F)(G)(H)(J) 12. (F)(G)(H)(J) 22. (F)(G)(H)(J) 32. (F)(G)(H)(J) 42. (F)(G)(H)(J) 52. (F)(G)(H)(J) 62. (F)(G)(H)(J) 72. (F)(G)(H)(J)
3. (A)(B)(C)(D) 13. (A)(B)(C)(D) 23. (A)(B)(C)(D) 33. (A)(B)(C)(D) 43. (A)(B)(C)(D) 53. (A)(B)(C)(D) 63. (A)(B)(C)(D) 73. (A)(B)(C)(D)
4. (F)(G)(H)(J) 14. (F)(G)(H)(J) 24. (F)(G)(H)(J) 34. (F)(G)(H)(J) 44. (F)(G)(H)(J) 54. (F)(G)(H)(J) 64. (F)(G)(H)(J) 74. (F)(G)(H)(J)
5. (A)(B)(C)(D) 15. (A)(B)(C)(D) 25. (A)(B)(C)(D) 35. (A)(B)(C)(D) 45. (A)(B)(C)(D) 55. (A)(B)(C)(D) 65. (A)(B)(C)(D) 75. (A)(B)(C)(D)
6. (F)(G)(H)(J) 16. (F)(G)(H)(J) 26. (F)(G)(H)(J) 36. (F)(G)(H)(J) 46. (F)(G)(H)(J) 56. (F)(G)(H)(J) 66. (F)(G)(H)(J)
7. (A)(B)(C)(D) 17. (A)(B)(C)(D) 27. (A)(B)(C)(D) 37. (A)(B)(C)(D) 47. (A)(B)(C)(D) 57. (A)(B)(C)(D) 67. (A)(B)(C)(D)
8. (F)(G)(H)(J) 18. (F)(G)(H)(J) 28. (F)(G)(H)(J) 38. (F)(G)(H)(J) 48. (F)(G)(H)(J) 58. (F)(G)(H)(J) 68. (F)(G)(H)(J)
9. (A)(B)(C)(D) 19. (A)(B)(C)(D) 29. (A)(B)(C)(D) 39. (A)(B)(C)(D) 49. (A)(B)(C)(D) 59. (A)(B)(C)(D) 69. (A)(B)(C)(D)
10. (F)(G)(H)(J) 20. (F)(G)(H)(J) 30. (F)(G)(H)(J) 40. (F)(G)(H)(J) 50. (F)(G)(H)(J) 60. (F)(G)(H)(J) 70. (F)(G)(H)(J)

MATH TEST

1. (A)(B)(C)(D)(E) 11. (A)(B)(C)(D)(E) 21. (A)(B)(C)(D)(E) 31. (A)(B)(C)(D)(E) 41. (A)(B)(C)(D)(E) 51. (A)(B)(C)(D)(E)
2. (F)(G)(H)(J)(K) 12. (F)(G)(H)(J)(K) 22. (F)(G)(H)(J)(K) 32. (F)(G)(H)(J)(K) 42. (F)(G)(H)(J)(K) 52. (F)(G)(H)(J)(K)
3. (A)(B)(C)(D)(E) 13. (A)(B)(C)(D)(E) 23. (A)(B)(C)(D)(E) 33. (A)(B)(C)(D)(E) 43. (A)(B)(C)(D)(E) 53. (A)(B)(C)(D)(E)
4. (F)(G)(H)(J)(K) 14. (F)(G)(H)(J)(K) 24. (F)(G)(H)(J)(K) 34. (F)(G)(H)(J)(K) 44. (F)(G)(H)(J)(K) 54. (F)(G)(H)(J)(K)
5. (A)(B)(C)(D)(E) 15. (A)(B)(C)(D)(E) 25. (A)(B)(C)(D)(E) 35. (A)(B)(C)(D)(E) 45. (A)(B)(C)(D)(E) 55. (A)(B)(C)(D)(E)
6. (F)(G)(H)(J)(K) 16. (F)(G)(H)(J)(K) 26. (F)(G)(H)(J)(K) 36. (F)(G)(H)(J)(K) 46. (F)(G)(H)(J)(K) 56. (F)(G)(H)(J)(K)
7. (A)(B)(C)(D)(E) 17. (A)(B)(C)(D)(E) 27. (A)(B)(C)(D)(E) 37. (A)(B)(C)(D)(E) 47. (A)(B)(C)(D)(E) 57. (A)(B)(C)(D)(E)
8. (F)(G)(H)(J)(K) 18. (F)(G)(H)(J)(K) 28. (F)(G)(H)(J)(K) 38. (F)(G)(H)(J)(K) 48. (F)(G)(H)(J)(K) 58. (F)(G)(H)(J)(K)
9. (A)(B)(C)(D)(E) 19. (A)(B)(C)(D)(E) 29. (A)(B)(C)(D)(E) 39. (A)(B)(C)(D)(E) 49. (A)(B)(C)(D)(E) 59. (A)(B)(C)(D)(E)
10. (F)(G)(H)(J)(K) 20. (F)(G)(H)(J)(K) 30. (F)(G)(H)(J)(K) 40. (F)(G)(H)(J)(K) 50. (F)(G)(H)(J)(K) 60. (F)(G)(H)(J)(K)

READING TEST

1. (A)(B)(C)(D) 6. (F)(G)(H)(J) 11. (A)(B)(C)(D) 16. (F)(G)(H)(J) 21. (A)(B)(C)(D) 26. (F)(G)(H)(J) 31. (A)(B)(C)(D) 36. (F)(G)(H)(J)
2. (F)(G)(H)(J) 7. (A)(B)(C)(D) 12. (F)(G)(H)(J) 17. (A)(B)(C)(D) 22. (F)(G)(H)(J) 27. (A)(B)(C)(D) 32. (F)(G)(H)(J) 37. (A)(B)(C)(D)
3. (A)(B)(C)(D) 8. (F)(G)(H)(J) 13. (A)(B)(C)(D) 18. (F)(G)(H)(J) 23. (A)(B)(C)(D) 28. (F)(G)(H)(J) 33. (A)(B)(C)(D) 38. (F)(G)(H)(J)
4. (F)(G)(H)(J) 9. (A)(B)(C)(D) 14. (F)(G)(H)(J) 19. (A)(B)(C)(D) 24. (F)(G)(H)(J) 29. (A)(B)(C)(D) 34. (F)(G)(H)(J) 39. (A)(B)(C)(D)
5. (A)(B)(C)(D) 10. (F)(G)(H)(J) 15. (A)(B)(C)(D) 20. (F)(G)(H)(J) 25. (A)(B)(C)(D) 30. (F)(G)(H)(J) 35. (A)(B)(C)(D) 40. (F)(G)(H)(J)

SCIENCE TEST

1. (A)(B)(C)(D) 6. (F)(G)(H)(J) 11. (A)(B)(C)(D) 16. (F)(G)(H)(J) 21. (A)(B)(C)(D) 26. (F)(G)(H)(J) 31. (A)(B)(C)(D) 36. (F)(G)(H)(J)
2. (F)(G)(H)(J) 7. (A)(B)(C)(D) 12. (F)(G)(H)(J) 17. (A)(B)(C)(D) 22. (F)(G)(H)(J) 27. (A)(B)(C)(D) 32. (F)(G)(H)(J) 37. (A)(B)(C)(D)
3. (A)(B)(C)(D) 8. (F)(G)(H)(J) 13. (A)(B)(C)(D) 18. (F)(G)(H)(J) 23. (A)(B)(C)(D) 28. (F)(G)(H)(J) 33. (A)(B)(C)(D) 38. (F)(G)(H)(J)
4. (F)(G)(H)(J) 9. (A)(B)(C)(D) 14. (F)(G)(H)(J) 19. (A)(B)(C)(D) 24. (F)(G)(H)(J) 29. (A)(B)(C)(D) 34. (F)(G)(H)(J) 39. (A)(B)(C)(D)
5. (A)(B)(C)(D) 10. (F)(G)(H)(J) 15. (A)(B)(C)(D) 20. (F)(G)(H)(J) 25. (A)(B)(C)(D) 30. (F)(G)(H)(J) 35. (A)(B)(C)(D) 40. (F)(G)(H)(J)

ENGLISH TEST

45 Minutes—75 Questions

> **Directions:** In the following five passages, certain words and phrases are underlined and numbered. In the right-hand column are alternatives for each underlined portion. Select the one that best conveys the idea, creates the most grammatically correct sentence, or is the most consistent with the style and tone of the passage. If you decide that the original version is best, select NO CHANGE. You may also find questions that ask about the entire passage or a section of the passage. These questions will correspond to small numbered boxes in the text. For these questions, decide which choice best accomplishes the purpose set out in the question stem. After you've selected the best choice, fill in the corresponding oval in your Answer Grid. For some questions, you'll need to read the context in order to answer correctly. Be sure to read until you have enough information to determine the correct answer choice.
>
> You will also find questions about a section of the passage or about the passage as a whole. These questions do not refer to an underlined portion of the passage, but rather are identified by a number or numbers in a box.
>
> For each question, choose the alternative you consider best and fill in the corresponding oval on your answer document. Read each passage through once before you begin to answer the questions that accompany it. For many of the questions, you must read several sentences beyond the question to determine the answer. Be sure that you have read enough ahead each time you choose an alternative.

Passage I

DUKE ELLINGTON, A JAZZ GREAT

[1]

By the time Duke Ellington published his autobiography, *Music is My Mistress*, in 1973 he had traveled to dozens of countries and every continent. "I pay rent in New York City," he answered when asked of his residence.

1. A. NO CHANGE
   B. 1973. He had
   C. 1973, it had
   D. 1973, he had

[2]

In the 1920s, though, Ellington pays more than rent in New York; he paid his dues on the bandstand. Having moved to Harlem from

2. F. NO CHANGE
   G. paid
   H. has to pay
   J. pay

GO ON TO THE NEXT PAGE

Washington, D.C., in 1923, Ellington <u>established:</u>
<u>his own</u> band and achieved critical recognition
with a polished sound and appearance. The
first New York review of the Ellingtonians in
1923 commented, "The boys look neat in dress
suits and labor hard but not in vain at their
music." As Ellington made a name for himself
as a <u>leader arranger and pianist,</u> his Harlem
Renaissance compositions and recordings highlighted two enduring characteristics of the man.
First, Ellington lived for jazz. Second, Harlem
sustained <u>it,</u> physically and spiritually.

[3]

Ellington himself admitted he was not a
very <u>good pianist. As a teenager</u> in Washington.

He missed more piano <u>lessons then he took</u>
with his teacher, Mrs. Clinkscales, and spent
more time going to dances than practicing the
the piano. <u>Mrs. Clinkscales was really the</u>
<u>name of his piano teacher!</u> In the clubs,

3. A. NO CHANGE
    B. established the following: his own
    C. established his own
    D. took the time and effort to establish
       his own

4. F. NO CHANGE
    G. leader arranger, and pianist,
    H. leader, arranger, and pianist
    J. leader, arranger, and pianist,

5. A. NO CHANGE
    B. him,
    C. them,
    D. itself,

6. F. NO CHANGE
    G. good pianist as a teenager
    H. good pianist, a teenager
    J. good pianist, as a teenager

7. A. NO CHANGE
    B. lessons then he had taken
    C. lessons; he took
    D. lessons than he took

8. F. NO CHANGE
    G. That was really the name of his
       piano teacher: Mrs. Clinkscales!
    H. Mrs. Clinkscales was really the
       name of his piano teacher.
    J. OMIT the underlined portion.

GO ON TO THE NEXT PAGE ⟶

therefore, Ellington and his friends eventually

    9

caught word of New York and the opportunities

that awaited and were there for young musicians.

         10

Ellington wrote, "Harlem, to our minds, did

indeed have the world's most glamorous

atmosphere. We had to go there." He left

                                    11

Washington with drummer Sonny Greer.

                11

Before they could even unpack in Harlem,

though, they found themselves penniless.

Not until Ellington was lucky enough to find

fifteen dollars on the street could he return

to Washington and recollect himself.

                 [4]

    Ellington eventually did return to Harlem,

and he achieved great success as the bandleader

at the Cotton Club from 1927 to 1932. Located

in the heart of Harlem at 142nd Street and Lenox

Avenue, he played at the Cotton Club, which was

                12

frequented by top entertainers and rich patrons.

    12

Harlem's nightlife, "cut out of a very luxurious,

royal-blue bolt of velvet," was an inspirational

backdrop, and Ellington composed, arranged,

and recorded prolifically to the rave of excited

critical acclaim. "Black and Tan Fantasy," "Hot

and Bothered," and "Rockin' in Rhythm" were

9. A. NO CHANGE
    B. however
    C. despite
    D. then

10. F. NO CHANGE
    G. awaiting and being there for
    H. that awaited
    J. that were there for

11. A. NO CHANGE
    B. With drummer Sonny Greer, it was
        Washington that he left.
    C. Leaving Washington, he, Ellington,
        left with drummer Sonny Greer.
    D. OMIT the underlined portion.

12. F. NO CHANGE
    G. he played at the Cotton Club, a club
        that was frequented
    H. the Cotton Club, which was
        frequented
    J. the Cotton Club was frequented

GO ON TO THE NEXT PAGE ⇒

Ellington's early hits during this period. [13] They exhibited his unique ability to compose music that animated both dancers in search of a good time and improvising musicians in search of good music. Before long, the once fumbling pianist from Washington, D.C., became the undisputed leader of hot jazz in decadent Harlem. [14]

13. The purpose of including the names of Ellington's songs is to:

   A. provide some details about Ellington's early music.
   B. contradict an earlier point that Ellington did not create his own music.
   C. illustrate the complexity of Ellington's music.
   D. discuss the atmosphere at the Cotton Club.

14. The purpose of paragraph 4, as it relates to the previous paragraphs, is primarily to:

   F. demonstrate how accomplished Ellington had become.
   G. suggest that Ellington did not like living in New York.
   H. remind us how difficult it is to be a musician.
   J. make us skeptical of Ellington's abilities.

Question 15 asks about
the preceding passage as a whole.

---

15. The writer wishes to insert the following detail into the essay:

   > The combination of fun and seriousness in his music led to critical acclaim and wide mass appeal.

   The sentence would most logically be inserted into paragraph:

   A. 1, after the last sentence.
   B. 3, before the first sentence.
   C. 4, after the first sentence.
   D. 4, before the last sentence.

GO ON TO THE NEXT PAGE ⟶

Passage II

COLORING AS SELF-DEFENSE IN ANIMALS

> The following paragraphs may or may not be in the most logical order. Each paragraph is numbered in brackets, and question 29 will ask you to choose the appropriate order.

[1]

Some animals change its coloring with the
16
seasons. The ptarmigan sheds its brown plumage

16. F. NO CHANGE
    G. their
    H. it's
    J. there

in winter, replacing it with white feathers. The
17

17. A. NO CHANGE
    B. winter and replacing
    C. winter: replacing
    D. winter replacing

stoat, a member of the weasel family is known
18
as the *ermine* in winter because its brown fur

changes to white. The chameleon is perhaps the

18. F. NO CHANGE
    G. weasel family known
    H. weasel family, which is known
    J. weasel family, is known

most versatile of all animals having changed
19
their protective coloration. The chameleon

changes its color in just a few minutes to

whatever surface it happens to be sitting on.

19. A. NO CHANGE
    B. who changes
    C. that change
    D. that changed

[2]

While animals like the chameleon use their
20
coloring as a way of hiding from predators,
20
the skunk uses its distinctive white stripe as a

way of standing out from its surroundings. Far

20. F. NO CHANGE
    G. their use coloring
    H. use coloring their
    J. coloring their use

GO ON TO THE NEXT PAGE ⇒

from placing it in danger; the skunk's visibility

              21

actually protects it. By distinguishing itself from

other animals. The skunk warns its predators

       22

to avoid its infamous stink. Think about it:

the question is would your appetite be whetted

                23

by the skunk's odor?

  23

[3]

    Researchers have been investigating how

               24

animal species have come to use coloring as a

means of protecting themselves. One study has

shown that certain animals have glands that

release special hormones, resulting in the change

of skin or fur color. Therefore, not all the animals

               25

that camouflage themselves have these glands.

The topic remains and endures as one of the

            26

many mysteries of the natural world.

[4]

    Animals have a variety of ways of protecting

themselves from enemies. Some animals adapt

---

21. A. NO CHANGE
    B. danger, the skunk's
    C. danger; the skunks'
    D. danger, it is the skunk's

22. F. NO CHANGE
    G. animals, therefore, the
    H. animals because
    J. animals, the

23. A. NO CHANGE
    B. would your appetite be whetted by
the skunk's odor?
    C. the question is as follows, would
your appetite be whetted by the
skunk's odor?
    D. the question is would your appetite
be whetted by the odor of the
skunk?

24. F. NO CHANGE
    G. investigated
    H. were investigating
    J. investigate

25. A. NO CHANGE
    B. Nevertheless,
    C. However,
    D. Finally,

26. F. NO CHANGE
    G. remaining and enduring as
    H remains and endures
    J. remains

GO ON TO THE NEXT PAGE ⟩

in shape and color to their environment. The tree frog, for example, blends perfectly into its surroundings. When it sits motionless, <u>a back-ground of leaves completely hides the tree frog.</u>
₂₇

This camouflage enables the tree frog to hide from
₂₈
other animals that would be interested in eating
₂₈
the tree frog.
₂₈

27. A. NO CHANGE
     B. the tree frog is completely hidden in a background of leaves.
     C. completely hidden is the tree frog in a background of leaves.
     D. a background of leaves and the tree frog are completely hidden.

28. F. NO CHANGE
     G. This camouflage enables the tree frog to hide from predators.
     H. This camouflage enables the tree frog to hide from other animals interested in eating the tree frog.
     J. OMIT the underlined portion.

Questions 29–30 ask about the preceding passage as a whole.

---

29. What would be the most logical order of paragraphs for this essay?

     A. 3, 1, 4, 2
     B. 1, 2, 4, 3
     C. 4, 1, 2, 3
     D. 2, 1, 3, 4

30. Suppose the author had been asked to write an essay on how animals use their colorings to protect themselves in the wild. Would this essay meet the requirement?

     F. Yes, because the author covers several aspects of how animals use their colorings to protect themselves.
     G. Yes, because the author thoroughly investigates how one animal protects itself with its colorings.
     H. No, because the author does not consider animals that exist in the wild.
     J. No, because the author does not include information from research studies.

GO ON TO THE NEXT PAGE ▷

Passage III

THE HISTORY OF CHOCOLATE

The word *chocolate* is used to describe a variety

of foods made from the beans of the cacao tree.
    31

The first people known to have made chocolate

31. A. NO CHANGE
    B. foods, which are made
    C. foods and made
    D. foods and are

were the Aztecs, a people who used cacao seeds
                  32

to make a bitter but tasty drink. However, it

was not until Hernan Cortez's exploration of

32. F. NO CHANGE
    G. Aztecs, and they used
    H. Aztecs a people that use
    J. Aztecs, who used

Mexico in 1519. That Europeans first learned
           33

of chocolate.

33. A. NO CHANGE
    B. 1519 that
    C. 1519, that
    D. 1519:

   Cortez came to the New World in search of

gold, but his interest was also fired by the Aztecs'

strange drink. When Cortez returned to Spain,

his ship's cargo included and held three chests of
                    34

cacao beans. It was from these beans that Europe

34. F. NO CHANGE
    G. included, held
    H. included
    J. including and holding

experienced its first taste of what seemed to be a
                                   35

very unusual beverage. The drink soon became

popular among those people wealthy enough to

35. A. NO CHANGE
    B. seems to be
    C. seemingly is
    D. seemed being

afford it. Over the next century cafes specializing
            36

36. F. NO CHANGE
    G. Over the next century cafes
       specialize
    H. Over the next century, cafes
       specializing
    J. Over the next century, there were
       cafes specializing

GO ON TO THE NEXT PAGE ⟶

in chocolate drinks began to appear throughout

Europe. 37

Of course, chocolate is very popular today.

People all over the world enjoy chocolate bars
                                       38
chocolate sprinkles and even chocolate soda.
         38

In fact, Asia has cultivated the delicacy of
   39
chocolate-covered ants! People enjoy this food

as a snack at the movies or sporting events. The

chocolate ant phenomenon has yet to take over

America, but enjoy their chocolate Americans do
            40
nonetheless.

Many chocolate lovers around the world

were ecstatic to hear that chocolate may actually

be good for you. Researchers say: chocolate
                            41
contains a chemical that could prevent cancer
   41
and heart disease. New research measures the

amount of catechins, the chemical thought to

37. The author is considering the addition
of another sentence here that briefly
describes one of the first European cafes
to serve a chocolate drink. This addition
would:

A. weaken the author's argument.

B. provide some interesting details.

C. contradict the topic of the
paragraph.

D. highlight the author's opinion of
chocolate.

38. F. NO CHANGE

G. chocolate, bars, chocolate, sprinkles,
and even chocolate soda.

H. chocolate bars chocolate sprinkles—
even chocolate soda.

J. chocolate bars, chocolate sprinkles,
and even chocolate soda.

39. A. NO CHANGE

B. Unfortunately

C. In spite of this

D. The truth is

40. F. NO CHANGE

G. but Americans enjoy their chocolate

H. but enjoy their chocolate is what
Americans do

J. but Americans do enjoy their
chocolate

41. A. NO CHANGE

B. have said the following: chocolate
contains

C. say that chocolate contains

D. say: chocolate contained

GO ON TO THE NEXT PAGE ⟹

be behind the benefits, in different types of

chocolate.

<u>The substance is also found in tea.</u> The
42
studies show that chocolate is very high in

catechins. The research is likely to be welcomed

<u>by those</u> with a sweet tooth, although dentists
43

<u>may less be pleased.</u>
44

42. F. NO CHANGE

    G. Another place where the substance is found is tea.

    H. Also, tea contains the substance.

    J. OMIT the underlined portion.

43. A. NO CHANGE

    B. with them

    C. by us

    D. to those

44. F. NO CHANGE

    G. pleased less they will be.

    H. may be pleased less.

    J. may be less pleased.

> Question 45 asks about
> the preceding passage as a whole.

45. Suppose the author had been given the assignment of writing about culinary trends in history. Would this essay satisfy the requirement?

    A. Yes, because the essay discusses many culinary trends in history.

    B. Yes, because the essay shows how chocolate has been used over time.

    C. No, because the essay focuses too much on chocolate in present times.

    D. No, because the essay only covers chocolate.

GO ON TO THE NEXT PAGE ⇨

Passage IV

THE MILITARY UNIFORM OF THE FUTURE

[1]

Scientists, in programs administers by the United
46
States Army, are experimenting to develop the
military uniform of the future. As imagined, it

would be light as silk, bulletproof, and able to
47
rapidly change at the molecular level to adapt to
biological or chemical threats. In response to a
detected anthrax threat, for example, it would
become an impermeable shield. The pant leg of a

soldier who's leg had been broken would have been
48   49

able to morph into a splint, or, even form an
50
artificial muscle. Nanosensors would transmit
vital signs back to a medical team or monitor
the breath for increased nitric oxide, a sign of
stress.

46. F. NO CHANGE
    G. administering by
    H. administered by
    J. administers with

47. A. NO CHANGE
    B. would: be light as silk, bulletproof, and able to
    C. would be light as silk bulletproof and able to
    D. light as silk, bulletproof, and was able to

48. F. NO CHANGE
    G. soldier whose
    H. soldier, who's
    J. soldier that's

49. A. NO CHANGE
    B. would be
    C. will have been
    D. is

50. F. NO CHANGE
    G. splint or even form
    H. splint, or even, form
    J. splint or, even, form

GO ON TO THE NEXT PAGE

[2]

The especially promising Invisible Soldier program aims to make the long-held dream of human invisibility a reality by using technology.
51
To create a covering capable of concealing a
51   52

soldier and making him invisible from most
52

wavelengths of visible light. 53 54

51. A. NO CHANGE
    B. technology to create
    C. technology, which were creating
    D. technology; create

52. F. NO CHANGE
    G. making a soldier invisible and concealing him
    H. concealing a soldier making that soldier invisible
    J. concealing a soldier

53. The writer's description of the U.S. Army's Invisible Soldier program seems to indicate that the army's opinion of the program is:
    A. skeptical.
    B. curious.
    C. enthusiastic.
    D. detailed.

54. What is the purpose of this paragraph, as it relates to the rest of the essay?
    F. To highlight one of the successes of the scientists' programs
    G. To predict the future of U.S. military uniforms
    H. To outline what will follow in the essay
    J. To introduce a specific example of the uniform of the future

GO ON TO THE NEXT PAGE

[3]

A solution proposed in the <u>early stages near</u>

₅₅

<u>the beginning of</u> the program's development

₅₅

would construct a suit or cape from fabric linked

to sensors that can detect the coloring and

pattern of the background. The sensors would

then send varying intensities of electrical current

to the appropriate areas of the fabric, <u>they</u> would

₅₆

be impregnated with chemicals sensitive to

electricity. The coveralls would change colors

continually as the soldier moved.

[4]

The problem with this solution from a

military standpoint, <u>you know, is</u> <u>power: the</u>

₅₇   ₅₈

<u>fact that the suit</u> would require a continuous

₅₈

flow of electricity means that a soldier would

have to carry a large number of batteries, which

would hardly contribute to ease of movement

and camouflage.

[5]

[1] To address this problem, army researchers

have developed a new kind of color-changing

pixel, known as the intererometric modulator or

i-mod. [2] The researchers hope that a flexible

suit made of i-mod pixels could completely blend

into any background. [3] In addition to matching

a background, the pixels could also be set to

show other colors, for example, a camouflage

mode that would render a soldier effectively

55. A. NO CHANGE
    B. beginning and the early stages of
    C. early stages of
    D. OMIT the underlined portion.

56. F. NO CHANGE
    G. that
    H. it
    J. which

57. A. NO CHANGE
    B. is, like,
    C. however, is
    D. therefore, is

58. F. NO CHANGE
    G. power; the fact that the suit
    H. power the fact that the suit
    J. power the fact that, the suit

GO ON TO THE NEXT PAGE

invisible in the forest and a flash mode that
would enhance a soldier's visibility in a rescue
situation. [4] Changing the distance between the
mirrors changes the color of the light that they
reflect. [5] Each i-mod pixel is made up of a pair
of tiny mirrors. 59

59. Which of the following sequences would
make paragraph 5 most logical?

A. 2, 4, 5, 3, 1

B. 2, 3, 1, 5, 4

C. 1, 4, 5, 2, 3

D. 1, 5, 4, 2, 3

> Question 60 asks about
> the preceding passage as a whole.

60. The writer wishes to insert the
following material into the passage:

> When H.G. Wells wrote *The Invisible
> Man*, there was no interest in
> camouflaging soldiers; the British
> army was garbed in bright red
> uniforms. Since that time, govern-
> ments have learned the value of
> making soldiers difficult to see,
> first by using camouflage fabrics,
> and today by envisioning something
> even more effective that would
> change color to match the terrain.

The new material would most logically
be placed in paragraph:

F. 2.

G. 3.

H. 4.

J. 5.

GO ON TO THE NEXT PAGE

Passage V

CALIFORNIA: A STATE BUILT ON DREAMS

It lasted fewer than ten years, but when it was over, the United States had been radically and forever changed. The population had exploded on the West Coast of the country, <u>fortunes had been made and those same fortunes were lost,</u> and a new state had entered the union—
61

a state that would become a state of mind for all <u>Americans: California.</u>
62

The United States <u>acquiring</u> the territory
63
that would later become California during the Mexican War (1846–1848). One of the many settlers who traveled to the new territory was <u>John Sutter who was a shopkeeper</u> from Switzer-
64
land who had left behind his wife, his children,

and his debts, in search of a new life. <u>Hired he did</u> a carpenter named James Marshall to build
65
a sawmill for him on the American River in the foothills of the Sierra Nevada mountains.

61. A. NO CHANGE
    B. fortunes had been made and lost,
    C. fortunes, which had been made, were then lost,
    D. made and lost were fortunes,

62. F. NO CHANGE
    G. Americans, and that place was called California.
    H. Americans, California.
    J. Americans. California.

63. A. NO CHANGE
    B. has acquired
    C. is acquiring
    D. acquired

64. F. NO CHANGE
    G. John Sutter, a shopkeeper
    H. John Sutter; a shopkeeper
    J. John Sutter, who was a shopkeeper

65. A. NO CHANGE
    B. He hired
    C. Hiring
    D. He did hire

GO ON TO THE NEXT PAGE ⟹

On January 24, 1848, <u>while inspecting the</u>
₆₆

<u>mill's runoff into the river</u>, Marshall saw two
₆₆

shiny objects below the surface of the water. He

took the nuggets to Sutter, who was annoyed

by the discovery; Sutter didn't want <u>them</u> mill
₆₇

workers distracted by gold fever. <u>Keeping the</u>
₆₈

<u>discovery</u> quiet for a while, but then he couldn't
₆₈

resist bragging about it. Word got out, and

workers began quitting their jobs and heading

into the hills to look for the source of the gold

that had washed down the river.

[69] Thousands of people poured into

California in search of fortune and glory. <u>This is</u>
₇₀

<u>similar to recent stock market increases</u>. During
₇₀

the two years after Marshall's discovery, more

than 90,000 people made their way to California,

looking for gold. In fact, so many people moved

---

66. F. NO CHANGE

G. (he was inspecting the mill's runoff into the river)

H. inspecting the mill's runoff into the river all the while

J. OMIT the underlined portion.

67. A. NO CHANGE

B. this

C. his

D. there

68. F. NO CHANGE

G. The discovery he was keeping

H. He kept the discovery

J. Keeps he the discovery

69. Which of the following would provide the best transition here, guiding the reader from the topic of the previous paragraph to the new topic of this paragraph?

A. Sutter and Marshall did not make a profit.

B. The gold rush had officially begun.

C. Can you image how a small discovery led to such a large state?

D. Most of the "gold" turned out to be a hoax.

70. F. NO CHANGE

G. The rush for gold was similar to recent stock market increases.

H. This was similar to recent stock market increases.

J. OMIT the underlined portion.

GO ON TO THE NEXT PAGE →

West in just <u>singularly one</u> of those years, 1849,
71
that all the prospectors, regardless of when they
arrived, became known as Forty-niners. By 1850,
so many people had moved to the California
territory that the United States Congress was
forced to declare it a new state. In 1854, the
population had increased by another 300,000
people. <u>In fact,</u> 1 out of every 90 people then
72
living in the United States was living in
California.

Even after all of the gold had been taken
from the ground, California remained a magical
place in the American imagination. The 31st
state had become a place <u>that</u> lives could change,
73
fortunes could be made, and dreams could come

true. For many <u>people, and California</u> is still
74
such a place.

71. A. NO CHANGE
    B. one
    C. one and only one
    D. singular

72. F. NO CHANGE
    G. In spite of this,
    H. Believe it or not,
    J. Therefore,

73. A. NO CHANGE
    B. where
    C. through which
    D. in

74. F. NO CHANGE
    G. Forty-niners, California
    H. people and California
    J. people, California

GO ON TO THE NEXT PAGE ⟱

> Question 75 asks about
> the preceding passage as a whole.

75. Suppose the writer had been assigned to write a brief essay detailing the life of a Forty-niner during the California gold rush. Would this essay successfully fulfill the assignment?

A. Yes, because the essay tells about the lives of John Sutter and James Marshall.

B. No, because the essay covers a historical rather than biographical perspective of the gold rush.

C. Yes, because one can imagine the life of a Forty-niner from the details provided in the essay.

D. No, because the essay does not discuss Forty-niners.

IF YOU FINISH BEFORE TIME IS CALLED, YOU MAY CHECK YOUR WORK ON THIS SECTION ONLY. DO NOT TURN TO ANY OTHER SECTION IN THE TEST. **STOP**

MATH TEST

60 Minutes—60 Questions

Directions: Solve each of the following problems, select the correct answer, and then fill in the corresponding oval on your Answer Grid.

Don't linger over problems that are too time-consuming. Do as many as you can, then come back to the others in the time permitted.

You may use a calculator on this test. Some questions, however, may be easier to answer without the use of a calculator.

Note: Unless the question says otherwise, assume all of the following:

1. Illustrative figures are *not* necessarily drawn to scale.

2. All geometric figures lie in a plane.

3. The term *line* indicates a straight line.

4. The term *average* indicates arithmetic mean.

1. The regular price for a certain bicycle is $125.00. If that price is reduced by 20%, what is the new price?

   A. $100.00
   B. $105.00
   C. $112.50
   D. $120.00
   E. $122.50

2. If $x = -5$, then $2x^2 - 6x + 5 = ?$

   F. -15
   G. 15
   H. 25
   J. 85
   K. 135

DO YOUR FIGURING HERE.

GO ON TO THE NEXT PAGE

3. How many distinct prime factors does the number 36 have?

   A. 2

   B. 3

   C. 4

   D. 5

   E. 6

DO YOUR FIGURING HERE.

4. In the figure below, what is the value of x ?

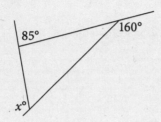

   F. 105°

   G. 115°

   H. 135°

   J. 245°

   K. 255°

5. What is the average of $\frac{1}{20}$ and $\frac{1}{30}$?

   A. $\frac{1}{25}$

   B. $\frac{1}{24}$

   C. $\frac{2}{25}$

   D. $\frac{1}{12}$

   E. $\frac{1}{6}$

GO ON TO THE NEXT PAGE ⟶

6. The toll for driving a segment of a certain freeway is $1.50 plus 25 cents for each mile traveled. Joy paid a $25.00 toll for driving a segment of the freeway. How many miles did she travel?

    F.   10

    G.   75

    H.   94

    J.   96

    K.   100

7. For all x, $3x^2 \times 5x^3 = ?$

    A. $8x^5$

    B. $8x^6$

    C. $15x^5$

    D. $15x^6$

    E. $15x^8$

8. How many units apart are the points $P(-1, -2)$ and $Q(2, 2)$ in the standard (x, y) coordinate plane?

    F.   2

    G.   3

    H.   4

    J.   5

    K.   6

9. In a group of 25 students, 16 are female. What percentage of the group is female?

    A.   16%

    B.   40%

    C.   60%

    D.   64%

    E.   75%

DO YOUR FIGURING HERE.

GO ON TO THE NEXT PAGE

10. For how many integer values of x will $\dfrac{7}{x}$ be greater than $\dfrac{1}{4}$ and less than $\dfrac{1}{3}$?

    F.   6

    G.   7

    H.   12

    J.   28

    K.   Infinitely many

DO YOUR FIGURING HERE.

11. Which of the following is a polynomial factor of $6x^2 - 13x + 6$?

    A. $2x + 3$

    B. $3x - 2$

    C. $3x + 2$

    D. $6x - 2$

    E. $6x + 2$

12. What is the value of a if $\dfrac{1}{a} + \dfrac{2}{a} + \dfrac{3}{a} + \dfrac{4}{a} = 5$?

    F. $\dfrac{1}{2}$

    G.   2

    H.   4

    J. $12\dfrac{1}{2}$

    K.   50

GO ON TO THE NEXT PAGE

13. In the figure below, $\overline{AD}$, $\overline{BE}$, and $\overline{CF}$ all
intersect at point G. If the measure of $\angle AGB$
is 40° and the measure of $\angle CGE$ is 105°, what
is the measure of $\angle AGF$?

DO YOUR FIGURING HERE.

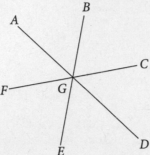

A. 35°

B. 45°

C. 55°

D. 65°

E. 75°

14. Which of the following is the solution
statement for the inequality $-3 < 4x - 5$?

F. $x > -2$

G. $x > \dfrac{1}{2}$

H. $x < -2$

J. $x < \dfrac{1}{2}$

K. $x < 2$

GO ON TO THE NEXT PAGE

15. In the figure below, *BD* bisects ∠*ABC*.
The measure of ∠*ABC* is 100° and the
measure of ∠*BAD* is 60°. What is the
measure of ∠*BDC* ?

DO YOUR FIGURING HERE.

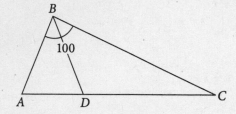

A. 80°

B. 90°

C. 100°

D. 110°

E. 120°

16. If $x + 2y - 3 = xy$, where x and y are positive,
then which of the following equations
expresses y in terms of x?

F. $y = \dfrac{3 - x}{2 - x}$

G. $y = \dfrac{3 - x}{x - 2}$

H. $y = \dfrac{x - 3}{2 - x}$

J. $y = \dfrac{x - 2}{x - 3}$

K. $y = \dfrac{6 - x}{x - 2}$

GO ON TO THE NEXT PAGE

17. In a group of 50 students, 28 speak English and 37 speak Spanish. If everyone in the group speaks at least one of the two languages, how many speak both English and Spanish?

    A. 11
    B. 12
    C. 13
    D. 14
    E. 15

18. A car travels 288 miles in 6 hours. At that rate, how many miles will it travel in 8 hours?

    F. 216
    G. 360
    H. 368
    J. 376
    K. 384

19. When $\frac{4}{11}$ is written as a decimal, what is the 100th digit after the decimal point?

    A. 3
    B. 4
    C. 5
    D. 6
    E. 7

20. What is the solution for x in the system of equations below?

    $$3x + 4y = 31$$
    $$3x - 4y = -1$$

    F. 4
    G. 5
    H. 6
    J. 9
    K. 10

DO YOUR FIGURING HERE.

GO ON TO THE NEXT PAGE

21. In the standard (x, y) coordinate plane, points P and Q have coordinates $(2, 3)$ and $(12, -15)$, respectively. What are the coordinates of the midpoint of $\overline{PQ}$?

    A. $(6, -12)$
    B. $(6, -9)$
    C. $(6, -6)$
    D. $(7, -9)$
    E. $(7, -6)$

22. In the figure below, $\angle B$ is a right angle, and the measure of $\angle C$ is θ. What is the value of $\cos \theta$?

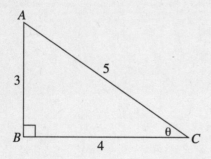

    F. $\dfrac{3}{4}$

    G. $\dfrac{3}{5}$

    H. $\dfrac{4}{5}$

    J. $\dfrac{5}{4}$

    K. $\dfrac{4}{3}$

DO YOUR FIGURING HERE.

GO ON TO THE NEXT PAGE

23. In the figure below, the circle centered at P is tangent to the circle centered at Q. Point Q is on the circumference of circle P. If the circumference of circle P is 6 inches, what is the circumference, in inches, of circle Q ?

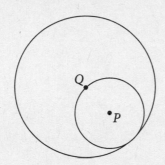

    A. 12

    B. 24

    C. 36

    D. 12π

    E. 36π

24. If $f(x) = x^3 - x^2 - x$, what is the value of $f(-3)$?

    F. −39

    G. −33

    H. −21

    J. −15

    K.   0

25. If the lengths, in inches, of all three sides of a triangle are integers, and one side is 7 inches long, what is the least possible perimeter of the triangle, in inches?

    A.   9

    B. 10

    C. 15

    D. 21

    E. 24

DO YOUR FIGURING HERE.

GO ON TO THE NEXT PAGE

26. What is the complete factorization of
    $2x + 3x^2 + x^3$?

    F. $x(x^2 + 2)$

    G. $x(x - 2)(x + 3)$

    H. $x(x - 1)(x + 2)$

    J. $x(x + 1)(x + 2)$

    K. $x(x + 2)(x + 3)$

27. If $xyz \neq 0$, which of the following is
    equivalent to $\dfrac{x^2 y^3 z^4}{(xyz^2)^2}$?

    A. $\dfrac{1}{y}$

    B. $\dfrac{1}{z}$

    C. y

    D. $\dfrac{x}{yz}$

    E. xyz

28. As a decimal, what is the sum of $\dfrac{2}{3}$ and $\dfrac{1}{12}$?

    F. 0.2

    G. 0.5

    H. 0.75

    J. 0.833

    K. 0.875

29. The formula for converting a Fahrenheit
    temperature reading to Celsius is
    $C = \dfrac{5}{9}(F - 32)$, where C is the reading
    in degrees Celsius and F is the reading in
    degrees Fahrenheit. Which of the following
    is the Fahrenheit equivalent to a reading
    of 95° Celsius?

    A. 35°F

    B. 53°F

    C. 63°F

    D. 203°F

    E. 207°F

DO YOUR FIGURING HERE.

GO ON TO THE NEXT PAGE

30. A jar contains 4 green marbles, 5 red marbles, and 11 white marbles. If 1 marble is chosen at random, what is the probability that it will be green?

    F. $\dfrac{1}{3}$

    G. $\dfrac{1}{4}$

    H. $\dfrac{1}{5}$

    J. $\dfrac{1}{16}$

    K. $\dfrac{5}{15}$

31. What is the average of the expressions $2x + 5$, $5x - 6$, and $-4x + 2$?

    A. $x + \dfrac{1}{3}$

    B. $x + 1$

    C. $3x + \dfrac{1}{3}$

    D. $3x + 3$

    E. $3x + 3\dfrac{1}{3}$

32. The line that passes through the points $(1, 1)$ and $(2, 16)$ in the standard (x, y) coordinate plane is parallel to the line that passes through the points $(-10, -5)$ and $(a, 25)$. What is the value of a?

    F. -8

    G. 3

    H. 5

    J. 15

    K. 20

DO YOUR FIGURING HERE.

GO ON TO THE NEXT PAGE

33. In the figure below, $\overline{QS}$ and $\overline{PT}$ are parallel, and the lengths of $\overline{QR}$ and $\overline{PQ}$, in units, are as marked. If the perimeter of $\triangle QRS$ is 11 units, how many units long is the perimeter of $\triangle PRT$?

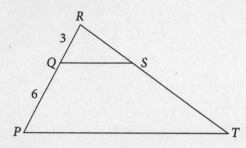

    A. 22
    B. 33
    C. 66
    D. 88
    E. 99

DO YOUR FIGURING HERE.

34. The figure shown below belongs in which of the following classifications?

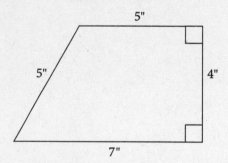

    I.   Polygon
    II. Quadrilateral
    III. Rectangle
    IV. Trapezoid

    F. I only
    G. II only
    H. IV only
    J. I, II, and III only
    K. I, II, and IV only

GO ON TO THE NEXT PAGE

35. If one solution to the equation
    $2x^2 + (a - 4)x - 2a = 0$ is $x = -3$,
    what is the value of a?

    A. 0
    B. 2
    C. 4
    D. 6
    E. 12

DO YOUR FIGURING HERE.

36. A menu offers 4 choices for the first course,
    5 choices for the second course, and 3 choices
    for dessert. How many different meals,
    consisting of a first course, a second course,
    and a dessert, can one choose from this
    menu?

    F. 12
    G. 24
    H. 30
    J. 36
    K. 60

37. If an integer is divisible by 6 and by 9, then
    the integer must be divisible by which of the
    following?

    I. 12
    II. 18
    III. 36

    A. I only
    B. II only
    C. I and II only
    D. I, II, and III
    E. None

GO ON TO THE NEXT PAGE

38. For all $x \neq 0$, $\dfrac{x^2 + x^2 + x^2}{x^2} = ?$

    F. 3

    G. $3x$

    H. x^2

    J. x^3

    K. x^4

DO YOUR FIGURING HERE.

39. Joan has q quarters, d dimes, n nickels, and no other coins in her pocket. Which of the following represents the total number of coins in Joan's pocket?

    A. $q + d + n$

    B. $5q + 2d + n$

    C. $.25q + .10d + .05n$

    D. $(25 + 10 + 5)(q + d + n)$

    E. $25q + 10d + 5n$

40. Which graph below represents the solutions for x of the inequality $5x - 2(1 - x) \geq 4(x + 1)$?

    F.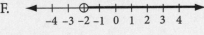

    G.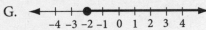

    H.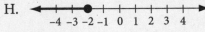

    J.

    K.

41. In the standard (x, y) coordinate plane, line m is perpendicular to the line containing the points $(5, 6)$ and $(6, 10)$. What is the slope of line m?

    A. -4

    B. $-\dfrac{1}{4}$

    C. $\dfrac{1}{4}$

    D. 4

    E. 8

DO YOUR FIGURING HERE.

42. In the right triangle below, $\sin \theta = $?

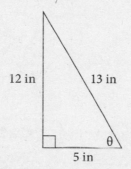

    F. $\dfrac{5}{13}$

    G. $\dfrac{5}{12}$

    H. $\dfrac{12}{13}$

    J. $\dfrac{13}{12}$

    K. $\dfrac{13}{5}$

43. If $9^{2x-1} = 3^{3x+3}$, then $x = $?

    A. -4

    B. $-\dfrac{7}{4}$

    C. $-\dfrac{10}{7}$

    D. 2

    E. 5

GO ON TO THE NEXT PAGE

44. From 1970 through 1980, the population of
City Q increased by 20%. From 1980 through
1990, the population increased by 30%. What
was the combined percent increase for the
period 1970–1990?

    F. 25%

    G. 26%

    H. 36%

    J. 50%

    K. 56%

DO YOUR FIGURING HERE.

45. Martin's average score after four tests is 89.
What score on the fifth test would bring
Martin's average up to exactly 90?

    A. 90

    B. 91

    C. 92

    D. 93

    E. 94

46. Which of the following is an equation for the
circle in the standard (x, y) coordinate plane
that has its center at $(-1, -1)$ and passes
through the point $(7, 5)$?

    F. $(x - 1)^2 + (y - 1)^2 = 10$

    G. $(x + 1)^2 + (y + 1)^2 = 10$

    H. $(x - 1)^2 + (y - 1)^2 = 12$

    J. $(x - 1)^2 + (y - 1)^2 = 100$

    K. $(x + 1)^2 + (y + 1)^2 = 100$

GO ON TO THE NEXT PAGE

47. Which of the following is an equation for the graph in the standard (x, y) coordinate plane below?

DO YOUR FIGURING HERE.

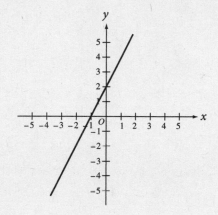

A. $y = -2x + 1$

B. $y = x + 1$

C. $y = x + 2$

D. $y = 2x + 1$

E. $y = 2x + 2$

48. What is $\frac{1}{4}$% of 16?

F. 0.004

G. 0.04

H. 0.4

J. 4

K. 64

49. For all s, $(s + 4)(s - 4) + (2s + 2)(s - 2) = ?$

    A. $s^2 - 2s - 20$

    B. $3s^2 - 12$

    C. $3s^2 - 2s - 20$

    D. $3s^2 + 2s - 20$

    E. $5s^2 - 2s - 20$

50. Which of the following is an equation of the parabola graphed in the (x, y) coordinate plane below?

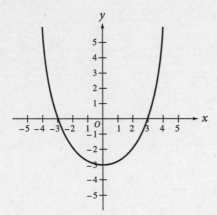

    F. $y = \dfrac{x^2}{3} - 3$

    G. $y = \dfrac{x^2 - 3}{3}$

    H. $y = \dfrac{x^2}{3} + 3$

    J. $y = \dfrac{x^2 + 3}{3}$

    K. $y = 3x^2 - 3$

DO YOUR FIGURING HERE.

GO ON TO THE NEXT PAGE

51. In the figure below, $\sin a = \dfrac{4}{5}$. What is $\cos b$?

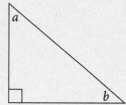

A. $\dfrac{3}{4}$

B. $\dfrac{3}{5}$

C. $\dfrac{4}{5}$

D. $\dfrac{5}{4}$

E. $\dfrac{4}{3}$

52. For all $x \neq 0$, $\dfrac{x^2 + x^2 + x^2}{x} = ?$

F. $3x$

G. x^3

H. x^5

J. x^7

K. $2x^2 + x$

DO YOUR FIGURING HERE.

53. One can determine a student's score S on a certain test by dividing the number of wrong answers (w) by 4 and subtracting the result from the number of right answers (r). This relation is expressed by which of the following formulas?

    A. $S = \dfrac{r - w}{4}$

    B. $S = r - \dfrac{w}{4}$

    C. $S = \dfrac{r}{4} - w$

    D. $S = 4r - w$

    E. $S = r - 4w$

54. What is the volume, in cubic inches, of the cylinder shown in the figure below?

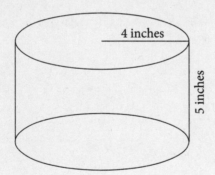

4 inches

5 inches

    F. 20π
    G. 40π
    H. 60π
    J. 80π
    K. 100π

DO YOUR FIGURING HERE.

GO ON TO THE NEXT PAGE

55. In the figure below, $\overline{AB}$ is perpendicular to $\overline{BC}$. The lengths of $\overline{AB}$ and $\overline{BC}$, in inches, are given in terms of x. Which of the following represents the area of $\triangle ABC$, in square inches, for all $x > 1$?

DO YOUR FIGURING HERE.

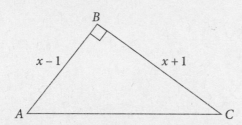

A. x

B. $2x$

C. x^2

D. $x^2 - 1$

E. $\dfrac{x^2 - 1}{2}$

56. In 1990, the population of Town A was 9,400 and the population of Town B was 7,600. Since then, each year, the population of Town A has decreased by 100, and the population of Town B has increased by 100. Assuming that in each case, the rate continues, in what year will the two populations be equal?

F. 1998

G. 1999

H. 2000

J. 2008

K. 2009

GO ON TO THE NEXT PAGE

57. In a certain club, the average age of the male
    members is 35 and the average age of the
    female members is 25. If 20% of the members
    are male, what is the average age of all the
    club members?

    A. 26
    B. 27
    C. 28
    D. 29
    E. 30

58. To determine the height h of a tree, Roger
    stands b feet from the base of the tree and
    measures the angle of elevation to be θ, as
    shown in the figure below. Which of the
    following relates h and b ?

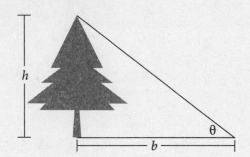

    F. $\sin \theta = \dfrac{h}{b}$

    G. $\sin \theta = \dfrac{b}{h}$

    H. $\sin \theta = \dfrac{b}{\sqrt{b^2 + h^2}}$

    J. $\sin \theta = \dfrac{h}{\sqrt{b^2 + h^2}}$

    K. $\sin \theta = \dfrac{\sqrt{b^2 + h^2}}{b}$

GO ON TO THE NEXT PAGE

59. The formula for the lateral surface area S of a right circular cone is $S = \pi r \sqrt{r^2 + h^2}$, where r is the radius of the base and h is the altitude. What is the lateral surface area, in square feet, of a right circular cone with base radius 3 feet and altitude 4 feet?

A. $3\pi\sqrt{5}$

B. $3\pi\sqrt{7}$

C. 15π

D. 21π

E. $\dfrac{75\pi}{2}$

60. In the figure below, line t crosses parallel lines m and n. Which of the following statements must be true?

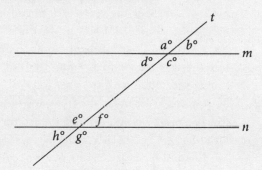

F. $a = b$

G. $a = d$

H. $b = e$

J. $c = g$

K. $d = g$

DO YOUR FIGURING HERE.

READING TEST

35 Minutes—40 Questions

Directions: This test contains four passages, each followed by several questions. After reading each passage, select the best answer to each question and fill in the corresponding oval on your Answer Grid. You may refer to the passages while answering the questions.

Passage I

PROSE FICTION

This passage is adapted from *Bleak House*, by Charles Dickens, which was first published in 1853. In this excerpt, Esther recounts some of her childhood experiences.

I can remember, when I was a very little girl indeed, I used to say to my doll when we were alone together, "Now, Dolly, I am not
Line clever, you know very well, and you must be
(5) patient with me, like a dear!"

…My dear old doll! I was such a shy little thing that I seldom dared to open my lips, and never dared to open my heart, to anybody else. It almost makes me cry
(10) to think what a relief it used to be to me when I came home from school of a day to run upstairs to my room and say, "Oh, you dear faithful Dolly, I knew you would be expecting me!" and then to sit down on
(15) the floor, leaning on the elbow of her great chair, and tell her all I had noticed since we parted…

I was brought up, from my earliest remembrance—like some of the prin-
(20) cesses in the fairy stories, only I was not charming—by my godmother. At least, I only knew her as such. She was a good, good woman! She went to church three times every Sunday, and to morning prayers on
(25) Wednesdays and Fridays, and to lectures whenever there were lectures, and never missed. She was handsome; and if she had

ever smiled, would have been (I used to think) like an angel—but she never smiled.
(30) She was always grave and strict. She was so very good herself, I thought, that the badness of other people made her frown all her life… It made me very sorry to consider how good she was and how unworthy of
(35) her I was, and I used ardently to hope that I might have a better heart; and I talked it over very often with the dear old doll, but I never loved my godmother as I ought to have loved her and as I felt I must have
(40) loved her if I had been a better girl…

I had never heard my mama spoken of… I had never been shown my mama's grave. I had never been told where it was…

Although there were seven girls at
(45) the neighboring school where I was a day boarder, and although they called me little Esther Summerson, I knew none of them at home. All of them were older than I, to be sure (I was the youngest there by a good
(50) deal), but there seemed to be some other separation between us besides that, and besides their being far more clever than I was and knowing much more than I did. One of them in the first week of my going to
(55) the school (I remember it very well) invited me home to a little party, to my great joy. But my godmother wrote a stiff letter declining for me, and I never went. I never went out at all.

GO ON TO THE NEXT PAGE ⇒

(60)   It was my birthday. There were holidays at school on other birthdays—none on mine. There were rejoicings at home on other birthdays, as I knew from what I heard the girls relate to one another—there were none (65) on mine. My birthday was the most melancholy day at home in the whole year...

Dinner was over, and my godmother and I were sitting at the table before the fire. The clock ticked, the fire clicked; not (70) another sound had been heard in the room or in the house for I don't know how long. I happened to look timidly up from my stitching, across the table at my godmother, and I saw in her face, looking gloomily at me, (75) "It would have been far better, little Esther, that you had had no birthday, that you had never been born!"

I broke out crying and sobbing, and I said, "Oh, dear godmother, tell me, pray do (80) tell me, did Mama die on my birthday?"

"No," she returned. "Ask me no more, child!"

...I put up my trembling little hand to clasp hers or to beg her pardon with what (85) earnestness I might, but withdrew it as she looked at me, and laid it on my fluttering heart. She...said slowly in a cold, low voice—I see her knitted brow and pointed finger—"The time will come—and soon (90) enough—when you will understand this better and will feel it too... I have forgiven her"—but her face did not relent—"the wrong she did to me, and I say no more of it, though it was greater than you will ever (95) know... Forget your mother and leave all other people to forget her... Now, go!"

...I went up to my room, and crept to bed, and laid my doll's cheek against mine wet with tears, and holding that solitary (100) friend upon my bosom, cried myself to sleep. Imperfect as my understanding of my sorrow was, I knew that I had brought no joy at any time to anybody's heart and that I was to no one upon earth what Dolly was (105) to me.

Dear, dear, to think how much time we passed alone together afterwards, and how often I repeated to the doll the story of my birthday and confided to her that I would (110) try as hard as ever I could to repair the fault I had been born with... I hope it is not self-indulgent to shed these tears as I think of it.

1. According to the passage, Esther only remembers:

   A. being brought up by her parents for a short time.

   B. being brought up by her mother for a short time.

   C. being brought up by her godmother for a short time.

   D. being brought up by her godmother.

2. It is most likely that Esther thought of her doll as:

   F. only an amusing plaything.

   G. her only friend and confidante.

   H. a princess in a fairy tale.

   J. a beautiful toy that was too fragile to touch.

3. As it is used in the passage, *stiff* (line 57) most closely means:

   A. difficult to bend.

   B. rigidly formal.

   C. unchanging.

   D. not moving easily or freely.

GO ON TO THE NEXT PAGE ⟹

4. Which of the following most likely contributed to Esther's belief that she had been born with a fault (lines 110–111)?

   F. She is not very clever.

   G. Her birthday was never celebrated.

   H. She did not have any friends at school.

   J. Her mother died in childbirth.

5. Esther's godmother's words, actions, and facial expression as described in paragraph 10 (lines 83–96) suggest that she:

   A. had a change of heart about celebrating Esther's birthday.

   B. did not know what had happened to Esther's mother.

   C. continued to resent Esther's mother.

   D. had truly forgiven Esther's mother.

6. According to the passage, Esther's childhood could be most accurately characterized as:

   F. an adventure.

   G. a time of loneliness and confusion.

   H. a period of dedication to education and self-improvement.

   J. a period of attempting to become more like her godmother.

7. From Esther's statement, "I was to no one upon earth what Dolly was to me" (lines 104–105), it is reasonable to infer that Esther:

   A. believed that her godmother loved her.

   B. believed that she would be able to become friends with the girls at school.

   C. believed that no one loved her.

   D. believed that her mother was alive.

8. In the passage, it is implied that all of the following contributed to separating Esther from the other girls at her school EXCEPT:

   F. the other girls were older than Esther.

   G. Esther's godmother did not allow Esther to socialize with the other girls outside of school.

   H. Esther believed that the other girls were much smarter.

   J. Esther was self-indulgent.

9. According to the passage, one reason that Esther thinks of her godmother as a "good, good woman" (lines 22–23) is:

   A. that when she smiles, she looks like an angel.

   B. that she forgave Esther's mother.

   C. that she frequently attends church services.

   D. that she gave Esther a doll.

10. In the passage, Esther describes herself as a child as:

   F. self-indulgent and not very clever.

   G. shy and not very clever.

   H. shy and faithful.

   J. self-indulgent and faithful.

GO ON TO THE NEXT PAGE ⟶

Passage II

SOCIAL SCIENCE

This passage is excerpted from "The Return of the Big Cats," by Mac Margolis, *Newsweek*, December 11, 2000, © 2000 by Newsweek, Inc. All rights reserved. Reprinted by permission.

Marcos Nunes is not likely to forget his first holiday in Brazil's Pantanal wilderness. One afternoon last October he was coaxing his
Line
(5) horse through a lonely tuft of woods when he suddenly found himself staring down a fully grown spotted jaguar. He held his breath while the painted cat and her cub paraded silkily through the grove, not 10 meters away... "Thank you," he wrote later
(10) in a hotel visitor's log, "for the wonderful fright!"

As Nunes and other ecotourists are discovering, these big, beautiful animals, once at the brink of extinction, are now
(15) staging a comeback. Exactly how dramatic a comeback is difficult to say because jaguars—*Panthera onca*, the largest feline in the New World—are solitary, secretive, nocturnal predators. Each cat needs to
(20) prowl at least 35 square kilometers by itself. Brazil's Pantanal, vast wetlands that spill over a 140,000-square-kilometer swath of South America the size of Germany, gives them plenty of room to roam. Nevertheless,
(25) scientists who have been tagging jaguars with radio transmitters for two decades have in recent years been reporting a big increase in sightings. Hotels, campgrounds, and bed-and-breakfasts have sprung up to
(30) accommodate the half-million tourists a year (twice the number of five years ago) bent on sampling the Pantanal's wildlife, of which the great cats must be the most magnificent example.

(35) Most sightings come from local cattle herders—but their jaguar stories have a very different ring. One day last September, ranch hand Abel Monteiro was tending cattle near the Rio Vermelho, in the southern Pantanal,
(40) when, he says, a snarling jaguar leaped from the scrub and killed his two bloodhounds. Monteiro barely had time to grab his .38 revolver and kill the angry cat. Leonelson Ramos da Silva says last May he and a group
(45) of field hands had to throw flaming sticks all night to keep a prowling jaguar from invading their forest camp... The Brazilian interior, famous for its generous spirit and cowboy *bonhomie*, is now the scene of a
(50) political cat fight between the scientists, environmentalists, and ecotourists who want to protect the jaguars and the embattled ranchers who want to protect themselves and their livelihood.

(55) The ranchers, to be sure, have enough headaches coping with the harsh, sodden landscape without jaguars attacking their herds and threatening their livelihoods. Hard data on cattle losses due to jaguars in
(60) the Pantanal are nonexistent, but there are stories. In 1995, Joo Julio Dittmar bought a 6,200-hectare strip of ideal breeding ground, only to lose 152 of his 600 calves to jaguars, he claims. Ranchers chafe at laws that forbid
(65) them to kill the jaguars. "This is a question of democracy," says Dittmar. "We ranchers ought to be allowed to control our own environment."

Man and jaguar have been sparring for
(70) territory ever since 18th-century settlers, traders, and herdsmen began to move into this sparsely populated serto, or back lands. By the 1960s, the Pantanal was a vast, soggy canvas, white with gleaming herds of Nelore
(75) cattle. Game hunters were bagging 15,000 jaguars a year in the nearby Amazon Basin (no figures exist on the Pantanal) as the worldwide trade in pelts reached $30 million a year. As the jaguars grew scarce, their
(80) chief food staple, the capybaras—a meter-long rodent, the world's largest—overran

GO ON TO THE NEXT PAGE ⟶

farmers' fields and spread trichomoniasis,
a livestock disease that renders cows sterile.

(85) Then in 1967, Brazil outlawed jaguar
hunting, and a world ban on selling pelts
followed in 1973. Weather patterns also
shifted radically—due most likely to global
warming—and drove annual floods to
near-Biblical proportions. The waters are
(90) only now retreating from some inundated
pasturelands. As the Pantanal herds shrank
from 6 million to about 3.5 million head,
the jaguars advanced. Along the way they
developed a taste for the bovine intruders.

(95) The ranchers' fear of the big cats is
partly cultural. The ancient Inca and Maya
believed that jaguars possessed supernatural
powers. In Brazil, the most treacherous
enemy is said to be *o amigo da onca*, a
(100) friend to the jaguar...

Some people believe there may be a way
for ranchers and jaguars to coexist. Sports
hunters on "green safaris" might shoot
jaguars with immobilizing drugs, allowing
(105) scientists to fit the cats with radio collars.
Fees would help sustain jaguar research and
compensate ranchers for livestock losses.
(Many environmentalists, though, fear
fraudulent claims.) Scientists are setting up
(110) workshops to teach ranchers how to protect
their herds with modern husbandry, pasture
management, and such gadgets as blinking
lights and electric fences.

Like many rural folk, however, the
(115) wetland ranchers tend to bristle at bureau-
crats and foreigners telling them what to do.
When the scholars go home and the greens
log off, the *pantaneiros* will still be there—
left on their own to deal with the jaguars as
(120) they see fit.

11. As it is used in the passage, *canvas*
(line 74) most closely means:

A. a survey of public opinion.

B. a background.

C. a coarse cotton fabric.

D. a painting.

12. According to the passage, one result
of the decline of the jaguar population
during the 1960s was:

F. the increase in the population of the
settlers.

G. an increase in Brazil's ecotourist
business.

H. an increase in the price of a jaguar
pelt.

J. an increase in the population of
their most common source of food,
the capybaras.

13. According to the passage, it is difficult
to determine the extent of the jaguar's
comeback because:

A. the area they inhabit is so large.

B. the stories that the local ranchers
tell about jaguars contradict the
conclusions reached by scientists.

C. jaguars are solitary, nocturnal
animals that can have a territory of
35 square kilometers.

D. scientists have only used radio
transmitters to track the movements
of the jaguar population.

GO ON TO THE NEXT PAGE ⟶

14. The information about ecotourism in the first and second paragraphs of the passage (lines 1–34) suggests that:

    F. the jaguars are seen as a threat to the safety of tourists.

    G. the jaguars are important to the success of Brazil's growing ecotourism industry.

    H. the growth of the ecotourism industry is threatening the habitat of the jaguars.

    J. it is common for ecotourists to spot one or more jaguars.

15. According to the passage, which of the following is NOT a method for protecting cattle herds that scientists are teaching ranchers?

    A. "Green safaris"

    B. Pasture management

    C. The use of blinking lights and electric fences

    D. Modern husbandry

16. It is most likely that the author of the passage included the jaguar stories of three ranchers (lines 35–47, 61–68) in order to:

    F. express more sympathy toward the ranchers than toward the environmentalists and scientists.

    G. illustrate the dangers and economic losses that the jaguars currently pose to ranchers.

    H. show the violent nature of the ranchers.

    J. provide a complete picture of the Pantanal landscape.

17. From information in the passage, it is most reasonable to infer that the cattle herds "shrank from 6 million to about 3.5 million head" (lines 91–92) because:

    A. the jaguars had killed so many cattle.

    B. environmentalists and scientists worked to convert pastureland into refuges for the jaguars.

    C. many cows had become sterile from trichomoniasis, and annual floods submerged much of the pastureland used by ranchers.

    D. the cattle could not tolerate the increase in the average temperature caused by global warming.

18. The main conclusion reached about the future of the relationship between the people and the jaguars in the Pantanal is that:

    F. the increase in ecotourism will ensure the continued growth in the jaguar population.

    G. the ranchers themselves will ultimately determine how they will cope with the jaguars.

    H. the jaguar population will continue to fluctuate with the number of tourists coming into the Pantanal.

    J. the scientists' new ranching methods will make it easy for the ranchers and jaguars to coexist.

GO ON TO THE NEXT PAGE

19. According to the passage, which of the following groups want to protect the jaguar?

    I. Ecotourists

    II. Environmentalists

    III. Scientists

A. I and II only

B. I and III only

C. II and III only

D. I, II, and III

20. According to the passage, there is no accurate data available on:

F. the number of cattle killed by jaguars.

G. the number of ranchers attacked by jaguars.

H. the growth rate of ecotourism in Brazil.

J. the percentage of the Pantanal wetlands inhabited by jaguars.

Passage III

HUMANITIES

This passage is excerpted from *Music Through the Ages* Revised Edition, © 1987 by Marion Bauer and Ethel R. Peyser, edited by Elizabeth E. Rogers, copyright © 1932 by Marion Bauer and Ethel R. Peyser, renewed copyright © 1960 by Ethel R. Peyser. Reprinted by permission of G.P. Putnam's Sons, a division of Penguin Group (USA), Inc.

Greek instruments can be classified into two general categories—string and pipe, or lyre and aulos. Our knowledge of them comes
Line
(5) from representations on monuments, vases, statues, and friezes and from the testimony of Greek authors. The lyre was the national instrument and included a wide variety of types. In its most antique form, the chelys, it is traced back to the age of fable and
(10) allegedly owed its invention to Hermes. Easy to carry, this small lyre became the favorite instrument of the home, amateurs, and women, a popular accompaniment for drinking songs and love songs as well as
(15) more noble kinds of poetry... Professional Homeric singers used a kithara, a larger, more powerful instrument, which probably came from Egypt. The kithara had a flat wooden sound box and an upper horizontal
(20) bar supported by two curving arms. Within this frame were stretched strings of equal length, at first but three or four in number. Fastened to the performer by means of a sling, the kithara was played with both
(25) hands. We are not sure in just what manner the instrument was used to accompany the epics. It may have been employed for a pitch-fixing prelude and for interludes, or it may have paralleled or decorated the vocal
(30) melody in more or less free fashion.

    ...Two types of tuning were used: the dynamic, or pitch method, naming the degrees "according to function"; and the

GO ON TO THE NEXT PAGE ⇒

thetic, or tablature, naming them "according
(35) to position" on the instrument.

As early as the eighth century B.C.,
lyres of five strings appeared. Terpander
(fl. c. 675 B.C.), one of the first innova-
tors, is said to have increased the number
(40) of strings to seven. He is also supposed to
have completed the octave and created the
Mixolydian scale. Aristoxenos claimed that
the poetess Sappho, in the seventh century
B.C., in addition to introducing a mode in
(45) which Dorian and Lydian characteristics
were blended, initiated use of the plectrum
or pick. At the time of Sophocles (495–406
B.C.), the lyre had eleven strings.

Another harplike instrument was the
(50) magadis, whose tone was described as
trumpetlike. Of foreign importation, it had
twenty strings, which, by means of frets,
played octaves. As some of the strings were
tuned in quartertones, it was an instru-
(55) ment associated with the enharmonic mode.
Smaller versions, the pectis and the barbitos,
were also tuned in quartertones. Greek men
and boys had a style of singing in octaves
that was called magadizing, after the octave-
(60) playing instruments.

The kithara was identified with Apollo
and the Apollonian cult, representing the
intellectual and idealistic side of Greek art.
The aulos or reed pipe was the instrument of
(65) Dionysians, who represented the unbridled,
sensual and passionate aspect of Greek
culture.

Although translated as "flute," the
aulos is more like our oboe. Usually found
(70) in double form, the pipes set at an angle,
the aulos was imputed to have a far more
exciting effect than that produced by the
subdued lyre. About 600 B.C., the aulos
was chosen as the official instrument of
(75) the Delphian and Pythian festivals. It was
also used in performances of the Dionysian
dithyramb as well as a supplement of the
chorus in classic Greek tragedy and comedy.

There was a complete family of auloi
(80) covering the same range as human voices.
One authority names three species of
simple pipes and five varieties of double
pipes. (The double pipe was the professional instrument.) An early specimen
(85) was supposed to have been tuned to the
chromatic tetrachord D, C sharp, B flat, A—
a fact that points to Oriental origin. Elegiac
songs called aulodia were composed in
this mode to be accompanied by an aulos.
(90) Although the first wooden pipes had only
three or four finger holes, the number later
increased so that the Dorian, Phrygian and
Lydian modes might be performed on a
single pair. Pictures of auletes show them
(95) with a bandage or phorbeia over their faces;
this might have been necessary to hold the
two pipes in place, to modulate the tone or,
perhaps, to aid in storing air in the cheeks
for the purpose of sustained performance.

21. The passage suggests that the aulos
was considered "the instrument of the
Dionysians" (lines 64–65) because:

A. it expressed the excitement and
passion of that aspect of Greek
culture.

B. it was chosen as the official instrument of the Delphian and Pythian
festivals.

C. it represented the intellectual and
idealistic side of Greek art.

D. it was invented around the time that
the Dionysian cult originated.

GO ON TO THE NEXT PAGE ⇒

22. The statement that the chelys can be "traced back to the age of fable" (line 9) implies that the chelys:

    F. was invented by storytellers.

    G. was used to accompany the epics.

    H. probably existed in legend only.

    J. was a particularly ancient instrument.

23. The main purpose of the passage is to describe the:

    A. use of the lyre in different musical settings.

    B. connection between the ancient Greek arts of music and drama.

    C. references to music in ancient Greek literature.

    D. origin and development of various Greek instruments.

24. According to the passage, the kithara was:

    F. most likely of Greek origin.

    G. played with one hand.

    H. used by professional musicians.

    J. less powerful than a chelys.

25. Which of the following is NOT cited as a change that occurred to the lyre between the eighth and fifth centuries B.C.?

    A. Musicians began to use a plectrum.

    B. Lyres featured increasing numbers of strings.

    C. Musicians began to use different scales and modes.

    D. Lyres were used to accompany dramatic productions.

26. It can be inferred from the passage that the chromatic tetrachord D, C sharp, B flat, A (line 86) was:

    F. not appropriate for elegaic songs.

    G. only used by professional musicians.

    H. impossible on the first wooden pipes.

    J. present in ancient Oriental music.

27. According to the passage, the most ancient form of the lyre was called a:

    A. magadis.

    B. kithara.

    C. chelys.

    D. barbitos.

28. According to the passage, one of Sappho's contributions to ancient Greek music was that she:

    F. completed the octave and created the Mixolydian scale.

    G. introduced a mode blending Dorian and Lydian characteristics.

    H. incorporated poetry into recitals of lyre music.

    J. helped increase the number of strings on the lyre.

GO ON TO THE NEXT PAGE

29. According to the passage, which of the following is/are characteristic of the aulos?

      I. It was used in performances of the Dionysian dithyramb.

      II. It sounded more exciting than the lyre.

      III. It resembles the modern-day flute more than it does the oboe.

A. I only

B. I and II only

C. II and III only

D. I, II, and III

30. Which of the following does the passage suggest is true about our knowledge of ancient Greek instruments?

F. Our knowledge is dependent on secondary sources.

G. Little is known about how instruments were tuned.

H. Very few pictures of ancient Greek instruments have survived.

J. More is known about string instruments than about pipe instruments.

Passage IV

NATURAL SCIENCE

This passage is an excerpt from "The Solar Inconstant," by John Horgan, *Scientific American*, September 1988, © 1988 by *Scientific American*. Reprinted by permission of *Scientific American*.

    Astronomers noted more than 150 years ago that sunspots wax and wane in number in an 11-year cycle. Ever since, people have
Line speculated that the solar cycle might exert
(5) some influence on the Earth's weather. In this century, for example, scientists have linked the solar cycle to droughts in the American Midwest. Until recently, however, none of these correlations has held up under
(10) close scrutiny.

    One problem is that sunspots themselves are so poorly understood. Observations have revealed that the swirly smudges represent areas of intense magnetic activity where
(15) the sun's radiative energy has been blocked and that they are considerably cooler than bright regions of the sun. Scientists have not been able, however, to determine just how sunspots are created or what effect they have
(20) on the solar constant (a misnomer that refers to the sun's total radiance at any instant).

    The latter question, at least, now seems to have been resolved by data from the *Solar Maximum Mission* satellite, which has
(25) monitored the solar constant since 1980, the peak of the last solar cycle. As the number of sunspots decreased through 1986, the satellite recorded a gradual dimming of the sun. Over the past year, as sunspots have
(30) proliferated, the sun has brightened. The data suggest that the sun is 0.1 percent more luminous at the peak of the solar cycle, when the number of sunspots is greatest, than at its nadir, according to Richard C.
(35) Willson of the Jet Propulsion Laboratory and Hugh S. Hudson of the University of California at San Diego.

GO ON TO THE NEXT PAGE ⟶

The data show that sunspots do not themselves make the sun shine brighter.
(40) Quite the contrary. When a sunspot appears, it initially causes the sun to dim slightly, but then after a period of weeks or months islands of brilliance called faculas usually emerge near the sunspot and more than
(45) compensate for its dimming effect. Willson says faculas may represent regions where energy that initially was blocked beneath a sunspot has finally breached the surface.

Does the subtle fluctuation in the
(50) solar constant manifest itself in the Earth's weather? Some recent reports offer statistical evidence that it does, albeit rather indirectly. The link seems to be mediated by a phenomenon known as the quasi-biennial oscillation
(55) (QBO), a 180-degree shift in the direction of stratospheric winds above the Tropics that occurs about every two years.

Karin Labitzke of the Free University of Berlin and Harry van Loon of the National
(60) Center for Atmospheric Research in Boulder, Colorado, were the first to uncover the QBO link. They gathered temperature and air-pressure readings from various latitudes and altitudes over the past three solar cycles.
(65) They found no correlation between the solar cycle and their data until they sorted the data into two categories: those gathered during the QBO's west phase (when the stratospheric winds blow west) and those
(70) gathered during its east phase. A remarkable correlation appeared: temperatures and pressures coincident with the QBO's west phase rose and fell in accordance with the solar cycle.

(75) Building on this finding, Brian A. Tinsley of the National Science Foundation discovered a statistical correlation between the solar cycle and the position of storms in the North Atlantic. The latitude of storms
(80) during the west phase of the QBO, Tinsley found, varied with the solar cycle: storms occurring toward the peak of a solar cycle

traveled at latitudes about six degrees nearer the Equator than storms during the cycle's
(85) nadir.

Labitzke, van Loon, and Tinsley acknowledge that their findings are still rather mysterious. Why does the solar cycle seem to exert more of an influence
(90) during the west phase of the QBO than it does during the east phase? How does the 0.1 percent variance in solar radiation trigger the much larger changes—up to six degrees Celsius in polar regions—observed
(95) by Labitzke and van Loon? Van Loon says simply, "We can't explain it."

John A. Eddy of the National Center for Atmospheric Research, nonetheless, thinks these QBO findings as well as the
(100) *Solar Maximum Mission* data "look like breakthroughs" in the search for a link between the solar cycle and weather. With further research, for example, into how the oceans damp the effects of solar flux, these
(105) findings may lead to models that have some predictive value. The next few years may be particularly rich in solar flux.

31. According to the passage, the main source of information about the effect of sunspots on the solar constant is provided by:

A. studies of droughts in the Midwest.

B. data from the *Solar Maximum Mission* satellite.

C. temperature and air pressure readings taken in Colorado.

D. discussions between various eminent astronomers.

GO ON TO THE NEXT PAGE ⟶

32. As it is used in the passage, the term *solar constant* refers to:

    F. magnetic activity.

    G. the sun's total radiance.

    H. the sun's surface temperature.

    J. wind direction.

33. The main purpose of this passage is to:

    A. explain why scientists have failed to find any direct correlation between sunspots and the Earth's weather.

    B. describe a possible correlation between the solar cycle and the Earth's weather.

    C. describe the solar cycle and its relation to the solar constant.

    D. prove conclusively that sunspots dramatically influence the Earth's weather.

34. As it is used in line 30, the word *proliferated* means:

    F. grown in size.

    G. brightened.

    H. decreased in number.

    J. increased in number.

35. Which of the following explains why the sun appears brighter during periods of sunspot activity?

    A. Energy that has been blocked is finally released.

    B. The sun shines brighter when sunspots first appear.

    C. Magnetic activity increases the sun's temperature.

    D. Air pressure in the Earth's atmosphere falls.

36. The shift in the direction of stratospheric winds that occurs every two years is known as:

    F. a facula.

    G. the solar flux.

    H. North Atlantic storms.

    J. the quasi-biennial oscillation.

37. Which of the following best summarizes the main point of the last paragraph?

    A. Scientists will soon be in a position to accurately predict the Earth's weather.

    B. Many findings of the *Solar Maximum Mission* cannot yet be explained.

    C. The relationship between the solar cycle and the Earth's weather may become clear with further research.

    D. Scientists disagree as to whether studying sunspots will ever have any practical value.

38. According to the passage, changes in the solar cycle may influence the Earth's weather in which of the following ways?

    I. Changing the direction of stratospheric winds

    II. Altering temperature and pressure levels

    III. Influencing the latitude of storms

    F. I only

    G. I and II only

    H. II and III only

    J. I, II, and III

GO ON TO THE NEXT PAGE

39. From the information in the first paragraph, it may be inferred that scientists now consider a correlation between the solar cycle and droughts in the American Midwest to be:

    A. probable.
    B. unlikely.
    C. confusing.
    D. useful.

40. According to the passage, which of the following statements best describes the current understanding of the relationship between sunspot activity and solar luminosity?

    F. At the peak of sunspot activity, the solar constant decreases in magnitude.
    G. At the peak of sunspot activity, the solar constant increases in magnitude.
    H. At the low point of sunspot activity, the sun is 0.1 percent brighter than it is at the peak of such activity.
    J. Scientists have yet to demonstrate a relationship between the two phenomena.

SCIENCE TEST

35 Minutes—40 Questions

Directions: This test contains seven passages, each followed by several questions. After reading each passage, select the best answer to each question and fill in the corresponding oval on your Answer Grid. You may refer to the passages while answering the questions. You may NOT use a calculator on this test.

Passage I

Acid-base indicators are used to determine changes in pH. The pH is a quantitative measure of the hydrogen ion concentration of a solution. For any solution, the pH ranges from 0 to 14. An acid-base indicator is a weak acid or base that is sensitive to the hydrogen ion concentration and changes color at a known pH. At any other pH, the acid-base indicator is clear.

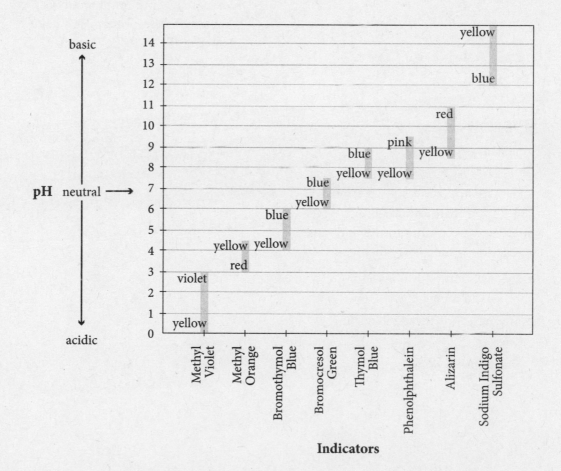

1. Which indicators undergo a color change in the region from pH 8 to pH 12?

   A. Bromocresol green, bromothymol blue, and thymol blue

   B. Thymol blue, phenolphthalein, and alizarin

   C. Phenolphthalein, alizarin, and sodium indigo sulfonate

   D. Phenolphthalein and bromothymol blue

2. Which of the following indicators undergoes a red-to-yellow or yellow-to-red color change?

      I. Alizarin

     II. Thymol blue

    III. Methyl orange

   F. I only

   G. II only

   H. I and III only

   J. I, II, and III

3. A chemist is running an experiment in a solution that becomes basic upon completion. According to the diagram, the reaction is complete when:

   A. the addition of bromocresol green results in a blue color.

   B. any indicator turns violet.

   C. a white solid appears.

   D. the addition of bromothymol blue results in a blue color.

4. Which of the following hypotheses is consistent with the information in the passage and the diagram?

   F. Color changes for any given acid-base indicator occur in a solution with a pH less than 7.

   G. Color changes for any given acid-base indicator occur in a solution with a pH greater than 7.

   H. Color changes for acid-base indicators always occur within the same pH range.

   J. Color changes for acid-base indicators vary within the pH range.

5. Compared to bromothymol blue, phenolphthalein undergoes a color change at:

   A. a higher pH.

   B. a lower pH.

   C. the same pH.

   D. Cannot be determined from the data provided.

GO ON TO THE NEXT PAGE

Passage II

The Brazilian tree frog (*Hyla faber*) exchanges gases through both its skin and lungs. The exchange rate depends on the temperature of the frog's environment. A series of experiments was performed to investigate this dependence.

EXPERIMENT 1

Fifty frogs were placed in a controlled atmosphere that, with the exception of temperature, was designed to simulate their native habitat. The temperature was varied from 5°C to 25°C, and equilibrium was attained before each successive temperature change. The amount of oxygen absorbed by the frogs' lungs and skin per hour was measured, and the results for all the frogs were averaged. The results are shown in Table 1.

Table 1

Temperature (°C)	Moles O_2 absorbed/hr	
	Skin	Lungs
5	15.4	8.3
10	22.7	35.1
15	43.6	64.9
20	42.1	73.5
25	40.4	78.7

EXPERIMENT 2

The same frogs were placed under the same conditions as in Experiment 1. For this experiment, the amount of carbon dioxide eliminated through the skin and lungs was measured. The results are averaged and given in Table 2.

Table 2

Temperature (°C)	Moles O_2 absorbed/hr	
	Skin	Lungs
5	18.9	2.1
10	43.8	12.7
15	79.2	21.3
20	91.6	21.9
25	96.5	21.4

6. The results of Experiment 1 suggest that the total amount of O_2 absorbed per hour is:

   F. affected by the temperature.

   G. independent of the temperature.

   H. an indication of how healthy a Brazilian tree frog is.

   J. always less than the total amount of CO_2 eliminated per hour.

7. According to Experiment 2, the total amount of CO_2 eliminated per hour at 17°C is closest to:

   A. 21 mol/hr.

   B. 85 mol/hr.

   C. 106 mol/hr.

   D. 115 mol/hr.

GO ON TO THE NEXT PAGE

8. Ectotherms are animals whose bodily functions are affected by the temperature of their environment. Which of the following results supports the conclusion that *Hyla fabers* is an ectotherm?

   F. The oxygen absorbed at 25°C

   G. The carbon dioxide released by the lungs

   H. The oxygen absorbed over the entire temperature range

   J. The results do not support this conclusion.

9. According to the results of Experiment 2, which of the following plots best represents the amount of carbon dioxide eliminated through the skin and lungs as a function of temperature?

   A.

   B.

   C.

   D.

10. On the basis of the experimental results, one could conclude that as temperature increases:

    F. O_2 absorbed by the lungs increases and CO_2 released by the skin decreases.

    G. O_2 absorbed by the lungs increases and CO_2 released by the skin increases.

    H. O_2 absorbed by the lungs decreases and CO_2 released by the lungs increases.

    J. O_2 absorbed by the lungs decreases and CO_2 released by the lungs decreases.

11. According to the results of these experiments, as the temperature rises above 15°C, which of the following phenomena can be observed?

    A. The Brazilian tree frog's ability to absorb oxygen through the skin decreases, as does its ability to release carbon dioxide through the lungs.

    B. The Brazilian tree frog's ability to absorb oxygen through the skin decreases, while its ability to release carbon dioxide through the lungs remains about the same.

    C. The Brazilian tree frog's ability to absorb oxygen through the skin remains about the same, as does its ability to release carbon dioxide through the lungs.

    D. The Brazilian tree frog's ability to absorb oxygen through the skin increases, while its ability to release carbon dioxide through the lungs remains about the same.

GO ON TO THE NEXT PAGE ⇨

Passage III

A scientist wants to use a certain organic reagent to develop a means of extracting valuable elements from radioactive nuclear power plant effluent. Using the organic reagent, she measured extraction curves for six different elements: tungsten (W), molybdenum (Mo), ytterbium (Yb), erbium (Er), thulium (Tm), and europium (Eu).

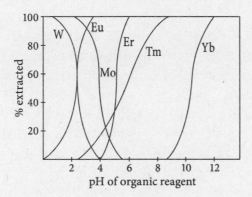

12. At which pH level is the organic reagent most effective in extracting molybdenum?

F. 3

G. 4

H. 5

J. 6

13. The engineers who run a power plant that ejects waste with high levels of erbium and tungsten isotopes would like to extract as much of both elements as possible. Assuming a single-step extraction, this could be accomplished by using the organic reagent at a pH of:

A. less than 1.5 or greater than 5.5.

B. 4.

C. 4.6.

D. It is impossible to extract large amounts of both elements using the reagent at any pH.

14. Based on the data given, which of the following conclusions can be drawn about the effect of pH on the percentage extracted?

F. The percentage of an element extracted increases as pH increases.

G. The percentage of an element extracted decreases as pH increases.

H. The percentage of an element extracted is independent of pH.

J. The effect of pH is different for different elements.

15. The researcher was able to extract 45% of the thulium from the plant's effluent. The pH level of the organic reagent was most likely between:

A. 4 and 5.

B. 5 and 6.

C. 6 and 7.

D. 7 and 8.

16. If erbium is among the elements being extracted by the organic reagent at a certain pH, which of the following cannot be among the other elements being extracted?

F. Europium

G. Thulium

H. Molybdenum

J. Ytterbium

GO ON TO THE NEXT PAGE

Passage IV

While the focus (point of origin) of most earthquakes lies less than 20 km below the Earth's surface, certain unusual seismographic readings indicate that some activity originates at considerably greater depths. Below, two scientists discuss the possible causes of deep-focus earthquakes.

SCIENTIST 1

Surface earthquakes occur when rock in the Earth's crust fractures to relieve stress. However, below 50 km, rock is under too much pressure to fracture normally. Deep-focus earthquakes are caused by the pressure of fluids trapped in the Earth's tectonic plates. As a plate is forced down into the mantle by convection, increases in temperature and pressure cause changes in the crystalline structure of minerals such as serpentine. In adopting a denser configuration, the crystals dehydrate, releasing water. Other sources of fluid include water trapped in pockets of deep-sea trenches and carried down with the plates. Laboratory work has shown that fluids trapped in rock pores can cause rock to fail at lower shear stresses. In fact, at the Rocky Mountain Arsenal, the injection of fluid wastes into the ground accidentally induced a series of shallow-focus earthquakes.

SCIENTIST 2

Deep-focus earthquakes cannot result from normal fractures because rock becomes ductile at the temperatures and pressures that exist at depths greater than 50 km. Furthermore, mantle rock below 300 km is probably totally dehydrated because of the extreme pressure. Therefore, trapped fluids could not cause quakes below that depth. A better explanation is that deep-focus

quakes result from the slippage that occurs when rock in a descending tectonic plate undergoes a phase change in its crystalline structure along a thin plane parallel to a stress. Just such a phase change and resultant slippage can be produced in the laboratory by compressing a slab of calcium magnesium silicate. The pattern of deep-quake activity supports this theory. In most seismic zones, the recorded incidence of deep-focus earthquakes corresponds to the depths at which phase changes are predicted to occur in mantle rock. For example, little or no phase change is thought to occur at 400 km, and indeed, earthquake activity at this level is negligible. Between 400 and 680 km, activity once again increases. Although seismologists initially believed that earthquakes could be generated at depths as low as 1,080 or 1,200 km, no foci have been confirmed below 700 km. No phase changes are predicted for mantle rock below 680 km.

17. Scientists 1 and 2 agree on which point?

    A. Deep-earthquake activity does not occur below 400 km.

    B. Fluid allows tectonic plates to slip past one another.

    C. Water can penetrate mantle rock.

    D. Rock below 50 km will not fracture normally.

GO ON TO THE NEXT PAGE ⟹

18. Which of the following is evidence that would support Scientists 1's hypothesis?

    F. The discovery that water can be extracted from mantle-like rock at temperatures and pressures similar to those found below 300 km

    G. Seismographic indications that earthquakes occur 300 km below the surface of the Earth

    H. The discovery that phase changes occur in the mantle rock at depths of 1,080 km

    J. An earthquake underneath Los Angeles that was shown to have been caused by water trapped in sewer lines

19. Both scientists assume that:

    A. deep-focus earthquakes are more common than surface earthquakes.

    B. trapped fluids cause surface earthquakes.

    C. the Earth's crust is composed of mobile tectonic plates.

    D. deep-focus earthquakes cannot be felt on the Earth's crust without special recording devices.

20. To best refute Scientist 2's hypothesis, Scientist 1 might:

    F. find evidence of other sources of underground water.

    G. record a deep-focus earthquake below 680 km.

    H. find a substance that doesn't undergo phase changes even at depths equivalent to 680 km.

    J. show that rock becomes ductile at depths of less than 50 km.

21. According to Scientist 1, the earthquake at Rocky Mountain Arsenal occurred because:

    A. serpentine or other minerals dehydrated and released water.

    B. fluid wastes injected into the ground compressed a thin slab of calcium magnesium silicate.

    C. fluid wastes injected into the ground flooded pockets of a deep-sea trench.

    D. fluid wastes injected into the ground lowered the shear stress failure point of the rock.

22. Scientist 2's hypothesis would be strengthened by evidence showing that:

    F. water evaporates at high temperatures and pressures.

    G. deep-focus earthquakes can occur at 680 km.

    H. stress has the same effect on mantle rock that it has on calcium magnesium silicate.

    J. water pockets exist at depths below 300 km.

23. According to Scientist 2, phase changes in the crystalline structure of a descending tectonic plate:

    A. occur only at the Earth's surface.

    B. are not possible.

    C. cause certain minerals to release water, which exerts pressure within the plate.

    D. cause slippage that directly results in an earthquake.

GO ON TO THE NEXT PAGE

Passage V

Astronomers want to know the effects of atmospheric conditions on the impact of an asteroid-to-Earth collision. The most common hypothesis is that the presence of moisture in the Earth's atmosphere significantly reduces the hazardous effects of such a collision. One researcher has decided to create a laboratory model of the Earth. The researcher has the ability to control the amount of moisture surrounding the model. The researcher has also created models of asteroids at various sizes. The researcher will use a collision indicator (see table below) based on the Torino Scale to measure the results of two experiments.

Collision Indicator	
0 to 0.9	A collision capable of little destruction
1 to 3.9	A collision capable of localized destruction
4 to 6.9	A collision capable of regional destruction
7 to 10	A collision capable of global catastrophe

EXPERIMENT 1

The researcher simulated collisions on the Earth model with asteroid models equivalent to mass ranging from 1,000 kg to 1,000,000 kg. The controlled moisture level of the model Earth's atmosphere was 86%. The effects of the collisions were recorded and rated according to the collision indicator.

EXPERIMENT 2

The researcher simulated collisions on the Earth model with asteroid models equivalent to the same mass as in Experiment 1. The controlled moisture level of the model Earth's atmosphere in this experiment was 12%. The effects of the collisions were recorded and rated according to the collision indicator. The results of both experiments are shown in the graph.

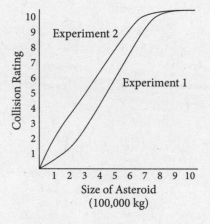

24. How was the experimental design of Experiment 1 different from that of Experiment 2?

    F. The impacts of more asteroids were measured.

    G. The impacts of larger asteroids were measured.

    H. There was more moisture in the atmosphere.

    J. There was a different collision indicator.

GO ON TO THE NEXT PAGE

25. If the atmospheric moisture in Experiment 2 was increased to 50%, the collision rating for an asteroid with a mass of 400,000 kg would most likely be between:

    A. 2 and 3.

    B. 4.5 and 5.5.

    C. 6 and 7.

    D. 9 and 10.

26. Based on the experimental results, one can generalize that an increase of moisture in the atmosphere would:

    F. decrease the impact of an asteroid-to-Earth collision, regardless of the size of the asteroid.

    G. decrease the impact of an asteroid-to-Earth collision with asteroids under 700,000 kg.

    H. increase the impact of an asteroid-to-Earth collision, regardless of the size of the asteroid.

    J. increase the impact of an asteroid-to-Earth collision with asteroids under 700,000 kg.

27. In a simulated asteroid-to-Earth collision, a 400,000 kg asteroid received a collision rating of 4. The amount of moisture in the atmosphere was most likely closest to:

    A. 0%.

    B. 12%.

    C. 86%.

    D. 100%.

28. According to the researcher's model, a 100,000 kg asteroid colliding in an atmosphere with a moisture level of 12% would be likely to have the same impact as an asteroid colliding in an atmosphere with a moisture level of 86% with a size closest to which of the following?

    F. 50,000 kg

    G. 120,000 kg

    H. 270,000 kg

    J. 490,000 kg

29. To be minimally capable of regional destruction, an asteroid entering an atmosphere with a moisture level of 86% would have to be roughly what percent larger than an asteroid capable of the same level of destruction entering an atmosphere with a moisture level of 12%?

    A. 20%

    B. 70%

    C. 150%

    D. 220%

GO ON TO THE NEXT PAGE

Passage VI

The electrical conductivity of a material determines how it will react to various temperature conditions in a consumer product. Product researchers need to know how a material will react in order to determine its safety for consumer use. The electrical conductivity of two different samples of a platinum dithiolate compound was measured from 10 K to 275 K. The results and general conductivity versus temperature plots for conductors and semiconductors are shown below.

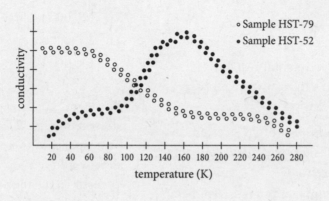

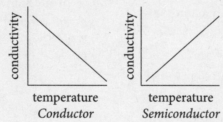

30. For Sample HST-52, which of the following describes its behavior when the temperature is dropped from 200 K to 100 K?

F. The sample remains a semiconductor.

G. The sample remains a conductor.

H. The sample undergoes a conductor to semiconductor transition.

J. The sample undergoes a semiconductor to conductor transition.

31. In a material exhibiting conductor-like behavior, the conductivity:

A. increases as the temperature increases.

B. decreases as the temperature increases.

C. decreases as the temperature decreases.

D. remains the same at all temperatures.

GO ON TO THE NEXT PAGE

32. A newly developed material has a semi-conductor to conductor transition at about 10 K as the temperature increases. Its conductivity versus temperature plot would resemble which of the following?

F.

G.

H.

J.

33. An industrial firm wishes to use HST-52 as a semiconductor in an assembly line component. The experimental results indicate that:

A. HST-52 is not a semiconductor; a new material will have to be chosen.

B. HST-52 is suitable for the planned application.

C. HST-52 is too brittle to be used in this manner.

D. HST-52 will be usable only if the assembly line is maintained at less than 150 K.

34. The temperature at which a compound's conductivity-versus-temperature plot declines most quickly is known as its "optimal conductor" temperature. Which of the following could be the optimal conductor temperature for Sample HST-52?

F.   20 K

G.   80 K

H.   160 K

J.   180 K

GO ON TO THE NEXT PAGE

Passage VII

Siamese cats have a genotype for dark fur, but the enzymes that produce the dark coloring function best at temperatures below the cat's normal body temperature. A Siamese cat usually has darker fur on its ears, nose, paws, and tail, because these parts have a lower temperature than the rest of its body. If a Siamese cat spends more than one hour a day for six consecutive days outdoors (an "outdoor" cat) during very cold weather, darker fur grows in other places on its body. If a Siamese cat does not spend this amount of time outdoors, it is an "indoor" cat. The amount of dark fur on its body remains constant throughout the year.

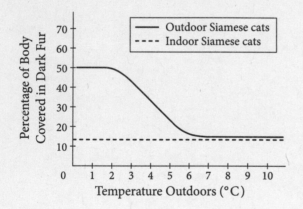

35. According to the graph, if the average temperature outdoors drops from 2°C to 0°C over the course of a month, what will most likely happen to the fur of an outdoor Siamese cat during the same time period? Over that time, the percentage of the cat's body covered in dark fur will:

A. increase.

B. decrease.

C. remain the same.

D. increase, then decrease.

36. A particular Siamese cat goes outdoors a total of three hours per week during the coldest part of the year. One could predict that the percentage of its body covered by dark fur would be closest to:

F. 0%.

G. 10%.

H. 40%.

J. 60%.

37. According to the graph, what is the most likely temperature outside if outdoor Siamese cats have 45% of their bodies covered in dark fur?

A. 0°C

B. 3°C

C. 6°C

D. 9°C

GO ON TO THE NEXT PAGE

38. If a Siamese cat that lived indoors was lost and later found with dark fur over 30% of its body, which of the following could be inferred about the period during which it was missing:

    I. It was living in an area where temperatures fell below 5°C.

    II. It spent more time outdoors than indoors.

    III. It was missing for at least six days.

F. I and II only

G. I and III only

H. II and III only

J. I, II, and III

39. If a Siamese cat has dark fur over 10% of its body, which of the following must be true about the cat?

A. It lives indoors.

B. It lives in an area where the temperature outdoors is usually 7°C or higher.

C. It either lives indoors or it lives in an area where the temperature outdoors is usually 7°C or higher.

D. None of the above

40. If a researcher wants to find out how fur color is affected by the amount of time a Siamese cat spends outside in cold weather, which experiment would be the most helpful?

F. The indoor cats in the original experiment should be used as the control group, and their fur color should be compared to a group of Siamese cats spending six hours or more a day outside in cold weather for six consecutive days.

G. A new group of Siamese cats should be formed and kept outside two or more hours a day at varying temperatures. Their fur color at different outdoor temperatures should be compared to the outdoor cats already charted.

H. Siamese cats should be split into two groups, one group spending only one hour per day outside for six consecutive days in cold weather and the other group spending at least two hours a day outside for six consecutive days in the same weather.

J. No new experiment is needed. The data already gathered shows that the more time a Siamese cat spends outside in cold weather, the darker its fur will be.

WRITING TEST

30 Minutes—1 Question

Directions: This is a test of your writing skills. You will have thirty (30) minutes to write an essay in English. Before you begin planning and writing your essay, read the writing prompt carefully to understand exactly what you are being asked to do. Your essay will be evaluated on the evidence it provides of your ability to express judgments by taking a position on the issue in the writing prompt; to maintain a focus on the topic throughout the essay; to develop a position by using logical reasoning and by supporting your ideas; to organize ideas in a logical way; and to use language clearly and effectively according to the conventions of standard written English.

You may use the unlined pages in this test booklet to plan your essay. These pages will not be scored. *You must write your essay in pencil on the lined pages in the answer folder.* Your writing on those lined pages will be scored. You may not need all the lined pages, but to ensure you have enough room to finish, do NOT skip lines. You may write corrections or additions neatly between the lines of your essay, but do NOT write in the margins of the lined pages. *Illegible essays cannot be scored, so you must write (or print) clearly.*

If you finish before time is called, you may review your work. Lay your pencil down immediately when time called.

DO NOT OPEN THIS BOOKLET UNTIL TOLD TO DO SO.

GO ON TO THE NEXT PAGE

ACT Writing Test Prompt

School athletics has become increasingly competitive in recent years, as professional athletes are drafted at younger ages and the money and fame that professional athletes enjoy have risen to astronomical levels. Some students and school administrators believe that all student athletes should be required to maintain a minimum grade point average or be barred from playing, to ensure that they still get a good education. Others believe this requirement would be unfair because athletics and academics are unrelated and because such a rule would make it too difficult for coaches to do their jobs. In your opinion, should student athletes be required to maintain a minimum grade point average?

In your essay, take a position on this question. You may write about either one of the two points of view given, or you may present a different point of view on this question. Use specific reasons and examples to support your position.

Use this space to *plan* your essay. Your work here will not be graded. Write your essay on the lined pages that follow.

GO ON TO THE NEXT PAGE

GO ON TO THE NEXT PAGE

Practice Test Two
ANSWER KEY

ENGLISH TEST

1. D	11. A	21. B	31. A	41. C	51. B	61. B	71. B
2. G	12. J	22. J	32. J	42. J	52. J	62. F	72. F
3. C	13. A	23. B	33. B	43. A	53. C	63. D	73. B
4. J	14. F	24. F	34. H	44. J	54. J	64. G	74. J
5. B	15. D	25. C	35. A	45. D	55. C	65. B	75. B
6. G	16. G	26. J	36. H	46. H	56. J	66. F	
7. D	17. A	27. B	37. B	47. A	57. C	67. C	
8. J	18. J	28. G	38. J	48. G	58. F	68. H	
9. B	19. C	29. C	39. A	49. B	59. D	69. B	
10. H	20. F	30. F	40. G	50. G	60. F	70. J	

MATH TEST

1. A	9. D	17. E	25. C	33. B	41. B	49. C	57. B
2. J	10. F	18. K	26. J	34. K	42. H	50. F	58. J
3. A	11. B	19. D	27. C	35. D	43. E	51. C	59. C
4. G	12. G	20. G	28. H	36. K	44. K	52. F	60. J
5. B	13. D	21. E	29. D	37. B	45. E	53. B	
6. H	14. G	22. H	30. H	38. F	46. K	54. J	
7. C	15. D	23. A	31. A	39. A	47. E	55. E	
8. J	16. F	24. G	32. F	40. K	48. G	56. G	

READING TEST

1. D	6. G	11. B	16. G	21. A	26. J	31. B	36. J
2. G	7. C	12. J	17. C	22. J	27. C	32. G	37. C
3. B	8. J	13. C	18. G	23. D	28. G	33. B	38. H
4. G	9. C	14. G	19. D	24. H	29. B	34. J	39. A
5. C	10. G	15. A	20. F	25. D	30. F	35. A	40. G

SCIENCE TEST

1. B	6. F	11. B	16. J	21. D	26. G	31. B	36. G
2. H	7. C	12. F	17. D	22. H	27. C	32. H	37. B
3. A	8. H	13. D	18. F	23. D	28. H	33. D	38. G
4. J	9. B	14. J	19. C	24. H	29. B	34. J	39. C
5. A	10. G	15. B	20. G	25. B	30. H	35. C	40. H

ANSWERS AND EXPLANATIONS

English Test

The questions fall into the following categories, according to the skills they test. If you notice that you're having trouble with particular categories, review the following:

1. REDUNDANCY: English Workout 1
2. RELEVANCE: English Workout 1
3. VERBOSITY: English Workout 1
4. JUDGING THE PASSAGE: English Workout 2
5. LOGIC: English Workout 2
6. MODIFIERS: English Workout 2
7. READING-TYPE QUESTIONS: English Workout 2
8. STRUCTURE AND PURPOSE: English Workout 2
9. TONE: English Workout 2
10. VERB USAGE: English Workout 2
11. COMPLETENESS: English Workouts 2 and 3
12. IDIOM: English Workouts 2 and 3
13. PRONOUNS: English Workouts 2 and 3
14. SENTENCE STRUCTURE: English Workouts 2 and 3
15. PUNCTUATION: English Workout 3

PASSAGE I

1. D
Punctuation

A comma is needed to set off the introductory phrase, so choice A cannot be correct. Choice B creates a sentence fragment, and the pronoun *it* in choice C does not match the subject of the sentence—Duke Ellington.

2. G
Verb Usage

The whole passage is in past tense, and there is no reason why this verb should not be in past tense as well. Also, the part of the sentence on the other side of the semicolon gives you a big clue by using *paid*.

3. C
Punctuation

The colon is used incorrectly in the original sentence, and choice B does not solve the problem. Choice D is unnecessarily wordy.

4. J
Punctuation

Commas are needed between items in a series, so eliminate choices F and G. A comma is also needed to set off the introductory phrase, so eliminate choice H.

5. B
Pronouns

In order to figure out the appropriate pronoun, identify the noun to which the pronoun refers. The only possible corresponding noun is *Ellington*; therefore, choice B is the correct answer.

6. G
Completeness

"As a teenager in Washington" is not a complete sentence. Choice H does not make sense, and choice J is incorrect because the comma is unnecessary.

7. D
Idiom
The word *then* should be *than*—D is the choice that makes this correction.

8. J
Relevance
Even though the piano teacher's name is mentioned in the preceding sentence, more information about her name is unnecessary to make the sentence relevant to the passage.

9. B
Structure and Purpose
There is a contrast between Ellington's not being a good pianist and his hearing about the opportunities for musicians in New York. The correct contrast is established by choice B.

10. H
Redundancy
Awaited and *were there for* mean the same thing, so one part of the underlined portion should be deleted—that eliminates choices F and G. Choice J is also unnecessarily wordy.

11. A
Logic
The sentence is logical in the flow of the paragraph, so eliminate choice D. The paragraph discusses Ellington's move to Harlem, and the *they* in the next sentence indicates Ellington wasn't alone. Choice A is the simplest and most correct way to phrase the sentence.

12. J
Pronouns
The subject of the sentence is the Cotton Club, so choices with the pronoun *he*—F and G— should be eliminated. Choice H creates a sentence fragment.

13. A
Structure and Purpose
This list of songs follows a description of Ellington's early musical career, so choice A is correct. The songs do not contradict anything, so eliminate choice B. The names of the songs themselves do not illustrate complexity; therefore, choice C is incorrect. This part of the paragraph is no longer about the Cotton Club, so eliminate choice D.

14. F
Structure and Purpose
The last paragraph of the essay lists the accomplishments of Ellington. Choice F is the only answer choice that makes sense.

15. D
Judging the Passage
Paragraph 4 is the only paragraph that covers elements of Ellington's music. The logical place for the insertion is before the last sentence of the essay where his musical ability is discussed.

PASSAGE II
16. G
Pronouns
The subject is *animals*, so a plural pronoun is needed. Choice F is a singular pronoun, choice H is a contraction, and choice J uses *there* instead of *their*.

17. A
Punctuation
The comma is needed to set off the second clause from the first, so eliminate choice B and D. Choice C incorrectly uses a colon.

18. J
Punctuation
The phrase "a member of the weasel family" is a nonessential clause and should be set off by commas. Eliminate choices G and H because they create sentence fragments.

19. C
Verb Usage

"Having changed" is the incorrect verb tense. Ermines are nonhuman, so choice B is incorrect; choice C uses *that* correctly. The whole passage is in present tense, so eliminate choice D because it is in past tense.

20. F
Sentence Structure

Choose the most logical order of the words. Choice F is the choice that makes the most sense.

21. B
Punctuation

"Far from placing it in danger" is an introductory phrase and should be set off by a comma. Eliminate choices A and C. D is unnecessarily wordy and doesn't make sense with the rest of the sentence.

22. J
Completeness

"By distinguishing itself from other animals" is a sentence fragment. These words make sense as an introductory phrase and should therefore be set off by a comma. J is the only choice that accomplishes this concisely.

23. B
Verbosity

The unnecessary phrase "the question is" should be eliminated. Choice B is the simplest and most correct way to phrase the question.

24. F
Verb Usage

The investigating has occurred in the past, and it is still occurring. The tense of the answer choice should be present perfect. Choices G and H only refer to the past, and choice J refers only to the present.

25. C
Logic

The previous sentence speaks of special glands, but this sentence says that some animals do not have these glands. This is a contrast, and *however* sets it up best.

26. J
Redundancy

Remains and *endures as* are the same thing, so the correct choice will eliminate one of them. choice J does just that.

27. B
Pronouns

The pronoun *it* refers to the tree frog, not a background of leaves. Choice B fixes this modifier error by placing "the tree frog" after the modifying phrase.

28. G
Logic

The information pertains to the paragraph's topic, so eliminate choice J. Choice G is a simple and logical way of rephrasing all of the excess words.

29. C
Structure and Purpose

Paragraph 4 begins with an introduction, and paragraph 3 ends with a conclusion. Choice C is the only choice that features this correct order.

30. F
Judging the Passage

The author covers a range of topics in the area and uses several animals as examples. All of the other answer choices are incorrect because they contradict things that the author does in the essay.

PASSAGE III

31. A
Verbosity

The other answer choices are unnecessarily wordy.

32. J
Verbosity

The other answer choices are unnecessarily wordy.

33. B
Completeness

The sentences on both sides of the period are fragments. The best way to fix this mistake is to simply combine the sentences as choice B does.

34. H
Redundancy

Included and *held* relay the same information. Choice H deletes one of the unnecessary words.

35. A
Verb Usage

The drink was unusual to the people who never experienced it before. In other words, the verb form should be past tense. Eliminate choices B and C. Choice D does not make sense, so eliminate it.

36. H
Sentence Structure

"Over the next century" is an introductory phrase and should be set off by a comma. Choices H and J add the comma, but J also adds unnecessary words.

37. B
Judging the Passage

This description would provide some "color" to the essay. It would not weaken or contradict anything, so eliminate choices A and C. It would

not say anything about the author's opinion of chocolate either, so eliminate choice D.

38. J
Punctuation

Commas are needed between items in a series. Choice G is incorrect because there are too many commas.

39. A
Logic

The sentence provides an example of the uses of chocolate worldwide. Choices B and C set up an unwarranted contrast. Choice D is not a good transition between the two sentences.

40. G
Verbosity

The word *do* is unnecessary in the sentence, especially with the presence of *nonetheless*. Choice G is the most concise statement of the information.

41. C
Punctuation

The colon is not used properly here, so eliminate choices A, B, and D.

42. J
Relevance

Tea has nothing to do with the topic, so the sentence should be eliminated.

43. A
Idiom

The research will be welcomed *by* people, not *to* or *with* them. Therefore, eliminate choices B and D. "Us with a sweet tooth" does not make sense, so choice A is the correct answer.

44. J
Logic
Choice F and G do not make any sense at all. Between choices H and J, the latter is the best style.

45. D
Judging the Passage
This essay is about only chocolate, and it does not cover any other culinary trends in history. Therefore, it would not meet the requirement.

PASSAGE IV

46. H
Idiom
Here, the verb is being used as part of a modifying phrase. Choice H is idiomatically correct.

47. A
Punctuation
Commas are needed in a series, so eliminate choice C. A colon is not appropriate; eliminate choice B. Choice D incorrectly switches to the past tense.

48. G
Modifiers
The form needed is the possessive of *who,* so choice G is correct.

49. B
Verb Usage
This sentence is part of a list of proposed "uniform of the future" developments. The other sentences in that list use the verbs *would be,* *would become,* and *would transmit;* the correct form is choice B.

50. G
Punctuation
No commas are needed in a list of only two items.

51. B
Completeness
Be wary of sentences that begin with *to;* they are often fragments like the one here. B is the best and most concise way to combine the two parts of the sentence.

52. J
Redundancy
Two words in the underlined portion of the sentence have closely related meanings: *concealing* means "keeping from being observed" or "hiding," and *invisible* means "hidden" or "impossible to see." Because these words convey the same idea, this is a simple redundancy that can be fixed by eliminating one of the two words. Therefore, we can eliminate choices F, G, and H and select choice J as the answer.

53. C
Judging the Passage
To determine the U.S. Army's opinion of the Invisible Soldier program, look at the words used to introduce and describe it: the army has dreamed of such a program and invested in it. So the army attitude is positive; we can eliminate the negative word *skeptical* in choice A and the neutral words *curious* and *detailed* in choice B and choice D, leaving *enthusiastic,* choice C.

54. J
Structure and Purpose
In context, this paragraph offers a specific example of the more general issues raised in paragraph 1.

55. C
Redundancy
Although the underlined segment is necessary, having *beginning* and *early stages* is redundant. Choice C is the most concise way to rephrase this.

56. J
Sentence Structure

As written, this is a run-on sentence, so eliminate choice F. To correct it, the new clause should be made subordinate by replacing the pronoun with a relative pronoun, so eliminate choice H. The correct form, since it follows a comma, is *which* rather than *that*, so eliminate choice G.

57. C
Tone

The passage has a formal, technical tone. It would, therefore, be inappropriate for the author to use the highly informal expressions "you know, is" or "is, like" eliminate choices A and B. The choice "however, is" is appropriate since this paragraph contrasts with the preceding one. Choice D would be appropriate if this paragraph drew a conclusion based on the prior paragraph, but it doesn't.

58. F
Punctuation

A colon is correct punctuation here because the material that follows it is an explanation of what precedes it.

59. D
Logic

Only sentence 2 and sentence 1 are choices for a first sentence. To put the sentences in logical order, first look for a good transition from paragraph 4, which discusses a problem. Sentence 1 explicitly refers to addressing the problem, so it's the better choice. Eliminate choices A and B. The second sentence should follow logically from sentence 1's description of the new color-changing pixel, and our choices are sentences 4 and 5. Sentence 4 in choice C refers to mirrors, which we haven't encountered before in the passage, rather than pixels, so we can eliminate this choice. That leaves us with

choice D, sentence 5, which refers to the pixels introduced in the first sentence.

60. F
Structure and Purpose

To answer this question, we need an idea of the purpose of each paragraph. Paragraph 1 introduces the "uniform of the future," paragraph 2 the Invisible Soldier program, paragraph 3 the program's early-stage solution, paragraph 4 a problem with that solution, and paragraph 5 a new advance that may solve that problem. The new sentences to be inserted do not discuss a problem with such a program. We can therefore eliminate choices G, H, and J. The material properly belongs in paragraph 2, choice F, because it introduces camouflage generally.

PASSAGE V

61. B
Verbosity

Choice A and C are too wordy, and choice D does not continue the verb tense established in the series.

62. F
Punctuation

The colon is used here to dramatically introduce California. The commas in choices G and H do not do this well, and the separate sentence in choice J does not work either.

63. D
Verb Usage

This paragraph is in the past tense, so the introductory sentence should be in the past tense as well.

64. G
Punctuation

This is a long nonessential clause that should be set off by a comma—eliminate choices F and H.

Choice J is incorrect because it unnecessarily adds more words.

65. B
Sentence Structure
The word order is incorrect in choice A. Choice C creates a sentence fragment, and *did* in choice D is unnecessary.

66. F
Logic
The information is pertinent to the topic, and choice F is the clearest way to express it.

67. C
Modifiers
The only choice that works here is choice C, which uses the correct possessive form. *Their* would have also worked, but it does not appear as one of the answer choices.

68. H
Sentence Structure
Choice F is a sentence fragment. Choice G and J are very awkward.

69. B
Logic
The last sentence of the previous paragraph talks about how workers began to quit their jobs to join the gold rush. The first sentence of this paragraph magnifies this point. Choice B is the only logical transition.

70. J
Relevance
This information is not pertinent to the gold rush back in 1849.

71. B
Redundancy
Singularly and *one* are redundant. Choice C is too wordy, and choice D is incorrect within the context of the sentence.

72. F
Logic
This sentence is a more specific detail that illustrates the preceding sentence. Choice F is the best transition between the two sentences.

73. B
Modifiers
Choice A makes it sound as though lives are changing the place rather than the other way around. Choice C does not make sense, and choice D is grammatically incorrect.

74. J
Sentence Structure
Choice H and F do not make sense because of the word *and*. Choice G is incorrect because the sentence is talking about people today, not the Forty-niners.

75. B
Judging the Passage
Though the Forty-niners are mentioned, the focus of the essay is on the history of the California gold rush. Therefore, the essay would not meet the requirements of the assignment.

Math Test

Answer explanations for the Math test refer to 100 Key Math Concepts for the ACT, found at the end of this book.

1. A
Percent Increase and Decrease
100 Key Math Concepts for the ACT, #33. To reduce a number by 20%, you could take 20% of the original number and subtract the result, or you could just take 80% of the original number:

New price = 80% of original price
= (.80)($125)
= $100

2. J
Evaluating an Algebraic Expression

100 Key Math Concepts for the ACT, #52. Plug in $x = -5$ and see what you get:

$$2x^2 - 6x + 5 = 2(-5)^2 - 6(-5) + 5$$
$$= 2 \times 25 - (-30) + 5$$
$$= 50 + 30 + 5$$
$$= 85$$

3. A
Prime Factorization

100 Key Math Concepts for the ACT, #11. The prime factorization of 36 is $2 \times 2 \times 3 \times 3$. That factorization includes two distinct prime factors, 2 and 3.

4. G
Exterior Angles of a Triangle

100 Key Math Concepts for the ACT, #81. The exterior angles of a triangle (or any polygon, for that matter) add up to 360°:

$$x + 85 + 160 = 360$$
$$x = 115$$

5. B
Average Formula,
Adding/Subtracting Fractions

100 Key Math Concepts for the ACT, #41, #22. Don't jump to hasty conclusions—don't just average the denominators. Do it right—add the fractions and divide by 2:

$$\text{Average of two numbers} = \frac{\text{Sum}}{2}$$

$$\frac{\frac{1}{20} + \frac{1}{30}}{2} = \frac{\frac{3}{60} + \frac{2}{60}}{2} = \frac{\frac{5}{60}}{2} = \frac{\frac{1}{12}}{2} =$$

$$\frac{1}{12} \times \frac{1}{2} = \frac{1}{24}$$

6. H
Rate

100 Key Math Concepts for the ACT, #39. Everyone pays $1.50, and the rest of the toll is based on the number of miles traveled. Subtract $1.50 from Joy's toll to see how much is based on distance traveled: $25.00 - $1.50 = $23.50. Then divide that amount by 25 cents per mile:

$$\frac{\$23.50}{\$0.25 \text{ per mile}} = 94 \text{ miles}$$

7. C
Multiplying and Dividing Powers,
Multiplying Monomials

100 Key Math Concepts for the ACT, #47, #55. Multiply the coefficients and add the exponents:

$$3x^2 \times 5x^3 = 3 \times 5 \times x^{2 + x^3} = 15x^5$$

8. J
Finding the Distance between Two Points

100 Key Math Concepts for the ACT, #71. You could use the distance formula, but it's easier here to think about a right triangle. One leg is the difference between the xs, which is 3, and the other leg is the difference between the ys, which is 4, so you're looking at a 3-4-5 triangle, and the hypotenuse, which is the distance from P to Q, is 5.

9. D
Percent Formula

100 Key Math Concepts for the ACT, #32. Percent times whole equals part:

$$(\text{Percent}) \times 25 = 16$$

$$\text{Percent} = \frac{16}{25} = 0.64 = 64\%$$

10. F
Comparing Fractions

100 Key Math Concepts for the ACT, #28. For $\frac{7}{x}$ to be greater than $\frac{1}{4}$, the denominator x has to be less than 4 times the numerator, or 28. And

for $\frac{7}{x}$ to be less than $\frac{1}{3}$, the denominator x has to be greater than 3 times the numerator, or 21. Thus, x could be any of the integers 22 through 27, of which there are 6.

11. B
Factoring Other Polynomials— FOIL in Reverse

100 Key Math Concepts for the ACT, #61. To factor $6x^2 - 13x + 6$, you need a pair of binomials whose "first" terms will give you a product of $6x^2$ and whose "last" terms will give you a product of 6. And since the middle term of the result is negative, the two last terms must both be negative. You know that one of the factors is among the answer choices, so you can use them in your trial-and-error effort to factor. You know you're looking for a factor with a minus sign in it, so the answer's either choice B or D.

Try choice B first: Its first term is $3x$, so the other factor's first term would have to be $2x$ (to get that $6x^2$ in the product). B's last term is -2, so the other factor's last term would have to be -3. Check to see if $(3x - 2)(2x - 3)$ works:

$$(3x - 2)(2x - 3)$$
$$= (3x \times 2x) + [3x\,(-3)] + [(-2)(2x)] + [(-2)(-3)]$$
$$= 6x^2 - 9x - 4x + 6$$
$$= 6x^2 - 13x + 6$$

It works. There's no need to check choice D.

12. G
Adding/Subtracting Fractions

100 Key Math Concepts for the ACT, #22. The four fractions on the left side of the equation are all ready to be added, because they already have a common denominator: a.

$$\frac{1}{a} + \frac{2}{a} + \frac{3}{a} + \frac{4}{a} = 5$$
$$\frac{1+2+3+4}{a} = 5$$

$$\frac{10}{a} = 5$$
$$10 = 5a$$
$$a = 2$$

13. D
Intersecting Lines

100 Key Math Concepts for the ACT, #78. $\angle CGE$ and $\angle BGF$ are vertical angles, since $\angle BGF$ measures 105°. If you subtract $\angle AGB$ from $\angle BGF$, you're left with $\angle AGF$, the angle you're looking for. So $\angle AGF$ measures 105° − 40°, or 65°.

14. G
Solving an Inequality

100 Key Math Concepts for the ACT, #69. You solve an inequality much the way you solve an equation: do the same things to both sides until you've isolated what you're solving for. (Just remember to flip the sign if you ever multiply or divide both sides by a negative number.) Here, you want to isolate x:

$$-3 < 4x - 5$$
$$2 < 4x$$
$$\frac{2}{4} < x$$
$$x > \frac{1}{2}$$

15. D
Interior Angles of a Triangle, Exterior Angles of a Triangle

100 Key Math Concepts for the ACT, #80, #81. Because BD bisects $\angle ABC$, the measure of $\angle ABD$ is 50°. Now you know two of the three angles of $\triangle ABD$, so the third angle measures 180° − 60° − 50° = 70°.

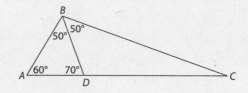

$\angle BDC$, the angle you're looking for, is supplementary to the 70° angle, so $\angle BDC$ measures $180° - 70° = 110°$.

16. F
Solving "In Terms Of,"
Factoring Out a Common Divisor
100 Key Math Concepts for the ACT, #64, #58. To express y in terms of x, isolate y:

$$x + 2y - 3 = xy$$
$$2y - xy = -x + 3$$
$$y(2 - x) = 3 - x$$
$$y = \frac{3 - x}{2 - x}$$

17. E
Identifying the Parts and the Whole
100 Key Math Concepts for the ACT, #31. If you add the number of English-speakers and the number of Spanish-speakers, you get $28 + 37 = 65$. But there are only 50 students, so $65 - 50 = 15$ of them are being counted twice—because those 15 speak both languages.

18. K
Rate
100 Key Math Concepts for the ACT, #39. Set up a proportion:

$$\frac{288 \text{ miles}}{6 \text{ hours}} = \frac{x \text{ miles}}{8 \text{ hours}}$$
$$6x = 288 \times 8$$
$$6x = 2{,}304$$
$$x = 384$$

19. D
Repeating Decimals
100 Key Math Concepts for the ACT, #30. To convert a fraction to a decimal, you divide the denominator into the numerator. Clearly, you don't have time to take the division out to 100 places after the decimal point. There must be a pattern you can take advantage of. Start

dividing and continue just until you see what the pattern is:

$$11\overline{)4.000000\ldots} = .363636\ldots$$

The 1st, 3rd, 5th, etc. digits are 3; and the 2nd, 4th, etc. digits are 6. In other words, every odd-numbered digit is a 3 and every even-numbered digit is a 6. The 100th digit is an even-numbered digit, so it's a 6.

20. G
Solving a System of Equations
100 Key Math Concepts for the ACT, #67. Since it's x you're looking for, eliminate y. Fortunately, the equations are all ready for you—just add them and the $+ 4y$ cancels with the $- 4y$:

$$3x + 4y = 31$$
$$3x - 4y = -1$$
$$6x = 30$$
$$x = 5$$

21. E
Finding the Distance between Two Points
100 Key Math Concepts for the ACT, #71. The coordinates of the midpoint are the averages of the coordinates of the endpoints. The average of the xs is $\frac{2 + 12}{2} = 7$, and the average of the ys is $\frac{3 + (-15)}{2} = -6$, so the coordinates of the midpoint are $(7, -6)$.

22. H
Sine, Cosine, and Tangent of Acute Angles
100 Key Math Concepts for the ACT, #96. Cosine is "adjacent over hypotenuse." Here, the leg adjacent to θ is 4 and the hypotenuse is 5, so $\cos \theta = \frac{4}{5}$.

23. A
Circumference of a Circle
100 Key Math Concepts for the ACT, #89. The center of Q is on P's circumference, and the radius of circle Q is twice the radius of circle P.

You could use the circumference of circle P to find the radius of circle P, then double that radius to get the radius of circle Q, and finally use that radius to calculate the circumference of circle Q. It's much easier and faster, however, if you realize that "double the radius means double the circumference." If the circumference of circle P is 6, then the circumference of circle Q is twice that, or 12.

24. G
Evaluating an Expression
100 Key Math Concepts for the ACT, #52. This looks like a functions question, but in fact it's just a "plug-in-the-number-and-see-what-you-get" question:

$$f(x) = x^3 - x^2 - x$$
$$f(-3) = (-3)^3 - (-3)^2 - (-3)$$
$$= -27 - 9 + 3$$
$$= -33$$

25. C
Integer/Noninteger, Miscellaneous Triangles
100 Key Math Concepts for the ACT, #3. If the two unknown side lengths are integers, and the sum of the two lengths has to be greater than 7, then the least amount the two unknown sides could add up to would be 8, which would make the perimeter $7 + 8 = 15$.

26. J
Factoring Other Polynomials—FOIL in Reverse, Factoring Out a Common Divisor
100 Key Math Concepts for the ACT, #61. First factor out an x from each term, then factor what's left:

$$2x + 3x^2 + x^3 = x(2 + 3x + x^2)$$
$$= x(x^2 + 3x + 2)$$
$$= x(x + 1)(x + 2)$$

27. C
Simplifying an Algebraic Fraction, Multiplying and Dividing Powers, Raising Powers to Powers
100 Key Math Concepts for the ACT, #62, #47, #48. Get rid of the parentheses in the denominator, and then cancel factors the numerator and denominator have in common:

$$\frac{x^2 y^3 z^4}{(xyz^2)^2} = \frac{x^2 y^3 z^4}{x^2 y^2 z^4} = \frac{x^2}{x^2} \cdot \frac{y^3}{y^2} \cdot \frac{z^4}{z^4} = y$$

28. H
Adding/Subtracting Fractions, Converting Fractions to Decimals
100 Key Math Concepts for the ACT, #22, #29. Normally you would have a choice: either convert the fractions to decimals first and then add, or add the fractions first and then convert the sum to a decimal. In this case, however, both fractions would convert to endlessly repeating decimals, which might be a bit unwieldy when adding. In this case, it seems to make sense to add first, then convert:

$$\frac{2}{3} + \frac{1}{12} = \frac{8}{12} + \frac{1}{12} = \frac{9}{12} = \frac{3}{4} = 0.75$$

29. D
Solving a Linear Equation
100 Key Math Concepts for the ACT, #63. This looks like a physics question, but in fact it's just a "plug-in-the-number-and-see-what-you-get" question. Be sure you plug 95 in for C (not F):

$$C = \frac{5}{9}(F - 32)$$
$$95 = \frac{5}{9}(F - 32)$$
$$\frac{9}{5} \times 95 = F - 32$$
$$F - 32 = 171$$
$$F = 171 + 32 = 203$$

30. H
Probability

100 Key Math Concepts for the ACT, #46. Probability equals the number of favorable outcomes divided by the total number of possible outcomes. In this problem, a favorable outcome is choosing a green marble—that's 4. The "total number of possible outcomes" is the total number of marbles, or 20:

$$\text{Probability} = \frac{\text{Favorable outcomes}}{\text{Total number of possible outcomes}}$$

$$= \frac{4}{20}$$

$$= \frac{1}{5}$$

31. A
Adding and Subtracting Polynomials, Average Formula

100 Key Math Concepts for the ACT, #54, #41. To find the average of three numbers—even if they're algebraic expressions—add them and divide by 3:

$$\text{Average} = \frac{\text{Sum of terms}}{\text{Number of terms}}$$

$$= \frac{(2x + 5) + (5x - 6) + (-4x + 2)}{3}$$

$$= \frac{3x + 1}{3}$$

$$= x + \frac{1}{3}$$

32. F
Using Two Points to Find the Slope

100 Key Math Concepts for the ACT, #72. Parallel lines have the same slope. Use the first pair of points to figure out the slope:

$$\text{Slope} = \frac{y_2 - y_1}{x_2 - x_1} = \frac{16 - 1}{2 - 1} = 15$$

Then use the slope to figure out the missing coordinate in the second pair of points:

$$\text{Slope} = \frac{y_2 - y_1}{x_2 - x_1}$$

$$15 = \frac{(25 - (-5))}{a - (-10)}$$

$$15 = \frac{30}{a + 10}$$

$$15a + 150 = 30$$

$$15a = -120$$

$$a = -8$$

33. B
Similar Triangles

100 Key Math Concepts for the ACT, #82. When parallel lines make a big triangle and a little triangle as they do here, the triangles are similar (because they have the same angle measurements). Side $\overline{PR}$ is three times the length of $\overline{QR}$, so each side of the big triangle is three times the length of the corresponding side of the smaller triangle, and therefore the ratio of the perimeters is also 3:1. So the perimeter of $\triangle PRT$ is 3 times 11, or 33.

34. K
Special Quadrilaterals

100 Key Math Concepts for the ACT, #86. It is a polygon because it's composed of straight line segments. It is a quadrilateral because it has four sides. It is not a rectangle because opposite sides are not equal. It is a trapezoid because it has one pair of parallel sides.

35. D
Evaluating an Algebraic Expression, Solving a Linear Equation

100 Key Math Concepts for the ACT, #52, #63.

Plug in $x = -3$ and solve for a:

$$2x^2 + (a - 4)x - 2a = 0$$

$$2(-3)^2 + (a - 4)(-3) - 2a = 0$$

$$18 - 3a + 12 - 2a = 0$$

$$30 - 5a = 0$$

$$-5a = -30$$

$$a = 6$$

36. K
Counting the Possibilities

100 Key Math Concepts for the ACT, #45. The total number of combinations of a first course, second course, and dessert is equal to the product of the three numbers:

Total possibilities = $4 \times 5 \times 3 = 60$

37. B
Prime Factorization,
Least Common Multiple

100 Key Math Concepts for the ACT, #11, #14. An integer that's divisible by 6 has at least one 2 and one 3 in its prime factorization. An integer that's divisible by 9 has at least two 3s in its prime factorization. Therefore, an integer that's divisible by both 6 and 9 has at least one 2 and two 3s in its prime factorization. That means it's divisible by 2, 3, $2 \times 3 = 6$, $3 \times 3 = 9$, and $2 \times 3 \times 3 = 18$. It's not necessarily divisible by 12 or 36, each of which includes two 2s in its prime factorization. You could also do this one by picking numbers. Think of a common multiple of 6 and 9 and use it to eliminate some options. $6 \times 9 = 54$ is an obvious common multiple—and it's not divisible by 12 or 36, but it is divisible by 18. The *least* common multiple of 6 and 9 is 18, which is also divisible by 18. It looks like every common multiple of 6 and 9 is also a multiple of 18.

38. F
Simplifying an Algebraic Fraction

100 Key Math Concepts for the ACT, #62.

$$\frac{x^2 + x^2 + x^2}{x^2} = \frac{3x^2}{x^2} = 3$$

39. A
Translating from English into Algebra

100 Key Math Concepts for the ACT, #65. Read carefully. This question's a lot easier than you might think. It's asking for the total number of coins, not the total value. q quarters, d dimes, and n nickels add up to a total of $q + d + n$ coins.

40. K
Solving an Inequality, Graphing
Inequalities

100 Key Math Concepts for the ACT, #69, #70. You solve an inequality much the way you solve an equation: do the same things to both sides until you've isolated what you're solving for. (Just remember to flip the sign if you ever multiply or divide both sides by a negative number.)

$$5x - 2(1 - x) \geq 4(x + 1)$$
$$5x - 2 + 2x \geq 4x + 4$$
$$5x + 2x - 4x \geq 4 + 2$$
$$3x \geq 6$$
$$x \geq 2$$

The "greater-than-or-equal-to" symbol is graphed as a solid circle.

41. B
Using Two Points to Find the Slope

100 Key Math Concepts for the ACT, #72. First find the slope of the line that contains the given points:

$$\text{Slope} = \frac{y_2 - y_1}{x_2 - x_1} = \frac{10 - 6}{6 - 5} = 4$$

Line m is perpendicular to the above line, so the slope of m is the negative reciprocal of 4, or $-\frac{1}{4}$.

42. H
Sine, Cosine, and Tangent of Acute Angles

100 Key Math Concepts for the ACT, #96. Sine is "opposite over hypotenuse." Here, the leg opposite θ is 12 and the hypotenuse is 13, so:

$$\sin \theta = \frac{12}{13}$$

43. E
Raising Powers to Powers,
Solving a Linear Equation

100 Key Math Concepts for the ACT, #48, #63. Express the left side of the equation so that both sides have the same base:

$$9^{2x-1} = 3^{3x+3}$$
$$(3^2)^{2x-1} = 3^{3x+3}$$
$$3^{4x-2} = 3^{3x+3}$$

Now that the bases are the same, just set the exponents equal:

$$4x - 2 = 3x + 3$$
$$4x - 3x = 3 + 2$$
$$x = 5$$

44. K

Combined Percent Increase and Decrease

100 Key Math Concepts for the ACT, #35. Be careful with combined percent increase. You cannot just add the two percents, because they're generally percents of different wholes. In this instance, the 20% increase is based on the 1970 population, but the 30% increase is based on the larger 1980 population. If you just added 20% and 30% to get 50%, you fell into the test maker's trap.

The best way to do a problem like this one is to pick a number for the original whole and just see what happens. As usual, the best number to pick is 100. (That may be a small number for the population of a city, but verisimilitude is not important—all that matters is the math.)

If the 1970 population was 100, then a 20% increase would put the 1980 population at 120. Now, to figure the 30% increase, multiply 120 by 130%:

New # = (Original #) + (30% of Original #)
New # = 130% of Original #
$$x = 1.3(120)$$
$$= 156$$

Since the population went from 100 to 156, that's a 56% increase.

45. E
Finding the Missing Number

100 Key Math Concepts for the ACT, #44. The best way to deal with changing averages is to go by way of the sums. Use the old average to figure out the total of the first four scores:

Sum of first 4 scores = $4 \times 89 = 356$

And use the new average to figure out the total he needs after the fifth score:

Sum of five scores = $5 \times 90 = 450$

To get his sum up from 356 to 450, Martin needs to score $450 - 356 = 94$.

46. K
Equation for a Circle

100 Key Math Concepts for the ACT, #75. If you find the distance from the center to the given point on the circle, you'll have the radius. The difference between the xs is 8, and the difference between the ys is 6. If 8 and 6 are the lengths of the legs of a right triangle, then the hypotenuse is 10. The radius, then, is 10. Now you can plug the radius and the coordinates of the center point into the general form of the equation of a circle:

$$(x - h)^2 + (y - k)^2 = r^2$$
$$(x + 1)^2 + (y + 1)^2 = 10^2$$
$$(x + 1)^2 + (y + 1)^2 = 100$$

47. E
Using Two Points to Find the Slope,
Using an Equation to Find the Slope
and the Intercept

100 Key Math Concepts for the ACT, #72, #73, #74. In addition to picking coordinates from the line and plugging them into the answer choices, use the points where the line crosses the axes—(–1, 0) and (0, 2)—to find the slope:

$$\text{Slope} = \frac{y_2 - y_1}{x_2 - x_1} = \frac{2 - 0}{0 - (-1)} = 2$$

The y-intercept is 2. Now plug $m = 2$ and $b = 2$ into the slope-intercept equation form:

$$y = mx + b$$
$$y = 2x + 2$$

48. G
Percent Formula

100 Key Math Concepts for the ACT, #32. Be careful. The question is not asking, "What is $\frac{1}{4}$ of 16?" It's asking, "What is $\frac{1}{4}$% of 16?" One-fourth of 1% is 0.25%, or 0.0025:

$$\tfrac{1}{4}\% \text{ of } 16 = 0.0025 \times 16 = 0.04$$

49. C
Multiplying Binomials—FOIL

100 Key Math Concepts for the ACT, #56. Use FOIL to get rid of the parentheses, and then combine like terms:

$$(s + 4)(s - 4) + (2s + 2)(s - 2)$$
$$= (s^2 - 16) + (2s^2 - 2s - 4)$$
$$= s^2 + 2s^2 - 2s - 16 - 4$$
$$- 3s^2 - 2s - 20$$

50. F
**Equation for a Parabola,
Evaluating an Algebraic Expression**

100 Key Math Concepts for the ACT, #76, #52. The easiest way to find the equation of a given parabola is to take a point or two from the graph and plug the coordinates into the answer choices, eliminating the choices that don't work. Start with a point with coordinates that are easy to work with. Here, you could start with (3, 0). Plug $x = 3$ and $y = 0$ into each answer choice, and you'll find that only F works.

51. C
Sine, Cosine, and Tangent of Acute Angles

100 Key Math Concepts for the ACT, #96. Since $\sin a = \frac{4}{5}$, you could think of this as a 3-4-5 triangle:

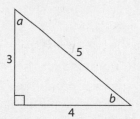

Cosine is "adjacent over hypotenuse." Here, the leg adjacent to b is 4, and the hypotenuse is 5, so $\cos b = \frac{4}{5}$. (Notice that the sine of one acute angle in a right triangle is equal to the cosine of the other acute angle.)

52. F
**Adding and Subtracting Monomials,
Simplifying an Algebraic Fraction**

100 Key Math Concepts for the ACT, #53, #62. Add the like terms in the numerator and then divide by the denominator:

$$\frac{x^2 + x^2 + x^2}{x} = \frac{3x^2}{x} = 3x$$

If you weren't careful, you might have confused this with problem 38 and missed the change in the denominator.

53. B
Translating from English into Algebra

100 Key Math Concepts for the ACT, #65. When you divide w by 4, you get $\frac{w}{4}$. When you subtract that result from r, you get $r - \frac{w}{4}$.

54. J
Volume of Other Solids

100 Key Math Concepts for the ACT, #95. The formula for the volume of a cylinder is $V = \pi r^2 h$, where r is the radius of the circular base and h is the height. Here $r = 4$ and $h = 5$, so:

Volume $= \pi r^2 h$

$\quad\quad\quad = \pi(4)^2(5)$

$\quad\quad\quad = \pi(16)(5)$

$\quad\quad\quad = 80\pi$

55. E
Area of a Triangle,
Multiplying Binomials—FOIL

100 Key Math Concepts for the ACT, #83, #56. With a right triangle, you can use the two legs as the base and the height to figure out the area. Here, the leg lengths are expressed algebraically. Just plug the two expressions in for b and h in the triangle area formula:

$$\text{Area} = \frac{1}{2}(x-1)(x+1) = \frac{1}{2}(x^2-1) = \frac{x^2-1}{2}$$

56. G
Rate

100 Key Math Concepts for the ACT, #39. The difference between the populations in 1990 was $9,400 - 7,600 = 1,800$. Each year, as the larger population goes down by 100 and the smaller population goes up by 100, the difference decreases by 200. Thus, it will take $1,800 \div 200 = 9$ years to erase the difference.

57. B
Miscellaneous Averages: Weighted Average

The overall average is not simply the average of the two average ages. Because there are a lot more women than men, women carry more weight, and the overall average will be closer to 25 than 35. Pick particular numbers for the females and males, say 4 females and 1 male. The ages of the 4 females total 4 times 25, or 100, and the age of the 1 male totals 35. The average, then, is $(100 + 35)$ divided by 5, or 27.

58. J
Sine, Cosine, and Tangent of Acute Angles,
Pythagorean Theorem

100 Key Math Concepts for the ACT #96, #84. The height h of the tree is the leg opposite θ.

The distance b from the base of the tree is the leg adjacent to θ. "Opposite over adjacent" is tangent, but all the answer choices are in terms of the sine. Sine is "opposite over hypotenuse," so you're going to have to figure out the hypotenuse. Use the Pythagorean theorem:

$$(\text{hypotenuse})^2 = (\text{leg}_1)^2 + (\text{leg}_2)^2$$
$$(\text{hypotenuse})^2 = b^2 + h^2$$
$$\text{hypotenuse} = \sqrt{b^2 + h^2}$$

Now, to get the sine, put the opposite h over the hypotenuse $\sqrt{b^2 + h^2}$: $\sin \theta = \dfrac{h}{\sqrt{b^2 + h^2}}$

59. C
Evaluating an Algebraic Expression

100 Key Math Concepts for the ACT, #52. This looks like a solid geometry question, but in fact it's just a "plug-in-the-numbers" question:

$$S = \pi r \sqrt{r^2 + h^2} = \pi(3)\sqrt{3^2 + 4^2} = 3\pi\sqrt{9 + 16} =$$
$$3\pi\sqrt{25} = 3\pi \times 5 = 15\pi$$

60. J
Parallel Lines and Transversals

100 Key Math Concepts for the ACT, #79. When a transversal crosses parallel lines, all the resulting acute angles are equal and all the resulting obtuse angles are equal. (You can generally tell at sight which angles are equal.) In this problem's figure, $a = c = e = g$ and $b = d = f = h$. Only J is true: c and g are both obtuse. In all the other choices, you'll find an obtuse and an acute angle.

Reading Test

Reading questions can be divided into four basic types: Detail questions, Inference questions, Big Picture questions, and Vocabulary-in-Context questions. As you review the answers and explanations, note which types you tend to answer correctly or incorrectly and tailor your studying to focus on areas where you need improvement.

PASSAGE I

1. D
Detail

Lines 18–21 provide the answer: "I was brought up, from my earliest remembrance…by my godmother."

2. G
Inference

From the description of Dolly in the first two paragraphs, it is clear that Esther viewed her doll as her only friend. "I was such a shy little thing that I seldom dared to open my lips, and never dared to open my heart, to anybody else" (lines 6–9). This idea is repeated in lines 97–101: "I went up to my room, and crept to bed, and laid my doll's cheek against mine wet with tears, and holding that solitary friend upon my bosom, cried myself to sleep."

3. B
Vocabulary-in-Context

In this case, *stiff* is used to describe the tone of the letter that Esther's godmother wrote to decline the invitation to another student's birthday party. Choice B, "rigidly formal," is the most appropriate definition in this context.

4. G
Big Picture

This is a Big Picture question. Esther mentions that her birthday was never celebrated and the pivotal scene in the passage happens on her birthday. In lines 3–4, Esther tells her doll that she is not very clever, but that is not the focus of the passage. In lines 54–57, she mentions being invited to a friend's home for a party so H is not correct. In lines 79–82, we find out that

Esther's mother did not die on her birthday, so choice J is not correct.

5. C
Detail

Although Esther's godmother says that she has forgiven Esther's mother, her facial expression directly contradicts this. "I see her knitted brow and pointed finger…her face did not relent…" (lines 88–92).

6. G
Inference

Esther is clearly lonely, as evidenced by her description of Dolly as her only friend and her explanation that there is a separation dividing her from the other girls at school. The birthday scene with her godmother also shows that Esther is quite confused about her own family past.

7. C
Inference

Her confrontation with her godmother gives Esther further reason to believe that no one loves her. The phrase before the cited line also points to choice C as the best answer: "I knew that I had brought no joy at any time to anybody's heart" (lines 102–103).

8. J
Detail

Choices F, G, and H are all mentioned in paragraph 5 (lines 44–59). At the end of the passage, Esther says, "I hope it is not self-indulgent to shed these tears as I think of it" (lines 111–112).

9. C
Detail

Esther's evidence that her godmother is a "good, good woman" is explained in lines 22–27: "She went to church three times every Sunday, and to morning prayers on Wednesdays and Fridays, and to lectures whenever there were lectures, and never missed."

10. G
Detail

In the first paragraph, Esther says, "Now, Dolly, I am not clever..." (lines 3–4). In the second paragraph, Esther describes herself as "such a shy little thing" (lines 6–7).

PASSAGE II

11. B
Vocabulary-in-Context

In the phrase "the Pantanal was a vast, soggy canvas, white with gleaming herds of Nelore cattle" (lines 73–75), *canvas* is used to mean "a background." None of the other choices makes sense.

12. J
Detail

The answer to this question can be found in lines 79–82: "As the jaguars grew scarce, their chief food staple, the capybaras—a meter-long rodent, the world's largest—overran farmers' fields..."

13. C
Detail

The answer to this question can be found in lines 15–20: "Exactly how dramatic a comeback is difficult to say because jaguars—*Panthera onca*, the largest feline in the New World—are solitary, secretive, nocturnal predators. Each cat needs to prowl at least 35 square kilometers by itself."

14. G
Inference

The last sentence of the second paragraph provides the answer. "Hotels, campgrounds, and bed-and-breakfasts have sprung up to accommodate the half-million tourists a year...

bent on sampling the Pantanal's wildlife, of which the great cats must be the most magnificent example" (lines 28–34). Tourists want to see the jaguars, and not having the jaguars might negatively affect the booming ecotourist business.

15. A
Detail

The "green safari" example is mentioned as a way for "scientists to fit the cats with radio collars" (lines 104–106). The other three examples provided are listed in lines 110–114 as methods the scientists are teaching the ranchers.

16. G
Big Picture

In lines 59–60, the author says, "Hard data on cattle losses due to jaguars in the Pantanal are nonexistent..." One reason for providing anecdotal information, then, is to tell the story of the hardships faced by the ranchers due to the jaguars. The author does not suggest that he empathizes with the ranchers more than the jaguars—in fact, he refers to the jaguars as "magnificent." The only example that shows rancher violence is Abel Monteiro shooting an attacking jaguar who had killed his two dogs (lines 43–47), an act of self-defense. The landscape of the Pantanal is not the focus of these two paragraphs, so choice J can be eliminated.

17. C
Inference

The passage explains that because of the decrease in the jaguar population, the capybara population increased. These rodents "spread trichomoniasis, a livestock disease that renders cows sterile" (lines 83–84). Lines 87–92 describe the effect of weather patterns and floods on the ranchers' land. "Weather patterns also shifted radically—due most likely to global warming—and drove annual floods to near-Biblical proportions. The waters are only now retreating from some inundated pasturelands."

18. G
Detail

The last sentence of the passage reads, "When the scholars go home and the greens log off, the *pantaneiros* will still be there—left on their own to deal with the jaguars as they see fit" (lines 118–121).

19. D
Detail

Evidence is given throughout the passage that all three groups support protecting the jaguars. It is most concisely stated in lines 49–53: "a political cat fight between the scientists, environmentalists, and ecotourists who want to protect the jaguars and the embattled ranchers…"

20. F
Detail

The answer to this question can be found in lines 59–61: "Hard data on cattle losses due to jaguars in the Pantanal are nonexistent, but there are stories."

PASSAGE III

21. A
Inference

This question asks you why the aulos was considered "the instrument of the Dionysians." In the fifth paragraph, you find out that the Dionysians "represented the unbridled, sensual and passionate aspect of Greek culture" (lines 65–67). The passage also says that the aulos had a "far more exciting effect" (lines 71–72) than the lyre. The suggestion here is clearly that the aulos must have been able to express the unbridled passion and excitement of the Dionysians, making choice A the best answer. Choice B is out because the fact that the aulos

was chosen as the official instrument of the Delphian and Pythian festivals doesn't explain why it was the instrument of the Dionysians. Choice C contradicts the passage: the kithara, not the aulos, represented the intellectual, idealistic side of Greek art. Finally, the author never says when the Dionysian cult originated, so choice D is also out.

22. J
Detail

All the author means by saying that the chelys can be "traced back to the age of fable" is that it is an ancient instrument. The chelys was an actual, not an imaginary, instrument, so choice H is wrong. Choice G is out because the kithara was used to accompany the epics, not the chelys.

23. D
Big Picture

Choice D is the only answer choice that adequately covers the entire passage. Choice A focuses only on the lyre. The connection between Greek music and drama, choice B, is mentioned only in passing, as are the references to music in ancient Greek literature, choice C. The passage is really all about the "origin and development of various Greek instruments," choice D.

24. H
Detail

The first thing the author says about the kithara is that it was used by "professional Homeric singers" (lines 15–16). The kithara, according to the author, probably came from Egypt, so choice F is wrong. Choice G and J contradict information in the paragraph to the effect that the kithara was more powerful than the chelys and was played with both hands.

25. D
Big Picture

Skim through the third paragraph to find the changes that occurred to the lyre between the eighth and fifth centuries B.C. Musicians began to use a plectrum in the seventh century B.C., choice A, lyres featured an increasing number of strings, choice B, during this period, and musicians also began to use different scales and modes, choice C. That leaves choice D. Nothing in the paragraph indicates that lyres were used to accompany dramatic productions.

26. J
Inference

The final paragraph says that "an early specimen" of the aulos was tuned to the chromatic tetrachord, "a fact that points to Oriental origin" (lines 86–87). From this, you can infer that the chromatic tetrachord must have been used in ancient Oriental music, choice J. Choice F is contradicted by the author's assertion that elegiac songs were composed in the mode of the chromatic tetrachord. There is no evidence to support either choice G or H.

27. C
Detail

In the fourth sentence of the first paragraph (lines 8–10), the author indicates that the chelys is the most antique form of the lyre.

28. G
Detail

Sappho did two things that we know about from lines 44–47. She introduced a mode "in which Dorian and Lydian characteristics were blended," and she "initiated the use of the plectrum."

29. B
Detail

All of the details you need to answer this question are in the sixth paragraph (lines 68–78). The first sentence states that the aulos is more like our oboe than our flute, so III is false. This means choices C and D can be eliminated. The second sentence of the paragraph confirms that the aulos sounded more exciting than the lyre (II). Since choice B is the only remaining answer choice that includes II, you know it has to be the best answer.

30. F
Big Picture

Greek instruments are discussed as a whole at the very beginning of the passage. The author says that our knowledge of Greek instruments comes from "representations on monuments, vases, statues, and friezes and from the testimony of Greek authors" (lines 4–6). These are all "secondary sources" of information about the instruments, so choice F is the best answer. Choice G is wrong because quite a bit is known about the tuning of the instruments, as represented in the second paragraph. Choice H is contradicted by the same sentence that supports choice F. Finally, there is no evidence to suggest that more is known about one type of instrument than the other, choice J.

PASSAGE IV

31. B
Detail

Lines 17–20 state that "Scientists have not been able, however, to determine just how sunspots are created or what effect they have on the solar constant..." This is followed by the statement that the question might be answered with "data from the *Solar Maximum Mission* satellite, which has monitored the solar constant since 1980" (lines 23–25).

32. G
Detail

The definition of *solar constant* is given in lines 20–21: "a misnomer that refers to the sun's total radiance at any instant."

33. B
Detail

The second sentence of the passage says, "people have speculated that the solar cycle might exert some influence on the Earth's weather" (lines 3–5). The concluding paragraph suggests that the findings discussed in the passage point to "a link between the solar cycle and weather" (lines 101–102).

34. J
Vocabulary-in-Context

From the sentence alone, it may be difficult to determine the answer. But the preceding sentence clarifies that *proliferated* means "increased in number."

35. A
Detail

The answer to this question can be found in lines 40–48: "When a sunspot appears, it initially causes the sun to dim slightly, but then after a period of weeks or months islands of brilliance called faculas usually emerge near the sunspot and more than compensate for its dimming effect. Willson says faculas may represent regions where energy that initially was blocked beneath a sunspot has finally breached the surface."

36. J
Detail

The answer to this question is found in lines 54–57: "the quasi-biennial oscillation (QBO), a 180-degree shift in the direction of stratospheric winds above the Tropics that occurs about every two years."

37. C
Big Picture

The last paragraph quotes a scientist as believing that there will be "breakthroughs" (line 101) in our understanding of the relationship between the solar cycle and the weather.

38. H
Big Picture

As described in the passage, the QBO changes directions every two years independently of the solar cycle. Lines 71–74 state that: "temperatures and pressures coincident with the QBO's west phase rose and fell in accordance with the solar cycle." Lines 79–82 state that: "The latitude of storms during the west phase of the QBO… varied with the solar cycle…"

39. A
Inference

Lines 8–10 read: "Until recently, however, none of these correlations has held up under close scrutiny." This suggests that recently they have begun to hold up under scrutiny.

40. G
Detail

The answer to this question can be found in lines 30–33: "The data suggest that the sun is 0.1 percent more luminous at the peak of the solar cycle, when the number of sunspots is greatest…"

Science Test

Science questions can be divided into three basic types: Figure questions, Patterns questions, and Scientific Reasoning questions. You may also see Basic Theory questions when you review the Conflicting Viewpoints passage. As you review the answers and explanations, note which types you tend to answer correctly or incorrectly, and tailor your studying to focus on areas where you need improvement.

PASSAGE I

1. B
Figure

Look at the *y*-axis of the graph between the region of pH 8 and pH 12 and then scan across at that level. The indicators that undergo color change at this pH range are thymol blue, phenolphthalein, and alizarin. These indicators correspond to choice B.

2. H
Figure

Looking carefully at the graph, you can see that methyl orange changes from red to yellow between pH 3 and pH 5, and alizarin changes from yellow to red between pH 9 and pH 11. Thymol blue undergoes a yellow to blue color change, so it is not correct.

3. A
Patterns

In order to determine when the reaction is complete and the solution is basic, the chemist should select an indicator that turns color when the pH has risen into the region of basicity (above 7). When bromocresol green inches above the pH of 7, it turns blue, so choice A is correct.

4. J
Scientific Reasoning

This question requires you to make a broad conclusion about acid-base indicators. Choices F and G are incorrect because there are plenty of indicators that change colors above or below pH 7. Choice H is incorrect because different indicators change colors at different pH levels, which explains why choice J is correct.

5. A
Figure

Compare the two indicators on the graph and you'll find that phenolphthalein undergoes a color change at a higher pH than bromothymol blue.

PASSAGE II

6. F
Figure

The quickest way to answer the question is to eliminate the wrong answer choices. A look at Table 1 rules out choice G because the total amount of oxygen absorbed is clearly affected by temperature. H is wrong because frog health is never an issue. The very mention of CO_2 makes choice J incorrect—Experiment 1 was only concerned with oxygen.

7. C
Patterns

There is no data for 17°C, so an estimate is necessary. The total (skin plus lungs) amount of carbon dioxide released per hour was about 100 mol/hr at 15°C and about 110 mol/hr at 20°C. The only choice that falls between these is choice C.

8. H
Scientific Reasoning

To show that *Hyla faber* is an ectotherm, one must find evidence demonstrating that changes in temperature cause changes in gas exchange. Table 1 demonstrates that as temperature increases, *Hyla faber*'s oxygen absorption increases, so H is correct. Choice F is not good evidence because data for only one temperature does not give an idea of how temperature changes affect gas exchange. Choice G is incorrect because the amount of carbon dioxide eliminated by the lungs is the same for 15°C, 20°C, and 25°C, which makes it look as though changes in temperature have little effect on gas exchange in the frog.

9. B
Figure

The amount of carbon dioxide eliminated by the skin increases over the range of temperatures; the increase levels off at the highest temperature. Carbon dioxide release by the lungs increases a bit over the lower temperatures and then levels off almost completely. The curve for skin release has to be much higher on the graph than the curve for lung release because the skin eliminated more carbon dioxide at each temperature than did the lungs. Choice B is the only graph that fits these patterns.

10. G
Patterns

When the answer choices all look similar like in this problem, find the differences between them and rule out the ones that cannot be correct. You can eliminate choice H and J right away because the results show that as temperature increases, O_2 absorbed by the lungs increases. F is not correct either—as temperature increases, CO_2 released by the skin increases, which is stated by choice G.

11. B
Figure

Here again, you want to be careful and refer to the answer choices as you review the tables to observe what happens as the temperature rises above 15°C. Since each of the answer choices refers to the tree frog's ability to absorb oxygen through the skin, start there. From Table 1, you can see that the skin's oxygen absorption rate goes down, so choices C and D are out. Now you need to refer to Table 2 to see what happens to the rate at which carbon dioxide is released from the lungs. It appears to remain about the same, so the correct answer is choice B.

PASSAGE III

12. F
Figure

A good way to approach this question would be to draw a vertical line on the graph from 100% extraction of molybdenum (Mo) to the x-axis. This line lands closest to the pH of 3. Therefore, choice F is correct.

13. D
Figure

To answer this question, you need to look at the extraction curves for both erbium and tungsten and observe how they change with pH. For tungsten, the percentage extracted decreases from 100% to 0% as the pH increases from 1 to 2. The percentage of erbium extracted increases from 0% to 100% as the pH increases from 4 to 6. There is no overlap between the two ranges. "A single-step extraction" could not remove both at the same time.

14. J
Figure

In the graph, there are two types of slopes: one in which the percentage of an element extracted increases as the pH increases, and one in which the percentage of an element extracted decreases with increasing pH. Since there are two types of slopes, choice J is the correct response. Choice F or G would be correct if the question pertained to a specific element, but the question asks you to consider the graph as a whole. If the percentage of an element extracted was independent of pH, you would expect to see the same percentage extracted at every pH. In other words, the graph for each element would be a horizontal line. This is not the case, so choice H is incorrect.

15. B
Figure

Draw a line on the graph from 45% to the line for thulium (Tm). Then draw a vertical line from that point to the *x*-axis. You should land on the *x*-axis between 5 and 6.

16. J
Figure

To answer this question, refer to the extraction curve for erbium. Erbium begins to be extracted when the pH level of the organic reagent is 4 or greater, and by a pH of 6, all of it is being extracted. Ytterbium, choice J, does not begin to be extracted until pH reaches approximately 9.

PASSAGE IV

17. D
Basic Theory

Scientist 1 states that "below 50 km, rock is under too much pressure to fracture normally." Scientist 2 gives the fact that "rock becomes ductile at the temperatures and pressures that exist at depths greater than 50 km" as the reason that "deep-focus earthquakes cannot result from normal fractures."

18. F
Scientific Reasoning

Scientist 1's theory is invalid unless water can be shown to exist in mantle rock at the level of deep-focus earthquakes. If researchers could subject mantle-like rock to those temperatures and pressures, and then extract water from it, choice F, their experimental results would support the hypothesis of Scientist 1.

19. C
Basic Theory

Both scientists believe that the Earth's crust (surface layer) is composed of mobile tectonic plates. In describing the plates as being "forced down into the mantle," Scientist 1 implies that they are normally in the crust, and Scientist 2 makes reference to "a descending tectonic plate." The introductory paragraph says that "most" earthquakes originate less than 20 km below the Earth's surface, so choice A is wrong. Neither scientist assumes that surface quakes are caused by trapped fluids, choice B; both state that such quakes are caused by normal fractures in the Earth's crust. Neither scientist discusses how deep-focus earthquakes are detected, so choice D is not an assumption made by either scientist.

20. G
Scientific Reasoning

Scientist 2 believes that deep-focus quakes are the result of slippage caused by phase changes. Scientist 2 would, therefore, not expect deep quakes to occur below 680 km where, according to the last sentence of the passage, "no phase changes are predicted." Recording a quake with an origin below that depth would send Scientist 2 back to the drawing board, or at least in search of deeper phase changes.

21. D
Basic Theory

The final sentence of Scientist 1's paragraph mentions that when fluids were injected into the ground at the Rocky Mountain Arsenal, the unintended result was "a series of shallow-focus earthquakes." The opening words *in fact* signal that this final sentence is meant to illustrate the previous sentence, which refers to experiments in which trapped fluids caused rock to fail at lower than normal shear stresses. The implication is that the quakes at the arsenal occurred because the fluid wastes lowered the shear stress failure point of the rock, choice D. Dehydration, choice A, is an important part of the hypothesis of Scientist 1 but is not specifically mentioned where Scientist 1 discusses the Rocky Mountain

Arsenal. The slab of calcium magnesium silicate, choice B, belongs in Scientist 2's paragraph. Choice C confuses the Rocky Mountain Arsenal incident with the deep-sea trenches that are mentioned in the previous two sentences.

22. H
Scientific Theory

Scientist 2 claims that the slippage involved in deep-focus quakes results from phase changes. To support this contention, she cites laboratory work that produced similar phase changes and slippage in a slab of calcium magnesium silicate. But neither scientist says that mantle rock is composed of calcium magnesium silicate. If the slippery slab is to serve as evidence for Scientist 2's theory, it must at least be similar to mantle rock, so choice H is correct. Choice F might help refute Scientist 1's viewpoint, but would not strengthen Scientist 2's theory. Choices G and J would tend to weaken Scientist 2's theory.

23. D
Scientific Reasoning

Phase changes are fundamental to the arguments of both scientists, and both agree that they occur deep beneath the Earth's surface, so you can eliminate choices choice A and B. The release of water from minerals is part of the explanation of Scientist 1, so choice C is out as well. Only choice D agrees with the logic of Scientist 2.

PASSAGE V

24. H
Figure

The one variable that changes is the amount of moisture. Choice G cannot be correct because Experiment 2 says that the researcher used models equivalent to the same mass as in Experiment 1. There is no evidence for choice F or J.

25. B
Scientific Reasoning

The moisture in Experiment 1 is 86%, and the moisture in Experiment 2 is 12%. If the moisture was changed to 50%, the collision rating would fall between the lines of the two experiments on the graphs. At 400,000 kg, the collision rating would be between 4.5 and 5.5.

26. G
Scientific Reasoning

The collision ratings for Experiment 1, with a high percentage of moisture in the atmosphere, were mostly lower than those in Experiment 2. Therefore, an increase in moisture would decrease the impact of a collision. Eliminate choices H and J. However, for asteroids over 700,000 kg, the lines on the graph meet—the presence of moisture loses its effect. Choice G is correct.

27. C
Figure

Feel free to draw on the graph (you can write on your test booklet during the ACT). Draw a line from 4 on the x-axis straight up. Draw a line from 4 on the y-axis straight across. Those two lines meet on the line for Experiment 1. The moisture level for Experiment 1 was 86%, so choice C is correct.

28. H
Figure

Again, it might help to draw on the graph to answer this question. Draw a vertical line up from 1 (100,000 kg) on the horizontal scale to see where it hits the curve representing Experiment 2. Then draw a horizontal line from this curve to the curve representing Experiment 1, and draw from that point down to the horizontal scale once again. You'll see that the size is closest to choice H, 270,000 kg.

29. B
Figure

To be minimally capable of regional destruction, an asteroid must have a collision rating of 4, so draw a horizontal line over from 4 on the vertical scale. If you do so, you'll see that size of an asteroid capable of such destruction goes from roughly 250,000 kg at a 12% moisture level to about 400,000 kg at an 86% moisture level. 400,000 is roughly 70% larger than 250,000, so choice B is the correct answer.

PASSAGE VI

30. H
Figure

Following HST-52 from right to left across the first figure (because the temperature is decreasing), conductivity increases and temperature decreases— just like the conductivity of a conductor—until 160 K, at which point HST-52's conductivity starts to decrease with decreasing temperature, like a semiconductor. With decreasing temperature, the sample undergoes a conductor to semiconductor transition, choice H.

31. B
Patterns

The plot for conductor-like behavior indicates that as the temperature increases, its conductivity decreases. Choices A and C describe the behavior of semiconductors, not conductors. Choice D is incorrect: if the conductivity of conductors were the same at all temperatures, the plot of conductivity vs. temperature for conductors would be a horizontal line.

32. H
Patterns

A material that has a semiconductor to conductor transition at 10 K will show a brief increase and then, starting at 10 K, a steady decrease as the temperature increases. H is the plot that shows this brief increase at low temperatures and then the decrease as the temperature rises.

33. D
Scientific Reasoning

The figure shows that HST-52 displays semiconductor behavior only up to about 150 K. Therefore, HST-52 will be usable as a semiconductor only at temperatures below about 150 K, choice D. Choice A is wrong because HST-52 is a semiconductor at certain temperatures, and B is wrong because HST-52 is not a semiconductor at all temperatures. The brittleness of HST-52 is never discussed in the passage, so choice C should be eliminated from the outset.

34. J
Patterns

You are looking for the temperature at which the downward slope for Sample HST-52 is the steepest. This is somewhat difficult to determine, but this much is clear: the slope does not begin to go down until the temperature rises above 160 K. Thus, the only answer that could make sense is choice J, 180 K.

PASSAGE VII

35. C
Figure

The graph shows no difference in the percentage of body covered in dark fur for outdoor temperatures less than or equal to 2°C, making choice C correct. The phrase "According to the graph" should remind you to extract data directly from the graph. Based on the passage alone, you might incorrectly assume that since the temperature drops over that month the percentage of body covered in dark fur would increase as in choice A. The graph shows, however, that this is only true for outdoor temperatures between 2°C and 7°C.

36. G
Scientific Reasoning

The key to this question is determining whether the cat in question is an outdoor or indoor cat. This cat goes outdoors a total of three hours per week, whereas an outdoor cat would spend at least six hours outdoors per week. Therefore, this cat is an indoor cat, and the percentage of dark fur on its body would remain just above 10%.

37. B
Figure

You can draw a line from 45% dark fur across to the solid line representing outdoor cats. If you draw a line from that intersection straight down to the *x*-axis, you will hit 3°C.

38. G
Patterns

If the cat grew dark fur over 30% of its body, it must have been an outdoor cat as defined in the passage, and according to the table, been exposed to temperature below 5°C (Statement I). To be an outdoor cat, a cat does not have to spend more time outdoors than indoors (Statement II), but it has to spend time outdoors for six consecutive days (Statement III).

39. C
Patterns

If a Siamese cat does not have dark fur over more than 10% of its body, then it must *either* be an indoor cat *or* live in an area where it is not regularly exposed to temperatures below 7°C.

40. H
Scientific Reasoning

Choice F is wrong because the indoor cats will not help us, since they don't go outside. Choice G is not a good choice because the outdoor cats of the original experiment cannot be used as a control group: the time they spent outside was not monitored—we only know that they spent more than one hour outside a day. Choice J is incorrect because the data already gathered only shows that outdoor cats turn darker in cold weather than indoor cats and doesn't provide any information about how varying the amount of time outdoors affects fur color. The correct answer is H: a completely new experiment would have to be set up.

Writing Test

MODEL ESSAY

Below is an example of what a high-scoring essay might look like. Notice the author states her position clearly in the introductory paragraph and supports that position with evidence in the following paragraphs. This essay also uses transitions, some advanced vocabulary, and an effective "hook" to draw in the reader.

While some people believe academics and athletics are not related, I think it is important to hold student athletes responsible for earning a minimum grade point average. We live in a sports-obsessed world, where professional athletes receive multi-million dollar contracts and where highly paid athletes are becoming younger and younger. For example, LeBron James, still in high school, obtained a lucrative endorsement deal with Nike and was a highly sought-after NBA draft pick. Sadly, when teams are recruiting young athletes, the last thing they often look at is grades. It is also unfortunate that, feeling the pressure from alumni and fans to have successful teams, schools are often willing to overlook poor grades in their high-performing athletes. With so much money and fame at stake, and with so many institutions turning a blind eye, is it any wonder that many young athletes will sacrifice anything to get ahead, even their academic performance? Requiring student athletes to maintain a minimum grade point average is important for several reasons.

As an educational institution, a school's number-one priority should be the education of its students. The school does its student athletes a disservice when it doesn't push them to do their best at academics and learn as much as they can. It is unfair to hold other students, who may not be lucky enough to have the same natural athletic abilities, to a higher academic standard than athletes, and devalues any effort they make to get good grades by showing them in effect that what really matters in life is how good you are at sports. Also, since sports place so many demands on students' time and energy, what incentive do athletes have to take the extra time to keep up with schoolwork if they aren't required to do so?

When a school does not require student athletes to achieve a specified grade point average, it sets them up for failure later in life. The hard truth is that there are not enough jobs in professional sports for every student athlete. If students don't get drafted to play sports once they finish school, or if they do get chosen and then get injured and can no longer play the sport as well or at all, they only will have their grades and grade point average to show for their time in school. If their grades aren't good, they will have difficulty finding a job and starting a new career.

I am not trying to say that high-school sports are bad, or that they don't offer benefits to students involved in them. Not only do those students get in shape, but they also get to be on a team and feel like a part of something important. I think, however, that when schools treat academics as secondary they are taking the focus off all the positive things students get by participating in sports. When students think their athletic performance is their best chance for a post-high school career, they no longer think about accomplishments like learning discipline and improving self-esteem. They only focus on winning at all costs. Schools encourage this by making athletic performance more important than academics. If students know that they have a high enough grade point average to succeed if their sport doesn't become their career, maybe sports can go back to being fun again.

Participating in sports is a great thing for students to do. It builds self-confidence, fosters school spirit, and teaches determination. However, high schoolers should be students first. Requiring student athletes to maintain a certain grade point average would ensure that students get the education they need whether or not they go on to play professional sports. Schools' number-one priority should be making sure that all of their students, whether they are athletes or not, have the education required to succeed in life.

You can evaluate your essay and the model essay based on the following criteria, covered in chapter 16:

- Does the author answer the question?
- Is the author's position clearly stated?
- Does the body of the essay support and develop the position taken?
- Are there at least three supporting paragraphs?
- Is the relevance of each supporting paragraph clear?
- Does the writer address the other side of the argument?
- Is the essay organized, with a clear introduction, middle, and end?
- Does the author start a new paragraph for each new idea?
- Is each sentence in a paragraph relevant to the point made in that paragraph?
- Are transitions clear?
- Is the essay easy to read? Is it engaging?
- Are sentences varied?
- Is vocabulary used effectively? Is college-level vocabulary used?

Practice Test Three

ACT Practice Test Three
ANSWER SHEET

ENGLISH TEST

1. Ⓐ Ⓑ Ⓒ Ⓓ   11. Ⓐ Ⓑ Ⓒ Ⓓ   21. Ⓐ Ⓑ Ⓒ Ⓓ   31. Ⓐ Ⓑ Ⓒ Ⓓ   41. Ⓐ Ⓑ Ⓒ Ⓓ   51. Ⓐ Ⓑ Ⓒ Ⓓ   61. Ⓐ Ⓑ Ⓒ Ⓓ   71. Ⓐ Ⓑ Ⓒ Ⓓ
2. Ⓕ Ⓖ Ⓗ Ⓙ   12. Ⓕ Ⓖ Ⓗ Ⓙ   22. Ⓕ Ⓖ Ⓗ Ⓙ   32. Ⓕ Ⓖ Ⓗ Ⓙ   42. Ⓕ Ⓖ Ⓗ Ⓙ   52. Ⓕ Ⓖ Ⓗ Ⓙ   62. Ⓕ Ⓖ Ⓗ Ⓙ   72. Ⓕ Ⓖ Ⓗ Ⓙ
3. Ⓐ Ⓑ Ⓒ Ⓓ   13. Ⓐ Ⓑ Ⓒ Ⓓ   23. Ⓐ Ⓑ Ⓒ Ⓓ   33. Ⓐ Ⓑ Ⓒ Ⓓ   43. Ⓐ Ⓑ Ⓒ Ⓓ   53. Ⓐ Ⓑ Ⓒ Ⓓ   63. Ⓐ Ⓑ Ⓒ Ⓓ   73. Ⓐ Ⓑ Ⓒ Ⓓ
4. Ⓕ Ⓖ Ⓗ Ⓙ   14. Ⓕ Ⓖ Ⓗ Ⓙ   24. Ⓕ Ⓖ Ⓗ Ⓙ   34. Ⓕ Ⓖ Ⓗ Ⓙ   44. Ⓕ Ⓖ Ⓗ Ⓙ   54. Ⓕ Ⓖ Ⓗ Ⓙ   64. Ⓕ Ⓖ Ⓗ Ⓙ   74. Ⓕ Ⓖ Ⓗ Ⓙ
5. Ⓐ Ⓑ Ⓒ Ⓓ   15. Ⓐ Ⓑ Ⓒ Ⓓ   25. Ⓐ Ⓑ Ⓒ Ⓓ   35. Ⓐ Ⓑ Ⓒ Ⓓ   45. Ⓐ Ⓑ Ⓒ Ⓓ   55. Ⓐ Ⓑ Ⓒ Ⓓ   65. Ⓐ Ⓑ Ⓒ Ⓓ   75. Ⓐ Ⓑ Ⓒ Ⓓ
6. Ⓕ Ⓖ Ⓗ Ⓙ   16. Ⓕ Ⓖ Ⓗ Ⓙ   26. Ⓕ Ⓖ Ⓗ Ⓙ   36. Ⓕ Ⓖ Ⓗ Ⓙ   46. Ⓕ Ⓖ Ⓗ Ⓙ   56. Ⓕ Ⓖ Ⓗ Ⓙ   66. Ⓕ Ⓖ Ⓗ Ⓙ
7. Ⓐ Ⓑ Ⓒ Ⓓ   17. Ⓐ Ⓑ Ⓒ Ⓓ   27. Ⓐ Ⓑ Ⓒ Ⓓ   37. Ⓐ Ⓑ Ⓒ Ⓓ   47. Ⓐ Ⓑ Ⓒ Ⓓ   57. Ⓐ Ⓑ Ⓒ Ⓓ   67. Ⓐ Ⓑ Ⓒ Ⓓ
8. Ⓕ Ⓖ Ⓗ Ⓙ   18. Ⓕ Ⓖ Ⓗ Ⓙ   28. Ⓕ Ⓖ Ⓗ Ⓙ   38. Ⓕ Ⓖ Ⓗ Ⓙ   48. Ⓕ Ⓖ Ⓗ Ⓙ   58. Ⓕ Ⓖ Ⓗ Ⓙ   68. Ⓕ Ⓖ Ⓗ Ⓙ
9. Ⓐ Ⓑ Ⓒ Ⓓ   19. Ⓐ Ⓑ Ⓒ Ⓓ   29. Ⓐ Ⓑ Ⓒ Ⓓ   39. Ⓐ Ⓑ Ⓒ Ⓓ   49. Ⓐ Ⓑ Ⓒ Ⓓ   59. Ⓐ Ⓑ Ⓒ Ⓓ   69. Ⓐ Ⓑ Ⓒ Ⓓ
10. Ⓕ Ⓖ Ⓗ Ⓙ   20. Ⓕ Ⓖ Ⓗ Ⓙ   30. Ⓕ Ⓖ Ⓗ Ⓙ   40. Ⓕ Ⓖ Ⓗ Ⓙ   50. Ⓕ Ⓖ Ⓗ Ⓙ   60. Ⓕ Ⓖ Ⓗ Ⓙ   70. Ⓕ Ⓖ Ⓗ Ⓙ

MATH TEST

1. Ⓐ Ⓑ Ⓒ Ⓓ Ⓔ   11. Ⓐ Ⓑ Ⓒ Ⓓ Ⓔ   21. Ⓐ Ⓑ Ⓒ Ⓓ Ⓔ   31. Ⓐ Ⓑ Ⓒ Ⓓ Ⓔ   41. Ⓐ Ⓑ Ⓒ Ⓓ Ⓔ   51. Ⓐ Ⓑ Ⓒ Ⓓ Ⓔ
2. Ⓕ Ⓖ Ⓗ Ⓙ Ⓚ   12. Ⓕ Ⓖ Ⓗ Ⓙ Ⓚ   22. Ⓕ Ⓖ Ⓗ Ⓙ Ⓚ   32. Ⓕ Ⓖ Ⓗ Ⓙ Ⓚ   42. Ⓕ Ⓖ Ⓗ Ⓙ Ⓚ   52. Ⓕ Ⓖ Ⓗ Ⓙ Ⓚ
3. Ⓐ Ⓑ Ⓒ Ⓓ Ⓔ   13. Ⓐ Ⓑ Ⓒ Ⓓ Ⓔ   23. Ⓐ Ⓑ Ⓒ Ⓓ Ⓔ   33. Ⓐ Ⓑ Ⓒ Ⓓ Ⓔ   43. Ⓐ Ⓑ Ⓒ Ⓓ Ⓔ   53. Ⓐ Ⓑ Ⓒ Ⓓ Ⓔ
4. Ⓕ Ⓖ Ⓗ Ⓙ Ⓚ   14. Ⓕ Ⓖ Ⓗ Ⓙ Ⓚ   24. Ⓕ Ⓖ Ⓗ Ⓙ Ⓚ   34. Ⓕ Ⓖ Ⓗ Ⓙ Ⓚ   44. Ⓕ Ⓖ Ⓗ Ⓙ Ⓚ   54. Ⓕ Ⓖ Ⓗ Ⓙ Ⓚ
5. Ⓐ Ⓑ Ⓒ Ⓓ Ⓔ   15. Ⓐ Ⓑ Ⓒ Ⓓ Ⓔ   25. Ⓐ Ⓑ Ⓒ Ⓓ Ⓔ   35. Ⓐ Ⓑ Ⓒ Ⓓ Ⓔ   45. Ⓐ Ⓑ Ⓒ Ⓓ Ⓔ   55. Ⓐ Ⓑ Ⓒ Ⓓ Ⓔ
6. Ⓕ Ⓖ Ⓗ Ⓙ Ⓚ   16. Ⓕ Ⓖ Ⓗ Ⓙ Ⓚ   26. Ⓕ Ⓖ Ⓗ Ⓙ Ⓚ   36. Ⓕ Ⓖ Ⓗ Ⓙ Ⓚ   46. Ⓕ Ⓖ Ⓗ Ⓙ Ⓚ   56. Ⓕ Ⓖ Ⓗ Ⓙ Ⓚ
7. Ⓐ Ⓑ Ⓒ Ⓓ Ⓔ   17. Ⓐ Ⓑ Ⓒ Ⓓ Ⓔ   27. Ⓐ Ⓑ Ⓒ Ⓓ Ⓔ   37. Ⓐ Ⓑ Ⓒ Ⓓ Ⓔ   47. Ⓐ Ⓑ Ⓒ Ⓓ Ⓔ   57. Ⓐ Ⓑ Ⓒ Ⓓ Ⓔ
8. Ⓕ Ⓖ Ⓗ Ⓙ Ⓚ   18. Ⓕ Ⓖ Ⓗ Ⓙ Ⓚ   28. Ⓕ Ⓖ Ⓗ Ⓙ Ⓚ   38. Ⓕ Ⓖ Ⓗ Ⓙ Ⓚ   48. Ⓕ Ⓖ Ⓗ Ⓙ Ⓚ   58. Ⓕ Ⓖ Ⓗ Ⓙ Ⓚ
9. Ⓐ Ⓑ Ⓒ Ⓓ Ⓔ   19. Ⓐ Ⓑ Ⓒ Ⓓ Ⓔ   29. Ⓐ Ⓑ Ⓒ Ⓓ Ⓔ   39. Ⓐ Ⓑ Ⓒ Ⓓ Ⓔ   49. Ⓐ Ⓑ Ⓒ Ⓓ Ⓔ   59. Ⓐ Ⓑ Ⓒ Ⓓ Ⓔ
10. Ⓕ Ⓖ Ⓗ Ⓙ Ⓚ   20. Ⓕ Ⓖ Ⓗ Ⓙ Ⓚ   30. Ⓕ Ⓖ Ⓗ Ⓙ Ⓚ   40. Ⓕ Ⓖ Ⓗ Ⓙ Ⓚ   50. Ⓕ Ⓖ Ⓗ Ⓙ Ⓚ   60. Ⓕ Ⓖ Ⓗ Ⓙ Ⓚ

READING TEST

1. Ⓐ Ⓑ Ⓒ Ⓓ   6. Ⓕ Ⓖ Ⓗ Ⓙ   11. Ⓐ Ⓑ Ⓒ Ⓓ   16. Ⓕ Ⓖ Ⓗ Ⓙ   21. Ⓐ Ⓑ Ⓒ Ⓓ   26. Ⓕ Ⓖ Ⓗ Ⓙ   31. Ⓐ Ⓑ Ⓒ Ⓓ   36. Ⓕ Ⓖ Ⓗ Ⓙ
2. Ⓕ Ⓖ Ⓗ Ⓙ   7. Ⓐ Ⓑ Ⓒ Ⓓ   12. Ⓕ Ⓖ Ⓗ Ⓙ   17. Ⓐ Ⓑ Ⓒ Ⓓ   22. Ⓕ Ⓖ Ⓗ Ⓙ   27. Ⓐ Ⓑ Ⓒ Ⓓ   32. Ⓕ Ⓖ Ⓗ Ⓙ   37. Ⓐ Ⓑ Ⓒ Ⓓ
3. Ⓐ Ⓑ Ⓒ Ⓓ   8. Ⓕ Ⓖ Ⓗ Ⓙ   13. Ⓐ Ⓑ Ⓒ Ⓓ   18. Ⓕ Ⓖ Ⓗ Ⓙ   23. Ⓐ Ⓑ Ⓒ Ⓓ   28. Ⓕ Ⓖ Ⓗ Ⓙ   33. Ⓐ Ⓑ Ⓒ Ⓓ   38. Ⓕ Ⓖ Ⓗ Ⓙ
4. Ⓕ Ⓖ Ⓗ Ⓙ   9. Ⓐ Ⓑ Ⓒ Ⓓ   14. Ⓕ Ⓖ Ⓗ Ⓙ   19. Ⓐ Ⓑ Ⓒ Ⓓ   24. Ⓕ Ⓖ Ⓗ Ⓙ   29. Ⓐ Ⓑ Ⓒ Ⓓ   34. Ⓕ Ⓖ Ⓗ Ⓙ   39. Ⓐ Ⓑ Ⓒ Ⓓ
5. Ⓐ Ⓑ Ⓒ Ⓓ   10. Ⓕ Ⓖ Ⓗ Ⓙ   15. Ⓐ Ⓑ Ⓒ Ⓓ   20. Ⓕ Ⓖ Ⓗ Ⓙ   25. Ⓐ Ⓑ Ⓒ Ⓓ   30. Ⓕ Ⓖ Ⓗ Ⓙ   35. Ⓐ Ⓑ Ⓒ Ⓓ   40. Ⓕ Ⓖ Ⓗ Ⓙ

SCIENCE TEST

1. Ⓐ Ⓑ Ⓒ Ⓓ   6. Ⓕ Ⓖ Ⓗ Ⓙ   11. Ⓐ Ⓑ Ⓒ Ⓓ   16. Ⓕ Ⓖ Ⓗ Ⓙ   21. Ⓐ Ⓑ Ⓒ Ⓓ   26. Ⓕ Ⓖ Ⓗ Ⓙ   31. Ⓐ Ⓑ Ⓒ Ⓓ   36. Ⓕ Ⓖ Ⓗ Ⓙ
2. Ⓕ Ⓖ Ⓗ Ⓙ   7. Ⓐ Ⓑ Ⓒ Ⓓ   12. Ⓕ Ⓖ Ⓗ Ⓙ   17. Ⓐ Ⓑ Ⓒ Ⓓ   22. Ⓕ Ⓖ Ⓗ Ⓙ   27. Ⓐ Ⓑ Ⓒ Ⓓ   32. Ⓕ Ⓖ Ⓗ Ⓙ   37. Ⓐ Ⓑ Ⓒ Ⓓ
3. Ⓐ Ⓑ Ⓒ Ⓓ   8. Ⓕ Ⓖ Ⓗ Ⓙ   13. Ⓐ Ⓑ Ⓒ Ⓓ   18. Ⓕ Ⓖ Ⓗ Ⓙ   23. Ⓐ Ⓑ Ⓒ Ⓓ   28. Ⓕ Ⓖ Ⓗ Ⓙ   33. Ⓐ Ⓑ Ⓒ Ⓓ   38. Ⓕ Ⓖ Ⓗ Ⓙ
4. Ⓕ Ⓖ Ⓗ Ⓙ   9. Ⓐ Ⓑ Ⓒ Ⓓ   14. Ⓕ Ⓖ Ⓗ Ⓙ   19. Ⓐ Ⓑ Ⓒ Ⓓ   24. Ⓕ Ⓖ Ⓗ Ⓙ   29. Ⓐ Ⓑ Ⓒ Ⓓ   34. Ⓕ Ⓖ Ⓗ Ⓙ   39. Ⓐ Ⓑ Ⓒ Ⓓ
5. Ⓐ Ⓑ Ⓒ Ⓓ   10. Ⓕ Ⓖ Ⓗ Ⓙ   15. Ⓐ Ⓑ Ⓒ Ⓓ   20. Ⓕ Ⓖ Ⓗ Ⓙ   25. Ⓐ Ⓑ Ⓒ Ⓓ   30. Ⓕ Ⓖ Ⓗ Ⓙ   35. Ⓐ Ⓑ Ⓒ Ⓓ   40. Ⓕ Ⓖ Ⓗ Ⓙ

ENGLISH TEST

45 Minutes—75 Questions

Directions: In the following five passages, certain words and phrases are underlined and numbered. In the right-hand column are alternatives for each underlined portion. Select the one that best conveys the idea, creates the most grammatically correct sentence, or is the most consistent with the style and tone of the passage. If you decide that the original version is best, select NO CHANGE. You may also find questions that ask about the entire passage or a section of the passage. These questions will correspond to small numbered boxes in the text. For these questions, decide which choice best accomplishes the purpose set out in the question stem. After you've selected the best choice, fill in the corresponding oval in your Answer Grid. For some questions, you'll need to read the context in order to answer correctly. Be sure to read until you have enough information to determine the correct answer choice.

You will also find questions about a section of the passage or about the passage as a whole. These questions do not refer to an underlined portion of the passage, but rather are identified by a number or numbers in a box.

For each question, choose the alternative you consider best and fill in the corresponding oval on your answer document. Read each passage through once before you begin to answer the questions that accompany it. For many of the questions, you must read several sentences beyond the question to determine the answer. Be sure that you have read enough ahead each time you choose an alternative.

Passage I

A SWIMMING CHANGE

[1]

Until three years ago, I had never considered myself to be athletically talented. I have never been able to hit, catch, throw, or kick a ball with any degree of confidence or accuracy. For years, physical education being often the worst

1. **A.** NO CHANGE
   B. education, was
   C. education was
   D. education,

part of the school day for me. Units on tennis, touch football, volleyball, and basketball were torturous. I not only dreaded fumbling a pass, so I also feared being hit in the face by a ball.

2. **F.** NO CHANGE
   G. and
   H. but
   J. though

GO ON TO THE NEXT PAGE

However, at the beginning of my freshman year of high school, my attitude toward sports changed.

[2]

Somehow, my good friend Gretchen convinced me to join <u>our schools</u> swim team.
3

<u>Knowing that I enjoyed swimming, over the</u>
4
<u>course of two summers, it was with Gretchen</u>
4
<u>that I practically had lived at the pool.</u> My
4

mother had <u>insisted</u> that I take swimming
5
lessons every summer since I was seven, so I was entirely comfortable in the water. I was also eager to start my high school experience with a new challenge and a new way to think of myself.

[3]

Of course, I had no idea what I was getting into when Gretchen and I showed up for the first day of practice. The team was made up of twenty

3. A. NO CHANGE
   B. our schools'
   C. our school's
   D. ours school

4. F. NO CHANGE
   G. Because we had spent two summers practically living at the pool, it was Gretchen who knew that swimming was enjoyed by me.
   H. Having practically lived at the pool over two summers, the two of us, Gretchen knew it was swimming that I enjoyed.
   J. Gretchen knew I enjoyed swimming, as we had spent two summers practically living at the pool.

5. Of the four choices, which is the only one that does NOT indicate that the narrator's mother decided that the narrator must take swimming lessons?
   A. NO CHANGE
   B. suggested
   C. required
   D. demanded

young women, most of these swimmers had
                    6

been participating in the community swim team

for years. I couldn't do a flip turn at the end of

of the lane without getting water up my nose. In

contrast, most of the other swimmers, who had
                                           7

been swimming competitively, since elementary
                    7

school, were able to gracefully somersault and
    7

begin the next lap. By the end of the first hour

of practice, I was exhausted and waterlogged.

[4]

However, I had no intention of giving up,
                                    8

which would mean quitting. I came back the
        8

next day and the next day for practice. Things

begun to get serious in the second week, when
   9

we started the regular schedule of four early

morning and five afternoon practices. Our

coach, whom had led the team to several state
        10

championships, demanded dedication from

everyone on the team. The hard work eventually
                                         11

paid off. By the end of the first month, I had
    11

discovered that I was good at the butterfly,

6. F. NO CHANGE
    G. women, the majority of them
    H. women most of them
    J. women, most of whom

7. A. NO CHANGE
    B. had been swimming competitively
        since elementary school,
    C. had been swimming, competitively
        since elementary school,
    D. had been swimming competitively
        since elementary school

8. F. NO CHANGE
    G. giving up and resigning myself to
        failure.
    H. giving up and quitting what I had
        set out to do.
    J. giving up.

9. A. NO CHANGE
    B. had been begun
    C. had began
    D. began

10. F. NO CHANGE
     G. for whom
     H. who
     J. which

11. A. NO CHANGE
     B. eventually paid off, so, as a result
     C. paid off eventually, however, by
     D. paid off, eventually, by

GO ON TO THE NEXT PAGE

a relatively new stroke that was first introduced
                    12

in the 1930s. I rarely won individual races, but I
        12

made a solid member of our team's medley relay.
                                         13

[5]

After that intimidating first season, I

continued swimming. I even will have earned
                            14

a varsity letter last year. Now I'm hoping to earn

a spot in the state competition my senior year. [15]

12. Assuming each of the following creates a true statement, which provides the information most relevant to the narrator's experience on the swim team?

F. NO CHANGE

G. a difficult stroke that interested few other members of our team.

H. which is faster than the backstroke but somewhat slower than the crawl.

J. which is still sometimes called the dolphin because it incorporates a two-stroke dolphin kick.

13. A. NO CHANGE

B. team's medley relay (it consists of four swimmers).

C. team's medley relay, which the person swimming backstroke always begins.

D. team.

14. F. NO CHANGE

G. would have earned

H. earned

J. earn

15. If inserted here, which of the following would be the most appropriate sentence to conclude the essay?

A. My coach continues to schedule demanding practices, but I have come to enjoy the early morning swims.

B. For someone who thought she didn't have any athletic talent, I have come a long way.

C. Gretchen is also still on the team, but she does not swim the medley relay.

D. I've always enjoyed swimming, so I'm not all that surprised by my success as an athlete.

GO ON TO THE NEXT PAGE

Passage II

EXPLORING DUBUQUE'S AQUARIUM

[1]

One lazy day last summer, my parents decided that my younger sister and I needed a break from our vacation from academics. They took us to the National Mississippi River Museum and Aquarium in Dubuque, Iowa. I was prepared to be bored by this family educational trip. However, from the first moment I walked through the museum's doors, I was captivated;
<u>16</u>
<u>by</u> all that there was to learn about life in the
16
Mississippi.

16. F. NO CHANGE
    G. captivated, by
    H. captivated by,
    J. captivated by

[2]

[1] A large tank stocked with fish and turtles <u>was there</u> to greet us as we walked into
17
the main hall. [2] There were also animals I had never before glimpsed, such as a fish called the long-nosed gar. [3] I was amazed by this fish in particular. [4] Its long, tubular shape and distinctive rod-shaped <u>nose that</u> made it appear like
18
something that lived in the dark depths of the ocean. [5] This first of five freshwater aquariums

17. A. NO CHANGE
    B. is there
    C. are there
    D. were there

18. F. NO CHANGE
    G. nose, which
    H. nose, and this
    J. nose

GO ON TO THE NEXT PAGE

offered a close-up view of <u>familiar animals that I</u>
                                              19

<u>had seen before,</u> such as ducks. [20]
       19

[3]

    In the next aquarium, I <u>see</u> a catfish bigger
                                                  21
than I had ever imagined this species could
be. According to the posted information, this
specimen weighed more than 100 pounds. With
its long whiskers and slow, lazy movements, this
catfish looked like the grandfather of all the
other fish in the tank.

[4]

    <u>I couldn't decide which I liked better, the</u>
                                                      22
<u>catfish or the long-nosed gar.</u> The next floor-to-
         22
ceiling tank, which represented the ecosystem
of the Mississippi bayou, held an animal I had
never seen: an alligator. At first, I had a hard
time spotting the creature—it blended in

19. A. NO CHANGE
    B. animals that were familiar sights to
       me,
    C. familiar animals to which I was no
       stranger,
    D. familiar animals,

20. To make paragraph 2 coherent and logical,
the best placement of sentence 5 is:
    F. where it is now.
    G. before sentence 1.
    H. after sentence 1.
    J. after sentence 2.

21. A. NO CHANGE
    B. had been seeing
    C. saw
    D. spot

22. Which sentence most effectively
connects this paragraph to the
preceding paragraph?
    F. NO CHANGE
    G. Although the catfish was impres-
       sive, it was not the biggest animal
       on display in the museum.
    H. After seeing the catfish, I was
       interested in exhibits that were a bit
       more hands-on.
    J. Until my visit to the museum, I had
       never really considered what the
       Mississippi River was like south of
       my home.

GO ON TO THE NEXT PAGE >

almost completely with a half-submerged log. [23]

Suddenly, though, it <u>slides into the water and</u>
                                          24
<u>aims</u> itself right at the glass separating me from
24
its ferocious claws and skin-tearing teeth. I had

a <u>slightly moment of</u> panic before I remembered
           25
that, try as it might, this alligator would never

successfully hunt tourists like me. As <u>much</u>
                                          26
of the on-lookers squealed in delight as the

alligator moved through the tank, I noticed

his companion. Far off in a corner slept an

enormous snapping turtle. I could imagine no

better roommate for the alligator than this hook-

beaked turtle with rough ridges running along

its shell.

23. At this point, the writer is considering removing the following phrase:

it blended in almost completely with a half-submerged log.

The primary effect of removing this phrase would be:

A. a smoother transition between sentences.

B. a greater contrast between images.

C. the loss of descriptive information.

D. an increased level of suspense.

24. F. NO CHANGE

G. slides into the water to aim

H. slid into the water and aiming

J. slid into the water and aimed

25. A. NO CHANGE

B. momentarily slight

C. moment of slight

D. momentarily of slight

26. F. NO CHANGE

G. a large amount

H. the many

J. many

GO ON TO THE NEXT PAGE ⟹

[5]

Despite my initial expectations, I happily spent the entire day soaking up information about creatures that live in the Mississippi River. In one section of the museum, I held a crayfish. [27] Later, I had the opportunity to touch the cool, sleek skin of a stingray, which can be found where the Mississippi empties into the Gulf of Mexico.

[6]

After seeing <u>all, I could inside the museum,</u>
                        28
I wandered outside, only to find even more

exhibits. <u>Having just enough time, it was that I</u>
                                                    29
<u>was able</u> to see the otters and watch a riverboat
    29
launching, but it was closing time before I was able to see the most impressive thing the museum had to offer. A football-field-sized steamboat from the 1930s is open to <u>tourists. And operates</u> as a
                                              30
"Boat and Breakfast" that hosts overnight guests. I'm hoping that my family will plan another educational trip to Dubuque soon so I can experience life on a steamboat.

27. The writer would like to insert a sentence describing the appearance of the crayfish at this point. Which sentence would best accomplish the writer's goal?

A. Also known as crawdads, crayfish are close relatives of the lobsters that live in freshwater.

B. At an average length of about three inches, the crayfish looks like a miniature lobster, complete with small but effective front pincers.

C. Although they are found throughout the United States, crayfish populations are densest in Kentucky and Mississippi.

D. At first, I was a bit nervous to touch the small creature, but then I relaxed and enjoyed the opportunity to look at it so closely.

28. F. NO CHANGE
    G. all I could inside the museum,
    H. all, I could inside the museum
    J. all I could inside the museum

29. A. NO CHANGE
    B. It was that I had just enough time, so I was able
    C. Having just enough time, it was possible
    D. I had just enough time

30. F. NO CHANGE
    G. tourists and that operates
    H. tourists, it operates
    J. tourists and operates

GO ON TO THE NEXT PAGE ⇒

Passage III

THE MYSTERY DINER

> The paragraphs in this essay may or may not follow the most logical order. Each paragraph is numbered, and question 45 will ask you to determine the best placement of paragraph 6.

[1]

Although secret identities and elaborate disguises are typically associated with the world of spies and villains, it has other uses. For six years,
$\underline{\text{31}}$

Ruth Reichl the restaurant critic for the *New*
$\overline{\text{32}}$
York Times, used aliases and costumes as a
$\overline{\text{32}}$
regular part of her job.

[2]

Dining is big business in New York City, from the neighborhood noodle shops and diners to the upscale steak houses and four-star French restaurants. [33] Many of the more than one million people who read the *Times* each day

31. A. NO CHANGE
    B. it does have
    C. they do have
    D. and they have

32. F. NO CHANGE
    G. Reichl, the restaurant critic, for the *New York Times*,
    H. Reichl, the restaurant critic for the *New York Times*,
    J. Reichl the restaurant critic for the *New York Times*

33. Should the following sentence be inserted into the passage at this point?

    The legendary French restaurant Le Bernardin received a four-star rating from the *Times* shortly after opening in 1986, an honor it has maintained ever since.

    A. Yes, because the added sentence emphasizes how important a positive review from the *Times* can be.
    B. Yes, because the specific information helps the reader develop a clearer picture of the type of restaurant reviewed by the *Times*.
    C. No, because it is unclear whether Reichl was responsible for reviewing this specific restaurant.
    D. No, because the specific information about one restaurant leads the reader away from the main topic of the essay.

GO ON TO THE NEXT PAGE ⟹

look to it for advice on where to eat. A positive
———
34

review from the *Times* could have brought a
                              ———————————
                                   35

restaurant unimagined success and month-long

waiting lists for reservations. A negative review,

on the other hand, can undermine a restaurant's

popularity and seriously cut into its profits.

Obviously, restaurant owners and workers have
          ————————————————————————
                      36

a lot at stake when the restaurant critic for the

Times walks in the door. Waiters and chefs often

pull out all of the stops to impress the writer

that the meal can make or break a restaurant.
————
37

[3]

Reichl was acutely aware that she received
                                   ———————————
                                        38

special treatment once restaurant staff recognized
———————————————
     38

her. She would be graciously greeted and led to

the best table in the restaurant, offered dishes

prepared specially by the head chef, and given

multiple courses of amazing desserts. In other

words, the dining experience of the restaurant

critic was nothing like that of the commonly
                                    ——————————
                                       39

ordinary person walking in from the street.
————————
   39

34. **F.** NO CHANGE
    G. look with
    H. look by
    J. looking to

35. **A.** NO CHANGE
    B. can bring
    C. will have brought
    D. will be bringing

36. **F.** NO CHANGE
    G. restaurant owners and workers;
    H. restaurant, owners and workers
    J. restaurant owners, and workers

37. **A.** NO CHANGE
    B. who's
    C. whose
    D. which

38. **F.** NO CHANGE
    G. special treatment was received by
       her
    H. she was the recipient of special
       treatment
    J. she was in the position of receiving
       special treatment

39. **A.** NO CHANGE
    B. common, representative, and
       average
    C. typical
    D. extravagant

GO ON TO THE NEXT PAGE ⟩

[4]

To remedy this, <u>Reichl decided a solution</u>
40

<u>would be to become,</u> for short periods of time,
40

someone else. <u>Transforming herself into different</u>
41

<u>personas, Reichl used wigs, special makeup, and</u>
41

<u>carefully selected clothing,</u> such as an attractive
41

blonde named Chloe, a redhead named Brenda,

and an older woman named Betty. 42

[5]

Sometimes, Reichl developed a different view
about the quality when she was not treated like

40.　F.　NO CHANGE
　　G.　she created a solution to the problem by becoming
　　H.　Reichl decided to become
　　J.　Reichl found a way to fix the problem, which involved becoming

41.　A.　NO CHANGE
　　B.　With wigs, special makeup, and carefully selected clothing, Reichl transformed herself into different personas,
　　C.　Transformed with wigs, special makeup, and carefully selected clothing, Reichl's different personas,
　　D.　Reichl used wigs, special makeup, and carefully selected clothing, that transformed herself into different personas,

42.　Which of the following true statements would make the most effective and logical conclusion for paragraph 4?
　　F.　Reichl found that she could quickly disguise herself as Betty, but it took more time to become Chloe.
　　G.　Her true identity hidden, Reichl would then dine at a restaurant she was currently evaluating.
　　H.　After six years at the *Times*, Reichl moved on to become the editor of *Gourmet* magazine.
　　J.　The former restaurant critic for the *Times* did not always agree with Reichl's methods or her selection of restaurants to review.

a very important person of a restaurant. Indeed,
                        _____
                            43

the difference between the treatment she received

as herself and as one of her characters was

occasionally so great that Reichl would revise

her initial impression of a restaurant and write

a more negative review. 44

[6]

By becoming an average customer, Reichl

encouraged even the most expensive and popular

restaurants to improve how they treated all of

their customers. After all, waiters could never

be certain when they were serving the powerful

restaurant critic for the *New York Times*.

43. For the sake of logic and coherence, the underlined portion should be placed:

A. where it is now.

B. after the word *developed*.

C. after the word *view*.

D. after the word *quality*.

44. Would deleting the word *occasionally* from the previous sentence change the meaning of the sentence?

F. Yes, because without this word, the reader would not understand that Reichl had different experiences when she dined in disguise.

G. Yes, because without this word, the reader would think that Reichl always changed her impression of restaurants when she received different treatment because she was not recognized.

H. No, because this word repeats an idea that is already presented in the sentence.

J. No, because this word is used only to show emphasis, and it does not contribute to the meaning of the sentence.

Question 45 asks about
the preceding passage as a whole.

---

45. To make the passage flow logically and smoothly, the best place for paragraph 6 is:

A. where it is now.

B. after paragraph 1.

C. after paragraph 3.

D. after paragraph 4.

GO ON TO THE NEXT PAGE

Passage IV

THE BENEFITS OF A SQUARE-FOOT GARDEN

[1]

[1] I used to start every spring with great hopes for my backyard vegetable garden. [2] After the last freeze in late March or early April, I devoted an entire weekend to preparing the soil in the garden. [3] I thinned out the rows that had too many plants and spent hours tugging out each weed that threatened to rob my little plants of the nutrients they needed to thrive. [4] Once spring truly arrived, I marked out my rows and scattered the packets of seeds that I hoped,
46
would develop into prize-winning vegetables.
46

[5] In the first few weeks of the season, I was almost always in the garden. 47

[2]

Despite my best intentions, my garden never lived up to the vision I had for it. After I had devoted several weekends to watering and weeding, the garden always started to become more of a burden less of a hobby. By July, the
48
garden was usually in disarray, and I didn't have

46. F. NO CHANGE
    G. hoped, would,
    H. hoped would,
    J. hoped would

47. To make paragraph 1 more logical and coherent, sentence 3 should be placed:
    A. where it is now.
    B. before sentence 1.
    C. after sentence 1.
    D. after sentence 4.

48. F. NO CHANGE
    G. burden:
    H. burden and
    J. burden, but,

GO ON TO THE NEXT PAGE

the energy or time to save it. July and August are
49

always the hottest parts of the year.
49

[3]

This past year, however, my garden was
50

finally the success I had imagined it could be.

Instead of planning the traditional garden of

closely planted rows that is modeled after large-
51

scale farming, I tried a new technique. My new
51

approach is called square-foot gardening.

[4]

A square-foot garden is designed for efficiency.
52

49. A. NO CHANGE

B. The hottest months are July and
August.

C. (July, along with August, provides
the hottest temperatures of the
year.)

D. OMIT the underlined portion.

50. Of the following choices, which would
be the LEAST acceptable substitution
for the underlined word?

F. on the other hand

G. indeed

H. though

J. in contrast

51. A. NO CHANGE

B. rows, which is modeled after large-
scale farming,

C. rows, which is based on the techniques for large-scale farming,

D. rows,

52. Which sentence most effectively links
the topic of paragraph 3 to the topic of
paragraph 4?

F. NO CHANGE

G. The technique of square-foot
gardening was pioneered by Mel
Bartholomew.

H. One of the benefits of a square-foot
garden is that it is less expensive to
maintain than a traditional garden.

J. My neighbor, who always has
a beautiful garden, introduced
me to the concept of square-foot
gardening, and I have been grateful
ever since.

GO ON TO THE NEXT PAGE ⇒

In a traditionally garden, you scatter a packet of
53

seeds down a row. When the plants emerge, they
54
spend hours thinning each row by pulling out at
54
least half of what was planted. In a square-foot

garden, you plant each seed individually, so there

is never a need for thinning in the garden. You
55
create the garden plan 1 square foot at a time,

until you have a block of 16 squares. Sturdy

pieces of lumber which could make effective
56
borders for each square. Walking paths that are

at least 2 feet wide separate each 16-square-

foot garden. The design is clean and simple, and

it eliminates the problem of getting to the rows

in the middle of a large garden. In fact, you can
57
do all the weeding, watering, and harvesting
57
from the walking paths.

[5]

In addition to being easier to weed and

water, a square-foot garden takes up much less

space than a regular garden. I was able to grow

an increased number of more vegetables in two
58
square-foot gardens, which took up a total of

32 square feet, than I ever had grown in my

traditional garden, which took up 84 square feet.

Preparing the soil for the smaller space only

53. A. NO CHANGE
B. conventionally
C. traditional
D. tradition

54. F. NO CHANGE
G. he spends
H. people spend
J. you spend

55. A. NO CHANGE
B. out the garden
C. in that garden
D. OMIT the underlined portion.

56. F. NO CHANGE
G. that make
H. make
J. OMIT the underlined portion.

57. A. NO CHANGE
B. you could have done
C. one can do
D. one is able to do

58. F. NO CHANGE
G. a larger quantity of more
H. an increased, bigger quantity
J. more

GO ON TO THE NEXT PAGE

required a few hours instead of a whole weekend. There was so much less weeding to do that the task never felt overwhelming. One season of using the square garden techniques <u>were all</u>
59
it took for me to convert to a completely new outlook on backyard gardening.

59. A. NO CHANGE
B. were just what
C. was all
D. could be

Question 60 asks about
the preceding passage as a whole.

---

60. If the writer had intended to write an essay detailing how to plan, prepare, and care for a square garden, would this essay meet the writer's goal?

F. No, because the writer relies on generalities rather than specifics when describing her square garden.

G. No, because the writer focuses on comparing two different types of gardens instead of explaining how to begin and care for one type of garden.

H. Yes, because the writer states specific measurements for her square garden.

J. Yes, because the writer maintains that square gardens are superior to traditional gardens.

GO ON TO THE NEXT PAGE

Passage V

THE IMPORTANCE OF MAINTAINING YOUR CAR

[1]

Most new car owners glance briefly at the owner's manual before depositing it in the glove compartment of their new automobile. Owners may dig out their manuals when something goes wrong, such as a flat tire or a flashing engine light but few car owners take the time to learn the basics about maintaining their new purchase. This is truly unfortunate, as a few simple and

routine steps improves the long-term performance of an automobile and decreases the possibility of a traffic accident.

[2]

One of the easiest and most overlooked maintenance steps is caring for a car's wiper blades. Most people don't notice a problem until the blades fail to clear the windshield during a rainstorm or heavy snowfall. When a driver's

vision being obscured, an accident is more likely

61. A. NO CHANGE
    B. wrong; such as a flat tire or a flashing engine light
    C. wrong, such as a flat tire, or a flashing engine light
    D. wrong, such as a flat tire or a flashing engine light,

62. F. NO CHANGE
    G. improve the long-term performance of an automobile and decreases
    H. improve the long-term performance of an automobile and decrease
    J. improves the long-term performance of an automobile and decrease

63. A. NO CHANGE
    B. notice a problem that causes trouble
    C. recognize that their wiper blades are the source of a problem
    D. realize that their blades are failing and will become a problem

64. F. NO CHANGE
    G. vision, has been
    H. vision is
    J. vision,

GO ON TO THE NEXT PAGE ⟹

to happen. Replacing the <u>set</u> blades at a time
65

each year greatly reduces this risk. In addition,
frequently refilling the windshield washer fluid
reservoir guarantees that there will always be
enough fluid to wash away grime that accumu-
lates on the windshield.

[3]

Much of car maintenance focuses on
preventing problems before they occur. For
example, checking the levels of coolant, oil, brake
fluid, and transmission fluid can avert serious
malfunctions. <u>In general,</u> these fluids should be
66
checked monthly and refilled whenever the need
is indicated.

[4]

<u>Cars are becoming more sophisticated every</u>
67
<u>year, but car owners without any expertise in</u>
67
<u>mechanics can still perform much of the basic</u>
67
<u>upkeep of their vehicle.</u> You should change the
67
oil in most cars every 3,000 to 7,000 miles. This

65. The underlined word would be most
logically placed:

A. where it is now.

B. before the word *time.*

C. before the word *year.*

D. before the word *risk.*

66. F. NO CHANGE

G. For generally,

H. With usual

J. By typically,

67. Which sentence is the most effective
way to begin paragraph 4?

A. NO CHANGE

B. Changing the oil and oil filter
regularly is another key to keeping
your car's engine performing at its
best.

C. An entire industry now focuses
on providing regular car maintenance, such as changing the oil and
rotating the tires.

D. Even if you haven't read your car
owner's manual, you probably know
that your car needs a tune-up every
so often.

GO ON TO THE NEXT PAGE

task requires a willingness to get a bit dirty, <u>so</u>
₆₈
you don't have to be a mechanic to change a car's
oil. Before you get started, read the oil change

<u>section, in your owner's manual</u> and collect all
₆₉

of the tools you will need. You <u>won't need many</u>
₇₀
<u>tools, but you will definitely need a car jack.</u>
₇₀
Never get under a car that is supported only by

car <u>jacks: you</u> do not want to risk being crushed
₇₁
by a car. After you've secured the car, changing
the oil is as straightforward as sliding under
the car with a drain pan to catch the oil and a
wrench to loosen the oil drain plug. Then follow
the instructions for changing the oil filter, and

68. F. NO CHANGE
    G. but
    H. for
    J. because

69. A. NO CHANGE
    B. section, in your owner's manual,
    C. section in your owner's manual;
    D. section in your owner's manual,

70. In paragraph 4, the writer wants to
    provide an explanation of how to
    change the oil in an automobile. Which
    of the following would most logically fit
    the writer's intention for this paragraph?

    F. NO CHANGE
    G. need to get under the car to open
       the oil drain, so use car jacks to
       raise the car and sturdy car jack
       stands to support it.
    H. may find it helpful to watch
       someone else change the oil before
       you try to perform the job on your
       own.
    J. only need to follow a few basic steps
       in order to successfully change your
       car's oil.

71. A. NO CHANGE
    B. jacks, you
    C. jacks you
    D. jacks you,

GO ON TO THE NEXT PAGE ⟹

fill the oil pan to the recommended level with

fresh oil. 72

[5]

These simple steps to maintaining the health of a car can be done by just about anyone. However, successfully changing a car's oil does not turn a car owner into a repair expert. More complicated tasks, such as adjusting a carburetor or installing

new brake pads, should be performed by a 73 qualified auto mechanic. 73

72. Paragraph 4 of the essay uses the second person (*you*, *your*). Revising this paragraph to remove the second-person pronouns would have the primary effect of:

   F. disrupting the logical flow of the essay.

   G. making paragraph 4 more consistent with the voice used in the rest of the essay.

   H. underscoring the direct advice given to the reader.

   J. lightening the essay's formal tone.

73. A. NO CHANGE

   B. professionally completed by a qualified

   C. performed by a certifiably qualified

   D. undertaken by qualifying

GO ON TO THE NEXT PAGE

Questions 74–75 ask about the preceding passage as a whole.

74. After reading back through the essay, the writer decided that the following sentence contains important information:

> The owner's manual provides instructions on how to test the levels of these different fluids used to lubricate and cool the engine.

Logically, this sentence should be placed:

F. after the last sentence of paragraph 2.

G. before the first sentence of paragraph 3.

H. after the last sentence of paragraph 3.

J. after the last sentence of paragraph 4.

75. If the writer had intended to write an essay persuading readers to familiarize themselves with the basic safety features and maintenance needs of their cars, would this essay meet the writer's goal?

A. Yes, because the essay repeatedly encourages readers to refer to the owner's manual for their car.

B. Yes, because the essay lists many basic maintenance steps that owners can independently accomplish.

C. No, because the essay encourages readers to go beyond learning about the features of their car and actually perform some of the basic upkeep.

D. No, because the essay does not discuss a car's safety features in any detail.

MATH TEST

60 Minutes—60 Questions

Directions: Solve each of the following problems, select the correct answer, and then fill in the corresponding oval on your Answer Grid.

Don't linger over problems that are too time-consuming. Do as many as you can, then come back to the others in the time permitted.

You may use a calculator on this test. Some questions, however, may be easier to answer without the use of a calculator.

Note: Unless the question says otherwise, assume all of the following:

1. Illustrative figures are *not* necessarily drawn to scale.

2. All geometric figures lie in a plane.

3. The term *line* indicates a straight line.

4. The term *average* indicates arithmetic mean.

---

1. Tanya used $3\frac{3}{8}$ yards of fabric to make her dress, and she used $1\frac{1}{3}$ yards of fabric to make her jacket. What was the total amount, in yards, that Tanya used for the complete outfit of dress and jacket?

    A. $4\frac{1}{8}$

    B. $4\frac{1}{6}$

    C. $4\frac{4}{11}$

    D. $4\frac{1}{2}$

    E. $4\frac{17}{24}$

2. $5x^3y^5 \times 6y^2 \times 2xy$ is equivalent to:

    F. $13x^3y^7$

    G. $13x^4y^8$

    H. $60x^3y^7$

    J. $60x^3y^{10}$

    K. $60x^4y^8$

DO YOUR FIGURING HERE.

GO ON TO THE NEXT PAGE

3. Brandon puts 6% of his $36,000 yearly salary into savings, in 12 equal monthly install-ments. Jacqui deposits $200 every month into savings. At the end of one full year, what is the difference, in dollars, between the amount of money that Jacqui saved and the amount of money that Brandon saved?

A.   20

B.   24

C.   240

D. 1,960

E. 2,800

4. Mikhail has received bowling scores of 190, 200, 145, and 180 so far in the state bowling tournament. What score must he receive on the fifth game to earn an average score of 180 for his five games?

F. 179

G. 180

H. 185

J. 200

K. Mikhail cannot earn an average of 180.

5. For steel to be considered stainless steel, it must have a minimum of 10.5% chromium in the metal alloy. If there are 262.5 pounds of chromium available, what is the maximum amount of stainless steel, in pounds, that can be manufactured?

A. 27.56

B. 252

C. 262.5

D. 2,500

E. 25,000

DO YOUR FIGURING HERE.

GO ON TO THE NEXT PAGE

6. A homeowner wants to put a wallpaper border on the top edge of all the walls of his kitchen. The kitchen measures 6.5 meters by 4 meters. What is the required length, in meters, of the border?

   F. 8
   G. 10.5
   H. 13
   J. 21
   K. 26

7. Which expression below is equivalent to $w(x - (y + z))$?

   A. $wx - wy - wz$
   B. $wx - wy + wz$
   C. $wx - y + z$
   D. $wx - y - z$
   E. $wxy + wxz$

8. Solve for n: $6n - 4 = 3n + 24$

   F. 28
   G. $\dfrac{28}{3}$
   H. $\dfrac{28}{9}$
   J. $\dfrac{20}{9}$
   K. $\dfrac{3}{28}$

DO YOUR FIGURING HERE.

GO ON TO THE NEXT PAGE

9. What two numbers should be placed in the blanks below so that the difference between successive entries is the same?

26, _____, _____, 53

A. 36, 43

B. 35, 44

C. 34, 45

D. 33, 46

E. 30, 49

DO YOUR FIGURING HERE.

10. What is the real number value of $m^3 + \sqrt{12m}$ when $5m^2 = 45$?

F. 5

G. 27

H. 33

J. 38.09

K. 739.39

11. The radius of a sphere is $3\frac{3}{5}$ meters. What is the volume of the sphere, to the nearest cubic meter? Use the formula $V = \frac{4}{3}\pi r^3$.

A. 42

B. 45

C. 157

D. 195

E. 3,429

GO ON TO THE NEXT PAGE ⟹

12. There are 10 peanuts, 6 cashews, and 8 almonds in a bag of mixed nuts. If a nut is chosen at random from the bag, what is the probability that the nut is NOT a peanut?

DO YOUR FIGURING HERE.

F. $\dfrac{5}{12}$

G. $\dfrac{7}{12}$

H. $\dfrac{5}{7}$

J. 10

K. 14

13. The number of people in the electronics store is shown in the matrix below.

Adolescents	Adults	Senior Citizens
[75	100	30]

The ratio of people from each age group who will purchase a product to the number of people in that age group in the store is shown in the following matrix:

Adolescents		0.20	
Adults	[	0.35	]
Senior Citizens		0.10	

Based on the matrices, how many people will make purchases?

A. 15

B. 41

C. 53

D. 133

E. 205

GO ON TO THE NEXT PAGE

Use the following table to answer questions 14 and 15:

The table below shows the genres of radio music, broken down by the medium (AM, FM, or satellite) on which they are aired. In addition, the table shows the number of hours in which there is a live disc jockey.

Genre	Medium	# of Hours Where There Is a Live Disc Jockey
Classical	AM	6
	FM	3
	Satellite	12
Country	AM	24
	FM	7
	Satellite	16
News	AM	24
	FM	24
	Satellite	24
Pop	AM	14
	Satellite	5
Rock	AM	12
	Satellite	24

14. What is the average number of hours, rounded to the nearest hour, that the country genre has a live disc jockey?

    F. 3

    G. 7

    H. 14

    J. 16

    K. 24

DO YOUR FIGURING HERE.

GO ON TO THE NEXT PAGE

15. The time of day in which there is a live disc jockey does not matter, as long as there is a live disc jockey for the number of hours listed in the table. Assume that a disc jockey can switch from any genre and medium to another with the flip of a switch. Based on the table, what is the minimum number of disc jockeys needed to cover all genres and mediums, if each works an eight-hour shift?

   A.   5
   B.   13
   C.   24
   D.   25
   E.   195

DO YOUR FIGURING HERE.

16. In the table below, every row, column, and diagonal must have equivalent sums. What is the value of the lower left cell in order for this to be true?

m	$-3m$	$3m$
$2m$	0	$-2m$
	$4m$	$-m$

   F. $-4m$
   G. $-3m$
   H. -3
   J. 0
   K. m

GO ON TO THE NEXT PAGE

17. The standard coordinate plane is shown below, with the four quadrants labeled. Point R, denoted by $R(x, y)$ is graphed on this plane, such that $x \neq 0$ and $y \neq 0$.

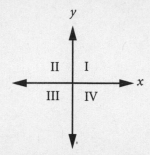

   If the product xy is a positive number, then point R is located in:

   A. quadrant I only.

   B. quadrant II only.

   C. quadrant III only.

   D. quadrant I or IV only.

   E. quadrant I or III only.

18. The cafeteria offers 7 different sandwiches, 3 different soups, and 4 different drink choices on the luncheon menu. How many distinct meals are available if a meal consists of 1 sandwich, 1 soup, and 1 drink?

   F. 7

   G. 14

   H. 21

   J. 84

   K. Cannot be determined from the given information.

DO YOUR FIGURING HERE.

GO ON TO THE NEXT PAGE

19. At the university, there are 5 females for every 3 males. If there are 6,000 male students, how many students are female?

    A. 10,000
    B. 12,000
    C. 16,000
    D. 18,000
    E. 30,000

20. What is the length, in inches, of the diagonal of a rectangle whose dimensions are 16 inches by 30 inches?

    F. 25
    G. 23
    H. 34
    J. 578
    K. 1,156

21. Which of the following expressions is NOT equivalent to $5n + 1$?

    A. $\dfrac{1}{5n + 1}$

    B. $5(n + 2) - 9$

    C. $\dfrac{1}{\dfrac{1}{5n + 1}}$

    D. $\dfrac{5n^2 + n}{n}$

    E. $\dfrac{25n^2 - 1}{5n - 1}$

DO YOUR FIGURING HERE.

GO ON TO THE NEXT PAGE

22. Which of the following equations is equivalent to $3x + 2y = 16$?

    F. $y = -\dfrac{3}{2}x + 16$

    G. $y = -\dfrac{2}{3}x + 8$

    H. $y = \dfrac{3}{2}x + 8$

    J. $y = -\dfrac{3}{2}x + 8$

    K. $y = -\dfrac{2}{3}x + 8$

DO YOUR FIGURING HERE.

23. A solution to the equation $x^2 - 20x + 75 = 0$ is:

    A. -15
    B. -5
    C. 0
    D. 3
    E. 5

24. Given right triangle $\triangle LMN$ below, what is the value of $\cos N$?

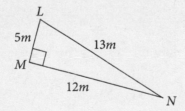

    F. $\dfrac{5}{13}$

    G. $\dfrac{5}{12}$

    H. $\dfrac{12}{13}$

    J. $\dfrac{13}{12}$

    K. $\dfrac{13}{5}$

GO ON TO THE NEXT PAGE

25. In the circle below, chord *AB* passes through the center of circle *O*. If the radius *OC* is perpendicular to chord *AB* and has length of 7 centimeters, what is the length of chord *BC*, to the nearest tenth of a centimeter?

DO YOUR FIGURING HERE.

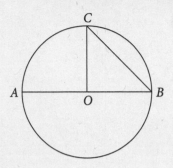

  A. 5.3

  B. 7.0

  C. 9.9

  D. 12.1

  E. 14.0

26. To convert a temperature in degrees Celsius to degrees Fahrenheit, the formula is $F = \frac{9}{5}C + 32$, where *C* is the degrees in Celsius. What temperature, to the nearest degree Celsius, equals a temperature of 86 degrees Fahrenheit?

  F. 30

  G. 54

  H. 80

  J. 86

  K. 187

GO ON TO THE NEXT PAGE

27. The Olympic-sized pool is 50 meters long, 25 meters wide, and holds 14,375 cubic meters of water. If the pool is the same depth in all parts, about how many meters deep is the water in the pool?

    A. Less than 9

    B. Between 9 and 10

    C. Between 10 and 11

    D. Between 11 and 12

    E. More than 12

28. In right triangle $\triangle DEF$ below, the measure of segment DE is 42 inches, and the tangent of angle D is $\frac{5}{8}$. What is the length of segment EF, to the nearest tenth of an inch?

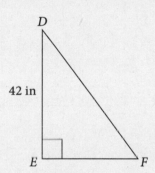

    F. 26.3

    G. 42.625

    H. 49.6

    J. 67.2

    K. 210.0

DO YOUR FIGURING HERE.

29. The bar graph below shows the number of people at the spring prom, according to their grade level at the high school. According to the graph, what fraction of the people at the prom were sophomores?

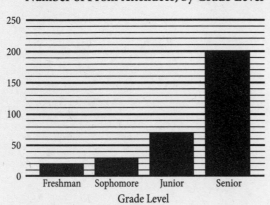

Number of Prom Attendees, by Grade Level

A. $\dfrac{1}{16}$

B. $\dfrac{3}{32}$

C. $\dfrac{3}{29}$

D. $\dfrac{3}{20}$

E. $\dfrac{3}{10}$

30. In the segment shown below, point X is the midpoint of segment WZ. If the measure of WY is 26 cm and the measure of WZ is 44 cm, what is the length, in centimeters, of segment XY?

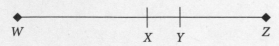

F. 4

G. 13

H. 18

J. 22

K. 70

DO YOUR FIGURING HERE.

GO ON TO THE NEXT PAGE

31. What is the *x*-coordinate of the intersection point, in the (*x*, *y*) coordinate system, of the lines $2x + 3y = 8$ and $5x + y = 7$?

    A.   −1

    B. $\dfrac{15}{7}$

    C.   1

    D.   2

    E.   3

DO YOUR FIGURING HERE.

32. For all pairs of real numbers *a* and *b*, where $a = 2b - 8$, *b* = ?

    F. $a + 4$

    G. $2a - 8$

    H. $2a + 8$

    J. $\dfrac{a - 8}{2}$

    K. $\dfrac{a + 8}{2}$

33. What is the area, in square millimeters, of the parallelogram *RSTU* shown below?

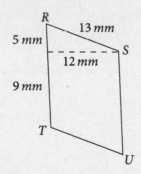

    A.   30

    B.   39

    C.   54

    D.   168

    E.   182

GO ON TO THE NEXT PAGE

34. If $x = -(y + 3)$, then $(x + y)^3 = ?$

    F.   –27

    G.   –9

    H.   9

    J.   27

    K. Cannot be determined from the given
        information.

DO YOUR FIGURING HERE.

35. Shown below is a partial map of Centerville,
    showing 80 square miles—a total of 8 miles
    of Main Street and a total of 10 miles of
    Front Street. There is a fire station at the
    corner of Main and Front Streets, shown as
    point *F*. The town wants to build a new fire
    station exactly halfway between the hospital,
    at *H*, and the school, at *S*. What would be
    the driving directions to get from the current
    fire station to the new fire station, by way
    of Main and Elm streets? All streets and
    avenues shown intersect at right angles.

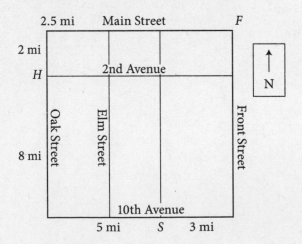

    A. 2.5 miles east, 4 miles north

    B. 2.5 miles west, 4 miles north

    C. 2.5 miles east, 6 miles south

    D. 5.5 miles west, 4 miles south

    E. 5.5 miles west, 6 miles south

GO ON TO THE NEXT PAGE

36. There are two consecutive odd integers. The difference between four times the larger and twice the smaller is 36. If x represents the smaller integer, which equation below can be used to determine the smaller integer?

    F. $4x - 2x = 36$

    G. $4(x + 1) - 2x = 36$

    H. $4(x + 2) - 2x = 36$

    J. $(x + 3) - 2x = 36$

    K. $36 - 4x = 2x$

37. A 15-foot supporting wire is attached to a telephone pole 12 feet from the ground. The wire is then anchored to the ground. The telephone pole stands perpendicular to the ground. How far, in feet, is the anchor of the supporting wire from the base of the telephone pole?

    A. 3

    B. 6

    C. 9

    D. 12

    E. 15

38. In the figure below, the sides of the square are tangent to the inner circle. If the area of the circle is 100π square units, what is the unit length of a side of the square?

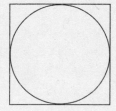

    F. 400

    G. 100

    H. 20

    J. 10

    K. π

39. The rectangles *ABCD* and *EFGH* shown below are similar. Using the given information, what is the length of side *EH*, to the nearest tenth of an inch?

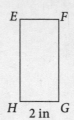
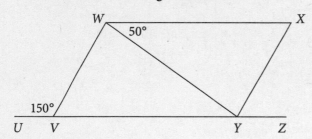

   A. 0.8

   B. 1.3

   C. 5.3

   D. 7.0

   E. 8.0

40. In the parallelogram *VWXY* below, points *U, V, Y,* and *Z* form a straight line. Given the angle measures as shown in the figure, what is the measure of angle $\angle WYX$?

   F.   25°

   G.   30°

   H.   50°

   J.   100°

   K.   150°

DO YOUR FIGURING HERE.

GO ON TO THE NEXT PAGE

41. In the figure below, all interior angles are 90°, and all dimension lengths are given in centimeters. What is the perimeter of this figure, in centimeters?

DO YOUR FIGURING HERE.

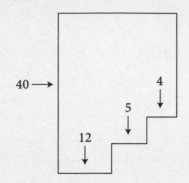

A. 40

B. 61

C. 82

D. 122

E. Cannot be determined from the given information.

42. In the mayoral election, $\frac{3}{4}$ of the eligible voters at one site cast a vote. Three-fifths of the votes at this site were for candidate Martinez. If there are 3,500 eligible voters at this site, how many of them voted for Martinez?

F. 417

G. 1,575

H. 2,100

J. 2,625

K. 4,725

43. Given that a and b are positive integers, and the greatest common factor of a^4b^2 and a^3b is 54, what is a possible value for b?

    A. 2
    B. 3
    C. 6
    D. 9
    E. 27

DO YOUR FIGURING HERE.

44. If 40% of x is 70, then what is 160% of x?

    F. 28
    G. 45
    H. 112
    J. 175
    K. 280

45. Point M (2, 3) and point N (6, 5) are points on the coordinate plane. What is the length of the segment MN?

    A. $\sqrt{2}$ units
    B. $2\sqrt{3}$ units
    C. $2\sqrt{5}$ units
    D. 6 units
    E. 20 units

46. The ratio of the sides of two squares is 5:7. What is the ratio of the perimeters of these squares?

    F. 1:2
    G. 1:12
    H. 1:35
    J. 5:7
    K. 25:49

GO ON TO THE NEXT PAGE

47. What is the equation of a circle in the coordinate plane with center (–2, 3) and radius of 9 units?

    A. $(x - 2)^2 + (y + 3)^2 = 9$
    B. $(x + 2)^2 + (y - 3)^2 = 9$
    C. $(x - 2)^2 + (y + 3)^2 = 81$
    D. $(x + 2)^2 + (y - 3)^2 = 3$
    E. $(x + 2)^2 + (y - 3)^2 = 81$

DO YOUR FIGURING HERE.

48. In the complex number system, $i^2 = -1$.
    Given that $\dfrac{3}{5 - i}$ is a complex number, what is the result of $\dfrac{3}{5 - i} \times \dfrac{5 + i}{5 + i}$?

    F. $\dfrac{3}{5 + i}$

    G. $\dfrac{15 + 3i}{24}$

    H. $\dfrac{15 + 3i}{26}$

    J. $\dfrac{15 + i}{26}$

    K. $\dfrac{15 + i}{24}$

49. The figures below show regular polygons and the sum of the degrees of the angles in each polygon. Based on these figures, what is the number of degrees in an n-sided regular polygon?

    180°   360°   540°   720°

    A. $60n$
    B. $180n$
    C. $180(n - 2)$
    D. $20n^2$
    E. Cannot be determined from the information given.

GO ON TO THE NEXT PAGE

50. Fifty high school students were polled to see if they owned a cell phone and an mp3 player. A total of 35 of the students own a cell phone, and a total of 18 of the students own an mp3 player. What is the minimum number of students who own both a cell phone and an mp3 player?

    F. 0
    G. 3
    H. 17
    J. 32
    K. 53

51. What is the solution set of all real numbers n such that $-4n + 3 > -4n + 1$?

    A. All real numbers
    B. All positive numbers
    C. All negative numbers
    D. All numbers such that $n > -\frac{1}{2}$
    E. All numbers such that $n < -\frac{1}{2}$

52. If 3 people all shake hands with each other, there are a total of 3 handshakes. If 4 people all shake hands with each other, there are a total of 6 handshakes. How many total handshakes will there be if 5 people all shake hands with each other?

    F. 7
    G. 9
    H. 10
    J. 11
    K. 12

DO YOUR FIGURING HERE.

GO ON TO THE NEXT PAGE

53. The chart below shows the percentages of the county budget expenses by category. The remainder of the budget will be placed in the category Miscellaneous. If this data is to be put into a circle graph, what will be the degree measure of the Miscellaneous wedge, rounded to the nearest degree?

DO YOUR FIGURING HERE.

Budget Category	Percentage of Budget
Salaries	23
Road Repair	5
Employee Benefits	22
Building Maintenance/ Utilities	18

A. 32
B. 58
C. 68
D. 115
E. 245

54. If $\tan \theta = -\frac{4}{3}$, and $\frac{\pi}{2} < \theta < \pi$, then $\sin \theta = ?$

F. $-\frac{4}{5}$

G. $-\frac{3}{4}$

H. $-\frac{3}{5}$

J. $\frac{3}{5}$

K. $\frac{4}{5}$

GO ON TO THE NEXT PAGE

55. Which of the following systems of inequalities is represented by the shaded region on the coordinate plane below?

DO YOUR FIGURING HERE.

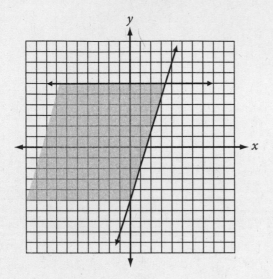

- A. $y < 6$ and $y > 3x - 5$
- B. $x < 6$ and $y > 3x - 5$
- C. $y < 6$ and $y < 3x - 5$
- D. $x < 6$ and $y < -3x - 5$
- E. $y < 6$ and $y > \frac{1}{3}x - 5$

56. If $f(x) = 2(x + 7)$, then $f(x + c) = ?$

- F. $2x + 2c + 7$
- G. $2x + c + 7$
- H. $2x + c + 14$
- J. $2x + 2c + 14$
- K. $2(x + 7) + c$

GO ON TO THE NEXT PAGE

57. Which graph below represents the solution set for the equation $y = \dfrac{2x^2 - 8}{x - 2}$?

DO YOUR FIGURING HERE.

A.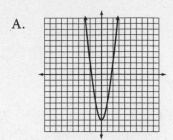

B.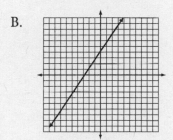

C.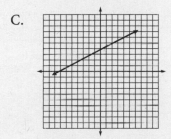

D.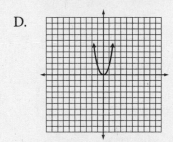

E.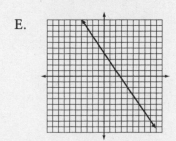

GO ON TO THE NEXT PAGE

58. What are the coordinates of Q', the reflection of the point $Q(r, s)$ after a reflection over the y-axis?

    F. $(-r, s)$

    G. $(-r, -s)$

    H. $(s, -r)$

    J. $(r, -s)$

    K. $(-s, r)$

59. If $g = 4q + 3$ and $h = 2q - 8$, what is g in terms of h?

    A. $g = \dfrac{h + 8}{2}$

    B. $g = \dfrac{4h + 11}{2}$

    C. $2h + 19$

    D. $2h + 11$

    E. $h = \dfrac{g - 3}{4}$

DO YOUR FIGURING HERE.

GO ON TO THE NEXT PAGE

60. Find the cos(75°) knowing that cos(75°) = cos(30° + 45°). Use the formula $\cos(\alpha + \beta) = \cos(\alpha)\cos(\beta) - \sin(\alpha)\sin(\beta)$ and the table of values below:

DO YOUR FIGURING HERE.

θ	$\sin\theta$	$\cos\theta$	$\tan\theta$
30°	$\dfrac{1}{2}$	$\dfrac{\sqrt{3}}{2}$	$\dfrac{\sqrt{3}}{3}$
45°	$\dfrac{\sqrt{2}}{2}$	$\dfrac{\sqrt{2}}{2}$	1
60°	$\dfrac{\sqrt{3}}{2}$	$\dfrac{1}{2}$	$\sqrt{3}$

F. $\dfrac{\sqrt{3} - \sqrt{2}}{4}$

G. $\dfrac{\sqrt{3} - \sqrt{2}}{2}$

H. $\dfrac{\sqrt{6} - \sqrt{2}}{4}$

J. $\dfrac{\sqrt{6} - \sqrt{2}}{2}$

K. $\dfrac{3 - \sqrt{2}}{4}$

READING TEST

35 Minutes—40 Questions

Directions: This test contains four passages, each followed by several questions. After reading each passage, select the best answer to each question and fill in the corresponding oval on your Answer Grid. You may refer to the passages while answering the questions.

Passage I

PROSE FICTION

This excerpt from a short story describes a conversation between a woman and her husband, who is a twin.

Emily couldn't help but grin broadly after answering the phone. She frequently called us "two peas in a pod," but I'd always felt
Line like any time we were mentioned outside
(5) of my presence he was "Bruce" and I was "Bruce's twin brother." Because of this, I wasn't surprised to hear my wife giggling uncontrollably and see her twirling the phone cord around her finger while talking
(10) to him. Despite the fact she was speaking to someone genetically identical to me, I couldn't help but wonder if she had ever responded so enthusiastically to one of my stories.
(15) "Okay, I'll tell him. Talk to you soon." After Emily hung up, I watched her take a deep, almost wistful breath before walking over to me.

"Bruce seems well," I said, trying to
(20) sound casual. "He told me about the new job and everything. What did you guys talk about?"

"Not much." Emily replied. She walked behind my chair and patted my shoulder
(25) before sitting on the couch and opening her magazine. It didn't appear as if she were really reading. She seemed to stop and start, pausing and reflecting about something

unrelated to the smiling celebrities featured
(30) in the article.

"It's funny to think that he knows some of these people," she said, pointing at her magazine.

I looked at the gleaming teeth and
(35) chiseled features of the actors, and then looked over at a picture of Bruce and me resting on the mantel. Looking closely at the photo always made my stomach turn; as with every picture of us, there was an
(40) unmistakable vitality in Bruce's face that wasn't present in mine. It were as if I were wearing a "Bruce" costume; I was trying to mimic one of his trademark smiles, but I always seemed to produce a different failed
(45) attempt.

"You all right?" Emily asked, noticing my expression.

I grabbed the picture from the mantel and brought it to her. She looked at it and
(50) looked up at me quizzically.

"Can you tell which one is me?" I asked.

She looked back at the picture and pushed her lip out as she looked from one face to the next. After about five seconds she
(55) pointed to my face, then turned and looked at me confidently.

"How could you tell?" I asked.

"Well, it wasn't very hard," she responded. "You are my husband, and I love
(60) the way you smile. Bruce looks exactly the

GO ON TO THE NEXT PAGE ⇨

same in every picture, it looks practiced, but
for you it always seems like you're thinking
about something, even concentrating, to
make sure you smile right."

(65)   "Really?" I was surprised by how much
thought she had put into this.

She took the picture and put it back on
the mantel. I could still see the perfection in
Bruce's smile and hesitation in mine, but at
(70) least Emily found a way to compliment my
insecurities.

Emily went back to perusing her
magazine.

"At least you ended up with a Fairholm,"
(75) I said, "even if it wasn't the famous one."

"Oh, was I supposed to pursue the
famous one?" she shot back.

She closed her magazine and put it
down on the coffee table. There wasn't an
(80) argument coming, but I saw her disappointment. The problem was not that she actually
would have married my brother before me;
it was the simple fact that I couldn't help but
believe that to be the case. I saw myself as
(85) second to him and always had. With embar-
rassing relatives, people will always point
out that one can't choose his or her family,
but when you're a twin, it's not the association that you fear, it's the comparison.

(90)   "Do you want to be where he is?" she
inquired, with an empty tone.

"This is exactly where I want to be,"
I replied. "I just never know how to explain
to people that I'm an insurance adjuster,
(95) not a Hollywood agent. They always want
to know how it happened when we had the
same upbringing and education. They look
at me as if I did something wrong."

"Do you ever call him?" she asked.
(100)   "I figure he's busy, and he calls enough,"
I said.

She cradled her chin in her hand, and
looked at me in mild disbelief. "You realize
that by not calling and turning down his
(105) invitations to visit you make him feel
rejected, right?"

"Come on, Emily. He's surrounded
by famous people, he doesn't need my
approval."
(110)   "Maybe not," she sighed, "but his favorite
stories to tell me aren't about Hollywood,
they're about you two growing up."

"Well, he was popular then, too," I said,
shrugging.
(115)   "He doesn't look at it that way," she
responded. "He would give up a lot to have
your approval, Dave. He wants to be your
brother, not a competitor."

"It's okay, Emily. I'll call him soon, but I
(120) think that he'll be okay either way."

1. Dave would probably agree with which
    of the following statements regarding
    his relationship with Bruce?

    A. They would be better off not talking
        at all.

    B. Their phone conversations are vital
        to their relationship.

    C. Their bond as twins is stronger due
        to Emily's effort.

    D. Their competition makes it harder
        for them to get along.

2. Emily is best described as:

    F. aloof and ineffectual.

    G. needling and meddlesome.

    H. caring and diplomatic.

    J. pained and inconsolable.

GO ON TO THE NEXT PAGE ⟹

3. Which of the following statements does NOT describe a feeling Dave has toward his brother?

   A. He is jealous of the reaction his brother gets from Emily during their phone conversation.

   B. He believes he would be better suited for his brother's type of work.

   C. He is resentful of his brother's superior social skills.

   D. He is skeptical of his brother's desire for his approval.

4. The primary focus of the first paragraph is:

   F. Emily's attempt to make her husband jealous.

   G. Emily's desire for the brothers to resolve their differences.

   H. Dave's hope to distance himself from his twin brother.

   J. Dave's feelings of inferiority to his twin brother.

5. Lines 99–120 ("Do you ever ... either way") suggest that Dave does not contact Bruce because Dave:

   A. believes that Bruce has great need for him but does not want to admit to Emily that she is right.

   B. feels guilty about being distant toward Bruce and worries that he will have to explain himself.

   C. wants to prove to Emily that he is not impressed by Bruce's high profile job.

   D. still harbors resentment over Bruce getting preferential treatment during their childhood.

6. According to the passage, when Dave looks at the photograph, he sees:

   F. his brother being cruel to him.

   G. two indistinguishable faces.

   H. a comparison unfavorable to him.

   J. his wife paying more attention to Bruce.

7. Which of the following best summarizes Dave's feelings when he asks Emily to pick him out in the picture?

   A. Dave is confident that Emily will prefer his image to Bruce's.

   B. Dave is insecure; he feels the picture compares him unfavorably to Bruce.

   C. Dave is worried, because he thinks Emily will want to talk more about Bruce after seeing a picture of him.

   D. Dave is angry because he did not want to talk about the picture in the first place.

8. It can be logically deduced from the passage that Dave and Bruce:

   F. tell Emily different sounding stories about their shared childhood.

   G. are frequently at odds regarding their different professions.

   H. have often fought over Emily's attention.

   J. were much closer shortly before Bruce moved.

GO ON TO THE NEXT PAGE

9. Both Emily and Dave conclude that when pictures are taken of the brothers:

   A. Bruce looks much better than Dave.

   B. Dave appears angry at Bruce.

   C. Pictures of Bruce are more consistent than those of Dave.

   D. Dave's expression makes a greater impression on the viewer than Bruce's.

10. According to the passage, the reason Emily tells Dave about the content of Bruce's stories is because Emily:

    F. wants to convince Dave that Bruce does not see himself as better than Dave.

    G. wishes to hear Dave's version of the stories.

    H. sees this as a way to make Dave more impressed with his brother.

    J. thinks that this will make Dave sympathetic to Bruce's loneliness.

Passage II

SOCIAL SCIENCE

This passage discusses the relationship between the media and public opinion.

Large-scale media would likely be traced back to ancient tribes sharing information about the edibility of berries or the
Line aggressiveness of animals. Despite constant
(5) evolution, the information most sought after is that regarding personal safety, personal opportunity, and the triumphs and misdeeds of others—the larger the persona and more laudatory or despicable the act,
(10) the better. When a story is of continued national interest, however, the focus shifts even further from facts and more to theater. To step back and compose an objective plot of goings on is a distant possibility, but
(15) establishing the hero or villain of the day is paramount. Ultimately, the public's desire to have cold, dry and correct facts is virtually nonexistent.

Current newscasts exacerbate this by
(20) delivering an assault on the senses with meaningless graphics and theatrical music; meanwhile, the monotone newscaster reads, verbatim from a teleprompter, often using phrases identical to those on other
(25) networks. Additionally, the viewer has probably already read the same story on the Internet earlier. When television was limited to three networks, rather than ubiquitous news-only channels, the newscaster
(30) was a national figure, audience members would eagerly await information that was new to them, and would expect a relatively thorough explanation of any complicated goings on. For example, to this day many
(35) people, in explaining the Watergate scandal to those too young to know of it, use Walter Cronkite's delineation as the basis for their understanding.

GO ON TO THE NEXT PAGE ⇨

The objective, trustworthy anchorperson
(40) has also given way to vociferous demagogues
promising truth but delivering oversimpli-
fied, bias-driven sound bites. The idea of
allowing individuals to draw their own
conclusions is notably absent; in fact, many
(45) personalities mock those with opinions
differing from those presented. The avail-
ability of neutral online sources mitigates
this slightly, but not to any large degree.
While the actual article may be impartial,
(50) electronic periodicals will still sensationalize
headlines in order to attract casual readers,
and those very headlines sway many readers
to certain opinions before the article is even
read. For example, if a headline mentions
(55) an "enraged public," the reader is far more
likely to both read and take umbrage with
the information than he or she would if
the article mentioned a subject that "irked
locals."
(60)   In truth, though, the public is as
desirous for dry and objective facts as
finicky children are for brussels sprouts. The
personalities willing to shrug off account-
ability in favor of wild accusations and
(65) bombastic slogans captivate a large demo-
graphic, while one would be generous by
saying that objective fact-based programs
occupy even a niche market. This not only
damages the general accuracy of so-called
(70) "news," but further polarizes the public.
People now have the option to receive their
news from hosts with a variety of political
leanings, and one almost invariably chooses
to watch the personality closest to one's own
(75) personal opinions. This is more harmful
than convenient, because it allows viewers
to simply parrot information they are
given, eliminating any thought or scrutiny.
It is this intellectual laziness that aids in
(80) distancing the general public from factual
information: as a growing number become
resigned to accept whatever their favorite
host tells them, the more freedom networks
have in passing sensationalist entertainment

(85) as news. It boils down to the unfortunate
truth that most are far more likely to accept
inaccurate information as fact rather than
question the legitimacy of something that
seems to fit with opinions a particular
(90) audience member holds.
     Those who make the news also obfuscate
objective facts. A legion of employees is
designated solely for the purpose of making
the decisions of political figures sound
(95) flawless. Oftentimes, important decisions
are made, and throughout a lengthy press
conference, not a single factual implication
is discussed. The meeting becomes nothing
more than an opportunity for political
(100) employees to test their infallible sounding
slogans, while the media dissects the
semantics rather than the facts. Semantics,
however, are all the media is presented with.
     Despite all these methods of prevarica-
(105) tion, people still are better informed than
they were in the past. Public knowledge of
events often occurs minutes after the fact,
rather than days or weeks. The populace
has a strong desire for news in general,
(110) and amid all the unscrupulous presentation methods, facts do exist. However, the
profitability of news has made presentation
premium, not trustworthiness. Complicating
matters further is the populace's impatience;
(115) the standard consumer would rather be
presented with a minute and potentially
inaccurate statement—one that may or may
not be retracted the following day—than
suffer through a lengthy treatise comprised
(120) of all the known facts and nuances of a
particular event. The desire to know still
exists, however; it just happens to be over-
shadowed by the public's desire for personal
consensus and the media's desire to reel in
(125) the public.

GO ON TO THE NEXT PAGE

11. One of the primary points the author attempts to make regarding the current news media is that:

    A. the media passes off made-up stories as facts.

    B. the news anchors are not as opinionated as they were in decades past.

    C. the media focuses more on presentation than substance.

    D. the media goes directly against what news audiences truly desire to see.

12. The author makes what claim about impartial news stories?

    F. They no longer exist.

    G. They can be sensationalized in ways other than article content.

    H. They often have headlines that correctly reflect the emotional level of the story.

    J. They all have headlines that attempt to make the reader feel involved in the story.

13. The author brings up Walter Cronkite's coverage of Watergate in order to assert that:

    A. Walter Cronkite was a particularly adept newsperson.

    B. a previous standard for news rightly included clarification of complex issues.

    C. current newscasters are far more forgettable than those before them.

    D. the expanding number of television channels has made individual newscasters less famous.

14. By stating that "personal consensus" is of great importance to the public (lines 123–124), the author is probably suggesting that members of the public:

    F. do not want information that contradicts their own beliefs.

    G. work hard to find the source closest to truth, despite the difficulties present.

    H. wish to resolve any moral conflicts they may have with practices in news reporting.

    J. have difficulty finding news sources reflecting their personal views.

15. According to the passage, what type of news stories are sensationalized the most?

    A. Those with a fairly clear chain of events

    B. Those that stay in the public's consciousness for long periods of time

    C. Those that clearly support one political view

    D. Those with the most scandalous information

16. As used in line 14 (paragraph 1), the word *distant* most nearly means:

    F. separated.

    G. different.

    H. reserved.

    J. unlikely.

GO ON TO THE NEXT PAGE

17. Based on the passage, which of the following headlines would the author be most likely to criticize?

   A. Earthquake Rocks Small Community, Arouses Questions Regarding Preparedness

   B. New Tax Protested by Idaho Farmers

   C. Parents Across Country Outraged at Offensive Song

   D. Governor Describes Proposed Legislation as "Monstrous"

18. The author asserts that individuals will often accept potentially inaccurate information because they:

   F. believe that most newscasters are honest.

   G. have no way to research correct facts.

   H. are forced to translate the guarded words of political employees.

   J. have similar political beliefs to specific media personalities.

19. In the fourth paragraph, the phrase "even a niche market" (line 68) expresses the author's feeling that:

   A. media companies are influenced greatly by public demand.

   B. cable television networks are unwilling to present objective facts.

   C. factual news media should look into better marketing practices.

   D. factual news would be profitable with greater exposure.

20. The author argues that in searching for a news source, audience members are most likely to choose the source that:

   F. features the most entertaining newscaster.

   G. validates the audience member's opinion.

   H. presents the shortest and simplest explanation for goings on.

   J. focuses on big stories rather than local ones.

GO ON TO THE NEXT PAGE

Passage III

HUMANITIES

This passage explores the relationship between the immigrant experience and one person's career choice.

My grandfather was born in a turbulent time in Russia. His non-communist lineage made him unwelcome, before he had left the womb. His father, an officer in the Russian
Line
(5) army, was considered an enemy of the communist Bolsheviks, so my grandfather lived less than a year in what was his native Moscow, and spent most of his younger years moving across Asia. Despite this, he
(10) had pride in being Russian, associated with Russians throughout his life, and would frequently quiz me on Russian history. This all in tribute to a country that ended up under different rule during the time his
(15) mother was pregnant with him.

As a child, exiled to Siberia, my grandfather heard his father tell of the greatness that existed within the country that had forced the family into exile. It was known
(20) that, first with his parents, and later as an adult, my grandfather was going to have to seek a new place to call home. Despite this foregone conclusion, Russia was still romanticized, and my grandfather learned
(25) to treat the country with reverence. This was in contrast to the sentiments found in other recently exiled Russians, who would not simply lament the actions taken by the country, but disparage all eight million
(30) square miles. In my family's search for a place to settle, attempting to forge a consistent identity was nearly impossible, as no one knew if the next location would hold for a month, let alone a year, all hoped for an
(35) unattainable "new Moscow."

The first elongated refuge was found, ironically, in China, which would later have its own communist revolution. After several years of relative stability, the revolution

(40) precipitated the move to the United States. Upon arrival in San Francisco, my grandfather, along with my grandmother and their young son, my father, found other Russian immigrants who were also new to the
(45) country. "*Ya amerikanets*" people would say, and despite the fact that they were recent immigrants who associated primarily with those of shared ethnicity and circumstance, they would play the role they desired, and
(50) repeat "*ya amerikanets*"—"I am American." They would share many stories about their native land, but did not repeat "*ya russkiy*," because being Russian went without saying.

While it was clear that this would be
(55) the last country my grandfather would reside in, and that he wished to become more American, it was perhaps the most confusing of times. It was less of a problem in acclimating to an adopted
(60) setting; the problem was dealing with a permanent setting at all. The only consistency throughout the first thirty years of my grandfather's life was the knowledge that every "home" was temporary, and now this
(65) was no longer the case. I often wonder if his successful career in the real estate business had anything to do with what must have been a rare transformation of circumstance.

Not only was my grandfather inter-
(70) ested in real estate, he was ardent about the importance of ownership, a naturally discordant view to that of the then Soviet Union, and thus selling homes became a purpose in addition to an occupation.

(75) Part of his success in real estate was owed to strategic compromise. Considering American sentiments regarding Russia during the Cold War, there were times that he was sure he lost certain house sales due
(80) to his last name and accent. However, to those willing to listen, he found advantages

GO ON TO THE NEXT PAGE →

informing people that he was an exiled Russian, and ardently disagreed with the communist government. He would
(85) also point out his pride in being a new American, and allow a potential buyer to degrade Russia without blinking.

Fortunately, the 1950s were a time of settling across the country, and this made
(90) real estate a very lucrative profession. It wasn't just this that attracted my grandfather, though; he also saw it as an opportunity to give tiny parts of the country to other people, returning the favor, in a way.
(95) Yet, it always seemed that something vital still rested in the opposite hemisphere. Once communism fell, he began returning to Russia yearly, and while he and my grandmother never showed the family
(100) pictures from Russia the way they would from the various cruise ships they traveled on, it could be deduced that returning to Russia was analogous to an adopted child traveling to meet his or her birth-parents:
(105) the journey is one of personal necessity rather than pleasure, and the encounter is one that elucidates one's very existence. In selling real estate, my grandfather had worked to make this unnecessary. I believe
(110) that he wished for people to keep those houses, and pass them down to later generations, giving the space a sort of familial permanence, rather than a fleeting stay.

For most, the thought of real estate
(115) agents conjures up images of smiling advertisements on benches and buses, and the skill of selling something so important. Many are wary of salespeople in general, questioning the practice of convincing
(120) people something is in their best interest when the salesperson stands to personally benefit. My grandfather did financially benefit from sales, but there was more to it; his realization of the American dream
(125) only made him want to be a part of others reaching for the same thing, whether their native home was around the block or thousands of miles away.

21. One of the main points the author attempts to convey in the passage is that:

A. immigrants would often rather live in their native land.

B. American-born people tend not to be able to understand how displacement affects immigrants.

C. immigrants that acclimate well to America still may have indelible ties to their native land.

D. immigrants are often shocked by the stability offered to them in America.

22. Based on the first three paragraphs, which of the following best describes the movements of the author's grandfather, prior to his emigration to America?

F. He grew up primarily in Siberia and then moved to China during the Russian revolution.

G. He grew up in Moscow, was exiled as an adult, and rapidly moved through Asia.

H. He was born in Moscow, moved rapidly through Asia, and settled for a while in communist China.

J. He was born in Moscow, exiled to Siberia with his family, and moved frequently before settling for a somewhat longer period in China.

GO ON TO THE NEXT PAGE ⇨

23. The author's grandfather's "purpose" (line 73) and desire to return "the favor" (line 94) are best described as:

    A. providing others with a sense of pride in being American.

    B. shedding light on injustices carried out by other countries.

    C. facilitating a stable situation for others.

    D. providing well for his family.

24. Which of the following actions contradicts a general attitude held by the author's grandfather?

    F. "He would also point out his pride in being a new American, and allow a potential buyer to degrade Russia without blinking" (lines 84–87).

    G. "They would share many stories about their native land, but did not repeat "*ya russkiy*," because being Russian went without saying" (lincs 51–53).

    H. "He was ardent about the importance of ownership, a naturally discordant view to that of the then Soviet Union" (lines 70–72).

    J. "Once communism fell, he began returning to Russia yearly" (lines 97–98).

25. The author classifies a "new Moscow" as "unattainable" (line 35) because:

    A. the family believed Moscow to be the most desirable city in the world.

    B. it was unlikely that communism would fall shortly after the revolution.

    C. cities in other countries are entirely unlike those in Russia.

    D. it would not be possible to find a new home that could still be considered a native home.

26. When the author refers to Russians playing "the role" (line 49), he most likely means that the Russians were:

    F. convincing themselves that they were ready to acclimate.

    G. joking with each other.

    H. naïve to the way Americans tend to act with each other.

    J. still hopeful that they would see Russia again.

27. The "strategic compromise" applied by the author's grandfather (line 76) would most likely involve:

    A. agreeing with the potential buyer, no matter what.

    B. ignoring offensive statements.

    C. acting as American as possible.

    D. taking America's side in international disputes.

GO ON TO THE NEXT PAGE

28. According to the passage, the grandfather's trip back to his native Russia provided him with:

   F. a greater understanding of the inner workings of his native land.

   G. greater motivation to sell homes in America.

   H. a greater sense of personal understanding.

   J. a necessary visit with estranged family members.

29. According to the first paragraph, the author's grandfather's birth happened:

   A. during the communist revolution.

   B. under communist rule.

   C. prior to the communist revolution.

   D. after the fall of communism.

30. When the author states that his grandfather "worked to make this unnecessary" (line 109), he is suggesting that his grandfather's occupation could potentially:

   F. help his grandfather feel more connected to America through his success.

   G. oversee a transaction that could give others a sense belonging.

   H. sell houses that would allow other recent immigrants stability.

   J. help others realize the American dream.

Passage IV

NATURAL SCIENCE

This passage discusses the degree to which rattlesnakes pose a threat to humans.

In both recorded and oral history, the rattlesnakes are categorized as malevolent beings. Their lance-shaped heads and angular brow-
Line lines make them look the perfect villain,
(5) and their venom cements this classification. Publicized reports of bite victims seem to prove their nefarious nature.

Unlike mammalian predators such as bears, rattlesnakes do not have the reputa-
(10) tion of an animal deserving human respect. One imagines the rattlesnake hiding in our backyards, waiting to strike.

In recent long-term studies, however, the social behavior of rattlesnakes has been
(15) found to be quite different than many would expect. Herpetologists, scientists who study snakes, had long suspected a more complex and thoughtful existence for the reptiles, and now have hard information to back up
(20) their theories. When examined, the sinister opportunist lurking in the shadows better resembles a mild-mannered domestic. Unlike the nonvenomous kingsnake, rattlesnakes are entirely noncannibalistic, and
(25) tend to spend their entire lives with a single mate. The mating ritual in which two males will extend almost half of their bodies off the ground to wrestle is not lethal, and, once bested, a rattlesnake peacefully retreats to
(30) find a new den of eligible mates. Female rattlesnakes give birth to live young, and rattlesnakes often share their dens, even hibernating with tortoises without incident.

Sadly, it seems that only those with an
(35) existing fascination with snakes are aware of this socially functional rattlesnake. Another discovery that made little stir in the public consciousness is an experiment in which herpetologists tracked snakes with radio
(40) transmitters, and saw their behavior when

GO ON TO THE NEXT PAGE →

humans entered their habitat. While a few snakes did hold their ground and rattle, most saw or sensed a disturbance (snakes cannot hear) and immediately headed in
(45) the opposite direction. Many of the snakes that were handled by herpetologists did not coil or strike. This is not to say that a snake will not bite a human if disturbed, but the tendency is to retreat first and give warning
(50) second, before striking becomes a possibility.

Describing a more docile nature does not imply that rattlesnakes would make good pets for children, but considering the aggressiveness often displayed by a South
(55) American pit viper, the fer-de-lance, one familiar with both would have far fewer trepidations in passing by a rattlesnake. For one thing, rattlesnakes do coil and rattle, giving humans an opportunity to move
(60) away, while fer-de-lances will often strike at passersby without warning. Further-more, when it comes down to statistics, American hospitals report an average of 7,000 snakebite patients a year; generally
(65) more than half are actually from nonven-omous snakes thought by victims to be venomous. On average, fewer than six people die of snake envenomation annually, and the vast majority of the serious bites are due
(70) to either handling the snake or stepping on it; most people bitten by snakes they were not engaging end up with very mild bites. Compare this with an average of over one million hospital visits for dog bites and
(75) twenty annual deaths at the jaws of man's best friend. With such miniscule statistics regarding snakebites, it is curious why they are still viewed as unfathomably dangerous, when bees, lightning—and yes, dogs—are
(80) responsible for far more human fatalities. The fer-de-lance, however, is responsible for thousands of annual deaths in Central and South America.

If one is looking for proof that rattle-
(85) snakes do not intend to harm humans, one should consider perhaps the most stunning

evidence regarding bite behavior. Over half of the bites rattlesnakes administer to humans are "dry," meaning the rattlesnake
(90) purposely does not release venom. While I will not posit that this is due to rattlesnakes possessing awareness for the well-being of their non-food-source bite victim, there is a great deal of thought present. The snake
(95) acknowledges that venom is needed for immobilizing and digesting prey (venom is actually saliva), producing venom takes time, and the human is not a food source. Therefore, if the snake is not surprised or
(100) fearing death, the damage of a rattlesnake bite will likely be far less severe than if the snake used all its venom. This has been known for some time, but, in many cases, it is probably better for humans to believe that
(105) the snakes are more liberal with venom than they are, simply because a frightened and cornered rattlesnake is very dangerous.

Unfortunately, some people take the traditional view of the rattlesnake and use
(110) it as an excuse to harm the animals. People in various areas use the fearsome reputation of rattlesnakes, along with the more docile reality, for profit. Rattlesnake roundups are held, where people collect snakes before-
(115) hand and join in a festival celebrating their conquest. The events are billed as both entertainment and as making surrounding residential areas safer for children; however, the vast majority of snakes are collected
(120) from uninhabited areas, and people are frequently bitten at the festivals while handling the snakes for the audience. Even-tually, the snakes are killed to make clothing or trophies, and these events are estimated
(125) to be responsible for 100,000 rattlesnake deaths annually, in comparison to fewer than six human deaths from rattlesnakes.

Behavior like this provides a better reason for *crotalid* mythology. With statis-
(130) tics categorically showing a low level of danger from rattlesnakes to humans, and an extremely high level vice versa, it would be

GO ON TO THE NEXT PAGE ⟶

a wonder to see what human-related folklore
would be like if rattlesnakes were able to
(135) speak or write.

31. In relation to the entire passage, the
phrase "the sinister opportunist lurking
in the shadows better resembles a mild-
mannered domestic" (lines 20–22) most
likely implies that:

   A. adult rattlesnakes are considerably
less aggressive than juveniles.

   B. recent studies regarding rattlesnakes
found few incidents of aggressive
behavior.

   C. rattlesnakes are more similar to
mammals than once thought.

   D. rattlesnakes are entirely predictable
in behavior.

32. The passage implies that the rattlesnake's fearsome reputation can be
beneficial because:

   F. it influences people to avoid or
move away from rattlesnakes.

   G. it protects the lives of rattlesnakes.

   H. it inspires medical advancement in
treating snakebites, despite a low
mortality rate.

   J. adventurous people may seek rattlesnakes as pets.

33. What evidence does the passage give
regarding the social ability of rattlesnakes?

   A. Rattlesnakes are aware of the uses
of their venom.

   B. Wrestling between males establishes
a social hierarchy.

   C. Rattlesnakes can share their habitat
with other species.

   D. Rattlesnakes rarely eat other snakes.

34. The statement "it would be a wonder to
see what human-related folklore would
be like if rattlesnakes were able to speak
or write" (lines 132–135) means that:

   F. humans and rattlesnakes both
present great risks to each other's
safety.

   G. humans and rattlesnakes behave in
many similar ways.

   H. humans are a much greater threat to
rattlesnakes than rattlesnakes are to
humans.

   J. humans have traditionally assigned
human emotions to rattlesnakes in
folklore.

35. According to the passage, what is the
correlation between human behavior
and serious rattlesnake bites?

   A. There is no statistical relationship.

   B. Humans that move in quick
motions attract strikes.

   C. Humans that actively seek interaction with snakes are less likely to
receive a "dry" bite.

   D. Rattlesnakes deliver a variable
amount of venom based on how
threatening humans act.

GO ON TO THE NEXT PAGE ⇒

36. What is suggested by lines 51–53 when the author states that the new evidence "does not imply that rattlesnakes would make good pets for children"?

    F. Only professional herpetologists should keep rattlesnakes.

    G. Dogs can also be dangerous pets.

    H. Nonaggressive behavior does not make a venomous animal harmless.

    J. Rattlesnakes in the wild are more docile than those in captivity.

37. The passage states that the relative likelihood of a human being killed by a rattlesnake bite is:

    A. greater than that of a dog bite.

    B. less than that of a bee sting.

    C. equal to that of a lightning strike.

    D. comparable to that of the South American fer-de-lance.

38. Which of the following correctly categorizes a rattlesnake's strategy in venom usage?

    F. The larger the prey or predator, the more venom is used.

    G. Even when threatened, a rattlesnake reserves venom to use on prey.

    H. Rattlesnakes are aware that they will wound larger animals.

    J. Rattlesnakes would rather use venom solely for prey.

39. The author states rattlesnake roundups use contradictory logic because:

    A. children are rarely bitten by rattlesnakes.

    B. the rattlesnakes that bite people at roundups would have been far less likely to bite someone in their natural habitat.

    C. organizers use erroneous statistics to make the rattlesnakes seem more dangerous and the events more impressive.

    D. many that go to the events are unaware of how many snakes are killed.

40. As used in line 129, the term *crotalid* is most likely:

    F. an unfavorable characterization of humans.

    G. a scientific word meaning "rattlesnakes."

    H. a word describing a herpetologist that specializes in rattlesnakes.

    J. a general word for a group unfairly accused of wrongdoing.

IF YOU FINISH BEFORE TIME IS CALLED, YOU MAY CHECK YOUR WORK ON THIS SECTION ONLY. DO NOT TURN TO ANY OTHER SECTION IN THE TEST. **STOP**

SCIENCE TEST

35 Minutes—40 Questions

> **Directions:** This test contains seven passages, each followed by several questions. After reading each passage, select the best answer to each question and fill in the corresponding oval on your Answer Grid. You may refer to the passages while answering the questions. You may NOT use a calculator on this test.

Passage I

Glaciers are large masses of ice that move slowly over the Earth's surface due to the force of gravity and changes in elevation. Glacial *calving* occurs when one edge of a glacier borders a body of water. A calving glacier's *terminus* (the lower edge) periodically produces icebergs as they break away from the glacier and into the water.

STUDY 1

A computer was used to create a model of a typical calving glacier. It was hypothesized that a primary factor determining the calving rate is the glacier's velocity at its terminus. Figure 1 shows the calving rate, in meters per year, and length of the computer-generated glacier over a period of 2,000 years.

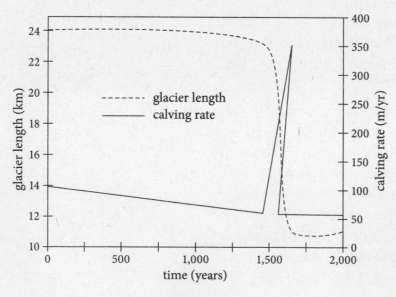

Figure 1

GO ON TO THE NEXT PAGE

STUDY 2

Four calving glaciers (A–D) were studied over a period of ten years. The average velocity at the terminus of each glacier was recorded for years 1–5 and again for years 6–10. The calving rate of each glacier was estimated for the same time periods. The results are recorded in Table 1.

Table 1

Glacier	Years 1–5		Years 6–10	
	Average velocity (m/yr)	Calving rate (m/yr)	Average velocity (m/yr)	Calving rate (m/yr)
A	72	72	63	64
B	51	52	45	47
C	98	106	256	312
D	160	189	53	54

STUDY 3

Meteorologists reported unusually high average temperatures in the regions of Glacier C and Glacier D during the same ten-year period examined in Study 2. It was hypothesized that the high temperatures were responsible for the relatively rapid variations in velocity and calving rates evident for Glacier C and Glacier D in Table 1.

1. If the glacier model used in Study 1 is typical of all calving glaciers, the scientists would draw which of the following conclusions about the relationship between glacier length and calving rate?

   A. As calving rate decreases, glacier length always increases.

   B. As glacier length decreases, calving rate always decreases.

   C. A sharp increase in calving rate results in a sharp decrease in glacier length.

   D. A sharp increase in calving rate results in a sharp increase in glacier length.

2. The meteorologists in Study 3 hypothesized that the faster the calving rate, the faster the sea level at a calving glacier's terminus would rise. If this hypothesis is correct, which of the following glaciers resulted in the fastest rise in sea level during years 6–10?

   F. Glacier A
   G. Glacier B
   H. Glacier C
   J. Glacier D

3. Based on the results of Study 2, a calving glacier traveling at a velocity of 80 m/yr would most likely have a calving rate:

   A. between 72 m/yr and 106 m/yr.
   B. between 106 m/yr and 189 m/yr.
   C. between 189 m/yr and 312 m/yr.
   D. over 312 m/yr.

4. Which of the following statements best describes the behavior of the glaciers observed during Study 2?

   F. All of the glaciers observed traveled faster during the first five years than during the last five years.

   G. All of the glaciers observed traveled faster during the last five years than during the first five years.

   H. The calving rate is always less than the average velocity for all of the glaciers observed.

   J. The calving rate is always greater than or equal to the average velocity for all of the glaciers observed.

GO ON TO THE NEXT PAGE

5. Which of the following graphs best represents the relationship between the calving rate and the average velocity of the glaciers observed in Study 2 for years 6–10?

A.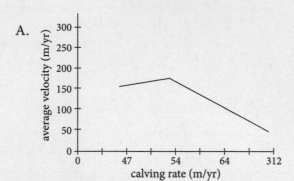

B.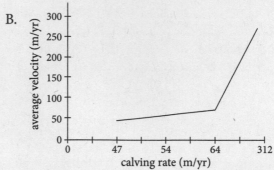

C.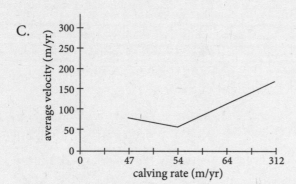

D.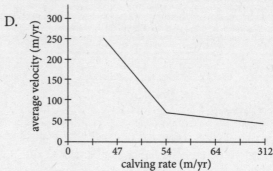

6. If the hypothesis made by the meteorologists in Study 3 is correct, the glacier modeled in Study 1 most likely experienced unusually high temperatures at approximately what time during the simulated 2,000-year study?

F.   500 years

G.   1,000 years

H.   1,500 years

J.   2,000 years

Passage II

Allergic rhinitis refers to a person's nasal reaction to small airborne particles called *allergens*. Table 1 shows the specific allergen, its type, and the approximate number of reported cases of allergic symptoms for a population of 1,000 people living in northern Kentucky during a single year.

Table 1

Month	Allergen type Specific allergen	Pollen			Mold		
		Trees	Grass	Weeds	Alternaria	Cladosporium	Aspergillus
January					❀	❀	❀
February					❀	❀	❀
March		❀❀			❀	❀	❀
April		❀❀❀❀			❀	❀	❀
May		❀❀❀	❀❀❀		❀	❀	❀
June			❀❀❀❀		❀	❀	❀
July			❀❀	❀	❀❀	❀	❀
August				❀❀❀	❀❀❀❀	❀❀❀	❀❀❀❀
September				❀❀	❀❀❀	❀❀❀❀	❀❀❀❀
October				❀❀	❀❀❀	❀❀	❀❀
November					❀❀	❀	❀
December					❀	❀	❀

Note: Each ❀ equals 100 reported cases of allergic rhinitis.

Weekly tree pollen and total mold spore concentrations were measured in grains per cubic meter (gr/m^3) for samples of air taken in southern Iowa for eight weeks. The pollen and mold spore counts are shown in Figures 1 and 2, respectively.

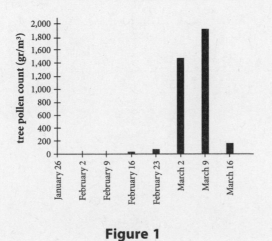

Figure 1

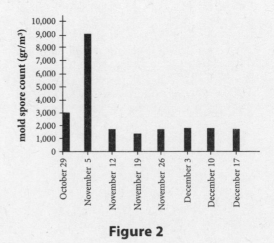

Figure 2

GO ON TO THE NEXT PAGE

7. Based on Figure 1, the tree pollen count on March 2 was closest to:

    A. 75 gr/m³.

    B. 150 gr/m³.

    C. 1,500 gr/m³.

    D. 1,900 gr/m³.

8. According to Figure 2, the mold spore count in the weeks after November 5:

    F. increased.

    G. decreased.

    H. varied between 1,000 gr/m³ and 2,000 gr/m³.

    J. remained above 2,000 gr/m³.

9. Based on the data in Figure 1, the tree pollen count increased the most between which two dates?

    A. February 9 to February 16

    B. February 23 to March 2

    C. March 2 to March 9

    D. October 29 to November 5

10. According to Figure 1, which of the following conclusions about the tree pollen count is most valid?

    F. The tree pollen count was highest on March 9.

    G. The tree pollen count was highest on March 16.

    H. The tree pollen count was lowest on February 23.

    J. The tree pollen count was lowest on March 16.

11. Based on Table 1, most of the cases of allergic rhinitis in May in northern Kentucky were caused by which of the following allergens?

    A. Tree and grass pollen

    B. Grass and weed pollen

    C. Alternaria

    D. Aspergillus

Passage III

Simple harmonic motion (SHM) is motion that is *periodic*, or repetitive, and can be described by a frequency of oscillation. Students performed three experiments to study SHM.

EXPERIMENT 1

The students assembled the pendulum shown in Diagram 1. The mass at the end of the arm was raised to a small height, *h*, and released. The frequency of oscillation was measured in oscillations per second, or Hertz (Hz), and the process was repeated for several different arm lengths. The results are shown in Figure 1.

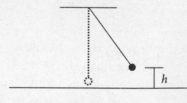

Diagram 1

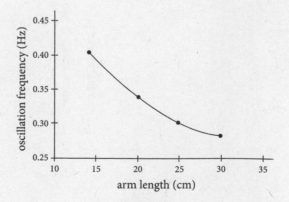

Figure 1

GO ON TO THE NEXT PAGE

EXPERIMENT 2

A spring was suspended vertically from a hook, and a mass was connected to the bottom of the spring, as shown in Diagram 2. The mass was pulled downward a short distance and released, and the frequency of the resulting oscillation was measured. The procedure was repeated with four different springs and four different masses, and the results are shown in Figure 2.

Diagram 2

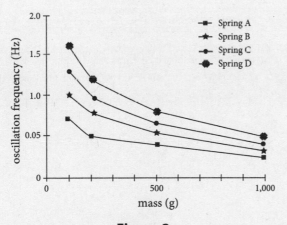

Figure 2

EXPERIMENT 3

Using the apparatus from Experiment 2, the mass-spring system was allowed to come to rest, and the *equilibrium length* of the spring was measured. The same four masses and four springs were used, and the results are shown in Figure 3.

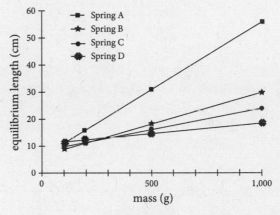

Figure 3

12. In Experiment 3, for which of the following masses would Spring B, Spring C, and Spring D have closest to the same equilibrium lengths?

F. 100 g

G. 270 g

H. 500 g

J. 1,000 g

GO ON TO THE NEXT PAGE

13. A student has hypothesized that as the length of the arm of a pendulum increases, the oscillation frequency of the pendulum during SHM will decrease. Do the results of Experiment 1 support her hypothesis?

   A. Yes; the oscillation frequency of the pendulum observed in Experiment 1 decreased as the arm length increased.

   B. Yes; although the longest pendulum arm resulted in the highest oscillation frequency, the frequency decreased with increasing arm length for the other three lengths tested.

   C. No; the oscillation frequency of the pendulum observed in Experiment 1 increased as the arm length increased.

   D. No; although the longest pendulum arm resulted in the lowest oscillation frequency, the frequency increased with increasing arm length for the other three lengths tested.

14. Based on the results of Experiment 2, if an engineer needs a spring that oscillates most slowly after being stretched and released, which of the following springs should be chosen?

   F. Spring A
   G. Spring B
   H. Spring C
   J. Spring D

15. Based on the results of Experiment 3, if a 700 g mass was suspended from Spring A, at what equilibrium length would the system come to rest?

   A. Less than 20 cm
   B. Between 20 cm and 30 cm
   C. Between 30 cm and 50 cm
   D. Greater than 50 cm

16. The students tested a fifth spring, Spring E, in the same manner as in Experiment 2. With a 100 g mass suspended from Spring E, the oscillation frequency was 1.4 Hz. Based on the results of Experiment 2, which of the following correctly lists the five springs by their oscillation frequency with a 100 g mass suspended from *fastest* to *slowest*?

   F. Spring E, Spring B, Spring C, Spring A, Spring D

   G. Spring D, Spring A, Spring C, Spring B, Spring E

   H. Spring A, Spring B, Spring C, Spring E, Spring D

   J. Spring D, Spring E, Spring C, Spring B, Spring A

GO ON TO THE NEXT PAGE

17. Experiment 1 was repeated using a larger pendulum mass. Which of the following figures best expresses the comparison between the results found using the larger pendulum mass and using the original mass?

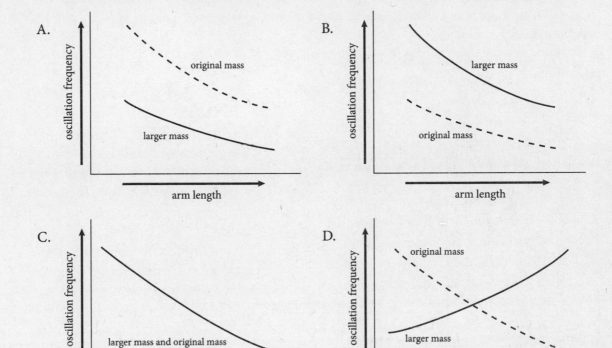

Passage IV

An *alloy* is a uniform mixture of two or more metals. When the melting point of an alloy is lower than the melting point of any of its metal components, the alloy is referred to as a *eutectic* system. Figure 1 is a *phase diagram* that illustrates the states of matter of the gold-silicon (Au-Si) eutectic system over a range of temperatures and alloy compositions. For the Au-Si system, 0% Si means pure Au, and 100% Si means pure Si.

Note: (Au) and (Si) represent the solid forms of gold and silicon, respectively.

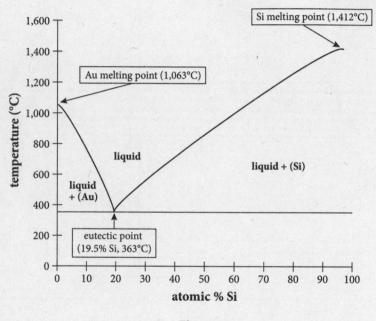

Figure 1

18. According to Figure 1, at what temperature will Au begin to boil?

    F.   363°C

    G. 1,063°C

    H. 1,412°C

    J.   The boiling point of Au is not included on the figure.

19. Based on Figure 1, an alloy that is atomically 50% Si and 50% Au will be in what state at a temperature of 600°C?

    A. Completely liquid

    B. Liquid with some amount of solid Si

    C. Liquid with some amount of solid Au

    D. Completely solid

GO ON TO THE NEXT PAGE

20. A *solder* is a metallic material designed specifically to have a very low melting point. To make a solder out of a Au-Si alloy, what atomic percentages of Au and Si would be most appropriate?

    F. 0% Si, 100% Au

    G. 19.5% Si, 80.5% Au

    H. 80.5% Si, 19.5% Au

    J. 100% Si, 0% Au

21. Based on the information in Figure 1, one could generalize that for Au-Si alloy compositions containing atomically less than 10% Si, the temperature at which the alloy becomes completely liquid decreases with:

    A. increasing Si atomic percentage.

    B. decreasing Si atomic percentage.

    C. increasing Au atomic percentage.

    D. neither increasing nor decreasing Si atomic percentage. The melting point is constant for all alloy compositions.

22. A liquid Au-Si alloy of unknown composition is gradually cooled from an initial temperature of 1,500°C. Solid particles are observed to begin forming as the temperature drops to 1,200°C. The particles must consist of which material, and what must be the approximate atomic composition of the alloy?

    F. The particles are Au, and the atomic composition of the alloy is 10% Si, 90% Au.

    G. The particles are Au, and the atomic composition of the alloy is 19.5% Si, 80.5% Au.

    H. The particles are Si, and the atomic composition of the alloy is 73% Si, 27% Au.

    J. The particles are Si, and the atomic composition of the alloy is 90% Si, 10% Au.

GO ON TO THE NEXT PAGE

Passage V

A person requires a certain percentage of oxygen in the blood for proper respiratory function. The amount of oxygen in the air varies enough with altitude that people normally accustomed to breathing near sea level may experience respiratory problems at significantly higher altitudes. Table 1 shows the average percentage of oxygen saturation in the blood, as well as the blood concentrations of three enzymes, GST, ECH, and CR, for three populations of high altitude (ha) dwellers and three populations of sea level (sl) dwellers. Enzyme concentrations are given in arbitrary units (a.u.). Figure 1 shows average oxygen partial pressure and average temperature at various altitudes.

Table 1

Population	Altitude range (m)	Oxygen saturation (%)	Enzyme concentration (a.u.)		
			GST	ECH	CR
ha 1	3,500–4,000	98.1	121.0	89.2	48.8
ha 2	3,300–3,700	99.0	108.3	93.5	45.6
ha 3	3,900–4,200	97.9	111.6	91.9	52.3
sl 1	0–300	98.5	86.7	57.1	44.9
sl 2	0–150	99.2	79.8	65.8	53.1
sl 3	0–200	98.7	82.5	61.4	47.0

Figure 1

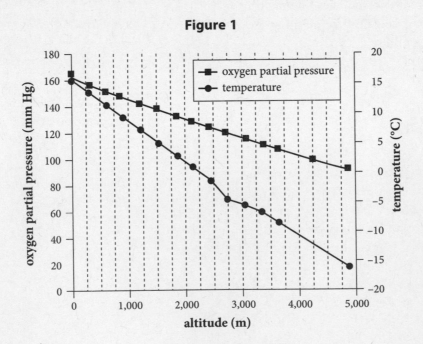

GO ON TO THE NEXT PAGE

23. Based on the data in Table 1, one would conclude that the blood of high altitude dwellers contains a higher concentration of:

A. CR than ECH.

B. CR than GST.

C. ECH than GST.

D. GST than CR.

24. Based on the information given, one would expect that, compared to the high altitude dwellers, the sea level dwellers:

F. have blood with a lower percentage oxygen saturation.

G. have blood with a lower GST concentration.

H. can tolerate lower oxygen partial pressures.

J. can tolerate lower temperatures.

25. According to Figure 1, an atmospheric sample found at an oxygen partial pressure of 110 mm Hg was most likely found at a temperature of about:

A. 8.1°C.

B. 0°C.

C. −5.4°C.

D. −12.5°C.

26. ECH is an enzyme that improves the efficiency of cellular energy production. Assume that people with higher ECH concentrations in the blood can function normally at higher altitudes without any respiratory difficulties. Based on Table 1, people from which population can function normally at the highest altitude?

F. sl 1

G. sl 2

H. ha 2

J. ha 3

27. Assume that a person's blood oxygen saturation percentage is determined only by the oxygen partial pressure at the location at which they live and the efficiency of the person's respiratory system at incorporating oxygen into the blood. Which of the following pieces of information supports the hypothesis that people from population ha 2 can incorporate oxygen into their blood more efficiently than people from population sl 1?

A. Population ha 2 lives where the oxygen partial pressure is lower than that of where population sl 1 lives, yet population ha 2 has a higher blood oxygen saturation percentage than does population ha 1.

B. Population ha 2 lives where the oxygen partial pressure is higher than that of where population sl 1 lives, yet population ha 2 has a lower blood oxygen saturation percentage than does population ha 1.

C. Population ha 2 has a higher CR concentration than does population sl 1.

D. Population ha 2 has an unusually high GST concentration.

GO ON TO THE NEXT PAGE

Passage VI

Two students explain why lakes freeze from the surface downward. They also discuss the phenomena of the melting of ice under the blades of an ice skater's skates.

STUDENT 1

Water freezes first at the surface of lakes because the freezing point of water decreases with increasing pressure. Under the surface, *hydrostatic pressure* causes the freezing point of water to be slightly lower than it is at the surface. Thus, as the air temperature drops, it reaches the freezing point of water at the surface before reaching that of the water beneath it. Only as the temperature becomes even colder will the layer of ice at the surface become thicker.

Pressure is defined as *force* divided by the *surface area* over which the force is exerted. An ice skater exerts the entire force of her body weight over the tiny surface area of two very thin blades. This results in a very large pressure, which quickly melts a small amount of ice directly under the blades.

STUDENT 2

Water freezes first at the surface of lakes because the density of ice is less than that of liquid water. Unlike most liquids, the volume of a given mass of water expands upon freezing, and the density therefore decreases. As a result, the *buoyant force* of water acting upward is greater than the force of gravity exerted downward by any mass of ice, and all ice particles float to the surface upon freezing.

Ice melts under an ice skater's skates because of friction. The energy used to overcome the force of friction is converted to heat, which melts the ice under the skates. The greater the weight of the skater, the greater the force of friction, and the faster the ice melts.

28. According to Student 1, which of the following quantities is *greater* for water molecules beneath a lake's surface than for water molecules at the surface?

    F. Temperature
    G. Density
    H. Buoyant force
    J. Hydrostatic pressure

29. When two ice skaters, wearing identical skates, skated across a frozen lake at the same speed, the ice under the blades of Skater B was found to melt faster than the ice under the blades of Skater A. What conclusion would each student draw about which skater is heavier?

    A. Both Student 1 and Student 2 would conclude that Skater A is heavier.
    B. Both Student 1 and Student 2 would conclude that Skater B is heavier.
    C. Student 1 would conclude that Skater A is heavier; Student 2 would conclude that Skater B is heavier.
    D. Student 1 would conclude that Skater B is heavier; Student 2 would conclude that Skater A is heavier.

30. Which student(s), if either, would predict that ice will melt under the blades of an ice skater who is NOT moving?

    F. Student 1 only
    G. Student 2 only
    H. Both Student 1 and Student 2
    J. Neither Student 1 nor Student 2

GO ON TO THE NEXT PAGE ⟩

31. A beaker of ethanol is found to freeze from the bottom upward, instead of from the surface downward. Student 2 would most likely argue that the density of frozen ethanol is:

    A. greater than the density of water.

    B. less than the density of ice.

    C. greater than the density of liquid ethanol.

    D. less than the density of liquid ethanol.

32. A toy boat was placed on the surface of a small pool of water, and the boat was gradually filled with sand. After a certain amount of sand had been added, the boat began to sink. Based on Student 2's explanation, the boat began to sink because:

    F. hydrostatic pressure became greater than the buoyant force of the water on the boat.

    G. atmospheric pressure became greater than the buoyant force of the water on the boat.

    H. the force of gravity of the boat on the water became greater than the buoyant force of the water on the boat.

    J. the force of gravity of the boat on the water became less than the buoyant force of the water on the boat.

33. According to Student 2, if friction between the ice and the blades of an ice skater's skates is reduced, which of the following quantities simultaneously decreases at the point where the blades and the ice are in contact?

    A. Pressure exerted by the blades on the ice

    B. Heat produced

    C. Force of gravity of the blades on the ice

    D. Freezing point of water

34. Based on Student 2's explanation, the reason a hot air balloon is able to rise above the ground is that the balloon and the air inside it are:

    F. less dense than the air outside the balloon.

    G. more dense than the air outside the balloon.

    H. at a higher pressure than the air outside the balloon.

    J. less buoyant than the air outside the balloon.

GO ON TO THE NEXT PAGE

Passage VII

In many communities, chemicals containing fluoride ions (F^-) are added to the drinking water supply to help prevent tooth decay. Use of F^- is controversial because studies have linked F^- with bone disease. Students performed two experiments to measure F^- levels.

EXPERIMENT I

Five solutions, each containing a different amount of Na_2SiF_6 (sodium silicofluoride) in H_2O were prepared. Five identical *electrodynamic cells* were filled with equal volumes of each of the five solutions, and a sixth identical cell was filled with a *blank* solution (one containing no added Na_2SiF_6). The cells were activated to measure the electrical *conductivity* for each. The conductivities were then corrected by subtracting the conductivity of the blank solution from each value (see Table 1 and Figure 1).

Table 1

Concentration of F^- (mg/L*)	Measured conductivity (μS/cm**)	Corrected conductivity (μS/cm**)
0.0	15.96	0.00
0.1	16.13	0.17
0.5	16.80	0.084
1.0	17.63	1.67
2.0	19.30	3.34
4.0	22.64	6.68

*mg/L is milligrams per liter.
**μS/cm is microsiemens per centimer.

Figure 1

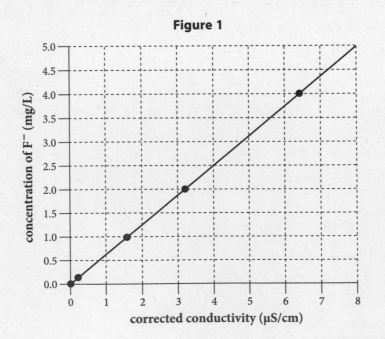

GO ON TO THE NEXT PAGE

EXPERIMENT 2

A water sample was taken directly from the drinking water supply of one community. An electrodynamic cell identical to those used in Experiment 1 was filled with water from this sample, and the cell was activated. The procedure was repeated for water samples from several communities, and the conductivities were measured (Table 2).

Table 2

Community	Measured conductivity (μS/cm**)	Concentration of F^- (mg/L)
Newtown	22.31	3.8
Springfield	16.46	0.3
Lakewood	18.63	1.6
Reading	19.47	2.1

35. Based on the results of Experiment 1, if the concentration of F^- in a solution is doubled, then the corrected conductivity of the solution will approximately:

    A. remain the same.
    B. halve.
    C. double.
    D. quadruple.

36. A sample was also taken from the drinking water supply of the community of Bluewater in Experiment 2, and its conductivity was measured to be 20.69 μS/cm. Which of the following correctly lists the drinking water supplies of Newtown, Lakewood, and Bluewater in *increasing* order of F^- concentration?

    F. Lakewood, Newtown, Bluewater
    G. Bluewater, Newtown, Lakewood
    H. Newtown, Bluewater, Lakewood
    J. Lakewood, Bluewater, Newtown

37. Based on the results of Experiment 1, if a solution with a concentration of 3.0 mg/L F^- had been tested, the corrected conductivity would have been closest to which of the following values?

    A. 1.3 μS/cm
    B. 3.3 μS/cm
    C. 5.0 μS/cm
    D. 6.5 μS/cm

38. If Experiments 1 and 2 were repeated to measure the concentration of chloride ions (Cl^-) in drinking water, then which of the following changes in procedure would be necessary?

    F. The solutions in Experiment 1 should be prepared by adding different concentrations of NaCl (or another chemical containing Cl^-) to H_2O.
    G. The conductivity of the blank solution should be added to the measured conductivities.
    H. The electrodynamic cells should be set to measure resistivity instead of conductivity.
    J. Both NaCl and Na_2SiF_6 should be added to all of the samples.

GO ON TO THE NEXT PAGE

39. Based on the results of Experiments 1 and 2, if the measured conductivities for the samples tested in Experiment 2 were compared with their corrected conductivities, the measured conductivities would be:

    A. lower for all of the samples tested.

    B. higher for all of the samples tested.

    C. lower for some of the samples tested, higher for others.

    D. the same for all of the samples tested.

40. The presence of other negative ions, such as Cl^-, results in an increase in the electrical conductivity of a solution. If all of the samples tested in Experiment 2 contained trace concentrations of Cl^-, how would the measurements have been affected? Compared to the actual F^- concentrations, the F^- concentrations apparently measured would be:

    F. higher.

    G. lower.

    H. the same.

    J. higher for some of the samples, lower for others.

WRITING TEST

30 Minutes—1 Question

Directions: This is a test of your writing skills. You will have thirty (30) minutes to write an essay in English. Before you begin planning and writing your essay, read the writing prompt carefully to understand exactly what you are being asked to do. Your essay will be evaluated on the evidence it provides of your ability to express judgments by taking a position on the issue in the writing prompt; to maintain a focus on the topic throughout the essay; to develop a position by using logical reasoning and by supporting your ideas; to organize ideas in a logical way; and to use language clearly and effectively according to the conventions of standard written English.

You may use the unlined pages in this test booklet to plan your essay. These pages will not be scored. *You must write your essay in pencil on the lined pages in the answer folder.* Your writing on those lined pages will be scored. You may not need all the lined pages, but to ensure you have enough room to finish, do NOT skip lines. You may write corrections or additions neatly between the lines of your essay, but do NOT write in the margins of the lined pages. *Illegible essays cannot be scored, so you must write (or print) clearly.*

If you finish before time is called, you may review your work. Lay your pencil down immediately when time called.

DO NOT OPEN THIS BOOKLET UNTIL TOLD TO DO SO.

GO ON TO THE NEXT PAGE

ACT Writing Test Prompt

In some cities, laws have been proposed that would restrict licensed drivers under 18 to driving alone or with an adult in the car. Parents and lawmakers who favor such laws point to the high incidence of car accidents with 16- and 17-year-old drivers, and claim that not allowing teenagers under 18 to ride together will help newer drivers to focus on driving safely. Teenagers and parents who are against the restriction argue that teenagers riding together isn't necessarily the cause of accidents and that more comprehensive driver training is a better way to reduce accidents. In your opinion, should cities pass laws that ban teenagers from riding in a car that is driven by a person under 18?

In your essay, take a position on this question. You may write about either one of the two points of view given, or you may present a different point of view on this question. Use specific reasons and examples to support your position.

Use this space to *plan* your essay. Your work here will not be graded. Write your essay on the lined pages that follow.

GO ON TO THE NEXT PAGE

GO ON TO THE NEXT PAGE

_____

_____

_____

_____

_____

_____

_____

_____

_____

_____

_____

_____

_____

_____

_____

_____

_____

_____

_____

_____

_____

_____

_____

Practice Test Three
ANSWER KEY

ENGLISH TEST

1. C	11. A	21. C	31. C	41. B	51. D	61. D	71. A
2. H	12. G	22. G	32. H	42. G	52. F	62. H	72. G
3. C	13. A	23. C	33. D	43. D	53. C	63. A	73. A
4. J	14. H	24. J	34. F	44. G	54. J	64. H	74. H
5. B	15. B	25. C	35. B	45. A	55. D	65. B	75. D
6. J	16. J	26. J	36. F	46. J	56. H	66. F	
7. B	17. A	27. B	37. C	47. D	57. A	67. B	
8. J	18. J	28. G	38. F	48. H	58. J	68. G	
9. D	19. D	29. D	39. C	49. D	59. C	69. D	
10. H	20. H	30. J	40. H	50. G	60. G	70. G	

MATH TEST

1. E	9. B	17. E	25. C	33. D	41. D	49. C	57. B
2. K	10. H	18. J	26. F	34. F	42. G	50. G	58. F
3. C	11. D	19. A	27. D	35. E	43. A	51. A	59. C
4. H	12. G	20. H	28. F	36. H	44. K	52. H	60. H
5. D	13. C	21. A	29. B	37. C	45. C	53. D	
6. J	14. J	22. J	30. K	38. H	46. J	54. K	
7. A	15. D	23. E	31. C	39. C	47. E	55. A	
8. G	16. G	24. H	32. K	40. J	48. H	56. J	

READING TEST

1. D	6. H	11. C	16. J	21. C	26. F	31. B	36. H
2. H	7. B	12. G	17. C	22. J	27. B	32. F	37. B
3. B	8. F	13. B	18. J	23. C	28. H	33. C	38. J
4. J	9. C	14. F	19. A	24. F	29. B	34. H	39. B
5. D	10. F	15. B	20. G	25. D	30. G	35. C	40. G

SCIENCE TEST

1. C	6. H	11. A	16. J	21. A	26. H	31. C	36. J
2. H	7. C	12. G	17. C	22. H	27. A	32. H	37. C
3. A	8. H	13. A	18. J	23. D	28. J	33. B	38. F
4. J	9. B	14. F	19. B	24. G	29. B	34. F	39. B
5. B	10. F	15. C	20. G	25. C	30. F	35. C	40. F

ANSWERS AND EXPLANATIONS

English Test

The questions fall into the following categories, according to the skills they test. If you notice that you're having trouble with particular categories, review the following:

1. REDUNDANCY: English Workout 1

2. RELEVANCE: English Workout 1

3. VERBOSITY: English Workout 1

4. JUDGING THE PASSAGE: English Workout 2

5. LOGIC: English Workout 2

6. MODIFIERS: English Workout 2

7. READING-TYPE QUESTIONS: English Workout 2

8. STRUCTURE AND PURPOSE: English Workout 2

9. TONE: English Workout 2

10. VERB USAGE: English Workout 2

11. COMPLETENESS: English Workouts 2 and 3

12. IDIOM: English Workouts 2 and 3

13. PRONOUNS: English Workouts 2 and 3

14. SENTENCE STRUCTURE: English Workouts 2 and 3

15. PUNCTUATION: English Workout 3

PASSAGE I

1. C
Verb Usage

Choice C forms a complete sentence by using the simple past tense *was*. Choice A creates a sentence fragment; an *-ing* verb needs a helping verb, such as *was* or *is*, to be the main verb in a sentence. Choice B incorrectly uses a comma to separate the subject from the main verb. Choice D omits the verb entirely, creating a sentence fragment.

2. H
Logic

The phrase *not only* in the beginning of the sentence is your clue to the correct answer. Logically, the phrase *not only* is always followed by *but also*. The other choices neither complete the idiom correctly nor convey the necessary contrast between the ideas in the two clauses.

3. C
Punctuation

Add an apostrophe and an *s* to a singular noun to show possession. The narrator and Gretchen attend one school, so choice C is correct. Choice A omits the apostrophe needed to show that the *swim team* belongs to the *school*. Choice B incorrectly treats *school* as a plural, placing the apostrophe after the *s*. Choice D incorrectly uses *ours* and does not make *school* possessive.

4. J
Verbosity

The test makers value simple and direct prose, so change passive constructions such as "it was with Gretchen that I" when you're given the opportunity. As is often the case on the English section of the ACT, the shortest answer—choice J—is correct. In addition to being verbose, choice F contains a sentence structure error: it is not clear who knows that the writer enjoyed swimming. Choices G and H are both also verbose.

5. B
Judging the Passage

Slow down and carefully read the Nonstandard-Format questions. You just may see a question such as this that tests vocabulary. Choice B indicates that the narrator's mother recommended swimming lessons but did not decide that the narrator *must* take them. Choices A, C, and D all indicate that the mother's mind was made up.

6. J
Pronouns

If a sentence seems to have too many ideas, then it is probably a run-on. By itself, a comma cannot separate two clauses that could be independent sentences, as in choice F. Choice G replaces *swimmers* with a pronoun but does not correct the run-on. Similarly, choice H removes the comma but does not address the problem of two complete thoughts that are incorrectly joined. Choice J solves the problem by using *whom*, which turns the second half of the sentence into a dependent clause that describes the *women*.

7. B
Punctuation

This sentence contains a parenthetical phrase. If you omitted "who had been swimming competitively since elementary school," you would still have a complete sentence. Like all parenthetical phrases, this needs to be set off from the rest of the sentence. A comma is used at the beginning of the phrase, so a comma must also be used at the end of the phrase. This makes choice D incorrect. Choices A and C insert unnecessary commas within the parenthetical phrase.

8. J
Redundancy

When in doubt, take it out. *Giving up,* by definition, means "quitting" or "failing." Choices F, G, and H create redundancies.

9. D
Verb Usage

Trust your ear. *Begin* is an irregular verb; the simple past tense *began* can be used by itself, but the past participle *begun* cannot. Instead, *begun* always appears with *has*, *have*, or *had*, as in "I *have begun* to prepare for the ACT." Choice D correctly uses the simple past tense *began*. Choice B creates another verb usage error by inserting *been*. Choice C incorrectly uses *began* with *had*.

10. H
Pronouns

Don't panic if you see a question that tests the use of *who* and *whom*. The pronoun *who* serves as a subject, just like the pronouns *he* and *she* replace subjects. The pronoun *whom* serves as an object, just like the pronouns *him* and *her* replace objects. Here, *coach* is the subject of the sentence, so *who* (choice H) is correct. Never refer to a person as *which* (choice J).

11. A
Verbosity

Don't force a change where one isn't needed. The correct answer for some of the underlined portions will be NO CHANGE. The sentence "The hard work eventually paid off" is correct and concise as it is written. Choice B is verbose, and choices C and D create run-on sentences.

12. G
Judging the Passage

Start by asking yourself, "Does this stuff belong here?" The question asks for a sentence that is relevant to the narrator's experience on the swim team. Only choice G is connected to the narrator and the swim team; the sentence explains that the narrator was one of the only swimmers on the team to be interested in the butterfly. The history of the stroke, F, the relative speed of the stroke, H, and an alternative name for the stroke, J, are not as related to the narrator's personal experience.

13. A
Relevance

The shortest answer is often, but not always, correct. Don't omit portions that add relevant information to the sentence. The sentence is about the narrator's swimming, so her participation in the medley relay is relevant. Choices B and C add descriptions of the medley relay that are not relevant to the topic.

14. H
Verb Usage

The four choices offer different tenses of the same verb. The clue *last year* indicates that the narrator earned the varsity letter in the past. Choice H, the simple past tense, is correct. Neither the future tense, F, nor the present tense, J, makes sense with the clue *last year*. Choice G would only make sense if something had prevented the narrator from earning the varsity letter.

15. B
Judging the Passage

Keep the main point of the passage in mind. Before beginning high school, the narrator had never thought of herself as an athlete. Then she joined the swim team and became successful at the sport. Choice B is most relevant to the central ideas of the passage. Choices A and C focus too narrowly on details in the passage, while choice D contradicts the main point of the passage.

PASSAGE II

16. J
Punctuation

Don't assume that a comma or semicolon is needed just because a sentence is long. Read the sentence aloud to yourself, and you should be able to hear that a comma is not needed in the underlined portion. A semicolon would only be correct if the second half of the sentence expressed a complete thought (choice F). Choices G and H both use an unnecessary comma.

17. A
Verb Usage

When a verb is underlined, check to see if it agrees with its noun. Watch out for descriptive phrases that separate a verb from its noun. Here, the verb *was* agrees with the singular noun *tank*. NO CHANGE is needed. Choice B uses the present tense, but the surrounding sentences use the past tense. Choices C and D incorrectly use a verb in the plural form.

18. J
Completeness

When the word *that* or *which* is underlined, watch out for an incomplete sentence. As it is written, this is a sentence fragment; a complete verb is missing. Removing *that*, as in choice J, turns *made* into the main verb of a complete and correct sentence. Choice G does not address the sentence fragment error, and choice H also fails to provide a clear and appropriate sentence.

19. D
Redundancy

If you are *familiar* with a type of animal, then you have almost certainly *seen it before*. Choice D creates a concise sentence that does not lose any of the original meaning. The other choices are redundant. Choice B repeats *sights* when *view* has already been used, and choice C uses the unnecessarily repetitive phrase "to which I was no stranger."

20. H
Logic

Scan the paragraph for connecting words and phrases that you can use as clues to determine the most logical order of sentences. In sentence 5, the word *first* suggests that the sentence should be placed close to the beginning of the paragraph. Sentence 2 says, "There were *also* animals I had never before glimpsed," which indicates that a preceding sentence discusses animals the writer had glimpsed. Sentence 5, which describes the writer's view of familiar animals, most logically belongs immediately after sentence 1.

21. C
Verb Usage

If an underlined verb agrees with its noun, then determine whether the verb's tense makes sense in the context of the passage. The surrounding verbs are in the past tense, so this sentence should use the simple past tense *saw* (choice C). Choices A and D use the present tense, and choice B illogically uses the past progressive "had been seeing."

22. G
Judging the Passage

An effective first sentence for a paragraph will introduce the topic of the paragraph and connect that topic to ideas that have come before. Paragraph 3 focuses on the catfish, while paragraph 4 describes the large alligator and snapping turtle in the bayou tank. Choice G is an effective connection between these paragraphs, referring to the catfish and introducing the idea that there were even bigger animals on display. Neither choice F nor choice H leads into the topic of paragraph 4. Choice J doesn't

provide a transition from the discussion of the catfish in paragraph 3.

23. C
Judging the Passage

The phrase in question provides a visual image; deleting the phrase would mean losing a description (choice C). The removal of the phrase would not affect the transition between sentences (choice A). Contrary to choice B, the contrast between images would be decreased. The level of suspense may be somewhat decreased by the loss of the description, but it would not be increased (choice D).

24. J
Verb Usage

The verbs *slides* and *aims* agree with the singular subject *it*, but they are in the wrong tense. The rest of the paragraph describes actions that took place in the past. For the sentence to make sense in context, these verbs should also be in the past tense (choice J). Choices F and G use present-tense verbs. Choice H creates a logically incomplete sentence.

25. C
Modifiers

If something sounds awkward or unusual, there is probably an error. Most words that end in -*ly* are adverbs; they are used to modify verbs, adjectives, or other adverbs. Adverbs cannot be used to describe nouns, such as *moment* (choice A). Choice C correctly uses the adjective *slight* to modify *panic*. The sentences formed by choices B and D don't make sense.

26. J
Idiom

The phrase "much of the onlookers" probably sounds strange to you. That's because *much* is used with noncountable things or concepts (as in "there isn't much time") or quantities (as in "there isn't much pizza left"). You could count the number of *onlookers*, so *many*, choice J, is correct. Choices G and H also create idiomatic errors.

27. B
Judging the Passage
The question tells you that the writer's goal is to describe the appearance of the crayfish, so eliminate any sentences that do not have details about how crayfish look (choice C). Choice A suggests that crayfish look like lobsters, and choice D describes the crayfish as small. Neither of these sentences offers the descriptive detail that is given in choice B.

28. G
Punctuation
Trust your ear. You naturally pause when a comma or semicolon is needed in a sentence. A pause between *all* and *I* just doesn't sound right; that's because the full introductory phrase "After seeing all I could inside the museum" should not be interrupted. A comma should not separate a verb (*seeing*) from its object (*museum*). This eliminates choices F and H. A comma is needed between an introductory phrase and the complete thought that follows, making choice G correct and choice J incorrect.

29. D
Verbosity
Say it simply. The shortest answer here is correct: it turns the passive construction "it was that" in choices A and B into the active "I had." Choice C is unnecessarily wordy.

30. J
Completeness
A sentence must have a subject and verb and express a complete thought. The sentence that begins "And operates" does not have a subject. Removing the period (choice J) creates a grammatically correct sentence. Choice G is awkwardly worded. Choice H creates a run-on sentence; a coordinating conjunction such as *and* needs to be used along with a comma to link two complete thoughts.

PASSAGE III
31. C
Pronouns
When a pronoun is underlined, check to see that it agrees in number with the noun it replaces or refers to. In this sentence, the underlined pronoun refers back to the plural "secret identities and elaborate disguises." Choice C uses the correct plural pronoun *they*. Choices A and B create pronoun agreement errors by using the singular pronoun *it*. Choice D creates a sentence fragment.

32. H
Punctuation
Many English questions will focus on the correct use of commas. Commas should be used to separate an appositive or descriptive phrase from the main part of the sentence. The phrase "the restaurant critic for the *New York Times*" describes the noun *Ruth Reichl,* so the phrase should be set off with commas (choice H). Choices F and J fail to use both necessary commas. On the other hand, choice G incorrectly inserts a third comma.

33. D
Structure and Purpose
Only add sentences that are directly connected to the topic of a paragraph. Paragraph 2 discusses the importance of a *Times* review to restaurants in New York City. The suggested sentence provides a specific detail about one restaurant without explaining how the review from the *Times* affected business. Choice D best explains why the sentence should not be added.

34. F
Idiom

Trust your ear. We look *to* someone or something for advice. No change is needed. Choice G suggests that the paper is looking along *with* its readers, while choice H suggests that the readers are looking near the newspaper. Choice J uses an *-ing* verb without a helping verb, which creates a sentence fragment.

35. B
Verb Usage

Verbs must make sense in the context of the passage. The next sentence says that a negative review "can undermine" a restaurant. Because the two sentences discuss possible results of a review, the underlined verb in this sentence should be in the same tense—"can bring" (choice B). Choice A illogically uses the conditional in the past tense, while choices C and D do not use the conditional at all.

36. F
Punctuation

The subject of the sentence is "restaurant owners and workers," and the verb is *have*. There isn't a descriptive phrase or clause separating the subject and verb, so no comma is needed. A semicolon should be used to connect two complete thoughts (choice G). Choice H incorrectly treats *restaurant* as the first item in a list; instead, *restaurant* identifies the type of *owners* and *workers*.

37. C
Pronouns

To whom does the meal belong? It belongs to the *writer,* so the possessive pronoun *whose* is correct. *Who's* is always a contraction for *who is* or *who has* (choice B). Choices A and D introduce sentence structure errors.

38. F
Verbosity

The shortest answer is often correct. The sentence is concise and direct as it is written. Each of the other choices adds unnecessary words to the underlined portion.

39. C
Redundancy

On the ACT, there's no need to say the same thing twice. *Common*, *ordinary*, *representative*, and *average* all have very similar meanings; choices A and B use redundant language. Choice C makes the sentence concise by using only *typical*. Choice D uses a word that does not make sense in the context of the sentence.

40. H
Redundancy

If you have *decided* to do something to solve a problem, you have found a *solution*—there's no need to use both words. Choice H eliminates the redundancy and verbosity errors of the other choices.

41. B
Modifiers

As a rule, modifying words, phrases, and clauses should be as close as possible to the things or actions they describe. For instance, the list beginning "such as an attractive blonde named Chloe" describes the *different personas*. Therefore, *different personas* should come right before the list. This eliminates choice A. Choice B correctly uses an introductory phrase and makes *Reichl* the subject of the sentence. Choice C is a sentence fragment; a complete verb is missing. Choice D inserts an unnecessary comma between *clothing* and *that*, and the pronoun *herself* is incorrect in context.

42. G
Logic

The most logical and effective sentence will be connected to the main topic of the paragraph and make a transition to the following sentence. Paragraph 4 describes how Reichl turned herself into different characters, and paragraph 5 describes the result of reviewing a restaurant while in disguise. The best link between these ideas is choice G. Choice F is a narrow detail that does not connect the two paragraphs, while choices H and J move completely away from the topic of Reichl's disguises.

43. D
Judging the Passage

Sometimes it helps to rephrase a question in your own words. For example, how this question could be rewritten: "What does the phrase *of a restaurant* describe?" Reichl focuses on the quality of a restaurant, so the best placement is D. The phrase does not describe *developed*, *view*, or *person*.

44. G
Logic

The word *occasionally* means "sometimes"; its placement in this sentence indicates that Reichl was sometimes treated very differently when she was in disguise, and sometimes she wasn't. Removing the word *occasionally* would indicate that Reichl always or typically had a different experience as one of her personas (choice G).

45. A
Judging the Passage

Paragraph 6 describes the effect of Reichl's use of disguises when she reviewed restaurants. Logically, this effect should follow the explanation of why and how Ruth dined as different people, the topics of paragraphs 3 and 4. Paragraph 6 should remain where it is.

PASSAGE IV

46. J
Punctuation

Trust your ear. A comma indicates a short pause, which you won't hear when you read this part of the sentence aloud. No comma is needed (choice J). A comma can be used to separate a descriptive phrase from the rest of the sentence (choices F and H), but neither "would develop into prize-winning vegetables" nor "develop into prize-winning vegetables" is a descriptive phrase. Choice G incorrectly treats the underlined portion of the sentence as part of a list.

47. D
Judging the Passage

The paragraph describes events in chronological order, from the last freeze of the year to the time that spring *truly arrived*. Sentence 3 describes thinning out the plants and pulling weeds so the new plants would grow; it would only make sense to do this *after* the seeds have been planted and have started to grow. Sentence 4 is about planting seeds, so sentence 3 must come after sentence 4 (choice D).

48. H
Sentence Structure

When you read this sentence aloud, you should be able to hear a short pause between *burden* and *less*. This pause indicates that the conjunction *and* is needed to separate the two descriptions (choice H). Choice G is wrong because a colon is used to introduce a brief definition, explanation, or list. Choice J uses the inappropriate conjunction *but*, which doesn't make sense in context.

49. D
Relevance

When "OMIT the underlined portion" is an option, consider whether the underlined portion is relevant to the topic of the sentence or paragraph. Paragraph 2 is about the writer's failure to maintain her garden, not about the weather in July and August. Choice D is correct.

50. G
Structure and Purpose

Always read the questions carefully! This one asks for the choice that would NOT work in the sentence. In other words, three of the answer choices would make sense in the sentence. The first sentence of paragraph 3 contrasts with paragraph 2, so the contrasting transitions in F, H, and J are all possible substitutions for the underlined word. *Indeed* (choice G), however, is a word used to show emphasis, not contrast.

51. D
Logic

The shortest answer is often correct. Choices A, B, and C all refer to large-scale farming, which is only loosely related to the topic of gardening. Choice D keeps the sentence focused on the topic of paragraph 3.

52. F
Judging the Passage

Before you answer this question, read enough of paragraph 4 to identify its main idea. Paragraph 3 introduces the topic of square-foot gardening, and paragraph 4 describes several of its advantages. The best link between these ideas is the original sentence (choice F). Paragraph 4 doesn't mention the history of square-foot gardening or the writer's neighbor, so choices G and J don't make sense. Choice H is a detail about square-foot gardening, but it does not function as a topic sentence for the paragraph.

53. C
Modifiers

If an underlined word ends in *-ly*, you can be pretty sure that it is an adverb. Remember that adverbs can be used to describe verbs,

adjectives, and other adverbs, but not nouns. The word *garden* is a noun, so choices A and B are incorrect. The adjective *traditional* (choice C) is correct. The phrase *tradition garden* (choice D) does not make sense.

54. J
Pronouns

Who spends hours thinning each row? From this sentence, it's unclear: you have no idea who *they* are. Other sentences in paragraph 4 use the pronoun *you*, so it makes sense to use *you* here.

55. D
Redundancy

"OMIT the underlined portion" is an option, so check to see if the information is irrelevant to the topic or repetitive. This sentence begins with the phrase "In a square-foot garden," so it is unnecessary to repeat "in the garden." Choice D is correct.

56. H
Completeness

"OMIT the underlined portion" isn't always the correct answer. As it is written, the sentence does not express a complete thought. To correct the error, remove *which could* so that *make* becomes the main verb of the sentence. Choices G and J create sentence fragments.

57. A
Pronouns

Don't look too hard for an error—many of the English questions will require NO CHANGE. The present tense and the pronoun *you* are used throughout paragraph 4, so this sentence is correct as it is written.

58. J
Verbosity

Remember that the ACT values economy. If you can express an underlined portion in fewer words without changing or losing the original meaning, then the shortest answer is probably correct. The only choice that does not use redundant language is J.

59. C
Verb Usage

The verb in this sentence is separated from its singular subject "one season" by the phrase "of using the square garden techniques." Choice C corrects the subject-verb agreement error of the original sentence. Incorrect choices use the plural form of the verb (A and B) or the future tense D, which does not make sense in the context of the sentence.

60. G
Judging the Passage

This question asks about the passage as a whole, so take a moment to think about the main idea of the passage. Paragraphs 1 and 2 describe the writer's failed attempts at a traditional garden, while paragraphs 3, 4, and 5 focus on the writer's success with a square-foot garden. The essay is not instructive; instead, it compares two types of gardens, choice G.

PASSAGE V

61. D
Punctuation

When a coordinating conjunction such as *but* or *and* combines two independent clauses (complete thoughts), a comma must come before it. In this sentence, a comma should be inserted after *light* (choice D). Choice C incorrectly places a comma in a compound and fails to add one before the coordinating conjunction, and choice B incorrectly uses a semicolon between an independent and a dependent clause. You'll likely see at least one semicolon question on the ACT, so remember that a semicolon is used to separate two complete thoughts or to separate

items in a series or list when one or more of those items already contains commas.

62. H
Verb Usage

The answer choices present different forms of the verbs *improves* and *decreases*, so you know the issue is subject-verb agreement. The two underlined verbs need to agree with the plural subject *steps*; only choice H puts both *improve* and *decrease* in the correct form.

63. A
Redundancy

The simplest way to say something is often the most correct way to say something. The original sentence is the most concise and correct version. Choice B is redundant, using both *problem* and *trouble*. Choices C and D are both unnecessarily wordy in comparison to A, which expresses the same meaning.

64. H
Verb Usage

An *-ing* verb needs a helping verb to function as the main verb in a clause or sentence. Changing *being* to *is*, as in choice H, corrects the sentence structure error. Choice G inserts an incorrect comma between *vision* and *has been*, while choice J creates a new sentence structure error by omitting the verb *being*.

65. B
Logic

Something that is *set* is established or predetermined. For the sentence to make sense, *set* should describe *time*; the wiper blades should be replaced at an *established* time each year. Choice B is correct. It does not make sense for the *blades* (choice A), the *year* (choice C), or the *risk* (choice D) to be *set*, or established.

66. F
Idioms
Trust your ear. With some idiom questions, you have to rely on your ear to hear what sounds correct. *In general* is an introductory phrase used to mean "usually" or "typically." Choice F provides the correct idiom for this context. The other choices contain idioms that are not typical of spoken English and do not fit this context.

67. B
Structure and Purpose
To pick the best first sentence for paragraph 4, you must be able to identify the main idea of the paragraph. If you scan a few sentences of paragraph 4 before you answer the question, you'll see that the topic of the paragraph is changing a car's oil and oil filter. Only choice B introduces this topic. Choice A is too general, while choices C and D refer to car maintenance procedures that are not discussed in paragraph 4.

68. G
Logic
The connecting word *so* is underlined, so consider the relationship between the two parts of the sentence. There is a slight contrast—the first part of the sentence explains what you *do* need, while the second part identifies what you *don't* need. The contrasting conjunction *but* (choice G) makes the most sense in context. The other choices indicate a cause-and-effect relationship that is not present in the sentence.

69. D
Punctuation
Information that is key to the main idea of a sentence should not be set off by commas. Here, it's important to know that the section is "in your owner's manual," so commas are incorrect. Choice D is correct. Choice C incorrectly uses a semicolon; a complete thought is not expressed by "and collect all of the tools you need."

70. G
Structure and Purpose
Carefully read the question so that you understand the writer's purpose. If the writer wants to explain how to change oil, then the sentence should explain at least one specific step in the process. Choice G provides the most detailed information about how to go about changing oil.

71. A
Punctuation
Use a semicolon to introduce or emphasize what follows. The warning "you do not want to risk being crushed by a car" is certainly worthy of emphasis, so the sentence is correct as it is written. The other choices create run-ons, as the sentence expresses two complete thoughts; additionally, D incorrectly separates a subject noun from its verb with a comma.

72. G
Tone
Paragraph 4 uses the informal *you* and *your*, while the rest of the essay uses the more formal third person. Therefore, eliminating the second-person pronouns from paragraph 4 would make the paragraph match the tone and voice of the rest of the essay (choice G). Choices H and J are opposite answers: eliminating *you* and *your* would make the advice less direct and would make the essay more formal.

73. A
Redundancy
Watch out for redundant language! A "qualified mechanic" will do a *professional* job, just as a "qualified mechanic" is likely *certified*; choices B and C use repetitive language. Choice D introduces a sentence structure error. The best version of the underlined portion is choice A.

74. H
Judging the Passage

Knowing the general topic of each paragraph will help you quickly answer a question like this one. The sentence refers to "these different fluids," so look for a part of the passage that discusses fluids. The second and third sentences of paragraph 3 refer to different fluids (*coolant, oil, brake fluid,* and *transmission fluid*), so the most logical placement for the sentence is at the end of paragraph 3 (choice H). Paragraph 2 and paragraph 4 each only refer to one fluid, so choices F and J are incorrect.

75. D
Judging the Passage

Use your Reading Comp skills to answer this question. Does the main idea of the passage fit with this purpose? Not really, as the passage focuses solely on basic maintenance that car owners can do themselves. The passage doesn't discuss the need to learn about a car's safety features. Choice D is correct.

Math Test

Answer explanations for the Math test refer to 100 Key Math Concepts for the ACT, found at the end of this book.

1. E
Adding/Subtracting Fractions

100 Key Math Concepts for the ACT, #22. To determine the total amount of fabric used, add the mixed numbers. To add mixed numbers, add the whole number parts, and then add the fractions. The whole number parts add to 4. To add the fractions, find the least common denominator of 8 and 3, which is 24. Convert each fraction to an equivalent fraction with a denominator of 24: $\frac{3 \times 3}{8 \times 3} = \frac{9}{24}$ and $\frac{1 \times 8}{3 \times 8} = \frac{8}{24}$.

Now, add the numerators, and keep the denominator: $\frac{9}{24} + \frac{8}{24} + \frac{17}{24}$. The total fabric used is $4\frac{17}{24}$. If you chose B, you found a common denominator, but you forgot to multiply the numerators by the same factor that you had multiplied the denominators by. A common error when adding fractions would result in choice C. This fraction was obtained by the incorrect procedure of adding the numerators, and then adding the denominators.

2. K
Multiplying and Dividing Powers, Multiplying Monomials

100 Key Math Concepts for the ACT #47, #55. To simplify this expression, first multiply the numerical coefficients to get $5 \times 6 \times 2 = 60$. To multiply the variable terms, keep the base of the variable and add the exponents. Remember that x denotes x^1. Multiply the x variable terms: $x^3 \times x = x^{3+1} = x^4$. Multiply the y variable terms: $y^5 \times y^2 \times y = y^{5+2+1} = y^8$. The resultant expression is $60x^4y^8$.

If your answer was J, you fell into the common trap of multiplying the exponents instead of the correct method of adding the exponents. If your answer was either F or G, you added the numerical coefficients instead of multiplying. If your answer was H, you did not include the exponents of 1 for the single terms of x and y.

3. C
Percent Formula

100 Key Math Concepts for the ACT, #32. First, find the amount each person saves yearly. Brandon saves 6% of his $36,000 salary, or $0.06 \times 36,000 = \$2,160$ each year. Jacqui saves $200 every month, or $12 \times 200 = \$2,400$ each year. The difference, in dollars, of their savings is therefore $2,400 - 2,160 = \$240$.

Answer choice A reflects the *monthly* difference in their savings. If you chose answer choice D, you incorrectly found the difference between Brandon's yearly savings and Jacqui's *monthly* savings. Choice E indicates Brandon's monthly *salary* minus Jacqui's monthly savings.

4. H
Average Formula,
Using the Average to Find the Sum,
Find the Missing Number
100 Key Math Concepts for the ACT, #41, #43, #44. An average is found by taking the total sum of the terms and dividing it by the total number of terms. Therefore, the sum = (average) × (number of terms). For Mikhail to have an average for the five games of 180, the sum = 180 × 5 = 900. The first four scores total 190 + 200 + 145 + 180 = 715. Therefore, his score for the fifth game must be 900 − 715 = 185.

Answer choice F is just the average of the first four scores. Choice G is the average of the first four scores added and averaged with 180.

5. D
Percent Formula
100 Key Math Concepts for the ACT, #32. The amount of chromium is a part of the whole alloy. Use the formula Part = Percent × Whole. There are 262.5 pounds of chromium available, which must reflect at least 10.5% of the whole. Let w represent the whole amount of alloy that can be manufactured and write the algebraic equation: $262.5 = 10.5\%w$ or $262.5 = 0.105w$. Divide both sides of the equation by 0.105: $w = \frac{262.5}{0.105}$ pounds of steel.

Choice A represents 10.5% of 262.5. If you chose answer choice B, you simply subtracted 10.5 from 262.5, without regard to the percent or the whole amount. Answer choice C is simply the amount of chromium. If you chose answer choice E, you set up the problem correctly but incorrectly converted 10.5% to the decimal 0.0105.

6. J
Special Quadrilaterals
100 Key Math Concepts for the ACT, #86. A wallpaper border is a strip that surrounds the perimeter of the kitchen. The perimeter of a rectangle = 2(length + width). The kitchen has a length of 6.5 meters and a width of 4 meters, so the amount of border needed is 2(6.5 + 4) = 2(10.5) = 21 meters.

Answer choice G is a common mistake made when calculating perimeter. This answer would result from just adding the two dimensions and not multiplying by 2. Answer choice K is the area, not the perimeter, of the kitchen.

7. A
PEMDAS
100 Key Math Concepts for the ACT, #7. To find an equivalent for the given expression, use the distributive property. First, evaluate the inner parentheses according to the order of operations, or PEMDAS. Distribute the negative sign to $(y + z)$ to get $w(x - y - z)$. Next, distribute the variable w to all terms in parentheses to get $wx - wy - wz$.

Answer choice B fails to distribute the negative sign to the z term. Answer choices C and D only distribute the w to the first term. Choice E incorrectly distributes wx to the $(y + z)$ term.

8. G
Solving a Linear Equation
100 Key Math Concepts for the ACT, #63. This is an equation with a variable on both sides. To solve, work to get the n terms isolated on one side of the equation and the numerical terms on the other side. Subtract $3n$ from both sides to get $6n - 3n - 4 = 3n - 3n + 24$. Combine like terms: $3n - 4 = 24$. Now, add 4 to both sides: $3n - 4 + 4 = 24 + 4$, or $3n = 28$. Finally, divide both sides by 3: $n = \frac{28}{3}$. Answer choice F reflects a common trap: forgetting to divide by 3. If

you chose answer choice H or J, you incorrectly added $6n$ and $3n$ and possibly subtracted 4 from 24 instead of adding 4. Dividing incorrectly at the last step would have led you to answer choice K.

9. B
Translating from English into Algebra, Solving a Linear Equation

100 Key Math Concepts for the ACT, #63, #65. In this arithmetic sequence, you can think of the terms as 26, $26 + s$, $26 + s + s$, and $26 + s + s + s$. In this example, s represents the difference between successive terms. The final term is 53, so set up an algebraic equation: $26 + s + s + s = 53$. Solve this equation for s, by first combining like terms: $26 + 3s = 53$. Subtract 26 from both sides to get $26 - 26 + 3s = 53 - 26$, or $3s = 27$. Divide both sides by 3 to find that s, the difference between terms, is 9. Therefore, the terms are 26, $26 + 9$, $26 + 9 + 9$, 53, or 26, 35, 44, 53.

Answer choice D results from taking $53 - 26$, dividing by 4, adding this value to each term, and rounding. In all of the incorrect answer choices, there is a common difference between second − first and then fourth − third, but it is different than the difference between the third and the second terms.

10. H
Evaluating an Expression, Solving a Linear Equation

100 Key Math Concepts for the ACT, #52, #63. First, solve the equation $5m^2 = 45$ for m. Once a value is obtained for m, substitute this into the expression to evaluate and find the answer. To solve the equation, divide both sides of the equation by 5 to get $m^2 = 9$. Take the square root of each side to get $m = 3$, or $m = -3$. Now, evaluate the expression. Because the expression contains the radical $\sqrt{12m}$, and the expression must be a real number, reject the value of $m = -3$. When a radicand, the expression under

the radical sign, is negative, the number does not have a value in the set of real numbers. Substitute 3 for m in the expression:

$$(3)^3 + \sqrt{12(3)} = 27 + \sqrt{36} = 27 + 6 = 33$$

If you chose answer choice G, you just found the value of m^3. You might have selected answer choice J if you interpreted the $12m$ under the radical sign as the number 12^3 instead of 12×3. If you chose answer choice K, you probably failed to take the square root of 9 when solving the equation and used the value of 9 for m.

11. D
Converting Fractions to Decimals, Volume of Other Solids

100 Key Math Concepts for the ACT, #29, #95. First, convert the mixed number radius to a decimal: $3\frac{3}{5} = 3.6$. Substitute 3.6 into the formula to get $V = \frac{4}{3} \times \pi \times (3.6)^3$. Use the π key on your calculator. If your calculator has fractional capability and follows the correct order of operations, type the entry in as listed above. Otherwise, first find 3.6 to the third power. Multiply the result by 4, and then divide by 3. Finally, multiply by π. In either case, the result is approximately 195.43, or 195 to the nearest cubic meter.

If you chose answer choices A or B, you multiplied the radius by 3, instead of taking the radius to the third power. For choice C, as well as choice A, you incorrectly converted $3\frac{3}{5}$ to 3.35, a common trap. If you arrived at answer choice E, you first multiplied $\frac{4}{3} \times \pi \times (3.6)$, and then raised this value to the third power.

12. G
Probability

100 Key Math Concepts for the ACT, #46. Probability is a ratio that compares the number of favorable, or desired, outcomes to the total number of outcomes. Probability is always a

number between 0 and 1, and is never greater than 1. In this question, the favorable outcome is the number of nuts that are NOT peanuts, or $6 + 8 = 14$. The total number of outcomes is $10 + 6 + 8 = 24$. The probability that the nut is NOT a peanut is $\frac{14}{24} = \frac{7}{12}$, in lowest terms.

Choice F is the probability that the nut IS a peanut. Choice H is the ratio that compares peanuts to other nuts.

13. C
Percent Formula
100 Key Math Concepts for the ACT, #32. The matrices outline the corresponding number of people in the store to the ratio, written as a decimal, of the number of people making purchases, *with reference to their age group*. A ratio written as a decimal is essentially a percentage. So following the correspondence yields $75 \times 0.20 = 15$ adolescent purchases, $100 \times 0.35 = 35$ adult purchases, and $30 \times 0.10 = 3$ senior-citizen purchases. This is a total of $15 + 35 + 3 = 53$ people making purchases.

Answer choice A represents the adolescent purchases. If you chose choice B, you took the total number of people in the store, 205, and multiplied by the ratio for adolescents, 0.20. Choice D adds the total number of people, 205, multiplies by the sum of the ratios, 0.65, and then rounds. Choice E is the total number of people in the store, not the total number of purchases.

14. J
Average Formula
100 Key Math Concepts for the ACT, #41. To find an average, calculate the sum of the data and then divide by the total number of data items. According to the table, the number of hours that the country genre has a live disc jockey is 24, 7, and 16. $24 + 7 + 16 = 47$. Divide: $47 \div 3 = 15.67$, which is 16 to the nearest hour.

Answer choice F is the number of *entries*, not hours, for the country genre. Choice G is the average number of hours for the classical genre. Answer choice K is the average number of hours for the news genre.

15. D
Remainders
100 Key Math Concepts for the ACT, #20. This problem tests your ability to read a table of information. You must study the wording in the problem and study the table to understand its structure. To determine the minimum number of disc jockeys needed given the information in the problem, add up all of the hours (the last column) and then divide by 8 (the number of hours a disc jockey works). From the table, the number of hours is: $6 + 3 + 12 + 24 + 7 + 16 + 24 + 24 + 24 + 14 + 5 + 12 + 24 = 195$ total hours. $195 \div 8 = 24.375$, which means you must have 25 disc jockeys, because you cannot have a fraction of a person.

A common trap would be answer choice C because the answer would round down to 24 disc jockeys, but this would fall short of the requirement to fulfill all of the hours.

Choice E reflects the total number of hours needed. Answer choice A is the number of 24-hour segments that require a live disc jockey.

16. G
Adding and Subtracting Signed Numbers, Adding and Subtracting Monomials
100 Key Math Concepts for the ACT, #5, #53. To find the missing value, add the monomials in the first row: $m + -4m + 3m = 0$. This first row sums to zero. To be sure, check the rightmost column: $3m + -2m + -m = 0$. Every row, column, and diagonal must sum to 0. The first column must therefore be $m + 2m + \square = 0$, or $3m + \square = 0$. Isolate the missing term on one side of the equation by subtracting $3m$ from both sides: $\square = -3m$.

If your choice was H, you ignored the *m* variable in the term. If your choice was F, J, or K, you may have just looked at the first column and the last row and found a value that would work with those, without considering the other rows, columns, and diagonals.

17. E
Multiplying/Dividing Signed Numbers

100 Key Math Concepts for the ACT, #6. The algebraic expression *xy* means to multiply the point's *x* value by its *y* value. If the product is positive, then the *x* and *y* factors are either both positive or both negative, according to the rules for multiplying signed numbers. Positive *x*-coordinates are to the right of the origin. Positive *y*-coordinates are above the origin. In quadrant I, both coordinates are positive, and in quadrant III, both coordinates are negative. In quadrant II, the *x*-coordinate is negative (to the left of the origin) and the *y*-coordinate is positive (above the origin). In quadrant IV, the *x*-coordinate is positive (to the right of the origin), and the *y*-coordinate is negative (below the origin).

18. J
Counting the Possibilities

100 Key Math Concepts for the ACT, #45. The number of distinct lunches is determined by the fundamental counting principle. The counting principle directs you to multiply the different choices together to find the total number of combinations: $7 \times 3 \times 4 = 84$. If you consider just the sandwiches and soups alone, each sandwich can be paired with one of three soups, so there would be $7 \times 3 = 21$ different alternatives. These 21 alternatives would then become $21 \times 4 = 84$ different meals, because each of these 21 meals could be combined with four different drink choices.

A common trap answer is choice G, where the numbers are added together, instead of multiplied. Choice F is the number of sandwiches available, not the number of distinct meals. Choice H reflects the number of distinct choices of just sandwich and soup.

19. A
Setting Up a Ratio, Solving a Proportion

100 Key Math Concepts for the ACT, #36, #38. The question describes a comparison of the number of female to male students. This is a ratio—the ratio of female to male students is 5 to 3, or $\frac{5}{3}$. Let *n* represent the number of female students. Set up the proportion $\frac{5}{3} = \frac{n}{6,000}$ and cross multiply to get $3n = 5 \times 6,000$, or $3n = 30,000$. Divide both sides by 3 to get $n = 10,000$ females.

If you chose answer choice B, you may have used rounding and incorrectly considered the ratio to be twice as many females as males. Answer choice C represents the total number of students at the university. If you chose choice D or choice E, you may have stopped after multiplying 6,000 by 3 or by 5, respectively.

20. H
Pythagorean Theorem,
Special Quadrilaterals

100 Key Math Concepts for the ACT, #84, #86. Draw a diagram of a rectangle:

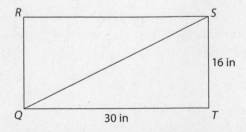

Because a rectangle has four right angles, you can treat the diagonal, *QS*, as the hypotenuse of a right triangle with legs of 16 and 30 inches. Use the Pythagorean theorem to solve for the length of the hypotenuse. If *c* represents the length of the hypotenuse and *a* and *b* represent the length of the legs, then $a^2 + b^2 = c^2$. Substitute into the formula:

$$c^2 = 16^2 + 30^2$$
$$c^2 = 256 + 900$$
$$c^2 = 1,156$$

Take the square root of both sides of the equation to find that $c = 34$ inches.

If you chose F, you used 30 inches for c (the hypotenuse) in the formula, and then solved for one of the legs. Choice G adds the two dimensions and divides by 2. If you chose choice J, you incorrectly divided by 2 instead of taking the square root; for choice K, you added the squares but did not take the square root of the sum.

21. A
Simplifying an Algebraic Fraction
100 Key Math Concepts for the ACT, #62. Answer choice A is not equivalent to $5n + 1$—it is the reciprocal. If you chose answer choice B, you may have incorrectly simplified by not multiplying 5×2. The expression simplifies as $5n + 10 - 9$, or $5n + 1$. Answer choice C is also equivalent to $5n + 1$—when you divide fractions, you multiply by the reciprocal of the denominator, and $\frac{1}{1} \div \frac{1}{5n + 1} = \frac{1}{1} \times \frac{5n + 1}{1} = 5n + 1$. If you chose either choice D or E, you may have thought that they could not be equivalent because they have a squared variable. But when choice D is factored and simplified, you can see it is equivalent: $\frac{n(5n + 1)}{n} = 5n + 1$. The same is true for choice E: $\frac{(5n + 1)(5n - 1)}{5n - 1} = 5n + 1$.

22. J
Solving "In Terms Of"
100 Key Math Concepts for the ACT, #64. Each of the answer choices is in the form $y = \ldots$, so solve for y in terms of x. Isolate y on one side of the equation. First, subtract $3x$ from both sides: $3x - 3x + 2y = -3x + 16$. Combine like terms to

get $2y = -3x + 16$. Now, divide all terms on both sides by 2: $y = -\frac{3}{2}x + 8$.

In answer choice F, the numeric term 16 is not divided by 2. Answer choices G and K have the reciprocal of the coefficient of x. In answer choice H, $3x$ was added to both sides of the equation instead of subtracted, to get the incorrect term of $+\frac{3}{2}x$.

23. E
Factoring Other Polynomials—FOIL in Reverse, Solving a Quadratic Equation
100 Key Math Concepts for the ACT, #61, #66. To solve a quadratic equation, first factor the trinomial in the form $ax^2 + bx + c$. Since the c term is positive and the b term is negative, the factors will be $(x - \#)(x - \#)$. Look for factors of 75 that when added together will equal 20, the b coefficient. Some factor possibilities for 75 are 1 and 75, 3 and 25, and 5 and 15. Only the factors 5 and 15 will add to 20. The equation, after factoring, becomes $(x - 5)(x - 15) = 0$. The solutions are the values of x that result in either of the factors equaling 0: $x = 5$ or $x = 15$.

The common error traps are choices A or B, where you might have quickly looked at the factors and thought the answers were either -5 or -15. If you chose choice D, you may have thought the only factors of 75 were 3 and 25, and therefore chose 3 as a solution. If you chose answer choice C, you may have ignored the term of 75 and found a solution of 0.

24. H
Sine, Cosine, and Tangent of Acute Angles
100 Key Math Concepts for the ACT, #96. The cosine (cos) ratio is the ratio of the side adjacent to angle N to the hypotenuse of the right triangle. The cos N $= \frac{12}{13}$.

Answer choice F is the sine (sin) ratio of angle N. Choice G is the tangent (tan) ratio of angle N. Choice J is the secant (sec), or the reciprocal of the cos to angle N. Choice K is the cosecant (csc), or the reciprocal of the sin to angle N.

25. C
Special Right Triangles

100 Key Math Concepts for the ACT, #85. Since chord AB passes through the center, it is a diameter of the circle, and segment OB is a radius, equal to 7 cm. Because OC is perpendicular to AB, a right angle is formed. To find the length of chord CB, note that it is the hypotenuse of right triangle $\triangle COB$, with legs that each measure 7 cm. Because the legs have the same measure, this is a special right triangle, the 45°-45°-90° right triangle, and the sides are in the ratio of $n:n:n\sqrt{2}$. Chord BC is therefore $7\sqrt{2} \approx 9.899$, or 9.9 to the nearest tenth of a centimeter. Alternately, you could have used the Pythagorean theorem, $a^2 + b^2 = c^2$, where $a = b = 7$:

$$7^2 + 7^2 = c^2$$
$$49 + 49 = c^2$$
$$c = \sqrt{98} \approx 9.9 \text{ cm}$$

If your answer was choice A, you used the Pythagorean theorem but evaluated 7^2 as 7×2, instead of 7×7. This is a common trap. Choice B is the length of the legs, not the hypotenuse. Choice D is $7\sqrt{3}$. Answer choice E is the length of the diameter of the circle.

26. F
Solving a Linear Equation

100 Key Math Concepts for the ACT, #63. Substitute the value of 86 into the formula for F, the degrees in Fahrenheit, to get $86 = \frac{9}{5}C + 32$. Subtract 32 from both sides:

$$86 - 32 = \frac{9}{5}C + 32 - 32$$
$$54 = \frac{9}{5}C$$

Now, multiply both sides by the reciprocal of $\frac{9}{5}$ to isolate C:

$$\frac{5}{9} \times 54 = \frac{5}{9} \times \frac{9}{5} \times C$$
$$30 = C$$

If you chose answer choice G, you forgot to multiply by the reciprocal to get rid of the fraction on the right side of the equation. Choice H incorrectly multiplies 86 by $\frac{5}{9}$ first, then adds 32. Choice J is the degrees in Fahrenheit. Choice K would be the degrees in Fahrenheit of 86 degrees Celsius.

27. D
Volume of a Rectangular Solid

100 Key Math Concepts for the ACT, #94. A swimming pool that is the same depth in all parts is a rectangular solid. The amount of water in the pool is the volume of the water. Use the formula $V = lwh$, and substitute in the volume, length, and width given in the problem. 14,375 = 50 × 25 × h, or 14,375 = 1,250h. Divide both sides of the equation by 1,250, to get 11.5 = h. The depth is between 11 and 12 meters.

28. F
Sine, Cosine, and Tangent of Acute Angles

100 Key Math Concepts for the ACT, #96. The tangent is the ratio of the side opposite to the given angle over the side adjacent to the given angle. Segment EF is the side opposite to angle D, so call this side m. Segment DE, the adjacent side to angle D, equals 42 inches. Set up the equation:

$$\frac{5}{8} = \frac{m}{42}$$
$$(42)(5) = 8m$$
$$210 = 8m$$
$$m = 26.3$$

If you chose G, you added 42 and $\frac{5}{8}$. Answer choice H reflects the length of side DF, the hypotenuse of the right triangle. Answer choice J incorrectly uses 42 as the opposite side and side EF as the adjacent side.

29. B
Setting Up a Ratio

100 Key Math Concepts for the ACT, #36. The fraction of the people who were sophomores would be the ratio of the number of sophomores to the total number of people at the prom. There were 30 sophomores and a total of $20 + 30 + 70 + 200 = 320$ people at the prom. The fraction is $\frac{30}{320} = \frac{3}{32}$.

Answer choice A is the fraction of the attendees who were freshmen. Answer choice C is the ratio of sophomores to those who are NOT sophomores. Answer choice D is the ratio of sophomores to seniors. Answer choice E is a common trap—it compares the number of sophomores to 100, instead of to the total number of students in attendance.

30. K
Adding/Subtracting Signed Numbers

100 Key Math Concepts for the ACT, #5. This problem requires you to understand that the sum of the parts of a segment is equal to the whole segment. It is given that X is the midpoint of segment WZ. Because the length of $WZ = 44$ cm, the length of WX is one-half of this, or 22 cm. From the relative positions of the points in the segment, $WX + XY = WY$, or alternately, $WY - WX = XY$. It is given that $WY = 26$ and calculated that WX is 22. Therefore, $XY = 26 - 22$, or 4 centimeters.

If you chose choice F, you just added the two numbers given in the problem. Answer choice G is the length of one-half of segment WZ, or the length of WX. If your answer was choice H, you subtracted the two numbers given in the problem. Choice J is one-half of segment WY.

31. C
Solving a System of Equations

100 Key Math Concepts for the ACT, #67. Find the point of intersection of two lines by solving the system of equations. Use the elimination method, by lining up the equations by like terms:

$$5x + y = 7$$
$$2x + 3y = 8$$

The problem asks for the x-coordinate, so look at the equations, and multiply one of them so that when the equations are combined, the y values are eliminated. If you multiply all terms in the top equation by -3, when you combine them, the y values will be eliminated:

$$-3(5x + y = 7) \Rightarrow -15x - 3y = -21$$
$$2x + 3y = 8 \Rightarrow 2x + 3y = 8$$

Combine like terms in the resulting equations: $(-15x + 2x) + (-3y + 3y) = -21 + 8$, or $-13x = -13$. Now, divide both sides of this simpler equation by -13 to get $x = 1$.

If you chose answer A, you probably divided the negative numbers incorrectly to get -1. Answer choice B may have resulted from only multiplying the y by -3 and not multiplying the terms of $5x$ and 7, and getting the result of $7x = 15$, or $x = \frac{15}{7}$. Answer choice D is the y-coordinate of the intersection of the two lines.

32. K
Solving "In Terms Of"

100 Key Math Concepts for the ACT, #64. To solve the equation for b, isolate b on one side of the equation. First, add 8 to both sides of the equation: $a + 8 = 2b - 8 + 8$, or $a + 8 = 2b$. Now, divide both sides by 2 to get $b = \frac{a + 8}{2}$.

If your answer was choice F, you forgot to divide a by 2. In choice G, you exchanged the variable a for the variable b, instead of solving for b.

Answer choice H is similar to choice G, but the subtraction was changed to addition. In choice J, you may have subtracted 8 from both sides instead of adding 8.

33. D
Areas of Special Quadrilaterals

100 Key Math Concepts for the ACT, #87. The area of a parallelogram is $A = bh$, where height h is the length of the perpendicular segment to one of the sides of the parallelogram. In the figure, segment RT, of length $9 + 5$, or 14 mm, is the base and the dotted segment, of length 12 mm, is the height. The area is $14 \times 12 = 168$ mm².

Answer choice A is the area of the little triangle at the top, not the parallelogram. If you chose answer choice B, you added the given numbers, without recognizing that the problem is asking for area. Answer choice C is the perimeter of the parallelogram. Answer choice E reflects a common error, where you multiplied the sides together, instead of the base times the height.

34. F
Evaluating an Expression,
Solving a Linear Equation

100 Key Math Concepts for the ACT, #52, #63. The problem asks for you to evaluate $(x + y)^3$, so manipulate the given equation to isolate $x + y$ on one side of the equation. Once you have this value, cube it to find the answer to the problem. For the given equation $x = -(y + 3)$, first distribute the negative sign on the right-hand side to get $x = -y - 3$. Now add y to both sides of the equation: $x + y = -y + y - 3$. Combine like terms to arrive at $x + y = -3$. Now substitute -3 for $(x + y)$ in the expression to get $(-3)^3 = -3 \times -3 \times -3 = -27$.

Answer choice G is a common trap: evaluating $(-3)^3$ as $-3 \times 3 = -9$. Answer choices H and J result from not applying integer multiplication rules for negative numbers.

35. E
Special Quadrilaterals

100 Key Math Concepts for the ACT, #86. Because all streets and avenues shown intersect at right angles, the map is a rectangle in which opposite sides have the same measures. To find the location halfway from H and S, first think of the corner of Oak and 10th to be the origin, or (0, 0). Just as in coordinate geometry, the first, ordered pair represents the east-west direction, and the second ordered pair represents the north-south direction. The distance from the origin at Oak Street to the school is 5 miles east. The distance from the origin at 10th Avenue to the hospital is 8 miles north. The new station will be halfway between these coordinates, or $\frac{5}{2} = 2.5$ miles east of the origin and $\frac{8}{2} = 4$ miles north of the origin.

To drive from F to the new fire station, you would have to drive $8 - 2.5 = 5.5$ miles west on Main Street, and then $10 - 4 = 6$ miles south on Elm Street (the first 2 miles south to get to 2nd Avenue, and then the 4 more miles south to be halfway from the hospital and the school). Choice A is the directions of the new fire station starting from the origin at Oak and 10th. Choice B is the directions of the new fire station starting from the school. Choice C is the directions from the corner of Main and Oak to the new station. If you answered choice D, you forgot to add in the 2 miles on Elm Street to get from Main to 2nd Avenue.

36. H
Translating from English into Algebra

100 Key Math Concepts for the ACT, #65. Consecutive integers are integers that differ by 1, such as 3, 4, 5... Consecutive odd integers are odd integers that differ by 2, such as 7, 9, 11, 13... Because the answer choices use the variable x, let x represent the smaller of the consecutive odd integers, so $(x + 2)$ would be the larger of

the integers. Four times the larger is represented by $4(x + 2)$, and twice the smaller by $2x$. The key word *difference* means to subtract the smaller from the larger, and the key word *is* means "equals." The equation is $4(x + 2) - 2x = 36$.

Choice F represents four times a number, minus twice the same number. Even though answer choices G and J are odd integers, they differ by an odd number, which would make the next number even. Choice K is an equation for the difference between 36 and four times the smaller integer.

37. C
Pythagorean Theorem
100 Key Math Concepts for the ACT, #84. The question states that the telephone pole is perpendicular to the ground and a wire is attached to the pole. This will result in a right triangle. It helps to draw a quick figure to represent the situation. The thicker side of the triangle represents the telephone pole, and the hypotenuse is the wire:

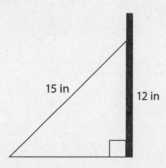

To find out how far the anchor of the supporting wire is from the base of the telephone pole, solve for the length of the missing leg. Use the Pythagorean theorem, which is $a^2 + b^2 = hypotenuse^2$. Let b represent the missing leg, and substitute in the given values to get $12^2 + b^2 = 15^2$, or $144 + b^2 = 225$. Subtract 144 from both sides: $b^2 = 81$. To solve for b, take the square root of both sides: $\sqrt{b^2} = \sqrt{81}$, so $b = 9$ or -9. A length cannot be negative, so the length is 9 ft.

Answer choice A subtracts $15 - 12$ to get 3. If you chose answer B, you may have thought that 15^2 meant 15×2 and calculated $30 - 24 = 6$. Choice D is the length up the pole, and choice E is the length of the wire.

38. H
Area of a Circle
100 Key Math Concepts for the ACT, #91. The area of a circle is $A = \pi r^2$, where r is the radius of the circle. Use the equation $100\pi = \pi r^2$, and solve for r by dividing both sides by π: $100 = r^2$. If you take the square root of both sides, then $r = 10$ or -10. Reject the -10 value, because a radius length cannot be negative. The radius of the circle is 10, so the diameter of the circle, which is the same as the length of a side of the square, is $2 \times 10 = 20$ units.

Answer choice F is the area of the square. Choice G is r^2. Choosing choice J is a common error that mistakes the radius of the circle for the side of the square.

39. C
Setting Up a Ratio, Solving a Proportion
100 Key Math Concepts for the ACT, #36, #38. When figures are similar, the side lengths are in proportion. Let x represent the missing side length, and set up the proportion of shorter side to longer side: $\frac{3}{8} = \frac{2}{x}$.

Cross multiply to get $3x = 16$. Divide both sides by 3 to get $x = 16 \div 3 \approx 5.3$, to the nearest tenth of an inch.

If you chose answer choices A or B, you set up the proportion incorrectly—make sure to match up the long sides and the short sides on the same side of the fraction. Answer choice D is the most common error made with similar figures, by assuming that since $3 - 1 = 2$, the missing side would be $8 - 1 = 7$. Similar figures have sides that are in proportion, which is not an additive relationship.

40. J
Parallel Lines and Transversals

100 Key Math Concepts for the ACT, #79. The figure shown is a parallelogram. Extend the top side out to make a parallel line to line *UZ*. Line *WY* is a transversal to the parallel lines, forming alternate interior angles, ∠*XWY* and ∠*WYV*, which have the same measures of 50°. Line *WV* is another transversal line to the parallel lines, forming alternate interior angles ∠*UVW* and ∠*VWX*. Because they have the same measure, ∠*VWX* = 150°. In addition, ∠*VWX* and ∠*VYX* have the same measure—they are opposite angles in a parallelogram. Now ∠*VYX* − ∠*WYV* = ∠*WYX*, or 150 − 50 = 100°.

If your answer was choice H, you incorrectly thought that ∠*WYX* had the same measure as ∠*XWY*. Answer choice K is the measure of ∠*VYX*, not ∠*WYX*.

41. D
Special Quadrilaterals

100 Key Math Concepts for the ACT, #86. The key to solving this problem is to simplify the drawing, knowing that you are looking for the perimeter. This figure, for perimeter purposes, can be thought of as a rectangle—just lower all the bottom pieces and move all left pieces to the right and you have a rectangle, with side lengths of 40 centimeters, and top/bottom lengths of 12 + 5 + 4 = 21 centimeters:

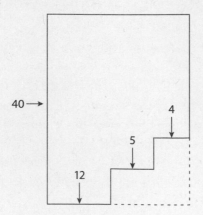

The perimeter is two times the length plus two times the width, or 2(40) + 2(21) = 80 + 42 = 122 centimeters.

Choice A is the measure of the length. Choice B is just the measure of two sides of the figure (just the numbers that are shown).

42. G
Convert Fractions to Decimals,
Translating from English into Algebra

100 Key Math Concepts for the ACT, #29, #65. Convert the fractions into decimal equivalents, and remember that the key word *of* means to multiply. Because $\frac{3}{4}$ of the 3,500 eligible voters cast a vote, this is 0.75 × 3,500 = 2,625 votes that were cast at the site. Three-fifths of these votes were for Martinez, or 0.6 × 2,625 = 1,575 votes for Martinez.

If you answered choice F, you followed the correct procedure, but incorrectly converted the fractions. Choice H is $\frac{3}{5}$ of all the eligible voters. Choice J is $\frac{3}{4}$ of the eligible voters. Answer K is the sum of choices H and J.

43. A
Greatest Common Factor,
Evaluating an Expression

100 Key Math Concepts for the ACT, #15, #52. To find the greatest common factor, find all factor pieces that the two expressions have in common. In this case, the factors in common are *a*, *a*, *a*, and *b*, or a^3b. It is given that the greatest common factor is 54, so think of a cubic number that is a factor of 54. The first cubic numbers are 1^3 (1), 2^3 (8), and 3^3 (27). Twenty-seven is a factor of 54: 27 × 2 = 54, so a possible value for *b* is 2.

Answer choice B is the value of the variable *a*. Answer choice C, 6, is a factor of 54, but that leaves the value of 9 for *a*, and 9 is not a perfect cube. The same reasoning would eliminate choice D. Choice E is the value of a^3.

44. K
Percent Formula

100 Key Math Concepts for the ACT, #32. To tackle this problem, break it up into its parts. First, find the value of x, given that 40% of x is 70. The key word *of* means to multiply. Write this as the equation $0.40x = 70$; divide both sides by 0.40 to get $x = 175$. Now find 160% of x, or $1.60 \times 175 = 280$.

Answer choice F is 40% of 70. Choice G is 160% of 28, the incorrect value from choice F. Answer choice H is 160% of 70. A common trap is answer choice J, which is the value of the variable x.

45. C
Simplifying Square Roots,
Finding the Distance between Two Points

100 Key Math Concepts for the ACT, #49, #71. To find the length of segment MN, use the distance formula: $d = \sqrt{(x_2 - x_1)^2 + (y_2 - y_1)^2}$. Substitute in the point values:

$$d = \sqrt{(6 - 2)^2 + (5 - 3)^2}$$
$$d = \sqrt{4^2 + 2^2}$$
$$d = \sqrt{20} = \sqrt{4} \times \sqrt{5} = 2\sqrt{5}$$

If you chose answer choice A, you may have used the distance formula incorrectly, using $(y_1 - x_1)$ and $(y_2 - x_2)$ instead of finding the difference between the x- and y-coordinates. Answer choice B multiplies by 2 instead of raising to the second power in the formula. Choice D is just the sum of the differences between the x- and y-coordinates. If your answer was choice E, you forgot to take the square root of 20, as indicated by the distance formula.

46. J
Setting Up a Ratio, Special Quadrilaterals

100 Key Math Concepts for the ACT, #36, #86. If the sides are in the ratio of 5:7, the perimeter will also be in this exact same ratio. When finding a perimeter, you add up the sides. Perimeter

is measured in single units, just as is the side length. Therefore, the ratio will not change. If you are unsure about this fact, assign values and actually calculate the perimeters. Consider the smaller square to have sides $5s$ in length and the larger square to have sides $7s$ in length. The smaller square has a perimeter of $4 \times 5s = 20s$, and the larger $4 \times 7s = 28s$. The ratio $20s:28s$ is equivalent to 5:7, after dividing both terms of the ratio by $4s$.

If you chose answer F, you may have thought you needed to subtract $7 - 5 = 2$, to get the (incorrect) ratio 1:2. Likewise, choice G adds $7 + 5 = 12$. Choice H multiplies $7 \times 5 = 35$. Choice K confuses area and perimeter—the ratio of the *areas* is 25:49.

47. E
Equation for a Circle

100 Key Math Concepts for the ACT, #75. The equation of a circle, when given the coordinates of the center (h, k) and the radius (r), is obtained by $(x - h)^2 + (y - k)^2 = r^2$. Substitute in the given values to get $(x - (-2))^2 + (y - 3)^2 = 9^2$. This simplifies to $(x + 2)^2 + (y - 3)^2 = 81$.

There are two common traps when finding the equation of a circle. One trap is to forget to square the radius, as in answer choice B. The other common trap is adding h and k to x and y, instead of subtracting, as in answer choice C. Choice A is both of these traps together. Choice D incorrectly takes the square root of the radius, instead of squaring the radius.

48. H
Adding/Subtracting Signed Numbers,
Multiplying Fractions

100 Key Math Concepts for the ACT, #5, #23. In the complex number system, i^2 is defined to be equal to -1, as you are told in the question stem. Use the distributive property to multiply the fraction:

$$\frac{3}{5-i} \times \frac{5+i}{5+i} = \frac{(3 \times 5) + 3i}{5^2 + 5i - 5i - i^2} =$$

$$\frac{15 + 3i}{25 - (-1)} = \frac{15 + 3i}{26}$$

If your answer was choice F, you may have cancelled incorrectly to simplify. Choice G reflects a common error when multiplying complex numbers—$25 - i^2$ was incorrectly interpreted to be $25 - 1 = 24$. In choice J, the 3 in the numerator was not distributed to the i term. Choice K is the result of two errors—the common error described in choice G and the error in choice J.

49. C
Interior Angles of a Polygon

100 Key Math Concepts for the ACT, #88. One way to solve this problem is to make a table. Each time the number of sides goes up by 1, the sum of the angles goes up by 180°. Make a third column in the table to discover a relationship.

Number of Sides	Sum of the Angles	
3	180°	180° × 1
4	360°	180° × 2
5	540°	180° × 3
6	720°	180° × 4

Notice that to find the sum of the angles, you can multiply 180 times 2 less than the number of sides of the polygon. This is choice C.

If you chose choice A, you may have just considered the triangle and assumed that the relationship was 60n. If your answer was choice B, you may have noticed that the number of degrees rose by 180°, but this did not consider the sides of the polygons. Choice D is a relationship that works for the three-sided and six-sided polygons, but not the other two.

50. G
Identifying Parts and the Whole

100 Key Math Concepts for the ACT, #31. This problem is a method of logical thinking. The key to solving this problem is to first assume that there are no students who have both a cell phone and an mp3 player. If this were the case, then there would be $35 + 18 = 53$ students polled. The problem states that 50 students were polled, so therefore at least 3 students have both electronic devices. This is the minimum number of students who own both.

If you chose choice F, you may have ignored the fact that 50 students were polled. Choice H is the difference between the number of cell phone owners and mp3 owners. Choice J is a possible number of students who own *only* a cell phone. Choice K is the sum of 35 and 18.

51. A
Solving an Inequality

100 Key Math Concepts for the ACT, #69. To solve this inequality, attempt to get the variable on one side of the inequality by adding 4n to both sides: $-4n + 4n + 3 > -4n + 4n + 1$. Combine like terms to get $3 > 1$. This inequality is always true for the set of real numbers.

If you chose answer B or C, you may have thought that the term $-4n$ would limit the set of solutions. If your answer was choice D or choice E, you may have mistakenly added $-4n$ to both sides and added 3 to both sides to get $-8n > 4$, and then solved for n.

52. H
Setting Up a Ratio

100 Key Math Concepts for the ACT, #36. This question tests your problem-solving strategies. Make a diagram of the situation in order

to understand. In the diagram, the people are represented as diamonds and the handshakes as connecting lines:

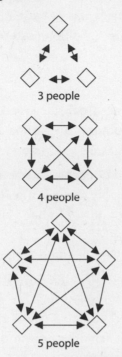

3 people

4 people

5 people

From the diagram, there are 10 total lines for 5 people, which represent 10 handshakes.

If you chose F, you may have considered that 4 people have 2 more handshakes than people and assumed this was the pattern for more people. If your answer was choice G, you may have incorrectly thought that the pattern in handshakes was multiples of 3. The key to the correct solution is to draw the picture.

53. D
Setting Up a Ratio, Solving a Proportion

100 Key Math Concepts for the ACT, #36, #38. First, determine the percentage in the category Miscellaneous. The total percentage must sum to 100%, so the percentage for Miscellaneous is $100 - 23 - 5 - 22 - 18 = 32\%$. To find the number of degrees in a circle graph that corresponds with 32%, set up the ratio, where x represents the number of degrees for the Miscellaneous category. Recall that there are 360° in a circle:

$\frac{32}{100} = \frac{x}{360}$. Cross multiply to get $32 \times 360 = 100x$, or $11{,}520 = 100x$. Divide both sides by 100 to get $x = 115°$, rounded to the nearest degree.

Choice A is a common trap that represents the percentage, not the number of degrees in a circle graph. If your answer was choice B, you thought that there were 180° in a circle. Answer choice C is the percentage of categories that are *not* Miscellaneous, and choice E is the number of degrees that are *not* Miscellaneous.

54. K
Special Right Triangles,
Sine, Cosine, and Tangent of Acute Angles

100 Key Math Concepts for the ACT, #85, #96. The information $\frac{\pi}{2} < \theta < \pi$ tells you that the angle is in quadrant II of the coordinate plane. In quadrant II, the sin values are positive. So the answer must be positive. Eliminate choices F, G, and H. You are given the value of tan θ, which is the ratio of the opposite side to the adjacent side of a right triangle. Sketch this triangle, using leg lengths of 4 and 3:

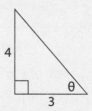

This is a special right triangle, the 3-4-5 Pythagorean triple, so the hypotenuse is 5 units in length. The sin of an angle is the ratio of the length of the opposite side to the length of the hypotenuse, or $\frac{4}{5}$.

If you chose choice F, you may have ignored the fact that the angle is in quadrant II and thought that the sin value would be negative. Choice G is the cotangent of the angle. Choices H and J are cosine values for the angle for quadrants II and I, respectively.

55. A
Using an Equation to Find the Slope,
Using an Equation to Find an Intercept
100 Key Math Concepts for the ACT, #73, #74. Look at the graphed boundary lines for the inequalities. Find the equation for these boundary lines and then determine if the shading represents less than or greater than these boundary lines. The horizontal line has a slope of 0 and a y-intercept (where the line crosses the y-axis) of 6, so the equation of this boundary line is $y = 6$. It is shaded below this line, so the inequality is $y < 6$. The slanted line has a slope with a change in y values of 3 and a change in x values of 1, so the slope is $\frac{3}{1} = 3$. The y-intercept is −5. The line is increasing, so the slope is positive. The shading is greater than, or above, this boundary line, so the inequality is $y > 3x − 5$. If you chose answer choice B, you fell into a common trap of interpreting the horizontal boundary line equation to be $x < 6$. Choice C is another common error, thinking that the shading represents less than, or below, the slanted line. Choice D interprets the slope as −3. Negative slopes decrease, or slant downwards, when going from left to right. Answer choice E represents a slope of $\frac{1}{3}$, not the correct slope of 3. A slope of $\frac{1}{3}$ would mean for every change of 1 in the y values, the x values would change by 3.

56. J
Evaluating an Expression
100 Key Math Concepts for the ACT, #52. The question asks you to evaluate the function $f(x)$, replacing x with $(x + c)$. Replace any instance of x in the function definition with $x + c$. This means that $2(x + 7)$ will be $2(x + c + 7)$. Use the distributive property and multiply each term in parentheses by 2 to get $2x + 2c + 2 \times 7$, or $2x + 2c + 14$.

In choice F, the 2 was not distributed to the constant term 7. Choice G only multiplies the 2 by the first term in the parentheses. In choices H and K, the c term was just added onto the end of the function definition, instead of replacing the x with $(x + c)$.

57. B
Simplifying an Algebraic Fraction,
Using an Equation to Find the Slope,
Using an Equation to Find an Intercept
100 Key Math Concepts for the ACT, #62, #73, #74. First, simplify the equation by simplifying the fraction on the right-hand side. Factor the numerator and then cancel the $(x − 2)$ factor from the numerator and denominator:

$$\frac{2x^2 − 8}{x − 2} = \frac{2(x^2 − 4)}{x − 2} = \frac{2(x + 2)(x − 2)}{x − 2} = 2(x + 2)$$

The simplified equation is $y = 2(x + 2)$, or $y = 2x + 4$. This equation is now in slope-intercept form, where the y-intercept is 4 and the slope is $\frac{2}{1}$. Choice B is the correct graph that has a slope of 2 and crosses the y-axis at 4.

If you ignored the denominator in the given equation, then you would have incorrectly chosen A, the graph of the quadratic $y = 2x^2 − 8$.

Choice C is the graph of the equation $y = \frac{1}{2}x + 4$. If this was your choice, you may have misinterpreted the slope of a line. Choice D is the graph of a quadratic function, not the correct linear function. You cannot assume a function is a quadratic just because you see a variable that is squared; you must first try to simplify the equation. Choice E is the graph of the linear function $y = −2x + 4$.

58. F
Line Reflections
This problem tests your knowledge of line reflections in the coordinate plane.

When you reflect a point or a figure over the y-axis, the x-coordinate of each point is the opposite sign and the y-coordinate stays the same. The reflection of the point Q(r, s) after a reflection over the y-axis is therefore Q'(–r, s).

Choice G would be the result of a reflection over the y-axis, followed by a reflection over the x-axis. Choice H is incorrect—the x- and y- coordinates were switched. Choice J is a common trap that represents a reflection over the x-axis.

59. C
Solving "In Terms Of"

100 Key Math Concepts for the ACT, #64. The problem is asking what is the value of g in terms of h. The two given equations do not show a direct relationship between g and h, so you must solve for q in the second equation to get q in terms of h, and then substitute this value in for q in the first equation. To solve for q in the second equation, isolate q by first adding 8 to both sides of the equation: $h + 8 = 2q – 8 + 8$, or $h + 8 = 2q$. Divide both sides by 2 to get $\frac{h+8}{2} = q$. Use this value of q in the first equation: $g = 4q + 3$ becomes $g = \frac{4(h+8)}{2} + 3$.

Factor out a 2 from the numerator and the denominator of the first term to get $g = 2(h + 8) + 3$. Multiply the terms in parentheses by 2, or $g = 2h + 16 + 3$, or $g = 2h + 19$.

Choice A is the value of q in terms of h from the second equation. In choice B, the constant term 3 in the first equation was incorrectly added to the numerator of the transformed first equation, and the 4 was not distributed to both terms of h and 8. In choice D, the 2 was factored out correctly, but the remaining 2 was not distributed to the constant term of 8. Choice E is the value of q, not h, in terms of g from the first equation.

60. H
Evaluating an Expression,
Trigonometric Functions of Other Angles

100 Key Math Concepts for the ACT, #52, #98. In this problem, you are asked to use the formula $\cos(\alpha + \beta) = \cos(\alpha)\cos(\beta) – \sin(\alpha)\sin(\beta)$ and the table of values to find the value of $\cos(75°) = \cos(30° + 45°)$. Substitute in 30° for α and 45° for β to get: $\cos(30°)\cos(45°) – \sin(30°)\sin(45°)$. Now use the table to replace each sin or cos with the corresponding values in the table: $\frac{\sqrt{3}}{2} \times \frac{\sqrt{2}}{2} – \frac{1}{2} \times \frac{\sqrt{2}}{2}$. Using order of operations, multiply and then subtract the numerators and keep the denominator: $\frac{\sqrt{6}}{4} – \frac{\sqrt{2}}{4} = \frac{\sqrt{6} – \sqrt{2}}{4}$. Alternately, you could use your calculator to find the value of the $\cos(75°) \approx 0.2588$, and then test each answer choice to find the answer closest to this value. Choice H will be the only value to equal the $\cos(75°)$.

If you chose F or K, you probably used the wrong values in the table. In choice G, you used the wrong values in the table and also forgot to multiply the denominators, resulting in a denominator of 2 instead of 4. Choice J is the common trap—you correctly used the table but did not multiply the denominators to get a denominator of 4.

Reading Test

Reading questions can be divided into four basic types: Detail questions, Inference questions, Big Picture questions, and Vocabulary-in-Context questions. As you review the answers and explanations, note which types you tend to answer correctly or incorrectly and tailor your studying to focus on areas where you need improvement.

PASSAGE I

1. D
Inference

The question is asking about Dave's opinion specifically. Throughout the passage, Dave describes the problems with comparison between twins, and many of his comments to Emily are also focused on comparing himself to his twin. Choice D is correct because it mentions this competition and implies that it makes their relationship more difficult. Choice A is extreme, choice B implies that their relationship is stronger than it is, and choice C is not supported by the text because Emily doesn't seem to be able to convince Dave to make more of an effort.

2. H
Detail

Emily has a good relationship with both brothers; she has an enjoyable conversation with Bruce and works to make Dave feel better. Also, she wants the brothers to be closer than they are. Because it reflects these details, choice H is the correct answer. Choice F is the opposite; Emily is very attentive, and choices G and J are both extreme and negative distortions of Emily's desire to help relations between the brothers.

3. B
Big Picture

This question is asking for an answer that is not found in the passage, so the first step is to eliminate choices that are contained in the passage. In the first paragraph, Dave is envious of the reaction his wife has when talking to Bruce, eliminating choice A. The paragraph about Dave's reaction to the picture captures his negative feelings regarding the difference in their popularity, eliminating choice C. The final conversation shows Dave as doubtful of Bruce's need for his approval, eliminating

choice D. This leaves choice B, which is not found in the passage and is therefore the correct answer.

4. J
Big Picture

The first paragraph starts with a description of Emily on the phone, but the focus quickly shifts to Dave's reaction. It then moves to Dave making some points about his brother's popularity and questioning if his own wife ever reacted so favorably to him. Choice J summarizes this well. Choices F and H are not found in the passage, and choice G occurs much later.

5. D
Inference

Emily attempts to make Dave believe that he is important to Bruce, but Dave still feels he is in Bruce's shadow. It is unclear whether or not Dave entirely believes Emily, but when she brings up Bruce's desire to talk about the brothers' childhood, Dave's response suggests that he does not want to talk about it because it again reminds him of how Bruce has always been the more popular of the two. This makes choice D the correct answer. Choice A is out of scope; the passage does not suggest that Dave does anything to spite Emily. Choice B is incorrect because Dave does not feel guilty; he sees Bruce's success as proof that it doesn't matter whether he calls Bruce or not. Choice C is out of scope; Dave's reasons for not calling Bruce have to do with his feelings toward his brother, not any feelings related to Emily.

6. H
Detail

In lines 39–42, Dave explicitly talks about how Bruce's image has positive aspects (vitality) that his image lacks. This is a perfect match for choice H, which restates this generally. Choices F and J are not found in the passage, and choice

G is contradicted by the fact that both Dave and Emily can tell the difference between the twins.

7. B
Detail

Dave is uncomfortable at this point, because Emily is clearly thinking about Bruce. The previous paragraph describes the picture as a source of insecurity for Dave, suggesting that he is nervous and seeking reassurance that Emily is with him for reasons other than his connection to Bruce. Only choice B describes these feelings. Choice A is the opposite of what Dave is feeling, and neither choice C nor D can be deduced from the information In the passage.

8. F
Inference

With an open-ended question like this, the answer choices must be individually tested. Choice F can be logically deduced, especially from the last exchange: Emily mentions that Bruce tells her stories about their childhood, and when Dave makes a comment about Bruce's popularity, Emily responds that "[Bruce] doesn't look at it that way" (line 115). This suggests that there is a difference between each brother's childhood stories. Choice G is too extreme and better describes the reaction other people have to the different professions of Bruce and Dave. Choice H is also too extreme: Dave feels competitive with Bruce, but that does not imply that they have fought. Choice J is not supported by the text; their childhood is the only time when it is stated that they spent time together.

9. C
Detail

Dave and Emily have different opinions regarding the picture. Dave is displeased with his image, while Emily professes to like his smile. However, Dave describes Bruce's smile as *trademark* (line 43), and Emily says that Bruce looks "exactly the same" (lines 60–61) in every picture. This makes choice C correct. Choices A and D depict opinions that are strictly Dave's and Emily's, respectively, and choice B is not supported by the passage at all.

10. F
Detail

Emily follows her comment about Bruce's stories by dismissing Dave's comment about Bruce's popularity, saying that Bruce "doesn't look at it that way" (line 115). This is in reaction to Dave's frequent comments suggesting that Bruce has been more successful socially and Dave's implication that Bruce feels superior to Dave. This matches choice F, which correctly restates this idea. Choice G is not supported by the passage; choice H is opposite because Emily wants Dave to focus less on his brother's successes; and choice J is extreme, since Bruce wants more attention from his brother but is not necessarily lonely.

PASSAGE II

11. C
Detail

The author is critical of the media throughout the passage and focuses mostly on ways in which the current media is not concerned enough with factual accuracy. Choice C matches this nicely. Choice A is too extreme; the author talks about distorting facts, not making them up. Choice B contradicts paragraph 2, which characterizes some news personalities as *demagogues* with biased views. Choice D contradicts paragraph 4; the public's desire for this type of news is one of the reasons for its existence.

12. G
Detail

In paragraph 3, the author mentions how impartial stories can sway the opinions of readers through headlines rather than content. Choices H and J both mention headlines, but choice H makes the opposite point, and J is far too specific, using the example as a basis for a point that the author does not explicitly make. Choice F is contradicted by the passage. Choice G is general, but correct: the headline is another method used to sensationalize the story, as illustrated by the example of the "enraged public" (line 55) versus the "irked locals" (lines 58–59).

13. B
Inference

The sentence preceding the Walter Cronkite example states that audience members expected to have complicated events explained to them; the Cronkite example follows this logic. Choice B matches this perfectly. Choice A may be inferred, but it is not the point the author is making—the author's concern is the treatment of the news, not specific news personalities. This reasoning also eliminates choice C. Choice D is never mentioned in or suggested by the passage.

14. F
Inference

In order to research this statement, it is a good idea to look back at paragraph 3 because it discusses the public. "Personal consensus" applies to the author's point about people looking for news reported with a political opinion similar to their own. Choice F matches this. Choices G and J are both contradicted by information given in paragraph 3. Choice H is not supported by the passage and contradicts the author's main point.

15. B
Detail

In paragraph 1, the author states that in stories of "continued national interest" (lines 10–11), the focus shifts from facts to *theater* (line 12). Choice B is the best match. Choices A, C, and

D are not explicitly mentioned as more or less likely to be sensationalized.

16. J
Vocabulary-in-Context

The sentence describes objective reporting as a "distant possibility." Questions like this are made easier if you pick a word that means the same thing in context. In this case, you can predict *improbable* or something similar. This matches choice J perfectly. Choices F, G, and H do not address the likelihood of objective reporting.

17. C
Inference

The author is most likely to criticize a headline that sensationalizes or makes a value judgment, and the end of paragraph 3 gives an example. Choices A, B, and D are all basically factual and specific. Choice C is correct because it uses a very inclusive group, like the example in paragraph 3 does, makes a value judgment by calling the song offensive, and uses emotional language.

18. J
Big Picture

The fourth paragraph focuses on the flaws of the public and states that individuals who agree with certain politically biased hosts are unlikely to question the validity of the "facts" presented. This matches choice J perfectly. Choices F and G are not explicitly stated by the author. Choice H describes accuracy problems for the media, not the public.

19. A
Detail

The author makes the point that fact-based news only captures a small minority of the news audience. Also, the beginning of paragraph 4 states that the public is not interested in dry facts. Choice A can be inferred because the media companies are providing the type of programs that the public seems to want. Choice B is extreme—in fact, it could be inferred that if the greater public was interested in objective facts, the media (including cable) would provide programs of that sort. Choices C and D cannot be deduced from the passage; the author seems to believe that factual news will not draw a large audience no matter what.

20. G
Inference

Because this question deals with the audience, paragraph 4 is a good place to look. The author states that audience members look for hosts who share their political opinions. Choice G is a general restatement of this idea, so it is correct. Choice F is not stated in the passage. Choice H distorts a detail from the last paragraph; audience members prefer short to lengthy, but there is no statement about audience members gravitating toward the shortest or most simple stories. Choice J misuses the detail about headlines from paragraph 3.

PASSAGE III

21. C
Big Picture

The author frequently describes his grandfather's actions and describes their relationship to his heritage. Choice C fits this, as the other Russians in paragraph 3 are also characterized as being naturally tied to Russia. Choice A distorts the grandfather's later visits to Russia; the passage does not imply that immigrants would prefer to be elsewhere. Choice B cites the opinions of American-born people, while the passage does not focus on those opinions. Choice D refers only to the grandfather, who was perpetually displaced; his story is addressed as being unique.

22. J
Inference

The three specific locations mentioned are Moscow, Siberia, and China, in that order. Also, the author mentions that China was the longest stay. Choices F, G, and H all have errors: F puts the Russian revolution in the wrong time period, G says he was exiled from Russia as an adult, and H says he settled in communist China, when he left during the revolution.

23. C
Inference

These line references both have to do with his work in real estate. You can deduce that he sees real estate as providing stability for people, something he did not have earlier in his life. Choice C matches this very well. Choice A is part of his sales strategy, not his purpose. Choices B and D are never discussed as tasks he specifically attempts.

24. F
Detail

The grandfather is proud to be Russian, and deeply influenced by his heritage, but is also proud to do his job and be a successful American. Choice F contradicts the grandfather's attitude, because while he criticizes the government, he loves the country itself. Choice G suggests an unspoken pride between Russians, which is in line with the grandfather's characterization. Choices H and J both fit because he is critical of the communist government but still reverent regarding the country.

25. D
Inference

The passage deals heavily with displacement, and its implications, along with its effects on people. Since Moscow was where the family was originally from, you can deduce that the answer will have something to do with belonging.

Choice D fits this classification well; Moscow is the family's native home, and all feel tied to Russia but are searching for places to live outside of Russia. Choices A and C are not implied at all in the passage. Choice B may be factually true but does not apply to the desires of the family.

26. F
Vocabulary-in-Context

This selection refers to Russians saying, "I am American" in Russian. It is contrasted with points about the fact that they are speaking Russian with other Russians, therefore suggesting that "playing the role" must mean becoming more accustomed to their new country. Choice F matches this perfectly. Choices G and H cannot be deduced from the information given, and choice J may be true, but does not apply to "playing the role."

27. B
Inference

"Strategic compromise" applies to the grandfather's desire to sell homes, in spite of the current stigma against Russians. The tactics mentioned by the author are informing the customer he was exiled and disagreed with the current Russian government, and not responding to negative remarks regarding the entire country of Russia. Choice B fits this final part, as negative statements about Russia as a whole would offend the grandfather. Choices A and D are too extreme and specific. Choice C is not mentioned.

28. H
Inference

According to the passage, this sort of trip "elucidates one's very existence" (line 107). This is the only result given; the rest of the details apply to the emotional strain involved. Choice H is the only choice that applies to this. Choices F and G are not even implied by the text, and choice

J applies to the adoption analogy rather than the grandfather.

29. B
Detail

The last sentence in the first paragraph states that the country came under new rule during the time his mother was pregnant with him. He was therefore born after the revolution and under communist rule. Choice B is correct. The other choices contradict that factual sentence.

30. G
Inference

The need to rediscover a lost native land is what would be made unnecessary so the correct answer would have to describe the opposite situation. Choice G fits this very well; having a sense of belonging would alleviate the need to search for it. Choice F is incorrect because the grandfather embodies the feelings he is potentially making unnecessary. Choice H describes people that may still desire to revisit their roots. Choice J describes a totally unrelated achievement possible in real estate.

PASSAGE IV

31. B
Big Picture

The passage is most concerned with discrediting the myth that rattlesnakes are aggressive and very dangerous, and the selection refers to exactly that: the "sinister opportunist" is the myth, while the "mild-mannered domestic" is closer to fact. Choice B can be deduced from this. Choice A is incorrect, as juvenile snakes are not even mentioned. Choice C misuses the detail about rattlesnakes giving live birth, which is not treated as a recent discovery. Choice D is too extreme; the author describes rattlesnakes as fairly docile but not entirely predictable.

32. F
Inference
At the end of paragraph 6, the author states that the reputation is good because a frightened and cornered rattlesnake is dangerous. Choice F fits this because if people did not avoid or move away from rattlesnakes, there would be more dangerous interaction between humans and snakes. Choices G and J are contradicted by the passage; in rattlesnake roundups, their reputation costs the snakes their lives, and the author, who is aware of their docile nature, would certainly never believe a rattlesnake should be a pet. Choice H misuses the detail about snakebite deaths.

33. C
Detail
The passage gives quite a few examples of the social behavior of rattlesnakes, so be prepared to find a restated fact among the answer choices. Choice C fits this nicely, because the second paragraph states that rattlesnakes have been known to hibernate with tortoises. Choice A is not a social behavior. Choice B goes beyond the text; the wrestling is used to claim a mate, but the losing snake will leave, rather than take a place within a hierarchy. Choice D also misuses a detail; rattlesnakes are described as "entirely noncannibalistic" (line 24), meaning they never eat other snakes.

34. H
Inference
The mythology referred to is that of the heartless, aggressive rattlesnake. This relates to rattlesnake roundups (line 113) to which the author clearly objects, so it would follow that the author sees this particular human behavior as heartless and aggressive. Choice H matches this perfectly, and the statistical comparison in paragraph 7 supports this. Choice F contradicts the author's belief that rattlesnakes are not as

dangerous as commonly thought. Choices G and J do not relate to the point the author is making.

35. C
Detail
The sixth paragraph states that serious bites can usually be traced to people that either handle or step on snakes, in contrast to those who were not engaging the snakes. Choice C fits this nicely, specifically focusing on those handling snakes, an example of individuals purposefully seeking interaction. Choice A is incorrect because a relationship is mentioned. Choice B is not mentioned in the text. Choice D is a distortion, because rattlesnakes deliver venom based on how threatened they feel, not necessarily based on how threatening humans act.

36. H
Inference
The selection's sentence starts with describing the docile behavior of rattlesnakes, as a follow-up to scientific findings in the previous paragraph. The implication is that snakes, while not as dangerous as often thought, can still be dangerous. Choice H matches this perfectly. Choice F is outside the scope of the passage; there is no mention of herpetologists keeping snakes. Choice G misuses a later detail; the author is not comparing the rattlesnake as a pet to dogs. Choice J states a comparison that is never made.

37. B
Detail
In paragraph 5, the author lists various statistics and states that dogs, bees, and lightning are all responsible for more annual deaths than rattlesnakes and that the fer-de-lance is responsible for substantially more. Choice B is the only answer that fits; every other choice is contradicted by the facts given.

38. J
Detail

In paragraph 6, the author explains that the rattlesnake knows that it needs its venom for food, and goes on to state that the only situation in which a rattlesnake would release all of its venom is when it feels threatened. Choice J fits with this; the rattlesnake wishes to conserve its venom, specifically for prey. Choice F is incorrect because humans are large in comparison and receive mostly "dry" bites. Choice G contradicts the statement about rattlesnakes potentially using all their venom if threatened. Choice H contradicts the statement that rattlesnakes are not aware of the well-being of non-food sources.

39. B
Big Picture

The author examines two pieces of contradictory logic. The first is that the organizers use the reputation of the rattlesnake to promote interest but rely on the more docile nature of the snakes. The second is the fact that most of the snakes are taken from areas without people and put into contact with people, thus making for a more dangerous situation. Choice B matches the second piece of information. Choice A is not stated as fact in the text. Choice C brings up erroneous statistics, when really it is the rattlesnake's erroneous reputation that is used. Choice D is not mentioned in the passage.

40. G
Vocabulary-in-Context

The answer lies in the last sentence, which speculates on the status of humans in rattlesnake folklore "if rattlesnakes were able to speak or write." This makes it clear that *crotalid* must have something to do with actual rattlesnakes. Choice G is the only choice that fits because the sentence is mocking the way that humans have characterized rattlesnakes within human mythology. Choices F, H, and J all are incorrect because they mention groups that are not specifically rattlesnakes.

Science Test

Science questions can be divided into three basic types: Figure questions, Patterns questions, and Scientific Reasoning questions. You may also see Basic Theory questions when you review the Conflicting Viewpoints passage. As you review the answers and explanations, note which types you tend to answer correctly or incorrectly, and tailor your studying to focus on areas where you need improvement.

PASSAGE I

The first passage requires a little basic understanding of the scientific method and a lot of figure interpretation. You don't need to grasp all of the details of the passage or the diagrams, but do take note of obvious trends or extremes in the given data. For example, the large changes in the data in Figure 1 at around 1,500 years are particularly worth noting.

1. C
Patterns

Be careful of extreme language, such as the use of *always* in choices A and B. While the general trend is that decreasing glacier length corresponds to decreasing calving rate, the opposite is true at the sharp peak in calving rate at around 1,500 years, which choice C correctly describes.

2. H
Figure

This question asks you to find the glacier with the largest calving rate for years 6–10 in Table 1. Make sure you are looking in the right place, which in this case is the far right column of Table 1.

3. A
Scientific Reasoning

This question requires a little deeper understanding of the data presented in Table 1. For all four glaciers during both time periods, the calving rate is slightly greater than or equal to the average velocity. To predict the calving rate of a glacier with a velocity of 80 m/yr, you must look for glaciers traveling at similar velocities. The closest values come from glaciers A and C during years 1–5, which had velocities of 72 m/yr and 98 m/yr, respectively. The corresponding calving rates for these two glaciers are 72 m/yr and 106 m/yr. The correct answer should fall within this range, as described by choice A.

4. J
Figure

With open-ended questions like this one, simple process of elimination is usually most efficient. Comparison of each choice with the data in Table 1 reveals that only choice J accurately reflects the "behavior of the glaciers."

5. B
Figure

Don't be too concerned with the strange scale of the horizontal axis of each choice. The values on the axis correspond exactly to the calving rates for years 6–10 given in Table 1. Simply find the graph that correctly plots the four points given by the data in the last two columns of Table 1.

6. H
Scientific Reasoning

The meteorologists in Study 3 hypothesized that high temperatures cause rapid variations in velocity and calving rate. Figure 1 shows a rapid change in calving rate at around 1,500 years. If the hypothesis is true, then the glacier modeled in Study 1 experienced a rapid change in temperature approximately 1,500 years ago, and choice H is correct.

PASSAGE II

This passage consists almost entirely of Table 1 and Figures 1 and 2, with very little descriptive language. Fortunately, the more complicated the diagram, the more likely the questions referring to that diagram will be straightforward. In other words, don't waste too much time trying to interpret Table 1 right away. As it turns out, only one question requires you to refer to Table 1.

7. C
Figure

Sometimes, you will be asked to simply read information directly from a graph. If you are careful to refer to the right part of the right graph, you will find correct answers to these kinds of questions very quickly. The bar for March 2 on Figure 1 rises to approximately 1,500 gr/m^3, as in choice C.

8. H
Patterns

You are asked to describe a trend in the data in Figure 1 beyond the high value given for November 5. After this value, the data maintains no discernable trend but does stay within a relatively small range of values, as is correctly described in choice H.

9. B
Figure

Be careful to answer the correct question. "Increased the most" doesn't necessarily mean the count increased to its largest value, which is the trap set in choice C. Choice D is also a trap, set for those who refer to the wrong figure.

10. F
Figure

This question asks about the tree pollen count, so you should refer to Figure 1. Process of elimination reveals that only choice F correctly reflects the data shown in the figure.

11. A
Figure
You are finally asked to refer to the rather complicated Table 1. Find the row for the month of May, and look for the corresponding column(s) containing the most reported cases of allergic rhinitis. In this case, that means the most ✿ symbols. Tree and grass pollens account for six of the nine total ✿ symbols in the May row, which indeed constitute most of the cases.

PASSAGE III

When a passage includes multiple experiments designed to study the same topic, look for key similarities and differences between the experiments. In Experiment 1, oscillation frequency of a pendulum is measured, and the only variable is the length of the pendulum arm. In Experiment 2, the oscillation frequencies of several springs are measured, and there are two variables: the spring and the suspended mass. Experiment 3 involves the same springs as does Experiment 2 but measures equilibrium length instead of oscillation frequency.

12. G
Figure
Notice that in Figure 3, the lines plotted for Springs B, C, and D intersect at approximately the same mass. The exact mass value is not completely clear from the figure, but it is definitely larger than choice F and smaller than choice H, which leaves choice G as the only possibility.

13. A
Figure
According to Figure 1, oscillation frequency does indeed decrease with increasing arm length, so you can eliminate choices C and D. The second part of choice B is simply false, which leaves only choice A.

14. F
Scientific Reasoning
This question requires a couple of steps of logic. First, you must realize what *slowly* means in terms of oscillation frequency. Recall from the passage that oscillation frequency is measured in "oscillations per second." The faster the spring oscillates, the more oscillations it will complete per second. Therefore, you are looking for the spring with the lowest value for oscillation frequency, which is Spring A.

15. C
Figure
Refer to the line plotted for Spring A in Figure 3. On that line, a mass of 700 g corresponds to an equilibrium length of just less than 40 cm. Only choice C includes this estimate.

16. J
Figure
According to Figure 2, an oscillation frequency of 1.4 Hz at a mass of 100 g would be represented by a data point that would fall in between the frequency values for Spring C and Spring D at that mass. Only choices H and J place Spring E correctly between Springs C and D, and only choice J correctly lists the springs in order of *decreasing* oscillation frequency.

17. C
Scientific Reasoning
The effects of mass are not mentioned in Experiment 1. Only the pendulum arm length affects the oscillation frequency, so the plots for the original mass and the larger mass should be identical, as in choice C.

PASSAGE IV

This passage is based almost entirely on Figure 1, which contains a great deal of information and deserves a few moments of your attention before attacking the questions. As always, it is important to understand what is represented on each axis. In this case, the vertical axis is straightforward, but the horizontal axis is a bit unconventional. The last sentence in the passage should help you to grasp that the horizontal axis represents the composition of the alloy, where the value (0–100%) is the atomic percentage of Si in the alloy. The farther to the right on the figure, the more Si and less Au there are in the alloy. The lines on the graph separate the different phases of the alloy, from completely solid at the bottom of the graph to completely liquid at the top. Play close attention to any notes included to help describe a figure. The note in this case tells you that parentheses around an element indicate that element's solid state.

18. J
Figure

Be careful to not confuse melting point with boiling point. Only the melting points are shown in Figure 1, so choice J is correct.

19. B
Figure

Draw a vertical line from the 50% mark on the horizontal axis and a horizontal line from the 600°C mark on the vertical axis. These lines intersect in the region of the diagram labeled "liquid + (Si)," which the note tells you means liquid plus Si in its solid state.

20. G
Figure

The lowest melting point is indicated by the section of the graph labeled "liquid" that reaches the farthest down on the graph. An arrow on the graph labels this point the "eutectic point" and gives the exact alloy composition there, which is reproduced correctly in choice G.

21. A
Scientific Reasoning

The question asks you to look at compositions with less than 10% Si, which means you can draw a vertical line from the 10% mark on the horizontal axis and ignore everything to the right of that line. In the portion of the graph to the left of this line, the temperature required for the alloy to become completely liquid decreases with increasing Si atomic percentage. Choice D is a trap set for those drawn to the wrong line on the figure. The horizontal line at a temperature of 363°C indicates the temperature at which the alloy becomes completely solid, not liquid.

22. H
Figure

Draw a horizontal line from 1,200°C on the y-axis to where it intersects the plot. Draw a line down from that point to the x-axis. It intersects somewhere between 70 and 80% Si. According to the figure, solid Si particles would also begin to form at this temperature. Choice H encompasses this information and is correct.

PASSAGE V

Don't be intimidated by unfamiliar language like the biological terms in this passage. Remember that no advanced scientific knowledge is assumed. As usual, here the important task is to be able to locate the appropriate information from the given figures. Note the trends in both figures, namely the decreases in temperature and oxygen partial pressure with increasing altitude in Figure 1 and the elevated GST and ECH concentrations of the high altitude dwellers in Table 1.

23. D
Figure

Make sure you refer to the correct part of Table 1 for the enzyme concentration values of populations ha 1, ha 2, and ha 3. The table shows that for all three high altitude populations, GST levels are highest, CR levels are lowest, and ECH levels are intermediate. Only choice D does not violate this relationship.

24. G
Figure

The process of elimination works best here. Choice F is not universally true; the oxygen saturation percentages are pretty similar for high altitude and sea level dwellers. Neither Table 1 nor Figure 1 shows a comparison between high or low altitude populations and temperature or partial oxygen pressure, so choices H and J cannot be correct. Only choice G is directly supported by the values in the table.

25. C
Figure

The answer to this question comes directly from Figure 1, but you must be careful to not confuse the two data sets. You can draw a horizontal line from 110 mm Hg on the left vertical axis until it intersects with the oxygen partial pressure data (squares). That intersection happens at about 3,200 m. To find the temperature at this altitude, draw a horizontal line from the temperature plot (circles) at 3,200 m to the right axis. It intersects at just under –5°C, choice C. Accidentally reversing the two data sets likely results in selecting answer trap A.

26. H
Figure

You are asked to find the highest ECH concentration for any of the six populations, which occurs for population ha 2.

27. A
Scientific Reasoning

Only choices A and C agree with the information in Table 1. You can eliminate choice C, though, because nothing in the passage or data suggests that CR concentration has anything to do with efficiency at incorporating oxygen into the blood.

PASSAGE VI

On passages that present two conflicting viewpoints, make sure you read the first passage and answer the questions associated with it before reading the second passage and answering the remaining questions. Note the fundamental similarities and differences between the two viewpoints. In this case, Student 1 attributes the fact that lakes freeze from the surface downward to the effects of pressure, while Student 2 credits a change in density. Both students are able to apply their explanations to the ice skating situation as well. You are not asked to determine the validity of either viewpoint, but instead to follow each argument separately and be able to apply each student's reasoning.

28. J
Basic Theory

Recall that Student 1 credits pressure for the freezing phenomenon. Choices G and H reflect elements of the viewpoint of Student 2 and can therefore be eliminated. If choice F were true, the temperature and pressure effects would work against each other, so only choice J makes sense.

29. B
Basic Theory

According to Student 1, pressure causes the ice to melt, and pressure increases with increasing weight. Student 2 states that friction causes the ice to melt and that the force of friction increases with increasing weight. Therefore, the students would agree that ice would melt faster under the heavier skater, as in choice B.

30. F
Basic Theory

In the explanation of Student 2, ice melts when heat is generated as the skater overcomes the force of friction by *moving* across the ice. If the skater is not moving, then, no heat should be generated. Student 1, though, explains that ice melts due to pressure, which is present whether or not the skater is moving, making choice F correct.

31. C
Scientific Reasoning

Student 2 explains that less dense materials float above more dense materials. Since the frozen ethanol remains below the liquid ethanol, choice C must be true.

32. H
Basic Theory

You can eliminate choices F and G due to the mention of pressure in both, which is a concept only Student 1 contemplates. Student 2 describes floating as the case in which the buoyant force exceeds the force of gravity, so the sinking boat is evidence of the opposite situation described in choice H.

33. B
Basic Theory

Eliminate choice A because only Student 1 considers pressure, and eliminate choice D because the only possible support for this explanation also comes from Student 1. Eliminate choice C because the force of gravity will only change as the mass of the skater changes. Student 2 states that heat is produced by overcoming friction, so less friction would mean less heat, as in choice B.

34. F
Basic Theory

Recall that the viewpoint of Student 2 focuses on a difference in *density*, and eliminate choice H. Choices G and J both actually mean the same thing, but the term *buoyant* is included in choice J to entice the unwary test taker. In either case, the balloon would remain on the ground. The less dense balloon described in choice F would indeed rise above the ground.

PASSAGE VII

The first paragraph of this research summary passage explains that the experiments were conducted to study F^- concentrations in water. Experiment 1 tested solutions prepared by the students to have specific F^- concentrations, and the solutions' electrical conductivities were measured. Table 1 shows a direct relationship between F^- concentration and conductivity, and Figure 1 further emphasizes the linearity of this relationship. Be careful to notice the difference between *measured* and *corrected* conductivities and that it is the corrected conductivities that are plotted in Figure 1. Don't worry if you don't recognize the units given for conductivity; knowledge of these units is not required to answer the questions.

Experiment 2 tested solutions taken from various communities' drinking water supplies. The direct relationship between F^- concentration and conductivity seen in Experiment 1 is confirmed.

35. C
Figure

Either Table 1 or Figure 1 can provide the answer here. Table 1 contains numerical examples of cases where the F^- concentration is indeed doubled (from 0.5 mg/L to 1 mg/L, for example) and gives the corresponding change in conductivity. Taking care to look in the *corrected* conductivity column, you can see that 2 times the concentration results in 2 times the corrected conductivity. Likewise, Figure 1 makes it clear that relationship between the two quantities is linear, which means that any multiplication of the concentration results in the same multiplication of the conductivity.

36. J
Figure

Compare the new conductivity value to those given in Table 2, specifically those for Newtown and Lakewood, and recall the direct relationship between conductivity and F^- concentration. Noticing that Bluewater's conductivity value lies between the values for Newtown and Lakewood allows you to eliminate choices F and G. Taking care to list the towns in order of *increasing* F^- leads you to choice J.

37. C
Figure

Refer to Table 1 to see where a value of 3.0 mg/L would fit in. This new concentration is between the 2.0 mg/L and 4.0 mg/L values given in the table, so the corrected conductivity should lie between 3.34 μS/cm and 6.68 μS/cm. Choices B and D are too close to the extremes of this range, but choice C is exactly in the middle as it should be. Alternatively, you could read the corrected conductivity for a concentration of 3.0 mg/L directly from Figure 1.

38. F
Scientific Reasoning

Questions that ask you to change the procedure of an experiment usually require you to review the original experiment before answering. In this case, the description of Experiment 1 tells you that F^- is added in the form of dissolved Na_2SiF_6. To study Cl^- concentrations, the students must use a chemical that contains Cl^- when preparing the solutions, as in choice F.

39. B
Scientific Reasoning

Experimental data is not required to answer this question. The last sentence of the description of Experiment 1 explains that the corrected conductivity is calculated by *subtracting* the measured conductivity of the blank solution. This always results in the corrected conductivity being less than the measured conductivity, as in choice B.

40. F
Scientific Reasoning

You are told that Cl^- results in an increase in conductivity, and the data shows that F^- results in an increase in conductivity. Therefore, in a solution containing both F^- and Cl^-, it would be impossible to distinguish the contributions to conductivity from each ion given only conductivity measurements. Conductivity would be increased by the presence of Cl^-, and the apparent values for F^- concentration would be falsely high, as in choice F. If you miss this point, you could at least eliminate choice J since the question asks only about the case where *all* of the samples have Cl^- concentrations. The effect of the Cl^- should not be different for different solutions.

Writing Test

MODEL ESSAY

Below is an example of what a high-scoring essay might look like. Notice the author states her position clearly in the introductory paragraph and supports that position with evidence in the following paragraphs. The essay also uses transitions, some advanced vocabulary, and an effective "hook" to draw in the reader.

The elevated rate of automobile accidents that occur when teenaged drivers are behind the wheel has driven some parents and legislators to lobby for laws that would ban drivers under 18 from driving with other teenagers in the car. Those who support these laws believe that driving alone or with an adult would minimize distraction for new drivers, helping them to drive more safely. Others disagree, pointing to the lack of evidence that groups of teenagers riding together are actually the cause of these accidents.

Everyone benefits from having more safe drivers on the road, but efforts to curb the freedoms of drivers under 18 are misguided and unfair. For example, elderly drivers may have impaired vision or motor skills, but are not subject to additional restrictions based only on their age. Male drivers are more prone to car accidents than female drivers, but one can only imagine the outcry if a restriction on the driving privileges of all men were proposed! A driver's license should provide the same responsibilities and freedoms to each person who receives one. If we don't believe that 16-year-olds are as capable of operating a car safely as 18-year-olds, we should not issue them driver's licenses at all.

If we want to promote safe driving, there are more evenhanded methods of doing so. In our state, all drivers who take their license exam must have completed 40 hours of classroom training, regardless of age. These classes are an effective way to ensure that everyone who takes the driver's exam has the same base level of knowledge about traffic laws, operation of a motor vehicle, and the importance of driving safely. This information is important for all new drivers. A requirement for licensed drivers to take a refresher course every five years could help to ensure that more drivers remain aware of new laws and safety issues.

Proponents of this law claim that preventing teenagers from riding in cars together will help to lower the number of accidents. However, no studies have been released that can isolate the presence of other teenagers in the car as a cause of accidents. Having a conversation with a friend in the passenger seat could certainly be distracting, but talking on a cell phone, or listening to loud music, might be equally or even more distracting—and again, all of these distractions can occur when an older person is driving, as well.

Safety and responsibility are important for drivers of all ages. The proposed laws target younger drivers unfairly, and there is no evidence that they would prevent accidents. Measures that attempt to promote safe driving should be aimed at all drivers, not the small percentage of them who are under 18 years old.

You can evaluate your essay and the model essay based on the following criteria, covered in chapter 16:

- Does the author answer the question?
- Is the author's position clearly stated?
- Does the body of the essay support and develop the position taken?
- Are there at least three supporting paragraphs?
- Is the relevance of each supporting paragraph clear?
- Does the writer address the other side of the argument?
- Is the essay organized, with a clear introduction, middle, and end?
- Does the author start a new paragraph for each new idea?
- Is each sentence in a paragraph relevant to the point made in that paragraph?
- Are transitions clear?
- Is the essay easy to read? Is it engaging?
- Are sentences varied?
- Is vocabulary used effectively? Is college-level vocabulary used?

Practice Test Four

ACT Practice Test Four
ANSWER SHEET

ENGLISH TEST

1. (A)(B)(C)(D) 11. (A)(B)(C)(D) 21. (A)(B)(C)(D) 31. (A)(B)(C)(D) 41. (A)(B)(C)(D) 51. (A)(B)(C)(D) 61. (A)(B)(C)(D) 71. (A)(B)(C)(D)
2. (F)(G)(H)(J) 12. (F)(G)(H)(J) 22. (F)(G)(H)(J) 32. (F)(G)(H)(J) 42. (F)(G)(H)(J) 52. (F)(G)(H)(J) 62. (F)(G)(H)(J) 72. (F)(G)(H)(J)
3. (A)(B)(C)(D) 13. (A)(B)(C)(D) 23. (A)(B)(C)(D) 33. (A)(B)(C)(D) 43. (A)(B)(C)(D) 53. (A)(B)(C)(D) 63. (A)(B)(C)(D) 73. (A)(B)(C)(D)
4. (F)(G)(H)(J) 14. (F)(G)(H)(J) 24. (F)(G)(H)(J) 34. (F)(G)(H)(J) 44. (F)(G)(H)(J) 54. (F)(G)(H)(J) 64. (F)(G)(H)(J) 74. (F)(G)(H)(J)
5. (A)(B)(C)(D) 15. (A)(B)(C)(D) 25. (A)(B)(C)(D) 35. (A)(B)(C)(D) 45. (A)(B)(C)(D) 55. (A)(B)(C)(D) 65. (A)(B)(C)(D) 75. (A)(B)(C)(D)
6. (F)(G)(H)(J) 16. (F)(G)(H)(J) 26. (F)(G)(H)(J) 36. (F)(G)(H)(J) 46. (F)(G)(H)(J) 56. (F)(G)(H)(J) 66. (F)(G)(H)(J)
7. (A)(B)(C)(D) 17. (A)(B)(C)(D) 27. (A)(B)(C)(D) 37. (A)(B)(C)(D) 47. (A)(B)(C)(D) 57. (A)(B)(C)(D) 67. (A)(B)(C)(D)
8. (F)(G)(H)(J) 18. (F)(G)(H)(J) 28. (F)(G)(H)(J) 38. (F)(G)(H)(J) 48. (F)(G)(H)(J) 58. (F)(G)(H)(J) 68. (F)(G)(H)(J)
9. (A)(B)(C)(D) 19. (A)(B)(C)(D) 29. (A)(B)(C)(D) 39. (A)(B)(C)(D) 49. (A)(B)(C)(D) 59. (A)(B)(C)(D) 69. (A)(B)(C)(D)
10. (F)(G)(H)(J) 20. (F)(G)(H)(J) 30. (F)(G)(H)(J) 40. (F)(G)(H)(J) 50. (F)(G)(H)(J) 60. (F)(G)(H)(J) 70. (F)(G)(H)(J)

MATH TEST

1. (A)(B)(C)(D)(E) 11. (A)(B)(C)(D)(E) 21. (A)(B)(C)(D)(E) 31. (A)(B)(C)(D)(E) 41. (A)(B)(C)(D)(E) 51. (A)(B)(C)(D)(E)
2. (F)(G)(H)(J)(K) 12. (F)(G)(H)(J)(K) 22. (F)(G)(H)(J)(K) 32. (F)(G)(H)(J)(K) 42. (F)(G)(H)(J)(K) 52. (F)(G)(H)(J)(K)
3. (A)(B)(C)(D)(E) 13. (A)(B)(C)(D)(E) 23. (A)(B)(C)(D)(E) 33. (A)(B)(C)(D)(E) 43. (A)(B)(C)(D)(E) 53. (A)(B)(C)(D)(E)
4. (F)(G)(H)(J)(K) 14. (F)(G)(H)(J)(K) 24. (F)(G)(H)(J)(K) 34. (F)(G)(H)(J)(K) 44. (F)(G)(H)(J)(K) 54. (F)(G)(H)(J)(K)
5. (A)(B)(C)(D)(E) 15. (A)(B)(C)(D)(E) 25. (A)(B)(C)(D)(E) 35. (A)(B)(C)(D)(E) 45. (A)(B)(C)(D)(E) 55. (A)(B)(C)(D)(E)
6. (F)(G)(H)(J)(K) 16. (F)(G)(H)(J)(K) 26. (F)(G)(H)(J)(K) 36. (F)(G)(H)(J)(K) 46. (F)(G)(H)(J)(K) 56. (F)(G)(H)(J)(K)
7. (A)(B)(C)(D)(E) 17. (A)(B)(C)(D)(E) 27. (A)(B)(C)(D)(E) 37. (A)(B)(C)(D)(E) 47. (A)(B)(C)(D)(E) 57. (A)(B)(C)(D)(E)
8. (F)(G)(H)(J)(K) 18. (F)(G)(H)(J)(K) 28. (F)(G)(H)(J)(K) 38. (F)(G)(H)(J)(K) 48. (F)(G)(H)(J)(K) 58. (F)(G)(H)(J)(K)
9. (A)(B)(C)(D)(E) 19. (A)(B)(C)(D)(E) 29. (A)(B)(C)(D)(E) 39. (A)(B)(C)(D)(E) 49. (A)(B)(C)(D)(E) 59. (A)(B)(C)(D)(E)
10. (F)(G)(H)(J)(K) 20. (F)(G)(H)(J)(K) 30. (F)(G)(H)(J)(K) 40. (F)(G)(H)(J)(K) 50. (F)(G)(H)(J)(K) 60. (F)(G)(H)(J)(K)

READING TEST

1. (A)(B)(C)(D) 6. (F)(G)(H)(J) 11. (A)(B)(C)(D) 16. (F)(G)(H)(J) 21. (A)(B)(C)(D) 26. (F)(G)(H)(J) 31. (A)(B)(C)(D) 36. (F)(G)(H)(J)
2. (F)(G)(H)(J) 7. (A)(B)(C)(D) 12. (F)(G)(H)(J) 17. (A)(B)(C)(D) 22. (F)(G)(H)(J) 27. (A)(B)(C)(D) 32. (F)(G)(H)(J) 37. (A)(B)(C)(D)
3. (A)(B)(C)(D) 8. (F)(G)(H)(J) 13. (A)(B)(C)(D) 18. (F)(G)(H)(J) 23. (A)(B)(C)(D) 28. (F)(G)(H)(J) 33. (A)(B)(C)(D) 38. (F)(G)(H)(J)
4. (F)(G)(H)(J) 9. (A)(B)(C)(D) 14. (F)(G)(H)(J) 19. (A)(B)(C)(D) 24. (F)(G)(H)(J) 29. (A)(B)(C)(D) 34. (F)(G)(H)(J) 39. (A)(B)(C)(D)
5. (A)(B)(C)(D) 10. (F)(G)(H)(J) 15. (A)(B)(C)(D) 20. (F)(G)(H)(J) 25. (A)(B)(C)(D) 30. (F)(G)(H)(J) 35. (A)(B)(C)(D) 40. (F)(G)(H)(J)

SCIENCE TEST

1. (A)(B)(C)(D) 6. (F)(G)(H)(J) 11. (A)(B)(C)(D) 16. (F)(G)(H)(J) 21. (A)(B)(C)(D) 26. (F)(G)(H)(J) 31. (A)(B)(C)(D) 36. (F)(G)(H)(J)
2. (F)(G)(H)(J) 7. (A)(B)(C)(D) 12. (F)(G)(H)(J) 17. (A)(B)(C)(D) 22. (F)(G)(H)(J) 27. (A)(B)(C)(D) 32. (F)(G)(H)(J) 37. (A)(B)(C)(D)
3. (A)(B)(C)(D) 8. (F)(G)(H)(J) 13. (A)(B)(C)(D) 18. (F)(G)(H)(J) 23. (A)(B)(C)(D) 28. (F)(G)(H)(J) 33. (A)(B)(C)(D) 38. (F)(G)(H)(J)
4. (F)(G)(H)(J) 9. (A)(B)(C)(D) 14. (F)(G)(H)(J) 19. (A)(B)(C)(D) 24. (F)(G)(H)(J) 29. (A)(B)(C)(D) 34. (F)(G)(H)(J) 39. (A)(B)(C)(D)
5. (A)(B)(C)(D) 10. (F)(G)(H)(J) 15. (A)(B)(C)(D) 20. (F)(G)(H)(J) 25. (A)(B)(C)(D) 30. (F)(G)(H)(J) 35. (A)(B)(C)(D) 40. (F)(G)(H)(J)

ENGLISH TEST

45 Minutes—75 Questions

Directions: In the following five passages, certain words and phrases are underlined and numbered. In the right-hand column are alternatives for each underlined portion. Select the one that best conveys the idea, creates the most grammatically correct sentence, or is the most consistent with the style and tone of the passage. If you decide that the original version is best, select NO CHANGE. You may also find questions that ask about the entire passage or a section of the passage. These questions will correspond to small numbered boxes in the text. For these questions, decide which choice best accomplishes the purpose set out in the question stem. After you've selected the best choice, fill in the corresponding oval in your Answer Grid. For some questions, you'll need to read the context in order to answer correctly. Be sure to read until you have enough information to determine the correct answer choice.

You will also find questions about a section of the passage or about the passage as a whole. These questions do not refer to an underlined portion of the passage, but rather are identified by a number or numbers in a box.

For each question, choose the alternative you consider best and fill in the corresponding oval on your answer document. Read each passage through once before you begin to answer the questions that accompany it. For many of the questions, you must read several sentences beyond the question to determine the answer. Be sure that you have read enough ahead each time you choose an alternative.

Passage I

THE PARTHENON

[1]

If you are like most visitors to Athens, you will make your way to the <u>Acropolis, the hill</u> that
1
once served as a fortified, strategic position overlooking the Aegean Sea—to see the Parthenon. This celebrated temple was dedicated in the fifth century B.C. to the goddess Athena. There is no more famous building in all of Greece; to climb up its marble steps is <u>to have beheld</u> a human
2
creation that has attained the stature of a natural

1. A. NO CHANGE
    B. Acropolis. The hill
    C. Acropolis—the hill
    D. Acropolis

2. F. NO CHANGE
    G. to behold
    H. beholding
    J. to be holding

GO ON TO THE NEXT PAGE →

phenomenon like the Grand Canyon. <u>You should</u>
₃

<u>also make an attempt to sample Athenian cuisine</u>
₃

<u>while you're there.</u>
₃

[2]

Generations of architects <u>have proclaimed</u>
₄

the Parthenon to be the most brilliantly

conceived structure in the Western world. The

genius of its construction is <u>subtle for example</u>
₅

the temple's columns were made to bulge

outward slightly in order to compensate for the

<u>fact, viewed from distance, that straight columns</u>
₆

<u>appear concave.</u> Using this and other techniques,
₆

the architects strove to create an optical <u>illusion</u>
₇

<u>of; uprightness,</u> solidity, and permanence.
₇

[3]

<u>Because of this,</u> the overall impression you'll
₈

get of the Parthenon will be far different from

the one the ancient Athenians had. Only by

standing on the marble steps of the Parthenon

and allowing your imagination to transport

3. A. NO CHANGE
   B. Also make an attempt to sample
      Athenian cuisine while you're there.
   C. While you're there, you should
      also make an attempt to sample
      Athenian cuisine.
   D. OMIT the underlined portion.

4. F. NO CHANGE
   G. has proclaimed
   H. proclaims
   J. are proclaiming

5. A. NO CHANGE
   B. subtle; for example
   C. subtle. For example
   D. subtle. For example,

6. F. NO CHANGE
   G. fact that straight columns, viewed
      from a distance, appear concave.
   H. view from a distance: straight
      columns appearing concave.
   J. fact, when viewed from far away,
      that straight columns appear
      concave.

7. A. NO CHANGE
   B. illusion of: uprightness
   C. illusion of, uprightness
   D. illusion of uprightness,

8. F. NO CHANGE
   G. Thus
   H. Rather
   J. Of course

you back to the Golden Age of Athens. You will
9
be able to see the temple's main attraction, the
legendary statue of Athena Parthenos. It was
38 feet high and made of ivory and over a ton of
pure gold. Removed from the temple in the fifth
10
century C.E., all that remains is the slight rectan-
10
gular depression on the floor where it stood.

[4]

Many of the ornate carvings and sculptures
that adorned the walls of the Acropolis is no
11
longer there, either. In the early nineteenth

century, the British diplomat Lord Elgins
12
decision to "protect" the ones that survived by
12
removing them from the Parthenon and carrying
them back to Britain (he had the permission of
the Ottoman Turks, who controlled Greece at the
time, to do so).

[5]

After they gained independence from the
Turks, they began to demand the sculptures and
13
carvings back from the British, to no avail. Thus,
if you want to gain a complete picture of what
the Parthenon once looked like, you'll have to
visit not only the Acropolis of Athens, but the
British Museum in London as well.

9. A. NO CHANGE
   B. Athens; you will
   C. Athens will you
   D. Athens. You may

10. F. NO CHANGE
    G. Having been removed from the
       temple in the fifth century C.E.,
    H. Given its removal from the temple
       in the fifth century C.E.,
    J. The statue was removed from the
       temple in the fifth century C.E.;

11. A. NO CHANGE
    B. will be
    C. have been
    D. are

12. F. NO CHANGE
    G. Elgin's deciding that
    H. Elgin decided to
    J. Elgin's decision to

13. A. NO CHANGE
    B. the Turks
    C. the Greeks
    D. who

Questions 14–15 ask about the preceding passage as a whole.

---

14. The writer wishes to insert the following material into the essay:

    > Some of them were destroyed in 1687 when attacking Venetians bombarded the Acropolis, setting off explosives that had been stored in the Parthenon.

    The new material best supports and therefore would most logically be placed in paragraph:

    F. 1.

    G. 2.

    H. 3.

    J. 4.

15. Suppose the editor of an architecture journal had requested that the writer focus primarily on the techniques the ancient Greek architects used in constructing the Parthenon. Does the essay fulfill this request?

    A. Yes, because the essay makes it clear that the Parthenon was an amazing architectural achievement.

    B. Yes, because the essay explains in the second paragraph the reason the temple's columns bulge outward slightly.

    C. No, because the Parthenon's construction is only one of several topics covered in the essay.

    D. No, because the author never explains what the architects who designed the Parthenon were trying to accomplish.

Passage II

THE LEGENDARY ROBIN HOOD

Although there is no conclusive evidence that a man named Robin Hood ever actually existed, the story of Robin Hood and his band of merry men has become one of the most popular traditional tales in English literature. Robin is the hero in a series of ballads dating from at least the fourteenth century. These ballads are telling
16
of discontent among the lower classes in the north of England during a turbulent era culminating in the Peasants' Revolt of 1381. A good deal of the rebellion against authority stemmed from restriction of hunting rights. These early ballads reveal the cruelty that was a part of medieval life. Robin Hood was a rebel, and many of the most striking episodes depict him and his companions robbing and killing representatives of authority and they gave the gains to the poor.
17

Their most frequentest enemy was the Sheriff of
18
Nottingham, a local agent of the central government. Other enemies included wealthy ecclesiastical landowners.

While Robin could be ruthless with those who abused their power, he was kind to the oppressed. He was a people's hero as King

16. F. NO CHANGE
    G. telling
    H. tell
    J. they are telling

17. A. NO CHANGE
    B. they were giving
    C. giving
    D. gave

18. F. NO CHANGE
    G. even more frequenter
    H. frequent
    J. frequently

GO ON TO THE NEXT PAGE

Arthur was a noble's. (The Broadway musical
                                    19
Camelot and Walt Disney's *The Sword in the*
                                    19
Stone are based on the legend of King Arthur.)
                                    19
   Some scholars have sought to prove that

there was an actual Robin Hood. However, refer-

ences to the Robin Hood legends by medieval

writers make it clear that the ballads were the

only evidence for Robin's existence available to

them. A popular modern belief that Robin was
20

of the time of Richard I probably stems from

the antiquary Richard Stukely's fabrication of a
                                    21

"pedigree." [22]

19. A. NO CHANGE
    B. (The Broadway musical and the
       movie, respectively, *Camelot* and
       Walt Disney's *The Sword in the
       Stone*, are based on the legend of
       King Arthur.)
    C. (Movies and musicals, including
       The Sword in the Stone and *Camelot*,
       are derived from the legend of King
       Arthur.)
    D. OMIT the underlined portion.

20. F. NO CHANGE
    G. him.
    H. it.
    J. those writing ballads about him.

21. A. NO CHANGE
    B. Stukelys fabrication
    C. Stukelys fabrication,
    D. Stukely's, fabrication

22. Suppose that at this point in the
    passage, the writer wanted to add more
    information about Richard Stukely.
    Which of the following additions would
    be most relevant to the passage as a
    whole?
    F. A discussion of relevant books
       on England during the realm of
       Richard I
    G. A definition of the term *antiquary*
    H. An example of Stukely's interest
       in King Arthur
    J. A description of the influence
       Stukely's fabricated pedigree has
       had on later versions of the Robin
       Hood tale

GO ON TO THE NEXT PAGE ⟩

In the eighteenth century, the nature of the legend was distorted by the suggestion that Robin was as a fallen nobleman. Writers adopted
23

23. A. NO CHANGE
    B. was like as if he was
    C. was a
    D. is as a

this new element as eagerly as puppies. Robin
24

24. F. NO CHANGE
    G. eagerly
    H. eagerly, like a puppy
    J. like a puppy's eagerness

was also given a love interest; Maid Marian.
25
Some critics say that these ballads lost much of their vitality and poetic value by losing the social impulse that prompted their creation.

25. A. NO CHANGE
    B. interests—Maid
    C. interest: Maid,
    D. interest—Maid

Consequently, in the twentieth century,
26
the legend of Robin Hood has inspired several movies and a television series. Even a Broadway

26. F. NO CHANGE
    G. (Do NOT begin new paragraph) In the twentieth century, on the one hand,
    H. (Begin new paragraph) In the twentieth century,
    J. (Begin new paragraph) In the twentieth century, therefore,

musical basing on the tale. So, whether or not a
27

27. A. NO CHANGE
    B. has been based
    C. to base
    D. OMIT the underlined portion.

Robin Hood actually lived in ancient Britain, and
28
the legendary Robin has lived in the popular imagination for more than 600 years.

28. F. NO CHANGE
    G. Britain,
    H. Britain, therefore
    J. Britain;

GO ON TO THE NEXT PAGE

Questions 29–30 ask about the preceding passage as a whole.

---

29. Suppose this passage were written for an audience that was unfamiliar with the legend of Robin Hood. The writer could most effectively strengthen the passage by:

    A. citing examples of legendary rebels from Spanish and French literature.

    B. including further evidence of Robin Hood's actual existence.

    C. quoting a few lines from a Broadway musical about ancient Britain.

    D. including a brief summary of the Robin Hood legend.

30. This passage was probably written for readers who:

    F. are experts on how legends are handed down.

    G. are authorities on ancient British civilization and culture.

    H. are convinced that Robin Hood was an actual historical personage.

    J. have some familiarity with the Robin Hood legends.

GO ON TO THE NEXT PAGE

Passage III

HOW MOTHER NATURE JUMP-STARTED MY CAREER

The following paragraphs may or may not be in the most logical order. Each paragraph is numbered in brackets, and question 45 will ask you to choose the most logical order of the paragraphs.

[1]

When Mt. St. Helens erupted, my training as a private pilot paid off. My editor asked me to write a feature story on the volcano. Only scientists and reporters were allowed within a ten-mile radius of the mountain. Eager to see
31
Mt. St. Helens for himself, my brother Jeff volunteered to accompany me as an assistant on the flight. He had never flown with me before, and
32
I looked forward at the opportunity to show off
32
my skills.
32

[2]

If I could read a newspaper, I entertained
33
thoughts of becoming a photojournalist. I always

31. A. NO CHANGE
    B. radius, consisting of ten miles,
    C. measurement of a ten-mile radius
    D. radius, measuring ten miles,

32. F. NO CHANGE
    G. but looked forward to the opportunity of showing off my skills.
    H. and I looked forward to the opportunity to show off my skills.
    J. nevertheless I anticipated being able to show off my skills.

33. A. NO CHANGE
    B. Since I found it easy to read a newspaper,
    C. Although I could read a newspaper,
    D. Ever since I could read a newspaper,

GO ON TO THE NEXT PAGE

envisioned myself in some faraway exotic place
34

performing dangerous deeds as a foreign

correspondent. I was thrilled when I was hired

for my first job as a cub reporter for the local

newspaper in my rural hometown. However,

some of the glamour began to fade after I

covered the umpteenth garden party. Then one

day, Mother Nature intervened, giving me the
35

opportunity to cover an international event.

[3]

When we arrived at the airport, filing my
36

flight plan; giving my credentials as a reporter
36

for the Gresham *Outlook*. As we departed

Troutdale airport, my Cessna 152 ascended

slowly on its way toward Mt. St. Helens. As we

neared the crater, I kept a careful watch for other
37

airplanes in the vicinity. A few other pilots were

also circling around the crater. I had to maintain

a high enough altitude to avoid both the smoke

being emitted from: the crater and the ashen
38

residue already in the atmosphere. Too much

exposure to the volcanic particles could put my

plane out of service. This element of danger

served to increase not only my awareness, but

also my excitement.

34. F. NO CHANGE
    G. I
    H. me
    J. it

35. A. NO CHANGE
    B. intervened:
    C. intervened;
    D. —intervened—

36. F. NO CHANGE
    G. I filed my flight plan and gave
    H. filing my flight plan, giving
    J. my flight plan was filed by me, and I gave

37. The best placement for the underlined portion would be:
    A. where it is now.
    B. after the word *other*.
    C. after the word *we*.
    D. before the word *crater*.

38. F. NO CHANGE
    G. (from: the crater)
    H. from, the crater,
    J. from the crater

GO ON TO THE NEXT PAGE ⇨

[4]

Jeff and I were at first speechless and mute
                                        39
at the awesome sight below us as we circled the
crater. It was as if the spectacular beauty of a
Fourth of July celebration were contained in one
natural phenomenon. Jeff helped me, steadying
                                       40
the plane and took notes, while I shot pictures
40

and dictated story ideas to him. 41

[5]

My story appeared as the front-page feature
the following day. However, I have realized
                    42
many of my early dreams, working as a foreign
correspondent in many different countries. And
yet none of my experiences has surpassed that
special pride and excitement I felt covering my
first "international" story.

39. A. NO CHANGE
    B. and also mute
    C. —and mute—
    D. OMIT the underlined portion.

40. F. NO CHANGE
    G. steadying the plane and taking
       notes,
    H. steadied the plane and taking notes,
    J. steadies the plane and takes notes

41. The writer could most effectively
    strengthen the passage at this point
    by adding which of the following?

    A. A description of Mt. St. Helens
    B. The sentence, "Jeff, take this plane
       lower!" to add excitement
    C. The statement, "A volcano is a vent
       in the earth's crust through which
       lava is expelled," to inform the
       reader
    D. A discussion of other recent volcanic
       eruptions to provide a contrast

42. F. NO CHANGE
    G. Since that time,
    H. Furthermore,
    J. Nevertheless,

GO ON TO THE NEXT PAGE

Questions 43–45 ask about the preceding passage as a whole.

---

43. Readers are likely to regard the passage as best described by which of the following terms?

    A. Optimistic

    B. Bitter

    C. Nostalgic

    D. Exhausted

44. Is the author's use of the pronoun *I* appropriate in the passage?

    F. No, because, as a rule, one avoids *I* in formal writing.

    G. No, because it weakens the passage's focus on volcanoes.

    H. Yes, because it gives immediacy to the story told in the passage.

    J. Yes, because *I* is, as a rule, appropriate in writing.

45. Choose the sequence of paragraph numbers that will make the passage's structure most logical.

    A. NO CHANGE

    B. 2, 1, 3, 4, 5

    C. 3, 4, 5, 1, 2

    D. 4, 5, 1, 2, 3

GO ON TO THE NEXT PAGE

Passage IV

SIR ARTHUR CONAN DOYLE

[1]

Sherlock Holmes, the <u>ingenious and extremely</u>
$\qquad$ 46

<u>clever</u> detective, with the deer-stalker hat, pipe,
46

and magnifying glass, is a universally recogniz-

able character. Everyone knows of Holmes's

ability to solve even the most bizarre mysteries

through the application of cold logic. <u>Therefore,</u>
$\qquad$ 47

<u>everyone</u> is familiar with the phrase "elementary,
47

my dear Watson," Holmes's perennial response to

the requests of his baffled sidekick, Dr. Watson,

for an explanation of his amazing deductions.

<u>Strictly speaking, of course, Holmes's "deductions"</u>
$\qquad$ 48

[2]

<u>were not deductions at all, but inductive inferences.</u>
$\qquad$ 48

But how many people know anything about

the creator of Sherlock Holmes, Sir Arthur Conan

Doyle? Fans of Holmes might be surprised to

discover that <u>he</u> did not want <u>to be engraved</u>
$\qquad$ 49 $\qquad$ 50

<u>forever in the memory of the people</u> as the
50

46. F. NO CHANGE
   G. ingenious
   H. ingenious, extremely clever
   J. cleverly ingenious

47. A. NO CHANGE
   B. Although everyone
   C. For this reason, everyone
   D. Everyone

48. F. NO CHANGE
   G. (Strictly speaking, of course,
      Holmes's "deductions" were not
      deductions at all, but inductive
      inferences.)
   H. Holmes's "deductions" were, strictly
      speaking, not deductions at all, but
      inductive inferences.
   J. OMIT the underlined portion.

49. A. NO CHANGE
   B. Conan Doyle
   C. they
   D. the detective

50. F. NO CHANGE
   G. to go down in the annals of history
   H. to be permanently thought of
      forever
   J. to be remembered

GO ON TO THE NEXT PAGE

author of the Sherlock Holmes stories. <u>In fact,</u>
₅₁
Conan Doyle sent Holmes to his death at the
end of the second book of short stories and
subsequently felt a great sense of relief. Having
had enough of his famous character by that time,
<u>Sherlock Holmes would never divert him again</u>
₅₂
<u>from more serious writing, he promised himself.</u>
₅₂
It took eight years and the offer of a princely
sum of money before Conan Doyle could be

persuaded to revive the detective. <u>Soap opera</u>
₅₃
<u>characters are sometimes brought back to life</u>
₅₃
<u>after they've been pronounced dead, too.</u>
₅₃
[1] Admirers of Holmes's coldly scientific
approach to his detective work may also be
taken aback when they learn that Conan Doyle

<u>has been deeply immersed</u> in spiritualism.
₅₄
[2] Convinced by these experiences of the

validity of paranormal <u>phenomena, that he</u>
₅₅
<u>lectured</u> on spiritualism in towns and villages
₅₅
throughout Britain. [3] For example, he and
his family attempted to communicate with the

51. A. NO CHANGE
    B. Despite this,
    C. Regardless,
    D. Yet

52. F. NO CHANGE
    G. the diversion of Sherlock Holmes,
       he promised himself, would never
       again keep him from more serious
       writing.
    H. more serious writing consumed all
       his time from then on.
    J. he promised himself that Sherlock
       Holmes would never again divert
       him from more serious writing.

53. A. NO CHANGE
    B. (Soap opera characters are
       sometimes brought back to life after
       they've been pronounced dead, too.)
    C. Sometimes you'll see soap opera
       characters who were dead being
       brought back to life, just like
       Holmes.
    D. OMIT the underlined portion.

54. F. NO CHANGE
    G. is deeply immersed
    H. was deeply immersed
    J. has been immersed deeply

55. A. NO CHANGE
    B. phenomena, he lectured
    C. phenomena was he that he lectured
    D. phenomena. He lectured

GO ON TO THE NEXT PAGE

dead by automatic writing, <u>thought to be a</u>
<u>   56</u>
<u>method of talking with those no longer among</u>
<u>   56</u>
<u>the living</u>, and through a spiritual medium, an
  56
individual who supposedly could contact those
in the world beyond. [4] Conan Doyle claimed
to have grasped materialized hands and watched
heavy articles swimming through the air during
sessions led by the medium. 57

[3]

Doyle seems never to have asked <u>himself: why</u>
                      58
<u>they</u> would manifest themselves in such curious
 58
ways, or to have reflected on the fact that many
of these effects are the standard trappings of
cheating mediums. One has to wonder, <u>what would</u>
                         59
<u>Sherlock Holmes have to say?</u>
    59

56. F. NO CHANGE

    G. a means of getting in touch with those beyond the grave

    H. thought to be a method of talking with the dead

    J. OMIT the underlined portion.

57. For the sake of unity and coherence, sentence 2 should be placed:

    A. where it is now.

    B. before sentence 1.

    C. after sentence 3.

    D. after sentence 4.

58. F. NO CHANGE

    G. himself—why they

    H. himself why those in the other world

    J. himself why they

59. A. NO CHANGE

    B. what would Sherlock Holmes have said?

    C. what is Sherlock Holmes going to say?

    D. what had Sherlock Holmes said?

Question 60 asks about
the preceding passage as a whole.

---

60. Which of the following would be the most appropriate subtitle for the passage?

    F. The Truth about Spiritualists

    G. Rational or Superstitious?

    H. The Secret Life of Sherlock Holmes

    J. His Religious Beliefs

GO ON TO THE NEXT PAGE

Passage V

FIRE IN YELLOWSTONE

[1]

During the summer of 1988, I watched Yellow-

stone National Park go up in flames. <u>Fires</u>

<u>ignited by lightning, in June,</u> had been allowed
61

to burn unsuppressed because park officials

expected that the usual summer rains would

douse them. But the rains never came, a <u>more</u>
62

plentiful supply of fuel <u>(fallen logs, branches, and</u>
63

<u>pine needles) were</u> available, and winds of up to
63

100 mph whipped the spreading fires along and

carried red-hot embers to other areas, creating

new fires.

[2]

By the time park officials succumbed to the

pressure of public opinion and decided to try to

extinguish the <u>flames. Its</u> too late. The situation
64

remained out of <u>control in spite of</u> the efforts
65

61. A. NO CHANGE
    B. Fires having been ignited by
       lightning, in June,
    C. Fires ignited by lightning in June
    D. Fires ignited by lightning in June,

62. F. NO CHANGE
    G. very much
    H. much more
    J. OMIT the underlined portion.

63. A. NO CHANGE
    B. (fallen logs, branches, and pine
       needles) was
    C. (fallen logs, branches, and pine
       needles) being
    D. (fallen logs, branches, and pine
       needles) having been

64. F. NO CHANGE
    G. flames. It's
    H. flames, it's
    J. flames, it was

65. A. NO CHANGE
    B. control. In spite of
    C. control; despite
    D. control; in spite of

GO ON TO THE NEXT PAGE

of 9,000 firefighters <u>employed</u> state-of-the-art
                          66
equipment. By September, more than 720,000

acres of Yellowstone <u>had been affected by fire.</u>

<u>Nature was only able to curb the destruction;</u>
                          67
the smoke did not begin to clear until the first

snow arrived on September 11.

[3]

<u>Having been an ecologist</u> who has studied
                  68
forests for 20 years, I knew that this was not

nearly the tragedy it seemed to be. <u>Many more</u>
                                        69
<u>acres of forest burned in Alaska in 1988 than</u>
                          69
<u>in Yellowstone Park.</u> Large fires are, after all,
          69

necessary <u>in order that the continued health in</u>
                          70
<u>the forest ecosystem be maintained.</u> Fires thin
                  70
out overcrowded areas and allow the sun to

reach species of plants stunted by shade. Ash

fertilizes the soil, and fire smoke kills forest

bacteria. In the case of the lodgepole pine, fire

66. F. NO CHANGE
    G. who employed
    H. which were employing
    J. which employed

67. A. NO CHANGE
    B. Nature able only to curb the
       destruction;
    C. Nature was able to curb only the
       destruction;
    D. Only nature was able to curb the
       destruction;

68. F. NO CHANGE
    G. As an ecologist
    H. I'm an ecologist
    J. Being an ecologist,

69. A. NO CHANGE
    B. The amount of acreage that burned
       in Yellowstone in 1988 was nowhere
       near as great as in Alaska.
    C. Many more acres of forest burned in
       Alaska in 1988, than in Yellowstone
       Park.
    D. OMIT the underlined portion.

70. F. NO CHANGE
    G. for the continued health of the
       forest ecosystem to be maintained.
    H. in order that the continued
       health of the forest ecosystem can
       persevere.
    J. for the continued health of the
       forest ecosystem.

GO ON TO THE NEXT PAGE ⇨

is essential to reproduction: the <u>pines' cone has</u>
71

<u>only opened</u> when exposed to temperatures
71

greater than 112 degrees.

[4]

The fires in Yellowstone did result in some loss of wildlife, but overall the region's animals proved to be fire-tolerant and fire-adaptive. <u>However,</u> large animals such as bison were often
72

seen grazing and bedding down in meadows near burning forests. Also, the fire posed little threat to the members of any endangered animal species in the park. 73

[5]

My confidence in the natural resilience of the forest has been borne out in the years since the fires ravaged Yellowstone. <u>Judging from the</u>
74

<u>recent pictures of the park,</u> the forest was not
74

destroyed; it was rejuvenated.

71. A. NO CHANGE
    B. pine's cone has only opened
    C. pine's cone opens only
    D. pines' cones have only opened

72. F. NO CHANGE
    G. Clearly,
    H. In fact,
    J. Instead,

73. The writer has decided that a better transition is needed between the previous paragraph and this one. Which of the following sentences could be added at the beginning of this paragraph to do that best?

    A. Although fire is an integral part of the long-term life of the forest, animals suffer in the short term.
    B. Since forest fires play such a natural role, I expected the impact on animal life to be minimal.
    C. One never knows what toll a fire will take on the wildlife, though.
    D. Temperatures greater than 112 degrees are indeed rather hot.

74. F. NO CHANGE
    G. Recent pictures of the park show that
    H. Judging by the recent pictures of the park,
    J. As judged according to pictures taken of the park recently,

GO ON TO THE NEXT PAGE ⇨

Question 75 asks about
the preceding passage as a whole.

75. If the writer wished to provide support
for the claim that the fire posed little
threat to the members of any endangered animal species in the park, he or
she would most likely:

A. list the endangered animal species
known to inhabit the park.

B. discuss the particular vulnerability
of endangered species of birds to
forest fires.

C. cite the reports of biologists who
monitored animal activity in the
park during the fire.

D. explain how infrequent such an
extensive series of forest fires
really is.

MATH TEST

60 Minutes—60 Questions

Directions: Solve each of the following problems, select the correct answer, and then fill in the corresponding oval on your Answer Grid.

Don't linger over problems that are too time-consuming. Do as many as you can, then come back to the others in the time permitted.

You may use a calculator on this test. Some questions, however, may be easier to answer without the use of a calculator.

Note: Unless the question says otherwise, assume all of the following:

1. Illustrative figures are *not* necessarily drawn to scale.

2. All geometric figures lie in a plane.

3. The term *line* indicates a straight line.

4. The term *average* indicates arithmetic mean.

---

1. What is the average of 230, 155, 320, 400, and 325?

    A. 205
    B. 286
    C. 300
    D. 430
    E. 490

2. Sarah has a wooden board that is 12 feet long. If she cuts three 28-inch pieces from the board, how much board will she have left?

    F. 14 inches
    G. 28 inches
    H. 36 inches
    J. 60 inches
    K. 72 inches

DO YOUR FIGURING HERE.

GO ON TO THE NEXT PAGE

3. If $4x + 18 = 38$, $x =$

A. 3

B. 4.5

C. 5

D. 12

E. 20

DO YOUR FIGURING HERE.

4. John weighs 1.5 times as much as Ellen. If John weighs 165 lb, how much does Ellen weigh?

F. 100 lb

G. 110 lb

H. 150 lb

J. 165 lb

K. 175 lb

5. What is the average of 237, 482, 375, and 210?

A. 150

B. 185

C. 210

D. 260

E. 326

6. If $\sqrt[3]{x} = 4$, $x =$

F. 4

G. 12

H. 36

J. 64

K. 256

7. $x^2 + 14 = 63$, $x =$

A. 4.5

B. 7

C. 14

D. 24.5

E. 2.8

GO ON TO THE NEXT PAGE

8. Which of the following is equivalent to $\sqrt{54}$?

   F. $2\sqrt{3}$

   G. $3\sqrt{6}$

   H. 15

   J. 9

   K. $9\sqrt{6}$

9. What whole number is closest to the solution
   of $\sqrt{90} \times \sqrt{32}$?

   A. 7

   B. 11

   C. 36

   D. 44

   E. 54

10. $5.2^3 + 6.8^2 =$

    F. 46.24

    G. 94.872

    H. 120.534

    J. 140.608

    K. 186.848

11. If x is a real number such that $x^3 = 512$,
    what is the value of x^2?

    A. 8

    B. 16

    C. 64

    D. 81

    E. 135

12. $3^3 \div 9 + (6^2 - 12) \div 4 =$

    F. 3

    G. 6.75

    H. 9

    J. 12

    K. 15

DO YOUR FIGURING HERE.

13. If bananas cost $0.24 and oranges cost $0.38, what is the total cost of x bananas and y oranges?

    A. $(x + y)(\$0.24 + \$0.38)$

    B. $\$0.24x + \$0.38y$

    C. $\$0.62(x + y)$

    D. $\dfrac{\$0.24}{x} + \dfrac{\$0.38}{y}$

    E. $\$0.38x + \$0.24y$

14. If $4x + 13 = 16$, what is the value of x?

    F. 0.25

    G. 0.50

    H. 0.55

    J. 0.70

    K. 0.75

15. What is 6% of 1,250?

    A. 75

    B. 208

    C. 300

    D. 500

    E. 750

16. On her first three geometry tests, Sarah scored an 89, a 93, and an 84. If there are four tests total and Sarah needs at least a 90 average for the four, what is the lowest score she can receive on the final test?

    F. 86

    G. 90

    H. 92

    J. 94

    K. 96

DO YOUR FIGURING HERE.

GO ON TO THE NEXT PAGE

17. The relationship between Fahrenheit and Celsius is $F = \frac{9}{5}C + 32$. If the temperature is 68° Fahrenheit, what is the temperature in degrees Celsius?

   A. 14°
   B. 20°
   C. 32°
   D. 68°
   E. 72°

DO YOUR FIGURING HERE.

18. The eighth grade girls' basketball team played a total of 13 games this season. If they scored a total of 364 points, what was their average score per game?

   F. 13
   G. 16
   H. 20
   J. 28
   K. 32

19. If $6x + 4 = 11x - 21$, what is the value of x?

   A. 2
   B. 3
   C. 4
   D. 5
   E. 6

20. A jacket with an original price of $160 is on sale for 15% off. What is the sale price?

   F. $120
   G. $136
   H. $140
   J. $148
   K. $155

GO ON TO THE NEXT PAGE

21. If the average of 292, 305, 415, and x is 343, what is the value of x?

    A. 315
    B. 337
    C. 360
    D. 382
    E. 396

DO YOUR FIGURING HERE.

22. A jar contains 8 red marbles, 14 blue marbles, 11 yellow marbles, and 6 green marbles. If a marble is selected at random, what is the probability that it will be green?

    F. $\frac{2}{39}$

    G. $\frac{2}{13}$

    H. $\frac{8}{39}$

    J. $\frac{11}{39}$

    K. $\frac{22}{39}$

23. Each day, Laura bikes to school in the morning and bikes home in the afternoon. If she bikes at an average speed of 12 miles per hour and the school is 3 miles from her house, how long does it take her to bike to school and back?

    A. 15 minutes
    B. 24 minutes
    C. 28 minutes
    D. 30 minutes
    E. 36 minutes

GO ON TO THE NEXT PAGE

24. A local high school is raffling off a college scholarship to the students in its junior class. If a girl has a .55 chance of winning the scholarship and 154 of the juniors are girls, how many of the juniors are boys? (Assume that every junior has an equal chance to win.)

    F.   85

    G. 126

    H. 154

    J.   161

    K. 168

25. For all x, $(x + 4)(x - 4) + (2x + 2)(x - 2) = ?$

    A. $x^2 - 2x - 20$

    B. $3x^2 - 12$

    C. $3x^2 - 2x - 20$

    D. $3x^2 + 2x - 20$

    E. $3x^2 + 2x + 20$

26. If $s^2 - 4s - 6 = 6$, what are the possible values of s?

    F. $-2, -6$

    G. $-2, 6$

    H. $2, -6$

    J. $2, 6$

    K. $2, 10$

DO YOUR FIGURING HERE.

GO ON TO THE NEXT PAGE

27. In the triangle below, if cos ∠BAC = .6 and the hypotenuse of the triangle is 15, what is the length of side BC?

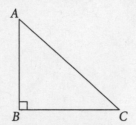

A.   3

B.   5

C. 10

D. 12

E. 15

28. If a car drives 80 miles per hour for x hours and 60 miles per hour for y hours, what is the car's average speed, in miles, for the total distance traveled?

F. $\dfrac{480}{xy}$

G. $\dfrac{80}{x} + \dfrac{60}{y}$

H. $\dfrac{80}{x} \times \dfrac{60}{y}$

J. $\dfrac{80x + 60y}{x + y}$

K. $\dfrac{x + y}{80x + 60y}$

29. If the first and second terms of a geometric sequence are 3 and 12, what is the expression for the value of the 24th term of the sequence?

A. $a_{24} = 3^4 \times 12$

B. $a_{24} = 3^4 \times 23$

C. $a_{24} = 4^3 \times 12$

D. $a_{24} = 4^{23} \times 3 - 3$

E. $a_{24} = 4^{23} \times 3$

DO YOUR FIGURING HERE.

GO ON TO THE NEXT PAGE

30. If $3^{3x+3} = 27^{\left(\frac{2}{3}x - \frac{1}{3}\right)}$, then $x = $?

    F. -4

    G. $-\dfrac{7}{4}$

    H. $-\dfrac{10}{7}$

    J. 2

    K. 4

DO YOUR FIGURING HERE.

31. The complex number i is defined as $i^2 = -1$.
    $(i + 1)^2(i - 1) = $

    A. $i - 1$

    B. $i - 2$

    C. $-2i$

    D. $-2i + 2$

    E. $-2i - 2$

32. A playground is $(x + 7)$ units long and $(x + 3)$ units wide. If a square of side length x is sectioned off from the playground to make a sandpit, which of the following could be the remaining area of the playground?

    F. $x^2 + 10x + 21$

    G. $10x + 21$

    H. $2x + 10$

    J. 21

    K. $21x$

33. If u is an integer, then $(u - 3)^2 + 5$ must be:

    A. an even integer.

    B. an odd integer.

    C. a positive integer.

    D. a negative integer.

    E. Cannot be determined by the information given.

GO ON TO THE NEXT PAGE

34. Which of the following is a solution to the inequality $-1 \geq -\frac{3}{5}x + 2$?

DO YOUR FIGURING HERE.

F.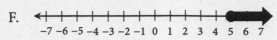

G.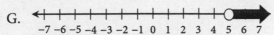

H.

J.

K.

35. If $f(x) = \frac{1}{3}x + 13$ and $g(x) = 3x^2 + 6x + 12$, what is the value of $f(g(x))$?

   A. $x^2 + 12x + 4$

   B. $\dfrac{x^2}{3} + 2x + 194$

   C. $x^2 + 2x + 17$

   D. $x^2 + 2x + 25$

   E. $x^2 + 2x + 54$

GO ON TO THE NEXT PAGE

36. What is the length of side *AC* in triangle *ABC* graphed on the coordinate plane below?

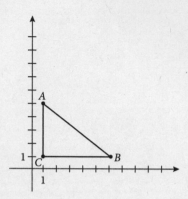

DO YOUR FIGURING HERE.

   F. 3

   G. 4

   H. 5

   J. 6

   K. 7

37. If $f(x) = 3\sqrt{x^2 + 3x + 4}$, what is the value of $f(4)$?

   A. 4

   B. $3\sqrt{2}$

   C. $4\sqrt{2}$

   D. $12\sqrt{2}$

   E. $25\sqrt{2}$

38. What is the equation of a line that is perpendicular to the line $y = \frac{2}{3}x + 5$ and contains the point $(4, -3)$?

   F. $y = \frac{2}{3}x + 4$

   G. $y = -\frac{2}{3}x + 3$

   H. $y = -\frac{3}{2}x + 3$

   J. $y = -\frac{3}{2}x - 9$

   K. $y = -\frac{3}{2}x + 9$

GO ON TO THE NEXT PAGE

39. Which of the following is the equation of the graph below?

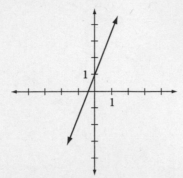

DO YOUR FIGURING HERE.

A. $y = 2x + 1$

B. $y = -2x + 1$

C. $y = \frac{1}{2}x + 1$

D. $y = -\frac{1}{2}x + 1$

E. $y = \frac{1}{4}x + 1$

40. In the figure below, at which point does $\overline{XZ}$ intersect with its perpendicular bisector?

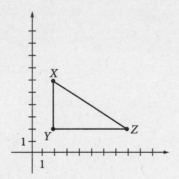

F. (4, 5)

G. (2, 4)

H. (4, 2)

J. (5, 2)

K. (5, 4)

41. What is the length of a line segment with endpoints (3, −6) and (−2, 6)?

    A. 1
    B. 5
    C. 10
    D. 13
    E. 15

DO YOUR FIGURING HERE.

42. What is the midpoint of the line segment in the graph below?

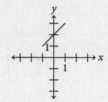

    F. (0, 1)
    G. (0, 2)
    H. (1, 2)
    J. (1, 1)
    K. (1, 3)

43. What is the volume of a sphere with a diameter of 6?

    A. 3π
    B. 9π
    C. 27π
    D. 36π
    E. 288π

44. A rectangle has a side length of 8 and a perimeter of 24. What is the area of the rectangle?

    F. 16
    G. 24
    H. 32
    J. 64
    K. 96

45. Isosceles triangle *ABC* has an area of 48.
    If $\overline{AB}$ = 12, what is the perimeter of *ABC*?

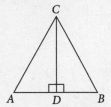

A. 32

B. 36

C. 48

D. 64

E. 76

46. The rectangular backyard of a house
    is 130 feet by 70 feet. If the backyard is
    completely fenced in, what is the length,
    in feet, of the fence?

F. 130

G. 200

H. 260

J. 400

K. 420

DO YOUR FIGURING HERE.

GO ON TO THE NEXT PAGE

47. In the figure below, lines *m* and *l* are parallel and $\angle a = 68°$. What is the measure of $\angle f$?

DO YOUR FIGURING HERE.

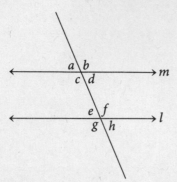

    A.   22°

    B.   68°

    C.   80°

    D. 112°

    E.   292°

48. A boy who is 4 ft tall stands in front of a tree that is 24 ft tall. If the tree casts a shadow that is 18 ft long on the ground and the two shadows end at the same point, what is the length of the boy's shadow?

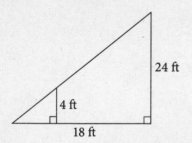

    F.   3 ft

    G.   4 ft

    H.   5 ft

    J.   6 ft

    K.   7 ft

GO ON TO THE NEXT PAGE

49. The hypotenuse of right triangle *RST* is 16. If the measure of ∠*R* = 30°, what is the length of *RS*?

DO YOUR FIGURING HERE.

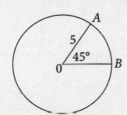

A. 4

B. 8

C. $8\sqrt{3}$

D. 12

E. 16

50. Circle *O* has a radius of 5 and ∠*AOB* = 45°. What is the length of arc *AB*?

F. 5

G. $\dfrac{4\pi}{5}$

H. 3

J. $\dfrac{3\pi}{4}$

K. $\dfrac{5\pi}{4}$

GO ON TO THE NEXT PAGE

51. What is the length of the diagonal of a square with sides of length 7?

    A. 7
    B. $7\sqrt{2}$
    C. 14
    D. 21
    E. 28

DO YOUR FIGURING HERE.

52. What is the perimeter of a regular hexagon with a side of 11?

    F. 33
    G. 44
    H. 66
    J. 72
    K. 78

53. A rectangle has a perimeter of 28, and its longer side is 2.5 times the length of its shorter side. What is the length of the diagonal of the rectangle, rounded to the nearest tenth?

    A. 4.0
    B. 10.0
    C. 10.8
    D. 12.4
    E. 14.2

GO ON TO THE NEXT PAGE

54. In the figure below, $\overline{MN}$ and $\overline{PQ}$ are parallel. Point A lies on $\overline{MN}$, and points B and C lie on $\overline{PQ}$. If $AB = AC$ and $\angle MAB = 55°$, what is the measure of $\angle ACB$?

DO YOUR FIGURING HERE.

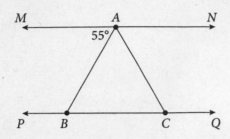

F. 35°

G. 55°

H. 65°

J. 80°

K. 125°

55. The chord below is 8 units long. If the chord is 3 units from the center of the circle, what is the area of the circle?

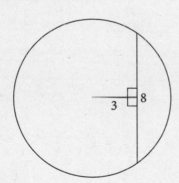

A. 9π

B. 16π

C. 18π

D. 25π

E. 28π

GO ON TO THE NEXT PAGE

56. If isosceles triangle *QRS* below has a base of
length 16 and sides of length 17, what is the
area of the triangle?

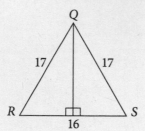

F.   50

G.   80

H. 110

J.   120

K. 180

57. In a high school senior class, the ratio of
girls to boys is 5:3. If there are a total of
168 students in the senior class, how many
girls are there?

A.   63

B. 100

C. 105

D. 147

E. 152

DO YOUR FIGURING HERE.

GO ON TO THE NEXT PAGE

58. What is the tangent of ∠*EFD* below?

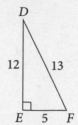

DO YOUR FIGURING HERE.

F. $\frac{5}{13}$

G. $\frac{5}{12}$

H. $\frac{12}{13}$

J. $\frac{13}{12}$

K. $\frac{12}{5}$

59. In the triangle below, what is the value of sin ∠*QRS*?

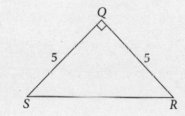

A. $\frac{\sqrt{2}}{6}$

B. $\frac{\sqrt{2}}{5}$

C. $\frac{\sqrt{2}}{2}$

D. $2\sqrt{2}$

E. $5\sqrt{2}$

GO ON TO THE NEXT PAGE

60. In the right triangle below, $JL = 17$ and $KL = 8$. What is the value of sin $\angle JLK$?

DO YOUR FIGURING HERE.

F. $\dfrac{8}{15}$

G. $\dfrac{8}{17}$

H. $\dfrac{8}{20}$

J. $\dfrac{3}{4}$

K. $\dfrac{15}{17}$

READING TEST

35 Minutes—40 Questions

> **Directions:** This test contains four passages, each followed by several questions. After reading each passage, select the best answer to each question and fill in the corresponding oval on your Answer Grid. You may refer to the passages while answering the questions.

Passage I

PROSE FICTION

This passage is an excerpt from the short story "Graduation," by John Krupp.

Rosemary sat at her kitchen table, working at a crossword puzzle. Crosswords were nice; they filled the time, and kept the mind
Line active. She needed just one word to complete
(5) this morning's puzzle; the clue was "a Swiss river," and the first of its three letters was "A." Unfortunately, Rosemary had no idea what the name of the river was, and could not look it up. Her atlas was on the
(10) desk, and the desk was in the guest room, currently being occupied by her grandson Victor. Looking up over the tops of her bifocals, Rosemary glanced at the kitchen clock: it was almost 10 A.M. *Land sakes!* Did
(15) the boy intend to sleep all day? She noticed that the arthritis in her wrist was throbbing, and put down her pen. At eighty-seven years of age, she was glad she could still write at all. She had decided long ago that
(20) growing old was like slowly turning to stone; you couldn't take anything for granted. She stood up slowly, painfully, and started walking to the guest room.

The trip, though only a distance of
(25) about twenty-five feet, seemed to take a long while. Late in her ninth decade now, Rosemary often experienced an expanded sense of time, with present and past tense intermingling in her mind. One minute she
(30) was padding in her slippers across the living room carpet, the next she was back on the farm where she'd grown up, a sturdy little girl treading the path behind the barn just before dawn. In her mind's eye, she could
(35) still pick her way among the stones in the darkness, more than seventy years later… Rosemary arrived at the door to the guest room. It stood slightly ajar, and she peered through the opening. Victor lay sleeping
(40) on his side, his arms bent, his expression slightly pained. *Get up, lazy bones,* she wanted to say. Even in childhood, Rosemary had never slept past 4 A.M.; there were too many chores to do. How different
(45) things were for Victor's generation! Her youngest grandson behaved as if he had never done a chore in his life. Twenty-one years old, he had driven down to Florida to visit Rosemary in his shiny new car, a
(50) gift from his doting parents. Victor would finish college soon, and his future appeared bright—if he ever got out of bed, that is.

Something Victor had said last night over dinner had disturbed her. Now what
(55) was it? Oh yes; he had been talking about one of his college courses—a "gut," he had called it. When she had asked him to explain the term, Victor had said it was a course that you took simply because it was
(60) easy to pass. Rosemary, who had not even had a high school education, found the term repellent. If she had been allowed to

GO ON TO THE NEXT PAGE ⇒

continue her studies, she would never have taken a "gut"… The memory flooded back
(65) then, still painful as an open wound all these years later. It was the first day of high school. She had graduated from grammar school the previous year, but her father had forbidden her to go on to high school
(70) that fall, saying that she was needed on the farm. After much tearful pleading, she had gotten him to promise that next year, she could start high school. She had endured a whole year of chores instead of books, with
(75) animals and rough farmhands for company instead of people her own age. Now, at last, the glorious day was at hand. She had put on her best dress (she owned two), her heart racing in anticipation. But her father was
(80) waiting for her as she came downstairs.

"Where do you think you're going?" he asked.

"To high school, Papa."

"No you're not. Take that thing off and
(85) get back to work."

"But Papa, you promised!"

"*Do as I say!*" he thundered.

There was no arguing with Papa when he spoke that way. Tearfully, she had trudged
(90) upstairs to change clothes. Rosemary still wondered what life would have been like if her father had not been waiting at the bottom of the stairs that day, or if somehow she had found the strength to defy him…
(95) Suddenly, Victor stirred, without waking, and mumbled something unintelligible. Jarred from her reverie, Rosemary stared at Victor. She wondered if he were having a nightmare.

1. According to the passage, Victor is Rosemary's:

   A. nephew.

   B. son.

   C. grandson.

   D. great-grandson.

2. It can be inferred from the passage that Rosemary is disturbed by Victor's:

   F. intention to drop out of college.

   G. disregard of her harsh upbringing.

   H. willingness to take courses that are easy to pass.

   J. inability to get out of bed in the morning.

3. The passage suggests that in the year after she finished grammar school, Rosemary most wanted:

   A. an escape from her father's company.

   B. the opportunity to go to college.

   C. the chance to study challenging subjects.

   D. the company of people her own age.

4. The passage suggests that Rosemary's attitude toward the physical afflictions of old age is generally one of:

   F. sadness.

   G. acceptance.

   H. resentment.

   J. optimism.

GO ON TO THE NEXT PAGE

5. According to the passage, Rosemary does crossword puzzles in order to:

   A. keep her mind active.

   B. practice her handwriting.

   C. learn new geographical facts.

   D. make her more aware of time.

6. The focus of the passage as a whole is on:

   F. Rosemary's concern at Victor's lack of motivation.

   G. the harsh treatment Victor received from his father.

   H. the contrast between Victor's and Rosemary's attitudes toward education.

   J. Rosemary's struggle to suppress painful memories.

7. It can be inferred from the passage that Victor's "shiny new car" (line 49) is mentioned in order to illustrate:

   A. the excessive generosity of Rosemary's parents.

   B. the contrast between Rosemary's generation and his.

   C. the strength of Victor's prospects for the future.

   D. the lack of physical hardship in Victor's life.

8. The third paragraph (lines 53–80) primarily portrays Rosemary in her youth as:

   F. resentful of her father's conduct.

   G. eager to continue her education.

   H. undecided about her future career.

   J. proud of her appearance.

9. Rosemary's recollection of growing up on the farm (lines 29–36) is mentioned as an example of her:

   A. nostalgia for her childhood experiences.

   B. determination to overcome her physical disabilities.

   C. ability to recall past and present events at the same time.

   D. disappointment at being denied an education.

10. The statement that Victor's "future appeared bright" (lines 51–52) most likely reflects the opinion of:

    F. Rosemary.

    G. Victor.

    H. Victor's parents.

    J. Rosemary's father.

GO ON TO THE NEXT PAGE

Passage II

SOCIAL SCIENCE

The following passage is an excerpt from "Architects and Power: The Natural Market for Architecture," by Robert Gutman, *Progressive Archictecture*, December 1992. Reprinted by permission of Penton Publishing.

Men and women for whom economic security is the prime consideration do not usually choose a career in architecture.

Line
(5) College graduates who focus on the issue of opportunity are more likely to get an MBA or a law or medical degree. The image of these other professions and how much better their members fare financially haunts architects. Not only do architects generally have

(10) lower incomes than those in other professions, but the demand for services of lawyers and physicians is more stable, and they are able to exercise more control over the domains in which they work. The differences

(15) are very apparent now as the privileged position of lawyers and physicians has come under scrutiny. Critics, however, are finding it difficult to reduce the autonomy of these professions, while architects are continually

(20) losing out to clients and other parties in the building industry in the battle for hegemony.

The use of these other professions as a reference group for architects in judging their own status in the hierarchy of social

(25) influence is a relatively new development. It begins in the middle of the nineteenth century, when a large number of middle-class occupations in Europe and America pressed governments to grant them special

(30) protected status, through a system of licensing. As a way of making sure they would be included under the licensing umbrella, architects began emphasizing those aspects of their work that most nearly

(35) resembled the thinking and skills of other fields. For example, architects, like physicians, argued that their work affected public

health and safety. The result was a shift in the definition of architecture from a focus

(40) on artistic accomplishment to expertise in dealing with the structural integrity of buildings, ventilation requirements, and the ability to interpret building and housing codes. The registration examinations still

(45) emphasize this component of architecture, even though this emphasis defines architecture in a way that parallels what others in the building industry are better at handling than architects.

(50) Should architects keep berating themselves because they do not enjoy many of the social and economic rewards of the other major professions? It might be worthwhile if there were a good chance that

(55) architecture could become more like law or medicine, that is, more science-based and more fully in control of its domain. A great deal of effort continues to go into programs intended to achieve these objectives, but I

(60) am doubtful that they can have much effect in transforming the fundamental existential condition of architecture. For example, even when architecture emphasizes its regard for the pragmatics of building, it still remains

(65) linked to the fate of the construction industry. Yet, as the current condition of the industry indicates, construction is notoriously volatile. Physicians face a much different situation, since illness and disease do not diminish

(70) during economic depression; indeed there is reason to believe that morbidity increases. And lawyers, like accountants, provide service to a wide range of industries, so that when business diminishes in one sector, they

(75) are supported by others.

At the same time, however, the attributes that first earned architecture its place as "the mother of all arts" are those that continue to set it apart today. There is no

GO ON TO THE NEXT PAGE ⇒

(80) other profession that is able to achieve what architects have historically accomplished in the realm of building. No other building profession is so learned about how to relate light, mass and structure to produce

(85) memorable visual and spatial experiences. Rare is the building not produced by an architect, that represents the supreme values of civilization. The design of the great seminal monumental buildings is the

(90) unique province of architecture, its "natural market." But many practitioners seem embarrassed to present themselves as artists. They seem to fear it may encourage clients to regard them as no different from painters,

(95) sculptors, and other visual artists. They also appear worried that to promote this image will create the impression that architecture is a luxury service, which, as the history of the profession's achievement shows, it

(100) usually is. Routine, ordinary buildings can be constructed without the benefit of architects. But instead of trying to compete in this market, where it is not particularly successful anyway, the profession should

(105) be making more effort to broaden what I have called its natural market. The question is how to stretch the profession's capacity, without at the same time injuring its fundamental strengths and its acknowledged

(110) cultural role. The strategy of emphasizing their skills in building, which so many firms have adopted, puts architects in competition with other professions and parties that can do it just as well, if not better. It also

(115) just discourages clients and the profession itself from recollecting the primary skill of the architect for which there is no peer; the design of buildings that have some value as art. This is the direction in which the

(120) profession must move if it is going to find greater employment in the decades ahead.

11. According to the passage, architects do not like being regarded as:

A. doctors.

B. artists.

C. builders.

D. accountants.

12. As it is used in the passage, the word *privileged* (line 15) most likely means:

F. authorized.

G. confidential.

H. superior.

J. aristocratic.

13. The passage suggests that architects were granted special protected status through a system of licensing partly because:

A. their market was threatened by other workers in the construction industry.

B. their work affected public health and safety.

C. many other middle-class occupations enjoyed similar protection.

D. fewer great monumental buildings were being designed.

GO ON TO THE NEXT PAGE

14. According to the passage, doctors and lawyers fare better financially than architects because:

    I. the demand for architects' services is less stable.

    II. doctors and lawyers are more able to exercise control over their fields.

    III. architects are forced to compete with other parties in the building industry.

  F. I and II

  G. II and III

  H. I and III

  J. I, II, and III

15. The main point the passage makes about architecture is that:

  A. architects should focus on designing buildings that have some artistic value.

  B. architects should possess as much economic security as doctors and lawyers do.

  C. architects should work to abolish the traditional system of licensing.

  D. architects should work to compete more with other building professions.

16. According to the passage, architecture is described as the "mother of all arts" (line 78) because:

  F. architects have been designing buildings since the beginnings of civilization.

  G. architecture is similar in nature to painting, sculpture, and other visual arts.

  H. architects relate light, mass, and structure to produce memorable artistic effects.

  J. architecture has survived the passage of time better than other art forms.

17. According to the passage, all of the following professionals thrive during periods of economic depressions EXCEPT:

  A. physicians.

  B. architects.

  C. lawyers.

  D. accountants.

18. Which of the following statements is best supported by the fifth paragraph?

  F. Architects want their clients to acknowledge their status as artists.

  G. Routine, ordinary buildings don't necessarily need the help of architects.

  H. Architects would like their profession to be regarded as a luxury service.

  J. Architects have been most successful in the housing market.

GO ON TO THE NEXT PAGE

19. According to the passage, college graduates are unlikely to choose a career in architecture because:

    A. there are fewer degrees offered in architecture than in other professions.

    B. architects are paid less than those in other professions.

    C. rising costs in education make architecture a less practical choice.

    D. other professions have a more glamorous image.

20. According to the passage, law and medicine are different from architecture in that they are:

    F. less based on scientific knowledge.

    G. more dependent on economic conditions.

    H. better protected by a licensing system.

    J. more fully in control of their domain.

Passage III

HUMANITIES

This passage is an excerpt from *A Short History of Western Civilization, Volume 1*, by John B. Harrison, Richard E. Sullivan, and Dennis Sherman, © 1990 by McGraw-Hill, Inc. Reprinted by permission of McGraw-Hill, Inc.

Enlightenment ideas were put forth by a variety of intellectuals who in France came to be known as the *philosophes*. *Philosophes*
Line is French for philosophers, and in a sense
(5) these thinkers were rightly considered philosophers, for the questions they dealt with were philosophical: How do we discover truth? How should life be lived? What is the nature of God? But on the whole
(10) the term has a meaning different from the usual meaning of "philosopher." The philosophes were intellectuals, often not formally trained or associated with a university. They were usually more literary than scientific.
(15) They generally extended, applied, popularized, or propagandized ideas of others rather than originating those ideas themselves. The philosophes were more likely to write plays, satires, pamphlets or simply participate in
(20) verbal exchanges at select gatherings than to write formal philosophical books.

It was the philosophes who developed the philosophy of the Enlightenment and spread it to much of the educated elite
(25) in Western Europe (and the American colonies). Although the sources for their philosophy can be traced to the Scientific Revolution in general, the philosophes were most influenced by their understanding of
(30) Newton, Locke, and English institutions.

The philosophes saw Newton as the great synthesizer of the Scientific Revolution who rightly described the universe as ordered, mechanical, material, and only originally
(35) set in motion by God, who since then has remained relatively inactive. Newton's synthesis showed to the philosophes that

GO ON TO THE NEXT PAGE

reason and nature were compatible: Nature functioned logically and discernibly, and (40) what was natural was also reasonable. Newton exemplified the value of reasoning based on concrete experience. The philosophes felt that his empirical methodology was the correct path to discovering truth.

(45) John Locke (1632–1704) agreed with Newton but went further. This English thinker would not exempt even the mind from the mechanical laws of the material universe. In his *Essay Concerning Human* (50) *Understanding* (1691), Locke pictured the human brain at birth as a blank sheet of paper on which nothing would ever be written except sense perception and reason. What human beings become depends on (55) their experiences—on the information received through the senses. Schools and social institutions could therefore play a great role in molding the individual from childhood to adulthood. Human beings were (60) thus by nature far more malleable than had been assumed. This empirical psychology of Locke rejected the notion that human beings were born with innate ideas or that revelation was a reliable source of truth.

(65) Locke also enunciated liberal and reformist political ideas in his *Second Treatise of Civil Government* (1690), which influenced the philosophes. On the whole Locke's empiricism, psychology and politics were appealing (70) to the philosophes.

England, not coincidentally the country of Newton and Locke, became the admired model for many of the philosophes. They tended to idealize it, but England did seem (75) to allow greater individual freedom, tolerate religious differences, and evidence greater political reform than other countries, especially France. England seemed to have gone furthest in freeing itself from traditional (80) institutions and accepting the new science of the seventeenth century. Moreover, England's approach seemed to work, for England was experiencing relative political

stability and prosperity. The philosophes (85) wanted to see in their own countries much of what England already seemed to have.

Many philosophes reflected the influence of Newton, Locke, and English institutions, but perhaps the most representative in (90) his views was Voltaire (1694–1778). Of all leading figures of the Enlightenment, he was the most influential. Voltaire, the son of a Paris lawyer, became the idol of the French intelligentsia while still in his early twenties. (95) His versatile mind was sparkling; his wit was mordant. An outspoken critic, he soon ran afoul of both church and state authorities. First he was imprisoned in the Bastille; later he was exiled to England. There he (100) encountered the ideas of Newton and Locke and came to admire English parliamentary government and tolerance. In *Letters on the English* (1732), *Elements of the Philosophy of Newton* (1738), and other writings, he (105) popularized the ideas of Newton and Locke, extolled the virtues of English society, and indirectly criticized French society. Slipping back into France, he was hidden for a time and protected by a wealthy woman who (110) became his mistress. Voltaire's facile mind and pen were never idle. He wrote poetry, drama, history, essays, letters, and scientific treatises—ninety volumes in all. The special targets of his cynical wit were the Catholic (115) church and Christian institutions. Few people in history have dominated their age intellectually as did Voltaire.

GO ON TO THE NEXT PAGE ⟶

21. The philosophes can best be described as:

    A. writers swept up by their mutual admiration of John Locke.

    B. professors who lectured in philosophy at French universities.

    C. intellectuals responsible for popularizing Enlightenment ideas.

    D. scientists who furthered the work of the Scientific Revolution.

22. Which of the following would most likely have been written by Voltaire?

    F. A treatise criticizing basic concepts of the Scientific Revolution

    G. A play satirizing religious institutions in France

    H. A collection of letters mocking the English Parliament

    J. A sentimental poem expounding the virtues of courtly love

23. According to the passage, Locke felt that schools and social institutions could "play a great role in molding the individual" (lines 57–58) primarily because:

    A. human beings were born with certain innate ideas.

    B. human nature becomes more malleable with age.

    C. society owes each individual the right to an education.

    D. the human mind is chiefly influenced by experience.

24. Based on the information in the passage, which of the following best describes Newton's view of the universe?

    I. The universe was initially set in motion by God.

    II. Human reason is insufficient to understand the laws of nature.

    III. The universe operates in a mechanical and orderly fashion.

    F. I only

    G. I and II only

    H. I and III only

    J. II and III only

25. According to the passage, which of the following works questioned the idea that revelation was a reliable source of truth?

    A. *Letters on the English*

    B. *Second Treatise of Civil Government*

    C. *Elements of the Philosophy of Newton*

    D. *Essay Concerning Human Understanding*

GO ON TO THE NEXT PAGE

26. The passage supports which of the following statements concerning the relationship between Newton and Locke?

    F. Locke's psychology contradicted Newton's belief in an orderly universe.

    G. Locke maintained that Newton's laws of the material universe also applied to the human mind.

    H. Newton eventually came to accept Locke's revolutionary ideas about the human mind.

    J. Newton's political ideas were the basis of Locke's liberal and reformist politics.

27. According to the passage, the philosophes believed that society should:

    I. allow individuals greater freedom.

    II. free itself from traditional institutions.

    III. tolerate religious differences.

    A. I only

    B. I and II only

    C. II and III only

    D. I, II, and III

28. It can be inferred from the passage that the author regards England's political stability and economic prosperity as:

    F. the reason why the philosophes did not idealize England's achievement.

    G. evidence that political reforms could bring about a better way of life.

    H. the result of Voltaire's activities after he was exiled to England.

    J. an indication that the Scientific Revolution had not yet started there.

29. The passage suggests that the French political and religious authorities during the time of Voltaire:

    A. allowed little in the way of free speech.

    B. overreacted to Voltaire's mild satires.

    C. regarded the philosophes with indifference.

    D. accepted the model of English parliamentary government.

30. How does the passage support the point that the philosophes were "more literary than scientific" (line 14)?

    F. It demonstrates how the philosophes' writings contributed to the political change.

    G. It compares the number of works that Voltaire authored to Newton's output.

    H. It traces the influences of English literary works on French scientists.

    J. It describes the kinds of literary activities the philosophes commonly engaged in.

GO ON TO THE NEXT PAGE ⟶

Passage IV

NATURAL SCIENCE

This passage explores the theory that a large asteroid collided with the Earth 65 million years ago.

Sixty-five million years ago, something triggered mass extinctions so profound that they define the geological boundary between
Line the Cretaceous and Tertiary periods (the K-T
(5) Boundary). Approximately 75 percent of all animal species, including every species of dinosaur, were killed off; those that survived lost the vast majority of their numbers. The Earth exists in a region of space teeming
(10) with asteroids and comets, which on collision have frequently caused enormous environmental devastation, including extinctions of animal species. Yet few traditional geologists or biologists considered the effect
(15) such impacts may have had on the geologic and biologic history of the Earth. Since gradual geologic processes like erosion or repeated volcanic eruptions can explain the topographical development of the Earth,
(20) they felt that there was no need to resort to extraterrestrial explanations.

An important theory proposed in 1980 by physicists Luis and Walter Alvarez challenged this view. The Alvarezes argued
(25) that an asteroid roughly six miles in diameter collided with the Earth in the K-T Boundary. Although the damage caused by the meteorite's impact would have been great, the dust cloud that subsequently
(30) would have enveloped the planet, completely blotting out the sun for up to a year—the result of soil displacement—would have done most of the harm, according to this theory. The plunge into darkness—and
(35) the resulting drastically reduced temperatures—would have interrupted plant growth, cutting off the food supply to herbivorous species, the loss of which in turn would have starved carnivores. Additional species

(40) would have perished as a result of prolonged atmospheric poisoning, acid rain, forest fires, and tidal waves, all initiated by the asteroid's impact.

Some subsequent research not only
(45) tended to support the Alvarez theory, but suggested that similar impacts may have caused other sharp breaks in Earth's geologic and biologic history. Research in the composition of the Earth revealed a
(50) 160-fold enrichment of iridium all over the world in a thin layer of sediments formed at the K-T Boundary. The presence of this element, which is extremely uncommon in the Earth's crust but very common in
(55) asteroids and comets, suggested that a meteorite must have struck Earth at that time. Additional physical evidence of such a strike was found in rock samples, which contained shocked quartz crystals and
(60) microtektites (small glass spheres)—both byproducts of massive collisions.

Observation of the lunar surface provided further evidence of the likelihood of a massive strike. Since the moon
(65) and the Earth lie within the same swarm of asteroids and comets, their impact histories should be parallel. Although some lunar craters were of volcanic origin, over the last four billion years at least five impact craters
(70) ranging from 31 to 58 miles in diameter have marred the lunar surface. Therefore, over the same time span, Earth must have experienced some 400 collisions of similar magnitude. Although such an impact crater
(75) had not been found, Alvarez supporters didn't consider finding it necessary or likely. They reasoned that geologic processes over 65 million years, like erosion and volcanic eruptions, would have obscured the crater,
(80) which in any case probably formed on the ocean floor.

GO ON TO THE NEXT PAGE →

Traditional biologists and geologists resisted the Alvarez theory. They pointed to the absence of any impact crater; to the
(85) fact that iridium, while rare at the Earth's surface, was common at its core and could be transported to the surface by volcanic activity; and to the fact that the Alvarezes, though eminent physicists, were not biolo-
(90) gists, geologists, or paleontologists.

31. According to the Alvarez theory, the mass extinctions of animal species at the end of the Cretaceous period were caused by:

   A. animals being crushed by an enormous asteroid.

   B. processes like erosion and repeated volcanic eruptions.

   C. extreme global warming causing a global firestorm.

   D. environmental conditions following a meteorite impact.

32. Based on the information in the passage, the author probably believes that those who held the traditional views about the topographical development of the Earth were:

   F. proven incorrect by the Alvarezes.

   G. unrivaled at the present time.

   H. correct in challenging alternative views.

   J. unreceptive to new evidence.

33. As it is used in line 50, the word *enrichment* most nearly means:

   A. wealth.

   B. improvement.

   C. increase in amount.

   D. reward.

34. The views of scientists who opposed the Alvarez theory would have been strengthened if:

   F. major deposits of iridium were found in the lava flows of active Earth volcanoes.

   G. iridium were absent in sediments corresponding to several episodes of mass extinction.

   H. iridium were absent in fragments of several recently recovered meteorites.

   J. the Alvarezes were biologists as well as physicists.

35. The author's attitude toward the Alvarez theory is best characterized as:

   A. dismissive.

   B. neutral.

   C. skeptical.

   D. supportive.

36. According to the passage, which of the following is the correct order of events in the Alvarez theory explaining the mass extinction of species at the end of the Cretaceous period?

   F. Soil displacement, disappearance of the sun, decline of plant life, fall in temperature

   G. Soil displacement, disappearance of the sun, fall in temperature, decline of plant life

   H. Fall in temperature, decline of plant life, soil displacement, disappearance of the sun

   J. Disappearance of the sun, fall in temperature, decline of plant life, soil displacement

GO ON TO THE NEXT PAGE ⟶

37. It can be inferred from paragraph 2 that the author discusses the Alvarezes' description of environmental conditions at the end of the Cretaceous period in order to:

   A. demonstrate that an immense meteorite hit the Earth.

   B. explain why no trace of an impact crater has yet been found.

   C. show that the Earth is vulnerable to meteorite collisions.

   D. clarify how a meteorite may account for mass extinctions.

38. The author's statement (lines 9–10) that "Earth exists in a region of space teeming with asteroids and comets" is important to:

   F. the Alvarezes' claim that an asteroid's impact caused atmospheric poisoning, acid rain, forest fires, and tidal waves.

   G. the Alvarezes' view that the resulting dust cloud, rather than the impact of the meteorite, did most of the harm.

   H. Alvarez supporters' argument based on the numbers of impact craters on the surface of the moon.

   J. traditionalists' view that topographical development of the Earth can be explained by gradual geologic processes.

39. Supporters of the Alvarezes' theory believe finding the impact crater is not necessary because:

   I. the crater probably is on the ocean floor.

   II. iridium occurs at the Earth's core.

   III. processes like erosion and volcanic eruptions obscured the crater.

   A. I only

   B. I and II only

   C. I and III only

   D. II and III only

40. According to the passage, species died in mass extinctions as a result of all of the following EXCEPT:

   F. shocked quartz crystals and microtektites.

   G. reduced sunlight for up to a year.

   H. loss of food supplies.

   J. prolonged atmospheric poisoning.

SCIENCE TEST

35 Minutes—40 Questions

Directions: This test contains seven passages, each followed by several questions. After reading each passage, select the best answer to each question and fill in the corresponding oval on your Answer Grid. You may refer to the passages while answering the questions. You may NOT use a calculator on this test.

Passage I

Optical fibers are strands of highly transparent glass used for communication transmissions. When light is transmitted through optical fibers, power is lost along the way. The power lost depends on the distance travelled, the wavelength of the light transmitted, the glass used, and any impurities present. The following attenuation (power loss in db/km) curve, which was recorded for a fluoride glass optical fiber, includes the attenuation caused by three different impurities commonly present in fluoride glass fibers.

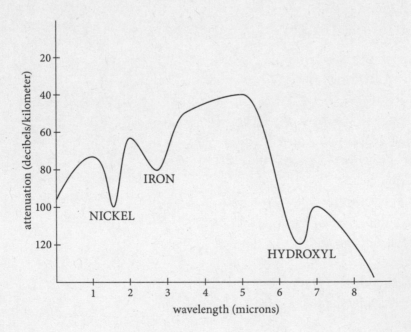

GO ON TO THE NEXT PAGE

1. In this fiber, copper impurities can lead to an attenuation of roughly 95 decibels per kilometer at wavelengths near 1.6 microns. Such impurities, if graphed as shown, would produce an attenuation response similar to that of:

   A. nickel.

   B. iron.

   C. hydroxyl.

   D. none of the impurities in the graph.

2. According to the graph, in a fiber without any impurities, as wavelength increases, power loss will:

   F. decrease then increase.

   G. increase then decrease.

   H. remain the same.

   J. fluctuate randomly.

3. If a researcher using a 6.6 micron laser wished to limit power loss, this fluoride glass fiber would be:

   A. ideal because attenuation is at a minimum at this wavelength.

   B. impossible because the fiber does not conduct light at this wavelength.

   C. inefficient because of interference from hydroxyl groups at this wavelength.

   D. unaffected by the laser's wavelength.

4. Suppose a scientist were able to develop a fluoride glass fiber without any hydroxyl impurities. Which of the following predictions would most likely be true?

   I. There will be less power lost in the range between six and seven microns.

   II. The attenuation due to iron impurities would increase.

   III. The fiber's overall power loss would decrease.

   F. I only

   G. I and III only

   H. II and III only

   J. I, II, and III

5. A certain computer communications system requires a cable five kilometers long. Based on the data in the graph, what is the minimum power loss that can be achieved using a fluoride glass fiber?

   A.   5 decibels

   B.   20 decibels

   C.   40 decibels

   D.   200 decibels

GO ON TO THE NEXT PAGE

Passage II

A *binary star system* consists of two stars that are gravitationally bound to each other. If two stars that orbit each other are viewed along a line of sight that is not perpendicular to the orbital plane, they will alternately appear to eclipse each other. The orbit of *eclipsing binary* System Q is shown in Figure 1 below.

Astronomers deduce that a given star is an eclipsing binary from its *light curve*—the plot of its surface brightness (observed from a fixed position) against time. The light curve of an eclipsing binary typically displays a deep primary minimum and a shallower secondary minimum. Figure 2 shows the light curve of System Q.

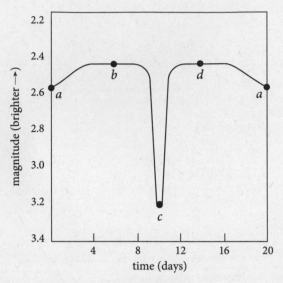

Figure 2

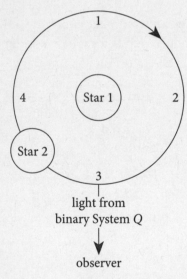

light from
binary System Q

↓

observer

Figure 1

Notes: Diagram is not drawn to scale. Star 1 is brighter than Star 2.

6. The point on the light curve labeled *c* corresponds to the position in Figure 1 labeled:

   F. 1.

   G. 2.

   H. 3.

   J. 4.

7. The period of revolution for eclipsing binary Q is about:

   A.   4 days.

   B. 10 days.

   C. 12 days.

   D. 20 days.

8. The stars in eclipsing binary Q alternately eclipse each other for periods of approximately:

   F. 2 days and 4 days.

   G. 2 days and 5 days.

   H. 2 days and 8 days.

   J. 5 days each.

GO ON TO THE NEXT PAGE ⟹

Light Curve of System X

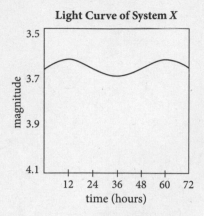

Light Curve of System Z

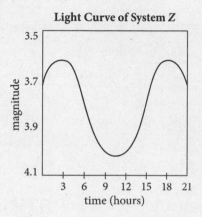

9. The light curves for two eclipsing binaries, Systems *X* and *Z*, are shown. Which of the following hypotheses would account for the deeper primary minimum of System *Z*?

    A. There is a more extreme difference between the magnitudes of the two stars of System *X* than between those of the two stars of System *Z*.

    B. There is a more extreme difference between the magnitudes of the two stars of System *Z* than between those of the two stars of System *X*.

    C. System *X* has a longer period of revolution than does System *Z*.

    D. System *Z* has a longer period of revolution than does System *X*.

10. The greatest total brightness shown on the light curve of an eclipsing binary system corresponds to the point in the orbit when:

    F. the brighter star in the binary pair is directly in front of the darker star.

    G. the larger star in the binary pair is directly in front of the smaller star.

    H. the brighter star in the binary pair is directly in front of the smaller star.

    J. both stars are visible.

Passage III

The utilization and replenishing of the Earth's carbon supply is a cyclic process involving all living matter. This cycle is shown below.

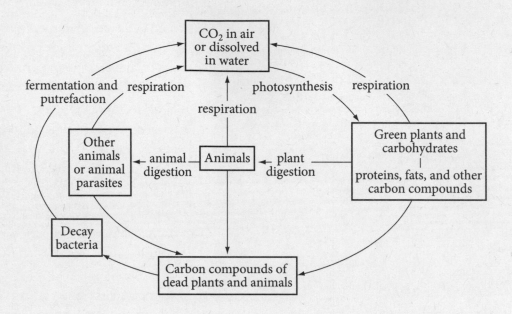

11. What effect would a sudden drop in the amount of the Earth's decay bacteria have on the amount of carbon dioxide in the atmosphere?

    A. The CO_2 level will drop to a life-threatening level since the bacteria is the sole source of CO_2.

    B. The CO_2 level will rise because the bacteria usually consume CO_2.

    C. The CO_2 level may decrease slightly, but there are other sources of CO_2.

    D. The CO_2 level will increase slightly due to an imbalance in the carbon cycle.

12. Which of the following statements are consistent with the carbon cycle as presented in the diagram?

    I. A non-plant-eating animal does not participate in the carbon cycle.

    II. Both plant and animal respiration contribute CO_2 to the earth's atmosphere.

    III. All CO_2 is released into the air by respiration.

    F. I only

    G. II only

    H. I and II only

    J. II and III only

GO ON TO THE NEXT PAGE

13. A direct source of CO_2 in the atmosphere is:

   A. the fermentation of green-plant carbohydrates.

   B. the photosynthesis of tropical plants.

   C. the digestion of plant matter by animals.

   D. the respiration of animal parasites.

14. Which of the following best describes the relationship between animal respiration and photosynthesis?

   F. Respiration and photosynthesis serve the same function in the carbon cycle.

   G. Animal respiration provides vital gases for green plants.

   H. Animal respiration prohibits photosynthesis.

   J. There is no relationship between respiration and photosynthesis.

15. The elimination of which of the following would cause the earth's carbon cycle to grind to a complete halt?

   A. Green plants

   B. Animals

   C. Animal predation

   D. Decay bacteria

Passage IV

Microbiologists have observed that certain species of bacteria are magnetotactic, i.e., sensitive to magnetic fields. Several species found in the bottom of swamps in the Northern Hemisphere tend to orient themselves toward magnetic north (the northern pole of the earth's magnetic field). Researchers conducted the following series of experiments on magnetotactic bacteria.

STUDY 1

A drop of water filled with magnetotactic bacteria was observed under high magnification. The direction of the first 500 bacterial migrations across the field of view was observed for each of five trials and the tally for each trial recorded in Table 1. Trial 1 was conducted under standard laboratory conditions. In Trial 2, the microscope was shielded from all external light and electric fields. In Trials 3 and 4, the microscope was rotated clockwise 90° and 180°, respectively. For Trial 5, the microscope was moved to another laboratory at the same latitude.

Table 1

Trial #	Direction			
	North	East	South	West
1	474	7	13	6
2	481	3	11	5
3	479	4	12	5
4	465	9	19	7
5	484	3	11	6

GO ON TO THE NEXT PAGE

STUDY 2

The north pole of a permanent magnet was positioned near the microscope slide. The magnet was at the 12:00 position for Trial 1 and was moved 90° clockwise for each of three successive trials. All other conditions were as in Trial 1 of Study 1. The results were tallied and recorded in Table 2.

Table 2

Trial #	Direction			
	12:00	3:00	6:00	9:00
1	472	6	15	9
2	8	483	3	6
3	17	4	474	5
4	5	19	9	467

16. The theory that light was not the primary stimulus affecting the direction of bacterial migration is:

    F. supported by a comparison of the results of Studies 1 and 2.

    G. supported by a comparison of the results of Trials 1 and 2 of Study 1.

    H. supported by a comparison of the results of Trials 3 and 4 of Study 1.

    J. not supported by any of the results noted in the passage.

17. If the south pole of the permanent magnet used in Study 2 had been placed near the microscope slide, what would the most likely result have been?

    A. The figures for each trial would have remained approximately the same, since the strength of the magnetic field would be unchanged.

    B. The bacteria would have become disoriented, with approximately equal numbers moving in each direction.

    C. The major direction of travel would have shifted by 180° because of the reversed direction of the magnetic field.

    D. The bacteria would still have tended to migrate toward Earth's magnetic north, but would have taken longer to orient themselves.

18. It has been suggested that magnetic sensitivity helps magnetotactic bacteria orient themselves downwards. Such an orientation would be most advantageous from an evolutionary standpoint if:

    F. organisms that consume magneto-tactic bacteria were mostly bottom-dwellers.

    G. the bacteria could only reproduce by migrating upwards to the water's surface.

    H. bacteria that stayed in the top layers of water tended to be dispersed by currents.

    J. the nutrients necessary for the bacteria's survival were more abundant in bottom sediments.

GO ON TO THE NEXT PAGE

19. Researchers could gain the most useful new information about the relationship between magnetic field strength and bacterial migration by repeating Study 2 with:

    A. incremental position changes of less than 90°.
    B. a magnet that rotated slowly around the slide in a counterclockwise direction.
    C. more and less powerful magnets.
    D. larger and smaller samples of bacteria.

20. Which of the following statements is supported by the results of Study 1?

    F. The majority of magnetotactic bacteria migrate toward the Earth's magnetic north pole.
    G. The majority of magnetotactic bacteria migrate toward the north pole of the nearest magnet.
    H. The majority of magnetotactic bacteria migrate toward the 12:00 position.
    J. The effect of the Earth's magnetic field on magnetotactic bacteria is counteracted by electric fields.

21. What is the control in Study 1?

    A. Trial 1
    B. Trial 2
    C. Trial 3
    D. Trial 5

Passage V

A process has been developed by which plastic bottles can be recycled into a clear, colorless material. This material, called *nu-PVC*, can be used to form park benches and other similar structures. A series of experiments was performed to determine the weathering abilities of *nu-PVC*.

EXPERIMENT 1

Fifteen boards of *nu-PVC*, each 150 × 25 × 8 cm in size, were sprayed with distilled water for ten hours a day for 32 weeks. All 15 boards remained within 0.1 cm of their original dimensions. The surfaces of the boards displayed no signs of cracking, bubbling, or other degradation.

EXPERIMENT 2

Fifteen sheets of *nu-PVC*, each 2 m × 2 m × 5 cm, were hung in a chamber in which the humidity and temperature were held constant. The sheets were irradiated with ultraviolet light for 12 hours a day for 32 weeks. At the end of the experiment, the sheets' flexibility had decreased by an average of 17.5%. The surface of the sheets showed no signs of degradation, but they had all become milky white in color.

EXPERIMENT 3

Fifteen boards, as in Experiment 1, were each found to be capable of supporting an average of 963 pounds for 15 days without breaking or bending. These same boards were then kept for 32 weeks at temperatures ranging from 5°C to –15°C. At the end of the experiment, the boards were able to support an average of only 400 pounds without bending or breaking.

GO ON TO THE NEXT PAGE

22. Based on the results of Experiment 1, which of the following conclusions concerning the effect of rain on *nu-PVC* is valid?

    F. The material absorbs water over time, causing it to permanently swell.

    G. The material will be useful only in areas where there is no acid rain.

    H. The material's surface does not appear to require a protective coating to avoid water damage.

    J. The material loses flexibility after prolonged exposure to precipitation.

23. Park benches in an often snow-covered region of Minnesota are to be replaced with new ones, made of *nu-PVC*. The experimental results indicate that:

    A. the benches will suffer little degradation due to weathering.

    B. the benches would have to be stored indoors during the winter to retain their initial strength.

    C. the benches should be varnished to prevent rain from seeping into the material.

    D. the benches will retain their initial flexibility.

24. A reasonable control for Experiment 1 would be:

    F. a *nu-PVC* board submerged in distilled water.

    G. a *nu-PVC* board stored in a dry warehouse.

    H. a wooden board subjected to the same conditions.

    J. a wooden board stored in a dry warehouse.

25. The purpose of the ultraviolet radiation used in Experiment 2 was to:

    A. simulate the effects of sunlight.

    B. avoid damage to the material's finish.

    C. turn the boards a uniform color.

    D. test the strength of the *nu-PVC*.

26. From the information given, it can be inferred that *nu-PVC*'s advantage over standard building materials, such as wood, is that it:

    F. is heavier and denser than other materials.

    G. can be developed in different colors and textures.

    H. is less subject to structural cracking and failure.

    J. is made from recycled plastic wastes.

27. Which of the following experiments would be the most likely to provide useful information concerning the weathering of *nu-PVC*?

    I. Repeating Experiment 1, increasing the length of the experiment from 32 weeks to 64 weeks

    II. Investigating the effects of sea water and salt-rich air on the material

    III. Repeating Experiment 3, decreasing the minimum temperature from $-15°C$ to $-40°C$

    A. II only

    B. III only

    C. I and II only

    D. I, II, and III

GO ON TO THE NEXT PAGE

Passage VI

Preliminary research indicates that dietary sugar may react with proteins in the body, damaging the proteins and perhaps contributing to the aging process. The chemical effects of glucose on lens proteins in the eye were investigated in the following experiments.

EXPERIMENT 1

A human tissue protein sample was dissolved in a glucose and water solution, resulting in a clear yellow solution. After 30 minutes, the solution became opaque. Spectrographic analysis revealed that an *Amadori product* had formed on the protein. It was determined that the Amadori products on one protein had combined with free amino groups on nearby proteins, forming brown pigmented cross-links between the two proteins. The cross-links are termed *advanced glycosylation end products* (AGE).

EXPERIMENT 2

Forty-six samples of human lens proteins taken from subjects ranging in age from 12–80 years were studied under an electron microscope. The lens proteins in the samples from older subjects occurred much more often in aggregates formed by cross-linked bonds than did the lens proteins in the samples from younger subjects. Fluorescent characteristics revealed the cross-links to be of two types: disulfide bonds and an indeterminate formation with brownish pigmentation.

EXPERIMENT 3

Two solutions containing lens proteins from cow lenses were prepared, one with glucose and one without. Only the glucose solution turned opaque. Analysis revealed that the lens proteins in the glucose solution had formed pigmented cross-links with the brownish color and fluorescence characteristics of those observed in Experiment 2.

28. It was assumed in the design of Experiment 3 that cow lens proteins:

    F. have a brownish pigment.

    G. react with sulfides.

    H. remain insoluble in water.

    J. react similarly to human lens proteins.

29. Based on the results in Experiment 1 only, it can be concluded that:

    A. proteins can form disulfide cross-links.

    B. glucose dissolved in water forms AGE.

    C. glucose can react with proteins to form cross-links.

    D. Amadori products are a result of glucose metabolism.

GO ON TO THE NEXT PAGE

30. As people age, the lenses in their eyes sometimes turn brown and cloudy (known as senile cataracts). Based on this information and the results of Experiment 2, which of the following hypotheses is the most likely to be valid?

    F. As people age, the amount of sulfur contained in lens proteins increases.

    G. Senile cataracts are caused by cross-linked bonds between lens proteins.

    H. Lens proteins turn brown with age.

    J. Older lens proteins are more fluorescent than younger lens proteins.

31. Which of the following hypotheses about the brown pigmented cross-links observed in Experiment 2 is best supported by the results of the three experiments?

    A. Their brownish color is caused by disulfide bonds.

    B. They are a natural formation which can be found at birth.

    C. They are caused by glucose in the diet reacting with lens proteins.

    D. They form when proteins are dissolved in water.

32. Based on the experimental results, lens proteins from a 32-year-old man would most likely have:

    F. more cross-links than lens proteins from a 32-year-old woman.

    G. more cross-links than lens proteins from an 18-year-old cow.

    H. more cross-links than lens proteins from an 18-year-old man.

    J. fewer cross-links than lens proteins from an 80-year-old man.

33. People with uncontrolled diabetes have excess levels of blood glucose. Based on this information and the results of the experiments, a likely symptom of advanced diabetes would be:

    A. senile cataracts, due to an increase of free amino groups in the urine.

    B. senile cataracts, due to glucose interacting with disulfide cross-links on lens proteins.

    C. senile cataracts, due to AGE cross-links of lens proteins.

    D. kidney failure, due to high levels of free amino groups in the urine.

GO ON TO THE NEXT PAGE

Passage VII

Two scientists discuss their views about the Quark Model.

SCIENTIST 1

According to the Quark Model, each proton consists of three quarks: two up quarks, which carry a charge of +2/3 each, and one down quark, which carries a charge of –1/3. All mesons, one of which is the p+ particle, are composed of one quark and one antiquark, and all baryons, one of which is the proton, are composed of three quarks. The Quark Model explains the numerous different types of mesons that have been observed. It also successfully predicted the essential properties of the Y meson. Individual quarks have not been observed because they are absolutely confined within baryons and mesons. However, the results of deep inelastic scattering experiments indicate that the proton has a substructure. In these experiments, high-energy electron beams were fired into protons. While most of the electrons incident on the proton passed right through, a few bounced back. The number of electrons scattered through large angles indicated that there are three distinct lumps within the proton.

SCIENTIST 2

The Quark Model is seriously flawed. Conventional scattering experiments should be able to split the proton into its constituent quarks, if they existed. Once the quarks were free, it would be easy to distinguish quarks from other particles using something as simple as the Millikan oil drop experiment because they would be the only particles that carry fractional charge. Furthermore, the lightest quark would be stable because there is no lighter particle for it to decay

into. Quarks would be so easy to produce, identify, and store that they would have been detected if they truly existed. In addition, the Quark Model violates the Pauli exclusion principle which originally was believed to hold for electrons but was found to hold for all particles of half-integer spin. The Pauli exclusion principle states that no two particles of half-integer spin can occupy the same state. The Δ^{++} baryon which supposedly has three up quarks violates the Pauli exclusion principle because two of those quarks would be in the same state. Therefore, the Quark Model must be replaced.

34. Which of the following would most clearly strengthen Scientist 1's hypothesis?

    F. Detection of the Δ^{++} baryon
    G. Detection of a particle with fractional charge
    H. Detection of mesons
    J. Detection of baryons

35. Which of the following are reasons why Scientist 2 claims quarks should have been detected, if they existed?

    I. They have a unique charge.
    II. They are confined within mesons and baryons.
    III. They are supposedly fundamental particles, and so could not decay into any other particle.

    A. I only
    B. II only
    C. I and III only
    D. I, II, and III

36. Which of the following could Scientist 1 use to counter Scientist 2's point about the Pauli exclusion principle?

    F. Evidence that quarks do not have half-integer spin

    G. Evidence that the Δ^{++} baryon exists

    H. Evidence that quarks have fractional charge

    J. Evidence that quarks have the same spin as electrons

37. If Scientist 1's hypothesis is correct, the Δ^{++} baryon should have a charge of:

    A. –1

    B. 0

    C. 1

    D. 2

38. Scientist 2 says the Quark Model is flawed because:

    F. the existence of individual baryons cannot be experimentally verified.

    G. the existence of individual quarks cannot be experimentally verified.

    H. particles cannot have fractional charge.

    J. it doesn't include electrons as elementary particles.

39. Scientist 1 says that some high-energy electrons that were aimed into the proton in the deep inelastic scattering experiments bounced back because they:

    A. hit quarks.

    B. hit other electrons.

    C. were repelled by the positive charge on the proton.

    D. hit baryons.

40. The fact that deep inelastic scattering experiments revealed a proton substructure of three lumps supports the Quark Model because:

    F. protons are mesons, and mesons supposedly consist of three quarks.

    G. protons are mesons, and mesons supposedly consist of a quark and an antiquark.

    H. protons are baryons, and baryons supposedly consist of three quarks.

    J. protons are baryons, and baryons supposedly consist of one quark and one antiquark.

WRITING TEST

30 Minutes—1 Question

Directions: This is a test of your writing skills. You will have thirty (30) minutes to write an essay in English. Before you begin planning and writing your essay, read the writing prompt carefully to understand exactly what you are being asked to do. Your essay will be evaluated on the evidence it provides of your ability to express judgments by taking a position on the issue in the writing prompt; to maintain a focus on the topic throughout the essay; to develop a position by using logical reasoning and by supporting your ideas; to organize ideas in a logical way; and to use language clearly and effectively according to the conventions of standard written English.

You may use the unlined pages in this test booklet to plan your essay. These pages will not be scored. *You must write your essay in pencil on the lined pages in the answer folder.* Your writing on those lined pages will be scored. You may not need all the lined pages, but to ensure you have enough room to finish, do NOT skip lines. You may write corrections or additions neatly between the lines of your essay, but do NOT write in the margins of the lined pages. *Illegible essay cannot be scored, so you must write (or print) clearly.*

If you finish before time is called you may review your work. Lay your pencil down immediately when time called.

DO NOT OPEN THIS BOOKLET UNTIL TOLD TO DO SO.

GO ON TO THE NEXT PAGE

ACT Writing Test Prompt

Some schools have instituted rules that forbid students from wearing any clothing with words other than the name of their school. Proponents of this rule argue that it prevents distractions in the classroom and allows teachers and students to focus on education. Opponents argue that such a rule violates students' freedom of expression and, therefore, should not be in place. Should schools forbid the wearing of all clothing that has words other than the name of the school?

In your essay, take a position on this question. You may write about either one of the two points of view given, or you may present a different point of view on this question. Use specific reasoning and examples to support your position.

GO ON TO THE NEXT PAGE ▷

_____

_____

_____

_____

_____

_____

_____

_____

_____

_____

_____

_____

_____

_____

_____

_____

_____

_____

_____

_____

_____

_____

_____

Practice Test Four
ANSWER KEY

ENGLISH TEST

1. C	11. D	21. A	31. A	41. A	51. A	61. C	71. C
2. G	12. H	22. J	32. H	42. G	52. J	62. J	72. H
3. D	13. C	23. C	33. D	43. C	53. D	63. B	73. B
4. F	14. J	24. G	34. F	44. H	54. H	64. J	74. G
5. D	15. C	25. D	35. A	45. B	55. B	65. A	75. C
6. G	16. H	26. H	36. G	46. G	56. J	66. G	
7. D	17. C	27. B	37. A	47. D	57. D	67. D	
8. J	18. H	28. G	38. J	48. J	58. H	68. G	
9. C	19. D	29. D	39. D	49. B	59. B	69. D	
10. J	20. F	30. J	40. G	50. J	60. G	70. J	

MATH TEST

1. B	9. E	17. B	25. C	33. C	41. D	49. C	57. C
2. J	10. K	18. J	26. G	34. F	42. G	50. K	58. K
3. C	11. C	19. D	27. D	35. C	43. D	51. B	59. C
4. G	12. H	20. G	28. J	36. G	44. H	52. H	60. K
5. E	13. B	21. C	29. E	37. D	45. A	53. C	
6. J	14. K	22. G	30. F	38. H	46. J	54. G	
7. B	15. A	23. D	31. E	39. A	47. D	55. D	
8. G	16. J	24. G	32. G	40. K	48. F	56. J	

READING TEST

1. C	6. H	11. B	16. H	21. C	26. G	31. D	36. G
2. H	7. B	12. H	17. B	22. G	27. D	32. H	37. D
3. D	8. G	13. B	18. G	23. D	28. G	33. C	38. H
4. G	9. C	14. J	19. B	24. H	29. A	34. F	39. C
5. A	10. F	15. A	20. J	25. D	30. J	35. D	40. F

SCIENCE TEST

1. A	6. H	11. C	16. G	21. A	26. J	31. C	36. F
2. F	7. D	12. G	17. C	22. H	27. A	32. J	37. D
3. C	8. H	13. D	18. J	23. B	28. J	33. C	38. G
4. G	9. B	14. G	19. C	24. G	29. C	34. G	39. A
5. D	10. J	15. A	20. F	25. A	30. G	35. C	40. H

ANSWERS AND EXPLANATIONS

English Test

The questions fall into the following categories, according to the skills they test. If you notice that you're having trouble with particular categories, review the following:

1. REDUNDANCY: English Workout 1

2. RELEVANCE: English Workout 1

3. VERBOSITY: English Workout 1

4. JUDGING THE PASSAGE: English Workout 2

5. LOGIC: English Workout 2

6. MODIFIERS: English Workout 2

7. READING-TYPE QUESTIONS: English Workout 2

8. STRUCTURE AND PURPOSE: English Workout 2

9. TONE: English Workout 2

10. VERB USAGE: English Workout 2

11. COMPLETENESS: English Workouts 2 and 3

12. IDIOM: English Workouts 2 and 3

13. PRONOUNS: English Workouts 2 and 3

14. SENTENCE STRUCTURE: English Workouts 2 and 3

15. PUNCTUATION: English Workout 3

PASSAGE I

1. C
Punctuation

At first glance, there may not seem to be anything wrong here. However, the dash after *Aegean Sea* alerts you that the writer has chosen to set off the parenthetical phrase describing *Acropolis* with dashes instead of commas. This means that you have to replace the comma after *Acropolis* with a dash, in order to have a matching pair. If there was a comma after *Aegean Sea*, this underlined part of the sentence would not need to be changed. Knowing that you need to "make it all match" will help you score points on ACT English.

2. G
Sentence Structure

This question tests your sense of parallelism. Your ear can often help you identify unparallel constructions. "To climb…is to have beheld" is unparallel. They should be in the same form: "to climb…is to behold."

3. D
Relevance

You have the option to OMIT in this question, which you should definitely take. Athenian cuisine has nothing to do with the subject of the paragraph or the passage, which is the Parthenon.

4. F
Verb Usage

This verb is appropriately plural—the subject, *generations,* is plural—and in the present perfect tense. Choices G and H are singular verbs, while choice J is wrong because generations of architects can't all be proclaiming at the present time.

5. D
Sentence Structure

Run-on sentences are common in the English section. There are a couple of ways to deal with this run-on sentence. You could put a semicolon after *subtle* to separate the clauses, or you could put a period after *subtle* and make the clauses into separate sentences. Since the choices offer you both options, there must be something more. And there is: you need a comma after *For example* to set it off from the rest of the sentence. Choice D fixes both errors.

6. G
Modifiers

This part of the sentence sounds strange; it seems that *the fact* is what is being "viewed from a distance," not the *straight columns*. "Viewed from a distance" is a misplaced modifier that has to be moved to a position where it clearly modifies *columns*. Choice G accomplishes this.

7. D
Punctuation

Read the sentence out loud and you'll hear that it has punctuation problems. There is no need for a semicolon or any other kind of punctuation mark between *of* and *uprightness*. Don't place a comma before the first element of a series, choice C, and don't place a colon between a preposition and its objects, choice B.

8. J
Logic

The phrase "because of this" doesn't make sense here. The optical illusion the architects created is not the reason you'll get a different impression of the Parthenon from the one the ancient Athenians had; the reason is that the statue of Athena Parthenos isn't there anymore. The introductory phrase that makes sense won't suggest conclusion or contrast, it will emphasize the information in the sentence, making choice J correct.

9. C
Completeness

"Only by standing...Golden Age of Athens" is a sentence fragment that has to be hooked up somehow to the sentence after it. You can't just use a semicolon to join the two, choice B, because then the first clause of the new sentence will still be only a fragment. You have to reverse the subject and verb of the second sentence to attach the fragment to it, as choice C does.

10. J
Modifiers

What was removed from the temple? The underlined part of the sentence is an introductory modifying phrase that you know describes the statue, but the word *statue* isn't anywhere in the sentence. As a result, the sentence doesn't make sense at all; it's impossible that "all that remains" in the temple was removed in the fifth century A.D. Choice J makes the sentence make sense.

11. D
Verb Usage

Quite a few words come between the subject and the verb of this sentence. You shouldn't be fooled, though; *many* is the subject of the sentence, not *carvings, walls*, or *Acropolis*. Since *many* is plural, the verb of the sentence has to be plural as well. *Is* has to be changed to *are*, choice D.

12. H
Completeness

This sentence is really only a sentence fragment; it has a subject, *decision*, but no verb. Choice H rewords the underlined portion to make *Lord Elgin* the subject and *decided* the verb.

13. C
Pronouns

They is an ambiguous pronoun because it's not immediately clear what group *they* refers to. You can figure out from the context that *they* is the Greeks; no other group could have won independence from the Turks and demanded the carvings back from the British. To make the first sentence clear, you have to replace *they* with the Greeks.

14. J
Reading-Type

What could have been destroyed by explosions in the Parthenon? Carvings. The fact that some of the carvings were destroyed during a war is another good reason that many of them can no longer be found in the Parthenon, as paragraph 4 states. Therefore, the new material belongs in paragraph 4.

15. C
Judging the Passage

The answer to the question is clearly "no." The writer did not fulfill the request because only the second paragraph discusses techniques of construction at all; even then, only one technique, the bulging of the columns, is described in any detail. The author covers several topics in the essay in addition to construction techniques, including the statue of Athena Parthenos and the fate of the carvings.

PASSAGE II

16. H
Verb Usage

The previous sentence tells you that "Robin is the hero"; look for a verb form that matches the present tense *is*, since the sentence continues the discussion of the ballads. Choice H's *tell* is in the right tense. Choice F switches to another tense, the present progressive, which makes it sound as if the ballads were literally speaking. Choice G lacks a main verb, creating a sentence fragment. Choice J has the same tense problem as choice F and compounds it by adding an extra, unnecessary subject, *they*.

17. C
Verb Usage

You need a verb that is parallel to *robbing* and *killing*, so *giving*, C, is the correct choice.

18. H
Modifiers

The adjective *frequent* is the correct choice to modify *enemy*. The underlined choice uses both the word *most* and the suffix *-est* to indicate the highest degree, or superlative form. Use one or the other, but not both. Likewise, choice G incorrectly uses *more* and the suffix *-er* together. Both of these express the comparative form—but again, you'd use one or the other, not both at once. In J, *frequently* is an adverb and so can't describe a noun.

19. D
Relevance

When you see the OMIT option, ask yourself if the underlined portion is really necessary. The parentheses are a clue that the underlined part isn't really relevant. It goes off on a tangent about modern adaptations of the King Arthur legend, whereas Robin Hood is the focus of the passage. Choices B and C reword the irrelevant sentence.

20. F
Pronouns

This is correct as is. *Them* matches the plural noun it's standing in for: *writers*. Choice G, *him*, and choice H, *it*, are singular, so they don't. Choice J is wordy.

21. A
Punctuation
This is correct because we need the possessive apostrophe. Choices B and C are wrong because they are the plural, not the possessive, form of Stukely, and there obviously aren't a lot of Stukelys running around. Choice D is wrong because if you read it out loud, you can tell that no pause—and so no comma—is called for.

22. J
Reading-Type
Since this passage is aimed at discussing the historical development of the Robin Hood legend, choice J is most in keeping with the subject matter. F goes way off track; you're asked to add more information on Stukely, not on English history. Choices G and H do relate their points to Stukely, but they pursue details. The main topic of the passage is Robin Hood, not antiquaries, G. (Remember, you want a choice that is most relevant to the passage as a whole.) As for H, King Arthur was mentioned earlier in the passage, but then only to make a point about Robin Hood. A discussion of Stukely's interest in King Arthur would stray from the topic of the passage.

23. C
Logic
The shortest answer is the best choice. Choices A and D wrongly imply a comparison between Robin and a nobleman, when the claim was that Robin was a nobleman. B is incoherent.

24. G
Tone
The comparison with a puppy is silly in this context since it jars with the matter-of-fact tone of this passage; all choices except G can be eliminated. (The ACT will sometimes use a phrase that simply doesn't go with the passage's tone.)

25. D
Punctuation
The only choice that will tie in both parts of the sentence is D. A dash in this context correctly makes an emphatic pause between *love interest* and its appositive, *Maid Marian*. All the rest of the choices have punctuation errors. Semicolons are used between independent clauses, and the part that would follow the semicolon in choice A isn't a clause. The plural form of the noun, *interests*, choice B, doesn't agree with the singular article. C can be ruled out because there is no reason to pause in the middle of a name, and so the comma is incorrectly placed.

26. H
Logic
All the choices, with the exception of H, have inappropriate connecting words. Since the passage moves to a discussion of a new time period, you should begin a new paragraph, ruling out choice G. In addition, "on the one hand" should be followed by "on the other hand." *Consequently*, choice F, and *therefore*, choice J, wrongly imply that what follows is a result of something in the previous sentence.

27. B
Verb Usage
The correct verb tense, and the only choice that doesn't create a sentence fragment, is B. *Basing*, choice A, and *to base*, choice C, create sentence fragments. Of course, the omission of the verb would also result in a sentence fragment, so choice D is incorrect.

28. G
Logic
G is the only choice that fits the rest of the sentence both logically and grammatically. *And* doesn't make sense as a connecting word in the original. Choice H also uses a connecting word that doesn't logically fit; *therefore* inaccurately suggests a

cause-and-effect relationship. Choice J is wrong because a semicolon should be used between independent clauses, and the first clause can't stand alone.

29. D
Reading-Type

Since we're told that the audience is unfamiliar with the story, it would make sense to include a summary of the Robin Hood legend, choice D, something the passage lacks. Choices A and C would do nothing for a reader curious about Robin Hood, since they go off on tangents about other issues. As the passage states that Robin Hood's existence is questionable (*legend-ary*), choice B doesn't fit in with the stance of the writer.

30. J
Reading-Type

Rarely are ACT English passages written for authorities or experts; they're usually written for the general public, as J correctly states in this question. If the passage were directed toward *experts*, choice F, or *authorities*, choice G, much of the basic information it presents would be unnecessary and not included. Since the passage states that the existence of Robin Hood is legendary, the passage can't be aimed at readers craving confirmation that he "was an actual historical personage," so choice H is wrong.

PASSAGE III

31. A
Verbosity

The shortest answer is correct. *Ten-mile* is cor-rectly punctuated: the hyphen makes it an adjective modifying *radius*. The other answers are wordy and awkward.

32. H
Idiom

You don't look forward *at* something. You look forward *to* something. Choice G wrongly implies that it is the brother who looks forward to the opportunity to show off the narrator's skills. J wrongly implies a contrast between the two parts of the sentence. Actually, it is precisely because she hasn't flown with her brother that the writer anticipates showing off her skills to him.

33. D
Logic

Ever since means from the time the narrator first could read to the present time of the narrative. This span of time makes sense, since the writer is telling us how long she had planned on a journalism career. *If* in A signals a hypothetical situation, rather than a period of time. *Since* in choice B implies a cause-and-effect relationship that doesn't hold up. Why would her ability to easily read a newspaper be a reason for her career decision? *Although* in choice C signals a contrast, but there isn't one.

34. F
Pronouns

It's true that you use *I* and *me*, in choices G and H, when you're writing about yourself. However, you can't say "I always envisioned I" or "I always envisioned me." Per the rules of grammar, you have to say "I always envisioned myself."

35. A
Punctuation

Choice A is correct because all you need to do is pause before the word *giving*, and this pause is signaled by the comma. You don't need a colon, as in choice B. Colons signal lists or defini-tions. You don't need a semicolon in choice C either—a semicolon should be placed between clauses that could stand alone as sentences, but the second part of this sentence can't. Choice D creates a sentence with no verb.

36. G
Modifiers

This is an example of a misplaced modifier. Choices F and H make it sound as if it is the airport, and not the pilot, that is filing the flight plan. Choice J is awkward (it uses a passive construction) and wordy. Choice G is concise, and the verbs *filed* and *gave* are parallel.

37. A
Modification

The adjective *careful* should be placed before *watch*, the noun it modifies. Choice B is wrong because the reference is not to "careful airplanes." *Neared* requires an adverb such as *carefully* before it, not an adjective. Choice D is wrong because it is the people, not the crater, that are *careful*.

38. J
Punctuation

The colon in the original interrupts the flow of the sentence. Colons often function like equal signs. ("Here's what we need for the picnic: salami, ham, cheese, and bread.") Colons signal lists or definitions, but nothing needs to be equated in this sentence.

39. D
Redundancy

Since *speechless* and *mute* mean the same thing, it's redundant to use both of them.

40. G
Verb Usage

Steadying and *took* should be in parallel form. This makes choice G right. The verbs in J are parallel, but they're in the present tense, which

doesn't fit with the past tense verbs *shot* and *dictated* in the nonunderlined part of the sentence.

41. A
Tone

Since Jeff and the narrator are circling the mountain, "a description of Mt. St. Helens" would be appropriate. Choice B contradicts the information in the passage; we're told that the plane must stay high enough to avoid smoke and ash. In any case, the tone of choice B doesn't suit the calm tone of the rest of the passage. Choice C sounds as if it belongs in a science textbook rather than in a story. Choice D wanders too far from the direct observation of the Mt. St. Helens volcano, which is the paragraph's focus.

42. G
Logic

"Since that time" is an appropriate transition. It makes clear the time shift between the day at Mt. St. Helens and the present. The other choices contain inappropriate connecting words. *However* in F and *nevertheless* in choice J signal contrasts, but there isn't one in the passage. *Furthermore* suggests an elaboration of what came before, but there is no elaboration in the passage.

43. C
Reading-Type

Since the author is favorably recalling a memorable past experience, *nostalgic* in choice C is the best choice. The passage is positive in tone. It's definitely not *bitter*, choice B, or *exhausted*, choice D. *Optimistic* is close but wrong. *Optimistic* means "hopeful." The passage focuses on the excitement of the past, not on the good things that might happen.

44. H
Judging the Passage

The use of *I* is appropriate because this is a firsthand account. First-person narratives do tend to draw the reader in. Choice J is not true, since *I* is not appropriate in all types of writing. The passage is personal and chatty; it's not an example of "formal writing." The passage isn't focused on volcanoes in general, as choice G says, but on the Mt. St. Helens eruption, the narrator's first international story.

45. B
Structure and Purpose

The passage reads best if the first and second paragraphs are switched. Choices A, C, and D confuse the time sequence of the narrative, which follows the narrator from her early dreams of becoming a photojournalist, to the memorable Mt. St. Helens story, to her present experience as a foreign correspondent.

PASSAGE IV

46. G
Redundancy

The description of Sherlock Holmes as "ingenious and extremely clever" is redundant because ingenious and extremely clever mean the same thing. You need to use only one of the two to get the point across.

47. D
Logic

Therefore is supposed to be a signal that the sentence that follows is a logical conclusion based on information from the preceding sentence or sentences. The use of *therefore* doesn't make any sense here because you can't conclude that everyone knows the phrase "elementary, my dear Watson" just because everyone knows of Holmes's detective abilities. Choice C is wrong for the same reason—"for this reason" and

therefore mean the same thing in this context. *Although*, B, indicates some sort of contrast; this would be wrong because there is no contrast within this sentence or between this sentence and the previous one. Really, there is no need for a structural signal here at all. Choice D is correct.

48. J
Relevance

Note that this question has an OMIT option—a strong clue that the underlined portion is irrelevant to the paragraph. The theme of the first paragraph is "everyone knows who Sherlock Holmes is (or was)." The last sentence has absolutely nothing to do with this main idea, so it should be omitted. Putting parentheses around the sentence (choice G) will not make it more relevant, so that is not the way to solve the problem.

49. B
Pronouns

He is an ambiguous pronoun because it's unclear whether *he* refers to Conan Doyle or to Sherlock Holmes. You know after reading the entire sentence that *he* is Conan Doyle, so you have to replace *he* with *Conan Doyle* for the sake of clarity.

50. J
Verbosity

From a grammatical point of view, there is nothing wrong here; it's just unnecessarily wordy. The ACT prizes clarity and simplicity in style, which often means that the shortest answer is the best one. "To be remembered" is the most concise, and therefore the correct, answer.

51. A
Logic

In fact is the appropriate signal phrase here. *Despite this*, *regardless*, and *yet* would all indicate a contrast between this sentence and the previous one. There is no contrast, however; Conan Doyle did not want to be remembered as the author of Sherlock Holmes stories, so he killed the detective off (at least for a while).

52. J
Modifiers
A modifying phrase that begins a sentence refers to the noun or pronoun immediately following the phrase. According to that rule, the phrase "having had enough of his famous character by that time" modifies *Sherlock Holmes*, which doesn't make sense at all. The sentence has to be rearranged so that the introductory phrase describes Conan Doyle. J is the choice that accomplishes this.

53. D
Relevance
Once again, take note of the OMIT choice. What do soap opera characters have to do with Arthur Conan Doyle and Sherlock Holmes? Nothing. This sentence disrupts the flow of the paragraph by being almost completely irrelevant, so it has to be omitted.

54. H
Verb Usage
The verb is in the wrong tense. "Has been deeply immersed" is in the present perfect tense, which is used to describe an action that started in the past and continues to the present or that happened a number of times in the past and may happen again in the future. Since Conan Doyle's immersion in spiritualism is over and done with, you have to use the simple past: "was deeply immersed."

55. B
Completeness
This is a sentence fragment because there is no subject and verb; all you have is an introductory phrase and a subordinate clause starting with

that. By omitting *that,* you can turn the subordinate clause into a main clause, making "he lectured" the subject and verb (choice B). Choice C would work if the sentence began with "so convinced." Choice D is wrong because the introductory phrase can't stand alone as a sentence.

56. J
Redundancy
Since this sentence says that Conan Doyle and his family attempted to communicate with the dead by automatic writing, it's redundant to explain that automatic writing was thought to be a means of communicating with "those no longer among the living." Omit the underlined portion of the sentence.

57. D
Structure and Purpose
The second sentence refers to "these experiences," so it should come directly after the sentence that describes the paranormal experiences Conan Doyle seemed to have had. The fourth sentence is the one that talks about materialized hands and heavy articles swimming through the air, so the second sentence should come after the fourth.

58. H
Pronouns
There are two problems with the underlined portion of the sentence: the colon does not belong there, and the pronoun *they* is ambiguous because it doesn't refer to anything in particular in the previous sentence. Choice H takes care of both of these problems by dropping the colon and by spelling out what the pronoun was supposed to refer to.

59. B
Logic
Here, you just have to pick the choice that makes sense. Sherlock Holmes is only a fictional

character, so choices A, C, and D are wrong; Holmes could not possibly have said anything about Conan Doyle's spiritualism, nor will he ever. You can still wonder, however, what the esteemed detective would have said, if he were real. This is the idea behind the last sentence.

60. G
Reading-Type

The passage contrasts the logical, deductive thinking used by Conan Doyle's fictional character, Sherlock Holmes, with Conan Doyle's own exploration of the paranormal. An appropriate subtitle must reflect this contrast. G is the only choice that does.

PASSAGE V

61. C
Punctuation

Read this sentence to yourself, pausing whenever you hit a comma. It doesn't sound right, does it? Now read the sentence again without pausing for the two commas. It should sound as though it flows a lot more smoothly and naturally. There is no reason to set off *in June* from the rest of the sentence because it is not a parenthetical phrase. The commas should be omitted.

62. J
Modifiers

There is no reason to use the comparative form of *plentiful* (*more plentiful*) because nothing is being compared here. In fact, no sort of adjective is needed in front of *plentiful* at all, so the OMIT choice is the correct one.

63. B
Verb Usage

The parenthetical phrase in the underlined portion is a clue that the noun immediately preceding the verb *were* is not its subject. The

subject is *supply,* and only choice B has a verb that agrees with the subject. Choice A uses the plural verb *were*. Choice C creates a fragment. Choice D uses the wrong tense.

64. J
Completeness

There are two problems here. One, the first sentence of this paragraph is really just a fragment because it forms a dependent clause. It should be the introductory clause for the second sentence. Two, the second sentence uses *its*, the possessive form of *it*, when it should use *it was*. Merely adding an apostrophe to *its* (as choices G and H do) would be wrong because *it's* means *it is*, not *it was*; you have to have the past tense here. Choice J takes care of both of these problems.

65. A
Punctuation

This part of the sentence is okay. No punctuation is necessary. It would be a mistake to try to break the sentence up into two parts with a period or semicolon after *control* because the part that started with "in spite of" would only be a fragment. Likewise, choice C creates a fragment.

66. G
Pronoun

The phrase "the efforts of 9,000 firefighters employed state-of-the-art equipment" doesn't make sense at all. You need a relative clause after *firefighters,* for example, "who employed state-of-the-art equipment." It is not correct to use the relative pronoun *which* when referring to a person or a group of people, so choice G is correct.

67. D
Modifiers

As you can see from the choices, the question here is where to put the modifier *only* so that the sentence makes sense. Since the fires did not stop until the first snow, you can infer that *only nature* was able to curb the destruction (choice D). All of the other choices state that nature had just a limited ability to curb the destruction, which is not what the writer means to say.

68. G
Sentence Structure

The introductory modifying phrase is unnecessarily wordy; drop the *having been* and the phrase becomes clearer and more concise. Choice H is wrong because it would produce a run-on sentence. Choice J is out because there is no reason to put a comma between *ecologist* and *who*.

69. D
Relevance

It seems at first that this sentence belongs in the paragraph because it follows the first sentence pretty naturally. Read further in the paragraph, however, and you realize that the fact that more acres burned in Alaska than in Yellowstone in 1988 is really irrelevant to the writer's argument in this paragraph. The writer is explaining that forest fires can be good for a forest, and that's why the Yellowstone fires were not such a great tragedy.

70. J
Redundancy

It's redundant to say "in order that continued health … be maintained"; if the health of the forest is maintained, obviously it will continue. J is the choice that avoids redundancy. Remember, the shortest choice is often the correct one.

71. C
Verb Usage

Use the present tense to describe things that are always true—"the sun comes up in the morning," "the cone only opens when exposed to great heat." Also, since the writer is talking about the cone of the lodgepole pine (which is singular), the possessive should be *pine's*, not *pines'*.

72. H
Logic

However is the wrong transition signal to use here because there is no contrast between this sentence and the previous one. This sentence actually supports the previous one. The fact that large animals were grazing and bedding down near the fire shows that they were indeed fire-tolerant and fire-adaptive, so the appropriate signal phrase is *in fact*.

73. B
Purpose

The third paragraph describes how the plant life of a forest benefits from a forest fire, while the fourth paragraph explains that the wildlife of Yellowstone survived the 1988 fires relatively well, as expected. A transition sentence between the two paragraphs is not going to say that "animals suffer from a forest fire," choice A, or that "one never knows what toll a fire will take," choice C; these choices contradict the author's tone and opinion. Choice D is an irrelevant statement. This leaves choice B, which is correct because it reflects the author's opinion in both paragraphs and provides a good introduction to the fourth.

74. G
Modifiers

The problem with "judging from the recent pictures of the park" is that the phrase is modifying *forest,* and a forest obviously can't judge anything. The phrase would have been okay if the sentence read "judging from the recent pictures of the park, I think that the forest was not destroyed." In this case, the phrase modifies *I*, the author, who is capable of judging. Choice G takes care of the problem by rewriting the sentence so that the modifying phrase is gone.

75. C
Reading-Type

Simply listing the endangered animal species in the park, choice A, would not show the fire to be relatively harmless to those species. Discussing the vulnerability of endangered birds to forest fires, choice B, would make the fire seem dangerous, so it's out, too. D may seem like an attractive choice, but it's not correct: even if the fires are infrequent, they could still be harmful to the endangered animals. Choice C is the correct answer. Reports of park biologists that the endangered animals were okay during the fire would be good evidence that they were not significantly threatened.

Math Test

Answer explanations for the Math test refer to 100 Key Math Concepts for the ACT, found at the end of this book.

1. B
Average Formula

Key Math Concepts for the ACT, #41. Plug the terms into the average formula and solve:

$$\text{Average} = \frac{\text{Sum of terms}}{\text{Number of terms}}$$

$$= \frac{230 + 155 + 320 + 400 + 325}{5}$$

$$= \frac{1,430}{5}$$

$$= 286$$

That's B.

2. J
Translating from English into Algebra

Key Math Concepts for the ACT, #65. Begin by converting Sarah's 12 feet of wood into inches. There are 12 inches in a foot, so Sarah has 12×12 inches = 144 inches. Cutting off three 28-inch pieces removes $3 \times 28 = 84$ inches, which leaves her with $144 - 84 = 60$ inches. That's choice J.

3. C
Adding and Subtracting Monomials

Key Math Concepts for the ACT, #53. To evaluate *x*, isolate it on one side of the equation, then solve.

$$4x + 18 = 38$$
$$4x = 20$$
$$x = 5$$

Choice C is correct.

4. G
Solving a Proportion

Key Math Concepts for the ACT, #38. Since John weighs *more* than Ellen, begin by eliminating choices J and K, as doing so will reduce the chance of a miscalculation error. According to the problem, John's 165 lb represents 1.5 times Ellen's weight. Therefore, Ellen's weight must be $\frac{165}{1.5} = 110$ lb. G is correct.

5. E
Average Formula

Key Math Concepts for the ACT, #41. To find the average of four numbers, plug them into the average formula and solve:

$$\text{Average} = \frac{\text{Sum of terms}}{\text{Number of terms}}$$

$$= \frac{237 + 482 + 375 + 210}{4}$$

$$= \frac{1,304}{4}$$

$$= 326$$

Choice E is correct.

6. J
Raising Powers to Powers Cube both sides to solve for *x*:

Key Math Concepts for the ACT, #48

$$\sqrt[3]{x} = 4$$
$$x = 64$$

7. B
Adding and Subtracting Polynomials

Key Math Concepts for the ACT, #54. Isolate the variable, then solve for *x*:

$$x^2 + 14 = 63$$
$$x^2 = 49$$
$$x = \pm 7$$

This is choice B.

8. G
Simplifying Square Roots

Key Math Concepts for the ACT, #49. You *could* use your calculator to solve this problem, but there's a much easier way. Begin by eliminating choice H, as it is not a perfect square. J can also be eliminated for the same reason. To simplify the radical, factor out a perfect square from 54. The largest factor of 54 that's also a perfect square is 9, so $\sqrt{54} = \sqrt{9 \times 6} = 3\sqrt{6}$.

9. E
Simplifying Square Roots

Key Math Concepts for the ACT, #49. You *could* punch the expression into your calculator, but it may actually be quicker to estimate. $\sqrt{90} \approx \sqrt{81} = 9$ and $\sqrt{32} \approx \sqrt{36} = 6$, so $\sqrt{90} \times \sqrt{32} \approx 9 \times 6 = 54$. With the calculator, the actual value is 53.6656. That's closest to choice E.

10. K
Multiplying and Dividing Roots

Key Math Concepts for the ACT, #51. When the choices are spaced far apart, estimation is generally the quickest way to the correct

answer. To estimate, round 5.2 to 5 and 6.8 to 7. Since $5^3 + 7^2 = 125 + 49 = 174$, the correct answer will be very close to 174. That would be choice K.

11. C
Raising Powers to Powers

Key Math Concepts for the ACT, #48. $x^3 = 512$, so $x = \sqrt[3]{512} = 8$. Be careful not to stop too soon. The problem asks for x^2, not *x*. $8^2 = 64$, which is choice C.

12. H
Evaluating an Expression

Key Math Concepts for the ACT, #52. To solve this problem, you'll need to follow the order of operations (PEMDAS).

First, evaluate the parentheses: $3^3 \div 9 + (6^2 - 12) \div 4 = 3^3 \div 9 + (36 - 12) \div 4 = 3^3 \div 9 + 24 \div 4$.

Next, simplify the exponent: $3^3 \div 9 + 24 \div 4 = 27 \div 9 + 24 \div 4$.

Then, take care of any multiplication and/or division, from left to right: $27 \div 9 + 24 \div 4 = 3 + 6$.

Finally, take care of any addition and/or subtraction, from left to right: $3 + 6 = 9$.

So H is correct.

13. B
Translating from English into Algebra

Key Math Concepts for the ACT, #65. Each banana costs \$.24, so the price of *x* bananas is \$.24*x*. Similarly, each orange costs \$.38, so the price of *y* oranges is \$.38*y*. Therefore, the total price of *x* bananas and *y* oranges is \$.24*x* + \$.38*y*. That's choice B.

14. K
Adding and Subtracting Monomials

Key Math Concepts for the ACT, #53. Isolate the variable, then solve for *x:*

$$4x + 13 = 16$$
$$4x = 3$$
$$x = \frac{3}{4}$$

K is correct, when you convert $\frac{3}{4}$ to the decimal 0.75.

15. A
Percent Formula

Key Math Concepts for the ACT, #32. The quickest way to solve this problem is to estimate. While you may or may not know 6% of 1,250 off the top of your head, 10% of 1,250 is 125. Since 6% < 10%, the correct answer must be less than 125. Only choice A works.

To solve this the math way, multiply 1,250 by the decimal form of 6%: $1,250 \times .06 = 75$.

16. J
Average Formula

Key Math Concepts for the ACT, #41. When an average problem involves variables, it often helps to think in terms of sum instead. For Sarah's exam scores to average at least a 90, they must sum to at least $90 \times 4 = 360$. She already has an 89, a 93, and an 84, so she needs at least $360 - (89 + 93 + 84) = 360 - 266 = 94$ points on her last test. Choice J is correct.

17. B
Adding and Subtracting Monomials

Key Math Concepts for the ACT, #53. You are given the equation to convert Fahrenheit to Celsius, so plug 68 in for F and solve for C:

$$F = \frac{9}{5}C + 32$$
$$68 = \frac{9}{5}C + 32$$
$$36 = \frac{9}{5}C$$
$$20 = C$$

This matches choice B.

18. J
Average Formula

Key Math Concepts for the ACT, #41. The basketball team scored 364 points in 13 games, so they scored an average of $\frac{364}{13} = 28$ points per game. Choice J is correct.

19. D
Adding and Subtracting Monomials

Key Math Concepts for the ACT, #53. Isolate the variable, then solve for x:

$$6x + 4 = 11x - 21$$
$$4 = 5x - 21$$
$$25 = 5x$$
$$5 = x$$

That's choice D.

20. G
Percent Formula

Key Math Concepts for the ACT, #32. The original price of the jacket is $160, so a 15% sale is a discount of $160 \times .15 = 24. Therefore, the sale price of the jacket is $160 - $24 = 136. This matches choice G.

21. C
Average Formula

Key Math Concepts for the ACT, #41. If the variable makes the average seem difficult to calculate, consider the sum instead. The average of four numbers is 343, so their sum must be $343 \times 4 = 1,372$. Three of the numbers are 292, 305, and 415, so the final number is $1,372 - (292 + 305 + 415) = 1,372 - 1,012 = 360$, or choice C.

22. G
Probability

Key Math Concepts for the ACT, #46. The probability of an event occurring is given by the formula:

$$\text{Probability} = \frac{\text{Number of desired outcomes}}{\text{Number of possible outcomes}}$$

In this problem, a desired outcome is getting a green marble while a possible outcome is simply getting any marble. There are 8 + 14 + 11 + 6 = 39 total marbles in the jar. Of these, 6 are green, so the probability of getting a green marble is $\frac{6}{39}$, which simplifies to $\frac{2}{13}$. That's choice G.

23. D
Rate
Key Math Concepts for the ACT, #39. Laura lives three miles from school, so biking to school and back means a total distance of 3 × 2 = 6 miles. Since Laura bikes at a speed of 12 miles per hour and 6 is half of 12, it must take her half an hour, or 30 minutes, to bike both legs of the journey. Choice D is correct.

24. G
Probability
Key Math Concepts for the ACT, #46. There's a lot going on in this problem, so find the most concrete point and begin there. You are told that the chance for a girl to win the scholarship is .55. Since this is more than half, there must be more girls than boys in the junior class, so eliminate H, J, and K. Now, .55 isn't much greater than .5, so if you were low on time on test day, choice G would be a great guess.

To solve this problem the math way, use the probability formula:

$$\text{Probability} = \frac{\text{Number of desired outcomes}}{\text{Number of possible outcomes}}$$

Since .55 is the probability that a girl would win, the 154 girls are the desired outcomes, and the total number of students (boys and girls) is the number of possible outcomes. Call x this total and use this formula to solve for x:

$$.55 = \frac{154}{x}$$

$$x = \frac{154}{.55}$$

$x = 280$

With 280 total students and 154 girls, there must be 280 − 154 = 126 boys. That's choice G.

25. C
Multiplying Binomials—FOIL
Key Math Concepts for the ACT, #56. This problem seems long, but it actually isn't that complicated. The order of operations says that all of the multiplication should be taken care of first. Let's begin with the first two terms:

$$(x + 4)(x - 4)$$

(If you noticed the difference of squares here, that will save you some time. If not, use FOIL.)

First: $x \times x = x^2$ Outer: $x \times -4 = -4x$
Inner: $4 \times x = 4x$ Last: $4 \times -4 = -16$

Combine like terms:
$$x^2 + (-4x) + 4x + (-16) = x^2 - 16$$

Now for the other two terms:
$$(2x + 2)(x - 2)$$

First: $2x \times x = 2x^2$ Outer: $2x \times -2 = -4x$
Inner: $2 \times x = 2x$ Last: $2 \times -2 = -4$

Combine like terms:
$$2x^2 + (-4x) + 2x + (-4) = 2x^2 - 2x - 4$$

Finally, add the two polynomials:
$$(x^2 - 16) + (2x^2 - 2x - 4) = 3x^2 - 2x - 20$$

Choice C is correct.

26. G
Solve a Quadratic Expression
Key Math Concepts for the ACT, #66. To solve a quadratic equation, first set it equal to 0. Begin by subtracting 6 from both sides of the equation to get $s^2 - 4s - 12 = 0$. To factor this, you will need two factors of −12 that add up to −4. The only pair of factors that meets this criterion is −6 and 2, so the equation factors to $(s + 2)(s - 6) = 0$. For this equation to be true, either $s + 2$ or $s - 6$ (or both) must be 0. Therefore,

the two possible solutions of s are -2 and 6. Choice G is correct.

27. D
Sine, Cosine, and Tangent of Acute Angles

Key Math Concepts for the ACT, #96. You are given the cosine of $\angle BAC$ and the hypotenuse of the triangle, so begin by using these to find the adjacent side:

$$\text{Cos } A = \frac{\text{Adjacent}}{\text{Hypotenuse}}$$

$$.6 = \frac{\text{Adjacent}}{15}$$

$$\text{Adjacent} = 9$$

So the adjacent side, $\overline{AB}$, is 9, and triangle ABC is a right triangle with a leg of 9 and a hypotenuse of 15. ABC must therefore be a 3-4-5 right triangle, and $\overline{BC}$ must be 12. Choice D is correct.

28. J
Translating from English into Algebra

Key Math Concepts for the ACT, #65. With variables in the question stem and the answer choices, this problem is perfect for picking numbers. Pick 2 for x and 3 for y. Now the problem reads: "If a car drives 80 miles per hour for two hours and 60 miles per hour for three hours, what is the car's average speed, in miles, for the total distance traveled?"

In this case, the car would have driven $80 \times 2 = 160$ miles and $60 \times 3 = 180$ miles, for a total of $160 + 180 = 340$ miles in five hours. The average speed is therefore $\frac{340}{5} = 68$ miles per hour. Plug 2 in for x and 3 in for y for each of the choices and see which comes out to 68:

F. $\frac{480}{2 \times 3} = \frac{480}{6} = 80.$ Eliminate.

G. $\frac{80}{2} = \frac{60}{3} = 40 + 20 = 60.$ Eliminate.

H. $\frac{80}{2} \times \frac{60}{3} = 40 \times 20 = 800.$ Eliminate.

J. $\frac{80(2) + 60(3)}{2 + 3} \times \frac{160 + 180}{5} = \frac{340}{5} = 68.$

Only choice J works, so it must be correct.

29. E
Geometric Sequences

In a geometric sequence, use the formula:

$$a_n = a_1(r^{n-1})$$

Where a_n is the *nth* term in the sequence, a_1 is the first term in the sequence, and r is the amount by which each preceding term is multiplied to get the next term.

The first two terms in this sequence are 3 and 12, so r is $\frac{12}{3} = 4$. Now that we have r, we can plug each known value in the equation and solve for a_{24}:

$$a_{24} = 3(4^{24-1}) = 3 \times 4^{23}$$

E is correct.

30. F
Raising Powers to Powers

Key Math Concepts for the ACT, #48 When an exponent equation looks difficult on test day, try to rewrite the problem so that either the bases or the exponents themselves are the same. In this problem, the two bases seem different at first glance but, since 27 is actually 3^3, you can rewrite the equation as:

$$3^{3x+3} = 3^{3\left(\frac{2}{3}x - \frac{1}{3}\right)}$$

This simplifies to $3^{3x+3} = 3^{2x-1}$. Now that the bases are equal, set the exponents equal to each other and solve for x:

$$3x + 3 = 2x - 1$$

$$x + 3 = -1$$

$$x = -4$$

Choice F is correct.

31. E
**Factoring Other Polynomials—
FOIL in Reverse**

Key Math Concepts for the ACT, #61. A complex number can seem scary on the ACT, but this problem defines it for you, so treat it like you would any other variable that you plug numbers into. In this problem, the key is swapping every i^2 with a -1. Begin by simplifying the first term in the expression:

$$(i + 1)^2 = (i + 1)(i + 1) = i^2 + 2i + 1$$
$$= -1 + 2i + 1 = 2i$$

Multiplying this by the second term gets you:

$$2i(i - 1) = 2i^2 - 2i = 2(-1) - 2i = -2 - 2i$$

Choice E is correct.

32. G
Translating from English into Algebra

Key Math Concepts for the ACT, #65. This is an area problem with a twist—we're cutting a piece out of the rectangle. To find the area of the remaining space, you will need to subtract the area of the sandpit from the area of the original playground. Recall that the area of a rectangle is length × width. The dimensions of the original playground are $x + 7$ and $x + 3$, so its area is $(x + 7)(x + 3) = x^2 + 10x + 21$. The sandpit is a square with side x, so its area is x^2. Remove the pit from our playground, and the remaining area is $x^2 + 10x + 21 - x^2 = 10x + 21$. Choice G is correct.

33. C
**Adding/Subtracting,
Multiplying/Dividing Signed Numbers**

Key Math Concepts for the ACT, #5, 6. When a problem tests a number property, the easiest way to solve it is to pick numbers. Since u is an integer, let's pick some integers for u. If $u = 2$, then $(u - 3)^2 + 5 = (2 - 3)^2 + 5 = (-1)^2 + 5 = 1 + 5 = 6$. This eliminates B, D, and E. If $u = 3$, then

$(u - 3)^2 + 5 = (3 - 3)^2 + 5 = 5$. This eliminates choice A, leaving choice C as the correct answer.

34. F
Solving an Inequality

Key Math Concepts for the ACT, #69. Ignore the number lines for now and focus on the inequality. Inequalities work like normal equations in all aspects except one—when multiplying or dividing by a negative number, remember to flip the inequality sign. To solve this inequality, isolate x:

$$-1 \geq -\frac{3}{5}x + 2$$
$$-3 \geq -\frac{3}{5}x$$
$$5 \leq x$$

"Greater than or equal to 5" is represented by a closed circle at 5 with the arrow pointing toward the right. Choice F is correct.

35. C
Multiplying Binomials—FOIL

Key Math Concepts for the ACT, #56. With nested functions, work from the inside out. To solve this problem, substitute the entire function of $g(x)$ for x in the function $f(x)$, then solve:

$$f(g(x)) = \frac{1}{3}(3x^2 + 6x + 12) + 13$$
$$f(g(x)) = x^2 + 2x + 4 + 13$$
$$f(g(x)) = x^2 + 2x + 17$$

C is correct.

36. G
Finding the Distance Between Two Points

Key Math Concepts for the ACT, #71 To find the length of a line segment on the coordinate plane, you would normally need to use the distance formula. This requires the coordinates of the segment's two endpoints. Since A (1, 5) and C (1, 1) have the same x-coordinate, a much faster way is to simply subtract the y-coordinate of C from the y-coordinate of A. The length of segment AC is $5 - 1 = 4$. Choice G is correct.

37. D
Evaluating an Expression

Key Math Concepts for the ACT, #52. To find $f(4)$, plug 4 in for x in the function $f(x)$, and solve:

$$f(x) = 3\sqrt{x^2 + 3x + 4}$$
$$= 3\sqrt{4^2 + 3(4) + 4}$$
$$= 3\sqrt{16 + 12 + 4}$$
$$= 3\sqrt{32}$$
$$= 3 \times 4\sqrt{2}$$
$$= 12\sqrt{2}$$

The correct answer is choice D.

38. H
Using Two Points to Find the Slope

Key Math Concepts for the ACT, #72. Perpendicular lines have negative reciprocal slopes. Since the line in the problem has a slope of $\frac{2}{3}$, the line we are looking for must have a slope of $-\frac{3}{2}$. The problem also says that this line contains the point (4, −3). Plugging all of this information into the equation of a line, $y = mx + b$, will allow us to find the final missing piece—the y-intercept:

$$y = mx + b$$
$$-3 = -\frac{3}{2}(4) + b$$

$$-3 = -6 + b$$
$$3 = b$$

With a slope of $-\frac{3}{2}$ and a y-intercept of 3, the line is $y = -\frac{3}{2}x + 3$. The correct answer is H.

39. A
Using Two Points to Find the Slope

Key Math Concepts for the ACT, #72. The line crosses the y-axis at (0, 1), so its y-intercept is 1. A quick look at the four choices reveals that each has a different slope, so finding the slope of our line will be enough to answer the question. We already have one point, (0, 1), so pick another point, such as (1, 3), and plug both into the two-point formula for slope:

$$\text{Slope} = \frac{y_2 - y_1}{x_2 - x_1}$$
$$= \frac{3 - 1}{1 - 0}$$
$$= \frac{2}{1}$$
$$= 2$$

The slope is 2 and the y-intercept is 1, so the line is $y = 2x + 1$. A is correct.

40. K
Finding the Distance Between Two Points

Key Math Concepts for the ACT, #71. Don't let the triangle fool you—its presence is wholly irrelevant, as you only need $\overline{XZ}$ itself to answer the question. A bisector of a line segment cuts the segment in half, so it must intersect that segment at its midpoint. Therefore, we are actually looking for the midpoint of $\overline{XZ}$. According to the figure, the coordinates of $\overline{XZ}$ are (2, 6) for X and (8, 2) for Z. Plug these points into the midpoint formula and solve:

$$\text{Midpoint} = \left(\frac{x_1 + x_2}{2}, \frac{y_1 + y_2}{2} \right)$$
$$= \left(\frac{2 + 8}{2}, \frac{6 + 2}{2} \right)$$

$$= \left(\frac{10}{2}, \frac{8}{2} \right)$$

$$= (5, 4)$$

K is correct.

41. D
Finding the Distance between Two Points

Key Math Concepts for the ACT, #71. To find the distance between two points, plug them into the distance formula and evaluate:

$$\text{Distance} = \sqrt{(x_2 - x_1)^2 + (y_2 - y_1)^2}$$

$$= \sqrt{(-2 - 3)^2 + (6 - (-6))^2}$$

$$= \sqrt{(-5)^2 + 12^2}$$

$$= \sqrt{25 + 144}$$

$$= \sqrt{169}$$

$$= 13$$

D is correct.

42. G

Finding the Distance Between Two Points

Key Math Concepts for the ACT, #71. Plug given points [(–1, 1) and (1, 3)] into the midpoint formula and solve:

$$\text{Midpoint} = \left(\frac{x_1 + x_2}{2}, \frac{y_1 + y_2}{2} \right)$$

$$= \left(\frac{1 + (-1)}{2}, \frac{3 + 1}{2} \right)$$

$$= \left(\frac{0}{2}, \frac{4}{2} \right)$$

$$= (0, 2)$$

G is correct.

43. D
Volume of a Sphere

Key Math Concepts for the ACT, #95.

Volume of a Sphere $= \frac{4}{3} \pi r^3$

Since you are told the diameter is 6, you know the radius of the sphere is 3. Watch out for this terminology on the ACT. If you knew the correct formula but use the diameter of the sphere instead of the radius, you would have selected choice E. If you don't recall the formula for the volume of a sphere, you should be able to eliminate some of the options and make an educated guess. Choice B is the area of a cross section of the sphere—too small—and choice A is even smaller, so you can eliminate both of these choices. Choice E seems pretty big (unless you fell for the trap), so you're down to choices C and D. Hopefully you'll remember that the volume of a sphere is a little bigger than the radius cubed times π (choice C) and will select D. But even if you guess between the two answers, you have a 50 percent chance of guessing correctly.

Choice D is correct.

44. H
Area of a Rectangle

Key Math Concepts for the ACT, #87. The perimeter of a rectangle is twice its length plus twice its width, or Perimeter = $2l + 2w$. To find the area, you must first determine the value of w, so plug in the values for perimeter and length to solve:

$$\text{Perimeter} = 2l + 2w$$

$$24 = 2(8) + 2w$$

$$24 = 16 + 2w$$

$$8 = 2w$$

$$4 = w$$

So the width is 4. The area of the rectangle is length × width, or 8 × 4 = 32. H is correct.

45. A
Area of a Triangle, Special Right Triangles

Key Math Concepts for the ACT, #83, #85. With only one known side, you cannot find the area directly, as you will need to figure out more sides first. Given the area of triangle *ABC* and its base, the first step is to find height $\overline{CD}$:

$$\text{Area} = \frac{1}{2}bh$$

$$48 = \frac{1}{2}(12)h$$

$$48 = 6h$$

$$8 = h$$

So $\overline{CD} = 8$. Triangle *ABC* is an isosceles triangle, so $\overline{CD}$ also happens to be the perpendicular bisector of $\overline{AB}$, meaning $\overline{AD} = \overline{DB} = 6$. With legs of 6 and 8, each of the smaller right triangles must be 3-4-5 right triangles, making the hypotenuse of each— $\overline{AC}$ and $\overline{CB}$—10. (You can also use the Pythagorean theorem; if *x* equals the hypotenuse, then $6^2 + 8^2 = x^2$ which simplifies to $36 + 64 = 100 = x^2$. Therefore, *x* equals 10.) Therefore, the perimeter of triangle *ABC* is $10 + 10 + 12 = 32$. Choice A is correct.

46. J
Perimeter of a Rectangle

Key Math Concepts for the ACT, #86. It may sound a bit more complex, but this problem is only asking you for the perimeter of a rectangle with the given dimensions, so plug them into the perimeter formula and solve:

$$\text{Perimeter} = 2l + 2w$$
$$= 2(130) + 2(70)$$
$$= 260 + 140$$
$$= 400$$

J is correct.

47. D
Parallel Lines and Transversals

Key Math Concepts for the ACT, #79. When two parallel lines are cut by a transversal, half of the angles will be acute and half will be obtuse. Each acute angle will have the same measure as each other acute angle. The same is true of every obtuse angle. Furthermore, the acute angles will be supplementary to the obtuse

angles. $\angle a$ is an acute angle measuring 68° while $\angle f$ is an obtuse angle, so $\angle a$ must be supplementary to $\angle f$. Therefore, $\angle f = 180° - 68° = 112°$.

D is correct.

48. F
Similar Triangles

Key Math Concepts for the ACT, #82. While this problem may *look* like a geometry problem at first glance, a closer look reveals that each of the three angles of one triangle is congruent to its corresponding angle in the other. The triangles are thus similar, and similar triangles have proportional sides, so this is actually a proportion problem. The boy's height is proportional to the tree's height in the same way that the boy's shadow is proportional to that of the tree, so call *x* the length of the boy's shadow, set up the proportion, and solve for *x*:

$$\frac{24}{18} = \frac{4}{x}$$

$$24x = 72$$

$$x = 3$$

So the boy's shadow is 3 ft long. That's choice F.

49. C
Special Right Triangles

Key Math Concepts for the ACT, #85. You are told that triangle *RST* is a right triangle and that one of its angles is 30°, so *RST* must be a 30-60-90 right triangle, meaning its sides must be in the proportion $x:x\sqrt{3}:2x$. Hypotenuse *RT* is 16, so *x* must be $\frac{16}{2} = 8$, and *RS* (the longer leg) must be $8\sqrt{3}$. (You can also use the Pythagorean theorem.) That matches choice C.

50. K
Length of an Arc

Key Math Concepts for the ACT, #90. To find the length of an arc, you will need the measure of the central angle as well as the circumference of the entire circle. In this problem, the central angle is 45°, and the circumference of the circle is $2\pi(5) = 10\pi$. Plug these values into the proportion and solve:

$$\frac{\text{Central angle}}{360°} = \frac{\text{Length of arc}}{\text{Circumference}}$$

$$\frac{45°}{360°} = \frac{\text{Length of arc}}{2\pi r}$$

$$\frac{1}{8} = \frac{\text{Length of arc}}{10\pi}$$

$$8 \times (\text{length of arc}) = 10\pi$$

$$\text{Length of arc} = \frac{10\pi}{8}$$

$$= \frac{5\pi}{4}$$

Choice K is correct.

51. B

Special Right Triangles

Key Math Concepts for the ACT, #85. A square has four right angles and four equal sides. Its diagonal cuts the square into two identical isosceles right triangles. The square in this problem has a side length of 7, so the base and height of each isosceles right triangle is also 7. The sides of an isosceles right triangle are in the proportion $x : x : x\sqrt{2}$, so the length of the diagonal (the hypotenuse of both triangles) is $7\sqrt{2}$. (Again, you can also use the Pythagorean theorem.) B is correct.

52. H

Perimeter of a Polygon

Key Math Concepts for the ACT, #86. A regular polygon is equilateral, so a regular hexagon is a hexagon with six equal sides. The regular hexagon in the problem has a side of 11, so its perimeter is $6 \times 11 = 66$.

H is correct.

53. C

Perimeter of a Rectangle, Pythagorean Theorem

Key Math Concepts for the ACT, #86, #84. The perimeter of the rectangle is 28, and one of its sides is 2.5 times the length of the other, so call x the shorter side. Our rectangle now has sides of x and $2.5x$. Draw a figure to help visualize this problem.

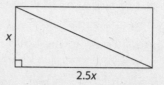

To find x, plug the information into the perimeter formula and solve:

$$\text{Perimeter} = 2l + 2w$$

$$28 = 2(x) + 2(2.5x)$$

$$28 = 2x + 5x$$

$$28 = 7x$$

$$4 = x$$

So $x = 4$, and the dimensions of the rectangle must be $4 \times 1 = 4$ and $2.5 \times 4 = 10$. These values are not parts of a special right triangle, so use the Pythagorean theorem to find the diagonal:

$$a^2 + b^2 = c^2$$

$$4^2 + 10^2 = c^2$$

$$16 + 100 = c^2$$

$$116 = c^2$$

$$\sqrt{116} = c$$

Since 116 isn't a perfect square but it lies between $10^2 = 100$ and $11^2 = 121$, $\sqrt{116}$ must be somewhere between 10 and 11 (it's approximately 10.77). The only choice that fits is C.

54. G

Parallel Lines and Transversals

Key Math Concepts for the ACT, #79. This is a pair of parallel lines cut by a transversal, but this time, there's also a triangle thrown into the mix. Begin with AB. This is a transversal, so

∠*MAB* and ∠*ABC* are alternate interior angles and ∠*MAB* = ∠*ABC* = 55°. Since triangle *ABC* is isosceles with *AB* = *AC*, ∠*ACB* is also 55°.

Choice G is correct.

55. D
Special Right Triangles Area of a Circle
Key Math Concepts for the ACT, #85, 91. The chord is perpendicular to the line segment from the center of the circle, so that line segment must be its perpendicular bisector. This allows us to add the following to the figure:

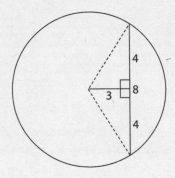

The two right triangles have legs 3 and 4, so they are both 3-4-5 right triangles with hypotenuse 5. This hypotenuse is also the radius of the circle, so plug that into the area formula to solve:

$$\text{Area} = \pi r^2$$
$$= \pi(5)^2$$
$$= 25\pi$$

The correct answer is choice D.

56. J
Special Right Triangles Area of a Triangle
Key Math Concepts for the ACT, #83, 85. Triangle *QRS* is an isosceles triangle, so its height is also the perpendicular bisector of *RS*. Each half of *RS* is $\frac{16}{2}$ = 8 units long, so each of the smaller right triangles has a leg of 8 and a hypotenuse of 17. They must therefore be 8-15-17 right triangles, making the height of *QRS* 15. Therefore, the

area of *QRS* is $\frac{1}{2} \times 16 \times 15 = \frac{1}{2} \times 240 = 120$. Choice J is correct.

57. C
Solving a Proportion
Key Math Concepts for the ACT, #38. The ratio of girls to boys is 5:3, so the ratio of girls to the total number of seniors is 5:(3 + 5), or 5:8. Call *x* the number of girls in the senior class. Set up the proportion and solve for *x*:

$$\frac{5}{8} = \frac{x}{168}$$
$$8x = 840$$
$$x = 105$$

There are 105 girls in the senior class, which is choice C.

58. K
Special Right Triangles
Key Math Concepts for the ACT, #85. The tangent of an angle is defined by $\text{Tan } A = \frac{\text{Opposite}}{\text{Adjacent}}$. The side opposite ∠*EFD* is 12 and the side adjacent to ∠*EFD* is 5, so $\tan \angle EFD = \frac{12}{5}$. K is correct.

59. C
Special Right Triangles Sine of Acute Angles
Key Math Concepts for the ACT, #85, 90. Since *QS* = *QR*, triangle *QRS* must be a 45-45-90 right triangle and the hypotenuse is $5\sqrt{2}$. Remember that $\sin \angle QRS = \frac{\text{opposite}}{\text{hypotenuse}}$. Therefore, $\sin \angle QRS = \frac{5}{5\sqrt{2}} = \frac{1}{\sqrt{2}} = \frac{\sqrt{2}}{2}$. Choice C is correct.

60. K
Special Right Triangles
Key Math Concepts for the ACT, #85. A right triangle with leg 8 and hypotenuse 17 must be an 8-15-17 right triangle, so *JK* = 15. Since *JK* is opposite ∠*JLK*, $\sin \angle JLK = \frac{15}{17}$. Choice K is correct.

Reading Test

Reading questions can be divided into four basic types: Detail questions, Inference questions, Big Picture questions, and Vocabulary-in-Context questions. As you review the answers and explanations, note which types you tend to answer correctly or incorrectly and tailor your studying to focus on areas where you need improvement.

PASSAGE I—PROSE FICTION

This passage, about an older woman called Rosemary and her grandson Victor, is essentially a story about the generation gap. Here's a road map:

In paragraph 1, Rosemary's awareness of the easy life Victor seems to be leading spurs a series of flashbacks in which she remembers her childhood experiences growing up on a farm.

Paragraph 2 relates her memories of getting up early in the morning.

In paragraph 3, Rosemary remembers her father preventing her from going to high school because he needed help on the farm. The author contrasts Rosemary's painful recollections with Victor's casual attitude toward education.

1. C
Detail
Line 11 explicitly states that Victor is Rosemary's grandson in line 11. Choice C is correct.

2. H
Inference
Rosemary's unease with Victor's behavior is the topic of paragraph 3. She is disturbed by his willingness to take a college course simply because it's "easy to pass," choice H. Choices G and J distort details from the wrong paragraph, while choice F brings up an idea that's not in the passage.

3. D
Inference
The answer is strongly implied in the passage. Paragraph 3 notes that Rosemary wanted to go to high school after finishing grammar school. Her father would not permit her to go, so she had to spend time "with animals and rough farmhands for company instead of people her own age," D. Choice B is flatly contradicted by paragraph 3, which indicates that Rosemary wanted to go to high school, not college. Choices A and C make inferences that are not supported by the passage.

4. G
Inference
Lines 19–20 say that Rosemary "had decided long ago that growing old was like slowly turning to stone." This sentiment suggests that she is resigned to the physical problems that accompany old age. *Acceptance*, choice G, therefore, is correct. *Sadness*, choice F, and *resentment*, choice H, are too negative in tone, while *optimism*, choice J, is too positive. Rosemary, in short, isn't at all emotional about the aging process.

5. A
Detail
Rosemary's interest in crossword puzzles is discussed in the opening sentences of paragraph 1. She does them for two reasons: to pass the time and to keep her mind active, choice A. The other choices distort details in paragraphs 1 and 2. Choice B plays on Rosemary's happiness at still being able to write at 87, choice C plays on her need to consult an atlas to look up the Swiss river, and choice D plays on her experience of "an expanded sense of time" as she grows older.

6. H
Big Picture

Most of the passage is about the different attitudes of Rosemary and Victor toward education, H. The first two paragraphs serve as a lead-in to this topic, while the remainder of the passage concentrates on Rosemary's thoughts and memories about education. Rosemary mentions Victor's laziness, choice F, but this isn't the main focus of the passage. Education is the primary focus. There's no information at all to suggest that Victor's father has mistreated him, choice G. Indeed, just the opposite is implied: Victor's "doting parents," after all, have given him a new car. Finally, choice J doesn't mention education. Moreover, Rosemary doesn't try to suppress her memories.

7. B
Inference

A question that contains a line reference requires you to understand the context in which the reference appears. In the lines that precede the mention of Victor's "shiny new car," Rosemary considers his easy upbringing, how he looks as if he's never done a chore. In other words, Victor's car is a symbol of his generation, which has had a much easier time of it than Rosemary's. So choice B is correct. Rosemary's parents, choice A—her father anyway—can't be described as generous. Besides, her parents have nothing to do with Victor's car. Similarly, while Rosemary seems to feel that Victor's future prospects are bright, choice C, and that his life lacks hardship, choice D, neither has anything to do with his car.

8. G
Detail

Paragraph 3 says that Rosemary is disturbed by Victor's dismissive attitude toward his education. She doesn't like the idea that his only reason for taking a course is that he can pass it. In contrast to Victor's attitude, Rosemary, in her youth, was eager to continue her education, choice G. Choices F and J refer to details from the wrong paragraphs, while choice H introduces an issue that the passage never tackles.

9. C
Detail

A few lines before Rosemary recalls what it was like growing up on the farm, the passage says that "Rosemary often experienced an expanded sense of time, with present and past tense intermingling in her mind," choice C. Choice D, on the other hand, alludes to recollections from the wrong paragraphs. Choices A and B distort details in paragraph 2.

10. F
Inference

The reference to Victor's bright future comes at the end of paragraph 2, which precedes Rosemary's opinion: "if he (Victor) ever got out of bed." It's clear from the text that it's Rosemary, choice F, who thinks that he has a good future. The passage never says what Victor thought about his own future, choice G. Nor does it say what his parents thought about his future, choice H. And it's extremely unlikely that Victor and Rosemary's father, choice J, were even alive at the same time.

PASSAGE II—SOCIAL STUDIES

Here's a road map to this social studies passage on architecture:

Paragraph 1 compares architects to other professionals, noting that in an economic and social sense they are worse off than doctors and lawyers.

Paragraph 2 goes into the historical background of architecture as a profession.

Paragraphs 3, 4, and 5 discuss the passage's big idea—whether architects should try to improve their professional status. This question is posed in paragraph 3, while in paragraphs 4 and 5, the author argues that architects should emphasize the artistic value of their profession (rather than try to improve their economic and social standing).

11. B
Detail

The first sentence in paragraph 5 says that architects "seem embarrassed to present themselves as artists," choice B. Choice A is wrong because paragraphs 1 and 2 show that architects want to be thought of in the same way as doctors. Although the passage mentions both builders, choice C, and accountants, choice D, there is no information that indicates that architects resent comparisons to them.

12. H
Detail

To determine the meaning of a word in the passage, it's necessary to understand the context in which that word appears. The word *privileged* comes up in the context of the author's point that doctors and lawyers, professionally speaking, are in a stronger position than architects. Thus, *privileged* in this case means "superior," choice H.

13. B
Inference

Since the question asks about how architects came to be regarded as professionals, your road map of the passage should have sent you to paragraph 2, the only paragraph that discusses historical matters. Lines 31–38 say that architects convinced governments to grant them a professional license by emphasizing architecture's effect on "public health and safety," choice B. Choices A, C, and D play on details that aren't linked to the licensing process.

14. J
Detail

The question asks why doctors and lawyers are in a better economic position than architects, so it's back to paragraph 1, where this issue is examined. The second half of the paragraph brings up three reasons why doctors and lawyers are better off: the demand for their services is "more stable," option I; they have more control over their fields, option II; and they aren't forced to deal with competitors, option III. Thus, choice J is correct.

15. A
Big Picture

The first part of the passage argues that architects are worse off economically and socially than other professionals. The second part of the passage argues that architects should concentrate on their art rather than try to improve their status. Choice A, therefore, is correct. Choice B, in contrast, goes against the spirit of the passage, which says that it isn't likely that architects will be able to achieve the status of doctors and lawyers. Choices C and D, finally, distort details in the passage.

16. H
Detail

Architecture is described as the "mother of all arts" because of the attributes that "set it apart" (lines 78–79). These attributes include its unrivaled ability to "relate light, mass, and structure to produce memorable visual and spatial experiences," choice H. Choice G runs counter to the thrust of the passage, which indicates that architecture is different from other arts. And choices F and J introduce issues not taken up in the text.

17. B
Detail

The effect of economic downturns on professionals is brought up toward the end of paragraph 3. Line 67 notes that the construction industry is "notoriously volatile," a clear indication that architects, B, face trouble in times of economic hardship. To the contrary, lines 68–75 say that doctors, choice A, lawyers, choice C, and accountants, choice D, are all assured of business in hard times.

18. G
Inference

Lines 100–102 state explicitly that architects aren't needed in the construction of routine, ordinary buildings, choice G. Choices F and H are flatly contradicted in the text, and choice J is not dealt with in the passage at all.

19. B
Detail

The information you need is in the first two sentences of the passage. These sentences say that college students who are interested in economic prosperity are probably not going to seek a career in architecture because other professions offer more opportunity for advancement. In other words, these professions pay better than architecture. Thus, choice B is correct. Choice D distorts a detail in paragraph 1, while choices A and C bring up issues that the passage does not deal with at all.

20. J
Detail

Lines 55–57 indicate that law and medicine are "more fully in control of [their] domain" than architecture, choice J. Choices F and G are flatly contradicted by paragraph 3, which says that law and medicine are more science-based and less dependent on economic conditions than architecture. Choice H is contradicted by

paragraph 2, which strongly implies that law, medicine, and architecture are all protected by a licensing system.

PASSAGE III—HUMANITIES

This passage tackles the philosophes, a group of mainly French intellectuals. Here's a road map:

Paragraph 1 defines the term *philosophes*—they were a group of thinkers who took the ideas of others and spread them through literary works.

Paragraph 2 says that the philosophes developed and spread the philosophy of the Enlightenment throughout Western Europe and the American colonies.

Paragraphs 3, 4, and 5 discuss the influence of Newton, Locke, and English institutions on the philosophes' thinking.

Paragraph 6 describes the ideas and career of perhaps the most famous philosophe, Voltaire.

21. C
Detail

This question asks for a description of the *philosophes*, so it's back to the first two paragraphs. Lines 15–17 say that they took the ideas of others and popularized them. The first sentence of paragraph 2 goes on to state that they "developed the philosophy of the Enlightenment and spread it to much of the educated elite in Western Europe (and the American colonies)." Thus, choice C is correct. Choices B and D are contradicted by information in the first paragraph, which states that the philosophes were generally neither professors nor scientists. Choice A, on the other hand, is too narrow in scope: true, the philosophes were influenced by Locke, but they were also influenced by Newton and English institutions.

22. G
Inference

Your road map of the passage should have sent you directly to the last paragraph, where Voltaire is discussed. This paragraph says that Voltaire criticized both French society and religious institutions, so you can infer that he might have attacked French religious institutions, choice G. Choice H is contradicted by information in the paragraph, which states that Voltaire "came to admire" English government. It's unlikely that he would have criticized the Scientific Revolution, F, because the philosophes were disciples of this revolution. Finally, the passage says nothing about Voltaire's views of "courtly love," choice J, so you can't infer what his position on this issue would have been.

23. D
Detail

The answer to a question that contains a line reference is found in the lines around that reference. Locke's idea that "schools and social institutions could…play a great role in molding the individual" comes up right after his belief that humans are shaped by their experiences, choice D. Choice A is contradicted by lines 50–53, while choices B and C distort details in paragraph 4.

24. H
Inference

Your road map should have pointed you to paragraph 3, where Newton is discussed. This paragraph says that Newton believed that "the universe [was]…originally set in motion by God," option I, and that "the universe operates in a mechanical and orderly fashion," option III. However, this paragraph doesn't say that Newton believed that "human reason is insufficient to understand the laws of nature," option II; if anything, it implies just the opposite. Choice H, options I and III only, is correct.

25. D
Detail

Lines 61–64 reveal that it was Locke who questioned the notion that "revelation was a reliable source of truth." Thus, you're looking for a work written by him, so you can immediately eliminate choice A, *Letters on the English*, and choice C, *Elements of the Philosophy of Newton*, both of which were authored by Voltaire. The remaining two works, *Second Treatise of Civil Government*, choice B, and *Essay Concerning Human Understanding*, choice D, were both written by Locke; but *Second Treatise of Civil Government*, choice B, is a political, not a philosophical, work, so it can be eliminated as well. That leaves choice D as the correct answer.

26. G
Inference

The first sentence of paragraph 4 states that Locke "agreed with Newton but went further." Specifically, Locke also thought that the human mind was subject to "the mechanical laws of the material universe" (lines 48–49), choice G. The other choices distort details in paragraphs 3 and 4.

27. D
Big Picture

The philosophes—as paragraph 5 shows—were greatly influenced by an England that allowed more individual freedom, was more tolerant of religious differences, and was freer of traditional political institutions than other countries, particularly France. Indeed, the philosophes wanted other countries to adopt the English model. Thus, choice D, options I, II, and III, is correct.

28. G
Big Picture

Since this question also asks about England, it's right back to paragraph 5. In the second-to-last sentence of the paragraph, the philosophes cite England's political stability and prosperity as evidence that England's system worked. The last sentence of the paragraph goes on to say that the philosophes "wanted to see in their own countries much of what England already seemed to have." Choice G, therefore, is correct. Choice F, on the other hand, flatly contradicts the gist of paragraph 5. Finally, choices H and J distort details from the wrong part of the passage.

29. A
Inference
The French political and religious authorities during the time of Voltaire are discussed in paragraph 6. Voltaire got in hot water with the authorities over his outspoken views, so it's safe to assume that they weren't advocates of free speech, choice A. Since they first imprisoned and then exiled him, they clearly didn't regard the philosophes with indifference, choice C. The passage doesn't say precisely what Voltaire was imprisoned and exiled for, so you can't infer that the authorities "overreacted to Voltaire's mild satires," choice B, which, in any case, weren't that mild. Finally, since Voltaire was an advocate of the English system of government, it's also safe to assume that the French hadn't accepted this model, making choice D wrong.

30. J
Big Picture
The notion that the philosophes were "more literary than scientific" appears in the middle of paragraph 1. A few lines further down, the paragraph furnishes a list of the types of literary works produced by the philosophes, so choice J is correct. The passage never mentions any "political change," choice F. Nor does it compare the literary outputs of Newton and Voltaire, choice G. Finally, choice H is out because the philosophes were not scientists.

PASSAGE IV—NATURAL SCIENCES

31. D
Detail
This question emphasizes the importance of reading all the choices before selecting one. The second paragraph tells us that the Alvarezes believe conditions created by the impact of a meteorite led to mass extinctions. The impact of the asteroid, choice A, caused great damage, but it didn't do "most of the harm"—see the third sentence. Processes like choices B and C are the explanations of the traditional scientists.

32. H
Inference
This isn't easy, but H is the only possible choice. The author is an objective scientist or science journalist who wouldn't want opponents to give up their view until the new theory has been fully tested against all their criticisms. The traditionalists' arguments are given only briefly, and the author clearly believes the Alvarezes have added something valuable to the study of mass extinctions, but the traditional view has not proven wrong conclusively, choice F. And as the last paragraph indicates, traditionalists have produced their own theories to account for new evidence, such as iridium reaching the Earth's surface via volcanic activity, choice J. Choice G is clearly not true; the author believes the new theory challenged the old one.

33. C
Detail
As it is used in the sentence, *enrichment* means "increase in amount." It wouldn't make sense for the Earth to have wealth, choice A, improvement, choice B, or reward of iridium, choice D.

34. F
Big Picture
The arguments of Alvarez-theory opponents are given in the last paragraph: no crater,

iridium comes from the Earth's core, and the Alvarezes are only physicists. If sufficient iridium deposits come from the Earth's core in lava flows, choice F, Alvarez supporters can't rely on them as evidence of impact. The Alvarezes didn't say extinctions never occurred without asteroid impact, choice G, or that all meteorites contain iridium, choice H. Choice J contradicts one of the opponents' arguments.

35. D
Big Picture
In the first sentence of paragraph 2, the author calls the Alvarez theory important. The bulk of the passage explains and supports this theory. The implication is that the author believes the Alvarezes were on the right track, so we want a positive answer. Choices A and C are negative, and choice B is neutral.

36. G
Detail
According to the information in the second paragraph, soil displacement was the immediate result of a meteorite's impact; it "blotted out" the sun, which reduced temperatures and caused plants to die.

37. D
Inference
Look back at the second paragraph; details there clarify how the impact led to extinctions—the crater didn't simply smash all species into extinction. Choice A uses the wrong verb. The lack of a known crater site, choice B, is mentioned at the end of paragraph 4, but that's not relevant to the discussion in paragraph 2. The conditions that result from meteorite collisions aren't evidence that the Earth is vulnerable to such collisions, choice C.

38. H
Big Picture
The large number of asteroids implied by *teeming* in paragraph 1 explains why Alvarez supporters believe frequent collisions must have occurred in Earth's history (paragraph 4). The fact that an impact would result in certain effects, F, or the idea that the dust cloud would do more harm than the impact itself, choice G, or the traditional view about gradual processes, choice J, are not related to the number of impacts that are likely.

39. C
Detail
The two sentences at the end of paragraph 4 offer the answer; only I and III explain this position. Iridium relates to a different argument entirely.

40. F
Detail
As we've seen, the disastrous consequences of an asteroid's impact are covered in paragraph 2, where choices G, H, and J are mentioned. Choice F is evidence of impact from paragraph 3.

Science Test

Science questions can be divided into three basic types: Figure questions, Patterns questions, and Scientific Reasoning questions. You may also see Basic Theory questions when you review the Conflicting Viewpoints passage. As you review the answers and explanations, note which types you tend to answer correctly or incorrectly, and tailor your studying to focus on areas where you need improvement.

PASSAGE I

The first passage describes the power loss (attenuation) in optical fibers due to impurities. The graph shows the attenuation curve for fluoride glass fibers. At certain ranges in wavelength, as you can see, impurities cause a sharp increase in attenuation; for example, nickel causes a power loss of about 95 db/km at 1.5 microns. The thing to note about this graph is that attenuation in db/km (the y-axis) increases as you move downward. This means, for example, that hydroxyl causes greater power loss than either of the other two impurities.

1. A
Figure
Take a look at the graph and locate the point that corresponds to 1.6 microns and 95 db/km. As it turns out, this is precisely where the line dips—and attenuation sharply increases—due to the presence of nickel impurities. Therefore, copper impurities have an attenuation response similar to that of nickel, choice A.

2. F
Figure
In order to answer this question, you have to envision what the attenuation curve would look like without the sharp dips due to the impurities. It looks as though the curve would rise steadily going from left to right until it reached five microns and 20 db/km, at which point it would start to fall. Once you saw this, you might have been tempted to answer that power loss will "increase then decrease," but remember that the power loss increases as you go down the y-axis. This means that power loss is actually decreasing and then increasing—choice F—as you move along the curve from left to right.

3. C
Scientific Reasoning Question
At 6.6 microns, according to the graph, hydroxyl impurities in a fluoride glass fiber cause an attenuation of nearly 120 db/km. That's quite a considerable loss of power. Someone who wished to limit power loss at this wavelength would

not choose to use fluoride glass fiber because of "the interference from the hydroxyl groups at this wavelength," choice C. This does not mean, though, that a fluoride glass fiber does not conduct any light at this wavelength at all, as B suggests; it's just that a lot of power is lost.

4. G
Scientific Reasoning
This question is a follow-up to the last one. You already know that hydroxyl impurities in fluoride glass fibers cause power loss in the range between six and seven microns. It stands to reason, then, that if you could get rid of these impurities, there would be less power loss both in the range of six to seven microns (Statement I) and in the fiber overall (Statement III). There is no reason to think that the attenuation due to iron impurities would increase, however, so Statement II is false. That makes choice G correct.

5. D
Figure
There are two steps to solving this problem. First, you have to figure out from the graph what the lowest attenuation could be for a fluoride glass fiber. The highest point on the curve—and the point of least power loss—is in the range of five microns, where the power loss is roughly 40 db/km. You could therefore transmit light at a wavelength of five microns and lose only 40 db/km. The second step to the problem is to multiply the power loss per kilometer (40 db/km) by five kilometers to determine what the power loss would be for a five-kilometer cable. The answer is 200 db, choice D.

PASSAGE II
This Data Representation passage is about binary star systems. Figure 1 shows how one star orbits around the other so that each appears to eclipse the other to the observer. The diagram is drawn so that you, the reader, are looking

down on the system from above—from this vantage point, you wouldn't see an eclipse. But the observer in the diagram is looking at the system from the side; from the observer's vantage point, one star can get in the way of the other and cause an eclipse.

Figure 2 is a light curve of the system. Note that the beginning and end points of the graph are the same point. In other words, when the system reaches the 20th day, it is right back where it started from, and it embarks on the cycle all over again. You can ignore the numbers on the y-axis; all you have to know is that as you go up the y-axis, brightness increases. The sharp drop in brightness between the 9th and 11th days is what the text refers to as a deep primary minimum. The secondary minimum is the shallower dip in brightness that goes from the 16th day all the way around to the 4th day of the cycle.

6. H
Figure

Point c is the point on the light curve at which the eclipsing binary is the darkest. Take a look at Figure 1. From the point of view of the observer, System Q is going to be darkest when the light from the brighter star, Star 1, is being blocked by the light from the less bright Star 2. Star 2 interposes itself between Star 1 and the observer when Star 2 is in position 3, choice H.

7. D
Figure

According to the x-axis of the light curve, the complete cycle of changes in the system's surface brightness (from point a through points b, c, and d and back to point a again) lasts 20 days. This means that it takes Star 2 20 days to complete its orbit around Star 1 (it is this orbit, after all, that is causing the changes in the system's brightness). Choice D is the correct answer.

8. H
Figure

The drops in brightness on the light curve (Figure 2) indicate when one star is eclipsing the other. The sharp drop known as the primary minimum—when the darker star eclipses the brighter star—lasts approximately two days. The secondary minimum—when the brighter star eclipses the darker star—goes from day 16 through day 20 to day 4, a total of eight days.

9. B
Scientific Reasoning

This question introduces two new light curve graphs. What gives System Z a deeper primary minimum than X? Well, the reason Q had a deep primary minimum was that one star was brighter than the other; during the time that the brighter star's light was eclipsed by the darker star, the whole system became much darker. You can safely assume that this is the reason Z has a deep primary minimum as well. X's lack of a deep primary minimum must mean, then, that neither of its stars is significantly brighter than the other. As you can see from X's light curve, the drop in brightness of the system is about the same no matter which star is being eclipsed, so the two stars must be equally bright. Since the more extreme difference in the magnitudes of System Z's stars is the reason for Z's deeper primary minimum, choice B is correct.

10. J
Scientific Reasoning

If either star in an eclipsing binary system is in front of the other, the brightness of the system is going to be reduced. The only time the system reaches maximum brightness is when both stars are completely visible—when the full brightness of one star is added to the full brightness of the other, choice J.

PASSAGE III

This is a passage with practically no text and one diagram that illustrates the carbon cycle. Each box of the diagram is a state in which naturally occurring carbon can be found (e.g., in carbon dioxide, in air, or in animals), and the arrows show how carbon can move from one state to another. For example, the carbon found in carbon dioxide can, through the process of photosynthesis, be taken up by green plants and incorporated into various carbon compounds (in fact, according to the diagram, this is the only way that the carbon in carbon dioxide can enter the carbon cycle). Pay attention to the direction of the arrows.

11. C
Figure

Decay bacteria, according to the diagram, gets carbon from the carbon compounds of dead plants and animals and adds to the supply of carbon dioxide in air and water through fermentation and putrefaction. Since there is no other way to get carbon from dead plants and animals back to carbon dioxide, you know that a drop in decay bacteria will reduce the amount of carbon available for forming carbon dioxide. The carbon dioxide level will not be greatly affected, though, because there are three other sources of carbon for carbon dioxide. Choice C is correct.

12. G
Figure

Let's take each of the statements one by one. Statement I is false because the diagram shows that the carbon in animals can move to "other animals" through the process of "animal digestion." An animal that only eats other animals is participating in the carbon cycle when it digests its prey. Statement II is clearly true; there are arrows labeled *respiration* going from the green plants, the animals, and the other animals stages back to the carbon dioxide stage. Statement

III, however, is not true, because some carbon dioxide is released into the air by fermentation and putrefaction. Since only Statement II is true, choice G is correct.

13. D
Figure

There are four direct sources of atmospheric carbon dioxide, according to the diagram: fermentation by decay bacteria and respiration by green plants, by animals, and by "other animals or animal parasites." Choice D correctly cites the respiration of animal parasites. If you were tempted by B, note the direction of the arrow for photosynthesis. Photosynthesis removes atmospheric carbon dioxide, using it as a source for carbon.

14. G
Figure

The arrow signifying animal respiration and the arrow signifying photosynthesis are linked in the diagram by the "carbon dioxide in air or dissolved in water" box. Animal respiration is one of the sources of carbon for carbon dioxide, and the carbon dioxide in turn provides carbon for the process of photosynthesis. In this sense, "animal respiration provides vital gases for green plants," choice G.

15. A
Figure

Look closely at the diagram. The only way that carbon dioxide can enter the carbon cycle is through the process of photosynthesis in which it is taken up by green plants. Note that green plants also emit carbon dioxide back into the air via the process of respiration. Therefore, if green plants were eliminated, the carbon cycle would come to a complete stop, and choice A is correct.

PASSAGE IV

The first paragraph of this Research Summary passage explains that the experiments were conducted on bacteria that are sensitive to magnetic fields. Study 1 tested to see whether these bacteria will migrate in the direction of magnetic north in various experimental conditions. The table of results indicates that the vast majority of bacterial migrations were in the direction of magnetic north no matter whether the microscope was in standard lab conditions, shielded, rotated, or moved to another laboratory.

Study 2 was conducted to determine whether the position of a nearby magnet would affect the direction of bacterial migration. In each experimental condition, according to the data, most of the bacterial migrations were in the direction of the north pole of the magnet. Clearly, you can conclude based on the evidence from this study and the previous one that the bacteria are sensitive to magnetic fields and tend to migrate in the direction of a magnet's north pole.

16. G
Scientific Reasoning

In order to be able to tell whether light was the stimulus affecting the direction of bacterial migration, you have to compare two trials, one with the light on and one with the light off. If there is no difference in the direction of bacterial migration in the two trials, then light does not have an effect and is not the primary stimulus. The two trials you need to compare are Trial 1 and Trial 2 of Study 1, because Trial 1 was conducted under standard lab conditions (with the light on), and in Trial 2 the microscope was shielded from all external light. Since the results of the trials differed only minimally, they support the theory that light was not the primary stimulus. Choice G is correct.

17. C
Scientific Reasoning

As we saw from the data, the bacteria are sensitive to magnetic fields and tend to migrate in the direction of magnetic north. In Study 2, this meant that the bacteria moved toward the magnet because the magnet's north pole was near the slide. If the magnet's south pole were placed near the slide, the magnetic field would be reversed and the bacteria would migrate in exactly the opposite direction, away from the magnet. That makes choice C the correct answer.

18. J
Scientific Reasoning

You don't need experimental data to answer this question; you just have to figure out which answer choice provides the best reason a bacteria should be able to move downward. Choices F and G are out immediately because both are good reasons a bacteria should move upward, not downward. While it may have been somewhat advantageous for bacteria not to be dispersed by currents, choice H, it would have been much more important for them to move downward to find food, so choice J is the best answer.

19. C
Scientific Reasoning

Here, you have to determine which new study would yield new and useful information about the relationship between magnetic field strength and bacterial migrations. You should try to determine the experimental condition that the researchers should vary before you look at the answer choices. To gain new information about magnetic field strength and bacterial migrations, the researchers should vary the magnetic field strength and observe the effect on bacterial migrations. Choice C is correct because it suggests using more and less powerful magnets, which would produce stronger and weaker magnetic fields than that of the magnet in Study 2.

20. F
Figure

In each of the trials of Study 1, bacterial migrations were largely found to be in the direction of magnetic north. Shielding from light and electric fields, rotation of the microscope, and movement of the microscope to another lab all had no distinct effect on the direction of migration. It is fairly easy to conclude from Study 1 that "the majority of magnetotactic bacteria migrate toward the earth's magnetic north pole," choice F.

21. A
Scientific Reasoning

In any experiment, the control condition is the one used as a standard of comparison in judging the experimental effects of the other conditions. In Study 1, there would be no way to know what the effect of, say, rotating the microscope was on bacterial migration if you didn't know how the bacteria migrated before you rotated the microscope. The control condition is the trial that is run without any experimental manipulations: in this case, Trial 1, choice A.

PASSAGE V

This Research Summary presents the results of three experiments that were done on the material *nu-PVC*. The purpose of the experiments was to "determine the weathering abilities of *nu-PVC*," so you can assume that each of the experimental conditions was designed to simulate some aspect of extreme weather. The method in Experiment 1 was to spray 15 boards of *nu-PVC* with distilled water 14 hours a day for 32 weeks; the boards were unaffected. The second experiment tested the ability of *nu-PVC* sheets to withstand ultraviolet light. Sheet flexibility decreased by 17.5% on average, and the sheets also turned white. In the third experiment, *nu-PVC* boards were tested for their ability to support weight before and after they were exposed for 32 weeks to cold temperatures. More than half of the boards' strength was lost as a result of this exposure.

22. H
Figure

According to the results of Experiment 1, *nu-PVC* does not suffer any kind of damage when exposed to water for a long period of time. It seems safe to say, then, that *nu-PVC* would not need a protective coating to avoid water damage, choice H.

23. B
Scientific Reasoning

The results that are relevant here are those from Experiment 3, in which *nu-PVC's* ability to withstand cold temperatures was tested. The *nu-PVC* boards did not fare well during this experiment; they lost more than half of their capacity to support weight without bending or breaking. In a cold environment, the benches could not be kept outside during the winter without sustaining damage. Choice B is correct.

24. G
Scientific Reasoning

Remember that a control is an experimental condition in which nothing special is done to the thing being tested. The control serves as a standard of comparison for the experimental effects found in other conditions. In Experiment 1, the *nu-PVC* boards were sprayed with distilled water for a long period of time to see what effect the water would have. In order to assess the water's effects accurately, though, you have to compare the results of Experiment 1 to the results of a condition in which *nu-PVC* boards are not exposed to water, choice G.

25. A
Scientific Reasoning

Although at first this question seems to require outside knowledge, it can be answered by the process of elimination using the information in the introduction. The introduction of the passage states that the series of experiments was performed to test the weathering abilities of *nu-PVC*. The only weather phenomenon in the answer choices is sunlight, choice A.

26. J
Scientific Reasoning

You know nothing in particular about standard building materials from the passage—you don't know how well they stand up to rain or ultraviolet radiation or how well they support weight after exposure to cold weather. This means you cannot compare *nu-PVC* to other materials at all, which rules out F and H. G is out because there is no information in the passage about the "different colors and textures" of *nu-PVC*. That leaves J. J is correct because it is an advantage of *nu-PVC* (perhaps the only one) that it is made of recycled plastic wastes. *Nu-PVC* helps to solve the garbage problem at the same time that it fills the need for building materials; wood and other standard building materials don't do that.

27. A
Scientific Reasoning

The conditions of the original experiments were clearly chosen so that *nu-PVC* would be subjected to extremes of water, radiation, and cold. There is little point in making the conditions even more extreme when a park bench would never have to survive such weather. It is unlikely, for example, that a park bench will be exposed to 32 weeks of continuous rain, much less 64 weeks, or that a bench will have to endure eight months of −40°C temperature. Thus, Statements I and III are not going to provide useful information. Statement II, on the other hand, is an

important experiment, because sea water and salt-rich air may well have a corrosive effect on *nu-PVC* whereas distilled water did not. Choice A is correct.

PASSAGE VI

The purpose of the three experiments described in this Research Summary was to investigate the effect of glucose on lens proteins in the eye. You should expect, after reading the first paragraph, that glucose would be found to react adversely with the lens proteins and damage them.

Experiment 1 showed that when human tissue protein is dissolved in glucose, an Amadori product forms that causes one protein to bind with another in a brown pigmented cross-link called an advanced glycosylation end product. Experiment 2 demonstrated that the lens proteins in older subjects are often bound to each other by cross-links; the cross-links are either disulfide bonds or "an indeterminate formation with brownish pigmentation" (you can guess from the color that it is the same type of cross-link as was found in Experiment 1). In Experiment 3, it was found that the lens proteins of cow lenses form brown cross-links when dissolved in glucose—the same type of brown cross-links found in Experiment 2 (and, you can infer, in Experiment 1).

28. J
Scientific Reasoning

The researcher who designed the experiments was interested in the effect of dietary glucose on lens proteins in the human eye, not the cow eye. There would be no reason to use cow lens proteins in Experiment 3 if cow lens proteins were expected to react any differently from human lens proteins, especially when human lens proteins were readily available for use—they were used, after all, for Experiment 1. Therefore, you know that the researcher assumed that cow lens proteins would react the same as human lens proteins, choice J.

29. C
Scientific Reasoning

Make sure that you stick to the results of Experiment 1 only when you answer this question. All you know from Experiment 1 is that when a human tissue protein was dissolved in a glucose and water solution, the proteins formed Amadori products that combined with other proteins to make brown cross-links. You can conclude from this that the glucose reacted with the proteins to form cross-links, choice C. Based on Experiment 1, though, you know nothing about disulfide cross links, choice A, or glucose metabolism, choice D. Choice B contradicts the results of Experiment 1 because it is protein, not glucose, that forms AGE.

30. G
Scientific Reasoning

Take another look at the results of Experiment 2. It was found that in the samples from older subjects, the lens proteins often formed cross-linked bonds, some of which were brown. The senile cataracts in the lenses of older people are also brown. The conclusion suggested by the identical colors of the cataracts and the cross-linked bonds is that the senile cataracts are made up of, or caused by, cross-linked bonds, choice G.

31. C
Scientific Reasoning

You don't know from the results of Experiment 2 how the brown pigmented cross-links developed among the lens proteins of older humans. Experiments 1 and 3 indicate, however, that glucose reacts with lens proteins in such a way that brown pigmented cross-links form among the proteins. And remember the main purpose of the experiments: the researcher is investigating the effects of glucose on lens proteins in order to see whether dietary sugar (glucose) damages proteins. The hypothesis that dietary sugar reacted with lens proteins to cause the brown pigmented cross-links found in older subjects would seem to be supported by the results of the three experiments, choice C.

32. J
Scientific Reasoning

The relevant results are those from Experiment 2: the lens proteins of younger subjects were found to have formed cross-linked aggregates much less frequently than the lens proteins of older subjects did. So you would expect that the lens proteins of a 32-year-old man would have fewer cross-links than the lens proteins of an 80-year-old man, choice J. H appears true, but the lens proteins appear "much more often" in older samples. The age difference is greater from 32 years to 80 than 18 years to 32; choice J is, thus, the most likely, and correct, answer.

33. C
Scientific Reasoning

String together the hypotheses that were the correct answers from questions 30 and 31, and you have the following overall hypothesis: dietary glucose causes brown pigmented (AGE) cross-links to form among lens proteins, and these brown cross-links in turn cause the formation of brown senile cataracts. According to this hypothesis, the excess glucose in an uncontrolled diabetic's blood should cause the formation of AGE cross-links among lens proteins and subsequently the development of senile cataracts, choice C.

PASSAGE VII

This passage contains a lot of scientific information and terms that you probably have never seen before. Just remember that you are not expected to recognize or understand everything in the passage. Your job is to answer questions, not to learn particle physics.

Scientist 1 explains the Quark Model—the structure of the proton, the structure of mesons and baryons in general—and then proceeds to give the reasons she thinks the Quark Model is correct. It explains the existence of the many different types of mesons, and it predicted the properties of at least one meson. Although individual quarks have not been observed, the deep inelastic scattering experiments indicated that the proton did indeed have a substructure of "three distinct lumps," which agrees with the Quark Model.

Scientist 2 asserts, however, that the Quark Model is flawed. He argues that if quarks really existed, they would have been found already; since they haven't been found, they don't exist. In addition, he says, the Quark Model violates the Pauli exclusion principle, which states that no two identical particles of half-integer spin can occupy the same state. The Δ^{++} baryon is cited as an example of a particle predicted by the Quark Model that violates the Pauli exclusion principle.

34. G
Scientific Reasoning
Scientist 1 is a proponent of the Quark Model, which says that baryons (including the proton) and mesons are made up of quarks, which have fractional charge. Quarks have never been observed, however. You find out from Scientist 2 that quarks should be easy to distinguish from other particles because they would be the only ones with fractional charge. If a particle with fractional charge was detected, then, it would most likely be a quark, and this would strengthen Scientist 1's hypothesis that the Quark Model is correct. Mesons, baryons, and the Δ^{++} baryon have all been detected, but mere detection of them does not tell us anything

about their substructure, so it cannot be used to support the Quark Model.

35. C
Basic Theory
Scientist 2 says that it should be easy to split the proton into quarks, that the quarks should be easy to distinguish because of their unique charge (Statement I), and that they should be stable because they can't decay into lighter particles (Statement III). Statement II is wrong because it is Scientist 1's explanation of why quarks cannot be detected. Therefore, choice C is correct.

36. F
Basic Theory
Scientist 2 says that the Quark Model is wrong because it violates the Pauli exclusion principle, which states that no two particles of half-integer spin can occupy the same state. He says that in the Δ^{++} baryon, for example, the presence of two up quarks in the same state would violate the principle, so the model must be incorrect. If Scientist 1 were able to show, however, that quarks do not have half-integer spin, F, she could argue that the Pauli exclusion principle does not apply to quarks and thus counter Scientist 2's objections. Evidence that the Δ^{++} baryon exists, choice G, or that quarks have fractional charge, H, isn't going to help Scientist 1 because neither has anything to do with the Pauli exclusion principle. Evidence that quarks have the same spin as electrons, choice J, would only support Scientist 2's position.

37. D
Scientific Reasoning
According to Scientist 2, the Δ^{++} baryon has three up quarks. Each up quark has a charge of $+2/3$ each, so the three quarks together have a total charge of 2, choice D.

38. G
Basic Theory

Scientist 2 thinks that the Quark Model is flawed for two reasons: 1) quarks have not been detected experimentally, and they would have been if they existed, and 2) the Quark Model violates the Pauli exclusion principle. The first reason is paraphrased in choice G, the correct answer. F is wrong because the existence of individual baryons, including protons, has been verified experimentally. Scientist 2 never says that he thinks particles cannot have fractional charge, nor does he complain that the Quark Model doesn't include electrons as elementary particles, so choices H and J are wrong as well.

39. A
Basic Theory

The deep inelastic scattering experiments, according to Scientist 1, showed that the proton has a substructure. The three distinct lumps that were found to bounce high-energy electrons back and scatter them through large angles were the three quarks that make up the proton (at least in Scientist 1's view), so choice A is correct.

40. H
Scientific Reasoning

This question is a follow-up of the last one. If the three lumps were indeed quarks, then this supports the Quark Model because in the Quark Model, the proton consists of three quarks. "Protons supposedly consist of three quarks" is not one of the choices, though, so you have to look for a paraphrase of this idea. Protons are baryons and not mesons, so choices F and G are out. Baryons, like protons, are all supposed to consist of three quarks, so this rules out choice J and makes choice H the correct answer.

Writing Test

MODEL ESSAY

Below is an example of what a high-scoring essay might look like. Notice the author states her position clearly in the introductory paragraph and supports that position with evidence in the following paragraphs. This essay also uses transitions, some advanced vocabulary, and an effective "hook" to draw in the reader.

The significance of clothing is important to many teenagers. A lot of us enjoy choosing clothing that expresses our own style. The color, fabric, shape, and design, and even a written message printed on an article of clothing can help one express a mood or an attitude, and help a person define himself. Because clothing choices are so individual and so personal, students should be given as much leeway as possible to wear what they want to. If this includes clothing with a written slogan or message, then such items should be allowed as long as the words are not judged to be rude, offensive, or distasteful to members of the school community. A rule forbidding "legible" clothing in our school would send students the message that they cannot be trusted to make appropriate choices about what others might find offensive. The majority of students do deserve that trust, and, therefore, I don't think legible clothing should be forbidden.

The first reason I don't support the banning of all legible clothing is that it sets up an authoritarian structure when there is no need for it. Teenagers are faced with many rules and restrictions, but schools should not implement regulations unnecessarily. In my own school, the teachers and staff work hard to create a climate that is tolerant and respectful of everyone. Most of the students appreciate this atmosphere and attempt to behave in ways that maintain it. Most of us do wear shirts with words or messages at some point during the school year, but I don't remember seeing a classmate's shirt that was offensive. If the administrators can trust students to make good judgments most of the time, then we do not need a rule forbidding clothing with messages. If, on occasion, a particular student does wear legible clothing with an offensive message, such an instance could be dealt with on an individual base.

A second reason I oppose forbidding legible clothing is that it is simply impractical. If the no words-on-clothing rule were in place, how far would administrators take it? Many, if not most, brands of clothing today have a label on the outside identifying the company. Would such clothing be forbidden? Where would administrators draw the line? Because of the impracticality of enforcing a rule against clothing with words, it would be better to leave clothing decisions up to the students and trust that we can make appropriate decisions.

It's understandable that some people might want to maintain a rule against legible clothing because they believe that clothing with any message at all, even if it's not an offensive message, might be distracting in school. While I can understand this concern, I would argue that distractions are a part of life, and students must learn to work around them.

Overall, the need for schools to encourage a climate of trust, tolerance, and support is a primary concern. Needless rules about what clothing students can and can't wear diminishes the sense of trust in a school. Respect and tolerance are important, but it's better to let students try to work out for themselves what these things mean than it is for administrators to try to prevent problems by implementing rules that may not actually be necessary.

You can evaluate your essay and the model essay based on the following criteria, covered in chapter 16:

- Does the author answer the question?
- Is the author's position clearly stated?
- Does the body of the essay support and develop the position taken?
- Are there at least three supporting paragraphs?
- Is the relevance of each supporting paragraph clear?
- Does the writer address the other side of the arguments?
- Is the essay organized, with a clear introduction, middle, and end?
- Does the author start a new paragraph for each new idea?
- Is each sentence in a paragraph relevant to the point made in that paragraph?
- Are transitions clear?
- Is the essay easy to read? Is it engaging?
- Are sentences varied?
- Is vocabulary used effectively? Is college-level vocabulary used?

Compute Your Score

1 **Figure out your score in each section.** Refer to the answer keys to figure out the number right in each test section. Enter the results below:

RAW SCORES		TEST 1	TEST 2	TEST 3	TEST 4
	English:	66			
	Math:	44			
	Reading:	34			
	Science:	29			

2 **Find your Practice Test scores.** Find your raw score on each section in the table below. The score on the far left column indicates your estimated scaled score if this were an actual ACT.

SCALED SCORE	RAW SCORES			
	English	Mathematics	Reading	Science
36	75	60	40	40
35	74	60	40	40
34	73	59	39	39
33	72	58	39	39
32	71	57	38	38
31	70	55–56	37	37
30	69	53–54	36	36
29	68	50–52	35	35
28	67	48–49	34	34
27	65–66	45–47	33	33
26	63–64	43–44	32	32
25	61–62	40–42	31	30–31
24	58–60	38–39	30	28–29
23	56–57	35–37	29	26–27
22	53–55	33–34	28	24–25
21	49–52	31–32	27	21–23
20	46–48	28–30	25–26	19–20
19	44–45	26–27	23–24	17–18

SCALED SCORE	RAW SCORES			
	English	**Mathematics**	**Reading**	**Science**
18	41–43	23–25	21–22	16
17	39–40	20–22	19–20	15
16	36–38	17–19	17–18	14
15	34–35	15–16	15–16	13
14	30–33	13–14	13–14	12
13	28–29	11–12	12–13	11
12	25–27	9–10	10–11	10
11	23–24	8	9	9
10	20–22	7	8	8
9	17–19	6	7	7
8	14–16	5	6	6
7	12–13	4	5	5
6	9–11	3	4	4
5	7–8	2	3	3
4	4–6	1	2	2
3	3	1	1	1
2	2	0	0	0
1	1	0	0	0

SCALED SCORES

	TEST 1	TEST 2	TEST 3	TEST 4
English:	27			
Math:	26			
Reading:	28			
Science:	24			

3 **Find your estimated composite score.** To calculate your estimated composite score, simply add together your scaled scores on each subsection and divide by four.

COMPOSITE SCORE

27			
TEST 1	TEST 2	TEST 3	TEST 4

100 Key
Math Concepts

NUMBER PROPERTIES

1. UNDEFINED

On the ACT, *undefined* almost always means **division by zero.** The expression $\frac{a}{bc}$ is undefined if either b or c equals 0.

2. REAL/IMAGINARY

A real number is a number that has a **location on the number line.** On the ACT, imaginary numbers are numbers that involve the square root of a negative number. $\sqrt{-4}$ is an imaginary number.

3. INTEGER/NONINTEGER

Integers are **whole numbers;** they include negative whole numbers and zero.

4. RATIONAL/IRRATIONAL

A **rational number** is a number that can be expressed as a **ratio of two integers. Irrational numbers** are real numbers—they have locations on the number line—they just **can't be expressed precisely as a fraction or decimal.** For the purposes of the ACT, the most important **irrational numbers** are $\sqrt{2}$, $\sqrt{3}$, and π.

5. ADDING/SUBTRACTING SIGNED NUMBERS

To **add a positive and a negative,** first ignore the signs and find the positive difference between the number parts. Then attach the sign of the original number to the larger number part. For example, to add 23 and –34, first we ignore the minus sign and find the positive difference between 23 and 34—that's 11. Then we attach the sign of the number with the larger number part—in this case, it's the minus sign from the –34. So 23 + (–34) = –11.

Make **subtraction** situations simpler by turning them into addition. For example, think of –17 – (–21) as –17 + (+21).

To **add or subtract a string of positives and negatives,** first turn everything into addition. Then combine the positives and negatives so that the string is reduced to the sum of a single positive number and a single negative number.

6. MULTIPLYING/DIVIDING SIGNED NUMBERS

To multiply and/or divide positives and negatives, treat the number parts as usual and **attach a negative sign if there were originally an odd number of negatives.** To multiply –2, –3, and –5, first multiply the number parts: $2 \times 3 \times 5 = 30$. Then go back and note that there were three—an odd number—negatives, so the product is negative: $(-2) \times (-3) \times (-5) = -30$.

7. PEMDAS

When performing multiple operations, remember **PEMDAS,** which means **Parentheses** first, then **Exponents,** then **Multiplication** and **Division** (left to right), then **Addition** and **Subtraction** (left to right).

In the expression $9 - 2 \times (5 - 3)^2 + 6 \div 3$, begin with the parentheses: $(5 - 3) = 2$. Then do the exponent: $2^2 = 4$. Now the expression is: $9 - 2 \times 4 + 6 \div 3$. Next do the multiplication and division to get $9 - 8 + 2$, which equals 3.

8. ABSOLUTE VALUE

Treat absolute value signs a lot like **parentheses.** Do what's inside them first and then take the absolute value of the result. Don't take the absolute value of each piece between the bars before calculating. In order to calculate $|(-12) + 5 - (-4)| - |5 + (-10)|$, first do what's inside the bars to get: $|-3| - |-5|$, which is $3 - 5$, or -2.

9. COUNTING CONSECUTIVE INTEGERS

To count consecutive integers, **subtract the smallest from the largest and add 1.** To count the integers from 13 through 31, subtract: $31 - 13 = 18$. Then add 1: $18 + 1 = 19$.

DIVISIBILITY

10. FACTOR/MULTIPLE

The **factors** of integer *n* are the positive integers that divide into *n* with no remainder. The **multiples** of *n* are the integers that *n* divides into with no remainder. Six is a factor of 12, and 24 is a multiple of 12. Twelve is both a factor and a multiple of itself.

11. PRIME FACTORIZATION

A **prime number** is a positive integer that has exactly two positive integer factors: 1 and the integer itself. The first eight prime numbers are 2, 3, 5, 7, 11, 13, 17, and 19.

To find the prime factorization of an integer, just keep breaking it up into factors until **all the factors are prime.** To find the prime factorization of 36, for example, you could begin by breaking it into 4 × 9:

$$36 = 4 \times 9 = 2 \times 2 \times 3 \times 3$$

12. RELATIVE PRIMES

To determine whether two integers are relative primes, break them both down to their prime factorizations. For example: 35 = 5 × 7, and 54 = 2 × 3 × 3 × 3. They have **no prime factors in common**, so 35 and 54 are relative primes.

13. COMMON MULTIPLE

You can always get a common multiple of two numbers by **multiplying** them, but unless the two numbers are relative primes, the product will not be the least common multiple. For example, to find a common multiple for 12 and 15, you could just multiply: 12 × 15 = 180.

14. LEAST COMMON MULTIPLE (LCM)

To find the least common multiple, check out the **multiples of the larger number** until you find one that's **also a multiple of the smaller.**

To find the LCM of 12 and 15, begin by taking the multiples of 15: 15 is not divisible by 12; 30 is not; nor is 45. But the next multiple of 15, 60, is divisible by 12, so it's the LCM.

15. GREATEST COMMON FACTOR (GCF)

To find the greatest common factor, break down both numbers into their prime factorizations, and take **all the prime factors they have in common.** 36 = 2 × 2 × 3 × 3, and 48 = 2 × 2 × 2 × 2 × 3. What they have in common is two 2s and one 3, so the GCF is 2 × 2 × 3 = 12.

16. EVEN/ODD

To predict whether a sum, difference, or product will be even or odd, just **take simple numbers like 1 and 2 and see what happens.** There are rules—"odd times even is even," for example—but there's no need to memorize them. What happens with one set of numbers generally happens with all similar sets.

17. MULTIPLES OF 2 AND 4

An integer is divisible by 2 if the **last digit is even.** An integer is divisible by 4 if the **last two digits form a multiple of 4.** The last digit of 562 is 2, which is even, so 562 is a multiple of 2. The last two digits make 62, which is not divisible by 4, so 562 is not a multiple of 4.

18. MULTIPLES OF 3 AND 9

An integer is divisible by 3 if the **sum of its digits is divisible by 3.** An integer is divisible by 9 if the **sum of its digits is divisible by 9.** The sum of the digits in 957 is 21, which is divisible by 3 but not by 9, so 957 is divisible by 3 but not 9.

19. MULTIPLES OF 5 AND 10

An integer is divisible by 5 if the **last digit is 5 or 0.** An integer is divisible by 10 if the **last digit is 0.** The last digit of 665 is 5, so 665 is a multiple of 5 but not a multiple of 10.

20. REMAINDERS

The remainder is the whole number left over after division. 487 is 2 more than 485, which is a multiple of 5, so when 487 is divided by 5, the remainder will be 2.

FRACTIONS AND DECIMALS

21. REDUCING FRACTIONS

To reduce a fraction to lowest terms, **factor out and cancel** all factors the numerator and denominator have in common.

$$\frac{28}{36} = \frac{4 \times 7}{4 \times 9} = \frac{7}{9}$$

22. ADDING/SUBTRACTING FRACTIONS

To add or subtract fractions, first find a **common denominator,** and then add or subtract the numerators.

$$\frac{2}{15} + \frac{3}{10} = \frac{4}{30} + \frac{9}{30} = \frac{4 \times 9}{30} = \frac{13}{30}$$

23. MULTIPLYING FRACTIONS

To multiply fractions, **multiply** the numerators and **multiply** the denominators.

$$\frac{5}{7} \times \frac{3}{4} = \frac{5 \times 3}{7 \times 4} = \frac{15}{28}$$

24. DIVIDING FRACTIONS

To divide fractions, **invert** the second one and **multiply.**

$$\frac{1}{2} \div \frac{3}{5} = \frac{1}{2} \times \frac{5}{3} = \frac{1 \times 5}{2 \times 3} = \frac{5}{6}$$

25. CONVERTING A MIXED NUMBER TO AN IMPROPER FRACTION

To convert a mixed number to an improper fraction, **multiply** the whole number part by the denominator, then **add** the numerator. The result is the new numerator (over the same denominator). To convert $7\frac{1}{3}$, first multiply 7 by 3, then add 1, to get the new numerator of 22. Put that over the same denominator, 3, to get $\frac{22}{3}$.

26. CONVERTING AN IMPROPER FRACTION TO A MIXED NUMBER

To convert an improper fraction to a mixed number, **divide** the denominator into the numerator to get a **whole number quotient with a remainder.** The quotient becomes the whole number part of the mixed number, and the remainder becomes the new numerator—with the same denominator. For example, to convert $\frac{108}{5}$, first divide 5 into 108, which yields 21 with a remainder of 3. Therefore, $\frac{108}{5} = 21\frac{3}{5}$.

27. RECIPROCAL

To find the reciprocal of a fraction, switch the numerator and the denominator. The reciprocal of $\frac{3}{7}$ is $\frac{7}{3}$. The reciprocal of 5 is $\frac{1}{5}$. The product of reciprocals is 1.

28. COMPARING FRACTIONS

One way to compare fractions is to re-express them with a **common denominator.**

$\frac{3}{4} = \frac{21}{28}$ and $\frac{5}{7} = \frac{20}{28}$; $\frac{21}{28}$ is greater than $\frac{20}{28}$, so $\frac{3}{4}$ is greater than $\frac{5}{7}$.

Another way to compare fractions is to convert them both to **decimals.** $\frac{3}{4}$ converts to .75, and $\frac{5}{7}$ converts to approximately .714.

29. CONVERTING FRACTIONS TO DECIMALS

To convert a fraction to a decimal, **divide the bottom into the top.** To convert $\frac{5}{8}$, divide 8 into 5, yielding .625.

30. REPEATING DECIMAL

To find a particular digit in a repeating decimal, note the **number of digits in the cluster that repeats.** If there are two digits in that cluster, then every second digit is the same. If there are three digits in that cluster, then every third digit is the same. And so on. For example, the decimal equivalent of $\frac{1}{27}$ is .037037037… which is best written $.\overline{037}$.

There are three digits in the repeating cluster, so every third digit is the same: 7. To find the 50th digit, look for the multiple of 3 just less than 50—that's 48. The 48th digit is 7, and with the 49th digit the pattern repeats with 0. The 50th digit is 3.

31. IDENTIFYING THE PARTS AND THE WHOLE

The key to solving most fraction and percent story problems is to identify the part and the whole. Usually, you'll find the **part** associated with the verb *is/are* and the **whole** associated with the word *of.* In the sentence, "Half of the boys are blonds," the whole is the boys ("*of* the boys"), and the part is the blonds ("*are* blonds").

PERCENTS

32. PERCENT FORMULA

Whether you need to find the part, the whole, or the percent, use the same formula:

Part = Percent × Whole

Example: What is 12% of 25?
  Setup: Part = .12 × 25

Example: 15 is 3% of what number?
  Setup: 15 = .03 × Whole

Example: 45 is what percent of 9?
  Setup: 45 = Percent × 9

33. PERCENT INCREASE AND DECREASE

To increase a number by a percent, **add the percent to 100%,** convert to a decimal, and multiply. To increase 40 by 25%, add 25% to 100%, convert 125% to 1.25, and multiply by 40. 1.25 × 40 = 50.

34. FINDING THE ORIGINAL WHOLE

To find the **original whole before a percent increase or decrease,** set up an equation. Think of a 15% increase over x as $1.15x$.

Example: After a 5% increase, the population was 59,346. What was the population *before* the increase?
  Setup: $1.05x = 59,346$

35. COMBINED PERCENT INCREASE AND DECREASE

To determine the combined effect of multiple percents' increase and/or decrease, **start with 100 and see what happens.**

Example: A price went up 10% one year, and the new price went up 20% the next year. What was the combined percent increase?

Setup: First year: 100 + (10% of 100) = 110. Second year: 110 + (20% of 110) = 132. That's a combined 32% increase.

RATIOS, PROPORTIONS, AND RATES

36. SETTING UP A RATIO

To find a ratio, put the number associated with the word *of* **on top** and the quantity associated with the word *to* **on the bottom,** and reduce. The ratio of 20 oranges to 12 apples is $\frac{20}{12}$, which reduces to $\frac{5}{3}$.

37. PART-TO-PART AND PART-TO-WHOLE RATIOS

If the parts add up to the whole, a part-to-part ratio can be turned into two part-to-whole ratios by putting **each number in the original ratio over the sum of the numbers.** If the ratio of males to females is 1 to 2, then the males-to-people ratio is $\frac{1}{1+2} = \frac{1}{3}$ and the females-to-people ratio is $\frac{2}{1+2} = \frac{2}{3}$. Or, $\frac{2}{3}$ of all the people are female.

38. SOLVING A PROPORTION

To solve a proportion, **cross multiply:**

$$\frac{x}{5} = \frac{3}{4}$$

$$4x = 5 \times 3$$

$$x = \frac{15}{4} = 3.75$$

39. RATE

To solve a rate problem, **use the units** to keep things straight.

Example: If snow is falling at the rate of one foot every four hours, how many inches of snow will fall in seven hours?

Setup: $\dfrac{1 \text{ foot}}{4 \text{ hours}} = \dfrac{x \text{ inches}}{7 \text{ hours}}$

$$\frac{12 \text{ inches}}{4 \text{ hours}} = \frac{x \text{ inches}}{7 \text{ hours}}$$

$$4x = 12 \times 7$$

$$x = 21$$

40. AVERAGE RATE

Average rate is *not* simply the average of the rates.

$$\text{Average } A \text{ per } B = \frac{\text{Total } A}{\text{Total } B}$$

$$\text{Average speed} = \frac{\text{Total distance}}{\text{Total time}}$$

To find the average speed for 120 miles at 40 mph and 120 miles at 60 mph, **don't just average the two speeds.** First figure out the total distance and the total time. The total distance is 120 + 120 = 240 miles. The times are three hours for the first leg and two hours for the second leg, or five hours total. The average speed, then, is $\frac{240}{5}$ = 48 miles per hour.

AVERAGES

41. AVERAGE FORMULA

To find the average of a set of numbers, **add them up and divide by the number of numbers.**

$$\text{Average} = \frac{\text{Sum of the terms}}{\text{Number of the terms}}$$

To find the average of the five numbers 12, 15, 23, 40, and 40, first add them: 12 + 15 + 23 + 40 + 40 = 130. Then divide the sum by 5: 130 ÷ 5 = 26.

42. AVERAGE OF EVENLY SPACED NUMBERS

To find the average of evenly spaced numbers, just **average the smallest and the largest.** The average of all the integers from 13 through 77 is the same as the average of 13 and 77: $\frac{13 + 77}{2} = \frac{90}{2} = 45$.

43. USING THE AVERAGE TO FIND THE SUM

Sum = (Average) × (Number of terms)

If the average of ten numbers is 50, then they add up to 10 × 50, or 500.

44. FINDING THE MISSING NUMBER

To find a missing number when you're given the average, **use the sum.** If the average of four numbers is 7, then the sum of those four numbers is 4 × 7, or 28. Suppose that three of the numbers are 3, 5, and 8. These numbers add up to 16 of that 28, which leaves 12 for the fourth number.

POSSIBILITIES AND PROBABILITY

45. COUNTING THE POSSIBILITIES

The fundamental counting principle: if there are *m* **ways** one event can happen and *n* **ways** a second event can happen, then there are *m* × *n* **ways** for the two events to happen. For example, with 5 shirts and 7 pairs of pants to choose from, you can put together 5 × 7 = 35 different outfits.

46. PROBABILITY

$$\text{Probability} = \frac{\text{Favorable outcomes}}{\text{Total possible outcomes}}$$

If you have 12 shirts in a drawer and 9 of them are white, the probability of picking a white shirt at random is $\frac{9}{12} = \frac{3}{4}$. This probability can also be expressed as .75 or 75%.

POWERS AND ROOTS

47. MULTIPLYING AND DIVIDING POWERS

To multiply powers with the same base, **add the exponents:** $x^3 \times x^4 = x^{3+4} = x^7$.

To divide powers with the same base, **subtract the exponents:** $y^{13} \div y^8 = y^{13-8} = y^5$

48. RAISING POWERS TO POWERS

To raise a power to an exponent, **multiply the exponents:** $(x^3)^4 = x^{3 \times 4} = x^{12}$

49. SIMPLIFYING SQUARE ROOTS

To simplify a square root, **factor out the perfect squares** under the radical, unsquare them, and put the result in front:

$$\sqrt{12} = \sqrt{4 \times 3} = \sqrt{4} \times \sqrt{3} = 2\sqrt{3}$$

50. ADDING AND SUBTRACTING ROOTS

You can add or subtract radical expressions only if the part under the radicals is the same:

$$2\sqrt{3} + 3\sqrt{3} = 5\sqrt{3}$$

51. MULTIPLYING AND DIVIDING ROOTS

The product of square roots is equal to the square root of the product:

$$\sqrt{3} \times \sqrt{5} = \sqrt{3 \times 5} = \sqrt{15}$$

The quotient of square roots is equal to the **square root of the quotient:**

$$\frac{\sqrt{6}}{\sqrt{3}} = \sqrt{\frac{6}{3}} = \sqrt{2}$$

ALGEBRAIC EXPRESSIONS

52. EVALUATING AN EXPRESSION

To evaluate an algebraic expression, **plug in** the given values for the unknowns and calculate according to PEMDAS. To find the value of $x^2 + 5x - 6$ when $x = -2$, plug in -2 for x:

$$(-2)^2 + 5(-2) - 6 = 4 - 10 - 6 = -12$$

53. ADDING AND SUBTRACTING MONOMIALS

To combine like terms, **keep the variable part unchanged while adding or subtracting the coefficients:** $2a + 3a = (2 + 3)a = 5a$

54. ADDING AND SUBTRACTING POLYNOMIALS

To add or subtract polynomials, **combine like terms:**

$$(3x^2 + 5x - 7) - (x^2 + 12) =$$
$$(3x^2 - x^2) + 5x + (-7 - 12) = 2x^2 + 5x - 19$$

55. MULTIPLYING MONOMIALS

To multiply monomials, **multiply the coefficients and the variables separately:**

$$2a \times 3a = (2 \times 3)(a \times a) = 6a^2$$

56. MULTIPLYING BINOMIALS—FOIL

To multiply binomials, use **FOIL.** To multiply $(x + 3)$ by $(x + 4)$, first multiply the **F**irst terms: $x \times x = x^2$. Next the **O**uter terms: $x \times 4 = 4x$. Then the **I**nner terms: $3 \times x = 3x$. And finally the **L**ast terms: $3 \times 4 = 12$. Then add and combine like terms: $x^2 + 4x + 3x + 12 = x^2 + 7x + 12$.

57. MULTIPLYING OTHER POLYNOMIALS

FOIL works only when you want to multiply two binomials. If you want to multiply polynomials with more than two terms, make sure you **multiply each term in the first polynomial by each term in the second:**

$$(x^2 + 3x + 4)(x + 5) =$$
$$x^2(x + 5) + 3x(x + 5) + 4(x + 5) =$$
$$x^3 + 5x^2 + 3x^2 + 15x + 4x + 20 =$$
$$x^3 + 8x^2 + 19x + 20$$

FACTORING ALGEBRAIC EXPRESSIONS

58. FACTORING OUT A COMMON DIVISOR

A factor common to all terms of a polynomial can be **factored out.** All three terms in the polynomial $3x^3 + 12x^2 - 6x$ contain a factor of $3x$. Pulling out the common factor yields $3x(x^2 + 4x - 2)$.

59. FACTORING THE DIFFERENCE OF SQUARES

One of the test maker's favorite factorables is the **difference of squares.**

$$a^2 - b^2 = (a - b)(a + b)$$

$x^2 - 9$, for example, factors to $(x - 3)(x + 3)$.

60. FACTORING THE SQUARE OF A BINOMIAL

Learn to recognize polynomials that are squares of binomials:

$$a^2 + 2ab + b^2 = (a + b)^2$$
$$a^2 - 2ab + b^2 = (a - b)^2$$

For example, $4x^2 + 12x + 9$ factors to $(2x + 3)^2$, and $n^2 - 10n + 25$ factors to $(n - 5)^2$.

61. FACTORING OTHER POLYNOMIALS— FOIL IN REVERSE

To factor a quadratic expression, **think about what binomials you could use FOIL on to get that quadratic expression.** To factor $x^2 - 5x + 6$, think about what **F**irst terms will produce x^2, what **L**ast terms will produce $+6$, and what **O**uter and **I**nner terms will produce $-5x$. Common sense—and trial and error—lead you to $(x - 2)(x - 3)$.

62. SIMPLIFYING AN ALGEBRAIC FRACTION

Simplifying an algebraic fraction is a lot like simplifying a numerical fraction. The general idea is to **find factors common to the numerator and denominator and cancel them.** Thus, simplifying an algebraic fraction begins with factoring.

To simplify $\dfrac{x^2 - x - 12}{x^2 - 9}$, first factor the numerator and denominator:

$$\frac{x^2 - x - 12}{x^2 - 9} = \frac{(x - 4)(x + 3)}{(x - 3)(x + 3)}$$

Canceling $x + 3$ from the numerator and denominator leaves you with $\dfrac{x - 4}{x - 3}$.

SOLVING EQUATIONS

63. SOLVING A LINEAR EQUATION

To solve an equation, do whatever is necessary to both sides to **isolate the variable.** To solve $5x - 12 = -2x + 9$, first get all the x terms on one side by adding $2x$ to both sides: $7x - 12 = 9$. Then add 12 to both sides: $7x = 21$, then divide both sides by 7 to get: $x = 3$.

64. SOLVING "IN TERMS OF"

To solve an equation for one variable **in terms of** another means to **isolate the one variable on one side of the equation,** leaving an expression containing the other variable on the other side. To solve $3x - 10y = -5x + 6y$ for x in terms of y, isolate x:

$$3x - 10y = -5x + 6y$$
$$3x + 5x = 6y + 10y$$
$$8x = 16y$$
$$x = 2y$$

65. TRANSLATING FROM ENGLISH INTO ALGEBRA

To translate from English into algebra, look for the key words and systematically turn phrases into algebraic expressions and sentences into equations. Be careful about order, especially when subtraction is called for.

Example: The charge for a phone call is r cents for the first 3 minutes and s cents for each minute thereafter. What is the cost, in cents, of a call lasting exactly t minutes? ($t > 3$)

Setup: The charge begins with r, and then something more is added, depending on the length of the call. The amount added is s times the number of minutes past 3 minutes. If the total number of minutes is t, then the number of minutes past 3 is $t - 3$. So the charge is $r + s(t - 3)$.

INTERMEDIATE ALGEBRA

66. SOLVING A QUADRATIC EQUATION

To solve a quadratic equation, put it in the $ax^2 + bx + c = 0$ form, **factor** the left side (if you can), and set each factor equal to 0 separately to get the two solutions. To solve $x^2 + 12 = 7x$, first rewrite it as $x^2 - 7x + 12 = 0$. Then factor the left side:

$$(x - 3)(x - 4) = 0$$
$$x - 3 = 0 \ \text{ or } \ x - 4 = 0$$
$$x = 3 \ \text{ or } \ 4$$

Sometimes the left side might not be obviously factorable. You can always use the **quadratic formula.** Just plug in the coefficients a, b, and c from $ax^2 + bx + c = 0$ into the formula:

$$\frac{-b \pm \sqrt{b^2 - 4ac}}{2a}$$

To solve $x^2 + 4x + 2 = 0$, plug $a = 1$, $b = 4$, and $c = 2$ into the formula:

$$x = \frac{-4 \pm \sqrt{4^2 - 4 \times 1 \times 2}}{2 \times 1}$$
$$= \frac{-4 \pm \sqrt{8}}{2} = -2 \pm \sqrt{2}$$

67. SOLVING A SYSTEM OF EQUATIONS

You can solve for two variables only if you have two distinct equations. Two forms of the same equation will not be adequate. **Combine the equations in such a way that one of the variables cancels out.** To solve the two equations $4x + 3y = 8$ and $x + y = 3$, multiply both sides of the second equation by -3 to get: $-3x - 3y = -9$. Now add the equations; the $3y$ and the $-3y$ cancel out, leaving $x = -1$. Plug that back into either one of the original equations and you'll find that $y = 4$.

68. SOLVING AN EQUATION THAT INCLUDES ABSOLUTE VALUE SIGNS

To solve an equation that includes absolute value signs, **think about the two different cases.** For example, to solve the equation $|x - 12| = 3$, think of it as two equations:

$$x - 12 = 3 \quad \text{or} \quad x - 12 = -3$$
$$x = 15 \quad \text{or} \quad 9$$

69. SOLVING AN INEQUALITY

To solve an inequality, do whatever is necessary to both sides to **isolate the variable.** Just remember that when you **multiply or divide both sides by a negative number,** you must **reverse the sign.** To solve $-5x + 7 < -3$, subtract 7 from both sides to get $-5x < -10$. Now divide both sides by -5, remembering to reverse the sign: $x > 2$.

70. GRAPHING INEQUALITIES

To graph a range of values, use a thick, black line over the number line, and at the end(s) of the range, use a **solid circle** if the point *is* **included** or an **open circle** if the point is *not* **included.** The figure here shows the graph of $-3 < x \le 5$.

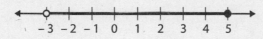

COORDINATE GEOMETRY

71. FINDING THE DISTANCE BETWEEN TWO POINTS

To find the distance between points, **use the Pythagorean theorem or special right triangles.** The difference between the xs is one leg and the difference between the ys is the other leg.

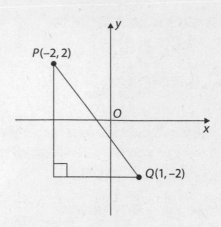

In the figure above, $\overline{PQ}$ is the hypotenuse of a 3-4-5 triangle, so $\overline{PQ} = 5$.

You can also use the **distance formula:**

$$d = \sqrt{(x_2 - x_1)^2 + (y_2 - y_1)^2}$$

To find the distance between $R(3, 6)$ and $S(5, -2)$:

$$d = \sqrt{(5 - 3)^2 + (-2 - 6)^2}$$
$$= \sqrt{(2)^2 + (-8)^2}$$
$$= \sqrt{68} = 2\sqrt{17}$$

72. USING TWO POINTS TO FIND THE SLOPE

In mathematics, the slope of a line is often called m.

$$\text{Slope} = m = \frac{\text{Change in } y}{\text{Change in } x} = \frac{\text{Rise}}{\text{Run}}$$

The slope of the line that contains the points $A(2, 3)$ and $B(0, -1)$ is:

$$\frac{y_2 - y_1}{x_2 - x_1} = \frac{-1 - 3}{0 - 2} = \frac{-4}{-2} = 2$$

73. USING AN EQUATION TO FIND THE SLOPE

To find the slope of a line from an equation, put the equation into the **slope-intercept** form:

$$y = mx + b$$

The slope is m. To find the slope of the equation $3x + 2y = 4$, reexpress it:

$$3x + 2y = 4$$
$$2y = -3x + 4$$
$$y = -\frac{3}{2}x + 2$$

The slope is $-\frac{3}{2}$.

74. USING AN EQUATION TO FIND AN INTERCEPT

To find the y-intercept, you can either put the equation into **$y = mx + b$ (slope-intercept)** form—in which case b is the y-intercept—or you can just plug $x = 0$ into the equation and solve for y. To find the x-intercept, plug $y = 0$ into the equation and solve for x.

75. EQUATION FOR A CIRCLE

The equation for a circle of radius r and centered at (h, k) is:

$$(x - h)^2 + (y - k)^2 = r^2$$

The figure below shows the graph of the equation $(x - 2)^2 + (y + 1)^2 = 25$:

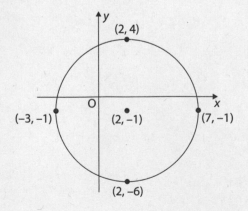

76. EQUATION FOR A PARABOLA

The graph of an equation in the form $y = ax^2 + bx + c$ is a parabola. The figure below shows the graph of seven pairs of numbers that satisfy the equation $y = x^2 - 4x + 3$:

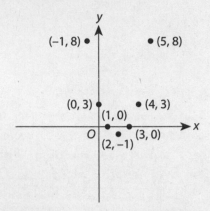

77. EQUATION FOR AN ELLIPSE

The graph of an equation in the form

$$\frac{x^2}{a^2} = \frac{y^2}{b^2} = 1$$

is an ellipse, with $2a$ as the sum of the focal radii and with foci on the x-axis at $(0, -c)$ and $(0, c)$, where $c = \sqrt{a^2 - b^2}$. The following figure shows the graph of $\frac{x^2}{25} + \frac{y^2}{16} = 1$:

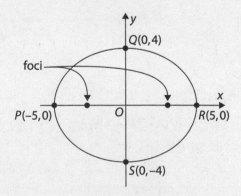

The foci are at $(-3, 0)$ and $(3, 0)$. $\overline{PR}$ is the **major axis,** and $\overline{QS}$ is the **minor axis.** This ellipse is symmetrical about both the x- and y-axes.

LINES AND ANGLES

78. INTERSECTING LINES

When two lines intersect, **adjacent angles are supplementary** and **vertical angles are equal.**

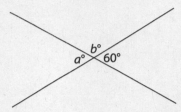

In the figure, the angles marked $a°$ and $b°$ are adjacent and supplementary, so $a + b = 180$. Furthermore, the angles marked $a°$ and 60° are vertical and equal, so $a = 60$.

79. PARALLEL LINES AND TRANSVERSALS

A transversal across parallel lines forms **four equal acute angles and four equal obtuse angles.**

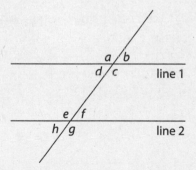

Here, line 1 is parallel to line 2. Angles a, c, e, and g are obtuse, so they are all equal. Angles b, d, f, and h are acute, so they are all equal.

Furthermore, **any of the acute angles is supplementary to any of the obtuse angles.** Angles a and h are supplementary, as are b and e, c and f, and so on.

TRIANGLES—GENERAL

80. INTERIOR ANGLES OF A TRIANGLE

The three angles of any triangle **add up to 180°.**

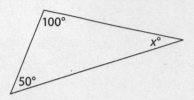

In the figure above, $x + 50 + 100 = 180$, so $x = 30$.

81. EXTERIOR ANGLES OF A TRIANGLE

An exterior angle of a triangle is equal to the **sum of the remote interior angles.**

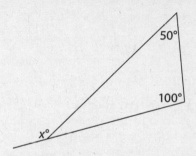

In the figure above, the exterior angle labeled $x°$ is equal to the sum of the remote interior angles:

$$x = 50 + 100 = 150$$

The three exterior angles of any triangle add up to 360°.

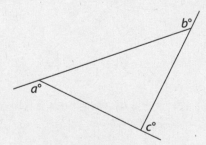

In the figure above, $a + b + c = 360$.

82. SIMILAR TRIANGLES

Similar triangles have the same shape: **corresponding angles are equal and corresponding sides are proportional.**

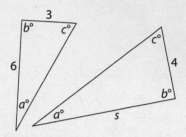

The triangles above are similar because they have the same angles. The 3 corresponds to the 4, and the 6 corresponds to the s.

$$\frac{3}{4} = \frac{6}{s}$$
$$3s = 24$$
$$s = 8$$

83. AREA OF A TRIANGLE

Area of Triangle $= \frac{1}{2}$(Base)(Height)

The height is the perpendicular distance between the side that's chosen as the base and the opposite vertex.

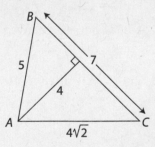

In the triangle above, 4 is the height when the 7 is chosen as the base.

$$\text{Area} = \frac{1}{2}bh = \frac{1}{2}(7)(4) = 14$$

RIGHT TRIANGLES

84. PYTHAGOREAN THEOREM

For all right triangles:

$(\text{leg}_1)^2 + (\text{leg}_2)^2 = (\text{hypotenuse})^2$

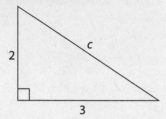

If one leg is 2 and the other leg is 3, then:

$$2^2 + 3^2 = c^2$$
$$c^2 = 4 + 9$$
$$c = \sqrt{13}$$

85. SPECIAL RIGHT TRIANGLES

3-4-5

If a right triangle's leg-to-leg ratio is 3:4 or if the leg-to-hypotenuse ratio is 3:5 or 4:5, then it's a 3-4-5 triangle, and you don't need to use the Pythagorean theorem to find the third side. Just figure out what multiple of 3-4-5 it is.

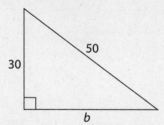

In the right triangle above, one leg is 30 and the hypotenuse is 50. This is 10 times 3-4-5. The other leg is 40.

5-12-13

If a right triangle's leg-to-leg ratio is 5:12 or if the leg-to-hypotenuse ratio is 5:13 or 12:13, then it's a 5-12-13 triangle, and you don't need to use the Pythagorean theorem to find the third side. Just figure out what multiple of 5-12-13 it is.

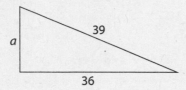

Here, one leg is 36 and the hypotenuse is 39. This is 3 times 5-12-13. The other leg is 15.

30°-60°-90°

The sides of a 30°-60°-90° triangle are in a ratio of $1:\sqrt{3}:2$. You don't need to use the Pythagorean theorem.

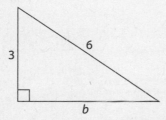

If the hypotenuse is 6, then the shorter leg is half that, or 3; and then the longer leg is equal to the short leg times $\sqrt{3}$, or $3\sqrt{3}$.

45°-45°-90°

The sides of a 45°-45°-90° triangle are in a ratio of $1:1:\sqrt{2}$.

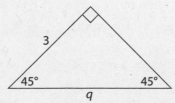

If one leg is 3, then the other leg is also 3, and the hypotenuse is equal to a leg times $\sqrt{2}$, or $3\sqrt{2}$.

OTHER POLYGONS

86. SPECIAL QUADRILATERALS

Rectangle

A rectangle is a **four-sided figure with four right angles.** Opposite sides are equal. Diagonals are equal.

Quadrilateral *ABCD* above is shown to have three right angles. The fourth angle therefore also measures 90°, and *ABCD* is a rectangle. The perimeter of a rectangle is equal to the sum of the lengths of the four sides, which is equivalent to 2(length + width).

Parallelogram

A parallelogram has **two pairs of parallel sides.** Opposite sides are equal. Opposite angles are equal. Consecutive angles add up to 180°.

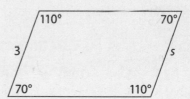

In the figure above, *s* is the length of the side opposite the 3, so *s* = 3.

Square

A square is a **rectangle with four equal sides.**

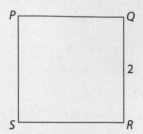

If *PQRS* is a square, all sides are the same length as *QR*. The perimeter of a square is equal to four times the length of one side.

Trapezoid

A **trapezoid** is a quadrilateral with one pair of parallel sides and one pair of nonparallel sides.

In the quadrilateral above, sides $\overline{EF}$ and $\overline{GH}$ are parallel, while sides $\overline{EH}$ and $\overline{FG}$ are not parallel. *EFGH* is therefore a trapezoid.

87. AREAS OF SPECIAL QUADRILATERALS

Area of Rectangle = Length × Width

The area of a 7-by-3 rectangle is $7 \times 3 = 21$.

Area of Parallelogram = Base × Height

The area of a parallelogram with a height of 4 and a base of 6 is $4 \times 6 = 24$.

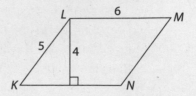

Area of Square = (Side)²

The area of a square with sides of length 5 is $5^2 = 25$.

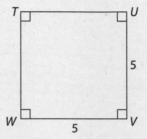

Area of Trapezoid = $\left(\dfrac{\text{base}_1 - \text{base}_2}{2}\right) \times$ Height

Think of it as the average of the bases (the two parallel sides) times the height (the length of the perpendicular altitude).

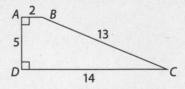

In the trapezoid *ABCD* above, you can use side *AD* for the height. The average of the bases is $\dfrac{2 + 14}{2} = 8$, so the area is 5×8, or 40.

88. INTERIOR ANGLES OF A POLYGON

The sum of the measures of the interior angles of a polygon is $(n - 2) \times 180$, where *n* is the number of sides.

Sum of the Angles = $(n - 2) \times 180$ degrees

The eight angles of an octagon, for example, add up to $(8 - 2) \times 180 = 1{,}080$.

To find **one angle of a regular polygon,** divide the sum of the angles by the number of angles (which is the same as the number of sides). The formula, therefore, is:

Interior Angle $= \dfrac{(n-2) \times 180}{n}$

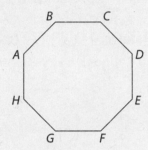

Angle A of the regular octagon above measures $\dfrac{1{,}080}{8} = 135$ degrees.

CIRCLES

89. CIRCUMFERENCE OF A CIRCLE

Circumference of a Circle $= 2\pi r$

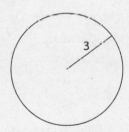

Here, the radius is 3, and so the circumference is $2\pi(3) = 6\pi$.

90. LENGTH OF AN ARC

An **arc** is a piece of the circumference. If n is the measure of the arc's central angle, then the formula is:

Length of an Arc $= \dfrac{n}{360}(2\pi r)$

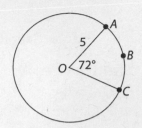

In the figure above, the radius is 5 and the measure of the central angle is 72°. The arc length is $\dfrac{72}{360}$, or $\dfrac{1}{5}$ of the circumference:

$$\left(\dfrac{72}{360}\right)2\pi(5) = \left(\dfrac{1}{5}\right)10\pi = 2\pi$$

91. AREA OF A CIRCLE

Area of a Circle $= \pi r^2$

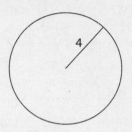

The area of the circle above is $\pi(4)^2 = 16\pi$.

92. AREA OF A SECTOR

A **sector** is a piece of the area of a circle. If n is the measure of the sector's central angle, then the formula is:

Area of a Sector $= \dfrac{n}{360}(\pi r^2)$

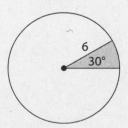

In the figure above, the radius is 6 and the measure of the sector's central angle is 30°. The sector has $\dfrac{30}{360}$, or $\dfrac{1}{12}$ of the area of the circle:

$$\left(\dfrac{30}{360}\right)(\pi)(6^2) = \left(\dfrac{1}{12}\right)(36\pi) = 3\pi$$

SOLIDS

93. SURFACE AREA OF A RECTANGULAR SOLID

The surface of a rectangular solid consists of three pairs of identical faces. To find the surface area, find the area of each face and add them up. If the length is l, the width is w, and the height is h, the formula is:

Surface Area = 2lw + 2wh + 2lh

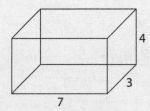

The surface area of the box above is:

$2 \times 7 \times 3 + 2 \times 3 \times 4 + 2 \times 7 \times 4 =$
$42 + 24 + 56 = 122$

94. VOLUME OF A RECTANGULAR SOLID

Volume of a Rectangular Solid = lwh

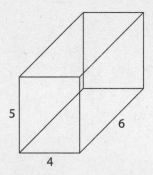

The volume of a 4-by-5-by-6 box is:

$4 \times 5 \times 6 = 120$

A cube is a rectangular solid with length, width, and height all equal. The volume formula if e is the length of an edge of the cube is:

Volume of a Cube = e^3

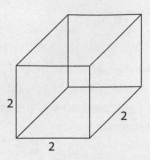

The volume of the cube above is $2^3 = 8$.

95. VOLUME OF OTHER SOLIDS

Volume of a Cylinder = $\pi r^2 h$

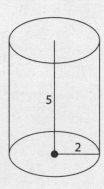

The volume of a cylinder where $r = 2$ and $h = 5$ is $\pi(2^2)(5) = 20\pi$.

Volume of a Cone = $\frac{1}{3}\pi r^2 h$

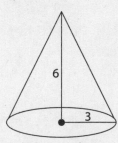

The volume of a cone where $r = 3$ and $h = 6$ is:

$$\text{Volume} = \frac{1}{3}\pi(3^2)(6) = 18$$

Volume of a Sphere = $\frac{4}{3}\pi r^3$

If the radius of a sphere is 3, then:

$$\text{Volume} = \frac{4}{3}\pi(3^3) = 36\pi$$

TRIGONOMETRY

96. SINE, COSINE, AND TANGENT OF ACUTE ANGLES

To find the sine, cosine, or tangent of an acute angle, use SOHCAHTOA, which is an abbreviation for the following definitions:

$$Sine = \frac{\text{Opposite}}{\text{Hypotenuse}}$$

$$Cosine = \frac{\text{Adjacent}}{\text{Hypotenuse}}$$

$$Tangent = \frac{\text{Opposite}}{\text{Adjacent}}$$

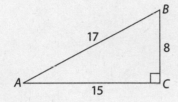

In the figure above:

$$\sin A = \frac{8}{17}$$

$$\cos A = \frac{15}{17}$$

$$\tan A = \frac{8}{15}$$

97. COTANGENT, SECANT, AND COSECANT OF ACUTE ANGLES

Think of the cotangent, secant, and cosecant as the reciprocals of the SOHCAHTOA functions:

$$Cotangent = \frac{1}{\text{Tangent}} = \frac{\text{Adjacent}}{\text{Opposite}}$$

$$Secant = \frac{1}{\text{Cosine}} = \frac{\text{Hypotenuse}}{\text{Adjacent}}$$

$$Cosecant = \frac{1}{\text{Sine}} = \frac{\text{Hypotenuse}}{\text{Opposite}}$$

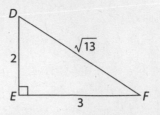

In the preceeding figure:

$$\cot D = \frac{2}{3}$$

$$\sec D = \frac{\sqrt{13}}{2}$$

$$\csc D = \frac{\sqrt{13}}{3}$$

98. TRIGONOMETRIC FUNCTIONS OF OTHER ANGLES

To find a trigonometric function of an angle greater than 90°, sketch a circle of radius 1 centered at the origin of the coordinate grid. Start from the point (1, 0) and rotate the appropriate number of degrees counterclockwise.

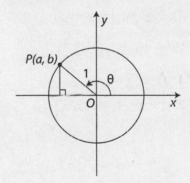

In the "unit circle" setup above, the basic trigonometric functions are defined in terms of the coordinates a and b:

$$\sin \theta = b$$
$$\cos \theta = a$$
$$\tan \theta = \frac{b}{a}$$

Example: $\sin 210° = ?$

Setup: Sketch a 210° angle in the coordinate plane:

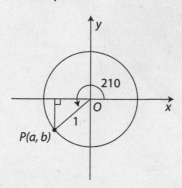

Because the triangle shown in the figure above is a 30°-60°-90° right triangle, we can determine that the coordinates of point P are $-\frac{\sqrt{3}}{2}, -\frac{1}{2}$. The sine is therefore $-\frac{1}{2}$.

99. SIMPLIFYING TRIGONOMETRIC EXPRESSIONS

To simplify trigonometric expressions, use the inverse function definitions along with the fundamental trigonometric identity:

$$\sin^2 x + \cos^2 x = 1$$

Example: $\dfrac{\sin^2 \theta + \cos^2 \theta}{\cos \theta} = ?$

Setup: The numerator equals 1, so:

$$\frac{\sin^2 \theta + \cos^2 \theta}{\cos \theta} = \frac{1}{\cos \theta} = \sec \theta$$

100. GRAPHING TRIGONOMETRIC FUNCTIONS

To graph trigonometric functions, use the x-axis for the angle and the y-axis for the value of the trigonometric function. Use special angles—0°, 30°, 45°, 60°, 90°, 120°, 135°, 150°, 180°, etc.—to plot key points.

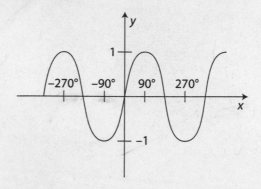

The figure above shows a portion of the graph of $y = \sin x$.